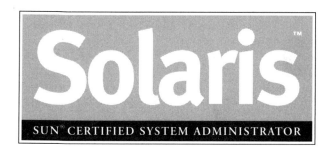

SUN® CERTIFIED SYSTEM ADMINISTRATOR

Sun® Certified System Administrator for Solaris™ 9.0 Study Guide

(Exam 310-014 & 310-015)

ABOUT THE CONTRIBUTORS

Author

Tim Gibbs is an independent computer consultant and has worked in the computer industry for nearly 25 years. He specializes in Relational Database Management Systems, Solaris, Linux, and 4GL Development and Training.

He has a vast experience with major international corporations and Government departments including NATO, The EU, Department of Industrial Relations (Australia / NSW), Department of Public Prosecutions (Australia / NSW), ICL Europe, Fujitsu Australia / Japan, Dresdner Bank, Barclays Global Investors, and The Australian Defense Force.

Technical Editor

Bill Kennedy has been a software engineer for nearly 20 years and has been designing and implementing database systems in UNIX environments for 10 years. As a senior database architect for a global outsourcing organization and sometimes-freelance consultant he has had extensive experience using UNIX in large-scale database environments across diverse industry sectors.

Bill can be reached at bill@wpkennedy.com.

Contributors

Brian Albrecht (SCSA, MCSE, CCNA, TCEC) is a solutions architect for Sprint E|Solutions. His specialty is designing and implementing complete business and network management solutions.

Brian lives in St. Louis, Missouri, and can be reached at brian.e.albrecht@mail.sprint.com.

Kevin Amorin (SCSA, SCNA, CCNA, MCSE) lives in the Boston area, where he works as a systems and network consultant. He holds a B.S. in computer science from Worcester Polytechnic Institute. Kevin has had the opportunity to work with and consult for a variety of organizations, including Motorola, Lucent, and

Microsoft, and he currently works at Harvard University. Kevin's interests include distributed computing, OS performance evaluation, and storage area networks.

In his spare time Kevin likes to travel and sail and is an avid sports enthusiast, as both a spectator and a competitor. He hopes to someday share his passion for computer science by teaching at the college level. Kevin can be contacted at kev@amorin.org.

Bill Bradford (SCSA, SCNA) is a system administrator for a large telecommunications company and has been using Sun systems since 1995.

In his spare time, Bill maintains Sunhelp.org, a web portal and information resource for users of Sun/SPARC computer systems and the Solaris and SunOS operating systems. He currently resides in Austin, Texas, with his wife, Amy. He can be reached at mrbill@mrbill.net.

Randy Cook (SCSA, MCSE) is currently the senior UNIX system administrator for the research and development department of one of the world's largest manufacturing facilities. He has written for IT magazines and interviewed on computing issues for radio and television. Randy was the technical editor for the first edition of this book as well as writing several chapters.

Ken Copas (HP OpenView Certified Consultant, Sentinel Services Certified Consultant) is a senior UNIX system administration consultant and the Midwest territory manager for DIS Research in Columbus, Ohio. He specializes in mission-critical computing, operations automation, and SAN architecture and implementation. Ken's contact information can be found at http://cbbc.net/copas/.

James A. (Jamie) Dennis (SCSA, Certified AIX System Administrator) is a native of Chillicothe, Ohio, and now lives and works in Columbus. He has worked in information technology since 1985 and in the UNIX environment since 1988. Jamie has worked for a variety of companies, from very small to large, as both a lead and a senior UNIX system administrator and as manager of a team of 12 UNIX system administrators. Jamie now consults as a lead UNIX system administrator and project manager. When not being a geek, Jamie loves to study Civil War history and genealogy and read John Grisham novels.

Fedil Grogan (SCSA, CCNA) lives in Corinth, Texas, and works as a UNIX system administrator for SBC Advanced Solutions, Inc. Fedil is working on obtaining Solaris 9 System and Network Certifications.

Umer Khan (SCSA, SCNA, CCIE, MCSE, CCA, CNX) obtained his bachelors degree in computer engineering from the Illinois Institute of Technology. He works as a senior network engineer at Broadcom Corporation (www.broadcom.com), where he enjoys the challenging and fast-paced IT environment. As the team lead for the Network Operations group, Umer is responsible for designing and deploying global LAN/MAN/WAN solutions that are available with 99.9 percent up time (planned and unplanned). Nearly ten years of experience in the IT industry have made him knowledgeable and certified in a wide range of technologies. Umer's personal web site is located at www.umer-khan.net, and he can be reached at umer.khan@mail.com.

David LaPorte (SCSA, SCNA, CCNA, MCSE) is a network engineer at Harvard University and has over six years of UNIX experience. He is a partner in NEPD, an independent consulting firm, and works with clients to secure and integrate their networks. David is interested in all aspects of enterprise computing, but current special interests include IPv6, VoIP, and video conferencing.

David lives in Framingham, Massachusetts, and can be contacted at dave@davidlaporte.org.

Hank Murphy has been programming since 1967 and has experience in IBM mainframes, VAXes, and PCs as well as Sun products. A senior software developer at Candle Corporation, he is also currently an adjunct instructor in computer science at Los Angeles Pierce College and taught at UCLA Extension from 1984–1993. His experience with Sun systems is predominantly software development and systems integration rather than system administration.

Hank lives with his wife in Agoura, California. When not writing code, he is involved in church activities and riding his Triumph Tiger motorcycle.

Stephen Potter (SCSA) has been tinkering with UNIX computer systems since 1985; he remembers the original VT100s and ADM3As. For nearly ten years, he has been consulting for Fortune 500 companies dealing with everything from migrations to rollouts, performance tuning, high availability design and architecture, and most everything in between. Stephen has been trained on Sun's E10K, HP/OpenView, and Veritas Cluster Server. He has an extensive background with Perl, having maintained the FAQ for several years, and was a coauthor of *Programming Perl,* second edition.

Now that Stephen is a father, he has cut back on his computing pursuits and much prefers spending time with his wife, Amanda, and son, John. Strangely, he finds watching his son discover new things to be far more interesting than anything having to do with computers.

Bret Sanders (SCSA, MCSE+I) began working with the Internet in 1990 while earning his business degree at the University of Redlands. Since then, he has gained more than 10 years of valuable experience in the computer industry. Working as the corporate Webmaster for Hughes Aircraft, Bret's primary mission was to connect parts of the company to the Internet as well as build and maintain the company's intranet systems. From Hughes, he moved north to Silicon Valley, where he began work for Sun Microsystems as a system/network manager. Wanting to focus his career on the Internet, he then moved on to GlobalCenter, where he built and maintained some of the largest Web sites on the Internet at the time, including sgi.com, playboy.com, and smartpages.com. With this experience under his belt, he moved on to a small Internet startup company, which was acquired by AOL in August 2000.

Andrew Seely (SCSA, LCP) has a B.S. in computer and information science from the University of Maryland University College, European Division, and a master's in computer science from Nova Southeastern University.

Andrew works for Computer Sciences Corporation as a senior systems analyst for a small but interesting UNIX network. After hours, he teaches UNIX classes at the University of Maryland University College, European Division, in southern Germany. In the past he has worked for Adarweb, the leading Web hosting company in Paris, France, as well as running his own consulting company, Soñador Internet Development. He spent seven years in the U.S. Air Force as a communications and computer systems operator.

Rob Sletten (SCSA, MCSE, CCSE/CCSA, MCP+I, CCNA) is a consultant for Lucent Technologies Worldwide Services in Charlotte, North Carolina, specializing in UNIX and Microsoft Consulting. Rob has over seven years of experience in the IT field, including UNIX, Microsoft, routing and switching, and network security. When he is not breaking ribs skiing, Rob's other hobbies include computer games, Web/database integration, programming, and gardening.

Ray Tran has over 15 years of experience as a system administrator on Sun platforms. He is employed at Broadcom Corporation in Irvine, California. His current focus is the heterogeneous infrastructure for the software source code management (SCM) for Broadcom.

Ray's experience has been primarily in the engineering environment, with exposure to different CAD/CAE tools. He also expanded his knowledge by consulting at a variety of companies to get exposure to different environments.

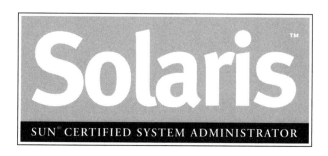

SUN® CERTIFIED SYSTEM ADMINISTRATOR

Sun® Certified System Administrator for Solaris™ 9.0 Study Guide

(Exam 310-014 & 310-015)

Tim Gibbs

McGraw-Hill/Osborne

New York   Chicago   San Francisco   Lisbon   London   Madrid
Mexico City   Milan   New Delhi   San Juan   Seoul   Singapore   Sydney   Toronto

The **McGraw·Hill** Companies

McGraw-Hill/Osborne
2600 Tenth Street
Berkeley, California 94710
U.S.A.

To arrange bulk purchase discounts for sales promotions, premiums, or fund-raisers, please contact **McGraw-Hill/Osborne** at the above address. For information on translations or book distributors outside the U.S.A., please see the International Contact Information page immediately following the index of this book.

Sun® Certified System Administrator for Solaris™ 9.0 Study Guide (Exam 310-014 & 310-015)

1234567890 DOC DOC 0198765432

Book p/n 0-07-222599-8 and CD p/n 0-07-222600-5
parts of ISBN 0-07-222598-X

Publisher
Brandon A. Nordin

Vice President & Associate Publisher
Scott Rogers

Acquisitions Editor
Timothy Green

Project Editor
Jennifer Malnick

Acquisitions Coordinator
Jessica Wilson

Technical Editor
Bill Kennedy

Copy Editor
Chrisa Hotchkiss

Proofreader
Linda Medoff

Indexer
David Heiret

Computer Designers
Lucie Ericksen,
Kelly Stanton-Scott

Illustrators
Michael Mueller,
Melinda Moore Lytle,
Lyssa Wald

Series Design
Roberta Steele

This book was composed with Corel VENTURA™ Publisher.

CONTENTS AT A GLANCE

Part I
Sun Certified System Administrator Examination for Solaris 9 Study Guide, Exam 310-011

Part II
Sun Certified Administrator Examination for Solaris 9 Study Guide,
Exam 310-012

Part III
Appendixes

TABLE OF CONTENTS

Solaris has a long and proud history at the forefront of open systems technology. As the best-selling UNIX system, Solaris is pervasive in the enterprise, and its legendary reputation for reliability and scalability is well deserved. The current release of Solaris—Solaris 9—represents both an incremental improvement and a major change in direction for the operating environment. Existing innovations and strengths are built upon in the core operating system, including support for IPv6, IPSec, new networking standards, improved threading and volume management. However, Solaris is much more than yet another operating system—it is the foundation for Sun ONE, the new platform for enterprise applications. Sun ONE provides support for directory services, enterprise Java applications, firewall security, Kerberos, and interoperability tools. Cross-platform integration is crucial for enterprises, which is why Solaris is well-positioned to become the Web Services platform for the next generation of enterprise services.

Dr. Tim Gibbs is a world-recognized expert in the area of enterprise systems. He has many years of practical experience working with operating systems and database servers, and he has crystallized this experience into a volume that will help you, the reader, become an expert Solaris system administrator. This book provides a pathway for you to learn all of the skills necessary to pass the Solaris certification exams as a system administrator. While no book can replace practical, hands-on experience, passing the exam will require detailed knowledge of some specific areas of administration. This volume presents this material in a concise, easy-to-read format, making it accessible to all readers. I recommend this book to you.

—Paul A. Watters, Ph.D.
Author, *Solaris 9: The Complete Reference*

ACKNOWLEDGMENTS

We would like to thank the following people:

- All the incredibly hard-working folks at Osborne: Gareth Hancock, Tim Green, and Jessica Wilson for their help in launching a great series and being solid team players

- Dr Paul Watters for a great foreword and introducing me to this writing lark in the first place

- Bill Kennedy for an absolutely fantastic job as technical editor

- David Thompson and Simon Rivett for spotting some mistakes

- Senri Oiso, Gillian Nelson, and Tech Pacific for letting me practice on them

- The cat for purring very loudly and walking all over the keyboard when I was working

- Susan for being as adventurous as me and for being a great friend

- Jennifer Malnick (yes, I do know it's a good day to die!)

This book's primary objective is to help you prepare for the Sun Certified System Administrator for Solaris 9 Exams, Parts I and II.

At the time of this book's publication all the exam objectives were posted on the Sun web site and the beta exam process had been completed. Sun announced its commitment to measuring real-world skills. This book is designed with that premise in mind: The author and contributors have practical experience in the field, using the Solaris operating environment in hands-on situations, and have followed the development of the product since early beta versions.

Because the focus of the exams is on application and understanding, as opposed to memorization of facts, no book by itself can fully prepare you to obtain a passing score on these exams. It is essential that you work with the operating environment to enhance your proficiency. Toward that end, this book includes many practical step-by-step exercises in each chapter that are designed to give you hands-on practice as well as guide you in truly learning the Solaris 9 operating environment, not just learning *about* it.

In This Book

This book is organized in such a way as to serve as an in-depth review for the Sun Certified System Administrator for Solaris 9 Exams, Parts I and II, for both experienced Solaris professionals and newcomers to the Solaris operating environment technologies. Each chapter covers a major aspect of each exam, with an emphasis on the "why" as well as the "how to" of working with and supporting Solaris 9 as a network administrator or engineer.

On the CD-ROM

For more information on the CD-ROM, please see Appendix B. You can access the additional bonus material covering the Solaris 9 upgrade exam using the Additional Training link on the CD-ROM and by completing the free online registration and logging in.

In Every Chapter

We've created a set of chapter components that call your attention to important items, reinforce important points, and provide helpful exam-taking hints. Take a look at what you'll find in every chapter:

- Every chapter begins with the **Certification Objectives**—what you need to know in order to pass the section on the exam dealing with the chapter topic. The Objective headings identify the objectives within the chapter, so you'll always know an objective when you see it!

- **Exam Watch** notes call attention to information about, and potential pitfalls in, the exam. These helpful hints are written by authors who have taken the exams and received their certification—who better to tell you what to worry about? They know what you're about to go through!

- **Practice Exercises** are interspersed throughout the chapters. These are step-by-step exercises that allow you to get the hands-on experience you need in order to pass the exams. They help you master skills that are likely to be an area of focus on the exam. Don't just read through the exercises; they are hands-on practice that you should be comfortable completing. Learning by doing is an effective way to increase your competency with a product.

- **On The Job** notes describe the issues that come up most often in real-world settings. They provide a valuable perspective on certification- and product-related topics. They point out common mistakes and address questions that have arisen from on-the-job discussions and experience.

- **From The Classroom** sidebars describe the issues that come up most often in the training classroom setting. These sidebars highlight some of the most common and confusing problems that students encounter when taking a live Solaris training course. You can get a leg up on those difficult-to-understand subjects by focusing extra attention on these sidebars.

- The **Certification Summary** is a succinct review of the chapter and a restatement of salient points regarding the exam.

- **Scenario and Solutions** sections lay out potential problems and solutions in a quick-to-read format:

SCENARIO & SOLUTION

Which command do you use to view a single entry in the table using a key?	/usr/bin/ypmatch -k *keyname mapname* Example: /usr/sbin/ypmatch -k sysadmin group
Which command do you use to view an entry in the table without using the key?	/usr/bin/ypcat *mapname* | grep *item* Example: /usr/sbin/ypcat passwd | grep sysadmin
Which command do you use to verify the /etc/nsswitch.conf configuration with NIS service?	/usr/bin/getent *service item* Example: /usr/bin/getent passwd sysadmin

■ The **Two-Minute Drill** at the end of every chapter is a checklist of the main points of the chapter. It can be used for last-minute review.

Q&A ■ The **Self Test** offers questions similar to those found on the certification exams. The answers to these questions, as well as explanations of the answers, can be found at the end of each chapter. By taking the Self Test after completing each chapter, you'll reinforce what you've learned from that chapter while becoming familiar with the structure of the exam questions.

■ The **Lab Question** at the end of the Self Test section offers a unique and challenging question format that requires you to understand multiple chapter concepts to answer correctly. These questions are more complex and more comprehensive than the other questions, as they test your ability to take all the knowledge you have gained from reading the chapter and apply it to complicated, real-world situations. These questions are aimed to be more difficult than what you will find on the exam. If you can answer these questions, you have proven that you know the subject!

Some Pointers

Once you've finished reading this book, set aside some time to do a thorough review. You might want to return to the book several times and make use of all the methods it offers for reviewing the material:

1. **Re-read all the Two-Minute Drills** or have someone quiz you. You also can use the drills as a way to do a quick cram before the exam. You might want

to make some flash cards out of 3 × 5 index cards that have the Two-Minute Drill material on them.

2. **Re-read all the Exam Watch notes.** Remember that these notes are written by authors who have taken the exam and passed. They know what you should expect—and what you should be on the lookout for.

3. **Review all the S&S sections** for quick problem solving.

4. **Re-take the Self Tests.** Taking the tests right after you've read the chapter is a good idea, because the questions help reinforce what you've just learned. However, it's an even better idea to go back later and do all the questions in the book in one sitting. Pretend that you're taking the live exam. (When you go through the questions the first time, you should mark your answers on a separate piece of paper. That way, you can run through the questions as many times as you need to until you feel comfortable with the material.)

5. **Complete the Exercises.** Did you do the exercises when you read through each chapter? If not, do them! These exercises are designed to cover exam topics, and there's no better way to get to know this material than by practicing. Be sure you understand why you are performing each step in each exercise. If there is something you are not clear on, re-read that section in the chapter.

SUN® CERTIFIED SYSTEM ADMINISTRATOR

Part I

Sun Certified
System
Administrator
Examination for
Solaris 9
Study Guide,
Exam 310-011

CHAPTERS

1

Understanding System Concepts

T o truly understand any machine, you must first understand its function and parts. Then you must understand how those parts work together to perform the machine's function.

This chapter touches on all three topics—function, parts, and how the parts work together—in very general terms. The rest of the book goes into specific detail, but first you need to understand some common terms. This chapter covers the basic terminology in system administration and the use of the man command. This command is a starting point designed to give you the foundation on which the rest of the book builds.

CERTIFICATION OBJECTIVE 1.01

Defining System Administration Terms

This section introduces you to the basic terminology that you'll need to understand in your role as system administrator.

Daemons

Many sysadmins are quick to point out that a *daemon* is not a *demon*. Even though it might sometimes seem like it, your server is not possessed by a devil. (Some of your users might be, but not your server.) A *daemon* is defined as a program that runs in the background, disconnected from a terminal or a particular login session. It is often used to manage system functions.

The term "daemon" is derived from Greek mythology. The ancient Greeks called a supernatural being that acted as an intermediary between the gods and man a daemon. This is an accurate description of what a UNIX daemon does for you. Basically, a daemon is always there, waiting to be called on to perform some action or service. Daemons are running on a system for every service the system provides. However, don't confuse the terms "daemon" and "process."

A *process* is an instance of a running program. So although a daemon is a process, a process isn't necessarily a daemon. You can see all the processes that are running on your system by using the ps command, which displays all the processes at once. These processes can comprise one big list, even on a little-used system. Naturally, with the use of command options, you can use the ps command to display only the information you're looking for. The ps command is covered in more detail in Chapter 7, but for now, let's take a look at some of the daemons that are running on your system.

EXERCISE 1-1

Viewing the Processes on a System

Let's first take a look at what is going on behind the scenes on your Solaris system. For this exercise, your system's hostname is *enterprise.timgibbs.net*.

1. Log in to the system:

```
Trying 192.168.0.2...
Connected to enterprise.
Escape character is '^]'.
SunOS 5.9
login:gibbst
password: *********
Last login: Tue Apr  3 19:12:13 from :0
Sun Microsystems Inc.   SunOS 5.9
Welcome to enterprise.timgibbs.net
[enterprise: gibbst] $
```

2. List the processes.

Now you've logged in to *enterprise* as the user *gibbst* and seen a message from the very conscientious system administrator regarding a planned outage.

3. Now look at the processes, including the daemons, that are currently running on *enterprise* by using the following ps command:

```
[enterprise: gibbst] $ ps -ef | more
    UID   PID  PPID  C    STIME TTY      TIME CMD
    root    0    0   0  Mar 20 ?        0:03 sched
root    196    1   0  Mar 20 ?        0:16 /usr/sbin/nscd
root    206    1   0  Mar 20 ?        0:00 /usr/lib/lpsched
root    177    1   0  Mar 20 ?        0:01 /usr/sbin/syslogd
root    268    1   0  Mar 20 console  0:00 /usr/lib/saf/ttymon -g -h
-p cc9972-b console login:  -T sun-color -d /dev/cons
root    158    1   0  Mar 20 ?        0:01 /usr/sbin/inetd -s
root    157    1   0  Mar 20 ?        0:00 /usr/lib/nfs/lockd
daemon  160    1   0  Mar 20 ?        0:00 /usr/lib/nfs/statd
root    186    1   0  Mar 20 ?        0:01 /usr/sbin/cron
--More--
```

The ps command is used here with the *e* and *f* options. This command displayed every process in a full listing. Because the list would easily cover more than one screen, we piped (|) the display into the more command. This way, you can see one screen at a time, and by pressing the SPACEBAR, you see more of the display. The ps command is covered in more detail in Chapter 7. For now, let's go daemon hunting!

4. Examine the following line, which is bolded in the preceding ps command output:

```
root    206    1  0    Mar 20 ?        0:00 /usr/lib/lpsched
```

This is one of the daemons running on the system named *enterprise*. It's the printer spooling daemon, lpsched. This daemon waits for print requests, and then sends the print job to the requested printer. The lpsched daemon is always running, waiting for a print job to come in.

Remember that most daemons end with the letter d. Most are started by initialization scripts at boot time, but this is configurable. Daemons can be stopped or restarted as needed. You often have to restart a daemon after making a configuration change to its service, or, to fix a stuck print queue, you might have to stop and start the print spooler daemon.

Shells

A *shell* is the interface between the user and the kernel. It's the means by which you communicate commands. There are many kinds of shells. This section focuses on three of the most popular: Bourne, C, and Korn.

The *Bourne shell* was written by S. R. Bourne and can be found on nearly all UNIX systems. It lacks some of the bells and whistles of others, but it remains one of the most prevalent shells in UNIX. The shell is located in /bin/sh and uses a dollar sign ($) at the user prompt. Shell scripts are most often written to be run by the Bourne shell because of its excellent input/output control and expression-matching features. However, many people feel it lacks strong interactivity features.

To answer this need, pioneers at the University of California at Berkeley developed the *C shell*. This shell, located in /bin/csh and using a percentage symbol (%) at the user prompt, provides features not found in Bourne, such as job control, command history, and aliasing. The C shell is designed to use command syntax that resembles C, the programming language used to write UNIX. However, many people feel that it lacks strong control of input and output.

In an effort to combine the best of both the Bourne and C shells, David Korn developed the *Korn shell,* which can be found in /bin/ksh and uses a dollar sign ($) at the command prompt. The Korn shell is a superset of the Bourne shell, but it adds features such as aliasing, history, and the popular command-line editing.

These three shells are provided as part of the Solaris operating environment. They are covered in more detail later in Chapter 14, but for now, let's take a look at how to try a new shell.

EXERCISE 1-2

Changing the Shell

When you create a user, the default shell assigned to that user is the Bourne shell. Let's walk through the steps you as the sysadmin can use to change a user's shell. Once again, we'll use a Solaris 9 system named *enterprise* as our example.

1. Log in to the system and find out which shell you are using:

```
Trying 192.168.0.2...
Connected to enterprise.
Escape character is '^]'.
SunOS 5.9
login:gibbst
password: **********
Last login: Tue Apr  4 17:22:10 from :0
Sun Microsystems Inc.   SunOS 5.9
Welcome to enterprise.timgibbs.net
[enterprise: gibbst] $ echo $SHELL
/bin/sh
```

Here we have logged in as the user named *gibbst.* Using the echo command, you can see that the SHELL variable is set to /bin/sh. This tells you that you are currently using the Bourne shell. Now, let's change the shell.

2. Switch to the root account:

```
Su -
password: **********
Sun Microsystems Inc.   SunOS 5.9
BUGGER - Not Happy Jan!
[enterprise: root] #
```

Now you are the superuser, or root, of *enterprise.* Notice how the command prompt has changed from the user prompt dollar sign ($) to the root prompt pound sign (#).

3. Execute the command passwd *-e* to change the shell from the user named *gibbst:*

```
[enterprise: root] # passwd -e gibbst
```

The current shell will be displayed and you will be prompted for the new shell:

```
old shell/bin/sh
New shell:/bin/csh
[enterprise: root] #
```

Now, the next time you log in as the user *gibbst,* you will use the C shell to do so.

---

on the
Job   *By default, users can't use the passwd -e command to change their shells; only the root user can do so. A user can, however, use another shell by changing the SHELL variable. This can be done by editing the user's .profile file in his or her home directory or from the command line.*

File Systems

A *file system* is a collection of directories and files organized in a hierarchical structure. A file system has a one-to-one correspondence with physical storage, such as a disk partition, or a virtual device presented by Solstice DiskSuite or Veritas Volume Manager (either of which may contain one or more physical devices). The *root directory* or root (/) file system is the absolute parent of all other directories and file systems.

Under the slash (/), other file systems are connected to the root file system. Before a disk partition or virtual disk can be accessed, it must first have a file system written on it. The newfs command does this for you. Once the partition contains a file system, the mount command attaches the new file system to the *mount point:* the location (directory) on the parent file system where a separate file system may be attached. File systems can be identified by the special *lost+found* directory that exists under the

SCENARIO & SOLUTION	
How can you tell which shell you're using?	Use the command echo $SHELL to see what your shell variable is set to.
How can you find out more about your shell's capabilities?	Use the man command. For example, man csh will give you a good overview of using the C shell.

mount point for every file system. One benefit of creating separate file systems is that data written to one cannot overflow into another. Having /export/home as a separate file system prevents users from filling up the root file system and crashing the server.

The UNIX file system is hierarchical; therefore, files are identified by their full path. Executing a command against the hosts file may produce unpredictable results. However, using the hosts file full path of /etc/inet/hosts guarantees that the operation is applied to the correct file. If you want to use the cp command to copy a file named foobar.tim to your home directory, you have to tell the cp command exactly where the file is located, and exactly where you want it to go:

```
[enterprise: root] # cp /export/home/gibbst/foobar.tim
/export/home/tim
```

on the

job

This is an actual conversation I had with a coworker recently:
Me: Hey, find /1st_floor -name "Scott."
Coworker: cd /1st_floor/breakroom; ls | grep coffee.
For this reason, it often seems like UNIX sysadmins are speaking another language.

Kernels

A *kernel* is the very heart of an operating system. It communicates instructions to the hardware and schedules and executes all the system commands. It manages all the daemons, devices, and system resources such as memory, swap space, and file systems. When you are running a shell program, such as the Bourne shell, you are using that program to communicate with the kernel.

The kernel is loaded during the boot process and must be running for the system to operate. The kernel-specific files can be found in the following directories:

- ■ **/kernel** This directory contains all the common kernel components that are needed for booting the system.

- ■ **/platform/***<platform-name>***/kernel** This directory contains the components that are needed for a *specific* type of platform. For example, on an Intel system, this directory is /platform/i86pc/kernel.

- ■ **/platform/***<hardware-class-name>***/kernel** This directory contains the kernel components specific to this hardware class.

- ■ **/usr/kernel** This directory contains kernel components common to all platforms within a particular instruction set.

on the

ⓙob

On occasion, you might have to reconfigure the parameters of a Solaris kernel to tweak it for optimal performance—the installation of a database application, for example. Make sure that you have read the instructions carefully and tested the changes on a test system before you do it on a mission-critical system! Without a bootable kernel, you don't have a bootable system, which could get you booted out the door.

Operating Systems

An *operating system* is a set of programs that manage all system operations and provide a means of communication between the user and the resources available to that user. An operating system consists of the kernel and the shell.

This chapter already defined the kernel and the shell. To fully understand operating systems, it is also essential that you understand hardware, which is discussed in later chapters.

exam

ⓦatch

The definitions of a shell and an operating system are similar. Both are used to communicate instructions, but remember that a shell is a component of an operating system.

Sun Microsystems refers to Solaris 9 as an operating environment. What's the difference between an operating environment and an operating system? Consider the analogy that both are like a shelter in which you live. An operating system provides you with the bare essentials. It's like a tent that contains food, a sleeping bag, and a T-1 connection to the Internet. If you're talking bare essentials, you could probably get by without the sleeping bag. In contrast, an operating environment is like a house with running water, electricity, home entertainment system, walk-in meat locker, hot tub, and so on. An operating environment includes all the bells and whistles that make running the system easier and more fun. Solaris 9 is designed from the ground up as a server operating environment. You won't find games, cute sound effects, or 3-D wallpapers included with the installation. However, it does have some very handy administrative applications and features, such as these:

- **IPv6 compatibility** The latest version of Internet Protocol allows for better security and increased available addresses.
- **Solaris smart card** This allows a sysadmin to add more security by requiring users to be validated with a personal ID card.

- **PDA synchronization**   Using this feature, users can transfer contact, calendar, and mail data between their Solaris 9 system and their personal digital assistants (PDAs).

- **GNU tools**   Perl, Apache, bash, and a few other GNU free popular utilities are now included with Solaris 9.

- **X Server**   This feature has been upgraded to allow for better mobility and ease of use, compatibility with EnergyStar, better power management, and web-based access.

These are just some of the features of the Solaris 9 operating environment that make it an industry standout.

on the **job**

Sun Microsystems announced it would drop the CDE and OpenWindows GUIs in favor of GNOME 2 in Solaris 9, but it may not be ready in time for the Solaris 9 release. Although these changes might affect how users access their workstations, you shouldn't get bogged down trying to learn how to use one kind of GUI over another. Your worth as a sysadmin will be measured at the command line, not among icons.

CERTIFICATION OBJECTIVE 1.02

Defining the Effects of Various man Command Options in Viewing Online Manual Pages

Without a doubt, no matter how far your journey into Solaris takes you, the beacon that you can depend on is the man command.

Short for *manual,* the man command is the way you access information about the commands and configuration files on your system. It's not a difficult command to learn or use.

The syntax of the man command is

```
man < command_name>
```

Let's look at how to use the command to get information on another helpful command, the ls command.

Using the man Command

1. Log in to the system:

```
[voyager: gibbst]$ telnet enterprise
Trying 192.168.0.2...
Connected to enterprise.
Escape character is '^]'.
SunOS 5.9
login:gibbst
password: **********
Last login: Tue Apr  8 11:44:12 from :0
Sun Microsystems Inc.    SunOS 5.9
Welcome to enterprise.timgibbs.net
[enterprise: gibbst] %
```

2. Use the man command to get information about the ls command:

```
[enterprise: gibbst] % man ls
Reformatting page.  Please Wait... done

User Commands                                                   ls(1)

NAME
ls - list contents of directory

SYNOPSIS
/usr/bin/ls [ -aAbcCdfFgilLmnopqrRstux1 ]  [ file ... ]

/usr/xpg4/bin/ls [ -aAbcCdfFgilLmnopqrRstux1 ]  [ file ... ]

DESCRIPTION
For each file that is a directory, ls lists the contents  of
the  directory;  for  each file that is an ordinary file, ls
repeats its name and any other  information  requested.  The
output is sorted alphabetically by default. When no argument
is given, the current  directory  is  listed.  When  several
arguments   are   given,   the  arguments  are  first  sorted
appropriately, but file arguments appear before  directories
and their contents.
--More--(10%)
```

The output of the man command is shown one screen at a time; the preceding excerpt shows the contents of the first screen. As you can see, the man command shows you a brief description of the command, its syntax, and more detailed information on its use. The man command also displays the revision history of the command and, in most cases, its author.

Man pages are marked with either nroff tags or Standard Generalized Markup Language (SGML). Both of these methods are used to mark a document with tags to describe how to read the text. For now, let's just say that they are similar to HTML, used to tell a web browser how to display a web page. That's why when you start the man command, it says, "Reformatting page. Please Wait…done" before displaying the page. The command reads the document's tags to display it on your screen correctly. The man pages are usually kept in /usr/share/man. The man pages using SGML tags are found in /usr/share/man/sman*; the man pages using nroff tags are kept in /usr/share/man/man*. The directories are searched in the order specified in the /usr/share/man/man.cf file.

The man command also includes some handy options you can use:

```
-k - The keyword switch
```

You use the *-k* switch to find information using a keyword search. The syntax for using this option is

```
man -k <keyword>
```

For example, say you wanted to find information on viewing documents in the PDF format. You would type

```
man -k PDF
```

Then the man command displays all the commands that deal with PDF documents. Actually, it displays all the commands that have *PDF* in their man pages. Here's another example:

```
-M - The path command
```

Use this option if you want the man command to search for a command in a directory not specified in the /usr/share/man/man.cf file. The syntax for using this option is

```
man -M <path_name>
```

For example, let's say you've loaded an application that has installed its man pages into a directory not specified by the MANPATH variable or in the /usr/share/man/man.cf file, but into the /opt/app/man directory. To view information on a command from the man pages in that directory, type the following:

```
man -M /opt/app/man <command_name>
```

This command forces the man command to look only in the named path for the man page on that command.

With the "all" option

```
-a
```

the *-a* option shows you all the man pages that match the name specified. The syntax is

```
man -a <command_name>
```

The man pages will be searched in the order in which they are specified in the MANPATH variable or as specified in the /usr/share/man/man.cf file. For example, if you type

```
man -a passwd
```

you will be able to scroll through first the man page for the passwd command, and then the man page for the passwd file.

To search for files, use the *-f* option.

```
-f
```

The *-f* option gives you a brief summary of man pages that fit the name of the file you specify. The syntax is

```
man -f <file_name>
```

For example, let's say you want to see which man pages exist for the passwd command. You would type

```
man -f passwd
```

and you would see the following:

```
passwd          passwd (1)      - change login password and password attributes
passwd          passwd (4)      - password file
```

This output tells you that there is not only a passwd command but a man page on the passwd configuration file as well.

To do a section search, use

```
-s <section number>
```

Now that you know that there's more than one man page on passwd, how do you display the one you want? Commands sometimes have more than one version of a man page. These different versions are separated into sections. As you've seen, there are two versions of a man page for passwd. By default, the man command displays the man page on the passwd command, not the man page on the /etc/passwd configuration file. The *-s* option allows you to specify a section of the available man pages for the specified command, for example,

```
man -s 4 passwd
```

This command displays the man page that deals with the passwd file, not the command. You saw that the passwd file was in the (4) section of the manual when we used the *-f* option.

FROM THE CLASSROOM

UNIX Isn't Always UNIX

I have had the opportunity to work with a wide variety of UNIX operating systems in my career. The variety of UNIX flavors out there can be confusing, but they share many similarities. I often hear fellow UNIX sysadmins use the phrase, "UNIX is UNIX," meaning that if you know one kind, you know them all. In some ways that's true, but for the most part, it's not. Every brand of UNIX has its own unique way of doing things. Solaris is no different.

To prepare for these exams, make sure you use the man command on a Solaris system often—even on simple, often-used commands.

A switch or option that performs one task on one kind of UNIX might not perform the same task on another. The man pages are like the hidden history of UNIX. Many of them are virtually the same as they were when they were first added to a UNIX server. However, they are updated to reflect any changes and pertain to the version of UNIX on which they've been installed. By browsing through man pages on a Solaris system, you'll be able to see all the available options for the commands on that system.

—Randy Cook, SCSA

CERTIFICATION SUMMARY

This chapter covered the basic terminology you'll need to get started with the material in the rest of the book. It's important that you completely understand the terms before moving on to the next chapter. You also learned about one of the most helpful tools you'll ever need in your career as a sysadmin: the man command. The man command is one of the tools you should use regularly to prepare for these exams.

✓ TWO-MINUTE DRILL

Defining System Administration Terms

❑ A daemon is a process that waits and listens for a request. The lpsched daemon waits for print requests and sends them to the correct printer.

❑ A shell is the program used to communicate your commands or the commands of an application or script to the kernel. Three basic shells are installed with Solaris 9: Bourne, Korn, and C.

❑ A file system is a collection of files and directories organized in a hierarchical structure.

❑ A kernel is the master program that communicates the requests of applications to the system hardware. It also manages all devices, memory, and processes.

❑ The operating system is a set of programs that govern all operations and acts as a means for the user to communicate instructions to system resources.

Defining the Effects of Various man Command Options in Viewing Online Manual Pages

❑ The man command provides several options to allow for specialized searching and displaying of the online manuals provided with Solaris.

❑ The *-k* switch is used for searching for keywords.

❑ The *-M* switch allows you specify a different path to a man page.

❑ The *-a* switch allows you to view all the available pages on a command.

❑ The *-f* option allows you to search and view brief summaries.

❑ The *-s* option allows you to view specified sections of available man pages for a command.

SELF TEST

The following questions will help you measure your understanding of the material presented in this chapter. Read all the choices carefully because there might be more than one correct answer. Choose all correct answers for each question.

Defining System Administration Terms

1. You've run the command ps *-ef.* Which of the following is an example of a daemon?

   A. /etc/hosts

   B. /usr/dt/bin/dtscreen -mode pyro

   C. /sbin/sh

   D. /usr/lib/nfs/lockd

2. A new user logs in to a system and sees a dollar sign ($) at the command prompt. Which shell is this user using?

   A. The Money shell

   B. The C shell

   C. The Korn shell

   D. The Bourne shell

3. Where did the C shell get its name?

   A. It's short for *Complete shell.*

   B. It's short for *Complicated shell.*

   C. Its syntax is based on the C programming language.

   D. It doesn't stand for anything.

4. What is the correct way for a user to change his or her shell from the following choices?

   A. Use the passwd -shell *<username>* command.

   B. Use the passwd -e *<username>* command.

   C. A user can't change his or her shell.

   D. Change the SHELL variable.

5. Which of the following is an example of a file's name?

   A. /etc/default

   B. /etc/hosts

   C. hosts

   D. /usr/man/man.cf

6. Which statement is true about a kernel?

   A. Once Solaris is installed, it's not required.

   B. It's a good idea to delete it occasionally to make sure it doesn't get too big.

   C. It is loaded during the booting of the system.

   D. It gets its name from the fact that, like a military officer, it's in charge of everything.

Defining the Effects of Various man Command Options in Viewing Online Manual Pages

7. The man command can be used to search for specific keywords. Which command would search for the keyword *login*?

   A. man login

   B. man *-a* login

   C. man *-k* login

   D. man *-s* login

8. The man command can be used to display all the available man pages on a command. Which of the following commands displays all the man pages on the name *passwd*?

   A. man *-all* passwd

   B. man I grep passwd

   C. man *-a* passwrd

   D. man *-a* passwd

LAB QUESTION

Solaris has a way or three to do just about anything. But what if you are trying to perform a particular action and don't know which command to use? For example, how would you find out which command to use to display the name of the system into which you're logged? How would you use the man command to help you find the command you need?

SELF TEST ANSWERS

Defining System Administration Terms

1. ☑ **D.** This is one of the daemons used to provide NFS service. Daemons are often recognized by having the letter *d* at the end.

   ☒ **A** is incorrect because this is the host file on the system, which you probably wouldn't see if you ran the ps *-ef* command. **B** indicates that the screen saver is running on the system—that really cool fireworks one. **C** indicates that the Bourne shell is running.

2. ☑ **C or D.** Although the user is new, the default system shell can be whatever the sysadmin set it to when the user account was created. Out of the box, the Bourne shell is the default system shell.

   ☒ **B** is incorrect because the C shell uses a percent sign (%) at the user prompt. **A** is incorrect because, as of now, there is no UNIX shell called the Money shell.

3. ☑ **C.** The wizards at Berkeley wanted a shell that would work like programming in C, so they made one.

   ☒ **B and A** are incorrect because the C shell is neither complete nor complicated. **D** is also incorrect.

4. ☑ **D.** The correct way for a user to change his or her shell is by changing the SHELL variable in the user's .profile.

   ☒ **A** is incorrect because there is no *-shell* option with the passwd command and a user won't have access to the passwd command. Same for **B**; although there is an *-e* option, only the root user has access to the passwd command. **C** is also incorrect.

5. ☑ **B.** This answer describes the complete pathname of a file, which is how UNIX names files.

   ☒ **A** is incorrect because it describes the location of a directory. **C** is incorrect because it could be a directory or a filename. **D** could be correct if you moved or copied the man.cf file to this location, but the default location of the man.cf file is /usr/share/man/man.cf.

6. ☑ **C.** A kernel is loaded during the booting of the system.

   ☒ **A and B** are incorrect because the kernel is what keeps the system running. **D** is incorrect because the name *kernel* has nothing to do with the military rank of colonel. Besides, everybody knows it's sergeants that really run things.

Defining the Effects of Various man Command Options in Viewing Online Manual Pages

7. ☑ **C.** This displays the man pages that have the keyword login in their description.
☒ **A** is incorrect because it displays the man page for login. **B** is incorrect because the *-a* option displays all pages upon login. **D** is incorrect because the *-s* option is used to display sections.

8. ☑ **D.** This command displays all the man page manuals that cover the passwd command, one after another.
☒ **A** is incorrect because there is no *-all* option. **B** is incorrect because it doesn't follow the man command syntax. **C** is incorrect because "passwd" is misspelled.

LAB ANSWER

1. Use the man command to search for a keyword:

```
# man -k name
```

Did it show you the command you're looking for? Possibly, but it's three or four screens of commands. How can you narrow your search? You can't use more than one keyword. Let's try another keyword. Because you're trying to determine the host's name, or hostname, try using that as a keyword.

2. Narrowing the search:

```
# man -k hostname
```

Is that a more manageable list? It's considerably smaller than the first one. The following command

```
check-hostname  check-hostname (1m) - check if sendmail
```

can determine the system's fully qualified hostname:

```
gethostname     gethostname (3c)    - get or set name of current host
gethostname     gethostname (3xnet) - get name of current host
hostname        hostname (1)    - set or print name of current host system
sethostname     gethostname (3c)    - get or set name of current host
```

In addition, you can see that one of the choices is a command called hostname. What were the odds? Now let's see how the hostname command works before you run it.

3. Investigate a command:

```
# man hostname
```

You can see from the output of the command that just by typing the hostname command, you will see the name of the system displayed. It's a good thing that you checked it out first, because the hostname command can also be used to change the hostname of the system.

This is an example of using the man command to help jog your memory or to research your options among all the available commands on a system. Naturally, you're unlikely to have root access to a system and not know its hostname or how to find it. This was just a simple exercise to demonstrate the use of the keyword search capabilities of the man command.

Solaris™
SUN® CERTIFIED SYSTEM ADMINISTRATOR

2

Administering the Boot PROM

T his chapter discusses Sun's unique OpenBoot software. *OpenBoot* is firmware that controls the boot process of a Sun workstation and provides useful diagnostic capabilities. The basic references for OpenBoot are the Sun manuals *OpenBoot 2.x Command Reference Manual* and *OpenBoot 3.x Command Reference Manual.* You can find these in the AnswerBook2 Library under "OpenBoot Collection."

OpenBoot provides literally hundreds of commands, and understanding all of them would be a difficult task. Fortunately, knowing only a few commands suffices for day-to-day use. Examples of these are the commands related to setting breakpoints and displaying Sparc registers.

Introduction to OpenBoot

If you come from an IBM Personal Computer (PC) background, OpenBoot is similar to PC BIOS. OpenBoot provides built-in commands and a limited programming environment that uses the Forth language.

"The OpenBoot firmware executes immediately after you turn on your system," and its purpose is to

- Test and initialize the hardware.
- Determine the configuration of the hardware.
- Boot the operating system from disk or network.
- Provide interactive debugging for testing hardware and software.

Because OpenBoot is firmware, it goes through a release cycle, just like software programs. The samples for this chapter were prepared using OpenBoot 2.9 on a Sun IPX and OpenBoot 3.19 on a Sun Ultra 5.

exam
ⓦatch
On the exam and in Sun documentation, you might sometimes see the acronym NVRAM, which stands for nonvolatile random access memory and is often used instead of OpenBoot. NVRAM actually refers to the chip on which OpenBoot system configuration variables are stored.

A note here could help clarify the examples in this chapter. OpenBoot is independent of the Solaris operating environment; output normally goes to the system console. The monitor is under the control of OpenBoot rather than the operating system because there might not be any operating system running yet.

There is no way to use a print screen utility to copy the output of OpenBoot; however, OpenBoot can also run from an attached ASCII terminal or a PC terminal emulator. The examples in this chapter were captured using this method.

Use of a terminal rather than a dedicated graphics monitor is common in production Sun environments. This configuration is the norm for environments such as large Internet service providers (ISPs) in which many Sun systems (for example, Netras) are mounted in racks. To set up such an environment, attach a terminal (or a PC using terminal emulation software such as HyperTerminal) to the Sun serial port using a null modem cable. Next, disconnect the Sun keyboard. Upon reboot, the machine will detect the absence of the regular keyboard and switch to the serial port. The serial communications characteristics are normally 9600 bits per second, 8 data bits, no parity, 1 stop bit (all of which is abbreviated 9600-8-N-1). You might need to press ENTER to let OpenBoot detect the terminal's presence.

exam
Ⓦatch

If you are running Solaris on an Intel processor to teach yourself Solaris, you will be at a disadvantage for this part of the examination. I strongly urge you to track down someone who will let you play around with OpenBoot for an hour or two, just to let this chapter's contents gel in your mind.

FROM THE CLASSROOM

Buying Your Own Sun Workstation

Some readers will be blessed with their own Sun workstations courtesy of their employers and will be free to play around and make mistakes on a segregated system that does not affect anyone else in their companies. But for many readers, access to a Sun system will be limited, in particular from the standpoint of issuing OpenBoot commands. Even though much of the Solaris operating environment can be learned on an Intel-based system, you really need access to a Sun workstation to become fully familiar with Solaris.

Fortunately, the prices of used Sun workstations have fallen in recent years, and a reasonable configuration should be available for under $500 (U.S. currency); careful shopping will probably get you an even lower price. There are several sources for Sun workstations:

- You might be successful in scrounging one for free if you are patient, but don't rely on this option. However, try to identify companies that are Sun users, and see if they are discarding any old servers. You could get lucky.

■ There is a Sun workstation section on eBay, the online auction site (www.ebay.com). This approach is probably the cheapest for most people. Be patient; avoid spending more money than you should by being drawn into a bidding war. Note that Sun itself sells some refurbished equipment on eBay as of early 2001. Watching the auction action for a few weeks will be useful.

■ The misc.forsale.computers.workstation newsgroup lists many UNIX workstations, including Sun machines. Expect to pay a little more than at eBay; however, you could obtain a better warranty or return policy in this newsgroup than on eBay. Watch the newsgroup for two or three weeks to get a flavor for prices, deals, and so forth.

■ The next step up is to locate a reseller of Sun equipment. Several of these exist, some of which are regular sellers on eBay or the newsgroup cited in the preceding bullet. Prices will be higher, and the $500 workable configuration could exceed $500. However, there are usually limited guarantees and some technical support, so this might be the best choice for some readers. A list of Sun resellers is available at the www.sunhelp.org web site; this is an excellent resource in any case.

■ Finally, Sun itself has been creating attractively priced packages, which have dropped the cost of a new Sun workstation below $2000. If you can afford this price, it could well be worth the investment. Watch the Sun web site for specials.

One very important factor to consider when you're shopping is the underlying architecture of the workstation. The Solaris 9 operating environment will not run on all Sun workstations! Before spending your own money, review the "Supported Sun Hardware" section in *The Solaris 9 4/01 Sun Hardware Platform Guide*. This section lists Sun workstations and servers that are supported under Solaris 8.

More recent Sun workstations work with PC monitors; older ones do not.

In general, being patient and getting a feel for the going price by watching these sources for a few weeks will help you save money and, at the very least, help avoid overpaying.

—Hank Murphy

Using OpenBoot PROM Commands

OpenBoot commands can be entered directly from only two sources. The first is the system console, which is the normal case. The second is from a serial terminal attached to the TTYA or TTYB port on a Sparc workstation. This situation is often seen when Sparc servers are run in *headless mode*—in other words, with no display or keyboard attached. We assume the first case for the examples in this chapter. (OpenBoot commands may also be entered indirectly with the Solaris EEPROM command.)

To get into OpenBoot mode on a running system, you must press STOP-A. (The STOP key is located in a set of ten keys at the far left of a Sun keyboard.) Alternatively, the Sparc server starts running in OpenBoot mode when it is first powered on. You can also enter OpenBoot mode by halting Solaris with the init command. OpenBoot will also be entered if the system hardware detects an error and causes a Watchdog Reset. Let's hope you don't come across this situation!

Before using STOP-A or the init command to enter OpenBoot, make sure no users are logged in to the system. This point is very important. If the Sun system is operating as a server and you interrupt users by executing these commands, you could suddenly have a lot of people angry at you!

If you are using a serial terminal in a headless configuration, use BREAK (CTRL-], then "send break" if connected through a telnet session) to enter OpenBoot instead of STOP-A.

The initial output of OpenBoot is a banner that describes the OpenBoot version and some details of the hardware on which it is running. Some form of logo bitmap is also displayed on the console. The type of Sparc processor, OpenBoot version, memory size, Ethernet address, and other configuration information is also displayed at this point. You can show this display again at any time when in the OpenBoot OK prompt using the banner command. Depending on the OpenBoot environment options set on the machine, the system might continue booting automatically (like a typical PC), or it could stop and wait for commands. In the latter case, the screen displays the messages shown here:

```
Type b (boot), c (continue), or n (new command mode)
>n
Type  help  for more information
ok
```

There is a little history behind the *b* and *n* options shown in the code. Early Sun workstations (before the Sun SPARCstation 1) did not include OpenBoot; instead, they had a very limited boot monitor. The *b* and *c* options operate in this mode, called *Restricted Monitor mode.* The *n* option will select full OpenBoot mode, also called *Forth Monitor mode,* which we assume for the rest of this chapter. After typing **n**, you will see the prompt change from >> to ok.

It's common to refer to this prompt as the *OK prompt* in much the same way as you refer to the C prompt on a PC.

Unlike a PC's BIOS, if you forget a command, OpenBoot provides help that often jogs your memory enough to remember it. Help is offered on two levels. The first, which you invoke by typing **help** and pressing ENTER at the OK prompt, provides a list of the categories of commands for which help is available. A typical OpenBoot help command output in shown here:

```
ok help
Enter 'help command-name' or 'help category-name' for more help
Use ONLY the first word of a category description) Examples:
help select   -or-   help line
     Main categories are:File download and boot
Resume execution
Diag (diagnostic routines)
Select I/O devices
System and boot configuration parameters
Line editor
Tools:(memory,numbers,new commands,loops)
Assembly debugging:(breakpoints,registers,disassembly,symbolic)
>-prompt
Power on reset
Floppy eject
Sync (synchronize disk data)
```

This method is useful when you are first learning OpenBoot; it helps you at least remember the commands. To get further information, enter the help command followed by the category name, as shown next. (The diag category covers various hardware testing options and is not one of the examination objectives. However, these options are useful in real life.)

```
ok help diag
Category: Diag (diagnostic routines)
test   device-specifier ( -- ) run selftest method for specified
device
Examples:
test /memory        - test memory
test /sbus/le       - test net
test net            - test net (device-specifier is an alias)
test floppy         - test floppy disk drive
watch-clock         (--)      show ticks of real-time clock
probe-scsi          (--)      show attached SCSI devices
```

For further information on help, refer to the OpenBoot manuals.

CERTIFICATION OBJECTIVE 2.02

Knowing the Combination of Actions Required to Interrupt a Nonresponsive System

Sometimes, despite the best system administration practices, you just have to reboot the system to clear up some error condition. This might be due to any number of circumstances beyond your control, such as memory leaks in heavily used applications. However, for whatever reason, to serve as a system administrator and to pass the Sun Solaris Certified Systems Administrator examination, you have to know the procedures related to booting and rebooting the system.

on the job

Rebooting a production server is not a decision to make lightly or hastily. Because many users or customers can be logged in to the system at the same time, an interruption in service can have expensive consequences. For servers used by highly paid professionals—for example, doctors—the cost of 15 minutes' delay at the hourly pay rate of 100 users could exceed the cost of the server. For e-commerce applications, the sales in a 15-minute period can also exceed the cost of the hardware being rebooted. Furthermore, for high-dollar-rate stock or currency trading systems, downtime costs can run in the millions of dollars per hour.

Before using the techniques in this chapter, be sure the Sun system is not actually still working. Check all evidence of activity, such as these:

1. Can users still log in?
2. Can users who are already logged in issue commands and get output?
3. Can you connect to the system with telnet, rlogin, or cu?
4. Can you ping the system?
5. For an e-commerce server, is the server web page still functioning?

You might be able to think of other details to check at your installation. The key point is to verify that the system in question is truly not operational before entering OpenBoot. Oh yes—check for dumb things like the keyboard being unplugged, too!

Unlike using PC-based systems, rebooting a Sun system involves more than locating the CTRL, ALT, and DELETE keys or the reset switch. Solaris provides a facility to save at least some of the work in process on the machine at the time of the reboot, and it's usually important to use this facility on production machines.

Several keyboard commands are available in this situation (aborting a hung system), as shown in Table 2-1. Of these, STOP-A and the go and sync commands are most frequently used.

TABLE 2-1	Action	Effect
OpenBoot Keyboard Commands	STOP-A	Aborts
	STOP	Bypasses POST
	STOP-D	Enters diagnostic mode (affected by diag-switch? setting)
	STOP-N	Resets NVRAM contents to their default values
	go	Commands to resume
	sync	Commands to synchronize disk data

Using the STOP-A Keyboard Combination

Sun keyboards have a key labeled STOP on the left side of the keyboard. This key is used much like a control (CTRL) key: in other words, in combination with other keys to obtain some desired altered action. When you encounter a phrase like STOP-N, it means to press and hold the STOP key, then the N key, and then release both.

Following the STOP-A command, your system console monitor should display the OK prompt.

When you are faced with a hung system, if you cannot get any response to normal Solaris commands, press STOP-A to revert to OpenBoot. At that point, it is advisable to attempt to save whatever data has not yet been written to disk. The command to accomplish this task is sync. sync passes control back to Solaris, which then attempts to write out any unwritten data blocks to disk. Solaris then attempts to make a core file (a dump for storage). If you do not want to create a core file, use STOP-A again after you see the message "Syncing File Systems...Done." This command interrupts the core file processing. At that point, you can boot again, correct any external hardware problems, or take whatever other action is appropriate based on what you know about the error situation.

You also might want to resume execution. For example, if your diagnosis determines that the problem was external to the Sun system (for example, if the network adapter was being flooded with messages due to malfunctioning network hardware outside the Sun system), it might be better to resume execution rather than rebooting. In such a case, you can use the go command to resume execution. Note that this practice is usually not recommended, because a reboot is typically safer. In general, using the Solaris shutdown and reboot commands is the preferred way to handle this situation.

With this information about interrupting a nonresponsive system, let's look at the following scenarios and their solutions.

SCENARIO & SOLUTION

Someone asks you where the STOP key is. What do you do?	Point to the left end of the keyboard.
Your mind has gone blank and you can't remember a command name. What do you do?	Type **help**.

SCENARIO & SOLUTION

A server appears to be hung. How do you attempt to recover, assuming no obvious cause is known?	First, press STOP-A to get into OpenBoot. Next, issue the sync command. Finally, reboot.
Just as you get ready to reboot following a hung system, someone discovers that the electricians have accidentally drilled through a network cable. Once that is fixed, how do you try to continue without the reboot?	Use the go command.

CERTIFICATION OBJECTIVE 2.03

Using Command Strings to Manipulate Custom Device Aliases

Sun systems often involve more hardware units than a typical PC-based server. To support this extra hardware, Sun hardware and OpenBoot provide a complicated naming system that is arcane, even to many system administrators. Because many commands, such as the boot command, permit multiple target devices, the need arises to be able to create simpler device names that are easier to remember. There are two ways to do this, depending on the version of OpenBoot you are using. From OpenBoot version 2.6 and later, the nvalias and nvunalias commands allow you to easily create your own device names. Older versions supported the devalias command. We'll cover both commands because OpenBoot still supports the older command.

TABLE 2-2	Command	Purpose
Some Additional OpenBoot Commands	.attributes	Lists device attributes.
	.properties	Lists device information (newer version of .attributes).
	cd	Changes directory. OpenBoot organizes its internal information, much like a simple file structure, and the cd command navigates this.

TABLE 2-2	Command	Purpose
Some Additional OpenBoot Commands *(continued)*	printenv	Displays environment variables.
	setenv	Assigns values to environment variables.
	show-disks	Lists disk devices on the system.

We will use several commands that are not part of the exam objectives. These are listed in Table 2-2, and all are issued from the OpenBoot OK prompt.

You might be wondering what an *environment variable* is. Basically, it is a value that controls OpenBoot's processing. For readers with a PC background, environment variables are something like BIOS option settings, but they are created as freeform text.

e x a m
ⓦa t c h

You might see the term configuration variable **used instead of environment variable. These are synonymous terms in the context of OpenBoot questions.**

The format of the setenv command, used to place values in environment variables, is

```
setenv environment_variable_name value
```

environment_variable_name is the environment variable you want to change, and *value* represents the desired new value. Note that the *environment_variable_name* is followed by a question mark. Here's an example of the setenv command:

```
setenv auto-boot? false
```

The auto-boot environment variable determines whether the OpenBoot PROM automatically boots up Solaris (or other operating system). If set to false, the variable causes OpenBoot to drop to the OK prompt after powering on rather than automatically starting Solaris. Another useful environment variable, boot-device, indicates which device will be used to boot the system. The output of a printenv command is shown next.

```
ok printenv
Variable Name          Value                 Default Value

tpe-link-test?         true                  true
scsi-initiator-id      7                     7
keyboard-click?        false                 false
keymap
ttyb-rts-dtr-off       false                 false
ttyb-ignore-cd         true                  true
ttya-rts-dtr-off       false                 false
ttya-ignore-cd         false                 true
```

```
ttyb-mode                9600,8,n,1,-            9600,8,n,1,-
ttya-mode                9600,8,n,1,-            9600,8,n,1,-
pcia-probe-list          1,2,3,4                 1,2,3,4
pcib-probe-list          1,2,3                   1,2,3
mfg-mode                 off                     off
diag-level               max                     max
#power-cycles            93
system-board-serial#
system-board-date
fcode-debug?             false                   false
output-device            screen:r1024x768x60     screen
input-device             keyboard                keyboard
load-base                16384                   16384
boot-command             boot                    boot
auto-boot?               true                    true
watchdog-reboot?         false                   false
diag-file
diag-device              net                     net
boot-file
boot-device              disk net                disk net
local-mac-address?       false                   false
ansi-terminal?           true                    true
screen-#columns          80                      80
screen-#rows             34                      34
silent-mode?             false                   false
use-nvramrc?             false                   false
nvramrc                  devalias pgx24 /pci@1f,0 ...
security-mode            none
security-password
security-#badlogins      0
oem-logo
oem-logo?                false                   false
oem-banner
oem-banner?              false                   false
hardware-revision
last-hardware-update
diag-switch?             false                   false
ok
```

But what does this have to do with device aliases, and what is a device alias, anyway?

One of OpenBoot's unique functions is to build a map of all devices connected to the system during a boot cycle. This map is called a *device tree*. Its purpose is to describe all the elements of the Sun computer's configurations in terms of four elements: properties, methods, children, and parent. *Properties* are characteristics of the device, such as its address. *Methods* are essentially the commands you can issue that involve the device. *Self-test* is an example of a method. The *children* and *parent* elements describe the devices below the hardware unit and the unit above it.

The top of the device tree is the Sun Sparc or UltraSPARC processor itself. The next lower level in the device tree comprises the hardware devices, which are typically always present on the main board in a workstation: memory; built-in controllers for mouse/keyboard/serial ports/network controller; and the bus used to connect other devices (Sbus or PCI bus, depending on the Sun model).

The next lower level in the tree is usually a controller attached to the bus. This is typically SCSI for many Sun machines, although PCI became the preferred bus beginning around 1998. The bus could have multiple controllers. (On many Sun workstations, controllers are built into the main board, so this explanation is not always true. However, from an architectural standpoint, the controllers behave as though they were independent of the main board.) The next lower level consists of the devices actually connected to the controllers: disks, tapes, high-speed network controllers, and so on.

An individual device description can have the following form (for Sbus Sparc systems):

```
/sbus@1f,0/esp@0,40000/sd@3,0:a
```

The pieces (nodes) of this description are as follows:

/sbus@1f,0	The Sbus address
/esp@0,40000	The external controller address
/sd@3,0:a	The unit attached to the controller

Note that labels such as sd, sd0, sd1, and so forth are used to specify SCSI disks in OpenBoot. So the key point is that every hardware device in the Sparc architecture has an entry in the device tree. Furthermore, the description of that entry is long, so we have to be very careful when typing a line like this:

```
/sbus@1f,0/esp@0,40000/sd@3,0:a
```

Of course, there is a shortcut: device aliases. The nvalias command creates a custom device alias. Its syntax is

```
nvalias alias device
```

The new custom device alias is specified by the *alias* operand. The *device* operand specifies the device address that the new alias represents. For example,

```
nvalias seedyrom  /pci@1f,0/pci@1,1/ide@3/cdrom@2,0:f
```

This operand adds a new alias named *seedyrom* for the CD-ROM drive on an Ultra 5. Here's another example:

```
nvalias newdisk /sbus/esp@0,800000/sd@3,0
```

This operand adds an alias *newdisk* as SCSI address 3 on an IPX. To list all your device aliases, change to the /aliases node within OpenBoot and issue the .properties command (or .attributes if you are running the older OpenBoot 2.*x*). For example,

```
ok cd /aliases
ok .attributes
newdisk                    /sbus/esp@0,800000/sd@3,0
screen                     /sbus@1,f8000000/cgsix@3,0
ttyb                       /zs@1,f1000000:b
```

(The rest of the output is not shown.) In addition, the show-disks command displays some of this information.

Using the devalias Command

A command named devalias allows you to create a device alias, just as nvalias does. However, devalias creates a temporary alias (until the next reset), whereas nvalias creates a permanent alias. The devalias command can also be used to list all the aliases instead of the OpenBoot .attributes or .properties commands.

If you are running with OpenBoot 2.5 and earlier, however, devalias is the only command available. To create a permanent alias using devalias, you must create an OpenBoot command that is executed whenever OpenBoot is reset. The method provided for this action is the nvedit command. This method provides a very simple line editor that edits a command kept in NVRAM.

EXERCISE 2-1

Using the nvedit Command

This exercise displays the use of nvedit:

1. Enter the nvedit command. Depending on the system, it could respond with a line number (0 to start).

2. Key in your desired command and press ENTER at the end of each line.

3. Use CTRL-C to exit nvedit.

4. You must follow this procedure with the nvstore command to save the buffer you just entered.

To use this facility to set up a permanent device alias, key in a devalias command for the aliases you want to add while in nvedit. You must also set the configuration variable use-nvramrc? to true.

TABLE 2-3	Command	Function
Commands Used with nvedit	CTRL-B	Moves back one character
	CTRL-C	Exits the editor
	CTRL-F	Moves forward one character
	CTRL-K	Used at the end of a line to join it with the next line (deletes the carriage return)
	CTRL-L	Lifts the buffer
	CTRL-N	Moves to the next line
	CTRL-O	Inserts a new line
	CTRL-P	Moves to the preceding line
	DELETE	Deletes

Before using nvstore, you can also test the new command with the nvrun command. The nvedit commands are listed in Table 2-3.

In general, nvalias is much easier to use than nvedit. Just be aware that nvedit can be used to fulfill the same function.

The following scenarios and solutions summarize some of the points in this part of the chapter.

SCENARIO & SOLUTION

How do you find out the boot device on a Sun workstation?	Use the printenv command; look for the boot-device configuration variable.
How do you see the disk names known to OpenBoot?	Use the show-disk (preferred), .attributes, or .properties commands.
How do you change a configuration variable?	Use the setenv command.
You are adding a new disk. You want to verify that everything is OK before booting up Solaris 8. How can you prevent Solaris 8 from booting up on the next power-on cycle?	Set setenv AUTO-BOOT? to false.
How do you add a device alias permanently?	Use nvalias. (The devalias command is temporary.)
You inherit an old SparcStation. How do you find out which device aliases have been defined?	Use devalias with no operands to display the device aliases.

CERTIFICATION SUMMARY

This chapter presented an overview of the OpenBoot PROM monitor, which controls booting, hardware diagnostics, and related hardware elements. You learned how to enter OpenBoot from a running Solaris system using the STOP-A key combination. This chapter also covered some diagnostic and recovery techniques, such as the sync command. All of these could appear on the Sun Solaris Certified Systems Administrator examination.

Additionally, the chapter discussed the process of defining device aliases with the nvalias and devalias commands. To use these aliases, you also had to learn the concept of the OpenBoot device map, the idea behind environment variables, and the OpenBoot device addressing scheme.

TWO-MINUTE DRILL

Using OpenBoot PROM Commands

❑ OpenBoot provides a limited operating command environment for booting and hardware control.

❑ OpenBoot commands are entered at the OK prompt for hardware-related actions such as booting the system.

❑ OpenBoot is normally run from the Sun system console, but it can also be run from an ASCII terminal if the Sun keyboard is disconnected.

❑ OpenBoot has Restricted Monitor (*b, n,* and go commands) and Forth Monitor (OK prompt) modes.

❑ OpenBoot provides help for the general command syntax.

Knowing the Combination of Actions Required to Interrupt a Nonresponsive System

❑ Check several Solaris operating environment or application services before deciding that the system is nonresponsive.

❑ Try less drastic measures, such as telnet, rlogin, or cu, to investigate and fix the problem, if possible.

❑ Use STOP-A to get into OpenBoot while Solaris is running (BREAK if using an ASCII terminal).

❑ Use STOP-A to interrupt a hung system, and then use the sync command to save work by writing disk buffers before rebooting.

❑ Use the Solaris operating environment commands shutdown and reboot where possible, and reserve OpenBoot for more difficult situations.

Using Command Strings to Manipulate Custom Device Aliases

❑ The Sun hardware configuration is organized as a device tree, with the processor as the top node, followed by buses, onboard controllers, and devices.

❑ Device addresses are structured this way:

```
/sbus@1f,o/esp@0,40000/sd@3,0
```

❑ Navigate the device tree with cd and ls commands, and get information with the .attributes (OpenBoot 2.*x*) or .properties (OpenBoot 3.*x*) commands.

❑ OpenBoot's default operation is controlled by environment or configuration variables.

❑ The printenv and setenv commands display and alter configuration variables.

❑ The nvalias and nvunalias commands let you create your own device aliases.

❑ OpenBoot versions before 2.6 use nvedit and nvstore instead of nvalias and nvunalias.

❑ The printenv command with no operands displays all OpenBoot environment variables.

SELF TEST

The following questions will help you measure your understanding of the material presented in this chapter. Read all the choices carefully because there might be more than one correct answer. Choose all correct answers for each question.

Using OpenBoot PROM Commands

1. You are sitting at the console of a running Solaris 9 system displaying the OpenBoot OK prompt. Which of the following commands would help you determine the memory size of the machine?

   A. mem

   B. banner

   C. memsize

   D. printenv

2. You are sitting at the console of a running Solaris system displaying the OpenBoot OK prompt. You key in the following command:
   who
   and OpenBoot responds
   who?
   What is OpenBoot trying to tell you?

   A. It cannot recognize you because you have not logged in.

   B. You should use the whoami command.

   C. OpenBoot does not recognize the who command.

   D. No users are logged in.

Knowing the Combination of Actions Required to Interrupt a Nonresponsive System

3. You are sitting at the console of a running Solaris system, logged in as root. What would you do to bring up the OpenBoot prompt?

   A. Press STOP-A.

   B. Press STOP-N.

   C. Enter the command init s.

   D. Press CTRL-BREAK.

4. Which OpenBoot command synchronizes the file system after a system is aborted?

   A. halt

   B. sync

   C. fsck

   D. dev-sync

5. After using STOP-A to interrupt a hung system, which command should you execute next to save unwritten disk buffers?

   A. boot -s

   B. go

   C. sync

   D. reset

6. A Sun server is not responding to commands issued at the system console. Which of the following steps should you attempt before entering OpenBoot mode? (Choose two answers.)

   A. Attempt to connect to the hung server with telnet.

   B. Power off the server, and then power it on again to reboot.

   C. Attempt to boot from the Solaris 9 installation CD-ROM.

   D. Try to determine if any logged-in users can issue commands successfully.

Using Command Strings to Manipulate Custom Device Aliases

7. Which command(s) would you use to change the value of an OpenBoot configuration variable?

   A. banner

   B. setenv

   C. set-env

   D. set

8. Which command will create a permanent device alias?

   A. devalias

   B. nvalias

   C. nvedit

   D. nvstore

9. You are sitting at the console of a Sun workstation at the OK prompt. Which command would you use to determine which device was being used for booting?

A. probe-scsi

B. setenv boot-device

C. devalias

D. printenv

10. Consider the following full device path:

```
/sbus/esp@0,800000/sd@3,0
```

What does *sd* indicate?

A. Selected disk

B. System disk (boot disk)

C. Show-disks

D. SCSI disk

LAB QUESTION

This lab exercise departs slightly from the format used in most of the other chapters in the book. Because you might have limited access to a Sun system for use of OpenBoot, this exercise has two parts. The first is a general familiarization section. The first ten steps will familiarize you with OpenBoot operation and output. These are followed by three optional steps that you might or might not be permitted to do at your work site. From a running Sun workstation, perform the following:

1. Use STOP-A to get into OpenBoot. Observe the change in the screen for this and the following step.

2. Use the go command to return to Solaris.

3. Use STOP-A again. Type in the letter **n** and press ENTER to go to Forth Monitor mode.

4. Issue the help command from the OK prompt.

5. Issue help again with *boot* as the second operand.

6. Issue the printenv command.

7. Issue the devalias command.

8. Issue cd /aliases followed by the .attributes command. (*Note:* Depending on your version of OpenBoot, either this step or Step 9 could present you with an error message or not recognize the command. This is normal and can be ignored.)

9. Issue the .properties command.

10. Issue the show-disks command.

The next three steps are optional. You should ensure that the system administrator knows what you are doing before proceeding. To prevent possible problems, perform the following steps only if assistance is available from a knowledgeable system administrator.

1. Issue a setenv command, such as setenv auto-boot? true.

2. Use nvalias to create a device alias. Ensure that the name chosen is not already a custom device name.

3. Use devalias to create a custom device name.

For the second part of the lab exercise, assume that you are booting over the network. (This is usually done with the boot net command.) Your installation has three servers, named Larry, Moe, and Curly. You are working on Moe. You want to set things up so that an assistant with little knowledge can boot from one of the other two systems over the network. How do you set things up so that your assistant can boot from Larry or Curly without you being there during the test session?

SELF TEST ANSWERS

Using OpenBoot PROM Commands

1. ☑ B. This command displays the OpenBoot startup banner, which includes the memory size of the machine.

☑ A and C are incorrect because they are nonsense commands. D is a valid command, but memory size is not a configuration variable.

2. ☑ C. When you enter a command OpenBoot cannot recognize, it echoes back the command followed by a question mark.

☑ A is incorrect because who is not a recognized command, which is also the error with B. D is not applicable; OpenBoot has no knowledge of logged-in usernames.

Knowing the Combination of Actions Required to Interrupt a Nonresponsive system

3. ☑ A. This key combination halts the machine and puts you into either the Forth Monitor mode or the Restricted Monitor mode. You might still have to issue the n command, but the other choices are clearly wrong.

☑ B is incorrect because STOP-N resets the NVRAM contents to their default values, which is not what the question asked for. C is incorrect because the init command with the s operand takes you only to single-user mode in Solaris, not to OpenBoot. Finally, D is incorrect because BREAK is used only on serial terminals to get into OpenBoot, and the question says that you are at the system console.

4. ☑ B. This is the command to synchronize files after an abort.

☑ A is incorrect because the halt command is a Solaris command, not an OpenBoot command. C is incorrect for the same reasons. D is incorrect because dev-sync is not even an OpenBoot command.

5. ☑ C. This is the purpose of the sync command.

☑ A is incorrect because a reboot will not perform any processing of unsaved buffers. The go command in B is incorrect because it will resume running the Solaris system, probably still in a hung condition. Finally, D is incorrect because it would be equivalent to A, assuming the default setting for auto-boot?.

6. ☑   A and D. If the problem is localized to the system console, but normal Telnet connections and user commands still work, a reboot might not be necessary, or a reboot could be deferred to a less inconvenient time.

   ☑   B is incorrect because it will automatically reboot the server, depending on the setting of the auto-boot? configuration variable. C is incorrect because it involves entering OpenBoot, which the question asks you to avoid.

Using Command Strings to Manipulate Custom Device Aliases

7. ☑   B. The setenv command is used to change the value of an OpenBoot configuration variable.

   ☑   A is incorrect because it has nothing to do with configuration variables. C is incorrect because it attempts to confuse the issue by putting a dash in the name of the correct command. Just plain set, D, is used within Solaris to set environment variables, not OpenBoot.

8. ☑   B. nvalias creates a device alias kept in nonvolatile storage.

   ☑   A is almost right, but it doesn't create a permanent alias. C is used in older Suns (before OpenBoot version 2.6) as part of creating a device alias but doesn't do everything by itself. The same applies to D.

9. ☑   D. The printenv command displays all the current OpenBoot configuration variables, and the boot-device variable determines which device is used.

   ☑   A is incorrect because the probe-scsi command displays all the SCSI devices connected to the Sun system. However, if there are multiple disks, you cannot determine which of these is the default boot device from the probe-scsi output by itself. B is incorrect because the setenv command is used to change variables, not display them, and the syntax is wrong here because the new choice is missing anyway. This command actually received the response "Usage: setenv option-name value." C is incorrect because it lists the device aliases currently assigned in the system. However, this still does not tell you which of the aliases is used as the default boot unit.

10. ☑   D. sd stands for SCSI disk.

   ☑   A is not the right choice because disk selection, in this context, would be done with the cd command. B is incorrect because the boot command or boot-device configuration variable selects the boot device. C gives the name of an OpenBoot command, not a description of sd.

LAB ANSWER

First, this problem requires a simple command for the assistant to enter. This involves a device alias. There are two methods for creating device aliases. The first is the devalias command. The second is the nvalias command. Which is preferable?

A reasonable case could be made for each. However, because you need this only for the duration of the test session, your choice should be devalias. (Remember that devalias creates a temporary device alias, whereas nvalias creates a permanent alias.)

Let's say the device alias is for Larry. Therefore, you want to create a device alias named Larry, which you will have the assistant use in commands such as

```
ok boot larry
```

Now, what will Larry be a device alias for? To boot over the network, you key in

```
ok boot net
```

How do you make Larry into an alias for "net"?

First, find out which device aliases you already have. The devalias OpenBoot command with no parameters gives you this alias, along with a long list of other device aliases. Enter the following at the OK prompt:

```
devalias
```

Find the line that looks something like this:

```
net /pci@1f,0/pci@1,1/network@1,1
```

(*Note:* This is on an Ultra 5, and Sun systems using Sbus will appear differently. Simply look for the *net* identifier on the left side of the screen.) The /pci@1f,0/pci@1,1/network@1,1 part is the device path. To create your device alias, enter the following command:

```
devalias larry /pci@1f,0/pci@1,1/network@1,1
```

and press ENTER. Now see if it's there. Enter

```
devalias
```

Review the output. Do you see "larry"? Is the device path correct—in other words, is it the same as the entry for the alias "net"?

Now for the acid test. (*Note:* If your network has a boot server, make sure you can boot from it successfully before trying this step. You can use boot net to try this beforehand.) Now try to boot from your new alias. Enter

```
boot larry
```

You should see a line that says something like this:

```
Boot device: /pci@1f,0/pci@1,1/network@1,1   File and args:
```

You did not specify any arguments, so this is normal. At this point, the system should boot up from the network. If you do not have a network boot server, expect to see this message:

```
Timeout waiting for ARP/RARP packet
```

Use STOP-A to terminate the boot sequence in this case.
Now let's see what happens across a power-off reset sequence. Enter

```
reset
```

The console screen will go blank, followed by the OpenBoot banner. Use STOP-A to interrupt the boot sequence. You should see an OK prompt at this point. Enter

```
ok devalias
```

You will see a screen similar to what you have seen earlier. But what happened to "larry"? (That alias should be gone.) Remember, again, that devalias creates a temporary device alias—and that is what you just did. The reset command and power-on sequence got rid of it for you.

Solaris™

SUN® CERTIFIED SYSTEM ADMINISTRATOR

3

Installing the Solaris Operating Environment

CERTIFICATION OBJECTIVES

S ome of the most fundamental skills a systems administrator needs are related to installing and maintaining the system and associated software. Systems that are improperly installed and improperly patched will suffer from instability, which will result in long downtimes. Systems without the necessary software or with improperly configured software will not be useful to the user community.

The deeper your understanding of these topics, the more effective you can be. A system installation can be a confusing nightmare of installation options and configurations. An administrator with a solid understanding of the installation process can quickly and effectively get a system up and running. Installing software can be a very tedious and time-consuming process, especially if the software must be installed on multiple machines throughout the enterprise. An administrator who understands how software is handled in the Solaris operating environment will be able to make the process completely automatic, saving time and reducing mistakes.

This chapter deals with the three main areas of installing and maintaining a system: the initial operating system installation, additional software installation, and operating system patches. Because hands-on experience with the Solaris operating environment is essential to passing the Solaris certification exam, this chapter is one of the most important in this book.

CERTIFICATION OBJECTIVE 3.01

Installing the Solaris Operating Environment Software on a Networked Standalone System

This section deals with the information and processes necessary to install the Solaris operating environment. It covers the various versions of Solaris, the options for installing Solaris, and the hardware requirements. It also covers the function of software packages, clusters, and groups. Finally, it details preinstallation planning and the Solaris operating environment installation.

Versions of Solaris

Solaris comes in several different versions. These versions are based on the platform on which you intend to install, your geographic location, and the age of the hardware you need to support. All versions of Solaris contain the following disks:

- Solaris Installation CD-ROM
- Solaris Software CD-ROM 1 of 2
- Solaris Software CD-ROM 2 of 2
- Solaris Documentation CD-ROM and DVD

Platform Editions

Solaris supports two platforms: the Scalable Processor Architecture (Sparc) platform and the Intel/x86 platform. (Originally, Solaris 9 was not going to be available on the x86 platform, but due to user pressure, it will be released.) Both editions are available from Sun, generally for the cost of the media and shipping. This chapter deals almost exclusively with the Sparc platform. Both editions are built from the same source tree, so knowledge of one should impart knowledge of the other. Many people preparing for the Solaris certification exam find it useful to be able to load the Intel version on commodity hardware that they already have at home.

International Edition

Solaris is available in two "regional" versions: the English Edition and the International Edition. The International Edition contains a multilingual version of the Solaris Installation CD-ROM as well as a Solaris Languages CD-ROM, to support languages other than English. The International Edition also contains a two-CD set of Solaris documentation, one for European languages (English, French, German, Italian, Spanish, and Swedish), and one for Asian languages (Simplified and Traditional Chinese, Japanese, and Korean).

Hardware Releases

From time to time, generally about once a quarter, Sun Microsystems comes out with new hardware releases. These hardware releases are labeled *mm/yy,* such as

Solaris Hardware 01/01 for the hardware release from January 2001. These updated editions provide drivers for newly released hardware, as well as generally bundling more patches with the environment. The patches are not integrated into the release; they are separate to make it easier to maintain consistency and keep patching easy between systems running the same environment but different hardware releases.

Installation Options

Solaris provides five installation options. Each option has its advantages and disadvantages. Some of them provide easy graphical user interface (GUI)–driven installation for a single system. Others provide a way of automating the installation of large numbers of systems for rapid deployment. Some provide a completely automatic, hands-free installation of a single system.

Interactive Installation

The interactive installation is a GUI-driven option. It guides you through all the steps required for the installation of Solaris. It does not allow you to install any additional software, only that software that is part of Solaris. You can install any other software you want after the interactive installation is completed.

Solaris Web Start

Solaris Web Start provides the installation process with a Java-powered GUI. It guides you step by step through the installation of Solaris, starting with the Solaris Installation CD-ROM. It also allows you to install other packaged software (see "Software Packages, Clusters, and Groups," later in this chapter), some of which comes bundled with Solaris. The installation can use a local or a remote CD-ROM drive.

exam
Ⓦatch

To fully prepare for the certification exam, make sure you are comfortable with all installation options. The best way to do this is to install the Solaris operating environment several times using all the different options.

Network Installation

A Solaris network installation allows you to install a large number of systems without using a local CD/DVD. The Solaris software is copied onto a network-accessible installation server and then installed across the network to the local clients.

This method allows multiple machines to be built in parallel and removes the need to insert the CD/DVDs into each system.

Default JumpStart

The default JumpStart installation allows a new system (only) to be installed, completely "hands-off." When you boot the system with the JumpStart Software Disk 1 installed, JumpStart begins automatically and installs a default setup. Based on the model and disk size of the system, JumpStart determines the software components that need to be installed.

Custom JumpStart

The custom JumpStart installation is the most powerful installation option. By setting up a JumpStart server, the system administrator can define every aspect of the system installation and configuration: the file system layouts, the software components to be installed, the patches that are installed, other software that will be installed, and all the customization of the environment. You can define profiles based on the type of user that will be using the machine, the type of duty the machine will perform, the location of the machine, or any other criteria.

on the
()ob   *Most likely, you will be concerned with only the Web Start and custom JumpStart options. Web Start is fine for a single machine or a small number of machines. In an enterprise environment, you will find that a custom JumpStart setup will save you a lot of time and headaches.*

Hardware Requirements

There are relatively few hardware requirements for installing a Solaris-based system. Basically, you need a computer from the supported platforms, disk space, memory, and either a CD/DVD drive or access to a network that includes an installation server.

Platforms

As mentioned, Solaris is supported on either the Sparc platform or the Intel/x86 platform. Intel/x86 systems are available from literally hundreds of vendors and run processors made by Intel, Advanced Micro Devices (AMD), and VIA Technologies

(Cyrix). Sparc systems are also available from many vendors, with Sun being the largest. You can also visit www.sparc.com for a list of other manufacturers.

Disk Space

A Solaris installation could require anywhere from around 600 megabytes (MB) of disk space (for a core workstation) to around 2.7 gigabytes (GB) of disk space (for the entire distribution on a server). Most servers require around 2GB of disk space. Other software that you might choose to install will obviously increase the required disk space, as shown in Table 3-1.

Memory

The minimum amount of memory required to install and run Solaris is 96MB. This is, however, the minimum to support the system. Performance will be much improved if you install at least 128MB, and preferably 256MB. A large server that supports multiple users will require even more memory.

Solaris will support up to 4 petabytes of memory, although the largest available system currently supports only 192GB of memory.

Other Hardware

The only other hardware that is strictly required to install Solaris is either a locally attached CD-ROM or DVD drive or a supported network interface card (NIC). Due to the amount of software that will be installed as part of Solaris, you should use either a fast CD-ROM or DVD drive, or a fast NIC. A 4x CD-ROM drive can take several hours just to install the base environment, whereas a 40x CD-ROM drive can take 15 to 20 minutes; of course, a DVD is even faster and easier. Similarly, a 10 megabit

TABLE 3-1	Software Group	Required Disk Space
Required Disk Space	Entire distribution plus original equipment manufacturer (OEM) support	2.4GB
	Entire distribution	2.3GB
	Developer system support	1.9GB
	End-user system support	1.6GB

(Mb) NIC can take a very long time, whereas a 100Mb NIC will go relatively quickly. Plan your time accordingly.

Software Packages, Clusters, and Groups

The Solaris software is organized into three components. The most basic component is the *software package:* a collection of all the files and information necessary to install software on a system or remove it. Built upon packages are *software clusters:* logical collections of software, such as a windowing environment or a development environment. The largest component is a *software group:* a collection of all the clusters and packages necessary to define a particular role for a system to perform, such as an end-user workstation or a network server.

Software Packages

The basic components of a software package can include the following:

- A file containing information about the package, its title, its purpose, the version, and other information. This is the pkginfo file.
- A file containing the names, locations, sizes, and permissions of all the files. This is the pkgmap file.
- A script that is run to query the installer about which components to install, where to install them, and how to configure them. This is the preinstall script.
- The files (executable binaries, man pages, and configuration controls) that make up the software.
- A script that is run during the removal of the software to ensure that everything is removed properly.

Software Clusters

A *cluster* is a collection of several packages that logically belong together. For example, the SUNWCdtrun cluster contains the packages that are related to the Common Desktop Environment (CDE) runtime environment. This includes the runtime libraries, the daemons required for the networking of the desktop, and the desktop login programs. Another example is SUNWCfwcp, which is a collection of freeware compression programs such as GNU zip, bzip, Info-zip, and the Zip compression library.

Software Groups

A *software group* basically determines what a particular system will be used for. In a real sense, the software groups are nothing more than megaclusters. They are clusters that contain other clusters as well as packages.

Solaris has five software groups:

- **Core operating environment**   This software group, referred to as *SUNWCreq*, is the minimum required software for a system to run. It includes the kernel, the network drivers, the standard command set, and the graphical interface drivers. It does not include any of the man pages, the graphical interface runtime system, Java, any of the development tools, or any other optional software. It requires only about 700MB of disk space.

- **End-user operating environment**   *SUNWCuser* is the software group that would generally be used on a desktop workstation, except for a software developer. It includes everything that the core includes plus man pages, the CDE and Open Windows graphical interfaces, the Java runtime, and other bundled optional software such as Netscape Communicator. This software group uses about 1.2GB of disk space.

- **Developer operating environment**   This package, *SUNWCprog*, includes everything from the end-user operating environment plus the software required for a developer. This includes developer libraries, include files, extra programming tools, and the man pages to go with them. These extras add about 300MB to the required disk space. This environment does not include a C compiler, though. The only C compiler available directly from Sun is an additional-cost item.

- **Entire distribution group**   *SUNWCall*, the entire Solaris distribution, contains everything that the developer operating environment contains, plus additional software that would be useful on a server. This software includes the Apache Web Server, a Dynamic Host Configuration Protocol (DHCP) server, a Network File System (NFS) server, and several freeware or open source utilities. This software group requires just under 2GB of disk space.

- **Entire distribution plus OEM support group**   This software group, *SUNWCXall*, adds support for hardware from OEMs. This software group requires a little over 2GB of disk space. Most of the extra drivers added might never be used, but you should install this group if the exact hardware configuration is unknown.

SCENARIO & SOLUTION

What if you are installing a desktop workstation for a user who needs to run only remote applications?	Install the end-user operating environment.
What if you are installing a desktop workstation for a software developer?	Install the developer operating environment.
What if you are installing a system to be used as a web server?	Install the entire distribution group or entire distribution plus OEM support group.
What if you are installing an old system, with only a 1GB hard disk, to be used by a desktop power user?	Install the core operating environment; you will need to NFS-mount CDE and other applications from another system.

Preinstallation Planning

Now that you've gathered the general information, it is time to move on to the preinstallation planning. The first item in the plan is to decide if the system is to be a client system, a standalone system, or a server system. A *client system* is one in which part or all of the Solaris operating environment is maintained on another system—an operating system server—and in which the client system cannot function without the OS server. A *standalone system* is one in which all necessary pieces of the Solaris operating environment are stored locally and the system can function normally without an OS server. A *server system* provides some form of service to other systems. If you have already chosen the software group to be installed, you probably have already made this decision. Because the setup of clients and servers can be complicated, the focus here is on standalone systems.

The next item to be decided is whether the system will be networked or nonnetworked. A *networked system* is one that can access other systems and services. It does not mean that the system necessarily relies on the other systems. By definition, a client or a server system must be networked. Standalone systems can be either networked or nonnetworked, depending on their use. An example of a system that might be standalone and nonnetworked is a security access control system—a system that controls who can get in and out of a building. An example of a standalone networked system is a desktop workstation. The user would want to be able to access a local area network, printers, and possibly even a corporate web server.

To set up a networked system, you need a few more pieces of information: the hostname to be assigned to the system, the Internet Protocol (IP) address to be assigned to the system, the name service type and related information, and the subnet mask. Let's look at these items in more detail:

■ The hostname must be a unique name to distinguish this machine from other machines. There are many naming conventions, including themes (fantasy worlds, band names, sports teams, and the like) or some kind of coded name. Theme names are generally easier to remember and can help distinguish the machines. However, they are often confusing for new users. Coded names, which often include location codes, manufacturer codes, operating system codes, and function codes, make it very easy to determine a great deal of information about a system very quickly. They might also have to change if any of the information about the system changes, which could be even more confusing in the end.

on the
ⓘob

It is very easy to go overboard with any naming convention. One place where I worked used mythological names for all their systems. The routers were named after the rivers around Hades. Although Styx and Acheron aren't too difficult to remember, Kokytos and Pyriplegethoin can be difficult! Another place that I worked used a coded naming scheme that included such easy-to-remember names as cmht3r205phpljivcps for an HP Laser Jet IV Color PostScript printer in Tower 3 Room 205 of the Columbus, Ohio, office; and cmht3r205ss10s251b for the second SPARC 10 running Solaris 2.5.1 in the same location.

■ The IP address must also be unique. It tells the network which subnet or segment the machine is on, as well as which particular system is on that network. Hostnames and IP addresses are usually mapped together because hostnames are easier for people to remember. They also don't necessarily have to change if the machine moves to a new location, whereas an IP address probably will.

■ Solaris supports a variety of naming services, including Network Information Service (NIS), NIS+, the Domain Naming Service (DNS), and DHCP. The options during the installation are NIS, NIS+, Other, LDAP, or None.

Other and None allow the person installing the system to configure his or her own naming service after he or she finishes building the system.

■ The subnet mask (commonly netmask) is used to determine which network a particular system is on. The netmask details how to break the IP address into the network address and the host address. For example, an IP address of 192.168.21.12 coupled with a netmask of 255.255.255.0 means that the host is on the 192.168.21.0 network and has the host address of 12 on that network.

During the installation, you will also need to know the geographic location of and time zone in which the system resides, the root password that will be assigned to the system, and any languages—other than English—that need to be supported.

The System Installation

This section explains the specific steps in installing the Solaris operating environment. It goes through the power-on sequence, booting the installation media, the basic system configuration, configuring internationalization and localization, selecting the software, configuring the disks, installing the software, and post-installation procedures.

The Power-On Sequence

The first step to install the Solaris operating environment is to turn on the power to the system. The system will go through a power-on self-test (POST) cycle, during which it tests all the installed hardware to ensure that it is working properly. After POST, if the Electrically Erasable Programmable Read-Only Memory (EEPROM) variable AUTO-BOOT? is set to true, the system will attempt to boot. If the EEPROM variable BOOT-DEVICE is set to cd and a CD-ROM is in the CD-ROM drive, it will run that CD-ROM. Otherwise, it will try to boot from the internal hard disk, and finally will end up at a prompt that looks like OK; in that case, type **boot cdrom**.

If the system has a graphical output device (a monitor as opposed to a character output device such as a terminal or a network console server), the installation will display a graphical interface. Otherwise, it will display a character-based interface. The information and responses will always be exactly the same. The only difference will be the navigation method. The mouse and the right mouse button will be used on the graphical interface; the UP-ARROW, DOWN-ARROW, and ENTER keys will be used on the character interface. On the graphical interface, to move to the next screen, there will be a button labeled Next; on the character interface, the sequence will be either F-2 or ESC-2.

Initial Configuration Options

After some information and welcome screens, the following sequence takes place:

1. Questions appear asking whether the system is to be networked. On the first screen, select Networked and click Next to continue to the next screen.

2. This question deals with DHCP. For now, select No and click Next.

3. The machine asks for the hostname of the system. Type the hostname and click Next.

4. The machine asks for the IP address. Enter the IP address and click Next.

5. The machine requests the subnet mask. Enter the appropriate subnet mask and click Next.

6. This screen determines whether to enable Internet Protocol version 6 (Ipv6). Enabling it is harmless, so choose Yes and click Next.

7. The last question in this group deals with the name service. Choose the appropriate name server (or None) and click Next.

The next four questions deal with geographic location, date, time, and the root password:

1. Choose Geographic Region and click Next.

2. Choose the closest region and click Next.

3. This screen prompts for the date and time. If the defaults are correct, click Next. Otherwise, change them as appropriate.

4. The last screen of this group requests the root password. Enter the root password, noticing that for security reasons, it will appear as a string of asterisks on the screen. Enter it the second time to verify that it was entered correctly, and click Next.

The last set of questions in this section relate to miscellaneous areas. The first one deals with power management. Solaris systems can save their current state and turn themselves off when they are not being used. This might be fine for a desktop workstation, but it probably is not OK for a server. This feature needs to be configured more after the installation is complete. (We will not use it.) Now do the following:

1. Choose the appropriate response, and select Don't Ask so that it won't prompt every time the system boots. Click Next.

2. This question deals with network proxy servers. A proxy server can provide a network with additional security as well as enhanced network traffic control. Choose whichever server is appropriate and fill in the requested information. Click Next.

3. This screen is a confirmation screen. It prints the information that it is using to define the system. After checking the information, either click Confirm or click Back to go back to the previous screens to correct any mistakes. Once the information is confirmed, the system displays a message stating that it is configuring and then moves into the installation parameters process. Once it starts the installation parameters process, it ejects the Installation CD-ROM and requests Solaris Software CD 1 of 2. Insert the CD-ROM and click Next.

Installation Options, Internationalization, and Localization

The Type Of Install screen begins the installation parameters process. The choices here are Default Install and Custom Install. The default installation is the easiest. It will make all the configuration decisions. The custom installation requires you to have more knowledge of the system, allows the choice of software to be installed, determines which disks to use, and determines how to configure those disks. For our purposes, select Custom Install and continue to the next screen.

The next two screens deal with internationalization of the system. Various language options and character fonts can be installed. Choose any extra options that are needed and continue to the Select Products screen.

Software Selection

The next couple of screens deal with some of the software products that are available to install. The specific options and screens might vary, but they include the Solaris Software CD 2 of 2 CD and the Solaris Documentation CD-ROM. There could also be options for installing other software, either through the local CD-ROM or through various network options. Choose the products as appropriate for the system.

The next screen prompts for either 32-bit or 64-bit software support. Enable 64-bit support if the hardware supports it. All recent Sun hardware supports 64-bit operations, but some older system might not. Sixty-four-bit operations allow for larger or more granular operations (such as file sizes or timings). They are generally useful, although they could come at a cost to some backward compatibility. Software that uses 64-bit support might not be usable on systems that support only 32-bit operations.

Then choose the appropriate software group to be installed. If the specific use of the system is unknown, it is recommended that the entire Solaris software plus OEM group be installed, if space is available.

Disk Configurations

Solaris does not necessarily look at a physical disk as a single object. In the base operating system, it is possible to define the disk as having from one to eight areas, called *slices* or, historically, *partitions*. Each of these slices can contain a *file system*, which is a logical layout and grouping of a directory structure.

Greater understanding of the system is required for configuring the disks. If the disks are improperly configured, it might be impossible to maintain the system. If the slices are too small, it could be difficult to install patches or extra software. If the slices are too large, space that could be used on another file system might be wasted.

The first screen has two windows. The window on the left shows the disks that are available to be used. The window on the right shows the disks on which you have been chosen to install Solaris. Disks can be moved from one window to the other by highlighting them and using the Add and Remove buttons. There is also an area to show how much disk space is required for the installation and how much is available. The default boot disk has already been selected; this is generally the disk labeled c0t0d0. Choose the appropriate disks and continue to the next screen.

After the system has gathered the disk space requirements, the next screen shows the default disk layout. By default, Solaris populates three disk slices: the root file system, which contains all installed software on slice 0; a swap area on slice 1; and the /export/home file system where user files will reside on slice 7. Solaris also uses slice 2 as the entire disk for certain operations. You cannot modify this through any of the default installation procedures, although you can by using the custom JumpStart. However, modification is not recommended.

Click Modify to change the disk layout, to add or delete file systems, or to resize the swap disk area. To create a new file system or increase the size of one of the currently defined file systems, you must decrease the size of one of the file systems. On this screen, Solaris shows the minimum required disk space for a particular file system, as well as the recommended size and the currently defined size. As new

FROM THE CLASSROOM

Defining Slices in the Solaris 9 Operating Environment

There are two schools of thought when it comes to disk slices. Solaris, by default, uses the "put almost everything on one slice" school. I prefer to break things up into separate slices to minimize system problems should a file start to grow without bounds. If the root file system fills, the system will crash. Log files are notorious for growing without being rotated, especially if a process is logging error messages. My standard slices usually include the following file systems: / (root) at 128MB on slice 0, /usr at 2GB on slice 3, /var at 1.5GB on slice 4, and /opt at 1.5GB on slice 5.

I usually do not allocate whatever is left to any slice. Leaving unallocated space is useful

for two reasons: first, this layout leaves two slices available for Volume Manager products, should I want to use them; and second, users don't see a great deal of low utilization of the existing file systems. I believe that user files should never reside on the root disk, so /export/home is placed on another disk completely, as are all user applications that require any kind of configuration. Common tools—things that can easily be installed using JumpStart or some other such automation—are installed into either /usr/local (part of the /usr file system) or /opt/local (part of the /opt file system).

—*Stephen P. Potter, Senior UNIX Engineer, Information Control Corporation*

file systems are defined, the minimum and recommended sizes of the other file systems could change. This screen also shows the capacity of the disk, how much of the disk has been allocated, and the free space that has not yet been allocated.

Installing

Once the file systems have been correctly defined, the Ready To Install confirmation screen appears, showing the chosen configuration. If all is well, click Install Now; otherwise, click Back to go back and fix any errors. During most of the rest of the installation, the Installing screen will be displayed. This screen shows status messages and two progress bars. The first bar is for each package being installed; the second bar is for the overall installation process. Several factors determine how long the installation process takes; it can range from several minutes to an hour or more.

This is especially true of a custom JumpStart that might include patches, extra software, and local customizations.

From time to time, an Installation Summary screen might appear, signaling the end of a particular part of the installation process. This screen provides an option to view a log of everything that occurred during the process. After each Installation Summary screen, there will be an option to install other software, either from a local CD-ROM or from a network file system. Choose as appropriate until the installation is complete and the screen to select the desktop environment is displayed.

EXERCISE 3-1

Installing the Solaris Operating System

Warning: The purpose of this exercise is to install a brand new operating environment on your system. Everything that is currently on the system will be destroyed. Ensure that the system you are using does not have anything that you do not want to be lost.

This exercise is a repeat of the preceding part of this section, "The System Installation." You can refer back to that section at any time for more information. The total time to complete this exercise is between one and two hours, depending on the hardware you are using. Perform the following steps:

1. If the system you will use is currently running a Solaris operating system, log in to the machine as root and shut it down. The command is shutdown and the options are $-i$ for the run level, $-g$ for the grace period before the shutdown begins, and $-y$ to verify, without asking, whether to continue:

   ```
   # shutdown -i 0 -g 0 -y
   ```

2. Make sure the Solaris Installation CD-ROM is in the CD-ROM drive. Start the installation process:

   ```
   ok boot cdrom
   ```

3. After several minutes, the system will boot and start to ask you for information. The following information is intended only as a guideline. You can modify these guidelines for your environment. You will be performing an initial installation, not an upgrade. Format the root disk, and make the swap size the minimum size. Allow the swap partition to start at the beginning of the disk.

4. At this point, Solaris will switch to the Web Start installation. Continue providing information as follows. Remember these are only guidelines. If you are setting up this machine on a real network, you should modify the information as appropriate. You are setting up a networked system. You will not be using DHCP. Choose a name of your liking and use the IP address 192.168.21.12 with a netmask of 255.255.255.0. This system will not need IPv6, but there is no harm in enabling it. You will not be using a name service.

5. Enter the appropriate information for your geographic region and time zone.

6. Choose a root password—something hard for others to guess but easy for you to remember. Enter your password twice and notice that it shows up on the screen as a line of asterisks.

7. This system will not use power management, and you don't want to be asked every time. Assume that the system is directly connected to the Internet.

8. When the system ejects the CD-ROM, insert the Solaris Software CD 1 of 2 .

9. Select a custom install and choose the appropriate language options.

10. Refer to the listing of software groups in the section "Software Packages, Clusters, and Groups," earlier in the chapter. Assuming that the available disk is large enough, this system will install the entire Solaris software plus OEM, and there will be no additional software installed, so clear all options. Select 64-bit operations if your hardware supports them. (Hardware built within the last couple of years supports 64-bit operations, but older hardware probably will not.) Be sure you check to see whether your system supports 64-bit operations. Giving the wrong answer here could cause your system to work incorrectly.

11. Select the boot disk to be used, if it is not already selected. Set up the slices any way you like, ensuring that you create separate slices for the root, /usr, /var, and /opt file systems. If you don't create separate slices, the file hierarchies will still be created in the root file system. You want to separate them for this exercise, though. Refer to the preceding "From the Classroom" sidebar for an example layout.

12. The rest of the installation is automatic. When the Solaris Software CD 1 of 2 is finished, insert the Solaris Software CD 2 of 2 . After both CDs are finished, reboot the system.

13. You should now have a workable system. Log in to the system as root using the password you specified during the configuration, and verify that the system is accessible.

CERTIFICATION OBJECTIVE 3.02

Understanding the Functions of Package Administration Commands

One of the most troublesome aspects of system administration is the maintenance of the installed software. What happens when a new version of the software is released? What happens when software becomes obsolete and needs to be removed? How is it possible to determine which software is installed? Operating system developers have come up with different ways to manage this process. For example, Microsoft Windows generally uses Install Shield, and RedHat Linux uses RPMs. Solaris uses packages. As you learned earlier, a package is a collection of all the files and information necessary to install or remove software on a system.

Four commands deal with using packages: pkgadd for adding packages to the system, pkginfo for finding out about a particular package, pkgchk to verify a package against its definition, and pkgrm to remove a package from the system. Other commands deal with creating packages, and they will be covered in Chapter 30.

The four package commands that are dealt with all reference certain common files and directories. One of these files is /var/sadm/install/contents. This file lists all the installed files on the system. It is queried by the pkginfo and pkgchk commands and is updated by the pkgadd and pkgrm commands when packages are added and deleted.

exam
ⓦatch

Although this chapter does not dwell on the Solaris admintool graphical interface, you should be familiar with how it works. It provides most, but not all, of the functionality that the individual commands provide. To start the admintool, type admintool& *at the command prompt. You will find the package-related commands under Browse | Software. Once you are in this section, you can select a package and select Show Details for the basic pkginfo functionality. Use Edit | Add and Edit | Delete to access the pkgadd and pkgrm functionality.*

The pkgadd Command

Use the pkgadd command to unpack a software package and install it on the system:

```
pkgadd [-n] [-a admin] [-d [dev|path]] [-s spool] instance [-r response]
```

By default, pkgadd runs in an interactive mode, requesting directives from the user to define how it should install the package *instance,* as well as verifying that the user wants to continue when pkgadd thinks a dangerous answer has been given. Once the directives are given, pkgadd will run any included installation scripts and then copy the package's files to their proper locations. The default location of the instance is /var/spool/pkg.

The *-n* option causes pkgadd to run in noninteractive mode; it stops only when certain directives are needed, such as whether to allow the use of setuid files or to change permissions on an existing file or directory. If the *-a* option and an argument are given, pkgadd uses the file given as an administrative file rather than the default. The administrative file contains answers to the directives, thus causing pkgadd to run completely noninteractively.

Although the *-n* and *-a* options cause pkgadd to run noninteractively, the included installation scripts might still be interactive. This can be troublesome if the same package is being installed on many machines at once. However, you can provide answers to the installation scripts so that they can run noninteractively as well, by using the *-r* option and its argument. This flag specifies a file that contains the responses that would normally be needed to complete the installation. The argument can be the name of a directory instead of an individual file. In this case, pkgadd searches for a response file with the same name as the package instance being installed and uses it. This file is useful when several packages are being installed with a single invocation of the pkgadd command.

If the *-d* option and an argument are passed to the command, pkgadd looks in that location for the instance instead of in the default spool directory. The argument can be either a full pathname to a directory containing the packages (such as /opt/admin/packages/), the name of a package *datastream* file (a single file that simulates a package install directory, such as /opt/admin/packages/perl5.6.0.pkg), or a device name or alias (such as /dev/rmt/0n or /cdrom/cdrom0).

The *-s* option and its argument are the final option covered. Generally, pkgadd is used to install software onto a system. Sometimes, the package needs to be copied only to a spool location. The *-s* option can be used to perform this action. This option takes as an argument the location of the spooling directory to be used. The default spool location in Solaris is /var/spool/pkg.

```
# pkgadd -n -d /cdrom/cdrom0/s0/Solaris_9/Product SUNWdoc
Processing package instance <NWdoc> from </cdrom/cdrom0/s0/solaris_9/Product>
Documentation Tools
(sparc) 11.8.0,REV=2000.01.08.18.17
Copyright 2001 Sun Microsystems, Inc.  All rights reserved.
Using </> as the package base directory.
## Processing package information.
## Processing system information
   1 package pathname is already properly installed.
## Verifying package dependencies.
## Verifying disk space requirements.
## Checking for conflicts with packages already installed.
## Checking for setuid/setgid programs.
Installing Documentation Tools as <NWdoc>
## Installing part 1 of 1.
Installation of <NWdoc> was successful.
```

The pkginfo Command

You use the pkginfo command to gain information about a package:

```
pkginfo [ -q | -x | -l ] [ -d [ dev | path ] ] instance
```

By default, pkginfo gives a one-line description of all installed packages. This line contains the category, the package instance, and the package name. The instance name(s) limits the return to only those packages listed. The various flags and arguments modify the other default behaviors.

The *-q, -x,* and *-l* options are mutually exclusive. They determine the level of detail that pkginfo returns. The *-q* option causes pkginfo to return no output, only a return code that signifies whether the package was found. This option is useful in scripting situations to ensure that an already installed package is not overwritten. The *-x* option returns the package instance, the package name, the architecture, and the version, if available. The *-l* option returns the long output format. This output contains all information that is known about the package, except an actual listing of the files included. It tells you how much disk space, approximately, the package uses, as well as the package instance, name, version, vendor, and status. The status is either fully installed or partially installed. A package is partially installed only if the installation failed to complete properly.

Similar to the pkgadd command, the *-d* option and argument cause pkginfo to look for an uninstalled package in the location provided. It then returns information about that package rather than about an installed package. As with pkgadd, the argument can be a full pathname to a directory, the name of a package datastream file, or a device name or alias.

```
Pkginfo -1 SUNWdoc
  PKGINST:    SUNWman
     NAME:    Documentation Tools
 CATEGORY:    system
     ARCH:    sparc
  VERSION:    11.8.0,REV=2000.01.08.18.17
  BASEDIR:    /
   VENDOR:    Sun Microsystems, Inc
DESC:         utilities and fonts for development, display, and
              production of documentation such as manual pages
              (nroff/troff)
PSTAMP:       catsup20000108183649
INSTRELEASE:  Mar 18 2001 16:45
HOTLINE:      Please contact your local support provider
STATUS:       Completely Installed
FILES:          384 installed pathnames
                  5 shared pathnames
                 25 directories
               2332 blocks used (approx)
```

The pkgchk Command

The pkgchk command verifies the installation of a package and checks files for correctness based on the information of the package to which they belong:

```
pkgchk [ options ] [ -p path ] [ instance ]
```

By default, the pkgchk command checks all packages installed on the system and prints any errors or discrepancies on the standard error. It checks file attributes, file contents, and pathnames. Options modify this default behavior.

It is possible, using the *-f* option, to have pkgchk try to correct any file attribute problems it finds. This option could be useful for checking the system's security or if someone has accidentally changed the permissions on an entire directory. If an instance name(s) is provided, pkgchk verifies only those packages, not the entire system. If a filename is given as the argument to the *-p* option, pkgchk checks that filename against its installed package database and verifies that file against the instance to which it belongs. The options *-a* and *-c* can be used to limit what pkgchk checks on each file; *-a* checks only file attributes, and *-c* checks only file contents. Another interesting option is *-n,* which causes pkgchk not to check files that are likely to change, such as the password file or log files.

This example shows the output of pkgchk against the password file on a system in use. Accounts have been added to the password file, so pkgchk returns an error.

```
pkgchk -p /etc/passwd
ERROR: /etc/passwd
File size <414> expected <963> actual
File cksum <34239> expected <34776> actual
```

Perhaps the most useful option for pkgchk is *-l,* which returns a long listing of all the information pkgchk can find about the file or package. It is not as useful for packages, on which pkgchk can be used. For individual files, it is quite handy, though.

```
pkgchk -1 -p /etc/passwd
Pathname: /etc/passwd
Type: regular file
Expected mode: 0644
Expected owner: root
Expected group: root
Expected file size (bytes): 414
Expected sum(1) of contents: 34239
Expected last modification: Sept 23 07:07:01 PM
Referenced by the following packages:
        SUNWcore
Current status: installed
```

The pkgrm Command

You use the pkgrm command to remove a previously installed package:

```
pkgrm [ -nvA ] [ -a admin ] instance
```

The software might no longer be necessary, it may be obsolete, or the installation might not have completed successfully. By default, pkgrm checks for other packages that depend on the package to be removed and warns the user before allowing the package to be removed.

As with the pkgrm command, the *-n* option is used to specify that pkgrm should be run in noninteractive mode. If pkgrm is being run in noninteractive mode and some form of user interaction is required, the command will fail. In addition, as with the pkgadd command, the *-a* option and argument will specify an administration file that controls how pkgrm behaves.

The pkgrm command generally will not remove a file if it is shared with another package. The *-A* option instructs pkgrm to absolutely remove the files, even if they are shared.

```
# pkgrm SUNWdoc
The following packages is currently installed:
   SUNWdoc          Documentation Tools
                    (sparc) 11.8.0,REV=2000.01.08.18.17
Do you want to remove this package? y
## Removing installed package instance <NWdoc>
## Verifying package dependencies.
Do you want to continue with the removal of this package [y,n,?,q] y
## Processing package information.
## Removing pathnames in class <none>
?.
?.
## Updating system information.
Removal of SUNWdoc was successful.
```

EXERCISE 3-2

Working with Package Commands

During this exercise, you will use the package commands to query the system about a software package, install a software package, and remove a software package. This exercise uses the pkginfo, pkgadd, and pkgrm commands and the SUNWdoc package that is found on the Solaris Software CD 1 of 2.

1. Insert the Solaris Software CD 1 of 2 into the CD-ROM drive.

2. Use pkginfo to determine which installed packages are related to the CDE. All the CDE packages start with SUNWdt (desktop). Unfortunately, they do not all necessarily have CDE in their description.

   ```
   # pkginfo | grep SUNWdt
   ```

   Which packages were listed?

3. Use pkginfo to find out all the information about the SUNWdoc package. If this package is not currently installed, skip Steps 4 and 5 and go to Step 6; then return to this step after Step 6.

   ```
   # pkginfo -l SUNWdoc
   ```

Which information was listed for this package?

4. If the SUNWdoc package was found in Step 3, use pkgrm to remove this package:

```
# pkgrm SUNWdoc
```

What was the output of the pkgrm command?

5. Use pkginfo to verify that the SUNWdoc package is no longer on the system:

```
# pkginfo SUNWdoc
```

6. Use pkgadd to install the SUNWdoc package from the directory /cdrom/cdrom0/Solaris_9/Product. Use pkginfo to verify that it is correctly installed:

```
# pkgadd -d /cdrom/cdrom0/Solaris_9/Product SUNWdoc
# pkginfo -l SUNWdoc
```

Notice in the results from pkginfo that the status is "Fully Installed."

7. If you need to return to Steps 3–5, do so now. Otherwise, eject the CD-ROM.

CERTIFICATION OBJECTIVE 3.03

Understanding the Steps to Install, Remove, and Verify Which Patches Are Currently Installed

Patches are used to keep the operating system up to date with the fixes to problems that have been encountered. Solaris has three levels of patches: recommended, security, and product-specific patches. *Recommended patches* are those that should be installed on all systems; they fix some kind of improperly operating software. *Security patches* are those that close security holes and make the system more secure. They are less severe than recommended patches, but they should still be installed if possible. *Product-specific patches* are fixes for either unbundled software or supplemental hardware drivers. These patches need be applied only if the specific software or hardware is installed on the system.

All three levels of patches use the same structure and functionality. The only differences are in availability and purpose.

Obtaining Patches

Sun supports a variety of options to obtain patches. The recommended and security patches can be obtained by anyone through the World Wide Web or through anonymous File Transfer Protocol (FTP) at sunsolve.sun.com. Product-specific patches are accessible only to Sun Service contract customers. They can be accessed via the World Wide Web or FTP from sunsolve.sun.com by using a valid SunSolve ID, or they can be requested on CD-ROM. The recommended and security patches are available in the "Public Patch Access" section. All patches are available to contract customers through "Contract Customer Patch Access."

Along with the individual patches, three other files are available. These files are a report of all the recommended and security patches, called Solaris9. PatchReport; a cluster, or bundled collection, of all the recommended patches, called 9_Recommended.zip; and installation instructions for the cluster, called 9_Recommended.README.

The patch report is useful for tracking the changes that have occurred to the recommended patch list. The cluster is an easier method of downloading and installing all the patches at once. The cluster contains a script, called install_cluster, to automatically install the entire cluster.

If patch downloads are automated, only the new or changed individual patches need be downloaded each time, not the entire cluster. The recommended cluster for older versions of Solaris, which is actually a compressed tar file instead of a zip archive, can approach 100MB in size and might not change as often; downloading individual patches can save considerable bandwidth and time.

on the
job

The recommended and security patches are also available from the University of North Carolina at www.ibiblio.org/pub/sun-info/sun-patches. This archive can also be reached through anonymous FTP and rsync. There are also several country-specific SunSolve sites. A complete list of the international SunSolve servers can be found via the SunSolve Servers link from the main SunSolve page at sunsolve.sun.com.

New to Solaris 9 is the patch management command smpatch. This command "manages patch installation on single or multiple machines, analyzes patch requirements, and downloads required patches."

Decomposing a Patch

A patch is a collection of all the information necessary to update a piece of software. This definition is similar to the definition of a package. In fact, patches consist of information files and packages. Patches are distributed as either compressed tar files or zip archives, depending on the version of Solaris for which the patch is prepared. Prior to Solaris 8, patches were distributed as compressed tar files. Solaris 7 distributed both tar and zip formats. Solaris 8 and 9 distribute patches only as zip archives.

exam
ⓦatch

Pay careful attention to the contents of a patch. Understanding the parts and their functions is crucial to understanding how patches work.

Patch names are mostly incomprehensible, being composed of a base code identifier and a revision number; for example, the main kernel patch for Solaris 8 Sparc edition is 108528-06. When the patch is unpacked, it creates a directory structure with this name. Within that directory structure will be the following:

- **README.108528-06**   This is a file that contains information about the patch, including the bug IDs resolved by this patch, a revision history, and installation instructions. Most of this file is useless without a service contract and access to the SunSolve Symptoms and Resolutions database.

- **Some packages, such as SUNWhea**   These packages are modifications to the base installed package of the same name. When the patch is installed, the files in these packages will replace those currently installed. If the files are not currently installed, they will be added.

- **installpatch and backoutpatch scripts**   Optionally, if the package is for an unbundled software product, it could also contain installpatch and backoutpatch scripts. Prior to Solaris 2.6, each patch contained its own individual install script. Since the release of Solaris 2.6, the install script has been added to the operating system itself. Patches for Solaris 8 and 9 no longer contain the installpatch and backoutpatch scripts.

- **Other optional information files**   These files can vary from patch to patch or might not even exist.

To unpack a zip archive, use /usr/bin/unzip:

```
# /usr/bin/unzip 108528-06.zip
```

To unpack a compressed tar file, use /usr/bin/zcat and /usr/bin/tar:

```
# /usr/bin/zcat 108528-06.tar.Z | tar xvf -
```

Once a patch has been installed on the system, a directory is created under /var/sadm/patch with the README file and the install log file. There is also a directory created under /var/sadm/pkg/ for each package that was part of the patch. Within that directory is a pkginfo file and a save directory to which the files that were replaced are copied. This copying is done so that the patch can be uninstalled, or backed out, later if a problem arises because of its installation.

These directory structures can grow very large if many patches are installed on the system. If multiple revisions of the same patch are installed, or if patches will never be backed out, it is possible to delete these copies. However, this is not recommended.

The patchadd Command

You use the patchadd command to install a patch(s) on the system and to check on the currently installed patches. The three forms of the command are shown here. One form installs just one patch, another form installs multiple patches, and the last form (the first one discussed earlier) displays installed patches. Historically, Solaris used the showrev command for this purpose. It still has that functionality for backward-compatibility purposes.

```
patchadd [-d] [-u] [-B backout_dir] [-C net_install_image| -R client_root_path| -S
service] patch
patchadd [-d] [-u] [-B backout_dir] [-C net_install_image| -R client_root_path| -S
service] -M patch_dir| patch_id......| patch_dir patch_list
patchadd [-C net_install_image| -R client_root_path| -S service] -p
```

The -d option stops patchadd from using /var/sadm/patch/ to copy the replaced files. This means the patch can never be backed out; the only way to remove this patch is to rebuild the entire system. The -u option causes patchadd to replace files unconditionally. Normally, if patchadd finds that a file to be replaced has been modified from its original state, it errors out. This option will override that behavior. The -B option and its argument tell patchadd to use a directory other than /var/sadm/patch/ to save its backups.

By default, patchadd installs only a single patch, specified as patch_id. To make patchadd install multiple patches, you must add the -M option. This option informs patchadd to expect multiple patches. It requires a directory of where to find the patches, and either a list of patch_ids or a file containing a list of the patches to be installed.

```
# patchadd /var/tmp/111023-01
Checking installed patches?
Verifying sufficient filesystem capacity (dry run method)
Installing patch packages?
Patch number 111023-01 has been successfully installed.
See /var/sadm/patch/111023-01/log for details.
Patch packages install:
SUNWcarx.u    SUNWcarx.us    SUNWcsr
```

The patchrm Command

You use the patchrm command to remove, or back out, a patch from a system:

```
patchrm [-f] [-B backout_dir] [-C net_install_image| -R client_root_path| -S service]
patch_id
```

You would normally do this only if you determined that a specific patch was causing a problem on the system. Generally, one revision of a patch, or a patch that supersedes an older patch, would simply be installed over the old patch.

The *-f* option specifies to patchrm that it should remove this patch, even if it has been superseded by another patch. Unlike patchadd, there is no option to patchrm to remove multiple patches. In general, if multiple patches need to be removed, there is something more fundamentally wrong.

```
# patchrm 111023-01
Checking installed packages patches?
Backing out patch 111023-01?
Patch 111023-01 has been backed out.
```

The showrev Command

The main purpose of mentioning showrev here is to demonstrate its use with patches:

```
showrev [ -a ] [ -p ] [ -w ] [ -c command ]
```

However, that is not its only use. In its simplest form, with no arguments, showrev prints information about the currently running system, including hostname, hosted, operating system version, platform and architecture, hardware provider, network domain name, and kernel version. The *-p* option shows information on the installed patches. The output lists the patch number and revision, if that patch obsoletes any other patches, if that patch has any prerequisites, if that patch is incompatible with anything, and the packages that it affects. This output is the same as the output from

```
patchadd -p
```

The *-w* option shows information about the Open Windows version installed. The *-a* option combines all the information that showrev knows about the system into one output. That output includes the information that would be returned from the lone showrev command, the *-w* option, and the *-p* option.

```
# showrev -p
Patch: 111023-01 Obsoletes: Requires: Incompatibles: Packages: SUNWcsu
Patch: 109529-02 Obsoletes: 110331-01 Requires: Incompatibles: Packages: SUNWluxop
Patch: 108921-08 Obsoletes: Requires: 108652-19 Incompatibles: Packages: SUNWdtwm
```

The other interesting use of showrev is to find information about a specific command. Given the *-c* option and a command name, showrev prints known information about that command.

EXERCISE 3-3

Installing and Removing Patches

In this exercise, you will use the showrev command to determine if a particular patch is installed. If it is installed, you will use patchrm to remove it and then add it using patchadd. If it is not installed, you will use patchadd to install it, then remove it using patchrm.

1. Using either FTP or the World Wide Web, obtain the current revision of patch 110662 from sunsolve.sun.com. This particular patch is a bug fix for the ksh shell. We use it because it should be a "safe" patch to install and uninstall. For example,

```
#ftp sunsolve.sun.com
Connected to sunsolve6.sun.com.
220 - Several welcome messages
Name (sunsolve.sun.com:spp): anonymous
     331 Guest login ok, send your complete e-mail address as password
     Password: tim@timgibbs.com
     230 - Disclaimer messages
     ftp>> cd pub/patches
     250 CWD command successful.
```

```
ftp>> bin
200 Type set to I.
ftp>> ls 110662*
200 PORT command successful.
150 Opening ASCII mode data connection for /bin/ls.
-rw-r-r- 1 15   116072 Mar    6  12:47      110662-02.zip
-rw-r-r- 1 15       1783 Mar    6  12:47      110662.readme
226 Transfer complete.
ftp>> get 110662-02.zip
local: 110662-02.zip remote: 110662-02.zip
200 PORT command successful
150 Opening BINARY mode data connection for 110662-02.zip (116072 bytes).
226 Transfer complete.
116072 byes receives in 2.37 seconds (48 Kbytes/sec).
ftp>> exit
221 Goodbye.
```

2. Use unzip to unpack the archive.

   ```
   # unzip 110662-02.zip
   ```

3. Use showrev -p or patchadd -p to see if this patch is already installed. If it is installed, skip to Step 7 and return to it after Step 9.

   ```
   # showrev -p | grep 110662
   ```

4. Perform this step only after you have verified that the patch is not currently installed. Use patchadd to install the patch.

   ```
   # patchadd 110662-02
   ```

5. Verify that the patch is installed using showrev -p or patchadd -p.

   ```
   # showrev -p | grep 110662
   ```

6. If you would like, you can browse /var/sadm/patch/110662-02 and /var/sadm/pkg/SUNWcsu to see which files are there.

7. Perform this step only after you have verified that the patch is installed. Using patchrm, remove the patch from the system.

   ```
   # patchrm 110662-02
   ```

8. Verify that the patch has been uninstalled using showrev -p or patchadd -p.

   ```
   # showrev -p | grep 110662
   ```

9. If you like, you can browse /var/sadm/patch and /var/sadm/pkg to see whether the patch and package directories are there. Return to Step 4 if you need to install the patch or if you would simply like more practice.

CERTIFICATION SUMMARY

This chapter discussed the processes necessary to install and maintain a system. It discussed installation, working with packages, and patching. You must be intimately familiar with these fundamental skills. Lack of such familiarity will lead to unstable systems and will decrease system availability.

In discussing installation, this chapter covered the contents of the Solaris Media Kit, the various releases of the Solaris operating environment, the installation options, hardware requirements, software groups and clusters, planning, and the actual installation. The releases include platform editions, international editions, and hardware releases. The five installation options are interactive, Web Start, network, default JumpStart, and custom JumpStart. The hardware requirements include a Sparc or Intel/x86 platform, between 600MB and 2.3GB of disk space, 64MB of memory, and a CD-ROM or NIC card.

This chapter described a cluster and a software group and listed the five software groups: core, end-user, developer, entire distribution, and entire distribution plus OEM. This chapter also presented a systematic installation of a system, including the preinstallation configuration gathering of the hostname, IP address, netmask, and naming service.

The section on packages defined a package as a collection of all the information necessary for a software component and the use of software packages. You learned about the pkgadd command, used to install packages. You also learned about the pkginfo and pkgchk commands as ways to query the package database in /var/sadm/install/contents. The last part of this section dealt with the pkgrm command for removing packages from the system.

The last part of the chapter dealt with patches and patching. The various patches supported by Sun were listed as recommended, security, and unbundled product. A patch was described as a collection of all the information necessary to update a piece of software. The makeup of a patch, a collection of packages, was explained. The patchadd and patchrm commands, for installing and uninstalling patches, respectively, were described. Finally, you looked at the showrev command, both for its general information-gathering abilities and also for its patch information.

TWO-MINUTE DRILL

Installing the Solaris Operating Environment Software on a Networked Standalone System

❑ The Solaris installation media consists of at least these four CD-ROMs: Installation, Software CD 1 of 2, Software CD 2 of 2, and Documentation.

❑ The five installation options are interactive installation, Solaris Web Start, network installation, default JumpStart, and custom JumpStart.

❑ The minimum hardware requirements for Solaris are a Sparc or Intel/x86-based system, 600MB to 2.3GB of disk space, 64MB of memory, and either a local CD-ROM drive or a supported network interface card (NIC).

❑ The five software groups are core, end user, developer, entire distribution, and entire distribution plus OEM.

❑ The pieces of information required before starting to install the system are the hostname, the Internet Protocol (IP) address, the name service to be used, and the subnet mask.

Understanding the Functions of Package Administration Commands

❑ A package is the complete collection of files, directories, scripts, and configuration information for a specific piece of software. It can reside in either a directory or a single file known as a package datastream.

❑ The /var/sadm/install/contents file lists every file on the system that is part of a package. This file can be useful for finding where another file resides.

❑ Most package commands have a default directory for their information. This default can generally be changed with the -d option and its argument, which is a full pathname or a device name or alias.

❑ The pkginfo command can briefly list all the software installed on a system; or if executed with the -l option, it can return detailed information about a specific software package.

❑ The Solaris admintool provides a graphical interface to all the package commands.

Understanding the Steps Required to Install a Patch, Verify Which Patches Are Currently Installed, and Remove a Patch

❑ Sun supports three types of patches: recommended, security, and product specific.

❑ A patch minimally consists of a README file and one or more packages to be updated.

❑ The recommended patch cluster can be installed with the install_cluster command that is distributed with the cluster.

❑ By default, patchadd places the README file and the installation log in a directory under /var/sadm/patch/ and copies the files to be replaced to /var/sadm/pkg. The directories in /var/sadm/patch are named after the patch ID; the directories in /var/sadm/pkg are named for the package with a subdirectory named for the patch ID.

❑ The showrev command with the *-p* option displays all patches that have been installed. The command has other uses, including displaying the version information for a specific command with *-c*.

SELF TEST

The following questions will help you measure your understanding of the material presented in this chapter. Read all the choices carefully because there might be more than one correct answer. Choose all correct answers for each question.

Installing the Solaris Operating Environment Software on a Networked Standalone System

1. The versions of the Solaris Operating Environment include which of the following?

   A. Platform editions, hardware releases, and regional (international) editions

   B. Standard Edition, Gold Edition, and Collectors Edition

   C. Sparc Edition, Intel/x86 Edition, and PA-RISC Edition

   D. Workstation Edition, Server Edition, and Enterprise Edition

2. You need to install a workstation for a software developer who will be doing the majority of his development on this workstation. You should install

   A. The core operating environment

   B. The entire distribution group

   C. The end-user operating environment

   D. The developer operating environment

3. To install a new standalone networked system, you must determine which of the following information during the preinstallation planning phase?

   A. The hostname, the IP address, the primary user, and the netmask

   B. The hostname, the IP address, the naming service, and the netmask

   C. The hostname, the day of the week, the naming service, and the netmask

   D. The root password, the IP address, the naming service, and the netmask

Understanding the Functions of Package Administration Commands

4. Which of the following package administration commands were discussed in this chapter?

A. installpkg, deletepkg, checkpkg, and infopkg

B. addpkg, rmpkg, checkpkg, and infopkg

C. pkgadd, pkgrm, pkgchk, and pkginfo

D. install_cluster, remove_cluster, cluster_check, and cluster_info

5. You have been instructed to install packages named SUNWpl, SUNWtcl, SUNWpyth, SUNWgnuc, and SUNWzope on a large number of machines. These packages reside on an NFS-available file system that is mounted on each machine as /local/software. Each of these packages requires additional information for the install. You know that this information will be the same for all the machines. What is the quickest way to install all these packages?

A. Create a single admin file and a response file for each package. Install the packages using

```
pkgadd -na /local/software/admin -d /local/software/ SUNWpl SUNWtcl\
SUNWpyth SUNWgnuc SUNWzope -r /local/software/response/
```

B. Use

```
pkgadd -n -d /local/software -s /var/spool/pkgs SUNWpl SUNWtcl\
SUNWpyth SUNWgnuc SUNWzope
```

C. Create a single response file and an admin file for each package. Install the packages using

```
pkgadd -na /local/software/admin/ -d /local/software SUNWpl SUNWtcl\
SUNWpyth SUNWgnuc SUNWzope -r /local/software/response
```

D. From each machine, run

```
pkgadd -d /local/software SUNWpl SUNWtcl\ SUNWpyth SUNWgnuc SUNWzope
```

and answer the questions for each one.

6. The pkgchk command is used for what purpose?

A. This command ensures that a package datastream is not damaged.

B. This command reads the contents file of a package and ensures that all those files are actually in the package. This is so that errors do not happen during an installation.

C. This command is used to verify the installation of a package and to check files for correctness based on the information of the package to which they belong.

D. This command is used for version control. When pkgchk is run on a file, it creates a snapshot of it to track changes.

Understanding the Steps to Install, Remove, and Verify Which Patches Are Currently Installed

7. You need to install several patches on a machine. To handle this task, you would do which of the following?

   A. Run the installpatch command for each individual patch.

   B. Run the patchadd command with *-M* and a list of patches to install.

   C. Run the installpatch command with a list of patches to install.

   D. Run the patchadd command for each individual patch.

8. You need to uninstall several patches on a machine. To perform this task, you would do which of the following?

   A. Run the backoutpatch command for each individual patch.

   B. Run the patchrm command with *-M* and a list of patches to uninstall.

   C. Run the backoutpatch command with a list of patches to uninstall.

   D. Run the patchrm command for each individual patch.

9. What are the two ways to determine the patches that are installed on a Solaris operating environment system?

   A. patchinfo *-p* or showrev *-p*

   B. patchadd *-p* or showrev *-p*

   C. patchinfo *-p* or patchadd *-p*

   D. patchchk *-p* or patchinfo *-p*

LAB QUESTION

You are planning an installation facility for an entire university computing environment. You will be responsible for installing and configuring all systems across the campus. These systems will include everything from workstations for professors and graduate students to public labs, research computing servers, and highly available servers in clustered environments for registration and billing. List the five software groups that are available and explain one or more reasons to use each group.

SELF TEST ANSWERS

Installing the Solaris Operating Environment Software on a Networked Standalone System

1. ☑ **A.** The platform editions are Sparc and Intel/x86, the hardware releases are generally quarterly, and the regional editions include English and International.

☒ **B** is incorrect because these editions usually relate to PC games or DVD/video releases. **C** is incorrect because Sun does not support the PA-RISC architecture. PA-RISC chips are generally found in UNIX systems built by Hewlett-Packard. Sun did support the PowerPC architecture in some older versions of Solaris, but that support has been discontinued. **D** is incorrect because Workstation, Server, and Enterprise editions are products in the Microsoft Windows 2000 family. Sun does offer a Workstation Edition and a Server Edition, with the only difference being the inclusion of some optional management software. It does not support an Enterprise Edition, however.

2. ☑ **D.** A software developer likely needs to have all the development tools and include files for builds.

☒ **A** is incorrect because the core environment is the minimum necessary to boot the system. It does not provide much functionality. **B** is incorrect because the entire distribution group includes software that is used on servers, such as the Apache Web Server, NFS server, and a DHCP server. **C** is incorrect because the end-user operating environment is missing some fundamental development tools, such as build tools and include files.

3. ☑ **B.** During the configuration stage, you will be asked to assign a hostname and an IP address. You will also be asked to choose a naming service and assign a netmask.

☒ **A** is incorrect because there really is no need to know who the primary user will be, unless you install different software for different users or you name the machines after the users. **C** is incorrect because, unless you have a very strange environment, the day of the week is a useless piece of trivia. **D** is incorrect because it is not the best answer, even though it could be a correct answer. You also need to know the root password that is being assigned, but the hostname is more important.

Understanding the Functions of Package Administration Commands

4. ☑ **C.** This chapter discussed the commands to install packages (pkgadd), remove packages (pkgrm), check the installation of packages (pkgchk), and get information about a package (pkginfo).

☒ **A** is incorrect because none of these commands exists. **B** is incorrect because the parts of the names (add/pkg, rm/pkg, and so on) are backward. **D** is incorrect because install_cluster is a command for installing the recommended patch cluster. The other commands do not exist.

5. ☑ **A.** An admin file can be used to provide all the necessary package directives, and a response file can be created for each package to provide responses to the installation scripts. Be sure that the response file is named after the package instance and resides in the response directory provided—for example, /local/software/response/SUNWpl.
☒ **B** is incorrect because this action will copy the package instance into the spool directory, but it will not do anything else. Actually, this answer is doubly wrong because mixing *-s* with *-n, -a,* or *-r* is a syntax error. **C** is incorrect because, although it looks almost identical to **A**, this answer specifies only a single response file and individual admin files. It is rarely necessary to create more than one admin file, but response files must be individualized for each package that uses them. **D** is incorrect because this method would work to install all the packages. However, it requires the same information to be repeated for each package on each machine. This process can be repetitive and tedious and is very error prone. It is not the best use of your time or of Solaris 8's capabilities.

6. ☑ **C.** The pkgchk command is used to verify the installation of a package or to check the correctness of files.
☒ **A** is incorrect because a package datastream is checked with the UNIX sum command, an MD5 checksum, or some other form of cyclic redundancy check (CRC). **B** is incorrect because there really is no preprogrammed way to check that a package contains all the files it is supposed to contain, although some chicanery with pkgadd might be able to do that. **D** is incorrect because version control is handled using the RCS (Revision Control System), SCCS (Source Code Control System), or other such tools.

Understanding the Steps to Install, Remove, and Verify Which Patches Are Currently Installed

7. ☑ **B.** Unlike many UNIX commands, you must provide the *-M* option to install multiple patches with a single command.
☒ **A** is incorrect because the command installpatch was for older versions of the Solaris operating environment. It was included with each patch. **C** is incorrect because the command installpatch was for older versions of the Solaris operating environment. Because it was included with each patch, it could be different with each patch, and therefore had to be run separately. **D** is incorrect, even though you could install patches this way. It would simply take more time and be more error-prone than using *-M* and providing a list of patches to be installed.

8. ☑ **D.** This is the only way to remove multiple patches. Unlike most UNIX commands that encourage performing multiple tasks at once, patchrm wants to make sure you know what you are doing before it lets you uninstall multiple patches.

   ☒ **A** is incorrect because the command backoutpatch was used in older versions of the Solaris operating environment. It was included with each patch. **B** is incorrect because the command patchrm cannot take a list of patches to remove. Removing multiple patches generally indicates a problem, and Solaris wants you to be sure you know what you are doing. **C** is incorrect because the command backoutpatch was used in older versions of the Solaris operating environment. Because it was included with each patch, it could be different with each patch, and therefore had to be run separately.

9. ☑ **B.** Either command returns a list of all the patches installed on the system.

   ☒ **A** is incorrect because there is no patchinfo command. There is a pkginfo command for packages. **C** is incorrect because there is no patchinfo command. **D** is incorrect because neither patchchk nor patchinfo is a valid command.

LAB ANSWER

The five software groups that are supported in the Solaris operating environment are core, end-user, developer, entire distribution, and entire distribution plus OEM support.

A system that has the core software group installed is one that does not have enough local disk space installed to be able to support a more complete installation. It is a system in which the rest of the operating environment could be served from a larger system. Some good examples of machines that might use the core software group are workstations in a publicly accessible computing center and library kiosks, such as online card catalogs.

A system that has the end-user software group is one that can stand on its own and not rely on another system for most functionality. A good example of this kind of machine is a workstation on a professor's desk or a system used to register for classes. You might think that a registration system could use the core group, but you probably would not want these systems to rely on an OS server, especially during registration week.

A system that has the developer software group is one that includes all the tools needed to develop software (minus the compiler itself). This system can function completely without access to an OS server. Good places to use this kind of system are the computer science or computer engineering college, on a CS/CE professor's desk, and in the system programming department for the university.

A system that has the entire distribution software group is one used specifically to serve some sort of application to other systems. This category includes web servers for various schools, database servers for billing and record keeping, and application or computer servers for the CS/CE department.

A system that has the entire distribution plus OEM software group is very similar to one using the entire distribution group. Specifically, this system would serve well as an OS server, where the hardware installed on the clients might be unknown. It would not hurt anything to use this group in all places where you might use the entire distribution group. It might take up a few more (hundred) megabytes of disk space, but having all the drivers available might save you a great deal of work in trying to figure out why a certain system doesn't work because an unknown or unexpected piece of hardware was installed.

4

Initialization
and Shutdown

Most people are familiar with DOS-based systems and how easily they start up and shut down. Flip the power switch, and a DOS system is on. Flip it again, and it is off. A system running the Solaris 9 operating environment is much more complex than that. The system could have hundreds of services for which it is responsible; it might have thousands of users on it at once. Those services and users can be using all sorts of data. Improperly stopping the system can lead to a loss of that data, potentially costing significant amounts of productivity or even revenue.

In most production environments, a system—and hence, a system administrator—is measured by the amount of time that system is available to the users. Systems can be defined as being 24/7 or as having to have 98 percent uptime. The speed with which a system can be shut down and restarted can strongly affect those metrics. The more a system administrator understands the system's processes, the better the administrator can be at debugging, finding, and fixing errors that could keep a system down. A mistake in modifying any of a number of files can cause a system to mysteriously stop during the boot process and can be very difficult to track down. The administrator's ability to automatically start services when a system boots can make the difference between a good night's sleep and a restless night of being paged because a system was rebooted.

This chapter will familiarize you with the process of booting a system and shutting it down. You will learn to maintain those 98-percent uptime metrics, saving you long hours tracking down improper modifications to the system and allowing you to get that good night's sleep.

CERTIFICATION OBJECTIVE 4.01

Understanding the Solaris 9 Operating Environment Bootstrap Process

For a system to be usable, it must have the Solaris 9 operating environment loaded into memory. To load the environment into memory, the system must first retrieve it from storage media (disk, tape, or CD-ROM). In the Solaris operating environment, the drivers in the operating system control the storage media. Therefore, to boot the operating environment, you need to have the environment available. This situation presents a catch-22.

By using a staged process of loading-dependent pieces of the operating environment in a particular order, Solaris can get around this seemingly impossible situation. In effect, it is able to "pull itself up by its own bootstraps." Because of this colloquialism, the process has come to be known as *bootstrapping*, or, more simply, *booting*.

The Boot Process

When a system is powered on, it goes through several phases before the Solaris 9 operating environment is properly running and will accept any users. The four main phases of the boot process are

- Boot PROM phase
- Boot programs phase
- Kernel phase
- INIT phase

Each of these phases is responsible for certain functions to ensure that the system is working correctly.

Boot PROM Phase

The *boot programmable read-only memory* (PROM) phase is primarily concerned with ensuring that the hardware is working properly and beginning the process of starting the Solaris 9 operating environment. First, it runs the *power-on self-test* (POST). POST scans the system to find the installed hardware, runs primary diagnostics on everything it finds, and builds a device tree.

Once POST is completed, the PROM displays the system *banner.* The banner consists of information such as the hardware type, processor type and speed, PROM version, the Ethernet (or MAC) address assigned to the system, the host ID assigned to the system, and the size of the installed memory. PROM then runs a few more thorough diagnostics on the processor and memory.

The final function of the boot PROM phase is to run the boot command, if appropriate. The nonvolatile RAM (NVRAM) variable AUTO-boot? controls whether the PROM automatically runs the boot. The boot command uses the NVRAM variable BOOT-DEVICE to locate the boot device. From the boot device, it reads the primary boot loader, boot block (BOOTBLK), and executes it. The boot block is always located at the beginning of the boot device and is of a fixed size. It is always located in sectors 1 through 15 of the boot device.

The boot program can be called with several options, which are used to determine the run level to which the system will be booted, how much interaction is required, and how much diagnostic information is printed. Table 4-1 lists some of the options that might be most useful.

exam
Watch

An excellent way to become familiar with the Solaris 9 operating environment boot process is to use the -i and -v options to boot the system.

Boot Programs Phase

When the boot block executes, its sole function is to load the secondary boot program, UFSBOOT, and execute it. The function of UFSBOOT is to locate and load the basic kernel, which controls the rest of the Solaris 9 operating environment. The location of UFSBOOT is encoded into the boot block. This location can change, so you might have to install a new boot block. You accomplish this task with the installboot command.

The purpose of this two-stage boot process is simplicity and flexibility. The *UFS* in UFSBOOT is short for UNIX file system. If the boot block were going to load the kernel directly, it would need to have knowledge of the file system structure that the operating environment is going to use. As a result, the boot block would have to be a much larger and more complex program. The partitioning of the disk slices would be limited, and UFS would be the only file system that could be used for booting the operating environment. As you will learn later, several other kinds of file systems exist. Potentially, one of these file system types could be used for the boot file system.

Kernel Phase

The *kernel* is the heart of the Solaris 9 operating environment. It is the process that remains running at all times and controls what happens on the system. It acts as the

	Boot Option	Function
TABLE 4-1 Solaris 9 Boot Options	*-a*	Boots from an alternate /etc/system file
	-s	Boots into single-user maintenance mode
	-r	Reconfigures devices during boot
	-w	Mounts the root file system as writeable for repair
	-i	Boots interactively; the system requests answers to many questions that normally have defaults
	-v	Prints verbose diagnostic messages during boot

conduit and gatekeeper between the applications and the hardware. It is responsible for making sure that two processes do not attempt to use the same resources at the same time.

The core kernel of the Solaris 9 operating environment is actually composed of two main static pieces: a platform-independent piece called generic UNIX (GENUNIX) and a platform-dependent piece called UNIX. The platform-dependent piece contains any code that relies on the underlying hardware of the system; the platform-independent piece contains the code that would be common across all architectures.

The UFSBOOT program loads the two main kernel pieces into memory, starts the kernel executing, and then turns control over to the kernel. The kernel uses the UFSBOOT program to locate and load modules necessary to begin controlling the system. Once UFSBOOT has loaded the modules necessary for the kernel to mount the root file system, it is unloaded and the kernel takes complete control.

Modules are pieces of software that are able to interface with and control a particular piece of hardware. These modules can be *dynamically loaded*—that is, loaded on demand, only when required by the kernel. They can also be unloaded when they are no longer needed. This feature allows the kernel to remain as small as possible, using the least amount of memory and processing as fast as possible.

exam
ⓦatch *Modules are a key element of the Solaris 9 operating environment. Knowing how to find and use various modules is an important skill for a system administrator.*

The kernel files, GENUNIX and UNIX, can be found in the directory /platform/ARCH/kernel or /platform/ARCH/kernel/sparcv9, where *ARCH* is the architecture of the system (as returned by uname -*i*), such as sun4u for the Ultra SPARC lines of systems. The sparcv9 directory is for systems based on the SPARC version 9 specifications, which support 64-bit operations. Modules are generally located in /kernel, /usr/kernel, /platform/ARCH/kernel, or /platform/MODEL/kernel, where *MODEL* is the model (as returned by uname -*m*), such as SUNW,Ultra5_10 on an Ultra 10.

Once the kernel has mounted the root file system, it reads its configuration file, /etc/system, and configures itself. The /etc/system file contains all the configurations that the kernel needs to operate. These include the path the kernel searches for modules, the root file system type and device if different from the default, and any kernel or module parameters that need to be changed from their default values. It also includes any modules that need to be loaded as part of the kernel initialization, rather than when they are first used, and any modules that are specifically not to be used. The system file is read once, at boot time. Any changes to the system file require the system to be rebooted.

In some UNIX variants, if the system behavior or parameters need to be changed, the kernel must be completely rebuilt and relinked. Because much of the Solaris operating environment kernel is built from dynamically loadable modules, modifying the system file is all that is needed. These modifications are read when the system is next booted. These modifications can allow the system administrator to change the way the kernel behaves, configure hardware drivers, or tune the performance of the operating system. Note that a mistake in the /etc/system file can make the system unbootable. Always make a backup copy of this file before modifying it.

The system file uses the asterisk (*) character to start a comment. Noncommented lines take one of two forms. The first form starts with one of the five commands followed by a colon (:) and an argument. The second form starts with the word *set* followed by a kernel parameter and its value. There is an 80-character limit on all lines within this file.

The search path for modules can be modified from its default using MODDIR and a space-separated list of directories to search for modules. Modules that are specifically not to be used can be excluded using the EXCLUDE directive. By default, modules are loaded when they are first referenced after the kernel initialization by either a user process or an application. Modules can be forced to be loaded during initialization with FORCELOAD.

The root file system type, if it is other than UFS, can be modified with the ROOTFS directive. If, for some reason, the root device is different from the device on which the boot loader resides, the root device can be specified using ROOTDEV.

On an unmodified system, the /etc/system file will be nothing more than comments. The following is an example of some of the commands that might be in the file if they were not already defaults:

```
moddir: /kernel /usr/kernel /platform/sun4u/modules
rootfs:ufs
rootdev:/sbus@1,f8000000/esp@0,8000000/sd@3,0:a
exclude:
forceload: fs/ufs fs/procfs fs/tmpfs
forceload: sys/pipe sys/kaio sys/doorfs
set maxusers=512
set nautopush=32
```

on the
Job

You can gain amazing performance by modifying the system parameters based on the expected use of the system. Recently, I was helping with a database server that was having trouble. Whenever there was any network problem, the system would not recover correctly and connections would be refused. Any time there was a network outage, the server had to be rebooted! The source of the problem was that when the network had a problem, many client connections would be left unterminated and the login IDs would be locked. You cut the tcp_close_wait_interval from the default of 30 minutes to 5 minutes. That way, the broken connections timed out quickly and the IDs were available for use again.

INIT Phase

Once the kernel is fully loaded and configured, it loads and executes the INIT process. The *INIT phase* is the last step before the system is fully functional. Once INIT is started, the system actually has all the requirements necessary to be functional, but none of the services has been started. INIT is the ancestor of all processes that run on the Solaris 9 operating environment. It is responsible for starting all the processes that prepare the system for use. These include mounting the nonroot file systems, starting the daemon services such as SENDMAIL or CRON, and, finally, starting the GETTY processes that allow users to access the system. Once INIT has started all these processes and the system is ready for use, it is INIT's responsibility to restart GETTY as users log out, clean up after any "orphaned" processes, and control the transitions between run levels.

The INIT process is controlled by a configuration file called /etc/inittab. This file is used to describe the run levels and set the default run level at which the system will operate. It defines the processes that are executed during the transition to a new run level. It is also used to define processes that should be started, monitored, and restarted if they fail. Because the run levels are defined by INIT, they are often referred to as *INIT levels* or *INIT states*.

Each noncommented line in the INITTAB is composed of four fields, separated by a colon (:). Comment lines begin with a hash mark (#) and are ignored by the INIT process. They are there to help the administrator better understand the file. The four fields of the INITTAB file are as follows:

- ■ **The ID field**   The ID is a unique string of one to four characters. It is used to identify the entry.

- **The RLEVEL field** The RLEVEL field describes the run levels when the entry is valid. This field can be any combination of 0 through 6 to correspond to the various run levels. If it is blank, it is interpreted as 0123456, or valid at all run levels. It must not be blank for the INITDEFAULT action.

- **The ACTION field** The ACTION field determines the action to be taken when this entry is activated. An entry is activated when INIT enters the appropriate run level and the INITTAB file is scanned. Some of the more common possible actions are as follows; others may be found in the INITTAB manual page:

  - **SYSINIT** A process with the SYSINIT action is run before a console login prompt is displayed. INIT pauses its execution until this process completes and terminates.

  - **INITDEFAULT** INITDEFAULT defines the default run level where the system will operate. This line is scanned only when INIT starts at boot time, and INIT will cycle through the run levels until it reaches this level. If the RLEVEL field is blank for this entry, it causes the system to continually reboot itself; as mentioned, it is interpreted as 0123456. If it is set to 0, the system immediately shuts itself down as soon as INIT is executed. If it is set to 5, the system immediately powers itself down when INIT is executed. If no INITDEFAULT entry is present in the INITTAB file, INIT prompts at the console during the boot. The default is 3.

  - **RESPAWN** RESPAWN defines a process that should be started, if it is not currently running, and monitored so that it will be restarted if it terminates for any reason. A RESPAWN process will not be waited for; INIT will continue processing the file.

  - **WAIT** A process that is a WAIT action will cause INIT to pause its scanning of the INITTAB file until this process completes and terminates.

  - **ONCE** When an entry is defined as ONCE, the process is started when this entry is activated, and INIT continues to the next entry. As with a RESPAWN, INIT does not wait for this process to finish. However, when the process does complete, it will not be restarted.

  - **BOOT** A BOOT entry is a process in which INIT first begins at boot time. It is not waited for, and when it completes, it is not restarted.

- **The PROCESS field**   The PROCESS field specifies the command or script that is to be run when this entry is activated. In particular, this is how the run-level scripts are started.

A couple of examples that might be found in the INITTAB file are described as follows. The first example is the entry that defines run level 2. The ID associated with this entry is *s2*. Because this defines run level 2, the RLEVEL is 2. The ACTION is WAIT, which means that INIT will pause its scanning of the file until this script returns. The PROCESS it starts is /sbin/rc2:

```
s2:2:wait:/sbin/rc2 >/dev/msglog 2<>/dev/msglog </dev/console
```

This next example is a little more complex. This entry initializes the console, starts the console monitor, and provides the console login prompt. The ID is co. The only run levels that have a console login are two, three, and four. (One and *s* or *S* can have only root login, so only the root password prompt, not the entire console login, is provided.) When the process exits (a user logs out), the console prompt needs to be redisplayed, so the process must be restarted. Therefore, the ACTION is RESPAWN:

```
co:234:respawn:/usr/lib/saf/ttymon -g -h -p "`name -n` console login: " \
-T sun -d /dev/console -l console -m ldterm,ttcompat
```

EXERCISE 4-1

The Solaris 9 Bootstrap Process

In this exercise, you will modify the /etc/system file and reboot the system. Make a backup copy of the file in case you make a mistake. Make sure no one is using the system before shutting it down and restarting it. Most people are not very happy if their processes suddenly disappear out from under them.

The purpose of this exercise is to familiarize you with the Solaris 9 boot process and with modifying the default behavior. Depending on the speed at which your system can reboot, this exercise can take anywhere from 15 minutes to 1 hour.

1. If the system is currently running, log in as root and shut it down to the boot PROM using the shutdown command:

```
# shutdown -i 0 -g 0 -y
```

2. Start the bootstrap procedure using the *-v* flag. This flag instructs the system to print a large amount of diagnostic information, which could help you determine when specific phases are entered:

   ```
   ok boot -v
   ```

3. Watch the diagnostic messages and see if you can determine when the boot programs phase, the kernel phase, and the INIT phase start.

4. When the system is completely booted, log in as root.

5. Change directory to the /etc directory:

   ```
   # cd /etc
   ```

6. Make a backup copy of the system file by copying it to another name:

   ```
   # cp system system.bak
   ```

7. Use the modinfo command to determine if the shared memory system (SHMSYS) module is loaded. If the module is not loaded, this command should return nothing:

   ```
   # modinfo | grep shmsys
   ```

8. Do you see anything from the previous command?

9. Edit the system file and add a line that reads

   ```
   forceload: sys/shmsys
   ```

10. Shut down the system.

    ```
    # shutdown -i 0 -g 0 -y
    ```

11. Boot the system.

    ```
    ok boot
    ```

12. Log in as root.

13. Use modinfo to determine if the SHMSYS module is loaded:

    ```
    # modinfo | grep shmsys
    ```

14. Do you see anything from the previous command? Unlike Step 11, this time, you should see a line similar to the following:

    ```
    95 1032f27b   23d8   52   1   shmsys (System V shared memory)
    ```

This line shows that the module is loaded. The information provided includes the ID assigned to the module, the memory address where it was loaded, the size of the module, some module-specific information, the name of the module, and the description.

CERTIFICATION OBJECTIVE 4.02

Understanding and Working with Solaris Run Levels

A system running the Solaris 9 operating environment can be in one of several defined states, known as run levels. A *run level* is a named operating state that defines the available resources and services. Run levels provide the system administrator with control over the uses of the system; the levels determine the number of users who can access the system and what is available to those users. By using different run levels, an administrator can disallow anyone else from accessing the system, allow multiple users to use the system without some networking services, allow full use of the system, or reboot the system.

Run levels are named with a single alphanumeric character, generally 0 through 6, *s,* or *S.* There is nothing particularly special about the predefined run levels other than that they are predefined. New run levels could be added if needed, and not all defined run levels are currently used. Table 4-2 lists the eight defined Solaris 9 operating environment run levels.

TABLE 4-2	Run Level	Function
Solaris 9 Run Levels	0	PROM mode. It is used to bring a running system to the OK prompt, either to turn the system off or to perform a PROM mode function.
	S or *s*	Single-user mode. If the system is booted into this mode, only the minimum number of file systems are mounted. Minimal services are started.
	1	Single-user administrative mode. All file systems are accessible. Minimal services are started.

TABLE 4-2	2	Standard multiuser mode. Generally, all normal services are started, except the Network File Service (NFS) and any service that relies on NFS being available.
Solaris 9 Run Levels *(continued)*	3	Default run level. All normal services are started, including NFS and any service that relies on NFS being available.
	4	Unused or user defined. This run level is not currently used. Some users define special services to start in this mode.
	5	Shutdown mode. It performs equivalently to run level 0, except that it also powers down the system, if the hardware supports it.
	6	Reboot mode. It performs equivalently to run level 0, except that it issues a boot command when it reaches the PROM level.

Note that run levels 0, 5, and 6 are not actually states in which the system can remain. Run level 0 is used to transition to the PROM mode, when the operating environment is not actually running. Run levels 5 and 6 use run level 0 to enter the PROM mode. Run level 5 then attempts to power down the system; run level 6 causes the system to return to the default run level when it is completed. These run levels are used to ensure that a system is properly shut down or restarted.

How Run Levels Work

As mentioned, run levels are named states of execution with defined services and resources available. The preceding section discussed the INIT process, the INITTAB file, and how those relate to naming the run levels. This section describes how the available resources and services are defined.

/sbin/rc# (Where # Falls in the Range of 0 to 6, s or S)

Each run level is controlled by a *run control script,* named /sbin/rc#, where the pound sign (#) is the level this script controls. These scripts can be thought of as *metascripts*: their major function is to run other scripts. The scripts that are run by the /sbin/rc# scripts are *service control scripts.* They are used to control various services, such as the mail service or the printing service. These service control scripts can be found in directories named /etc/rc#.d, where the pound sign (#) is the run level.

When the run control script starts, it first defines the environment it needs to operate. This could include setting variables, such as PATH. It could also include making sure that certain resources, such as mounting the /usr file system, are available. Once its environment is set, the script then runs any shutdown scripts found in the /etc/rc#.d directory. Next, it runs any startup scripts for the new run level. Finally, it performs any cleanup activities it might need.

These scripts are executed by INIT whenever a new run level is entered. For example, if the system is to move from run level 3 to run level 1, the /sbin/rc1 script is run. During the boot process, the system moves through all run levels until it reaches the default run level. So, before the system enters run level 3 (generally the default run level), it will go through run levels 1 and 2 as well. Note that, as described in Table 4-2, run level 0 is used to bring a running system to PROM mode; so during the boot process, /sbin/rc0 would not be run.

In the Solaris 1.*x* operating environment (more commonly known as SunOS 4.*x*), these commands lived in the /etc directory. For backward-compatibility reasons, these scripts are still linked into the /etc directory and are sometimes called from there.

on the
Job

Understanding the material from this section has been very useful in my duties as a consultant. I was once called to help bring a major production system back to life. During an upgrade, something had corrupted one of the configuration files, and the boot process was hanging. The person doing the upgrade had been trying for several hours to debug the problem; an upgrade that had been scheduled to take two hours was in its tenth hour, and it was becoming a critical problem. Because I knew the order in which the run control scripts and service control scripts run, I was able to quickly pinpoint the process that was hanging. After that, it took only a couple of minutes, a little work with the od command, and one minor change to get the system back in running order.

/etc/init.d

The directory /etc/init.d is the true location of the service control scripts that are run by the run control metascripts. This is a centralized location where all the scripts can be kept for maintainability. Rather than being spread out over several directories or having multiple copies, the scripts can all be kept in one location and links can be made to the run levels that require them.

The service control scripts are written to both start and stop the services they control. When they are linked into the run-level directories, they will be named in such as way as to define which function should happen. In addition, a system administrator might need to stop and/or start a process directly, either during a run level when it doesn't normally run or if there is a problem with the service. In this case, the script can be called directly from this location with either START or STOP as an argument.

For example, here is a script to control the automatic mounting of file systems (AUTOFS) service:

```
#!/sbin/sh
#
# Copyright (c) 1993-1998 by Sun Microsystems, Inc.
# All rights reserved.
#
#ident    "@(#)autofs      1.6      98/12/14 SMI"

case "$1" in
'start')
        /usr/lib/autofs/automountd </dev/null >/dev/msglog 2>&1
        /usr/sbin/automount &
        ;;

'stop')
        /sbin/umountall -F autofs
        /usr/bin/pkill -x -u 0 automountd
        ;;

*)
        echo "Usage: $0 { start | stop }"
        ;;
esac
exit 0
```

FROM THE CLASSROOM

Going Further with Service Control Scripts

The service control scripts that are part of the base Solaris 9 operating environment will have only the start and stop functionality. Some third-party scripts have also added functionality to restart the service, to reconfigure the service, or to provide status information about the service. This functionality can be very useful to save the administrator from having to remember extra commands that might rarely be used. This way, the administrator can remember the service name and the arguments START, STOP, RESTART, CONFIGURE, and STATUS.

—*Stephen P. Potter, Senior UNIX Engineer,*
Information Control Corporation

/etc/rc#.d (Where # Falls in the Range of 0 to 6, s or S)

As we've seen, /etc/init.d is the centralized location for all service control scripts; /etc/rc#.d is the run-level–specific directory where the links are kept. The /sbin/rc# script looks in this directory to find the scripts to start and stop the services. Files in here are linked to /etc/init.d and are named K##service or S##service. The *K* and *S* tell the run control script whether the service should be killed (stopped) or started. The double pound (##) is a number from 00 to 99 that determines the order in which the service is started. These numbers are arbitrary to allow flexibility in terms of when a process is started or stopped. If a service, such as AUTOFS, relies on another service, nfs.client in this case, the dependent service needs to have a later start number (or an earlier termination number).

For example, in /etc/rc3.d, you might find S15nfs.server. This script starts the NFS server when run level 3 is entered. It is run after any scripts named S00 through S14 but before any scripts named S16 through S99. Another example that can be found in /etc/rc0.d is K36sendmail. This script stops the SENDMAIL service when run level 0 is entered (when the system is being shut down). It would be run before most other shutdown scripts.

Working with Run Levels

Several commands are available that deal with run levels. These commands include init, telinit, shutdown, halt, reboot, and poweroff. The commands init, telinit, and shutdown provide a general means for switching between run levels. The commands halt, reboot, and poweroff are used to move from a specific run level to another specific run level.

init and telinit

```
init [ rlevel ]
telinit [ rlevel ]
```

The main function of the INIT process was described in Chapter 2. However, if it is called by something other than the kernel when it is already running, it is used to instruct the main INIT process to change to another run level. After it has instructed the original instance, it will terminate itself. The telinit command is also provided for this purpose, to "tell" init what to do. In fact, this other command is implemented as a hard link to the init binary, not actually as a separate command. Using init or telinit will change to the new run level in an orderly manner. (It will run the /sbin/rc# script for the level it is entering.)

There appears to be a great deal of redundancy in the commands discussed here. Pay particular attention to how the commands interact with init and with the /sbin/rc# scripts.

shutdown

```
shutdown [ -i init level ] [ -g grace period ] [ -y ] [ message ]
```

You use the shutdown command to transition a running system to another run level nicely, using the init process. It is called with two arguments, the new run level to transition to (the default is run level S), and a grace period before actually performing the change. When shutdown is called, it sends a warning message to all users on the system. This warning message details when the shutdown will happen. If the optional message is supplied, it will also be sent. If the optional message is more than one word, it must be enclosed in quotation marks (either single or double). By default, the process pauses at the end of the grace period and waits for confirmation before changing the run level. The option *-y* can be used to direct shutdown not to ask for confirmation and to complete the transition. This is the normal way to shut down a system.

halt

```
halt
```

Think of the halt command as the opposite complement of the shutdown command. It immediately transitions the system to the PROM mode without running the /sbin/rc0 script. Instead of stopping the processes through the run control scripts, it signals init to send a termination signal to all processes. You generally use this command only in emergency situations, when it is essential to bring the system down quickly, or when you are certain that nothing will be adversely affected by the quick termination.

reboot

```
reboot [ -- ] [ boot options ]
```

You use the reboot command to immediately reboot the system. In other words, it performs a halt and a boot. It does not run the /sbin/rc0 script, and it is immediate. This command is not normally called with any arguments. However, the special argument consisting of two dashes can be used to protect arguments to be passed to the boot command at the PROM level.

SCENARIO & SOLUTION

You've modified the /etc/system file and need to reload it.	Use reboot -r to reboot the system and pass the reconfigure option to the boot command.
You've been informed of a physical environment emergency. The system needs to be shut down immediately.	Use halt to shut the system down as quickly as possible.
The system is currently running in a multiuser mode and you need to bring it into single-user mode for maintenance.	Use init 1 or telinit 1 to transition the system to the maintenance mode.
You need to shut the system down gracefully to perform a hardware upgrade.	Use shutdown -i 0 -g 300 -y to shut the system down gracefully in 5 minutes (300 seconds) to give users a chance to log off.

poweroff

```
poweroff
```

You use the poweroff command to immediately shut down the system and turn off the power, if the hardware supports it. It does not run /sbin/rc0, and it is immediate. You should probably use this command only in drastic situations.

EXERCISE 4-2

Working with Solaris Run Levels

This exercise will familiarize you with Solaris run levels and the commands for transitioning between them.

1. If the system is not currently running, boot it into the default run level with the boot command and log in as root.

```
ok boot
```

2. Use the telinit command to change from the default run level to run level 2.

```
# telinit 2
```

Did you notice any changes when you changed level? When you go from run level 3 to run level 2 on most systems, you should not notice any difference. If the system is an NFS server, the server will be shut down.

3. Use the reboot command to restart the system.

```
# reboot
```

What happened? You should see the system shut down all processes, enter the PROM mode, and then reboot to the default run level.

4. Use the shutdown command to bring the system to the PROM mode.

```
# shutdown -i 0 -g 30 -y
```

5. Boot the system using the *-a* flag. If you still have the /etc/system.bak file created in Exercise 4-1, use it to answer the question "Name of system file."

```
ok boot -a
```

6. Shut the system down using the halt command.

```
# halt
```

7. How did halt differ from shutdown? The shutdown command was an orderly shutdown. It provided a warning message and a grace period before it shut down. The halt command was a "dirty" shutdown. It was immediate with no warning, and the run control and service control scripts were not run.

CERTIFICATION SUMMARY

This chapter detailed how a system boots and how it shuts down. It described the stages of the bootstrap process. It also discussed the function of run levels and how to work with them. This knowledge is essential to a system administrator who is responsible for production-level systems.

This chapter described the four stages of the bootstrap process: the boot PROM phase, the boot programs phase, the kernel phase, and the INIT phase. The boot command and some of the more common and useful options were discussed as part of a brief description of the boot PROM phase. Full coverage of the boot PROM itself has been left for Chapter 2. The purpose of the primary boot loader, BOOTBLK, and the secondary boot program, UFSBOOT, were covered.

Also discussed were the pieces of the kernel, the static GENUNIX and UNIX files, as well as the dynamically loaded modules and the /etc/system configuration file. Detail was provided for the INIT phase and the process and files of that phase. These included the INIT process itself and the /etc/inittab file.

The second half of the chapter discussed the eight Solaris run levels and their purposes. The /sbin/rc# run control scripts, the /etc/init.d directory, the service control scripts contained within, and the /etc/rc#.d directories and links to the service control scripts were described. Finally, the six commands used to boot, reboot, and halt the system were detailed, as well as how they interact with INIT and the run levels.

TWO-MINUTE DRILL

Understanding the Solaris 9 Operating Environment Bootstrap Process

❑ The four phases of the bootstrap process are the boot PROM phase, the boot programs phase, the kernel phase, and the INIT phase.

❑ POST, the power-on self-test, scans the system to find the installed hardware, runs primary diagnostics, and builds a device tree.

❑ The boot PROM command boot uses the NVRAM variable BOOT-DEVICE to locate the primary bootloader, BOOTBLK.

❑ The primary bootloader loads the file system boot program, called UFSBOOT. UFSBOOT loads the core kernel.

❑ The Solaris 9 kernel is composed of two static pieces, called GENUNIX and UNIX, and dynamically loaded modules.

❑ The kernel pieces can be found in /platform/ARCH/kernel or /platform/ARCH/kernel/sparcv9. Modules can generally be found in /kernel, /usr/kernel, /platform/ARCH/kernel, or /platform/MODEL/kernel.

❑ The INIT process is the ancestor of all other processes. It is controlled by the file /etc/inittab.

❑ The /etc/inittab file is composed of lines with four fields separated by colons. The four fields are the ID field, the RLEVEL field, the ACTION field, and the PROCESS field.

Understanding and Working with Solaris Run Levels

❑ Run levels are named operating states that define the resources and services available to the system.

❑ Solaris 9 defines eight run levels: s, S, and 0 through 6.

❑ The INIT process controls the run levels. When a new run level is entered, INIT runs the /sbin/rc# script that corresponds to the level being entered.

❑ Run levels 0, 5, and 6 are not permanent states, like run levels s, S, and 1 through 3. Run level 4 is available to be defined as an alternative multiuser environment configuration, but it is not necessary for system operation and is usually not defined.

❏ The /sbin/rc# scripts call service control scripts that live in /etc/init.d and are linked into the /etc/rc#.d directories.

❏ The service control scripts are coded to take both a START and a STOP parameter when they are called. The links in the /etc/rc#.d directories begin with K## or S## to instruct the /sbin/rc# script to call them with either the START or STOP parameter.

❏ The commands init, telinit, and shutdown are all "clean" commands; they warn the users that the system is about to change and execute the proper /sbin/rc# scripts. The commands halt, reboot, and poweroff are immediate and send the users no warning of imminent system changes.

SELF TEST

The following questions will help you measure your understanding of the material presented in this chapter. Read all the choices carefully because there might be more than one correct answer. Choose all correct answers for each question.

Understanding the Solaris 9 Operating Environment Bootstrap Process

1. Which of the following lists the four phases of the Solaris 9 bootstrap process, in order of execution?

   A. INIT, boot PROM, kernel, boot programs

   B. Boot programs, boot PROM, INIT, kernel

   C. Boot PROM, boot programs, kernel, INIT

   D. Kernel, boot programs, boot PROM, INIT

2. When UFSBOOT loads the kernel, it loads which parts?

   A. The static core, GENUNIX and UNIX.

   B. The UFS file system module and then GENUNIX.

   C. The MMU memory system module, the UFS file system module, and then UNIX.

   D. It loads the whole kernel.

3. If you were installing a dynamically loaded module for the Veritas file system (VSFS), where would you place it? (Choose all that apply.)

   A. /usr/modules

   B. /kernel

   C. /platform/ARCH/kernel

   D. /usr/local/kernel

4. To change the default run level to which the system boots from 3 to 2, you would change which line in the /etc/inittab file?

   A. The sysinit line si:2:sysinit:

   B. The boot line db:2:boot:init

   C. The initdefault line is:2:initdefault:

   D. The once line on:2:once:default

Understanding and Working with Solaris Run Levels

5. Which of the following describes a run level?

   A. A named operating state that defines the available resources and services

   B. A speed at which you have defined the processor to run

   C. A particular version of the Solaris 9 operating environment that is installed on a system

   D. The variable in /etc/system that determines the maximum number of users who can access the system at once

6. If you use the command telinit to change from run level 3 to run level 2, which changes will occur on the system?

   A. You will change from multiuser mode to single-user mode, and all users will be logged out.

   B. You will reboot the system.

   C. Probably not much, unless the system is an NFS server. Run level 3 is defined for NFS serving. In that case, NFS will be stopped.

   D. Probably not much, unless the system runs a database. Run level 3 is defined for databases to operate in. In that case, the database will shut down.

7. If you were to install a new service, such as the OpenSSH (Secure Shell) service, how would you configure it to start automatically when the system booted?

   A. Add a line to /etc/inittab that defined a WAIT action for the OpenSSH server at run level 2.

   B. Create a service control script in /etc/init.d and link it into /etc/rc2.d.

   C. Modify the /etc/rc.local script to start the OpenSSH server when it is run.

   D. Create a CRON job that runs every 5 minutes. If the system has been up for less than 5 minutes, start the OpenSSH server. If the system has been up for longer than 5 minutes, do nothing.

8. The six common Solaris commands for dealing with changing run levels are which of the following?

   A. hup, stop, kill, int, term, and halt

   B. freeze, halt, stop, down, drop, and fire

   C. boot, reboot, halt, kill, shutdown, and init

   D. shutdown, halt, init, poweroff, telinit, and reboot

9. In which order are the scripts in /etc/rc2.d run by the /sbin/rc2 script?

   A. They are run in the order in which they are stored on the disk. So the longer a script has been around, the earlier it will run.

   B. The start scripts are run first, then the kill scripts are run. They run in alphabetical order—for example, AUTOFS would start before nfs.client.

   C. The kill scripts run first, and then the start scripts run. They run in ASCII sorting order, so the lowest-numbered script runs first. For example, S20foo would run before S30bar.

   D. They run in numerical order, so S20foo would run before K30bar.

LAB QUESTION

You have just installed a web server on a machine. You want the server to start automatically when the system enters run level 2. You also want the server to stop when the system enters run level *s*, 0, or 1. The web administrator is not very familiar with the Solaris 9 operating environment and wants you to make it easy for her to recycle the server if she makes a change to the configuration. She also wants you to make it easy for her to determine whether the server is running. Using the information from this chapter, describe the steps you would take to accomplish these tasks.

SELF TEST ANSWERS

Understanding the Solaris 9 Operating Environment Bootstrap Process

1. ☑ **C.** The boot PROM phase uses the boot command to load the BOOTBLK. The BOOTBLK loads UFSBOOT in the boot programs phase. The UFSBOOT loads the kernel during the kernel phase, and the kernel executes init during the INIT phase.
☒ **A** is incorrect because INIT is the last phase of the process. **B** is incorrect because boot PROM is the first phase of the process. **D** is incorrect because kernel is the last phase.

2. ☑ **A.** The UFSBOOT program loads the two main kernel pieces into memory, starts the kernel executing, and then turns over control to the kernel.
☒ **B** is incorrect because the kernel uses UFSBOOT to load the UFS module after it has taken control. Once the UFS module is loaded, the kernel unloads UFSBOOT. **C** is incorrect because the kernel loads most modules, including the MMU memory module. **D** is incorrect because once UFSBOOT has loaded the static core and the modules necessary for the kernel to mount the root file system, it is unloaded and the kernel takes complete control.

3. ☑ **B** and **C.** /kernel is one location where modules are found; /platform/ARCH/kernel is another.
☒ **A** is incorrect because modules can be found in /usr/kernel but not /usr/modules. **D** is incorrect because the /usr/local directory (if it exists) is usually used for locally installed software but not kernel modules.

4. ☑ **C.** The INITDEFAULT action defines the default run level where the system will operate.
☒ **A** is incorrect because the SYSINIT action is for processes to be run before the console login prompt is displayed. **B** is incorrect because the BOOT action is for processes to be run when INIT first starts. **D** is incorrect because the ONCE action is for processes that are started as soon as the line is parsed and then forgotten about.

Understanding and Working with Solaris Run Levels

5. ☑ **A.** A run level is a named operating state that defines the available resources and services.
☒ **B** is incorrect because you cannot change the speed at which a processor runs; that is determined when the processor is manufactured. **C** is incorrect because Solaris 9 is itself a version of the Solaris operating environment. There are quarterly hardware releases of the Solaris 9 operating environment, but they are generally equivalent functionally. **D** is incorrect because the variable in /etc/system that controls the number of users is MAXUSER. Generally a misnomer these days, MAXUSER is the basis for some system settings, but the system will allow more than MAXUSER users on the system.

6. ☑ **C.** Run level 3 is where some network services, such as NFS, are started.

   ☒ **A** is incorrect because both run level 2 and run level 3 are multiuser states. Run level 3 is the run level where some network services, such as NFS, are started. **B** is incorrect because run level 6 reboots the system. **D** is incorrect because databases are not defined to run at any particular level. They could be started in either run level 2 or run level 3.

7. ☑ **B.** Create a service control script that has START and STOP parameters and place it in /etc/init.d. Then create a link in /etc/rc2.d called S##sshd. You can also create a link in /etc/rc0.d or /etc/rc1.d called K##sshd to stop the process when it enters that run level, but doing so is not really necessary.

   ☒ **A** is incorrect because the WAIT action in /etc/inittab will cause INIT to wait for the process to complete. The OpenSSH server is a daemon and should run as long as the system is up. **C** is incorrect—at least, it is incorrect in Solaris 9. This used to be correct in Solaris 1, also known as SunOS 4. Solaris 2 through 9 now use individual service control scripts for each service. **D** is incorrect because, even though this action could work, it does not use the design of the Solaris 9 operating environment. Having a script run every 5 minutes when that script does something only if the system booted in the last 5 minutes is a waste of processing power.

8. ☑ **D.** init, telinit, and shutdown are commands to cleanly change run levels. halt, poweroff, and reboot are commands to quickly change run levels without running the /sbin/rc scripts.

   ☒ **A** is incorrect because these are all signals that can be sent to a process by the kill command (sighup, sigstop, sigkill, sigint, sigterm, and sighalt). **B** is incorrect because you would likely hear these words if you are a criminal fleeing from the police. **C** is incorrect because boot is a PROM-level command for starting the system. kill is a command used with individual processes to send signals.

9. ☑ **C.** The kill scripts run, using the two-digit number to determine the order. Then the start scripts run, again using the two-digit number to determine the order.

   ☒ **A** is incorrect because the age of the script or the order in which the scripts were placed on the disk has no bearing on when they will run. **B** is incorrect because the kill scripts have to run first; otherwise, the kill scripts would terminate processes that were just started by the start scripts. All scripts have two digits following the *S* or *K,* and they run in numerical order. **D** is incorrect because the kill scripts run before the start scripts.

LAB ANSWER

The first task is to have the web server start automatically when the system enters run level 2. This brings to mind the /etc/rc2.d directory. Your first thought might be to place a script in there to start the server. However, the second task is to stop the server when the system enters certain other run levels. With multiple copies of the similar scripts, it could be a headache to keep them updated. A better idea is to have a single script and link it to the places you need. This means you want to create a script in /etc/init.d.

The next task is to make it easy for the web administrator to recycle the web server. Recycling the web server is the same as stopping it and starting it. You are already writing a script to do that; it is easy to tack this functionality on.

The last task you need to accomplish is to make it easy for the web administrator to check the status of the web server. Because she is unfamiliar with the Solaris 9 operating environment, the fewer commands you need to teach her, the better. Because you are already going to write a script that starts, stops, and restarts the web server, you might as well also make it check the status. Then you can teach her one command and four options.

The final script would look something like the following. (For the sake of brevity, some parts are not completed.) This script should live in /etc/init.d as webserver and be linked into /etc/rc2.d as S45webserver and into /etc/rcS.d, /etc/rc0.d, and /etc/rc1.d as K55webserver:

```
#!/bin/sh
case "$1" in
    start)
            echo -n "Starting httpd: "
             /opt/www/server/start
            ;;
    stop)
            echo -n "Stopping httpd: "
            if [ -f /var/run/httpd.pid ]
                    /opt/www/server/stop
            fi
            ;;
    restart)
            $0 stop
            $0 start
            ;;
    status)
            if [ -f /var/run/httpd.pid ]
                    pid=`head -1 /var/run/httpd.pid`
            else
```

```
        pid=`ps -afe | grep httpd | awk '{print $2}''
fi
if [ "$pid" != "" ]
        echo "httpd running as $pid"
else
        echo "No httpd found"
fi
;;
    *)
        echo "usage: $0 [ start | stop | restart | status ]"
        ;;
esac
```

5

User
Administration

This chapter explores user account management and login procedures. You will learn how to add accounts using both the GUI-based Admintool and the command line, and how to customize a user's environment using various shell initialization files. You will also learn how to identify who is currently logged in, where each user is logged in from, and what each user is doing.

CERTIFICATION OBJECTIVE 5.01

Understanding Login Procedures

There are multiple methods of logging in to a UNIX server, including a login at the console, Telnet to the server, and rlogin to the server. Login processing consists of identifying yourself to the system and having your working environment configured by a set of system initialization files. These files vary depending on your default shell. (Refer to the section "Initialization Files," later in the chapter.)

As the user logs in, the userid, groupid, home directory, and default shell are parsed from the password file, /etc/passwd.

The user's base environment is set as follows:

- **HOME**   The login directory; for example, /home/gibbst
- **LOGNAME**   The login name; for example, gibbst
- **PATH**   /usr/bin:
- **SHELL**   The last field of the password entry; for example, /bin/ksh (default is /bin/sh)
- **MAIL**   The login name; for example, /var/mail/gibbst
- **TZ**   The time zone specification; for example, EST5EDT

Here is a sample of the /etc/passwd file:

```
root:x:0:1:Super-User:/:/sbin/sh
daemon:x:1:1::/:
bin:x:2:2::/usr/bin:
sys:x:3:3::/:
adm:x:4:4:Admin:/var/adm:
lp:x:71:8:Line Printer Admin:/usr/spool/lp:
```

```
smtp:x:0:0:Mail Daemon User:/:
uucp:x:5:5:uucp Admin:/usr/lib/uucp:
nuucp:x:9:9:uucp
Admin:/var/spool/uucppublic:/usr/lib/uucp/uucico
listen:x:37:4:Network Admin:/usr/net/nls:
nobody:x:60001:60001:Nobody:/:
noaccess:x:60002:60002:No Access User:/:
nobody4:x:65534:65534:SunOS 4.x Nobody:/:
ingres:x:100:100:Ingres DBA:/opt/app/ingres:/bin/ksh
```

In this example, the fields are, from left to right, user account (name), password, UID, GID, GECOS (comment), home directory, and initial program (shell). On systems with shadow passwords, the password is replaced with an *x* in /etc/passwd.

Logging in to a System

Before you can do any work on a Solaris system, you need to log in. Each user should have a unique user account, and accounts should never be shared. Once you establish your connection—whether by logging in to a directly attached terminal or monitor, or connecting remotely via telnet or rlogin—a login prompt will appear on your screen. Type in your user (account) name and press ENTER. Next, you will receive a password prompt. Type in your password and press ENTER. The sequence is shown in Figure 5-1.

FIGURE 5-1

A Telnet connection to a remote system

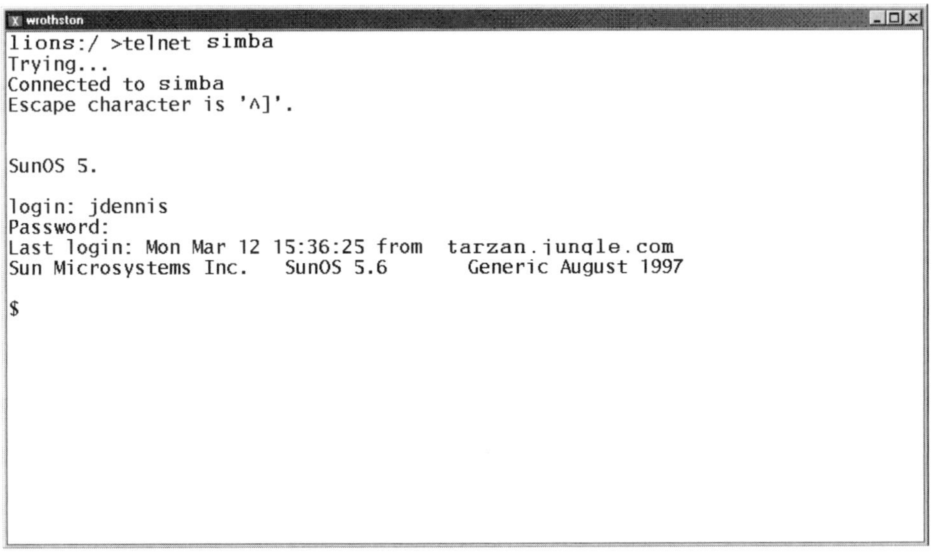

```
X wrothston                                                    _□×
lions:/ >telnet simba
Trying...
Connected to simba
Escape character is '^]'.


SunOS 5.

login: jdennis
Password:
Last login: Mon Mar 12 15:36:25 from   tarzan.jungle.com
Sun Microsystems Inc.    SunOS 5.6        Generic August 1997

$
```

If a user fails to enter the correct user ID and password five times, the failed login will be written to /var/adm/loginlog, if it exists, and the connection (TTY) will be dropped. By default, the file /var/adm/loginlog does not exist and can be created using the touch command so that login attempts can be logged.

Restricting Root-Level Access from Remote Connections

One of the great features of UNIX is its ability to be accessed from anywhere. However, this feature can also be a huge security risk.

Having said that, it is possible to prohibit a user from logging in directly as root unless the user is on the system console. (A *system console* is a terminal connected to the serial port of the server.) This is enabled using the variable CONSOLE in the /etc/default/login file. This file also controls other aspects of logging in to the system.

The CONSOLE variable's value determines how the root user accesses the system. The default setting is

```
CONSOLE=/dev/console
```

This means that the only way to log in as root is while sitting at the system. No user can Telnet or dial in remotely and log in as root. The only way to allow remote login as root is to comment the line out by adding the pound sign (#). It would look like this:

```
#CONSOLE=/dev/console
```

This configuration allows anyone who knows the root password to log in either remotely or at the system console. This is the least secure of the possible settings.

The other acceptable value is

```
CONSOLE=
```

The null value means that no user can log in as root either locally or remotely. However, a user can log in as any user with a valid account on the system, and then SU to root. The user will need to know the root password to switch to root successfully. All attempts to switch user—whether the user is SUing to root or to another user— are logged in /var/adm/sulog, if the file /etc/default/su has logging enabled. (SULOG=/var/adm/sulog will be uncommented in this file.)

I highly recommend that you keep the default setting of CONSOLE= /dev/console. If you know you will need remote root access, you can always comment it out. When you are done, make sure you uncomment the CONSOLE= line.

Logging Off of a System

To log off of a Solaris system, simply type **exit** at the shell prompt, or press CTRL-D.

Changing Login Passwords

To change a password, a user need only log in, then execute the passwd command. Figure 5-2 shows the sequence of changing a user's password.

Of course, the root user can change any other user's password as well as his or her own. This functionality (changing other users' passwords) is limited to the root user. No other user on the system has this capability. Any user can change his or her own password.

FIGURE 5-2	
| Changing a user's password | ```
X wrothston                                                    _ □ ×
$ passwd jdennis
Changing password for "jdennis"
jdennis's New password:
Re-enter jdennis's new password:
$
``` |
```

To change any given user's password, type the following:

```
passwd {login name}
```

For example, passwd gibbst would allow the root user to change the password of the user gibbst.

It is also advisable from a security perspective to enforce *password aging*—setting a limit for the number of days the password is valid—at which time, the password must be changed. The system administrator can perform this task by using the *min* and *max* parameters:

- **min** Sets the minimum number of days required between password changes for a specific user. The parameter *minweeks* in /etc/default/passwd controls this and, by default, is set to null.

- **max** Sets the maximum number of days the current password is valid for a specific user. The parameter *maxweeks* in /etc/default/passwd controls this and, by default, is set to null.

- **warn** Notifies a user *x* number of days before the password expires if *max* is set.

For example, using passwd *-s {username}* shows present password attributes for the user:

```
simba01# passwd -s gibbst
gibbst   PS
```

This output from passwd *-s* is formatted as username status. The status of *PS* means the account is passworded. Other statuses you might see are *LK* for locked or *NP* for no password. In the example case, password aging has not been enabled. We can then modify the password attributes:

```
enterprise# passwd -r files -n 7 -w 7 -x 30 gibbst
enterprise01# passwd -s gibbst
enterprise  PS     04/19/01    7   30   7
```

The format of the passwd *-s* display when password aging is enabled is as follows:

```
name status mm/dd/yy min max warn
```

The date displayed (*mm/dd/yy*) is the date the password was last changed for the user.

Note: All password aging dates are determined using Greenwich Mean Time (Universal Time) and could differ by as much as a day in other time zones.

In our example, we have modified the *min* (the *-n* option) to 7 days, the *max* (the *-x* option) to 30 days, and the *warn* (the *-w* option) to 7 days. Consequently, the user cannot change his or her password more often than 7 days, must change it every 30 days, and will be warned 7 days in advance that it must be changed.

The *-r* option identifies the repository to apply these changes to, as in files (/etc/passwd), nis, nisplus, or ldap.

CERTIFICATION OBJECTIVE 5.02

Identifying Users Who Are Currently Logged in to the System

In all versions of Solaris, several commands allow you to identify users who are currently logged in. The w command (see Figure 5-3), the who command (see Figure 5-4), and the finger command (see Figure 5-5) are used most frequently.

FIGURE 5-3	
Output of the w command	

```
simba :/ >w
   2:53pm  up 8 day(s), 12:47,  3 users,  load average: 0.07, 0.14, 0.26
User     tty          login@  idle   JCPU   PCPU  what
root     pts/1        2:49pm                       w
oracle   pts/2        8:36am   18    6:03          -ksh
oracle   pts/5        8:47am   12     54           -ksh
simba :/ >_
```

```
X wrothston                                                                    _ □ ×
simba :/ >who
root        pts/1        Mar 12 14:49        (simba.jungle.com)
oracle      pts/2        Mar 12 08:36        (192.168.0.3)
oracle      pts/5        Mar 12 08:47        (192.168.0.6)
simba :/ >_
```

The first command, w, tells more than just the users who are logged in. On the
first line, you see the uptime of the system, the time of day according to the system,

```
X wrothston                                                                    _ □ ×
simba :/ >finger
Login        Name                  TTY      Idle    When      Where
root                 Super User    pts/1            Mon 14:49  simba.jungle.com
oracle       Oracle@ lions         pts/2    20      Mon 08:36  192.168.0.3
oracle       Oracle@ lions         pts/5    14      Mon 08:47  192.168.0.6
simba :/ >_
```

how many users are logged in currently, and the load average (number of runnable processes) of the system over the past 1-, 5-, and 15-minute intervals.

Under user information, you see multiple headings:

- **User**   The user who is logged in
- **tty**   The name of the TTY the user is on
- **login@**   The time of day the user logged in
- **idle**   The number of minutes since a program last attempted to read from the terminal
- **JCPU**   The system unit time used by all processes and their children on that terminal
- **PCPU**   The system unit time used by the currently active process
- **what**   The name and arguments of the current process

Options to the w command are as follows:

- *-h*   Suppresses the heading.
- *-l*   Produces a long form of output, which is the default.
- *-s*   Produces a short form of output. In the short form, the TTY is abbreviated, and the login time and CPU times are left off, as are the arguments to commands.
- *-u*   Produces the heading line, which shows the current time, the length of time the system has been up, the number of users logged in to the system, and the average number of jobs in the run queue over the last 1, 5, and 15 minutes.
- *-w*   Produces a long form of output, which is the same as the default.

The who command identifies the users who are logged in, which TTY they are logged in on, the time they logged in, and which host or IP address they logged in from. If DNS is being used in your organization, the login location will resolve to a hostname, if it is identified in the DNS tables or in the local host table. If it is not, it will be identified by the IP address. The who command has considerably more power than merely identifying who is currently logged in, as referenced by the options available:

- *-a* Processes /var/adm/utmp or the named file with *-b, -d, -l, -p, -r, -t, -T,* and *-u* options turned on. /var/adm/utmp is the user accounting database. User login accounting information is stored in this file. The who command references this file, which is touched whenever a user logs in, to see which users are active on the system at this time, where they logged in from, and so on.

- *-b* Indicates the time and date of the last reboot.

- *-d* Displays all processes that have expired and not been respawned by init. The EXIT field appears for dead processes and contains the termination and exit values of the dead process. This can be useful in determining why a process terminated.

- *-H* Outputs column headings above the regular output.

- *-l* Lists only those lines on which the system is waiting for someone to log in. The name field is LOGIN in such cases. Other fields are the same as for user entries, except that the STATE field does not exist.

- *-m* Outputs information about only the current terminal.

- *-n x* Takes a numeric argument, *x,* which specifies the number of users to display per line. *x* must be at least 1. The *-n* option may be used only with *-q*.

- *-p* Lists any other process that is currently active and has been previously spawned by init. The NAME field is the name of the program executed by init, as found in /sbin/inittab. The STATE, LINE, and IDLE fields have no meaning. The COMMENT field shows the ID field of the line from /sbin/inittab that spawned this process.

- *-q* Displays the names and the number only of users currently logged in (quick who). When this option is used, all other options are ignored.

- *-r* Indicates the current run level of the init process.

- *-s* Lists only the NAME, LINE, and TIME fields. This is a default option.

The last command, finger, shows the login account, the name that TTY was logged in on, the amount of idle time, when the user logged in, and where the user logged in from.

Note: The GECOS field is from the password file /etc/passwd; GECOS is a seldom-used term that is a holdover from the early days of UNIX at Bell Labs. Today, it is a field that holds personal information about each user, such as full name, office phone number, and so on.

The finger command also has various options:

- *-b*   Suppresses printing the user's home directory and shell in a long format printout

- *-f*   Suppresses printing the header that is normally printed in a nonlong format printout

- *-h*   Suppresses printing of the .project file in a long format printout

- *-i*   Forces "idle" output format, which is similar to short format except that only the login name, terminal, login time, and idle time are printed

- *-l*   Forces long output format

- *-m*   Matches arguments only on username (not first or last name)

- *-p*   Suppresses printing of the .plan file in a long format printout

- *-q*   Forces quick output format, which is similar to short format except that only the login name, terminal, and login time are printed

- *-s*   Forces short output format

- *-w*   Suppresses printing the full name in a short format printout

CERTIFICATION OBJECTIVE 5.03

Adding, Modifying, or Deleting User and Group Accounts on the Local System

In addition to being able to use Admintool for user account management, a system administrator must know the underlying command structure and syntax, in the event that the GUI is not available for whatever reason (system resources, network resources, and so on).

Job *Command-line knowledge is highly valued by most employers. I have interviewed many system administrators over the past five years, and I rarely ask them how to add a user or display installed software using a GUI. Knowledge of the operating system is infinitely more important than being able to point and click.*

The useradd Command

The useradd command creates a new user account, adding information as appropriate to the /etc/passwd, /etc/group, and /etc/shadow files and creating the user home directory if requested. The command has various options.

```
useradd [ -c comment ] [ -d dir ] [ -e expire ] [ -f inactive ] [ -g group ]
[ -G group [, group...]] [ -m [ -k skel_dir ]] [ -u uid [ -o]] [ -s shell ] login
```

Use of the options is as follows:

- *-c* Allows the system administrator to enter comments or information that will identify the user. Also known as the GECOS field.

- *-d* Defines the location of the user's home directory.

- *-e* Expires the account after a given time frame.

- *-f* Defines the period (in days) after which, if the account is not used, it will be marked inactive.

- *-g* Defines the primary group membership for the user.

- *-G* Defines the supplementary group set for the user.

- *-m* Creates the user's home directory, if it does not already exist.

- *-k* Uses the directory {skel_dir} as a model for the user's home directory. This directory may contain a .profile and any other information that is applicable to a user account. (We will explore use of skeleton directories in the Scenarios and Solutions later in this chapter.)

- *-u* Assigns the user ID (numeric).

- *-o* Allows a UID to be duplicated (nonunique).

- *-s* Defines the user's default shell.

Let's look at the next example:

```
useradd -u 101 -c "Tim Gibbs" -d /export/home/gibbst -m -s /bin/ksh -g dba gibbst
```

In the example, we are adding login id gibbst (last field of the line) to the system, with UID 101 (*-u* option) and a comments field (*-c* option) stating the user's full name, creating a directory in /export/home/gibbst (*-d* and *-m* options), creating a default shell of /usr/bin/ksh (*-s* option—the Korn shell), and setting the user's primary group (*-g* option) as dba.

Additionally, to display the default values for the useradd command, you may use the *-D* option:

```
useradd -D [ -b base_dir ] [ -e expire ] [ -f inactive ] [ -g group ]
```

■ *-D* Displays default values for group, base_dir, skel_dir, shell, inactive, and expire. When used in conjunction with the *-g, -b, -f,* or *-e* options, the *-D* option sets the default values for the specified fields. The default values are the following:

Group	Other (GID of 1)
base_dir	/home
skel_dir	/etc/skel
Shell	/bin/sh
Inactive	0
Expire	Null (unset)

■ *-b* The default base directory for the system, base_dir, if *-d* dir is not specified. base_dir is concatenated with the user's login to define the home directory. If the *-m* option is not used, base_dir must exist.

As a system administrator, you need to know the various options for commands such as useradd, userdel, and usermod. Expect the exam to contain some questions on various options for these commands.

Now that you have a better idea of how to add users, here are some possible scenario questions and their answers.

SCENARIO & SOLUTION	
You've been given the assignment of creating a new user account for Joe Developer, utilizing the existing /home/devel directory as the home directory. Our corporate standard is the Korn shell, and all user accounts begin with the first initial of the first name and up to five characters of the last name. What command would be used to accomplish adding this user?	`useradd -g devel -d /home/devel -s /bin /ksh -c "Joe Developer" jdevel`
Given the scenario described, how would the command change if you were creating a home directory specific to this user?	`useradd -g devel -d /home/jdevel -m -s /bin/ksh -c "Joe Developer" jdevel`
Again, given the previous scenario, how would the command change if you were using /etc/skel/devel to populate the user's home directory with a common set of initialization files?	`useradd -g devel -d /home/jdevel -m -s /bin/ksh -c "Joe Developer" -k /etc/skel /devel jdevel`

The groupadd Command

Groups allow a system administrator to group together multiple users who perform similar functions, thereby allowing the members of the group to more easily share files. The groupadd command adds a new group definition to the system and modifies the /etc/group file as appropriate. Usage is

```
/usr/sbin/groupadd [-g gid [-o]] group
```

To create a new group on the system named *dba*, assigning it the group id of 101, the command syntax would be

```
groupadd -g 101 dba
```

If you wanted to create a new group using the same GID as an existing group, you could use the *-o* option, which allows GID to be nonunique.

The usermod Command

The usermod command modifies existing user accounts, and it has many options. Usage is as follows:

```
usermod [ -u uid [ -o ] ] [ -g group ] [ -G group [ , group ... ] ] [ -d dir [ -m ] ]
[ -s shell ] [ -c comment ] [ -l new_logname ] [ -f inactive ] [ -e expire ] login
```

Given the user account created earlier for Tim Gibbs, if you wanted to modify his UID from 101 to 102, the command would simply be

```
usermod -u 102 gibbst
```

Note that to make this modification, the user account cannot be in use and that any files previously owned by *gibbst* will now show as being owned by UID 101, because the association between *gibbst* and UID 101 has been removed. This problem can be corrected with a combination of the find command and chown.

on the job

In many environments, a user has accounts on multiple servers, none of which have the same UID. This presents a problem because it is common for a DBA or a developer to need to port those files from system to system; with the UID being different, the user can lose control of his or her own files. This situation can be corrected using usermod to change the UID to be common on all systems for the user, and then using a combination of find and chown to find all the user's files and give the user ownership. The find command used for this purpose is

```
find / -user [uid] -print -exec chown [new-user-account] {} \;
```

or, as in the previous example:

```
find / -user 101 -print -exec chown gibbst {} \;
```

The groupmod Command

The groupmod command modifies information pertinent to a given group in the system. Usage is as follows:

```
/usr/sbin/groupmod [ -g gid [ -o ]] [ -n name ] group
```

Given the group created earlier—the *dba* group with GID 101, you can modify the GID using the following command:

```
groupmod -g 102 dba
```

You could also modify the group name using the command as follows:

```
groupmod -n ingres dba
```

The userdel Command

The userdel command deletes a user's login from the system and makes the appropriate modifications to the /etc/passwd, /etc/group, and /etc/shadow files, as well as deleting the user's home directory, if requested. Usage is as follows:

```
userdel [ -r ] login
```

The *-r* option deletes the user's home directory. It would be advisable to make a backup copy of the directory prior to using this option.

Given the user *gibbst* created earlier, if you now want to remove him from the system but keep his directory until you can verify whether you need his files, you would run the command

```
userdel gibbst
```

If you know you don't need his files, you can use the command

```
userdel -r gibbst
```

on the **!** **o b**

I rarely use the -r option and remove a user's home directory. It is often difficult to know who, besides the removed user, may have used or needed to use a file in that user's home directory, especially in a development environment. In most environments I have worked in, I have a separate file system (a luxury some sites do not provide) for temporary storage of transient files, such as home directories of removed users. Normally, I create a TAR file, and then compress it to save space. I keep these on the system for up to six months, if space allows. If space is at a premium, I create a tape backup and retain these for up to one year (not in the normal tape rotation, but with the location documented in case of emergency).

The groupdel Command

The groupdel command deletes a group from the system. Usage is

```
/usr/sbin/groupdel group
```

Given the group *dba* created earlier, if you now want to remove it from the system, you can run the command

```
groupdel dba
```

SCENARIO & SOLUTION

Continuing the previous scenario, our corporate standard for UIDs for the development staff are numbers 500–599. The next available number in this series is 551. What command would you use to modify the UID associated with Joe Developer's account?	`usermod -u 551 jdevel` (Keep in mind that Joe can't be logged in when you run this command.)
Joe Developer has gotten a better job offer and moved on. His boss has come to you to remove Joe's account but wants to retain any files in his home directory. What command would be used to accomplish this chore?	`userdel jdevel`
Continuing the scenario, how would the command change if Joe's boss had already verified that none of Joe's files were needed, and he wanted to remove not only the user account but the home directory, too?	`userdel -r jdevel` (Remember our earlier On the Job note? It would be a good idea to make a special backup of the directory before removing it. Maybe Joe's boss was simply upset and didn't really think things through. When he calms down and comes to you a week later and asks for Joe's files, he'll be impressed by your foresight.)

This command modifies only the /etc/group file and deletes no files that were previously owned by this group.

CERTIFICATION OBJECTIVE 5.04

Listing the Shell Initialization Files Used to Set Up a User's Work Environment at Login

The *Bourne shell* is the original UNIX shell environment, in use since the advent of the UNIX operating system. The Bourne shell was created by the experts at AT&T Bell Labs—specifically, Stephen Bourne—in the early days of UNIX (the '80s). The *Korn shell* was created by David G. Korn, also of Bell Labs, in the early 1980s.

Initialization Files

The system's *initialization files* are files that define environment variables when a shell is started. Two types of initialization files exist: system and user. The system environment files set user defaults systemwide.

The Bourne and Korn shells both use /etc/profile to set their default environment. The C shell uses /etc/.login for its default environment.

When a user logs in, the systemwide initialization files will be read first to set up the default user environment. Once these files have been parsed by the login process, the user-specific initialization files will be read to set up the individual user environment. Note that any variables set in the user-specific initialization files will override variables set in the systemwide files.

Skeleton files, which may be used to populate a user's directory, are kept in /etc/skel. These files are especially helpful in creating a common environment for a group of users, such as a group of developers.

This system allows a system administrator to customize the user's environment as needed—maybe to set a specific environment for development staff, another environment for quality assurance staff, and yet another for system administration staff. A user may also customize his or her own environment, provided that the user has the ability to write to the initialization files in his or her home directory.

The initialization files for each shell are as follows:

- Bourne shell:
  - /etc/profile
  - $HOME/.profile
- Korn shell:
  - /etc/profile
  - $HOME/.profile
  - $HOME/.kshrc
- C shell:
  - /etc/.login
  - $HOME/.cshrc
  - $HOME/.login

The default /etc/profile and /etc/.login files check quotas, print the message of the day (MOTD) file (/etc/motd), and check for mail. Note that if the file $HOME/.hushlogin exists, the message of the day will not be printed. In this case, only the banner command will print a message to the screen.

exam
ⓦatch

It would behoove you to know the various initialization files for each shell, their locations, and the order in which they are sourced. These are common exam questions.

Defining a Variable in the .profile File

Each user can make changes to his or her environment by editing the .profile file located in his or her home directory. These settings, such as which shell to use or which path to use for executable commands, will be used over the same settings in /etc/profile.

For example, in my normal environment, programs that I use are located in /usr/local/bin. Other users do not need these same programs. I set the PATH statement in /etc/profile (the systemwide profile) for all the essential paths, then add my specific needs to the path in my $HOME/.profile. For example,

In /etc/profile PATH=/usr/bin:/usr/sbin**In $HOME/.profile** PATH=$PATH:/usr/local/bin

The PATH statement in my $HOME/.profile picks up the systemwide variables, then adds my specifics, so my path now is /usr/bin:/usr/sbin:/usr/local/bin.

Maintaining the /etc/profile File

The system initialization file, /etc/profile, has several important functions. They include exporting environmental variables to the shell, such as the user login name. The file exports the default path for all executable commands. It displays the contents of the ever-popular MOTD. The message displayed is found in /etc/motd. This variable is a good one to use to let users know about upcoming systemwide events. For example, if you are planning to take the system down for maintenance for a few hours on a Wednesday night, you can remind users of this upcoming event when they log in. If you edit the /etc/motd file, the /etc/profile file will display your warning to all the users of the system at login.

on the
Job

Many system administrators use the /etc/motd file to display a short message on the proper use of the system and/or short systemwide event messages. This process can be much more effective than sending out massive amounts of e-mail. Don't abuse this feature by creating a huge narrative. That is not what e-mail is for. Make sure you keep your messages short and relevant so that users avoid the tendency to yawn or read the paper while MOTD displays.

The /etc/profile file also sets default permissions and automatically checks to see whether you have mail waiting for you in your inbox.

Customizing the Templates in the /etc/skel Directory

The user initialization file, .profile, starts as a template. The templates are stored in the /etc/skel directory.

The Bourne and Korn shells both use the template /etc/skel/local.profile. The C shell uses both the /etc/skel/local.cshrc and /etc/skel/local.login.

When a user account is created, these files are modified based on the information provided and are renamed. The renamed files are then saved in the new user's home directory.

The Bourne and Korn shells' user initialization file is named .profile. The C shell's user initialization files are renamed to .cshrc and .login.

You can edit these templates in the /etc/skel directory to suit the environment you want for your users. For example, you can add a default printer to all users by adding to the /etc/skel/local.profile the line

```
LPDEST=printer1;export LPDEST
```

Modifying the skeleton files distributed with the operating system is not recommended. The recommended procedure is to create a new directory to contain the site-specific files, and add the site modified files to that directory. Then, when you create users, use that template to customize their environment. For example:

1. Become root on the system.

2. Make a site-specific directory:

```
# mkdir /usr/local/skel/devel
```

3. Copy the OS-supplied files to your directory:

```
# cp /etc/skel/local.cshrc /usr/local/skel/devel/.cshrc
# cp /etc/skel/local.login /usr/local/skel/devel/.login
# cp /etc/skel/local.profile /usr/local/skel/devel/.profile
```

4. Give the files the appropriate permissions:

```
# chmod 744 /usr/local/skel/devel/.*
```

Then use your favorite editor (mine is still vI) to modify these files to meet your users' needs.

FROM THE CLASSROOM

Expect the Unexpected

In this chapter, you have learned how to create user accounts, modify user accounts, delete user accounts, customize a user's environment, and much more. You've seen a number of On the Job examples from my years of experience. In a certification test, you need to expect the unexpected. In my experience with certification exams, they ask questions about rarely used options of commands. These questions truly do test your experience level and the extent to which you have drilled yourself on the commands used in a system administration environment.

—James Dennis, SCSA, IBM Certified Specialist AIX 4.1 System Administrator

CERTIFICATION SUMMARY

This chapter delved into the various options for adding, modifying, and deleting users and groups. It explored how to customize a user's environment using a shell environment, and how to customize the skeleton files to standardize new user setups. Various UNIX commands were discussed to determine who is on the system and where they logged in from. Finally, the use of password aging and the options available for a system administrator were explored. Careful reading and rereading of this material should give you a sound foundation on which to draw when taking the Solaris certification exams.

TWO-MINUTE DRILL

Understanding Login Procedures

■ When logging in, the system will read the input of the user account and password combination, validate and authenticate the user login, read the /etc/passwd file for user-specific information such as group information and default user shell, and initialize the user's environment accordingly.

Identifying Users Who Are Currently Logged In to the System

■ Three popular programs identify which users are logged in to the system and provide specific information, such as where the user logged in from, how long the user has been on the system, how long the system has been up, and the load on the system. These commands are w, who, and finger.

Adding, Modifying, or Deleting User and Group Accounts on the Local System

■ The useradd command allows you to create new user accounts.

■ The usermod command allows you to modify an existing user account.

■ The userdel command allows you to delete an existing user account.

■ The groupadd command allows you to add groups to the system.

■ The groupmod command allows you to modify existing groups.

■ The groupdel command allows you to delete groups from the system.

Listing the Shell Initialization Files Used to Set Up a User's Work Environment at Login

■ In the Bourne shell, /etc/profile and $HOME/.profile are used to set up a user's environment. In the Korn shell, /etc/profile, $HOME/.profile, and $HOME/.kshrc are used. Finally, in the C shell, /etc/.login, $HOME/.login, and $HOME/.cshrc are used.

SELF TEST

The following questions will help you measure your understanding of the material presented in this chapter. Read all the choices carefully because there might be more than one correct answer. Choose all correct answers for each question.

Understanding Login Procedures

1. Which of the following commands would not log you in to the remote system *voyager*?

    A. telnet -l gibbst voyager

    B. rlogin voyager -l gibbst

    C. rlogin -l voyager gibbst

    D. rlogin voyager

2. Which file contains failed login attempt information?

    A. /var/adm/lastlogin

    B. /var/adm/sulog

    C. /var/adm/failedlogins

    D. /var/adm/loginlog

Identifying Users Who Are Currently Logged in to the System

3. Which command will give you the number of users logged in to the system?

    A. numusers

    B. who -q

    C. who -a

    D. who

4. Which command will *not* show you which users are logged in to the system?

    A. finger

    B. who

    C. w

    D. whodo

Adding, Modifying, or Deleting User and Group Accounts on the Local System

5. Which of the following commands would allow you to delete a user account while keeping the user's files intact?

   A. userdel *-keep* gibbst

   B. userdel *-preserve* gibbst

   C. userdel gibbst

   D. userdel *-r* gibbst

Listing the Shell Initialization Files Used to Set Up a User's Work Environment at Login

6. Assuming that user Tim Gibbs has the Korn shell as his default shell, which of the following files is not accessed when he logs in?

   A. $HOME/.kshrc

   B. $HOME/kshrc

   C. $HOME/.profile

   D. /etc/profile

7. Which file contains all attempts to switch to the root user?

   A. /var/adm/switchroot

   B. /var/adm/sulog

   C. /var/adm/chroot

   D. /var/adm/suroot.log

LAB QUESTION

List the commands you would use to create a new user account for user *gibbst* (Tim Gibbs), creating his home directory, and giving him the default shell of /bin/ksh. How would you modify this user's environment to add /usr/local/bin to the path and add the default printer destination of COLORPR?

Once you've created the user account, you realize that you've assigned the wrong UID to the user. How do you correct this mistake, and which criteria must be met to accomplish this task?

SELF TEST ANSWERS

Understanding Login Procedures

1. ☑ C. The *-l* option must be immediately followed by the username, not the remote system name.
   ☒ A is incorrect because the syntax shown is correct for Telnet. B is incorrect because the syntax shown is for rlogin. D is incorrect because this is good syntax for rlogin.

2. ☑ D. If the file exists, failed login attempts will be written to /var/adm/loginlog.
   ☒ A is incorrect because lastlogin is one of the user accounting programs, not a log file. B is incorrect because it contains information about SU attempts, not login information. C is incorrect because there is no such filename as /var/adm/failedlogins.

Identifying Users Who Are Currently Logged in to the System

3. ☑ B. This command will give you the names and number of users logged in.
   ☒ A is incorrect because it is not a valid Solaris command. C and D are incorrect because they will give you longer listings of who is logged in, from where, and more detail than was wanted in this question.

4. ☑ D. This is not a valid Solaris command.
   ☒ A, B, and C are incorrect because they will all give you this information.

Adding, Modifying, or Deleting User and Group Accounts on the Local System

5. ☑ C. userdel with no options deletes only the user account.
   ☒ A is incorrect because *-keep* is not a valid option. B is incorrect because *-preserve* is not valid. D is incorrect because it will delete the user directory.

Listing the Shell Initialization Files Used to Set Up a User's Work Environment at Login

6. ☑ B. The correct file is .kshrc, not kshrc.
   ☒ A, C, and D are incorrect because all are accessed when a Korn shell user logs in.

7. ☑ B. All SU (switch user) command usage is logged in /var/adm/sulog.
   ☒ C and D are incorrect because neither is a valid log file in Solaris.

LAB ANSWER

You would use the following command to create the new user account, home directory, and default shell:

```
useradd -d /home/gibbst -m -s /bin/ksh -c "Tim Gibbs" gibbst
```

Using the text editor of your choice, you would add the following lines to /home/gibbst/.profile:

```
PATH=$PATH:/usr/local/bin;export PATH
LPDEST=COLORPR;export LPDEST
```

To change the UID, the user cannot be logged in. The following will change his UID:

```
usermod -u {newuid} gibbst
```

6

Solaris
File Security

I n today's highly complex computing environment, the ability to implement varying levels of security based on business requirements has increased the need for system administrators to use more than the standard UNIX file and directory permissions. In this chapter, we explore how to display and modify these permissions, as well as how to augment these permissions through the use of access control lists (ACLs).

CERTIFICATION OBJECTIVE 6.01

Using Regular Expressions to Search the Contents of Files

Regular expressions are one of the many tools available to help a system administrator find information. Regular expressions are used in combination with commands such as sed, awk, ed, vi, and grep, and they provide a consistent method of pattern matching. We could spend several chapters exploring these features, but we'll stick with the basics for now:

- The asterisk (*) allows selection of zero or more characters (wildcard).

- The question mark (?) allows selection of any single character, such as ?J. In that example, any occurrences of *J* will be selected.

- The period (.) following any character will match that character. For example, if you do grep x. {*filename*}, grep will match the *x* followed by any other single character.

To help you understand how this works, consider the following example, which has two dbf files in this directory. Doing an ls *-la* command, you see both files. If you pipe (|) the output of ls *-la* into grep x., then you see only the file that has a character after the *x* in the filename.

```
# ls -la dbf*
-rw-r-r-   1 root     other          31 Apr 24 10:59 dbf-files.tx
-rw-r-r-   1 root     other          31 Apr 23 16:36 dbf-files.txt
# ls -la dbf* | grep x.
-rw-r-r-   1 root     other          31 Apr 23 16:36 dbf-files.txt
```

- The carat (^) specifies matching the character(s) that follow it if they are at the beginning of the line. For example, ^J would select any line beginning with *J*.

■ The dollar sign ($) specifies to match the character(s) that follow it if they are at the end of the line.

■ The bracket ([...]) construct allows you to search for any pattern that is enclosed in the brackets.

As mentioned earlier, many UNIX commands use regular expressions. This chapter looks only at grep and how to use regular expressions with grep to search text files for a pattern, and print all lines that contain or match the pattern.

In Solaris, the standard implementation of grep has the following options:

■ *-b* Prints the block number on which the pattern was found.

■ *-c* Prints only the count of lines matching the pattern.

■ *-h* Suppresses printing the filename containing the matching line.

■ *-i* Turns off case sensitivity.

■ *-l* Prints only the filenames of those matching the pattern, separated by newline characters. Does not repeat the filenames when the pattern is found more than once in a given file.

The following example is searching for the string *open* in all files in a given directory:

```
$ grep -l open *
local.login
local.profile
```

As shown, two files were found that had the matching string.

■ *-n* Prints the line number on which the matching string was found.

■ *-s* Suppresses error messages about nonexistent or unreadable files.

■ *-v* Suppresses lines that match the string (does not mean verbose).

The following example is searching for a specific process in a process listing and doesn't want the grep command to show in the output:

```
$ ps -aef | grep ora | grep -v grep
    oracle   714    1  0 16:32:43 ?        0:00 ora_pmon_finance
    oracle   716    1  0 16:32:44 ?        0:00 ora_dbwr_finance
    oracle   718    1  0 16:32:44 ?        0:00 ora_lgwr_finance
    oracle   720    1  0 16:32:44 ?        0:00 ora_ckpt_finance
    oracle   722    1  0 16:32:44 ?        0:00 ora_smon_finance
    oracle   724    1  0 16:32:44 ?        0:00 ora_reco_finance
```

The grep *-v* grep part of this command sequence removes any output line that has the word "grep" in it.

■ *-w* Searches for the expression as a word, as though surrounded by a slash and less-than symbol (\<) and a period (.)

This example is searching for the word "openwin" in any file starting with *local*:

```
$ grep -w openwin local*
local.login:                    setenv OPENWINHOME /usr/openwin
local.login:             $OPENWINHOME/bin/openwin
local.profile:                   OPENWINHOME=/usr/openwin
local.profile:           $OPENWINHOME/bin/openwin
```

Additionally, the xpg4 implementation of grep has these options:

■ *-e pattern_list* Specifies one or more patterns to be used during the search for input. Patterns must be separated by a newline character. A null pattern can be specified by two adjacent newline characters in *pattern_list*. Unless the *-E* or *-F* option is also specified, each pattern will be treated as a basic regular expression. Multiple *-e* and *-f* options are accepted by grep. All the specified patterns are used when matching lines, but the order of evaluation is unspecified.

■ *-E* Matches using full regular expressions. Each pattern specified will be handled as a full regular expression. If any entire full regular expression pattern matches an input line, the line will be matched. A null full regular expression matches every line.

■ *-f pattern_file* Reads one or more patterns from the file named by the pathname *pattern_file*. Patterns in *pattern_file* are terminated by a newline character. A null pattern can be specified by an empty line in *pattern_file*. Unless the *-E* or *-F* option is also specified, each pattern will be treated as a basic regular expression.

■ *-F* Matches using fixed strings. Treats each pattern specified as a string instead of a regular expression.

■ *-q* Enables quiet mode. Does not write anything to standard out, regardless of matching lines. Exits with zero status if an input line is selected.

■ *-x* Considers only input lines that use all characters in the line to match an entire fixed string or regular expression to be matching lines.

EXERCISE 6-1

Using the grep Command

1. Imagine that you store copies of your error logs in your system administration home directory, under /home/sysadm/logs. You are looking for a memory parity error that was detected by one of your shell scripts on server *voyager* to determine how many occurrences you have of this specific error:

```
voyager:/home/sysadm/logs#  grep -c -E -i 'memory parity error' *
errorlog.0301:1
errorlog.0302:0
errorlog.0303:1
errorlog.0304:1
errorlog.0305:0
errorlog.0306:1
```

You are looking for the string *memory parity error* in all files, so you turn off case sensitivity (using the *-i* option) and look for an exact match (the *-E* option); you want to count only the occurrences, suppressing printing of all lines (the *-c* option). Notice in the output that each file that was checked was printed out, regardless of whether it had a pattern match. Three files matched the pattern and reported one error; the other three had no error and reported 0 occurrences. You could use the *-l* option to suppress the filenames that did not have the pattern, but you cannot count the lines with the *-c* option if you do so.

2. Next, you want to print each line that has the string in it and print the line number so you can easily find it in the file:

```
voyager:/home/sysadm/logs#  grep -n -i -E 'memory parity error' *
errorlog.0301:1:Memory Parity Error: Corrected
errorlog.0303:1:Memory Parity Error: Corrected
errorlog.0304:1:Memory Parity Error: Corrected
errorlog.0306:1:Memory Parity Error: Uncorrectable
```

3. Now you know more about your problem. If you wanted to report only those lines searching for the pattern *Memory Parity Error: Uncorrectable,* you would do so using the following expression:

```
voyager:/home/sysadm/logs# grep -E 'Memory Parity Error: Uncorrectable' *
errorlog.0306:Memory Parity Error: Uncorrectable
```

As you can see, only the one filename was returned, with the exact error message you were looking for.

In my many positions as a system administrator, I've relied heavily on regular expressions in my shell scripts and on the command line. Many of the places I've worked have not had the budget (nor, in some cases, the inclination) to implement expensive monitoring solutions, so the burden of trapping errors and monitoring the systems came down to me and my scripting abilities. I give some examples in this chapter, but these examples only scratch the surface. It's up to you to dive in and make regular expressions work for you.

CERTIFICATION OBJECTIVE 6.02

Using Command Sequences to Display or Modify File and Directory Permissions

Many times, system administrators don't dig into the commands and options available to them. Some commands have considerably more power than you might think. This section explores the ls and chmod commands—two of the system administrator's staples to survive in the UNIX environment.

exam
Watch

Commands such as ls are common areas that trip up exam takers. Options that are not commonly used in actual practice often appear on exams to test whether a system administrator has researched available options or possibly has landed on one or two options and never explored further.

The ls Command

The ls command has a great deal of power but is often underused. This section does not delve into every available option for the command, but be aware that the syntax for ls is as follows:

```
ls -{option} {operand}
```

as in

```
ls -la {filename}
```

or

```
ls -la {directory name}
```

Options for ls are as follows:

- *-a* Lists all entries, including those that begin with a dot (.), which are normally not listed.

- *-A* Lists all entries, including those that begin with a dot (.), with the exception of the working directory (.) and the parent directory (..).

- *-b* Forces printing of nonprintable characters to be in the octal *ddd* notation.

- *-c* Uses time of last modification of the inode (file created, mode changed, and so forth) for sorting (*-t*) or printing (*-l* or *-n*).

The following is an example of ls *-lc* output:

```
voyager:examples$ ls -lc
total 9
drwxr-xr-t   4 gibbst    users         1024 Apr  5 10:01 proddata/
-rwsr-xr-x   1 gibbst    users          979 Apr  5 09:57 add-user.ksh*
-rwsr-sr-t   1 gibbst    users            0 Apr  5 09:38 origin.txt*
-rwx-S--     1 gibbst    users         2559 Apr  5 09:37 datafile.dbf*
drwxr-xr-x   2 gibbst    users         1024 Apr  5 09:37 Mail/
lrwxrwxrwx   1 gibbst    users           19 Apr  5 09:30 web ->> /home/sysadm/www/
drwxr-xr-x   2 gibbst    users         1024 Apr  5 09:29 logs/
drwxr-xr-x   2 gibbst    users         1024 Apr  5 09:28 progs/
-rwxr-xr-x   1 gibbst    users          403 Apr  5 09:27 menu*
```

- *-C* Is the default output; multicolumn with entries sorted down the columns.

- *-d* Lists only the name (not contents) if an argument is a directory. Commonly used with *-l* to get the status of a directory.

- *-f* Forces each argument to be interpreted as a directory and lists the name found in each slot. This option turns off *-l, -t, -s,* and *-r* and turns on *-a;* the order is the order in which entries appear in the directory.

- *-F* Marks directories with a trailing slash (/), doors with a trailing double greater-than sign (>>), executable files with a trailing asterisk (*), FIFOs with a trailing pipe symbol (|), symbolic links with a trailing at sign (@), and AF_UNIX address family sockets with a trailing equal sign (=).

- *-g* Works the same as *-l* except that the owner is not printed.

- *-i* For each file, prints the inode number in the first column of the report.

- **-l**   Lists in long format, giving mode (permissions), ACL indication, number of links, owner, group, size in bytes, and time of last modification for each file (see previous description). If the file is a special file, the SIZE field instead contains the major and minor device numbers. Files modified within six months show *month date time*. If the file is a symbolic link, the filename is printed followed by double quote marks ("") and the pathname of the referenced file.

- **-L**   If an argument is a symbolic link, lists the file or directory the link references rather than the link itself.

- **-m**   Streams output format; files are listed across the page, separated by commas.

- **-n**   Works the same as *-l* except that the owner's UID and group's GID numbers, rather than the associated character strings, are printed.

- **-o**   Works the same as *-l* except that the group is not printed.

- **-p**   Puts a slash (/) after each filename if the file is a directory.

The following is an example of ls *-lp* output:

```
voyager:/home/gibbst$ ls -lp
total 12
drwxr-xr-t   6 gibbst  users       1024 Apr  5 09:30 ./
drwxr-xr-t  11 gibbst  users       1024 Apr  5 09:26 ../
-rwxr-xr-x   1 gibbst  users        165 Apr  5 09:27 .profile*
drwxr-xr-x   2 gibbst  users       1024 Apr  4  1996 Mail/
-rwxr-xr-x   1 gibbst  users        979 Feb  1  1998 add-user.ksh*
-rwx-S--     1 gibbst  users       2559 Apr  4 15:24 datafile.dbf*
drwxr-xr-x   2 gibbst  users       1024 Apr  5 09:27 logs/
-rwxr-xr-x   1 gibbst  users        403 Apr  5 09:27 menu*
-rwsr-sr-t   1 gibbst  users          0 Apr  3 12:43 origin.txt*
drwxr-xr-x   4 gibbst  users       1024 Apr  5 09:28 proddata/
drwxr-xr-x   2 gibbst  users       1024 Apr  5 09:28 progs/
lrwxrwxrwx   1 gibbst  users         19 Apr  5 09:30 web ->> /home/sysadm/www/
```

- **-q**   Forces printing of nonprintable characters in filenames as the character question mark (?).

- **-r**   Reverses the sort order to reverse alphabetic or oldest first, as appropriate.

- **-R**   Recursively lists subdirectories encountered.

- **-s**   Gives size in blocks, including indirect blocks, for each entry.

- **-t**   Sorts by timestamp (latest first) instead of name. The default is the last modification time. (See *-u* and *-c*.)

The following is an example of ls -*lt* output:

```
voyager:/home/sysadm/examples# ls -lt
total 9
lrwxrwxrwx   1 gibbst   users           19 Apr   5 09:30 web ->> /home/sysadm/www/
drwxr-xr-x   2 gibbst   users         1024 Apr   5 09:28 progs/
drwxr-xr-t   4 gibbst   users         1024 Apr   5 09:28 proddata/
-rwxr-xr-x   1 gibbst   users          403 Apr   5 09:27 menu*
drwxr-xr-x   2 gibbst   users         1024 Apr   5 09:27 logs/
-rwx-S--     1 gibbst   users         2559 Apr   4 15:24 datafile.dbf*
-rwsr-sr-t   1 gibbst   users            0 Apr   3 12:43 origin.txt*
-rwsr-xr-x   1 gibbst   users          979 Feb   1  1998 add-user.ksh*
drwxr-xr-x   2 gibbst   users         1024 Apr   4  1996 Mail/
```

- ■ **-u** Uses time of last access instead of last modification for sorting (with the -*t* option) or printing (with the -*l* option).

The following is an example of ls -*lu* output:

```
voyager:examples# ls -lu
total 9
drwxr-xr-x   2 gibbst   users         1024 Apr 16 01:30 Mail/
-rwsr-xr-x   1 gibbst   users          979 Apr 14 03:12 add-user.ksh*
-rwx-S--     1 gibbst   users         2559 Apr 14 03:12 datafile.dbf*
drwxr-xr-x   2 gibbst   users         1024 Apr 16 01:30 logs/
-rwxr-xr-x   1 gibbst   users          403 Apr 14 03:12 menu*
-rwsr-sr-t   1 gibbst   users            0 Apr   5 09:28 origin.txt*
drwxr-xr-t   4 gibbst   users         1024 Apr 16 01:30 proddata/
drwxr-xr-x   2 gibbst   users         1024 Apr 16 01:30 progs/
lrwxrwxrwx   1 gibbst   users           19 Apr 16 23:17 web ->> /home/sysadm/www/
```

- ■ **-x** Produces multicolumn output with entries sorted across rather than down the page.

The following is an example of ls -*x* output:

```
voyager:/home/sysadm# cd examples
voyager:/home/sysadm/examples# ls -x
Mail/          add-user.ksh*  datafile.dbf*  logs/          menu*
origin.txt*    proddata/      progs/         web@
```

- ■ **-1** Prints one entry per line of output.

Specifying more than one of the options in the following mutually exclusive pairs is not considered an error: -*C* and -*1* (one), -*c* and -*u*. The last option specified in each pair determines the output format.

EXERCISE 6-2

Using Various Options of the ls Command

To understand the output of the ls command using various options, take a look at the following exercise.

1. Most system administrators probably know the output derived from the ls *-la* command the way they know the backs of their hands. However, it also provides the best starting point in understanding the ls command, so that is where we begin:

```
voyager:/home/gibbst$ ls -la
total 12
drwxr-xr-t    6 gibbst users        1024 Apr  5 09:30 ./
drwxr-xr-t   11 gibbst users        1024 Apr  5 09:26 ../
-rwxr-xr-x    1 gibbst users         165 Apr  5 09:27 .profile*
drwxr-xr-x    2 gibbst users        1024 Apr  4  1996 Mail/
-rwxr-xr-x    1 gibbst users         979 Feb  1  1998 add-user.ksh*
-rwx-S--      1 gibbst users        2559 Apr  4 15:24 datafile.dbf*
drwxr-xr-x    2 gibbst users        1024 Apr  5 09:27 logs/
-rwxr-xr-x    1 gibbst users         403 Apr  5 09:27 menu*
-rwsr-sr-t    1 gibbst users           0 Apr  3 12:43 origin.txt*
drwxr-xr-x    4 gibbst users        1024 Apr  5 09:28 proddata/
drwxr-xr-x    2 gibbst users        1024 Apr  5 09:28 progs/
lrwxrwxrwx    1 gibbst users          19 Apr  5 09:30 web ->> /home/sysadm/www/
```

In this exercise, we explore the files that are bold in the above code. First, the file datafile.dbf has an interesting entry in the Group Execute Bit column. Normally, this will be an *x* if execute has been enabled or an *s* if the setgid bit has been enabled. What has occurred here is that someone has enabled setgid, but the group has no execute permissions on the file. Finally, the file web is a symbolic link to /home/sysadm/www. When a symbolic link is present, the first character of the permission set is an *l* (lowercase *L*).

2. The following is the output of ls *-lutr*, in the same directory as the previous example. This is simply a reverse alpha-ordered sort, but it excludes the dot (.) files (.profile and directory entries).

```
/home/gibbst$ ls -lr
total 9
lrwxrwxrwx   1 gibbst users          19 Apr  5 09:30 web ->> /haus/j/gibbst/www/
drwxr-xr-x   2 gibbst users        1024 Apr  5 09:28 progs/
drwxr-xr-x   4 gibbst users        1024 Apr  5 09:28 proddata/
-rwsr-sr-t   1 gibbst users           0 Apr  3 12:43 origin.txt*
-rwxr-xr-x   1 gibbst users         403 Apr  5 09:27 menu*
drwxr-xr-x   2 gibbst users        1024 Apr  5 09:27 logs/
-rwx-S--     1 gibbst users        2559 Apr  4 15:24 datafile.dbf*
-rwxr-xr-x   1 gibbst users         979 Feb  1  1998 add-user.ksh*
drwxr-xr-x   2 gibbst users        1024 Apr  4  1996 Mail/
```

3. Use ls *-li* to show the inode numbers for each file (the leftmost column):

```
/home/gibbst$ ls -li
total 9
1503236 drwxr-xr-x   2 gibbst users      1024 Apr  4  1996 Mail/
 591887 -rwxr-xr-x   1 gibbst users       979 Feb  1  1998 add-user.ksh*
 591888 -rwx-S--     1 gibbst users      2559 Apr  4 15:24 datafile.dbf*
1687581 drwxr-xr-x   2 gibbst users      1024 Apr  5 09:27 logs/
 591889 -rwxr-xr-x   1 gibbst users       403 Apr  5 09:27 menu*
 591890 -rwsr-sr-t   1 gibbst users         0 Apr  3 12:43 origin.txt*
1835022 drwxr-xr-x   4 gibbst users      1024 Apr  5 09:28 proddata/
1427459 drwxr-xr-x   2 gibbst users      1024 Apr  5 09:28 progs/
 591891 lrwxrwxrwx   1 gibbst users        19 Apr  5 09:30 web ->>
/haus/j/gibbst/www/
```

4. Use the ls *-s* option to show number of blocks, both direct and indirect, used by each file:

```
voyager:/home/gibbst$ ls -s
total 9
    1 Mail/              1 logs/              1 proddata/
    1 add-user.ksh*      1 menu*          1 progs/
    3 datafile.dbf*      0 origin.txt*     0 web@
```

We could go on for quite some time about the options available, but suffice it to say that there are many options, and ls has considerably more capability than simply listing a directory. Explore the various options and see how you might benefit from their use.

Given the output of ls *-la* on a directory, what conclusions can you draw about the following entries?

SCENARIO & SOLUTION

lrwxrwxrwx 1 jdennis users 20 Apr 5 00:24 .profile ->> home/usercommon/.profile	The .profile in this user's home directory is a symbolic link to the .profile in /home/usercommon. This is one way to keep the .profile consistent across users.
drwxr-sr-x 2 jdennis users 1024 Apr 4 14:31 temp	The temp directory has the setgid bit enabled.

on the job

As a system administrator working in a group of administrators, you will often find that a file's permissions have been changed and, unless a backup copy was made of the file prior to the change, it is difficult to know what the correct permissions should be. Whenever you install or take over administration of a server, it's a good idea to list all directories and files on the system and save the output in your personal sysadm directory. Then, if for some reason a file does get changed and you need to recover the original permission set, you can simply look at this file. In a very dynamic environment, you might want to script this process and run it in roots cron daily, searching for differences from your baseline and capturing any changes that have been made.

The chmod Command

You use the chmod command to modify permissions of existing files and directories. It is important to understand what the permission bits are before you use this command. It is also critical to understand the systemwide ramifications of using chmod, especially using its recursive abilities.

Syntax for chmod is

```
Chmod [-fR] {absolute mode} file
Chmod [-fR] {symbolic-mode-list} file
```

Options for chmod are as follows:

- *-f* Stands for force. If chmod cannot change the mode of a file, the *-f* option will suppress the warning messages, as in the following example:

```
$ ls -la
total 32
drwxr-xr-x+  2 gibbst staff          512 Apr 24 12:39 .
drwxr-xr-x   4 gibbst staff         1024 Apr 20 08:54 ..
-rw-r-r-     1 root    staff        1024 Apr 24 12:39 weekly.dbf
$ chmod +w weekly.dbf
chmod: WARNING: can't change weekly.dbf
```

Here you see the warning message. Try it with the *-f* option:

```
$ chmod -f +w weekly.bdf
$ ls -la
total 32
drwxr-xr-x+  2 gibbst staff          512 Apr 24 12:39 .
drwxr-xr-x   4 gibbst staff         1024 Apr 20 08:54 ..
-rw-r-r-     1 root    staff        1024 Apr 24 12:39 weekly.dbf
```

There was no warning message, but chmod still didn't change the file permissions.

- *-R* Recursively descends through directory arguments, setting the mode for each file as described previously. When symbolic links are encountered, the mode of the target file is changed, but no recursion takes place.

Chmod has two modes. One is the *absolute mode,* whereby you identify the changes to be made by supplying the octal representation of the file attributes, as in

```
chmod 775 {directory-name}
```

There is also the *symbolic mode,* whereby you identify the changes to be made by supplying the character representation of the change to be made, as in

```
chmod u=rwx,g=rw,o=rw {filename}
```

As you can see, the absolute mode is easier to use when you're making more than one change to a file.

The Absolute Mode of chmod

Table 6-1 shows how octal permissions are constructed for use with the absolute mode of chmod.

TABLE 6-1		Owner	Group	Other	Resulting Permission (If All Set)
Absolute Mode Definitions for the chmod Command	Read, Write, Execute	00700	00070	00007	00777
	Read	00400	00040	00004	00444
	Write	00200	00020	00002	00222
	Execute (search if a directory)	00100	00010	00001	00111
	Set User ID on execution (setuid)	04000			
	Set Group ID on execution (setgid)	02000			
	Save text image on exit (enable sticky bit)	01000			

EXERCISE 6-3

Using chmod

Given the information in Table 6-1, let's look at a few permission sets:

1. You have a file with 755 permissions. You want to enable the setuid on execution bit on this program. To do so, execute this command:

```
chmod 4755 <file>

/home/ gibbst$ ls -la add-user.ksh
-rwxr-xr-x   1 jdennis  users          979 Feb  1  1998 add-user.ksh*
/home/ gibbst$ chmod 4755 add-user.ksh
/home/ gibbst$ ls -la add-user.ksh
-rwsr-xr-x   1 gibbst users           979 Feb  1  1998 add-user.ksh*
```

2. As shown, to change a file in absolute mode, supply the octal value of the permission to the chmod command. Octal 04000 enables the setuid bit.

3. You have a directory that currently does not have its sticky bit enabled, but you want it enabled:

```
/home/ gibbst$ ls -ld proddata
drwxr-xr-x   4 gibbst users        1024 Apr  5 09:28 proddata/
/home/ gibbst$ chmod 01755 proddata
/home/ gibbst$ ls -ld proddata
drwxr-xr-t   4 gibbst users        1024 Apr  5 09:28 proddata/
```

Again, looking at the octal table, enabling the sticky bit requires adding the 01000 permission to the file.

The Symbolic Mode of chmods

In the other mode of chmod, symbolic mode, you represent the permissions as their abbreviations, as shown in Table 6-2.

FROM THE CLASSROOM

Sticky Bits

"Sticky bit" is a widely misused term. Many people mistake the setuid/setgid bits for the sticky bits. The purpose of a sticky bit is to prevent files in a directory from being removed or renamed. If a sticky bit is enabled, one or more of the following conditions must be met for a user to delete files:

- The user must own the file.
- The user must own the directory.
- The file must be writable by the user.
- The user is a privileged (root) user.

—*James Dennis, SCSA, IBM Certified Specialist
AIX 4.1 System Administrator*

TABLE 6-2	Permission Set	Applies to User	Applies to Group	Applies to Other	Applies to All
	read	u+r	g+r	o+r	a+r
Symbolic Mode Options for chmod		u−r	g−r	o−r	a−r
		u=r	g=r	o=r	a=r
	write	u+w	g+w	o+w	a+w
		u−w	g−w	o−w	a−w
		u=w	g=w	o=w	a=w
	execute	u+x	g+x	o+x	a+x
		u−x	g−x	o−x	a−x
		u=x	g=x	o=x	a=x

The syntax for symbolic mode is

```
chmod -[fR] [applies to who?]=[symbolic mode] {filename}
```

Let's look at an example for applying permissions using symbolic mode. Currently, the file permissions are as follows:

```
voyager:/home/sysadm$ ls -la fixprog.sh
-rw-r-r-   1 gibbst   users          475 Apr  4 22:08 fixprog.sh
(644 permissions)
```

When you run the chmod command

```
voyager:/home/sysadm$ chmod u=rwx,g=rx,o=r fixprog.sh
```

the resulting permissions are

```
voyager:/home/sysadm$ ls -la fixprog.sh
-rwxr-xr-   1 gibbst users           0 Apr  4 22:08 fixprog.sh
(754 permissions)
```

If you omit the *Applies to* information when running chmod in symbolic mode, the default is *a*, but umask is taken into account. When *who* is omitted, chmod will not override the restrictions of your user mask. The next section of this chapter discusses umask.

Pay close attention to the syntax for chmod for both symbolic and absolute modes. These areas commonly trip people up on the exams.

Occasionally, you will be presented with a challenge such as how to change permissions on all your data files at once. If they are not in the same directory, but you need to remove write permission from the other or world permission set, what do you do? Using the find command in conjunction with the chmod command works well for this purpose, as in

```
find / -name "*.dbf" -print -exec chmod o-w {} \;
```

It's a good idea to run the find command first without chmod, just to ensure that you are getting the right fileset:

```
find / -name "*.dbf" -print)
```

SCENARIO & SOLUTION

Given the directory listing `-rwxr-xr-x   1 jdennis  users 695 Apr 3  12:43 origin.txt` what are the octal permissions of the file origin.txt?	755

What effect would the command chmod +s have on this file?	Chmod +s turns on the setuid and setgid bits on the file, effectively making its listing look like this:
	 `$ ls -l origin.txt`
	 `-rwsr-sr-x   1 jdennis  users  695 Apr  3 12:43 origin.txt`

How can you tell if a directory has its sticky bit enabled?	When looking at an ls *-la* output, the file permissions will be represented as follows:
	 `$ chmod +t /home/jdennis`
	 `(chmod +t enables the sticky bit)`
	 `$ ls -la /home/jdennis`
	 `drwsr-sr-t   1 jdennis  users 0 Apr  3 12:43 /home/jdennis`

CERTIFICATION OBJECTIVE 6.03

Understanding the Effects of Selected umask Values on the Permissions Assigned to Newly Created Files and Directories

You use the umask command to define the permissions on newly created files. Normally, you will find the umask command in /etc/profile because this file is referenced by all login attempts. Therefore, any command or environmental setting in /etc/profile will affect all users on the system:

```
# sample /etc/profile
umask 022
PATH=/usr/bin:/usr/sbin
export PATH
```

The baseline for new files or directories is to assign full permissions; umask defines the offset. Directories, by default, are created with the execute bit on and therefore have a default permission set of 777 (read/write/execute for owner/group/world), whereas files are created with the execute bit off, so the default permission set for files begins at 666.

To refresh your memory, octal permissions are derived as follows:

- read = 4
- write = 2
- Execute = 1

(*Note:* This is a simplistic viewpoint of how permissions are set. See the prior discussion on chmod and octal permissions for full coverage of this concept.)

So, in an ls *-la* listing, given a file that shows

```
drwxr-xr-x
```

the octal permissions for this directory would be 755.

In the example /etc/profile shown, any file created will be created with octal permissions of 644, whereas a directory will be created with octal permissions of 755.

Table 6-3 gives an example of an 022 umask applied to the default file creation permissions.

TABLE 6-3		File	Directory
An 022 umask Applied to the Default File Creation	Default	666	777
	umask	022	022
	Resulting octal permission set	644	755

CERTIFICATION OBJECTIVE 6.04

Creating, Modifying, and Deleting Access Control Lists

Access control lists (ACLs) are used in the Solaris environment to provide granular control of file permissions. In today's complex computing environments, UNIX administrators have found the standard UNIX file and directory permissions to be insufficient. Using *file system ACLs* (FACLs) helps solve this problem. ACLs allow a system administrator to define extended permissions for files and/or directories. For example, you can specify a certain group ownership for a file and allow multiple other groups to have equal or lesser permissions based on ACLs.

Using getfacl to Display ACLs

To display FACLs, you use the command getfacl:

```
getfacl [-ad] file
```

Options for getfacl are the following:

- *-a* Displays the filename, the file owner, the file group owner, and the ACL of the file
- *-d* Displays the filename, the file owner, the file group owner, and the default ACL of the file, if it exists

If the file specified is a regular file, special file, or named pipe, getfacl displays the owner, the group, and the ACL. If a directory name is specified, getfacl displays the owner, the group, the ACL, and/or the default ACL. Only directories may contain default ACLs.

getfacl may be executed on a file system that does not support or have ACL enabled. In this case, getfacl reports the ACL based on the base permission bits, as discussed previously.

If no options are specified, getfacl displays the filename, the file owner, the file group owner, and both the ACL and the default ACL, if it exists:

```
# file: filename
# owner: uid
# group: gid
user::perm
user:uid:perm
group::perm
group:gid:perm
mask:perm
other:perm
default:user::perm
default:user:uid:perm
default:group::perm
default:group:gid:perm
default:mask:perm
default:other:perm
```

When multiple files are specified on the command line, a blank line separates the ACLs for each file.

The ACL entries are displayed in the order in which they are evaluated when an access check is performed. The default ACL entries that exist on a directory have no effect on access checks.

The user entry without a user ID (user::perm) indicates that the permissions are granted only to the file owner. If additional user entries are present, user: gibbst:perm indicates the permissions that are granted to the specified users.

The group entry without a group ID (group::perm) indicates that the permissions are granted to the file group owner. If additional group entries are present, group:staff:perm indicates the permissions that are granted to the specified groups.

The mask entry indicates the ACL mask permissions. These are the maximum permissions allowed to any user entries except the file owner and to any group entries, including the file group owner. These permissions restrict the permissions specified in other entries. For example, if the mask is *rw* and you attempt to specify that a user should have *rwx* permissions, the maximum permission granted will be *rw*. To indicate the ACL mask is restricting an ACL entry, getfacl displays a tab character, pound sign (#), and the actual permissions granted following the entry, similar to a comment in a shell script.

The other entry indicates the permissions that are granted to those who are not listed in the user or group permissions areas. Default entries may exist only for directories and indicate the default ACLs that are added to a file or directory created within that directory.

Displaying File Information

1. Given file datafile.dbf, running getfacl produces the following output:

```
voyager% getfacl datafile.dbf
# file: datafile.dbf
# owner: gibbst
# group: staff
user::tag
user:wpkennedy: - - -
user:srivett:r - -
group::r - -
mask::rw -
other:: - - -
```

2. After running the command

```
chmod 700 datafile.dbf
```

the resulting ACL will be the following:

```
voyager% getfacl datafile.dbf
# file: datafile.dbf
# owner: gibbst
# group: staff
user::rwx
user:spy: - - -
user:gibbst:r - -      #effective: - - -
group:: - - -
mask:: - - -
other:: - - -
```

(*Note:* If you are using ACLs, it is best to use setfacl rather than chmod to change the permissions.)

3. To display information when ACL contains default entries, the directory proddata has default ACL entries:

```
uxsdb01% getfacl -d proddata
# file: proddata
# owner: wpkennedy
# group: staff
default:user::rwx
default:user:spy: - - -
default:user:gibbst:r - -
default:group::r - -
default:mask:: - - - -
default:other:: - - - -
```

e x a m

Ⓦ@tch

Although ACLs are not widely used, such topics often trip up a system administrator on the exam.

Using setfacl to Set ACLs

Now that you've explored how to display ACLs, you need to know how to set them. To set FACLs, you use the setfacl command:

```
setfacl [-r] -s acl_entries file
setfacl [-r] -md acl_entries file
setfacl [-r] -f acl_file file
```

For each file specified, setfacl does one of the following:

■ Replaces its entire ACL, including the default ACL on a directory

■ Adds, modifies, or deletes one or more ACL entries, including default entries on directories

Note that if you have defined ACLs, it is advisable to use setfacl instead of chmod to change the permissions on the files from that time forward. Doing so does add administration overhead, but it also enables you to effectively use ACLs.

Directories may contain default ACL entries. If a file or directory is created in a directory that contains default ACL entries, the newly created file will have permissions based on the requested permissions weighed against the default value. For example, if the default value is read/write, but you request read/write/execute, the permissions granted will be read/write. The default ACL is the maximum permissions that may be given. Table 6-4 shows the syntax and description of the available ACLs.

| TABLE 6-4 | Syntax of ACL Options |

ACL Entry	Description
u[ser]::perms	File owner permissions.
g[roup]::perms	File group owner permissions.
o[ther]:perms	Permissions for users other than the file owner or members of file group owner.
m[ask]:perms	The ACL mask. The mask entry indicates the maximum permissions allowed for users (other than the owner) and for groups. The mask can be used to quickly change permissions on all the users and groups.
u[ser]:uid:perms	Permissions for a specific user. *uid* can be specified as either a username or a numeric UID.
g[roup]:gid:perms	Permissions for a specific group. *gid* can be specified as either a group name or a numeric GID.
d[efault]:u[ser]::perms	Default file owner permissions.
d[efault]:g[roup]::perms	Default file group owner permissions.
d[efault]:o[ther]:perms	Default permissions for users other than the file owner or members of the file group owner.
d[efault]:m[ask]:perms	Default ACL mask.
d[efault]:u[ser]:uid:perms	Default permissions for a specific user. *uid* can be specified as either a username or a numeric UID.
d[efault]:g[roup]:gid:perms	Default permissions for a specific group. *gid* can be specified as either a group name or a numeric GID.

For the *-d* option, acl_entries are one or more comma-separated ACL entries without permissions. Note that the entries for file owner, file group owner, ACL mask, and others may not be deleted.

Options to setfacl are the following:

■ **-s acl_entries**   Sets a file's ACL. All existing ACL entries are replaced with the newly specified ACL. You do not need to specify the entries in any certain order because they will be sorted by the command before being applied to the file.

The following entries are required:

■ There is one user entry for the file owner.

- There is one group entry for the file group owner.

- There is one other entry for nonfile owner/nongroup owner.

If there are additional user and group entries, the following applies:

- There is one mask entry for the ACL mask that indicates the maximum permissions allowed for users (other than the owner) and groups.

- You may not duplicate user entries with the same UID.

- You may not duplicate group entries with the same GID.

If the file is a directory, the following default ACL entries may be specified:

- There is one default user entry for the file owner.

- There is one default group entry for the file group owner.

- There is one default mask entry for the ACL mask.

- There is one default other entry.

Additional default user entries and additional default group entries might be specified, but you might not have duplicate additional default user entries with the same UID or duplicate default group entries with the same GID:

- *-m acl_entries*   Adds or modifies one or more ACL entries on the file. If an entry already exists for a specified UID or GID, the requested permissions will replace the current permissions. If an entry does not exist for the specified UID or GID, one will be created.

- *-d acl_entries*   Deletes one or more entries from the file. The entries for the file owner, the file group owner, and others may not be deleted from the ACL. Note that deleting an entry does not necessarily have the same effect as removing all permissions from the entry.

- *-f acl_file*   Uses the file *acl_file* as input to setfacl. *acl_file* may contain ACL entries to set another file's ACL. The same constraints on specified entries hold as with the *-s* option. The entries in *acl_file* are not required to be in any certain order. You may also specify a hyphen (-) for *acl_file*, in which case, standard input is used to set the file's ACL.

■ *-r* Recalculate the permissions for the ACL mask entry. The permissions specified in the ACL mask entry are ignored and replaced by the maximum permissions necessary to grant the access to all additional user, file group owner, and group entries in the ACL. The permissions in the additional user, file group owner, and group entries are left unchanged.

EXERCISE 6-5

Using ACL Entries

1. The following example adds one ACL entry to file fixprog.sh, which gives user *gibbst* only read permission:

```
setfacl -m user:gibbst:r-- /home/sysadm/fixprog.sh
```

2. The following example replaces the entire ACL for the fixprog.sh file, which gives *gibbst* full access, the file owner all access, the file group owner only read/write access, the ACL mask only read access, and others no access:

```
setfacl -s user:gibbst:rwx,user::rwx,group::rw-,mask:r—,other:--- fixprog.sh
```

Note that after this command, the file permission bits are *rwxr– – –*. Even though the file group owner was set with read/write permissions, the ACL mask entry limits it to only read permissions. The mask entry also specifies the maximum permissions available to all additional user and group ACL entries. Once again, even though the user *gibbst* was set with all access, the mask limits the user to read permissions. The ACL mask entry is a quick way to limit or open access to all the user and group entries in an ACL. For example, by changing the mask entry to read/write, both the file group owner and user *gibbst* would be given read/write access.

3. The following example gets the ACL from file fixprog.sh and sets the same ACL on the file newprog.sh:

```
getfacl fixprog.sh | setfacl -f - newprog.sh
```

Now that you have a better idea of ACLs, some scenario questions and their answers are next.

SCENARIO & SOLUTION	
Given the command getfacl -d {*filename*}, what data would you expect to see?	The filename, the file owner, the file group owner, and the default ACL of the file, if it exists.
Which command would you use to set permissions on the file newprog.sh the same as they are on fixprog.sh?	getfacl fixprog.sh | setfacl -f – newprog.sh.
After running setfacl, you see that the permissions you intended to grant have not been granted. The command that was run was setfacl -m user:jdennis:rwx /home/sysadm/fixprog.sh; yet when you look at the ACL, you see the user *jdennis* with file permissions of rw. What happened?	To troubleshoot this problem, run the getfacl fixprog.sh command. Upon looking at the file ACL, you see that the fixprog.sh file has a mask of rw. *jdennis* does not own the file, so his permissions are calculated using the mask; therefore, his maximum permissions are *rw*.

CERTIFICATION SUMMARY

This chapter used grep to explore the standard UNIX regular expression set. You also learned about the standard Solaris commands for displaying and changing file permissions (ls and chmod), as well as some enhanced commands (getfacl and setfacl). You've also learned the variety of options for chmod and how umask can affect permissions at the creation of files and directories.

This chapter by no means covered every available option in depth, but you've been exposed to the topics and expanded your knowledge.

TWO-MINUTE DRILL

Using Regular Expressions to Search the Contents of Files

■ Regular expressions give a system administrator more power when it comes to finding information in multiple files.

Using Command Sequences to Display or Modify File and Directory Permissions

■ File and directory permissions can be displayed in a variety of formats using the ls command.

■ You use chmod to modify file and directory permissions.

Understanding the Effects of Selected umask Values on the Permissions Assigned to Newly Created Files and Directories

■ You can set umask values systemwide using the umask command in /etc/profile.

■ You can set umask values on a user- or group-specific basis using the umask command in the local ($HOME)/.profile.

Creating, Modifying, and Deleting Access Control Lists

■ ACLs give you far greater granularity for file and directory permissions than the standard UNIX structure.

■ You can use getfacl to view the existing ACL prior to making a change. You can also use it as input to setfacl.

■ You can use setfacl to set, modify, or delete an ACL on a file or directory.

SELF TEST

The following questions will help you measure your understanding of the material presented in this chapter. Read all the choices carefully because there might be more than one correct answer. Choose all correct answers for each question.

Using Regular Expressions to Search the Contents of Files

1. You are searching for the string *Octavius* in a directory full of text files. Which command would you use to find this information?

   A. `grep -E 'Octavius' *`

   B. `grep -E 'Octavius`

   C. `grep -E 'Octavius'`

   D. None of the above

2. Given the command

   ```
   grep -i -n 'octavius' *
   ```

   which of the following output lines would you expect to see?

   A. `datafile.dbf:40:Octavius`

   B. `datafile.dbf:Octavius`

   C. No output; the regular expression string does not match the text in the file.

   D. None of the above.

Using Command Sequences to Display or Modify File and Directory Permissions

3. You need to get a listing of all files owned by a specific user (*gibbst*) on the system. You want not only the filenames, but the permissions of the files as well. Which of the following options would best accomplish this goal?

   A. From the root directory, execute the command

   ```
   ls -laR | grep gibbst
   ```

B. Execute the command

```
find / -user gibbst -exec ls -la {} \;
```

C. From the root directory, execute the command

```
ls -lar | grep gibbst
```

D. Execute the command

```
ls -la | grep gibbst
```

4. Given the output of the following ls command, what are the octal permissions of the file /home/gibbst/datafile.dbf?

```
-rwsr-sr-x   1 gibbst   users        0 Apr  3 12:43 datafile.dbf
```

A. 7655

B. 6755

C. 755

D. 655

5. You need to change the permissions on all .DBF files in the /proddata directory to enable the setgid bit. Which command will accomplish this task?

A. `chmod -R g+s *.dbf`

B. `chmod -R g+s /proddata/*.dbf`

C. `chmod -R g+s /proddata`

D. `find /proddata -name "*.dbf" -exec chmod g+s {} \;`

Understanding the Effects of Selected umask Values on the Permissions Assigned to Newly Created Files and Directories

6. You have the command umask 022 in your /etc/profile, and your $HOME/.profile has the command umask 026. Given these circumstances, which permissions would you expect to see on any newly created files?

A. 644 (*rw-r--r--*)

B. 664 (*rw-rw-r--*)

C. 640 (*rw-r---*)

D. None of the above

7. Your umask value is set to 022. If you run the umask *-S* command, which output would you expect?

   A. 022

   B. No output

   C. u=rwx,g=rx,o=rx

   D. u=rwx,g=r,o=r

Creating, Modifying, and Deleting Access Control Lists

8. You've modified file permissions on the file /home/sysadm/newprog.sh, using setfacl to set the permissions for user *gibbst* to have read/write/execute access on the file. However, when you list the permissions given by the command, you realize the user has only read permissions on the file. What possible explanation can you find for this discrepancy?

   A. Apparently when you typed in the command, you supplied the command arguments incorrectly.

   B. Someone modified the ACL after you set it up.

   C. The ACL for this file has a mask on it, not allowing this user to have permissions beyond read access.

   D. The user's scripting abilities were suspect, so subconsciously, you gave the user the permissions you felt he or she deserved.

9. You are trying to display the ACL for the file /home/sysadm/fixprog.sh. You've given it the command multiple times, but you still get the same result: the filename, the file owner, the file group owner, and the default ACL of the file. You don't see any of the ACL permission set. What could be wrong with this situation?

   A. You need the latest Solaris Jumbo Kernel patch.

   B. You accidentally deleted the ACL by using setfacl *-d* instead of getfacl.

   C. There are no ACLs on the file.

   D. You've been giving the command as getfacl *-d.* The *-d* option for getfacl displays only that information, not the complete ACL.

10. Given the following command

```
setfacl -m user:gibbst:rw- /home/sysadm/fixprog.sh
```

which permissions would you expect *gibbst* to have?

A. That depends on the mask setting.

B. The user would have read and write permissions.

C. All of the above.

D. None of the above.

LAB QUESTION

You've been given the task of determining why a certain script is not running on the system. Which commands covered in this chapter would you use to troubleshoot the reason the script is not running, and which command would you use to correct the situation? (*Note:* The user attempting to run the script is not the owner of the file.)

SELF TEST ANSWERS

Using Regular Expressions to Search the Contents of Files

1. ☑ **A.** When searching for any file in the directory that has the string you are searching for, you must supply either a filename or a wildcard.
   ☒ **B** is incorrect because it would try to read the current directory and return an error *grep: .: Is a directory.* **C** is incorrect because this command would try to read from the standard input in the absence of a filename or wildcard.

2. ☑ **A.** The *-i* option makes your search case insensitive, and the *-n* option tells you in which line number in the file the text was found.
   ☒ **B** is incorrect because the *-n* option gives you the line number, which is absent from the output. **C** is incorrect because you know the file contains the string, and you've allowed for case sensitivity with the *-i* option. You set the example up yourself. **D** is incorrect because **A** is correct.

Using Command Sequences to Display or Modify File and Directory Permissions

3. ☑ **B.** Combining the find command and the ls command in this manner would be the simplest and cleanest method to accomplish this task.
   ☒ **A** is incorrect because it would not list *all* files on the system owned by gibbst as the question requested. **C** is incorrect because the lowercase *r* option to ls is used for sorting the output in reverse alphabetic order or by oldest files first, as in ls *-lr* or ls *-ltr.* **D** is incorrect because you are limiting the search to the user's home directory.

4. ☑ **B.** 6755 is correct because the setuid and setgid bits are enabled. 4000 enables setuid, 2000 enables setgid, and the remaining permissions prior to enabling the setuid/setgid bits were 755.
   ☒ **A** is incorrect because the permissions in this case would be *rwsr-sr-t.* **C** is incorrect because it would show permissions as *rwxr-xr-x,* and **D** would show permissions as *rw-r-xr-x.*

5. ☑ **D.** Using the combination of find and the chmod commands will provide the desired result.
   ☒ **A** and **B** are incorrect because they will not recurse the directory tree when supplied with a filename wildcard. **C** is incorrect because it would effect the change on the /proddata directory and all files underneath it.

Understanding the Effects of Selected umask Values on the Permissions Assigned to Newly Created Files and Directories

6. ☑ **C.** Keep in mind that the starting permissions for any file, by default, are 666, and umask reduces the permission set accordingly. If you subtract 026 from 666, you get 640.
☒ **A** or **B** would be correct if your umask were set to 002, but it isn't, so they are incorrect. **D** is incorrect because there is a correct answer.

7. þ **C.** Symbolic mode output (*-S* option) shows you the permission set you would use in the chmod command.
☒ **A** is incorrect because it would be the result of umask without the *-S* option. **B** is incorrect because there would be output. **D** is incorrect because the default permission set is full permissions, with umask subtracting to achieve the resulting permission set.

Creating, Modifying, and Deleting Access Control Lists

8. ☑ **C.** The reason for the discrepancy is that the ACL for this file has a mask on it, meaning that the user has only read access.
☒ **D** does have some merit, although **C** is the more definitive answer. **A** is a distinct possibility, but a conscientious system administrator would not type in the command incorrectly. **B** is incorrect because nobody else had the permissions to change the ACL after you created it.

9. ☑ **D.** You've been giving the command as getfacl *-d.* The *-d* option for getfacl displays only that information, not the complete ACL.
☒ **A** is incorrect because it is doubtful the lack of a kernel patch would cause this problem. **B** is incorrect because you would not use setfacl *-d* to set the ACLs. **C** is incorrect because you actually *are* getting ACL information returned to you. If no ACL were set, the output would not show ACL information.

10. ☑ **C.** Given the small amount of data supplied in the question, both answers would be considered correct. The command itself, in the absence of the mask data, would set the user's permissions to read/write. If a mask were present, you could answer this question clearly.
☒ **A** is incorrect because it is not the only correct answer. **B** is incorrect for the same reason. **D** is incorrect because both **A** and **B** are incorrect.

LAB ANSWER

ls *-la* will show you the file permissions. In this case, you can see that the user *gibbst* owns the file and is the only user with execute permissions:

```
voyager:/home/sysadm# ls -la /home/sysadm/sar-start.sh
-rwxr-r-   1 gibbst users            345 Apr  3 12:43 sar-start.sh
```

To correct this situation, you could use the command

```
chmod g+x sar-start.sh
```

or the command

```
chmod 754 sar-start.sh
```

SUN® CERTIFIED SYSTEM ADMINISTRATOR

7

Understanding Process Control

CERTIFICATION OBJECTIVES

S olaris is an advanced multitasking, multiuser operating environment. Basically, this means that multiple users can be on the system at any one time, each running his or her own set of processes. The means by which these processes are controlled and the methods to monitor them are the subjects of this chapter.

Each running instance of a demand for system resources is known as a *process*. The *kernel* tracks this process by a unique integer known as the *process identifier* (PID). Processes can be managed using either their names or the associated PIDs. Both management methods are detailed in this section.

CERTIFICATION OBJECTIVE 7.01

Using Commands to Display Information for All Active Processes on the System

Solaris provides several methods of viewing process information. The ps and prstat commands allow you to list all active processes on the system from the command line; the Process Manager (located at /usr/dt/bin/sdtprocess) provides a graphical front end to the process list. Because the output of these commands can be overwhelming to heavily loaded systems, methods to eliminate extraneous data are also discussed here.

Using the ps Command to View Process Information

The ps command displays a listing of processes running on the system. This listing is a "snapshot" of the process table at the time the command was run and might not reflect its current state, even just a few seconds after execution. When called without arguments, the ps command lists only those processes running as the current user and attached to the current terminal, but other options are also available, as listed in Table 7-1.

| **TABLE 7-1** | PS Command Options |

Option	Description
-c	Prints scheduler information in a priocntl-compatible format.
-e, -A	Lists information about each process running.
-f	Shows additional information about each process.
-l	Shows a long process listing.
-G gidlist	Lists information for processes for which the real group ID numbers are given in gidlist. The list must be comma delimited.
-U uidlist	Shows information only about processes with a real user identification number (UID) given in the list that follows it. The list must be comma delimited.

on the
() o b

There are actually two versions of the ps command on a Solaris 9 system. The one described in this section can be found at /usr/bin/ps and is the System V version of the command. The BSD-compatible variant can be found at /usr/ucb/ps and may be a better choice for administrators more familiar with BSD-based systems (such as SunOS 4.x or FreeBSD). The exam does not include the BSD version, so we don't discuss it here. If you prefer the BSD version of ps, be aware that /usr/ucb is not listed in the PATH variable. You can add /usr/ucb before /usr/bin in the PATH, but you risk "preferring" the BSD version of other commands that you might not want (e.g., shutdown, ls, or chmod). Another solution is to add a shell alias mapping ps to /usr/usb/ps. Under the sh shell, the alias command would be

```
alias ps="/usr/ucb/ps"
```

This can be placed in /etc/profile or in .profile of a user's home directory.

Running ps without arguments results in output similar to the following:

```
$ ps
   PID TTY       TIME CMD
7470 pts/3    0:00 sh
```

The column headings represent the process identifier, the controlling terminal, the total execution time, and the command that was executed. (Note that command arguments are not printed.) You can also combine the various options to suit your needs. For instance, to show a long listing of all processes owned by user *don*, execute the following:

```
$ ps -lU don
 F S   UID   PID  PPID  C PRI NI     ADDR     SZ    WCHAN TTY      TIME CMD
8 S   111  7590  7589  0  51 20      ?       297      ? pts/3     0:00 sh
8 S   111  7591  7590  0  41 20      ?       227      ? pts/3     0:00 vi
```

This code doesn't show everything you might want to see, such as the file Don is editing with vi. To see the argument passed to vi (or, more specifically, to see the first 80 characters of the arguments passed), use the *-f* option.

```
$ ps -fU don
   UID   PID  PPID  C     STIME TTY      TIME CMD
   don  7590  7589  0 21:24:51 pts/3    0:00 -sh
   don  7591  7590  0 21:24:53 pts/3    0:00 vi /etc/hosts
```

Notice that the *-f* option also maps the UID to an actual account name. This makes reading the output of ps much easier, especially when viewing the processes of multiple users. To view all processes running on the system, use the *-e* option. Used in combination with the *-f* option, it provides an easy way to determine what is happening on the system:

```
$ ps -ef
          UID  PID  PPID  C    STIME TTY      TIME CMD
   root     0    0  0    Jan 07 ?      0:18 sched
   root     1    0  0    Jan 07 ?      0:09 /etc/init -
   root     2    0  0    Jan 07 ?      0:00 pageout
   root     3    0  0    Jan 07 ?     89:47 fsflush

(output deleted)
       don  7602  7598  0 21:41:04 pts/3     0:00 -sh
  dlaporte  7470  7468  0 20:38:30 pts/3     0:00 -sh
       don  7606  7602  0 21:41:09 pts/3     0:00 vi /etc/hosts
```

Tweaking the Output

On a busy system, the preceding listing can scroll over several pages, which makes finding a particular process a time-consuming task. By piping output from ps into the more command, you can get a nice page-by-page display of the data. The syntax for this command is as follows:

```
ps -ef | more
```

The same type of output redirection can be used to reduce the amount of output when you know what process you are interested in. For instance, if you would like to view all processes with the substring *ssh* in the command name, you can use the grep command:

```
$ ps -ef|grep ssh
  root    202     1  0   Jan 07 ?         0:57 /usr/local/sbin/sshd
root   7468   202  0 20:38:26 ?          0:01 /usr/local/sbin/sshd
root   7686   202  0 08:47:32 ?          0:00 /usr/local/sbin/sshd
root   7567   202  0 21:22:29 ?          0:00 /usr/local/sbin/sshd
dlaporte  7698  7688  0 08:48:08 pts/5   0:00 grep ssh
```

Notice that not only do you see the processes that were running on the system, but you also see the grep command you executed to view them! This seems strange, but it goes back to the idea that ps provides a snapshot of the system. At the time the ps command runs, the grep command is waiting for its input, and therefore shows up in the listing. The pgrep command, discussed in the section "Using kill to Terminate a Process," does not exhibit this behavior.

Column Headers

So far, we've dealt with only the UID, PID, and CMD fields of the ps command. You'll notice in the preceding examples that, depending on the options given, the output varies. Table 7-2 details the meaning of each column header and the options that must be given to view them.

The value of each field is typically a numerical value, with the exception of one: the STATE (S) field.

Process States

The values in the STATE field are simply letters, as described in Table 7-3.

TABLE 7-2 PS Column Headers

Header	Required Option	Description
S	-*l*	The process state.
UID	-*f* or -*l*	The effective user ID number of the process. (Use the -*f* option to have the UID map to an account name.)
PID	None	The process identifier.
PPID	-*f* or -*l*	The process identifier of the parent process.
C	-*f* or -*l*	The processor utilization for scheduling (obsolete). Not printed when the -*c* option is used.
PRI	-*l*	The priority of the process. Without the -*c* option, higher numbers mean lower priority. With the -*c* option, higher numbers mean higher priority.
NI	-*l*	A nice value used in priority computation. Not printed when the -*c* option is used. Only processes when certain scheduling classes have a nice value.
ADDR	-*l*	The memory address of the process.
SZ	-*l*	The total size of the process in virtual memory (in pages).
WCHAN	-*l*	The address of an event for which the process is sleeping.
STIME	-*f*	The starting time of the process.
TTY	None	The controlling terminal for the process.
TIME	None	The cumulative execution time of the process.
CMD	None	The command name.

TABLE 7-3

Process States

State	Description
O	The process is running.
S	The process is sleeping.
R	The process is runnable and on the run queue.
Z	The process is in a zombie state.
T	The process is stopped due to being traced or because of a job control signal.

The O state simply means that the process is currently executing on the processor. When executing ps, you will see the following line in the output:

```
# ps -el
 F S    UID    PID  PPID  C PRI NI     ADDR     SZ    WCHAN TTY      TIME CMD
8 O      0    582 27239  1  51 20        ?    237           pts/2    0:00 ps
```

Run the command several times, and you will see that ps always has an O state. When ps takes a snapshot, it is executing on the processor. The S state signifies that a process is sleeping. Typically, the process is blocked waiting for resources or input. When a process is ready to resume execution, it enters the runnable (R) state. In this state, the process waits in a queue to be executed on the processor. Although a multitasking operating system such as Solaris appears to be running processes simultaneously, it is actually running each for only a short period of time. The zombie (Z) state occurs when a child process dies and the parent fails to "clean up" after it. A zombie process no longer wastes CPU resources, but it still occupies a space in the process table. The T state describes a process stopped by job control. Two ways a process can enter this state are when a user executes a ^Z on a running process within his or her shell (assuming the shell supports job control) or via the pstop command.

Using the prstat Command to View Process Information

The prstat command provides process information at a configured interval. The output provided is similar to ps, although its dynamic nature is a valuable added benefit. When executed with output parameters, prstat displays process statistics on all processes on the system and refreshes them every five seconds. Other parameters are listed in Table 7-4.

Sorting Output

Unlike the ps command, prstat provides a built-in sorting mechanism. The process listing can be sorted on several criteria, which are listed in Table 7-5.

TABLE 7-4	The prstat Options

Option	Description
-a	Shows process information and summarized statistics per user.
-n num	Shows only the first *num* processes matching the sort criteria.
-p pidlist	Shows information only about processes with a process ID in the given list. The list must be comma delimited.
-s key	Sorts output in descending order according to key.
-v	Provides additional process usage data.
-G gidlist	Lists information for processes for which the real group ID numbers are given in *gidlist*. The list must be comma delimited.
-U uidlist	Shows information only about processes with a real UID given in the list that follows it. The list must be comma delimited.
-S <key>	Sorts output in ascending order according to the key. (Keys are listed in Table 7-5.)
interval [count]	Specifies the sampling interval in seconds. Optional *count* determines how many times the statistics are to be updated before prstat exits.

For instance, to view all processes on a system sorted in descending order of CPU usage, execute the following:

```
# prstat -s cpu

   PID USERNAME  SIZE   RSS STATE  PRI NICE     TIME  CPU PROCESS/NLWP
2014 root      2360K 1592K cpu0    53    0  0:00.00 0.6% prstat/1
 2009 root      3488K 2640K sleep   58    0  0:00.00 0.2% sshd/1
 2008 dlaporte 7352K 4680K sleep   54    0  0:00.00 0.1% emacs-20.4/1
 2011 dlaporte 2464K 1904K sleep   58    0  0:00.00 0.1% bash/1
  175 dns       6376K 4896K sleep   58    0  0:00.09 0.0% named/6
 1947 root      1584K 1400K sleep   48    0  0:00.00 0.0% bash/1
27222 root      1776K 1344K sleep   58    0  0:00.00 0.0% inetd/1
27238 dlaporte 2464K 1904K sleep   48    0  0:00.00 0.0% bash/1
27207 root      2672K 1776K sleep   58    0  0:00.00 0.0% sendmail/1
  163 root      1920K 1232K sleep   45    0  0:00.00 0.0% cron/1
  160 root      3792K 2072K sleep   48    0  0:00.00 0.0% syslogd/10
  348 root      1760K 1320K sleep   59    0  0:00.00 0.0% ttymon/1
   58 root      1392K 1072K sleep   53    0  0:00.00 0.0% syseventd/6
  345 root      1752K 1256K sleep   59    0  0:00.00 0.0% sac/1
    1 root       792K  256K sleep   58    0  0:00.17 0.0% init/1

Total: 42 processes, 70 lwps, load averages: 0.01, 0.01, 0.02
```

TABLE 7-5	Key	Description
The prstat Sort Keys	cpu	Sorts by process CPU usage (default)
	time	Sorts by process execution time
	size	Sorts by process image size
	rss	Sorts by resident set size
	pri	Sorts by process priority

Notice that the prstat command uses the most CPU time of any process on the system. Granted, the machine on which the preceding code was run was not under heavy load, but prstat can noticeably affect system performance. For this reason, it is best not to run prstat continuously with a low sampling interval.

One very useful function of the prstat command is to provide summarized statistics per user. This function can be very helpful in determining the resources each user consumes. For instance, the following code shows that *root* is using far more resources than any other user:

```
# prstat -a
PID USERNAME   SIZE    RSS STATE   PRI NICE      TIME  CPU PROCESS/NLWP
 2137 root     2248K 1392K run      30    0    0:43.41  96% prstat/1
 2279 jsmith   2544K 1624K sleep    58    0    0:00.00 1.0% top/1
 2281 dlaporte 2376K 1616K cpu0     58    0    0:00.00 0.6% prstat/1
 2282 root     1992K 1584K run      28    0    0:00.00 0.3% in.rlogind/1
 2284 root     1840K 1336K sleep    38    0    0:00.00 0.2% login/1

 NPROC USERNAME  SIZE    RSS MEMORY      TIME  CPU
    35 root      112M    63M    17%   0:44.09  97%
     2 jsmith   4952K  3480K   0.9%   0:00.00 1.2%
     8 dlaporte   15M    12M   3.2%   0:00.00 0.7%
     1 dns      6376K  4896K   1.3%   0:00.09 0.0%
     4 nobody     23M    14M   3.9%   0:00.00 0.0%

Total: 50 processes, 79 lwps, load averages: 1.04, 1.02, 0.97
```

Additional information is provided by using the *-v* option of prstat. The additional headers, as well as the base headers, are detailed in Table 7-6.

Using the sdtprocess Command to View Process Information

Solaris 9 has a new tool (introduced in Solaris 8) called the Process Manager. This tool, unlike prstat and ps, is a GUI tool and must be run in a graphical environment

TABLE 7-6	The prstat Column Headers	

Header	Required Option	Description
PID	None	Process identifier
USERNAME	None	Login name of the process owner
SIZE	None	Total virtual memory size of the process
RSS	None	Resident set size of the process
STATE	None	Process state
PRI	None	Process priority
NICE	None	Nice value of the process
TIME	None	Execution time of the process
CPU	None	Percentage of CPU used by the process
PROCESS/NLWP	None	Name of the process and number of LWPs in use
USR	-v	Percentage of time spent in user mode
SYS	-v	Percentage of time spent in system mode
TRP	-v	Percentage of time spent processing system traps
TFL	-v	Percentage of time spent processing text page faults
DFL	-v	Percentage of time spent processing data page faults
LCK	-v	Percentage of time spent waiting for user lock
SLP	-v	Percentage of time spent sleeping
VCX	-v	Number of voluntary context switches
ICX	-v	Number of involuntary context switches
SCL	-v	Number of system calls
SIG	-v	Number of signals received

such as CDE or displayed back to another machine running one. The Process Manager is a very robust tool, providing all the options available in prstat plus several others, at the click of a mouse. Figure 7-1 shows sdtprocess in action. A filter of *dlaporte* has already been applied to the process listing, leaving only those processes owned by user *dlaporte*.

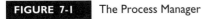

FIGURE 7-1   The Process Manager

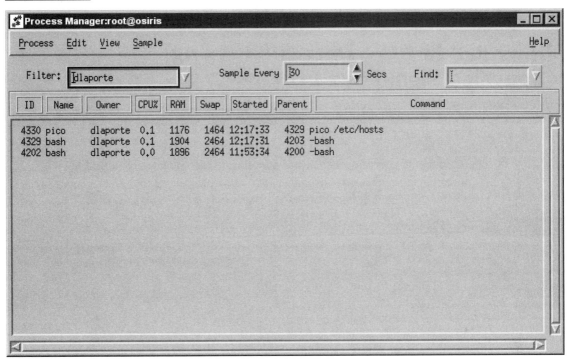

The output can be sorted on any of the column headers by simply clicking them; the sampling interval can be tweaked by changing the Sample Every field value. The Find field is useful for finding a specific process among a large amount of output. Typing a string into the field and pressing ENTER will highlight the first instance of the string in the output. Subsequent returns will show additional matches within the output. The Process Manager is also an effective way to send signals and kill processes, which are discussed in upcoming sections.

exam
ⓦatch

Don't be too concerned with the intricacies of the sdtprocess command. Sun administration exams are notorious for grilling you on command-line options. As such, concentrate on the options for ps and prstat. You can be sure you'll get a question on one of them.

CERTIFICATION OBJECTIVE 7.02

Understanding the Effect of Sending a Specified Signal to a Process

A *signal* is a message sent to a process to affect its operation. For instance, if a process is out of control and consuming large amounts of system resources, it might be useful to send a signal to terminate the process.

Signals do much more than simply kill processes, however. Solaris 9 has 42 different signals that can be sent, many of which are listed in Table 7-7.

| TABLE 7-7 | Solaris Signals |

Signal	Number	Description
SIGHUP	1	Hangs up
SIGINT	2	Interrupts
SIGQUIT	3	Quits
SIGILL	4	Illegal instruction
SIGTRAP	5	Trace trap
SIGABRT	6	Used by abort
SIGEMT	7	EMT instruction
SIGFPE	8	Floating-point exception
SIGKILL	9	Kill (cannot be caught or ignored)
SIGBUS	10	Bus error
SIGSEGV	11	Segmentation violation
SIGSYS	12	Bad argument to system call
SIGPIPE	13	Writes on a pipe with no one to read it
SIGALRM	14	Alarm clock
SIGTERM	15	Software termination
SIGUSR1	16	User-defined signal 1
SIGUSR2	17	User-defined signal 2

TABLE 7-7 Solaris Signals *(continued)*

Signal	Number	Description
SIGCHLD	18	Child status change alias (POSIX)
SIGPWR	19	Power-fail restart
SIGWINCH	20	Window size change
SIGURG	21	Urgent socket condition
SIGPOLL	22	Pollable event occurred
SIGIO	22	Socket I/O possible (SIGPOLL alias)
SIGSTOP	23	Stop (cannot be caught or ignored)
SIGTSTP	24	User stop requested from TTY
SIGCONT	25	Stopped process has been continued
SIGTTIN	26	Background TTY read attempted
SIGTTOU	27	Background TTY write attempted
SIGVTALRM	28	Virtual timer expired
SIGPROF	29	Profiling timer expired
SIGXCPU	30	Exceeded CPU limit
SIGXFSZ	31	Exceeded file size limit
SIGWAITING	32	Process' LWPs are blocked
SIGLWP	33	Special signal used by thread library
SIGFREEZE	34	Special signal used by CPR
SIGTHAW	35	Special signal used by CPR
SIGCANCEL	36	Thread cancellation signal used by libthread
SIGLOST	37	Resource lost
SIGRTMIN	38	Highest priority real-time signal
SIGRTMAX	45	Lowest priority real-time signal

Trapping Signals

When a process receives a signal, it can do one of three things:

- Ignore the signal.
- Take a specified action, such as closing all open files and exiting.
- Take the default action for the signal.

To ignore the signal or take special action, a process must have signal handlers specified. A *signal handler* allows a process to intercept the signal and do what the handler wants with it. For instance, on receiving a SIGHUP (1), many system daemons reread their configuration files, effectively restarting themselves with no downtime.

To view how a process handles each signal, use the psig command, part of the proc tools now included in Solaris. The psig command takes one or more PIDs as parameters and prints a list showing each signal and the process' response to it. For instance, the following shows the sample output using the syslog daemon as an example. (It has been trimmed for clarity.) The output you will see from the psig command will vary depending on the process you choose:

```
# psig 3530
3530:     /usr/sbin/syslogd
HUP       ignored
INT       ignored
QUIT      ignored
ILL       default
TRAP      default
ABRT      default
EMT       default
FPE       default
KILL      default
BUS       default

(output deleted)
```

All signals, except for two, can be handled in this manner. The first, SIGKILL (9), can be sent to a process to force it to release any resources it is using and then die unceremoniously.

on the **Job**

Use SIGKILL only when a process has refused to respond to any other methods of shutting it down. A SIGKILL does not allow a process to properly shut down and can lead to corrupted data files, especially in I/O-intensive applications such as databases. Use SIGKILL with extreme caution!

The second signal that cannot be caught is SIGSTOP (23). A SIGSTOP is used in shell-based job control. Typically, executing a ^Z on an active process sends the process a SIGSTOP, which suspends the process. (Execute a stty -*a* and examine the SUSP field to find out the exact value on your system.) The same result can be achieved using the pstop command, which accepts a PID as a parameter.

The complement to SIGSTOP is SIGCONT (25). This signal returns a stopped process to its previous state. The prun command can be used to send a SIGCONT to a stopped process. Both prun and pstop are part of the proc tools now included with Solaris. Because it's unlikely that many proc tools will appear on the test, they are not covered here. Please view the proc tools man page by executing man proc if you want to view a full listing.

Changing Process Priorities

Until now, you've learned how to manage processes by starting and stopping them. These tools are very useful, but they lack the granular control you often need on a day-to-day basis. If a process is using more than its fair share of system resources, stopping it outright is usually not an option. It would be nice to be able to manipulate the importance of the process to force the system to provide it with fewer resources to use in the first place. Fortunately, Solaris provides a method of doing exactly that. Remember, though, that this material is not included as part of the exam objectives; it is intended only to reinforce your process management skills.

Setting Process Priority with the nice Command   The nice command provides an administrator with a simple method to change the priority of a process. By default, the nice value of a process is set to 20. You can verify this by executing

```
ps -elf
```

and examining the NI field. This value is used as a modifier to the actual process priority specified in the PRI field. As the system administrator, you can set the nice value of any process to a value in the range of 0 to 39 by using the nice command:

```
/usr/bin/nice [ -increment| -n increment] <command>
```

The increment supplied to nice isn't the exact value to be set; rather, it is added to the current value. For instance, the command

```
nice -n 10 <process>
```

would result in the nice value of the process being set to 30 (because 20 is the default). Negative increments can also be used to increase the nice value of a process, but only the system administrator may do so.

The renice command is very similar to the nice command except that it works on processes already executing on the system. Table 7-8 lists the options available to renice.

The *-g, -p,* and *-u* options are mutually exclusive, meaning that you can use only one at a time. For instance, the following command raises the scheduling priority on PIDs 2834 and 24357:

```
# renice -n -8 -p 2834 24357
```

The following command sets the scheduling priority lower for processes run by *dlaporte:*

```
# renice -n 5 -u dlaporte
```

Although the nice and renice commands are useful, they are now considered deprecated. The priocntl command is a more robust (and therefore more complex) utility for setting and viewing scheduling priorities. The priocntl command is not part of the exam objectives, but you can read more about it by executing man priocntl.

Common Signals

You will rarely, if ever, use many of the signals shown in Table 7-7. Several are worth remembering, however. The signals in Table 7-9 are fairly common and perform useful actions that you should be aware of.

TABLE 7-8	Option	Description
The renice Options	*-n increment*	Schedules priority adjustment.
	-g gidlist	Lists groups for which to set adjustment. The list must consist of GIDs, not group names, and must be space delimited.
	-p pidlist	Lists processes for which to set adjustment. The list must be space delimited.
	-u uidlist	Lists users for which to set adjustment. The list must consist of UIDs or usernames and must be space delimited.

FROM THE CLASSROOM

Everyday Signals

Don't be intimidated by the large number of signals listed in Table 7-7. In day-to-day administration, you will see only a very small subset of these signals in use. For the test itself, you should prepare to see SIGHUP, SIGINT, SIGQUIT, SIGKILL, SIGTERM, SIGSTOP, and SIGCONT. Those signals and the effect they have on active processes are described in depth throughout this section.

In all my years of administration experience, I have rarely needed to use signals other than those listed. Some daemons (older versions of the BIND name server come to mind) used some uncommon signals for things such as statistics generation, but typically those are well described in the program documentation.

The use of signals in Solaris allows an administrator to finely control the operation of the processes running on a system. If a process runs amok, it is not necessary to reboot the machine—simply kill the offending process. This ability to solve problems on-the-fly truly separates UNIX, and therefore Solaris, from many other operating systems.

—*David LaPorte, SCSA, SCNA, MCSE, CCNA*

exam
Watch

Signals can be referred to by either name or number. Make sure you are able to map the signal name to its number as well as define what the signal is used for.

Now that you are aware of the signals you could see on the test and in day-to-day administration, the scenarios shown on the next page present a quick reference about when to use each.

As Table 7-9 shows, a SIGHUP is sent to all processes when a controlling terminal is disconnected—for instance, when a user logs off. This is a slight problem if you have a process that you would like to remain running once you've logged off. The nohup command allows a process to ignore the SIGHUP signal and continue operation even after a user logs off. The nohup command is located

SCENARIO & SOLUTION	
Which signal do you use to gracefully terminate a process?	Send a SIGTERM (15) to the process.
Which signal do you use if you would like to stop, not terminate, a process to reclaim CPU resources for another process?	Send a SIGSTOP (23) to the process.
Which signal do you use if a process refuses to respond to SIGHUP (1), SIGINT (2), and SIGTERM (15)?	Send a SIGKILL (9) to the process. Do this only if all other attempts have failed.
Which signal do you use if a stopped process needs to be returned to the runnable state?	Send a SIGCONT (25) to the process.

at /usr/sbin/nohup and takes only one option, the command to be executed. For instance, to nohup a command named import_data, you would execute

```
# nohup ./import_data &
```

This example would leave a file named nohup.out containing all output of the command in the current directory. If the user did not have write permissions to the current directory, it would instead be created in the user's home directory. The nohup command can be very useful for running commands with a long execution time, especially when those commands are run in the evening just before you log off and go home.

TABLE 7-9   Common Signals

Signal	Number	How Generated
SIGHUP	1	Generated when controlling terminal is disconnected. Used by many system daemons to trigger a reread of the configuration file.
SIGINT	2	Generated when a user executes a ^C on the current process (execute STTY -a and examine the INTR field for the exact value on your system) in a shell that supports job control.
SIGQUIT	3	Generated when a user executes a ^\ on the current process (execute STTY -a and examine the QUIT field for the exact value on your system) in a shell that supports job control.
SIGKILL	9	Terminates a process with extreme prejudice. The process is not allowed to clean up after itself; open files could be corrupted.

TABLE 7-9	Common Signals *(continued)*	

Signal	Number	How Generated
SIGTERM	15	Gracefully allows a process to exit. Default signal sent by kill and pkill.
SIGSTOP	23	Stops a process.
SIGCONT	25	Starts a stopped process.

CERTIFICATION OBJECTIVE 7.03

Using Commands to Terminate an Active Process

We've talked about the signals that are available, but we have yet to discuss how those signals are actually sent. Processes are always sending signals among themselves, but we're more concerned with how an administrator can send signals and terminate processes. Solaris provides three utilities to do this: kill, pkill, and sdtprocess. In all these utilities, a user may kill only processes that he or she owns. The one exception to this rule is the root user, who may kill any process on the system. There are four processes—sched, init, pageout, and fsflush—that cannot be terminated. These processes must be running on any functioning Solaris system.

Using kill to Terminate a Process

The kill utility provides an administrator with a mechanism to send a signal to a running process. Its name is actually a misnomer; the kill command can send almost any signal to a process. For it to function, you must supply kill with at least one function—the PID of the process you want to signal—but you should be aware of a few other options, which are listed in Table 7-10.

TABLE 7-10	Option	Description
The kill Options	*-l*	Lists all signals available to kill
	-s signal	Specifies signal to send
	-signal	Specifies signal to send
	pid	The PID to send signal to

For example, to view all signals supported by kill, execute the following:

```
# kill -l
 1) SIGHUP       2) SIGINT      3) SIGQUIT     4) SIGILL
 5) SIGTRAP      6) SIGABRT     7) SIGEMT      8) SIGFPE
 9) SIGKILL     10) SIGBUS     11) SIGSEGV    12) SIGSYS
13) SIGPIPE     14) SIGALRM    15) SIGTERM    16) SIGUSR1
17) SIGUSR2     18) SIGCHLD    19) SIGPWR     20) SIGWINCH
21) SIGURG      22) SIGIO      23) SIGSTOP    24) SIGTSTP
25) SIGCONT     26) SIGTTIN    27) SIGTTOU    28) SIGVTALRM
29) SIGPROF     30) SIGXCPU    31) SIGXFSZ    32) SIGWAITING
33) SIGLWP      34) SIGFREEZE  35) SIGTHAW    36) SIGCANCEL
37) SIGLOST     38) SIGRTMIN   39) SIGRTMIN+1 40) SIGRTMIN+2
41) SIGRTMIN+3  42) SIGRTMAX-3 43) SIGRTMAX-2 44) SIGRTMAX-1
45) SIGRTMAX
```

This listing can be helpful when you are trying to remember which signal to send. To send a SIGHUP (1) to a process with a PID of 1212, use one of the following commands:

```
kill -s HUP 1212
kill -HUP 1212
kill -1 1212
```

The kill command allows you to use several different syntaxes to accomplish the same goal. Note that when specifying the signal name rather than the signal number, you must drop the SIG suffix.

exam
Ⓦatch

Remember, the default signal sent by kill and pkill is SIGTERM (15), not SIGKILL (9). Don't let the names of the utility confuse you.

Unfortunately, kill will not accept a process name, only a process identifier. This adds an extra step because you must grep the output of ps to get the PID from the process name. Fortunately, Solaris 9 includes a utility called pgrep. Table 7-11 lists the options available to pgrep.

The pgrep utility allows you to quickly retrieve the PID of a process based on a substring of the process name. For instance, to retrieve the PID of the syslogd process, execute

```
# pgrep syslog
3527
```

TABLE 7-11   The pgrep Options

Option	Description
substring	String to match against processes.
-l	Long output format.
-v	Negation option; matches any process *except* those that match the expression.
-x	Matches *substring* against processes exactly.
-G grouplist	Specifies processes owned by any group in *grouplist*. The list must be comma delimited and may include GIDs or group names.
-U userlist	Specifies processes owned by any group in *userlist*. The list must be comma delimited and may include UIDs or usernames.

This works well for cases in which only one process is returned, but what if several processes match the substring? For example,

```
# pgrep sys
58
3527
```

It is impossible to tell which is the PID of the process you're looking for. Using the *-l* option will show not only the PID of the process, but its name as well:

```
root@osiris:~$ pgrep -l sys
   58 syseventd
3527 syslogd
```

You can now call kill on the appropriate PID. This process still seems awkward, as though you should be able to do these actions all in one step. Fortunately, you can! The next section shows you how.

Using pkill to Terminate a Process

The pkill utility is very similar to pgrep except that it eliminates the *-l* option and replaces it with an option to specify a signal to pass. For instance, using the preceding situation as an example, you can quickly send a SIGHUP to the syslog daemon by executing the following:

```
pkill -HUP -x syslogd
```

The *-x* option is fairly redundant, given that it is unlikely that another process would include the substring *syslogd*, but it's better to be safe than sorry.

Using sdtprocess to Terminate a Process

The sdtprocess utility provides methods for sending signals and killing processes via its GUI.

EXERCISE 7-1

Killing a Process with the Process Manager

1. Load the Process Manager application by executing /usr/dt/bin/sdtproccess in a terminal window.

2. Highlight the process and open the Process menu. It should look like this:

The two options you are interested in are Signal and Kill. The Signal option allows you to specify the signal you would like to send to the process; the Kill option sends a SIGKILL to the process. Note that this is different from the operation of kill and pkill! For this reason, you should avoid using the Kill option as much as possible and use Signal instead.

3. Select the Signal option. You will be presented with the dialog box shown next.

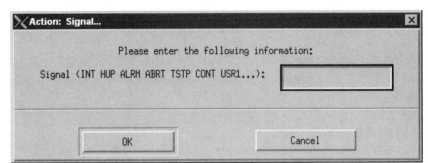

4. Enter the signal you would like to send (without the SIG prefix) and click OK.

This process is several steps longer than using pkill, but it could be preferable to users who are more inclined to use a GUI.

CERTIFICATION SUMMARY

The Solaris operating environment provides several methods to view process information and control. Utilities such as ps, prstat, and the Process Manager allow you to view all active processes on a system. The information provided by each tool and the method by which that information is displayed differ slightly among tools. Your own preferences and the information you require will determine the tool that is necessary for a given task.

Solaris provides 42 signals that can be used to control processes. Under normal circumstances, you will come in contact with only a small subset of this number. Processes can react to a signal by acting on it, ignoring it, or performing the default action. The SIGKILL signal cannot be trapped and is used to terminate an unresponsive process.

The Process Manager (sdtprocess), kill, and pkill allow a user to send a signal to processes they own. The root user may send a signal to any process, regardless of its ownership, except for sched, init, pageout, and fsflush.

TWO-MINUTE DRILL

Using Commands to Display Information for All Active Processes on the System

❑ The prstat command provides built-in sorting and summarization facilities.

❑ The Process Manager (sdtprocess) provides a user-friendly method of viewing and filtering process information.

❑ Use the *-fl* or *-v* options, respectively, to have ps and prstat display more verbose information.

❑ Without arguments, ps shows only processes owned by the user, whereas prstat and sdtprocess show the entire process table.

❑ The grep command can be used to provide basic filtering of ps output.

Understanding the Effect of Sending a Specified Signal to a Process

❑ Solaris provides 42 signals that can be sent to processes.

❑ The SIGKILL signal should be sent only if a process refuses to respond to anything else.

❑ The pstop and prun commands start and stop processes by sending SIGSTOP and SIGCONT signals, respectively.

❑ Many daemons reread their configuration files when they receive a SIGHUP.

❑ A process has three options upon receiving a signal: ignore it, take a specified action, or take the default action defined for the signal.

Using Commands to Terminate an Active Process

❑ The kill command requires the PID of the process to which you want to send a signal.

❑ The pgrep command will quickly map a process name to a PID.

❑ The pkill command is very similar to the pgrep command but includes an additional option to specify a signal to be sent to matching processes.

❑ If a specific signal is not specified, kill and pkill default to sending a SIGTERM.

❑ The Process Manager provides a simple method for sending signals for the GUI-inclined.

SELF TEST

The following questions will help you measure your understanding of the material presented in this chapter. Read all the choices carefully because there might be more than one correct answer. Choose all correct answers for each question.

Using Commands to Display Information
for All Active Processes on the System

1. After receiving several complaints from users about a slow-performing system, you run an uptime on the machine and find that it has a very high load. You would like to view a summary of users who are consuming particular resources. What is the best way to accomplish this task?

   A. Run `procinfo -I`.

   B. Run `prstat -a`.

   C. Select the Summary option from the Process menu in Process Manager.

   D. Execute `ps -elf`.

2. Which of the following commands will show all processes owned by users *bob* and *joe*? (Choose all that apply.)

   A. `ps -fU bob,joe`

   B. `prstat -U bob,joe`

   C. `ps -fU bob joe`

   D. Typing **bob OR joe** into the filter field of Process Manager

3. A colleague has set up the text-only console of a server to run prstat 0. You notice that the command is taking up a huge amount of system resources. How can you lower resource utilization and still get updated process data?

   A. Run the Process Manager with a large sampling interval.

   B. Use ps instead.

   C. Increase the sampling interval prstat uses.

   D. prstat uses large amounts of system resources and should not be run for extended periods of time.

Understanding the Effect of Sending a Specified Signal to a Process

4. A user reports that he accidentally killed an important process that was running on his system. Executing a ps *-IF* on a machine, you see the following:

```
F S   UID   PID  PPID  C PRI NI      ADDR     SZ    WCHAN TTY      TIME CMD
8 T   100 25394 25348  1  99 20        ?     129          pts/1    0:01 job2
```

Process 25394 has a T (for traced) listed in the state column. What do you tell the user?

A. The process is operating normally; it must be waiting on keyboard input from the user.

B. The process has been terminated; there is nothing you can do.

C. The process was stopped.

D. The process is unresponsive, so a SIGKILL must be sent.

5. A process on a system you maintain needs to be killed. It does not appear to be hung, but it does not respond to a SIGTERM, SIGINT, SIGHUP, or SIGKILL. Which command would you use to see if the process is ignoring those signals?

A. psig

B. prstat

C. pgrep

D. procinfo

6. A computationally intensive process has been running on a machine for several days. A user has requested that she be able to use the machine for an afternoon. Her process will need a fair amount of CPU resources. Which command pair would you use to stop and start the existing process?

A. pstop, pstart

B. pgrep, prun

C. pstop, prun

D. prstat, pstart

Using Commands to Terminate an Active Process

7. After receiving reports of a slow system, you run prstat on the affected machine and notice that a single user, *jsmith,* is running several wasteful processes. After a little research, you determine

that the processes are meant only to consume resources, not for any legitimate work. How would you terminate all processes owned by *jsmith*?

A. `ps -fU jsmith`

B. `pkill -9 -U jsmith`

C. `prstat -kU jsmith`

D. `pgrep -lU jsmith`

8. A user, *mjones*, approaches you complaining that she is unable to kill a process. As the root user, you run ps *-ef* to view all processes on the system. The PID of the process she is complaining about is 23405. (The relevant line is listed as follows.) What should you tell her the problem is?

```
    UID   PID  PPID  C   STIME   TTY       TIME CMD
bjenkins 23405     1  0 21:10:38 pts/1      0:01 /usr/bin/pico
```

A. The process is stopped.

B. The controlling terminal has disconnected.

C. The process is unresponsive.

D. She does not own the process.

9. Which of the following commands will successfully kill this process?

```
dlaporte 25976 25348  0 20:00:14 pts/1     0:00 pico /etc/hosts
```

A. `kill -s TERM 25976`

B. `pgrep -k 25976`

C. `pkill 25976`

D. `kill pico`

LAB QUESTION

You have received several complaints from users about extremely slow system performance. This is not the first time this has happened, unfortunately. It seems that the stat_maker process run by one of the users runs amok when it is fed very large datasets. After getting the user's approval to remedy the problem, you log in to the machine and begin to look around.

From the following list, identify the correct actions to take in solving this problem, and then place a number to the left of each step, indicating the correct order in which the steps should be completed. Note that some steps might not be valid.

____ Reboot the machine to terminate the runaway process.

____ View a process listing sorted by CPU usage produced by the prstat command.

____ Raise the process priority using the nice command.

____ Confirm that CPU usage has returned to normal levels.

____ Stop the process using pstop and confirm that CPU usage falls accordingly.

____ Send the process a SIGKILL signal using kill, if necessary.

____ Isolate the offending process and note its PID.

____ Send the process a SIGTERM signal using the kill command.

SELF TEST ANSWERS

Using Commands to Display Information for All Active Processes on the System

1. ☑ **B.** The *-a* option of the prstat command provides per-user process reports. These reports are very useful in determining which users are abusing resources.
   ☒ **A** and **C** are incorrect because neither actually exists. **D** does provide information on all active processes, but the data is not summarized as required by the question.

2. ☑ **A** and **B.** The ps and prstat commands both accept a list of UIDs or usernames.
   ☒ **C** is incorrect because this list must be comma delimited. The Process Manager does allow you to filter, but typing **bob OR joe** into the field will match only processes with that exact string in the output—most likely not what you are looking for.

3. ☑ **C.** Running prstat with a very small sampling interval can quickly eat up valuable system resources. Given that the console will probably be looked at only in passing, there is no need for such a small interval. Increasing the interval to 30 or more seconds will provide fairly up-to-date statistics and dramatically lessen prstat's effect on the system.
   ☒ **B** is very close to correct because the Process Manager does provide updating statistics and has a configurable sampling interval. However, the server had only a text-based console attached to it, and the Process Manager requires a windowing environment to run. Therefore, this answer is incorrect because ps cannot provide updating statistics.

Understanding the Effect of Sending a Specified Signal to a Process

4. ☑ **C.** The process was stopped (most likely by the user pressing ^Z in a shell that supports job control), not killed. Send a SIGCONT (25) to the process to start it again. The prun command can be used to send the signal, or you can use kill or pkill with a -CONT argument.
   ☒ **A** is incorrect because a process operating normally should have an O, R, or S value in the STATE field. **B** is also incorrect because if the process had been terminated, it wouldn't even show up in the process listing. **D** is also incorrect because the user reported that he was working with the process before it was killed.

5. ☑ **A.** The psig command will print a listing of each signal and how the process handles it. From this output, you can examine each of the signals and see if the action is listed as "ignore."
   ☒ **B** is incorrect because it shows only a listing of active processes on the box. **C** is incorrect because it will map a PID to a process name. The procinfo tool does not exist, so **D** is also incorrect.

6. ☑ C. The prun and pstop commands are used to start and stop processes. These actions are done via the SIGSTOP (23) and SIGCONT (25) signals. Stopping processes is an easy way to reclaim CPU resources and is also used in shell job control mechanisms.

☒ A and D are incorrect because the pstart command does not exist. The pgrep command is used to map a process name to a PID, so **B** is also incorrect.

Using Commands to Terminate an Active Process

7. ☑ B. The pkill command will kill all processes owned by user *jsmith.* You can safely send a SIGKILL because you have judged that the processes are doing nothing useful.

☒ A and D will show all processes owned by *jsmith,* but they will not kill them. C is also incorrect because prstat does have a -*k* option; the command will fail and display only its usage information.

8. ☑ D. The process the user is trying to kill is owned by user *bjenkins.* Users are allowed to kill only processes that they own. The user might be confused; there is probably no reason she would want to terminate another user's text editor.

☒ A and C are incorrect because the output does not provide you with enough information to make either assumption. B is incorrect because the process does appear to have a controlling terminal. When the controlling terminal disconnects, all processes attached to it are typically sent a SIGHUP, which should terminate them.

9. ☑ A. The kill command specified is correct. Although it is redundant (because kill sends a SIGTERM by default), it is perfectly legal to specify the signal with the -*s* option.

☒ D is incorrect because the kill command will accept only a PID. B is incorrect because the pgrep command does not support a -*k* option. C is also incorrect because the pkill command accepts a process name, not a PID, as a parameter.

LAB ANSWER

You are likely to encounter the situation described in this lab in the course of day-to-day administration. Although it is not a common occurrence, processes sometimes get out of control and need to be killed. It is therefore very important to know the process. The following procedure is only one way to do things:

1. View a process listing sorted by CPU usage.

2. Isolate the offending process and note its PID.

3. Stop the process using pstop and confirm that CPU usage falls accordingly.

4. Send the process a SIGTERM signal.

5. Send the process a SIGKILL signal, if necessary.

6. Confirm that CPU usage has returned to normal levels.

You could have, for instance, sent a SIGSTOP signal directly rather than using the pstop command, or you could have used the pkill command and not bothered to remember the process ID. The beauty of Solaris is that it allows you to follow different paths to the same goal. As your habits become entrenched, you will begin to favor some commands over others, much the way that this exercise reflects the commands I would use to diagnose this problem.

8

Working with File Systems

T
his chapter takes an in-depth look at Solaris file systems. It discusses the basic types of file systems, exactly what constitutes a file system, the standard Solaris file system structure, creating file systems, and how to use and administer file systems effectively.

The hierarchical structure of file systems, referred to as a *file system tree,* was designed to facilitate the organization of directories and files and provides a convenient way to administer data on a system. All the important data on your system is contained in files that are organized in file systems. Specific file systems and directories exist for the sole purpose of grouping together directories and files that are related.

The Solaris operating environment uses the Virtual File System (VFS) architecture. This architecture enables the kernel to handle basic file system operations, such as reading and writing files within a specific file system, without requiring the user or program to know which file system type is actually being used.

It is extremely important to have a thorough working knowledge of file systems to properly administrate a UNIX system. The system communicates to all its devices, including its disks, monitor, keyboard, and mouse, through special files called *device files* that exist on the root file system under the /dev directory. Every function that your system performs with regard to the input or output of data takes place through the use of file systems, directories, and files.

CERTIFICATION OBJECTIVE 8.01

Knowing the Types of File Systems in the Solaris Operating Environment

This section discusses basic file systems. Then it looks at the various types of Solaris 9 file systems and their specific uses.

File Systems in General

The term *file system* refers to a mounted directory and a file hierarchy. It is used to store and organize groups of related directories and files. The most common file systems exist as collections of data blocks and control structures on a disk partition.

File systems can exist locally, where they are accessed by the system via disk controllers, or remotely, where they are accessed via the network. Keep in mind that a remote file system to one server is just a local file system shared out by another server.

Solaris File System Types

Several types of file systems exist in the Solaris 9 operating environment. These different file system types facilitate different file storage and retrieval needs. There are three divisions of file system types: disk-based file systems that exist on physical disk drives local to the system; virtual or RAM-based file systems that exist in the memory of the system; and network-based file systems that are mounted remotely, over the network, from another system.

Let's take a closer look at each type.

Disk-Based File Systems

File systems that exist on a physical disk partition (excluding swap areas) are referred to as *disk-based file systems.* There are four types of standard disk-based file systems:

- UFS
- HSFS
- PCFS
- UDF

Table 8-1 shows the four types of disk-based Solaris file systems and describes the way the system uses each type.

exam
ⓦatch
When taking your exam, remember that there are now four types of disk-based file systems. UDF was new in Solaris 8.

File System Logging

UNIX File System (UFS) logging is the process of storing transactions (changes that make up a complete file or directory operation) in a log before they are applied to the file system. Once a transaction is stored, the complete transaction can be applied or reapplied to the file system later.

| TABLE 8-1 | Disk-Based File System Types |

Type	Description
UFS	The UNIX File System (UFS) type is the default type of file system for the Solaris operating environment. This file system type is based on the Berkeley Software Distribution (BSD) Fast File System.
HSFS	The High Sierra and ISO or International Standards Organization 9660 File System (HSFS) standard type is used for mounting media with read-only data, such as CD-ROMs.
PCFS	The Personal Computer File System (PCFS) type is used for reading and writing disk operating system (DOS)–formatted floppy disks.
UDF	The Universal Disk Format (UDF) file system is new in Solaris 8. UDF is the industry-standard format used to store information on optical media technology. This UDF file system type is mainly used for reading information from DVDs, but it can also be used for CD-ROMs and floppy disks that contain UDF file systems.

exam
Ⓦatch

File system logging was new in Solaris 8.

UFS logging offers two advantages. It prevents file systems from becoming inconsistent, therefore eliminating the need to run fsck. Furthermore, because fsck can be bypassed, UFS logging reduces the time required to reboot a system when it is stopped other than via an orderly shutdown.

Virtual File Systems

Virtual or *RAM-based file systems* are used to improve I/O performance. This is accomplished by providing access to data in physical memory rather than on a disk-based file system. Table 8-2 displays the types of virtual file systems and describes the way each type is used by the system.

on the
Ⓙob

Never delete files from the /proc directory. These files are used by the system to keep track of running processes. Deleting process files from the /proc directory will not kill the processes. Remember, /proc is a virtual file system and therefore uses no disk space.

TABLE 8-1	Virtual File System Types

Type	Description
CACHEFS	The Cache File System (CACHEFS) type is used as a disk cache area to speed access to slower file systems such as CD-ROMs (HSFS) or network-based file systems (NFS).
FDFS	The File Descriptor File System (FDFS) type provides specific names for opening files using file descriptors.
LOFS	The Loopback File System (LOFS) type is used to create a virtual file system that allows the system to access files using an alternative path.
NAMEFS	The Name File System (NAMEFS) type is used by STREAMS for dynamically mounting file descriptors over files.
PROCFS	The Process File System (PROCFS) type is used by the system to maintain a list of all the active processes by process ID number under /proc. This makes it possible for debuggers and other similar tools to access process information and address space through the use of file system calls.
SPECFS	The Special File System (SPECFS) type provides access to character special and block devices.
SWAPFS	The Swap File System (SWAPFS) type is used to provide swap space to the system.
TMPFS	The Temporary File System (TMPFS) type is used by the /tmp file system and uses local memory for file system operations. It is much faster than a disk-based file system.

Network-Based File Systems

The Network File System (NFS) is the only network-based file system currently supported by the Solaris operating environment. The following describes the way the system uses NFS:

NFS	The Network File System (NFS) type is used by the system to mount remote file systems from other servers over the network.

NFS Server Logging

NFS server logging provides a method for the NFS server to create a record of all file operations performed on its exported file systems. This feature is especially useful for sites that make anonymous FTP archives available via NFS and WebNFS protocols.

Understanding Solaris File System Types

This exercise tests your knowledge of the types of file systems that exist in the Solaris 9 operating environment.

How many file system types exist under Solaris 9? What are they, and on which part of the system are they based?

Answer: There are three types of file systems in Solaris 9:

1. Disk-based file systems exist on a physical disk partition.

2. Virtual file systems are RAM-based and exist in the system memory.

3. Network file systems are network-based file systems that are accessed remotely across a network.

CERTIFICATION OBJECTIVE 8.02

Performing Common File System Administration Tasks

This section discusses common file system administration tasks that you'll need to perform periodically. You'll examine several different tools and walk through a few real-life scenarios that will surely pop up on the job for you sometime in the near future.

Creating New UFS File Systems

Once you identify a disk partition that you would like to mount as a file system, you must run the newfs command to make it usable to the operating system. The newfs command is a user-friendly front-end program that actually runs the mkfs command to create a file system on a disk partition. Figure 8-1 shows newfs being used to create a new UFS file system on the raw disk partition /dev/rdsk/c0d0s6.

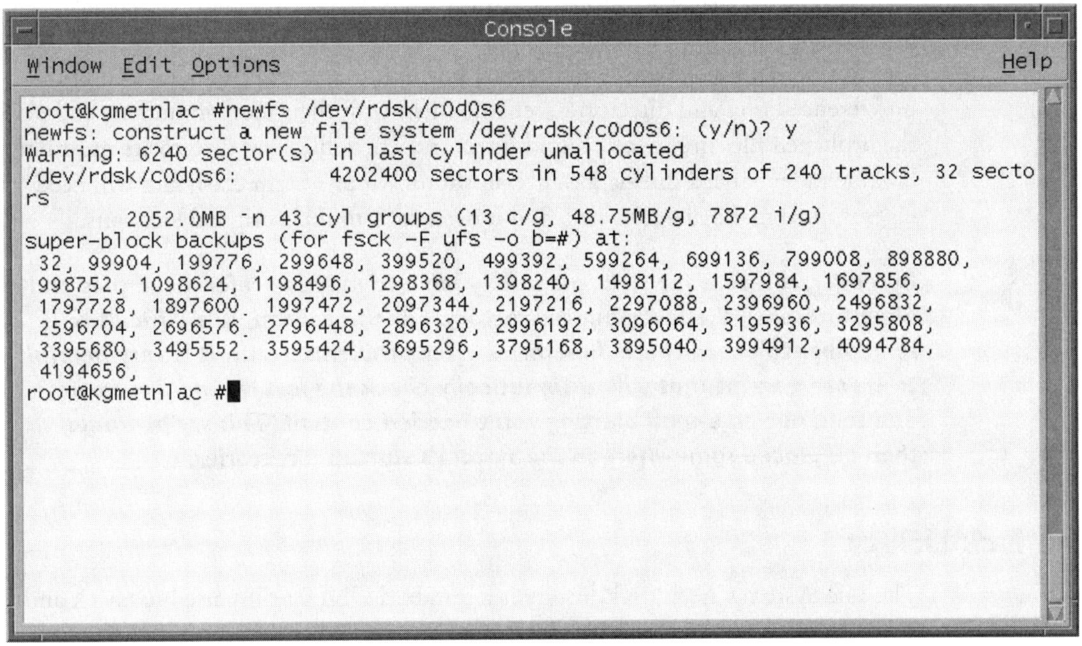

FIGURE 8-1   Using the newfs command to create a new UFS file system

```
┌─                              Console                              ▫ □
 Window  Edit  Options                                            Help
 root@kgmetnlac #newfs /dev/rdsk/c0d0s6
 newfs: construct a new file system /dev/rdsk/c0d0s6: (y/n)? y
 Warning: 6240 sector(s) in last cylinder unallocated
 /dev/rdsk/c0d0s6:        4202400 sectors in 548 cylinders of 240 tracks, 32 secto
 rs
          2052.0MB ·n 43 cyl groups (13 c/g, 48.75MB/g, 7872 i/g)
 super-block backups (for fsck -F ufs -o b=#) at:
  32, 99904, 199776, 299648, 399520, 499392, 599264, 699136, 799008, 898880,
  998752, 1098624, 1198496, 1298368, 1398240, 1498112, 1597984, 1697856,
  1797728, 1897600. 1997472, 2097344, 2197216, 2297088, 2396960, 2496832,
  2596704, 2696576. 2796448, 2896320, 2996192, 3096064, 3195936, 3295808,
  3395680, 3495552. 3595424, 3695296, 3795168, 3895040, 3994912, 4094784,
  4194656,
 root@kgmetnlac #█
```

The newfs command asks for confirmation before continuing. Once it receives confirmation, it displays sector, cylinder, and track information for the entire disk:

```
4202400 sectors in 548 cylinders of 240 tracks, 32 sectors
```

Then it displays the size in megabytes and the number of cylinder groups for the file system it is about to create:

```
2052.0MB in 43 cyl groups (13 c/g, 48.75MB/g, 7872 i/g)
```

Notice the information in the parentheses in Figure 8-1. This information indicates that there are 13 cylinders in a cylinder group, 48.75 megabytes of disk space in each cylinder group, and 7872 inodes available in each cylinder group.

Now the actual file system creation begins. As the file system is created, backups are made of the superblock information, and the location of the backups is displayed.

Note two points about the new file system that newfs has just created. First, 3 percent of the actual space available has been reserved for system maintenance. Second, the file system is created with a lost+found directory that the fsck command uses during file system check and repair. The fsck utility will find allocated but unreferenced files and directories, rename them with their inode numbers, and place the orphaned files in the lost+found directory. These files and directories most likely became unreferenced during an unclean shutdown or system crash and will need to be examined manually, renamed, and moved back to their original locations.

on the
ⓙob

In reality, it is rare for fsck to actually have to move unreferenced files and directories into the lost+found directory. For this reason, it is difficult to remember to check these directories after problems occur. It is very helpful to create a script that will automatically check the lost+found directories and send out an e-mail alerting you to added content. This script would then be placed somewhere in the system's startup directories.

The fsck Utility

The File System Check (fsck) utility is a standard UNIX utility used to check and, if necessary, repair the integrity of file systems before they are mounted. The fsck utility can be used in interactive or noninteractive mode. It is a very useful tool for troubleshooting disk and file system problems.

exam
ⓦatch

Avoid running fsck on a mounted file system. Not only can this cause erroneous results, but it could actually cause damage to the file system and result in the loss of data.

Why fsck Is Necessary

The fsck utility is necessary to ensure file system consistency and therefore data integrity. Each time just before a file system is mounted, the fsck utility is executed and checks for and repairs several possible problems with the disk, file system, superblock, and inodes.

Problems in these areas generally occur as a result of a system crash or improper shutdown. Such problems could be caused by human error, hardware failure, or loss of power. Possible disk problems include these:

- Free data blocks claimed by files

■ Free data block count

■ Free inode count

How to Check and Repair a File System

During the boot process, the fsck utility checks the status of each file system that is automatically mounted at boot time, just before it is mounted. This is an example of its noninteractive mode execution. The fsck command can also be executed from the command line in interactive mode. Figure 8-2 shows the fsck command being executed interactively from the command line for the file system just created.

Notice in Figure 8-2 the information that fsck displays about the file system. First, it verifies the raw device path to the file system. Then it displays that mount point to which the file system was last mounted. Note that there is no mount point displayed. This makes sense because this file system was just created and it has not yet been mounted. Then each phase of the fsck verification is displayed. If problems were found, they would also be displayed and a prompt would be presented asking

FIGURE 8-2   Using the fsck command to check and repair a file system

```
                             Console
 Window  Edit  Options                                    Help
root@kgmetnlac #fsck /dev/rdsk/c0d0s6
** /dev/rdsk/c0d0s6
** Last Mounted on
** Phase 1 - Check Blocks and Sizes
** Phase 2 - Check Pathnames
** Phase 3 - Check Connectivity
** Phase 4 - Check Reference Counts
** Phase 5 - Check Cyl groups
2 files, 9 used, 2058174 free (14 frags, 257270 blocks,  0.0% fragmentation)
root@kgmetnlac #
```

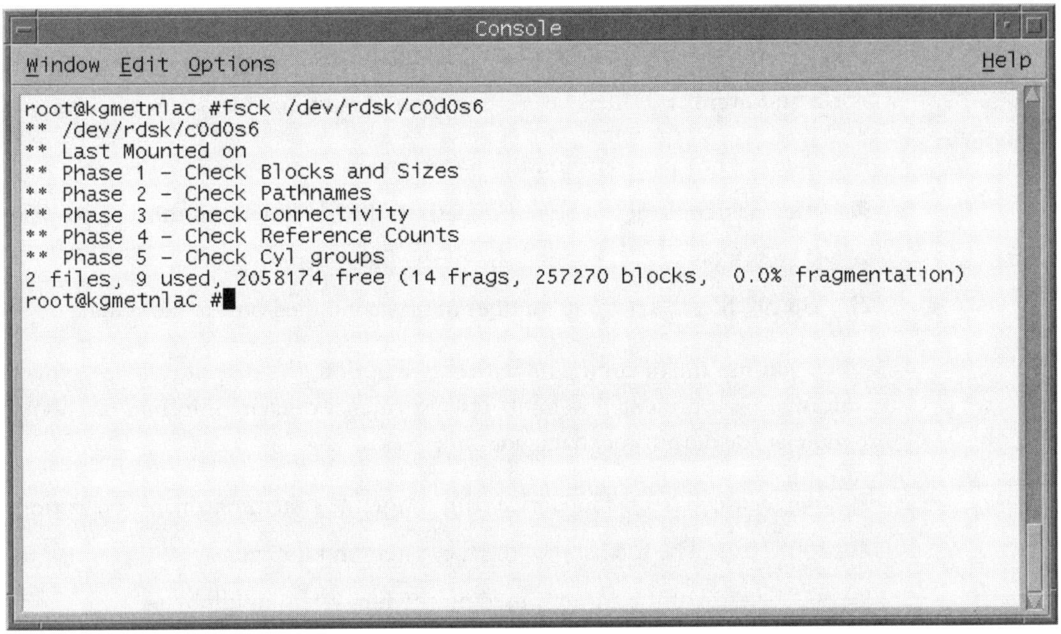

for verification to proceed with a repair. This file system was just created, so it should not have inconsistencies.

on the
job

The most common situation in which you can use the fsck command is when the system is in single-user mode and the file systems being checked are unmounted. A very common option to use with fsck is the -y option. This option causes fsck to automatically take default corrective actions when file system problems are discovered and will save you a great deal of time by removing the need to continually answer yes to each step of the corrective process.

Displaying Disk Space Usage by File Systems

Now that you know how to create, check, mount, and unmount file systems, let's take a look at gathering information about and monitoring file systems. When you log in to a system the first time, you can run the mount command or look at the /etc/mnttab file to see which file systems are currently mounted. Then you might wonder which file systems are the largest or which ones have more space available. These questions are best answered by using the df command. Figure 8-3 shows the df command being used, first with no option, and second with the *-k* option.

As you can see in Figure 8-3, the df command provides a wealth of information. By running the df command with no options, you get output with size information in blocks and number of files. Let's examine the output for /data.

- **/data**   The directory mount point name
- **(/dev/dsk/c0d0s6)**   The device path to the file system on the disk partition
- **4116348 blocks**   The total size of the file system in blocks
- **338492 files**   The total number of files contained on the file system

When you run the df command with the *-k* option, the output changes. Now the size information is presented in kilobytes and you get capacity information. Looking once more at the output for /data, you find

- **/dev/dsk/c0d0s6**   The device path to the file system on the disk partition
- **2058183**   The total size of the file system in kilobytes
- **9**   The size of the amount used on the file system in kilobytes

FIGURE 8-3   Using the df command to display disk space usage by a file system

```
┌──────────────────────────────── Console ────────────────────────────────┐
│ Window   Edit   Options                                             Help │
├──────────────────────────────────────────────────────────────────────────┤
│ root@kgmetnlac #df                                                       │
│ /proc              (/proc            ):       0 blocks    1894 files      │
│ /                  (/dev/dsk/c0d0s0  ): 2873402 blocks  297041 files      │
│ /dev/fd            (fd               ):       0 blocks       0 files      │
│ /admin1            (/dev/dsk/c0d0s3  ): 4116312 blocks  338476 files      │
│ /admin2            (/dev/dsk/c0d0s4  ): 2456118 blocks  337699 files      │
│ /admin3            (/dev/dsk/c0d0s5  ): 4116348 blocks  338492 files      │
│ /web               (/dev/dsk/c0d0s7  ):11744700 blocks  715765 files      │
│ /tmp               (swap             ):  626736 blocks   20957 files      │
│ /data              (/dev/dsk/c0d0s6  ): 4116348 blocks  338492 files      │
│ root@kgmetnlac #df -k                                                     │
│ Filesystem          kbytes     used    avail capacity  Mounted on        │
│ /proc                    0        0        0      0%   /proc              │
│ /dev/dsk/c0d0s0    2058183   621482  1374956     32%   /                  │
│ fd                       0        0        0      0%   /dev/fd            │
│ /dev/dsk/c0d0s3    2058183       27  1996411      1%   /admin1            │
│ /dev/dsk/c0d0s4    2058183   830124  1166314     42%   /admin2            │
│ /dev/dsk/c0d0s5    2058183        9  1996429      1%   /admin3            │
│ /dev/dsk/c0d0s7    5881710     9360  5813533      1%   /web               │
│ swap                318428     5064   313364      2%   /tmp               │
│ /dev/dsk/c0d0s6    2058183        9  1996429      1%   /data              │
│ root@kgmetnlac #█                                                         │
└──────────────────────────────────────────────────────────────────────────┘
```

- **1996429**   The size of the space still available for use in kilobytes
- **1%**   The percentage of used capacity on the file system
- **/data**   The directory mount point name

on the *Job*   *You can verify the conversion from blocks to kilobytes with this formula:*

```
<size in blocks> * 512 / 1024 = <size in kilobytes>
```

Displaying the Size of a Directory

Suppose now that you don't want to display the size of an entire file system. You want to display the size of a single subdirectory contained on a file system. This is where the du command works quite well. The du command has the following format:

```
# du [-a] [-s] [-k] [<directory name>]
```

Similar to the df command, the du command, if given no options, reports sizes in blocks. However, another characteristic of the du command issued with no options is that it displays the size of every directory under the directory on which it is executed. Figure 8-4 shows the du command executed with various parameters on the /data directory.

Looking at Figure 8-4, notice that if you issue du with no options for the /data directory, your directory size is reported in blocks and size output is provided for every directory under /data, as well as /data itself.

Next, the du command is issued with the -*k* option. This produces very similar output, except now the sizes are reported in kilobytes instead of blocks.

FIGURE 8-4   Using the du command to display the size of a directory

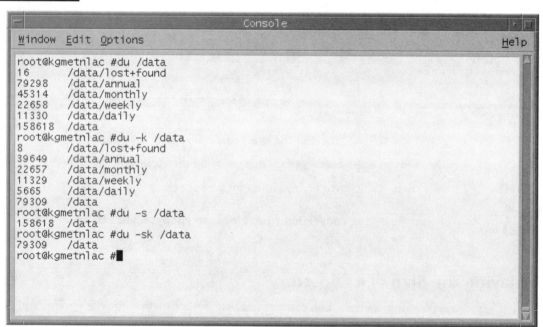

```
root@kgmetnlac #du /data
16        /data/lost+found
79298     /data/annual
45314     /data/monthly
22658     /data/weekly
11330     /data/daily
158618    /data
root@kgmetnlac #du -k /data
8         /data/lost+found
39649     /data/annual
22657     /data/monthly
11329     /data/weekly
5665      /data/daily
79309     /data
root@kgmetnlac #du -s /data
158618    /data
root@kgmetnlac #du -sk /data
79309     /data
root@kgmetnlac #
```

Every now and then, a file system will become 100 percent full and cause a system, program, or user error to occur. Once you have identified the file system that is full by using the df command, you can use the du -k command to determine which directory under that file system is taking up all the space.

If the only information desired was the total size of a directory and you did not care about the size of each directory beneath it, you would issue the du command with the *-s* option. This simply reports the total size of the specified directory in blocks.

By far the most common way of issuing the du command is with both the *-s* option and the *-k* option to report the size of only the specified directory in kilobytes.

The directory chosen for this illustration was also a file system. The du command discerns no difference between a file system and a directory.

The possibility of a file system becoming 100 percent full is the very reason for breaking file systems into separate mount points. For instance, if /var were not a separately mounted file system but was simply a directory under root (/), it could easily cause the root file system to become 100 percent full, which would eventually force a system crash.

It is very easy to confuse the uses of the du and df commands. Remember the f in df is for file system; therefore, the df command is valid only for mounted file systems. In contrast, the du command can be executed on any directory, including a file system.

Displaying Disk Usage by Username

Once you have taken on the responsibility of administrating a UNIX system, you will inevitably be required to monitor the amount of disk space being consumed by the users on that system. The Solaris operating environment provides a means of displaying how much disk space each user is using in each file system. You can use the quot command to display this information. The quot command has the following usage format:

```
# quot [-a] [-f] [<file system name>]
```

The options for this command are

- *-a* Instructs quot to report on all mounted file systems.
- *-f* Instructs quot to report the number of files.

Examining Disk Space Usage by User

Let's walk through the process of monitoring the amount of disk space being used by each user on the system.

By default, the quot command always shows the amount of disk space used in kilobytes. Figure 8-5 shows the quot command used with both the *-a* and the *-f* options.

In the output displayed by the quot command in Figure 8-5, first it lists the device path to the file system and the mount point directory name of each file system it is about to report on. Then it proceeds to list, by user, the amount of disk space, in kilobytes, and the number of files owned by the user. So the output of the quot command for the /data file system illustrates three points:

- Only the root user owns space on this file system.
- The total amount of space owned by the root user is 79,309 kilobytes.
- All the space that the root user owns on this file system is consumed by a total of 20 files.

Because the command was issued with the *-a* option, it was not necessary to also give it a file system name.

Unlike the du command, the quot command discerns a big difference between a file system and a directory. In fact, the quot command can be executed only on a file system.

FIGURE 8-5   Using the quot command to display disk usage by username

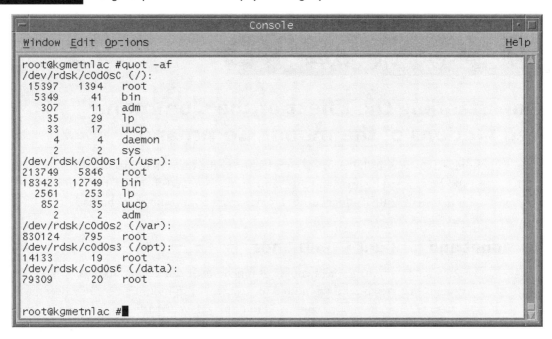

```
                                    Console
 Window  Edit  Options                                             Help
 root@kgmetnlac #quot -af
 /dev/rdsk/c0d0s0 (/):
  15397    1394    root
   5349      41    bin
    307      11    adm
     35      29    lp
     33      17    uucp
      4       4    daemon
      2       2    sys
 /dev/rdsk/c0d0s1 (/usr):
 213749    5846    root
 183423   12749    bin
   2561     253    lp
    852      35    uucp
      2       2    adm
 /dev/rdsk/c0d0s2 (/var):
 830124     795    root
 /dev/rdsk/c0d0s3 (/opt):
  14133      19    root
 /dev/rdsk/c0d0s6 (/data):
  79309      20    root

 root@kgmetnlac #
```

Now that you have looked at some common file system administration commands, let's take a quick look at these question-and-answer pairs.

SCENARIO & SOLUTION

How can you create a new file system on your disk partition?	Use the newfs command.
Why does the system run fsck on each file system it mounts during the boot process?	The fsck utility makes sure that all the information on the file system is synchronized to ensure data integrity.
How can you get a report that shows all the disk space available on the system?	Use the df command.

CERTIFICATION OBJECTIVE 8.03

Understanding the Effect of the Commonly Used Options of the mount Command

File systems must be *mounted,* or attached to the file system hierarchy, before they can be accessed by users and programs on the system. Of course, the root file system is always mounted, and all other file systems mount somewhere beneath it.

The mount and umount Commands

The mount command has a couple of functions. It can be used to display file systems that are currently mounted on a system or to mount an entirely new file system. To use the mount command to display the currently mounted file systems, simply issue the command with no arguments. Figure 8-6 shows an example of using the mount command to display the file systems that are currently mounted.

The output of the mount command, when the command is used to display the currently mounted file systems, is arranged as follows. Looking at the last entry in Figure 8-6 for /data, you see

- **/data**   The directory mount point for the file system
- **/dev/dsk/c0d0s6**   The disk partition on which the file system exists
- **read/write/setuid**   The options with which the file system was mounted
- **Wed Jan 12 15:24:20 2000**   The date and time that the file system was mounted

Commonly Used mount Options

The mount command can be given several different options with the *-o* option. Options are given to the mount command in the following syntax:

```
$ mount -o <option> <file system>
```

FIGURE 8-6   Using the mount command to display currently mounted file systems

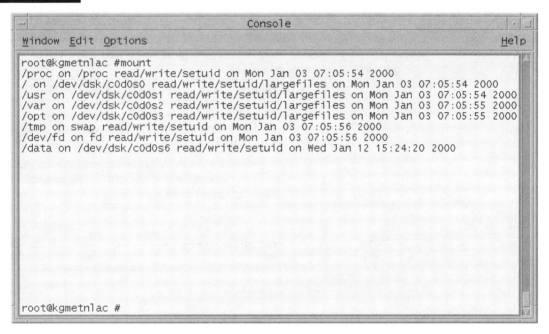

```
                                  Console
Window  Edit  Options                                                  Help
root@kgmetnlac #mount
/proc on /proc read/write/setuid on Mon Jan 03 07:05:54 2000
/ on /dev/dsk/c0d0s0 read/write/setuid/largefiles on Mon Jan 03 07:05:54 2000
/usr on /dev/dsk/c0d0s1 read/write/setuid/largefiles on Mon Jan 03 07:05:54 2000
/var on /dev/dsk/c0d0s2 read/write/setuid/largefiles on Mon Jan 03 07:05:55 2000
/opt on /dev/dsk/c0d0s3 read/write/setuid/largefiles on Mon Jan 03 07:05:55 2000
/tmp on swap read/write/setuid on Mon Jan 03 07:05:56 2000
/dev/fd on fd read/write/setuid on Mon Jan 03 07:05:56 2000
/data on /dev/dsk/c0d0s6 read/write/setuid on Wed Jan 12 15:24:20 2000




root@kgmetnlac #
```

Table 8-3 shows some commonly used mount options. (Bold options indicate default behavior.)

TABLE 8-3   Mount Time Options

Option	File System	Description
largefiles | nolargefiles	UFS	Determines whether the file system can contain files larger than 2GB.
logging | **nologging**	UFS	Determines whether logging for the file system is turned on. Logging helps prevent UFS file systems from becoming inconsistent, which means fsck can be bypassed. Bypassing fsck reduces the boot time after an unclean shutdown.
atime | noatime	UFS	Determines whether the access time is updated on files. Turning this option off can greatly reduce disk activity and improve performance.
remount	All	Allows changing the mount options of a file system that is already mounted.

TABLE 8-3	Mount Time Options *(continued)*	

Option	File System	Description
ro | **rw**	CacheFS, NFS, PCFS, UFS	Determines whether the file system is read-only (RO) or read-write (RW).
suid | nosuid	CacheFS, HSFS, NFS, UFS	Allows (suid) or prohibits (nosuid) setuid execution.
bg | **fg**	NFS	In case the first mount attempt fails, dictates whether mount retries occur in the background (bg) or in the foreground (fg).
hard | soft	NFS	In case the server does not respond to the mount command, dictates whether an error is returned (soft) or the mount is retried until the server responds (hard).
intr | nointr	NFS	Determines whether keyboard interrupts are delivered to a process that is hung while waiting for a response on a hard-mounted file system.
retry=n	NFS	Determines how many times a failed mount operation will retry.

Mounting and Unmounting Local File Systems

File systems may be mounted and unmounted by users, provided that the users have the proper system privileges to perform the task. Generally, the root user will be performing these types of tasks. An unmounted disk partition that contains a file system may be attached to the file system hierarchy using the mount command. Likewise, a mounted file system can be unmounted using the umount command.

To use the mount command to mount a file system, you must provide it with two parameters:

■ The device path to the file system on the disk partition

■ The mount point directory

on the

job

The mount point directory must be created prior to issuing a mount command, or it will fail. The umount command requires only one parameter: the device path to the file system on the disk partition or the mount point directory.

EXERCISE 8-3

Using mount and umount

Now let's walk through an example of using the mount and umount commands to actually modify which file systems are attached to the file system hierarchy. Figure 8-7 shows an example of unmounting and remounting the /data directory. Each time, the df command was used to verify that the procedure was successful.

Figure 8-7 shows that the umount command was used to unmount the /data file system. In unmounting a file system, the umount command needs only one parameter, which can be either the mount point directory or the device path of the file system on the disk partition. However, in mounting a file system, the mount command requires both parameters (unless the mount point has already been defined in the /etc/vfstab file).

FIGURE 8-7   Unmounting and remounting a file system

```
┌─                              Console                              ·  □
 Window  Edit  Options                                              Help
┌────────────────────────────────────────────────────────────────────┐
│root@kgmetnlac #umount /data                                          │
│root@kgmetnlac #df -k                                                 │
│Filesystem          kbytes     used    avail capacity  Mounted on     │
│/proc                     0        0        0     0%   /proc          │
│/dev/dsk/c0d0s0     2058183   620885  1375553    32%   /              │
│fd                        0        0        0     0%   /dev/fd        │
│/dev/dsk/c0d0s1     2058183   830124  1166314    42%   /usr           │
│/dev/dsk/c0d0s2     2058183   830124  1166314    42%   /var           │
│/dev/dsk/c0d0s3     2058183   830124  1166314    42%   /opt           │
│swap                 311792     5064   306728     2%   /tmp           │
│root@kgmetnlac #mount /dev/dsk/c0d0s6 /data                           │
│root@kgmetnlac #df -k                                                 │
│Filesystem          kbytes     used    avail capacity  Mounted on     │
│/proc                     0        0        0     0%   /proc          │
│/dev/dsk/c0d0s0     2058183   620885  1375553    32%   /              │
│fd                        0        0        0     0%   /dev/fd        │
│/dev/dsk/c0d0s1     2058183   830124  1166314    42%   /usr           │
│/dev/dsk/c0d0s2     2058183   830124  1166314    42%   /var           │
│/dev/dsk/c0d0s3     2058183   830124  1166314    42%   /opt           │
│swap                 311792     5064   306728     2%   /tmp           │
│/dev/dsk/c0d0s6     2058183    79309  1917129     4%   /data          │
│                                                                      │
│root@kgmetnlac #                                                      │
└────────────────────────────────────────────────────────────────────┘
```

exam
⓪atch

Be careful to note that umount is the command, not unmount.
These two words are easily mistaken for one another.

Mounting a File System of a Specified Type

The mount command accepts several mount type options. One of the options allows the administrator to specify the type of file system being mounted. When the mount command is used in this fashion, the format looks like this:

```
# mount -F <FS Type> <FS DEVICE PATH> <Mount Point Directory>
```

So, for example, to mount a CD-ROM, you might type this:

```
# mount -F hsfs /dev/dsk/c1t5d0 /cdrom
```

This mount type option is required only if the type of file system being mounted is not the default UFS or the NFS type.

Now that you have examined the mount and umount commands and common options to use with these commands, consider the following scenarios and solutions.

SCENARIO & SOLUTION

How can you see all the file systems mounted on the system?	Run the mount command with no arguments.
If booting as fast as possible after a system crash is important, which option can be used with the mount command to facilitate this?	If you use the logging option when mounting a UFS file system, the fsck process can be skipped, which can greatly reduce the amount of time it takes the system to boot.
For security reasons, you have been asked to mount /home such that any programs that might be on that file system would not run setuid. Which option do you use?	This would require the use of the nosuid mount time option.

Differentiating Between the /etc/mnttab and /etc/vfstab Files

This section examines two very important files:

■ The mounted file system table (/etc/mnttab)

■ The virtual file system table (/etc/vfstab)

/etc/mnttab is a system-generated file that contains information about each file system that is currently mounted on the Solaris 9 system. /etc/vfstab is a manually edited text file, owned by root, that determines which file systems will be mounted (and with what mount time options) during system startup.

EXERCISE 8-4

The Mounted File System Table

This exercise shows the exact makeup and use of each of the /etc/mnttab system table entries. When a file system is mounted either manually or automatically, it creates an entry in the /etc/mnttab file. Figure 8-8 shows an example of what the /etc/mnttab file might look like on a system.

This file contains several pieces of information regarding the currently mounted file systems. Let's look at the entry for /data again:

■ **/dev/dsk/c0d0s6**   The device path to the file system on the disk partition

■ **/data**   The mount point directory

■ **ufs**   The file system type

■ **largefiles,dev=1980006**   The mount time options and device number

■ **947708660**   The time the file system was mounted

FIGURE 8-8   The mounted file system table/etc/mnttab file

```
                                    Console
 Window  Edit  Options                                                    Help
 root@kgmetnlac #cat /etc/mnttab
 /proc    /proc    proc    rw,suid,dev=2940000      943877154
 /dev/dsk/c0d0s0 /       ufs      rw,suid,dev=1980000,largefiles  943877154
 /dev/dsk/c0d0s1 /usr    ufs      largefiles,dev=1980001  943877158
 /dev/dsk/c0d0s2 /var    ufs      largefiles,dev=1980002  943877158
 /dev/dsk/c0d0s3 /opt    ufs      largefiles,dev=1980003  943877158
 swap     /tmp     tmpfs   rw,dev=1      943877158
 fd       /dev/fd  fd      rw,suid,dev=2a00000      943877154
 auto_home         /home   autofs  ignore,indirect,nobrowse,dev=2b80002  943877164
 /dev/dsk/c0d0s6 /data   ufs      largefiles,dev=1980006  947708660




 root@kgmetnlac #
```

Notice that the information contained in the /etc/mnttab file is very similar to the output of the mount command shown in Figure 8-6. This makes sense because the information that the mount command reports is obtained from the /etc/mnttab file.

The /etc/mnttab file is an MNTFS read-only file system that provides mounted file system information directly from the kernel. Prior to Solaris 8, /etc/mnttab was a simple text file. This was changed because the text-based /etc/mnttab could be modified and become in sync with the actual state of the mounted file systems.

on the
job   *This change will cause existing programs or scripts to fail if they attempt to write to /etc/mnttab or if they use the -m option with the mount command to fake /etc/mnttab entries.*

exam
Watch *Watch for questions that imply manually editing the /etc/mnttab file, since this is no longer possible under Solaris 8 or 9.*

Setting Up Your System to Mount a Local File System Automatically at Boot Time

During the boot process, several file systems are mounted automatically. By default, these are the following:

- /
- /usr
- /var
- /opt
- /proc
- /tmp
- /home or /export/home

These file systems are automatically mounted when the system boots because they have entries in the virtual file system table, or /etc/vfstab, file. Once a new file system has been created using the newfs command on a selected disk partition and a mount point directory has been created to which the file system can be mounted, this file system can be added to the /etc/vfstab file so that it will be mounted automatically by default when the system boots.

EXERCISE 8-5

Using the Virtual File System Table

Let's add the file system created earlier, /dev/dsk/c0d0s6, so that it will automatically be mounted to the /data mount point directory when the system boots. Figure 8-9 shows what the modified /etc/vfstab file might look like on your system.

The /etc/vfstab file contains all the information necessary for the system to automatically mount file systems at boot time. Again, let's look at the line for /data to get an idea of the format for this file:

- **/dev/dsk/c0d0s6**   The device path to the file system to be mounted
- **/dev/rdsk/c0d0s6**   The raw device path to the disk partition to fsck

FIGURE 8-9   The virtual file system table/etc/vfstab file

```
root@kgmetnlac #cat /etc/vfstab
#device            device           mount    FS     fsck  mount    mount
#to mount          to fsck          point    type   pass  at boot  options
#
/proc              -                /proc    proc   -     no       -
swap               -                /tmp     tmpfs  -     yes      -
fd                 -                /dev/fd  fd     -     no       -
/dev/dsk/c0d0s4    -                -        swap   -     no       -
/dev/dsk/c0d0s0    /dev/rdsk/c0d0s0 /        ufs    1     no       -
/dev/dsk/c0d0s1    /dev/rdsk/c0d0s1 /usr     ufs    2     yes      -
/dev/dsk/c0d0s2    /dev/rdsk/c0d0s2 /var     ufs    2     yes      -
/dev/dsk/c0d0s3    /dev/rdsk/c0d0s3 /opt     ufs    2     yes      -
/dev/dsk/c0d0s6    /dev/rdsk/c0d0s6 /data    ufs    2     yes      -



root@kgmetnlac #
```

- **/data**   The mount point directory
- **ufs**   The file system type
- **2**   The order or preference for fsck to follow
- **yes**   The mount at boot parameter; where the nondefault mount time options are listed

---

on the job

In the example shown in Figure 8-9, only local file system types are used. However, it is very common to have a file server dedicated to serving out NFS file systems for remote mount by other systems. Usually, it is desirable to have those systems that mount NFS file systems over the network do so during their boot process. So, the /etc/vfstab file can also contain entries that cause the system to automatically mount NFS file systems during bootup as well. Here is an example of an NFS entry for the /etc/vfstab file:

```
Remotehost1:/usr/local/share  -   /usr/local/share  nfs   -    yes   -
```

Note that the hostname of the system that is serving the remote NFS file system, followed by a colon (:), is precluded just before the name of the device to mount. In addition, the "device to fsck" and the "fsck pass" columns both contain a hyphen (-) because NFS is not local to this system and therefore cannot be fscked.

Now that you are aware of the /etc/vfstab file and how it works, let's look at the final two mount commands. Every now and then an administrator needs to perform maintenance on a system. Usually, the system is put into single-user mode while the maintenance is accomplished. However, in single-user mode, only those file systems critical for system operation are mounted. So the mountall command comes in handy. This command, issued without arguments, will mount all the file systems listed in the /etc/vfstab file.

Likewise, the umountall command will unmount all the file systems listed in the /etc/vfstab file, with the following exceptions:

- /
- /usr
- /var
- /var/adm
- /var/run
- /proc
- /dev/fd

These file systems will not be unmounted when a umountall command is issued, since they are generally necessary for the system to function properly.

on the **Job**

When it comes to a normal system shutdown or reboot, it does not matter if a file system was mounted automatically at boot time or manually after the system was up and running, because all file systems that are mounted will automatically be unmounted as part of this process.

Now that you understand the uses and differences of the mounted and virtual file system tables, take a look at two common scenarios and their appropriate solutions.

SCENARIO & SOLUTION

How do you configure the system to automatically mount your new file system when it boots?	Add an entry for the new file system in the /etc/vfstab file.
How can you take a look at all the file systems currently mounted without using the mount command?	Simply cat the /etc/mnttab file.

CERTIFICATION OBJECTIVE 8.05

Understanding the Intended Purpose of Directories

This section takes a look at standard directories and file systems in the Solaris operating environment. Understanding the intended purpose of each directory is of great value to you.

The Contents and Purpose of the Default Solaris 9 File Systems

Now let's examine each of the Solaris 9 default file systems and directories and get a better understanding of their intended purpose. Table 8-4 shows each file system and directory, identifies the file system type, and describes the file contents.

/var/run

A new tmpfs-mounted file system, /var/run (introduced in Solaris 8), is the repository for temporary system files that are not needed across system reboots in this Solaris release and future releases. The /tmp directory continues to be a repository for nonsystem temporary files. Because /var/run is mounted as a memory-based file system rather than a disk-based file system, updates to this directory do not cause unnecessary disk traffic that would interfere with systems running power management software. The /var/run directory requires no administration. You might notice that it is not unmounted with the umount *-a* or the umountall command. For security reasons, /var/run is owned by root.

TABLE 8-4	The Default Solaris File Systems

File System or Directory	File System Type	Description
/ (the root)	ufs	The root directory is the beginning of the hierarchical file tree. This file system contains all the files and directories that are necessary for the system to boot properly. It is also the base file system that contains the mount point directories for every other standard file system that is mounted at boot time.
/etc	ufs	The /etc directory is not a file system by default; rather, it is a part of the root directory's file system. It contains host-specific system administrative configuration files and databases.
/export	ufs or NFS	The /export directory is not a file system by default; rather, it is a part of the root directory's file system. It holds alternative versions of the operating system. These alternative versions, accessed via NFS, are required by client systems whose architectures differ from that of the server.
/export/home or /home	ufs or NFS	The standard home file system is mounted at either of these two directory mount points and is automounted by default. This file system is generally a locally mounted ufs file system but could be an NFS file system mounted remotely from an NFS file server.
/opt	ufs or NFS	The opt file system is provided for optional, third-party software products. This file system is generally a locally mounted ufs but could be an NFS mounted remotely from an NFS file server.
/proc	procfs	The proc file system is a special file system type called procfs. This file system is mounted and used by the system specifically for maintaining a list of active processes, by process ID number.
/tmp	tmpfs	The tmp file system is a special file system type called tmpfs. This file system is actually mounted swap space used for the temporary storage of files. All files are deleted each time the system is booted or the file system is unmounted.
/usr	ufs	The usr file system is a locally mounted standard ufs-type file system used to store system files and directories. This file system contains files that are specific to the architecture of the system, such as Sparc executables.
/var	ufs	The var file system is a locally mounted, standard ufs-type file system used to store files and directories that have variable sizes. This is where the system log files are located.

Accessing Data on Disks or CD-ROMs

This section looks at using floppy disks and CD-ROMs in the Solaris 9 operating environment. Whether you are working with workstations or servers, understanding how to access data on removable media is extremely important.

How to Format a Floppy Disk

After making sure that you have inserted a blank, write-enabled floppy disk in the floppy drive, you use the fdformat command to format the disk.

The fdformat command

The fdformat command is used to format floppy disks and accepts the following options:

- *-v* Verifies proper formatting
- *-U* Unmounts the disk (if it is mounted)
- *-D* Formats at 720Kb instead of default 1.44Mb
- *-e* Ejects the disk when formatting finishes
- *-f* Forces format without confirmation
- *-b* Labels the newly formatted disk with the provided name of eight characters or fewer
- *-z* Lists all fdformat command options but does not actually format the disk

Here is an example of the syntax to use when formatting a standard floppy disk:

```
$ fdformat -v -U
```

When the fdformat command completes, you now have a DOS-formatted disk ready for use.

How to Place a ufs on a DOS-Formatted Disk

Once your floppy disk has been DOS formatted, to have a ufs placed on it, you must use the volcheck and newfs commands.

The volcheck Command

The volcheck command verifies that you have a properly formatted floppy disk inserted into the disk drive. Execute this command with the following syntax:

```
$ volcheck -v
```

This command indicates that the disk is ready to have a ufs placed on it by responding with the message, "Media was found." Once this check has completed successfully, you can continue by using the newfs command.

The newfs Command

The newfs command allows you to create a new file system. Used with the *-v* option, which makes the command *verbose* to display status messages, the syntax is as follows:

```
$ newfs -v /vol/dev/aliases/floppy0
```

When the newfs command finishes creating the ufs on your floppy disk, the disk is ready to be loaded as a ufs.

How to Load a Disk

Once you have a properly formatted disk, either DOS or ufs, you can load the disk for use with the volrmmount command.

The volrmmount Command

The volrmmount command is used to mount or unmount removable media such as floppy disks. It accepts the following options:

- *-i*   Mounts a newly inserted disk
- *-e*   Unmounts a currently mounted disk.

The standard syntax to use when mounting a floppy disk is as follows:

```
$ volrmmount -i floppy0
```

After this command completes, your floppy disk will be available to the system for reading and writing data.

Likewise, the standard syntax to use when unmounting a floppy disk is

```
$ volrmmount -e floppy0
```

Once this command completes, you will be able to remove your media from the system.

How to Examine the Contents of a Disk

Now that you have a floppy disk inserted and mounted, you can examine the disk's contents using the ls command. The ls command has many options; only two frequently used options are presented here.

The ls command

The ls command can provide a listing of the files and directories on a floppy disk. This command accepts, among many others, these two frequently used options:

- *-L* Shows symbolic links
- *-l* (**long format**) Shows information such as ownership, permissions, and date

A listing of the contents of the currently mounted floppy disk can be obtained using the following syntax:

```
$ ls -l /floppy/floppy0
```

How to Read and Write Information on a Disk

A mounted floppy disk can be read from or written to in exactly the same way you read from or write to any other mounted file system. Files and directories can be copied from or to the floppy disk using the cp command, and moved from or to the floppy disk using the mv command.

The cp Command

You use the cp command to copy files or directories from one location to another. You use the cp command without options to copy files and with the *-r* option to copy a directory and its contents.

The following syntax shows how to copy a file to a floppy disk:

```
$ cp /home/ken/notes.txt /floppy/floppy0/
```

This syntax demonstrates how to copy a directory and its contents from a floppy disk:

```
$ cp -r /floppy/floppy0/marysslides /home/ken/
```

When the cp command finishes, the original file or directory will still be intact, and a new, identical version of the file or directory will exist in the specified location.

The mv Command

You use the mv command to move files or directories from one location to another. Unlike the cp command, the mv command operates identically on files and directories, with no additional options.

The following is an example of how to move a file from a floppy disk:

```
$ mv /floppy/floppy0/larasfile.doc /home/ken/
```

This command moves a directory and all its contents to a floppy disk:

```
$ mv /home/ken/tarasdocs /floppy/floppy0/
```

When the mv command finishes, the original file or directory no longer exists in the original location but has been created in the specified location.

How to Find Out If a Disk Is Still in Use

For a file system to be unmounted, which is necessary before a floppy disk can be ejected, no users can be accessing it. You can use the fuser command to determine if any users are currently accessing a file system.

The fuser Command

The fuser command displays and/or kills the processes of users who are currently accessing a file system. This command accepts the following options:

- *-u* Displays the names of users who own processes currently accessing the specified file system
- *-k* Kills all the processes currently accessing the specified file system

The following is an example of how to display the names of all the users who own processes that are currently accessing the floppy disk:

```
$ fuser -u /floppy/floppy0
```

Once the users and their processes have been identified, it might be necessary to kill the processes to unmount the file system by using this command:

```
$ fuser -k /floppy/floppy0
```

Once all the processes accessing the file system have been stopped, the file system can be unmounted.

How to Eject a Disk

Once you have ensured that no one is currently using a floppy disk, you can eject the disk, simply by typing

```
$ eject floppy0
```

EXERCISE 8-6

Using a Floppy Disk

The following series of commands demonstrate what you just learned about using floppy disks in the Solaris 9 operating environment. In this exercise, you want to format a blank floppy disk, create a ufs on it, copy a directory and all its content onto it, list the new contents of the floppy, and then eject the disk.

Insert the blank write-enabled disk, and then issue these commands:

1. fdformat -v -U
2. volcheck -v

3. newfs -v /vol/dev/aliases/floppy0

4. volrmmount -i floppy0

5. cp -r /home/ken/homework /floppy/floppy0/

6. ls -l /floppy/floppy0/homework

7. eject floppy0

How to Load a CD-ROM

If Volume Management is running (and it is by default), a CD-ROM is extremely easy to load because, shortly after it is inserted into the CD-ROM drive, it is automatically mounted to /cdrom. However, if Volume Management is not running, a CD-ROM can be manually mounted as follows:

```
$ mount -F hsfs -o ro /dev/dsk/c0t6d0s0 /cdrom/cdrom0
```

on the
Job *Volume Management can be turned on and off easily with the following commands:*

```
# /etc/init.d/volmgt start
```

or

```
# /etc/init.d/volmgt stop
```

How to Examine the Contents of a CD-ROM

The procedure for examining the contents of a CD-ROM is identical to that of examining the contents of a floppy disk.

You can use the following syntax to obtain a listing of the contents of the currently mounted CD-ROM:

```
$ ls -l /cdrom/cdrom0
```

How to Copy Information from a CD-ROM

Unlike a floppy disk, a CD-ROM is read-only. Therefore, information cannot be moved to or from a CD-ROM using the mv command. Likewise, information cannot be copied to a CD-ROM using the cp command. However, the process of copying information from a CD-ROM is identical to copying information from a floppy disk.

The following illustrates how to copy a file from a CD-ROM:

```
$ cp /cdrom/cdrom0/cheat-codes.txt /home/ken/games/
```

Likewise, an entire directory can be copied from a CD-ROM, like this:

```
$ cp -r /cdrom/cdrom0/games /home/ken/
```

How to Determine Whether a CD-ROM Is Still in Use

This procedure is also identical to that used with a floppy disk. You can use the fuser command to identify the users accessing a CD-ROM and display or kill their processes.

The following is an example of how to display the names of all the users who own processes that are currently accessing a CD-ROM:

```
$ fuser -u /cdrom/cdrom0
```

Once you have identified the users and their processes, you might need to kill the processes to unmount the file system. You can accomplish this with the following command:

```
$ fuser -k /cdrom/cdrom0
```

Once all the processes accessing the file system have been stopped, the file system can be unmounted.

How to Eject a CD-ROM

Once you have ensured that no one is currently using the CD-ROM, you can eject the disk, simply by typing this:

```
$ eject cdrom0
```

FROM THE CLASSROOM

Closing Comments

This section of the exam was created to fully test your knowledge of file systems and administering those file systems under the Solaris 9 operating environment. Every other function the system serves depends directly on the ability of the system to store and retrieve information on file systems.

Working with file systems and administering those file systems is foundational to the UNIX systems administrator. Having a thorough, practical, working knowledge of file systems will be invaluable to you as your systems administration career develops.

One of the most common problems for students in the area of working with file systems is conceptualizing the difference between a file system and a directory. This problem exists because a file system, by default, is a directory, but most directories are not file systems. For example, /var is a mounted file system, as well as a directory that logically groups together files and other directories. However, /var/adm is just a directory that exists on the /var file system. Logically, file systems and directories appear the same to the system, programs, and users. The difference is that a file system can be mounted and unmounted, and a single directory cannot.

I trust that you have studied this chapter diligently and therefore am convinced that you will do well on this portion of the exam. I wish you the very best in your systems administration career and in life in general.

—Ken Copas, HP Open View Certified Consultant, HP Network Node Manager, Certified Consultant, Sentinel Services Certified Consulting Team

CERTIFICATION SUMMARY

This chapter took an in-depth look at Solaris file systems. It discussed the basic types of file systems, exactly what constitutes a file system, the standard Solaris file system structure, the process of creating file systems, and how to use and administer file systems effectively.

You looked at the hierarchical structure of file systems and discovered how this structure facilitates the organization of directories and files and provides a convenient way to administer data on a system. You followed a case study in which a new file system was created with the newfs command, verified with the fsck utility, and mounted to your system with the mount command. You studied several commands that allow for file system monitoring and administration.

Understanding file systems is fundamental to properly administrating your Solaris operating environment. This chapter includes a great deal of information that will not only help you pass the Solaris 9 certification test, but will help you perform countless system administration tasks throughout your career.

✓ TWO-MINUTE DRILL

Knowing the Types of File Systems in the Solaris Operating Environment

❑ Network-based file system type: NFS

❑ Virtual file system types: cachefs, fdfs, lofs, namefs, procfs, specfs, swapfs, and tmpfs

❑ Disk-based file system types: ufs, hsfs, pcfs, and udf

Performing Common File System Administration Tasks

❑ **newfs**   Command used to create a new file system

❑ **fsck**   Utility used to verify file system synchronization and data integrity

❑ **df**   Command used to display disk space usage by file system

❑ **du**   Command used to display disk space usage by directory

❑ **quot**   Command used to display disk space usage by username

Understanding the Effect of Commonly Used Options of the mount Command

❑ **ro**   Mounts file system in read-only mode

❑ **noatime**   Turns off file access time recording, which improves disk performance

❑ **largefiles**   Mount time option that allows files of 2GB or more on file systems

Differentiating Between the /etc/mnttab and /etc/vfstab Files

❑ **/etc/mnttab**   Shows currently mounted file systems

❑ **/etc/vfstab**   Controls which file systems are mounted automatically at system boot

❑ **mnttab**   System generated

❑ **vfstab**   Root administered

Understanding the Intended Purpose of Directories

❑ **/opt**   Provided for optional, third-party software products

❑ **/usr**   Contains files that are specific to the architecture of the system

❑ **/etc**   Contains host-specific system administrative configuration files and databases

Accessing Data on Disks or CD-ROMs

❑ **eject**   Command used to eject a floppy disk or CD-ROM

❑ **fdformat**   Command used to format floppy disks

❑ **ls**   Command used to list contents of floppy disks or CD-ROMs

SELF TEST

The following questions will help you measure your understanding of the material presented in this chapter. Read all the choices carefully because there might be more than one correct answer. Choose all correct answers for each question.

Knowing the Types of File Systems in the Solaris Operating Environment

1. What is the default Solaris 9 file system type?

    A. WYSIWYG

    B   ufs

    C. NFS

    D. defaultfs

2. Which file system types are virtual? (Choose all that apply.)

    A. cachefs

    B. nfs

    C. procfs

    D. swapfs

3. What is the name of the Solaris 9 file system architecture that enables the kernel to handle basic file system operations, such as reading and writing files, with a specific file system without requiring the user or program to know which file system type is actually being used?

    A. Journal File System (JFS)

    B. Kernel File System (KFS)

    C. Virtual File System (VFS)

    D. Basic File System (BFS)

Performing Common File System Administration Tasks

4. Your new boss wants a report that lists the percentage of disk space that is currently used on your Solaris 9 system. Pick the best way to produce the information requested.

    A. ls *-al*

    B. ps *-ef*

C. df *-k*

D. du *-sk*

5. A call just came in from the help desk. It seems that a user is complaining about a "File system full" error message when he tries to save files to his home directory under /home. Pick the best way to get a disk usage report by username for the /home file system.

A. quot /home

B. quot *-af*

C. f *-k* /home

D. du *-sk* /home

Understanding the Effect of Commonly Used Options of the mount Command

6. What is the command syntax to use to mount a file system?

A. mount /dev/dsk/c0d0s6 /data

B. mount /data /dev/dsk/c0d0s6

C. mountall /data

D. mount /dev/rdsk/c0d0s6 /data

7. Which command would mount the /data file system in such a way as *not* to allow the creation of files that were 2GB or larger in size?

A. mount nolargefiles /dev/dsk/c0d0s6 /data

B. mount *-o* nolargefiles /dev/dsk/c0d0s6 /data

C. mount *-o* largefiles /data /dev/dsk/c0d0s6

D. mount /data /dev/dsk/c0d0s6 -nolargefiles

8. Which of the following file systems would be unmounted if the umountall command were executed? (Choose all that apply.)

A. /var

B. /data

C. /opt

D. /usr

Differentiating Between the /etc/mnttab and /etc/vfstab Files

9. Where would you look on a Solaris 9 system to find out which file systems are currently mounted?

   A. /etc/vfstab

   B. /etc/mountfs

   C. /etc/mnttab

   D. /var/adm/syslog

10. How might you determine to which mount point directory the unmounted /dev/dsk/c0d0s6 file system was last mounted?

    A. ls -*ald* /dev/dsk/c0d0s6

    B. fsck /data

    C. fsck /dev/rdsk/c0d0s6

    D. mount /dev/dsk/c0d0s6 /data

Understanding the Intended Purpose of Directories

11. Which of the following file systems is used primarily for third-party software applications?

    A. /usr

    B. /data

    C. /var

    D. /opt

12. Which of the following file systems is always the top of the file system hierarchy?

    A. /

    B. /top

    C. /home

    D. /tmp

Accessing Data on Disks or CD-ROMs

13. Which command will allow you to view the contents of a CD-ROM that has been inserted into your Solaris 9 system? (Choose all that apply.)

    A. ls /cdrom/cdrom0

    B. ls -*l* /cdrom/cdrom0

    C. ls -*L* /cdrom/cdrom0

    D. lscdrom cdrom0

14. How would you go about copying a directory named games from a floppy disk to the /var/tmp directory?

    A. cp -*r* /var/tmp/games /floppy/floppy0/

    B. cp /floppy/floppy0/games /var/tmp

    C. cp -*r* /floppy/floppy0/games /var/tmp/

    D. mv /floppy/floppy0/games /var/tmp/

LAB QUESTION

As the new Solaris 9 UNIX system administrator for KMTL, Inc., you have just been assigned the task of installing a new third-party application that will allow users to render 3-D drawings. Determine in which file system you will install this application and explain why. Describe the process you would use to ensure that there is enough disk space available in the file system to hold the application before proceeding with the installation. If there were almost enough space, but not quite, how would you determine which directory in that file system was consuming the most disk space?

SELF TEST ANSWERS

Knowing the Types of File Systems in the Solaris Operating Environment

1. ☑ **B.** The ufs, or UNIX File System, type is the default type of file system for the Solaris operating environment. This file system type is based on the Berkeley Software Distribution (BSD) Fast File System.

   ☒ **A, C,** and **D** are incorrect because WYSIWYG is not a file system type, the Network File System (NFS) system type is used by the system to mount remote file systems from other servers over the network, and defaultfs does not exist.

2. ☑ **A, C,** and **D.** The Cache File System (cachefs) type is used as a disk cache area to speed access to slower file systems such as CD-ROMs (hsfs) or network-based file systems (NFS). The Process File System (procfs) type is used by the system to maintain a list of all the active processes by process ID number under /proc. This makes it possible for debuggers and other similar tools to access process information and address space through the use of file system calls. The Swap File System (swapfs) type is used to provide swap space to the system.

   ☒ **B** is incorrect because the Network File System (NFS) type is used by the system to mount remote file systems from other servers over the network.

3. ☑ **C.** The Virtual File System architecture enables the kernel to handle basic file system operations, such as reading and writing files within a specific file system, without requiring the user or program to know which file system type is actually being used.

   ☒ **A, B,** and **D** are incorrect because they do not exist under the Solaris 8 operating environment.

Performing Common File System Administration Tasks

4. ☑ **C.** The df command is the correct command to issue, and executing it with the *-k* option will cause the output to include the percentage of disk space that is currently being used in each file system.

   ☒ **A** is incorrect because this command will simply give you a long listing of all the files in the current directory. **B** is incorrect because this command will simply give you a full listing of every process running on your system. **D** is incorrect for two reasons. First, the du command will not report the percentage of disk space that is currently being used in each file system. Second, it requires an argument that is the directory name on which you want the command to execute.

5. ☑ **A.** The quot command will report the amount of disk space used by username and in kilobytes.
☒ **B** is incorrect because it issues quot with the *-a* option and therefore will report on all file systems. Although this will eventually lead to the pertinent information, it is not the best way to quickly retrieve the answer. **C** is incorrect because this command reports disk space usage for the entire file system and not by username. **D** is incorrect because this command reports the total amount of disk space used by the /home file system.

Understanding the Effect of Commonly Used Options of the mount Command

6. ☑ **A.** The proper command to use is the mount command, which requires two arguments: first, the device path of the disk partition that contains the file system; second, the mount point directory name.
☒ **B** is incorrect because the arguments are given in the wrong order. **C** is incorrect for two reasons. First, mountall is not the correct command to use; second, only one argument is given. **D** is incorrect because the first argument given is a raw device path.

7. ☑ **B.** The mount command is given; *-o* specifies mount time options; and nolargefiles is the option that prevents the creation of files of 2GB or more, a device path, and a mount point directory.

8. ☒ **A** is incorrect because the *-o* was not included to indicate a mount time option. This command would fail. **C** is incorrect for two reasons. First, the wrong option has been specified (largefiles will allow the creation of files of 2GB or more); second, the device path and mount point directory have been reversed. This command would also fail. **D** is incorrect because the device path and mount point directory have been reversed and the mount time option has been specified incorrectly. Again, this command would fail.

Differentiating Between the /etc/mnttab and /etc/vfstab Files

9. ☑ **B and C.** The umountall command will unmount all file systems listed in the /etc/vfstab file with the following exceptions: /, /usr, and /var.
☒ **A and D** are incorrect because they would not be unmounted.

10. ☑ **C.** The mounted file system table (/etc/mnttab) file maintains a list of all the file systems that are currently mounted on a system.
☒ **A** is incorrect because the virtual file system table (/etc/vfstab) file contains all the information necessary for the system to automatically mount file systems at bootup time.

B is incorrect because the file does not really exist. **D** is incorrect because the /var/adm/syslog file is where system messages are logged.

Understanding the Intended Purpose of Directories

11. ☑ **C.** Running fsck on an unmounted file system will report the name of the last mount point directory on which the file system was mounted.
☒ **A** is incorrect because this command will simply list information about the device path. **B** is incorrect because the fsck command requires a raw device path as an argument. **D** is incorrect because mounting the file system will not display the desired information. It will also prevent you from ever displaying the desired information because the last place the file system was mounted is where it was just mounted.

12. ☑ **D.** The /opt file system is provided for optional, third-party software products. This file system is generally a locally mounted ufs but could be an NFS mounted remotely from an NFS file server.
☒ **A** is incorrect because the usr file system is a locally mounted standard ufs type used to store system files and directories. This file system contains files that are specific to the architecture of the system, such as SPARC executables. **B** is incorrect because /data is not a standard Solaris 9 file system. **C** is incorrect because the var file system is a locally mounted standard ufs type used to store files and directories that have variable sizes. This is where the system log files are located.

Accessing Data on Disks or CD-ROMs

13. ☑ **A, B,** and **C.** The ls command is the correct command used to list the contents of the CD-ROM and requires no additional options. However, using the ls command with the -*l* option will show additional information about each file and the -*L* option will show symbolic links.
☒ **D** is incorrect because there is no lscdrom command.

14. ☑ **C.** The cp command is the correct command to use and it must be given the -*r* option in order to copy a directory.
☒ **A** is incorrect because it is copying the games directory from /var/tmp to the floppy drive instead of vice versa. **B** is incorrect because the -*r* option is missing from the cp command. **D** is incorrect because using the mv command will remove the directory from the floppy disk, and you simply want another copy of it in /var/tmp.

LAB ANSWER

Determining in which file system the application should be installed is a simple matter of understanding the intended purpose of each of the default Solaris 9 file systems. The /opt file system is the correct location for the application to be installed because it was specifically provided for optional, third-party software products.

To determine if enough disk space is available in the /opt file system for the application installation, issue the following command:

```
$ df -k /opt
```

This command will display the total amount of disk space, disk space used, and disk space still available.

If there were almost enough space, but not quite, you would determine which directory in that file system was consuming the most disk space in the following way:

```
$ du -k /opt
```

This command will give you a detailed listing of each directory under /opt and how much disk space is consumed by each directory, in kilobytes.

SUN® CERTIFIED SYSTEM ADMINISTRATOR

9

Working with Files and Directories

F iles are an integral part of the Solaris operating environment. Literally everything you encounter on a system running Solaris is a file. Every user owns files; the system itself owns files. A system can contain thousands or even millions of files at any particular time.

Files take storage space. Storage space costs money and must be shared by all users. An old axiom says, "Data will expand to fill the available storage space." Short of constantly adding more storage space to a system, the only way to manage the available storage space is to understand the different types of files and the options available for minimizing the storage requirements of each file and for determining which files can be safely removed from the system.

This chapter discusses the options for reducing the storage space required for files. You will learn about commands to consolidate many files into a single file, as well as commands to shrink the size of an individual file. This chapter also describes the kinds of files and what they are used for. The central theme of this chapter is, "Everything in a system is a file." You will learn how to differentiate one file from another.

CERTIFICATION OBJECTIVE 9.01

Reducing the Size of Files and Directories for Tape Storage

The size of disk drives has increased much faster than the size of tape drives. Huge disks are now extremely inexpensive, whereas large tape drives are rare and expensive. This increase in storage capacity has led to increased storage demand and increased archival capacity. A backup that can fit on a single tape (or a small number of tapes in a jukebox) reduces the chances of someone forgetting to change the tape or of the backup running over the maintenance window because it waited too long for someone to change the tape. Furthermore, hardware reliability issues increase as more and more tapes are loaded and unloaded.

on the
job

A previous client used an antiquated backup system—dumping database log files to a 4MM tape drive every night. This backup took three tapes and about eight hours to complete each night. It was common for the system administrator on call to be paged because the operators were having a problem changing the tape, the operators had forgotten to change a tape, and/or the backup was running long and holding up other jobs. I recommended that the client switch to a DLT drive, which holds about ten times the data that the 4MM drive did, and switch to a weekly backup schedule. I felt the DLT was more than capable of handling a week's worth of logs, which would reduce their backup times and cost tremendously. The client decided that weekly was not often enough but that the DLT might save some time. Once the new DLT was in place, backup time decreased to less than two hours. Almost three years later, the client is still using a single DLT per night (even with the growth of database usage), and backups still take under five hours.

There are also situations (such as software distribution, data warehouses, and FTP sites) when files need to be transferred from machine to machine. Reducing the size of the files to be transferred makes the transfers go more quickly. A large file transferred by FTP over a 56K modem can take several hours to complete. The longer the transfer takes, the more chance for dropped connections and corrupted files. Making the transfers smaller can reduce the transfer times and improve the chances for success.

exam
Watch

Many common system administration tasks require knowledge of the tar, compress, uncompress, zcat, and zip commands.

The tar Command

The tar command, short for *tape ar*chive, is not so much a command to be used to decrease the size of the files to be saved as it is a way to collect all the files together in a single place:

```
tar [c|x|t|r|u] [plv] [f archive] [ file list ]
```

The tar command has five modes:

- c (**create**) Creates a new tar archive, named archive, containing file list.
- x (**extract**) Extracts the files in *file list* from *archive*.
- t (**list**) Lists the files, the table of contents, of *archive*.
- r (**append**) Appends the files in *file list* to the end of *archive*.
- u (**update**) Appends the files in *file list* to the end of *archive* if they are already in the archive and have been modified since the archive was created. Note that the original file is not removed from the archive, so the archive will continue to grow with multiple copies of the updated files.

Normally when tar extracts files from an archive, they are created with the ownership and permissions of the user running the command. The *-p* option instructs tar to preserve the ownership and permissions as specified in the archive. The *-l* option directs tar not to cross a file system boundary when it is adding files to an archive. The *-v* option tells tar to produce verbose output. In the insert, extract, and append modes, this means to print the name of each file the command processes. In the table of contents mode, it means to output information similar to an ls *-l.*

As its name suggests, tar was originally designed to copy files to and from a tape drive. tar has several options that go along with this history. Some of them include *-b* to specify the tape block size, *-L* to specify the tape length, and *-M* to warn tar that the files will take more than one tape.

When used to create an archive file (as opposed to tape), the file is conventionally named with a .tar extension. The tar command itself does not do this naming, though.

The following two examples show how to create a tar archive and how to extract a single file from a tar archive. To extract all files in an archive, simply do not provide a file list:

```
$tar cf book.tar ch1.doc ch2.doc ch3.doc ch4.doc ch5.doc
$ tar xf book.tar ch3.tar
```

The compress, uncompress, and zcat Commands

The compress command attempts to make a single file take up less room by using the Lempel-Ziv encoding format. If the command is able to successfully compress a file, the file is renamed with a .Z extension; all other inode information is unchanged.

If the command is unable to compress the file, it leaves the file untouched. The compress command is often used in conjunction with tar to distribute software and patches. Prior to Solaris 2.7, all patches from Sun came compressed in a tar archive.

The compress command can take one of four options, shown in the following code listing: -c instructs compress to write its output to standard output (the screen) rather than modifying the file on disk. This might be useful in a situation where the output is to be piped into another command. By default, if the compression will not decrease the file size, the compress will fail. If the new name (either with the .Z for a compress or without for an uncompress) already exists, compress stops and asks for verification before overwriting the file. The -f option forces the compress command to run without asking for verification in either of the previously described cases. Compress reports no output except errors when it runs. The -v option instructs compress to report the percentage of compression achieved to standard error. Compress works by replacing common sets of bits with a memory offset. The -b option and its argument, a number between 9 and 16, determine how large a set of bits the command attempts to replace. The larger the number of bits that can be replaced, the more compressed the file will be.

```
compress [-cfv] [-b bits] file
uncompress [-cfv] [-b bits] file
zcat file
```

Compress has two links (see the section "Understanding Regular Files, Directories, Symbolic Links, Device Files, and Hard Links") to other filenames. The first link is to uncompress. Uncompress is a program that performs the opposite function of compress; it takes a compressed file (named with a .Z extension) and uncompresses it, saving it without the extension. The second link is to zcat. The zcat command is exactly the same as calling uncompress with the -c option; it uncompresses the file in memory, sending the output to standard output and leaving the original file untouched.

The following examples show how to compress a file, how to use zcat to read a compressed file, and how to uncompress a file:

```
$ compress -f README
$ zcat README.Z
$ uncompress README.Z
```

FROM THE CLASSROOM

Avoiding Problems with the tar Archive

Improperly collecting files in a tar archive or zip file can lead to strange errors that are hard to troubleshoot. One of the most common problems is tar archives created with this command line:

```
tar cplf file.tar .
```

When a tar file is created this way, the first file in the archive is the current directory (.) and all files are added with the path of *./filename.* It is very common for someone to extract an archive in either /tmp or /var/tmp. This becomes an issue because those directories have special permissions that allow everyone full write access but limited delete access. When this archive is extracted by root, the permissions on the directory will be changed to whatever the permissions of the current directory (.) are

in the archive, which generally does not have the special permissions. The proper way to create a tar archive is to back up to the parent directory and make the archive relative to the target directory. Instead of the previously mentioned problem tar command, use these two commands:

```
cd ..
```

and

```
tar cplf dir/file.tar dir
```

which will ensure that dir is created when the archive is extracted. The zip command discussed later in the chapter does not suffer from this problem, so it can safely be used right in the directory.

—Stephen P. Potter, Senior UNIX Engineer, Information Control Corporation

The pack, unpack, and pcat Commands

The pack command is a functional equivalent to compress. pack attempts to store individual files in a more compact fashion. If pack is able to compact a file, it is saved with a .z extension. Pack can take a single option, *-f,* to force the compacting, as shown in the following code listing. Unlike compress, which can have pathname (directory plus filename) lengths of 1024 bytes, pack is limited to use on files where the filename is 12 bytes (usually characters) or shorter.

```
pack [ -f ] file
unpack file
pcat file
```

Along with pack, there is an unpack command. Like uncompress, the unpack command restores a file to its original size and saves it as its original name. A symbolic link (see the section "Understanding Regular Files, Directories, Symbolic Links, Device Files, and Hard Links") is provided from unpack to pcat. The pcat command is like zcat: it uncompacts the file in memory, sends the output to standard output, and leaves the original file untouched.

The following examples show how to pack a file, how to use pcat to read a packed file, and how to unpack a file:

```
$ pack README
pack: README: 39.9% Compression
$ pcat README.z
$ unpack README.z
unpack: README: unpacked
```

The zip Command

The zip command is a recent addition to the Solaris operating environment. It implements the common PKZIP (Paul Katz's zip) format often found on MS-DOS–based systems. Whereas compress or pack work on an individual file, zip works on any number of files. It encodes each file to be as small as possible and then bundles the files together in a compact form. This process can be thought of as similar to a compress and a tar command in reverse order, using a single command.

Although zip is a recent addition to the Solaris operating environment, patches are now distributed only in zip format.

The zip command uses a highly optimized algorithm to encode files. Text files can be compressed to a half to a third their original size. By default, zip searches the current directory only for files. The *-r* option tells zip to recursively search in subdirectories for files.

```
zip [ -dfmu ] [ -r ] file [ file list ]
unzip [ -lt ] [ -fnou ] [ -d dir ] file [ file list ]
```

zip files can be modified once they are created. New files can be added to them, old files can be deleted, and modified files can be updated. If zip is given the *-f* option, it replaces (freshens) any files in it if they have a more recent modification date than the one stored in the zip file. The *-u* option is similar, except that it also adds any new files to the zip file that are not already there. If a file is freshened from either *-f* or *-u,* the old file will be removed from the zip file. If zip is passed the *-d* option and a list of files, it deletes those files from the named zip file. The *-m* option is used to move the file into the zip file; once the files are compressed and copied, they are deleted from the directory.

The companion program to zip is unzip. You can use the unzip command to extract files from a zip file, list the files in a zip file, or check a zip file for errors. If unzip is given no options, it extracts all files in the zip file to the local directory. It creates subdirectories as needed. If unzip is given the *-l* option, it provides a list of all the files in the zip file. When the *-t* option is used, the files will be unzipped in memory and their cyclic redundancy check (CRC) will be compared with the CRC stored in the zip file. If the CRCs match, the file is fine. If all files are fine, the zip file is fine.

The *-f* and *-u* options to unzip are similar to the same options for zip, except that they refer to the unzipped files. The *-f* option causes files that already exist to be updated if necessary. The *-u* option also causes new files to be created if they do not already exist. The *-n* option can be used to stop existing files from being overwritten by *-u.* Used together, they will cause only new files to be created. Files that already exist will not be touched. The *-o* option is used to cause unzip to do unsafe overwriting of files; files that already exist are overwritten without prompting for verification.

The following examples show how to zip several files into a single zip file and how to extract a single file from a zip file. To extract all files from the zip file, do not provide a file list:

```
$ zip part1.zip ch1.doc ch2.doc ch3.doc
  adding: ch1.doc (deflated 24%)
  adding: ch2.doc (deflated 31%)
  adding: ch3.doc (deflated 12%)
$ unzip part1.zip ch3.doc
Archive:  part1.zip
  inflating: ch3.doc
```

EXERCISE 9-1

Reducing File Size for Storage to Tape

This exercise provides an opportunity to use some of the commands discussed in this section. To complete it, you need to have some files to work with. You can copy files from /var/adm, or you can use any files you want. This exercise causes files to be changed and erased, so do not use files you want to keep, or make copies of the files first. Because the files used in the example and the files you use might be different, your results could vary from those shown in the exercise.

1. Determine the files that you are going to use and the directory you will work in. It's a good idea to copy the files in the /var/adm directory to another location, such as /var/tmp/Sol9_SG/ch9.

2. Use the du -sk command to determine how many disk blocks the files in the directory use:

```
$ du -sk .
879    .
```

3. Using the tar command, create an archive file of all the files:

```
$ tar cf ex91.tar *
```

4. Use the du -sk command to determine how many disk blocks the archive uses:

```
$ du -sk ex91.tar
856    ex91.tar
```

5. Compare the two numbers. Can you think of any reason they might be different? The end of most files will not match up exactly with the end of a disk block. For this reason, there will be some wasted space at the end of each file. When the files are added to a tar archive, they can be aligned more efficiently to use the space in the archive file. This will save at least a partial block per file.

6. Use the compress command to compress the archive file, and use the du -sk command to see how many blocks the compressed file takes:

```
$ compress ex91.tar
$ du -sk ex91.tar.Z
680    ex81.tar.Z
```

7. Uncompress the file and then pack it. How many blocks does it take now?

```
$ uncompress ex91.tar.Z
$ pack ex91.tar
pack: ex91.tar: 15.8% Compression
$ du -sk ex91.tar.z
 720    ex91.tar.z
```

8. Unpack the file and zip it. Now how many blocks does it take?

```
$ unpack ex91.tar.z
unpack: ex91.tar: unpacked
$ zip -m ex91.tar.zip ex91.tar
  adding: ex91.tar (deflated 41%)
$ du -sk ex91.tar.zip
512   ex91.tar.zip
```

9. Delete the zip file and create a zip file of all the files without using tar first. How many blocks does it take?

```
$ rm ex91.tar.zip
$ zip ex91.zip *
  adding: ?.
$ du -sk ex91.zip
  616 ex91.zip
```

How do the storage requirements of the two zip files compare? Why do you think this is? In general, using tar and zip should provide better compression than zip alone. Because zip works on each individual file, it cannot take advantage of duplication between the files to improve its efficiency. When it compresses the single tar file, it can take advantage of this duplication.

CERTIFICATION OBJECTIVE 9.02

Understanding Regular Files, Directories, Symbolic Links, Device Files, and Hard Links

A *file* in the Solaris operating environment is a related set of bits on some form of storage device, such as a disk, CD-ROM, or tape. This very low-level concept allows the operating system to treat various types of bit sets similarly. In the Solaris operating environment, a file can be a regular file, a directory, a link, a device, or one of several other types. For the most part, the system and the users treat them exactly the same.

exam
ⓦatch

It is very important to understand the relationship among a filename, an inode, and the data blocks a file contains.

The Solaris file system can be thought of as a database of sorts. Each record contains an inode (index node) and data blocks. An *inode* contains information about a file: the type of file, the owner, the access and modification times, the access permissions, the number of links to the file, the size of the file, and the physical location of the data blocks. Note that the filename and directory locations are *not* contained in the inode; this information is contained in the directory entry. The *data blocks* contain the actual information in the file.

Inodes are numbered and kept in groups that are evenly spaced out across the file system. The space where the inode group lives is called a *cylinder group*. Initially, the data blocks for each group of inodes immediately follow the group. When a process accesses a file, the operating system can quickly go to the location of the inode, gather information about the file, and move to the disk location where the actual data is stored.

As the file system is used, data blocks for one inode group could end up in the space for another inode group. This process is known as *fragmentation*. If a file system becomes highly fragmented, performance will degrade. The only way to reduce fragmentation is to copy all the files from the file system, re-create it, and replace the files. This is rarely an issue, except in some file systems that have very high file creation and destruction rates, such as mail or news spools.

The ls command determines most of the information contained in the inode about a file. ls -*i* lists the inode and the name of a file. ls -*l* lists the type and permissions, the links, the owner, the size, the last modification time, and the name of the file. Other options to ls list other information. To system administrators, the most important information shown is the file type. The type is the first character of the first column of the ls -*l* listing. Table 9-1 lists the file types.

Regular Files

A *regular file* is a way of storing data. Regular files can be either text or binary. Text files can be viewed with standard commands, such as cat, and will be legible if not understandable. Binary files are used to store data in either a compact or a machine-readable form.

TABLE 9-1

Determining File
Type from ls -l

Symbol	File Type
d	Directory
D	Door
l	Symbolic link
b	Block Special File
c	Character Special File
p	FIFO (or named pipe) special file
s	AF_UNIX address family socket
-	Ordinary file

Text files generally use the American Standard Code for Information Interchange (ASCII) set of characters, although Universal Text Format (UTF) is becoming increasingly popular. Text files are used in an almost infinite number of ways. They can be used like a piece of paper or a notebook and contain notes, meeting minutes, and stories. They can have format information—such as HTML, PostScript, or LaTeX—so that when they are rendered, they will look a certain way. They can be an image format. They can be scripts written in any of several programming languages. They can even be simple databases.

Binary files generally are not legible. The binary data structures do not map well into the normal ASCII or UTF code sets. Even if they did, they would be completely unreadable. Binary files can be used in all the same ways that regular files can be used, but they usually require some kind of interpreter to make them understandable. A binary file might be a word processed file or a spreadsheet. It might be an image. It might be a compiled program, in which case, the interpreter is built in to the file. Or it might be a full-featured database.

Directories

A *directory* is a file that contains information about other files. Like the file system, it can be thought of as another simple database. Each entry in this "database" contains a filename and the inode associated with that name. A directory does not actually contain files. The files are spread out all over the storage device. This name-to-inode mapping is one way. An inode has no knowledge of the filename or the directory in which the file is located. A file has no knowledge of its name, which inode describes it, or which directory it lives in.

This arrangement provides a lot of flexibility to the operating system. Because a directory is a file, it can be contained within other files (directories), creating a treelike structure. A file can be moved from one directory to another simply by adding the filename and inode to one directory file and removing it from another. It is also possible to have a single file that has multiple names and possibly multiple directory entries.

Symbolic Links

A *symbolic link* is a special kind of file that is an alias to another file. In essence, it is a regular file that contains the path to another file. Because it points to a path, it can be used to point to a file that resides on another file system. This is useful to make a file appear to be somewhere it really is not. Most actions performed on the link are actually performed on the real file. The most notable exception is deleting. If you delete a symbolic link (using rm), the original file is not touched, just the symbolic link. If you delete the original file but not the symbolic link, the symbolic link is left pointing to a file that no longer exists. This is sometimes called a *dangling link.*

A symbolic link takes up some disk space. It also takes up an inode. The disk space is equal to the number of characters in the pathname to which the link points. This is exactly the same amount of space a regular file would take up if it contained the pathname. As mentioned, it is essentially a regular file with some special treatment. Because the symbolic link points to a filename (not an inode), if a file is deleted (causing a dangling link) and a new file with the same name is created, the dangling link will point to the new file.

Because everything is a file, a symbolic link can point to a regular file, a directory file, or a device. A symbolic link can even point to another symbolic link; this kind of multiple level of indirection is not recommended, though. It can lead to performance problems, difficulty in tracking down missing files, and *link loops,* where a link points to a link that points to a link that points back to the original link.

on the **job**   *While on assignment for a large Fortune 500 company, I was given the task of cleaning up a server that had been in place for several years. Over the years, the department had gone through several different administration teams, different software products, and hundreds of user requirements. As I started trying to determine everything that was there, I found that a previous admin had a disturbing habit of making symbolic links at apparently random locations. In one case, I found he had created symbolic links for every file in /usr/local/bin in /nds/proj/bin! I'm not sure that anyone (except the previous administrator) even knew the /nds/proj/bin directory existed; certainly no one had been trying to keep it up in over four years. In another case, I found a link loop that was seven levels deep.*

Device Files

Device files are a symbolic way to reference a specific hardware device. Device files allow devices to be manipulated in ways similar to other files. Treating devices as files is a very powerful concept. It allows devices to be written to or read from with standard Solaris 8 commands. For example, the following command writes the specified file directly to the lp (line printer) device:

```
$ cat book/chapter9/devices.txt >> /dev/lp
```

Device files can either be *character devices* or *block devices*. This designation refers to the way in which the device is accessed, either unbuffered (character) or buffered (block). Character devices are sometimes known as *raw devices;* they are accessed based on the smallest addressable hardware unit, the sector. Generally, sectors are 512 bytes. Character devices are often used for databases and other activities that involve high-volume access, such as tape-based backups.

A buffered device is one in which access is done based on a fixed-size logical area of the disk. This logical area, the *disk block*, is defined by, for example, a file system. By default, UFS defines a disk block as 8 kilobytes, although this number is tunable when the file system is created. The entire block is read or written before the kernel returns control to the parent process. Because the device has been prepared in some way (such as by creating a file system), block devices are sometimes referred to as *cooked devices*.

A listing of one of the partitions of the root disk in /devices/pci@1f,0/pci@1,1/ sd@3 is provided here. Note the *c* in the first column; this is a character device. The block device is where the file system would be created and accessed. Most types of devices have both block and character versions:

```
crw---- 1    root sys    136,   0 Apr 25 09:31    sd@0,0:a,raw
```

Device files do not use data blocks the way other files do. Where other files store the size and data block list in their inode, devices store a reference to the device driver associated to them and the particular instance of that kind of device. These two numbers are called the *major* and *minor* device numbers. In this example, the major device is 136 and the minor device is 0. This is the first ("zeroth") instance of the device referenced by driver 136 (the sd, or SCSI device, driver).

Hard Links

A *hard link* is a directory entry to reference a specific file. A hard link is not a file type in and of itself; it is the name-to-inode mapping contained in the directory file. Every file has at least one hard link: the filename by which it is known. You can tell how many hard links there are to a particular file with the ls -*l* command. The second column contains the number of links to that filename. Most files have only one there. All directories have at least two links. In their parent, they have the link for the name by which they are known. Inside them, they have another hard link, simply called ".". Directories that contain other directories will also have a hard link in each of their subdirectories called "..".

Because hard links are simply directory entries pointing to the same inode, any changes to the inode or the data are visible in both links. For example, because a file's permissions are contained within its inode, both links have the same permissions. If you change the permissions using one link, the permissions on the other link also change. Like symbolic links, one exception to this is deleting. If you delete one link to a file, the file is not actually deleted; all the other links still exist. Hard links cannot span file systems, since each file system has its own set of inodes. Hard links to directories can be created only by the operating system.

There is only one concrete way to determine if two seemingly identical files are links or copies. You know that ls -*l* shows the link count, so if the link count on both files is one, they must be copies. If you extend the ls command with the -*i* option, it prints the inode associated with each file. If two files have the same inode, they are links to each other. If they have different inodes, they are copies.

exam
Ŵatch

Hard links and soft (symbolic) links behave very similarly. The differences between them can be subtle and difficult to understand. Pay careful attention to how each relates to an inode and the information stored within the inode.

Here is a more concrete example of the differences between hard and soft (symbolic) links. In the ls *-li* example output that follows, there are three filenames. Two of the files are hard links to the same inode. One of the files is a soft link to one of the hard links:

```
18804 -r-r-r-  2 spp    spp    6723 May  1 19:18 README
18804 -r-r-r-  2 spp    spp    6723 May  1 19:18 README.2
18813 lrwxrwxrwx 1 spp  spp       6 May  1 19:19 README.s ->>README
```

Notice that the two files README and README.2 are exactly the same in every way. They have the same inode (18804), permissions, owner, size, and modification date. The only difference between them is the name. Notice that the symbolic link, README.s, has a different inode (18813), permissions, and size.

EXERCISE 9-2

Working with Different Types of Files

In this exercise, you will create and delete several types of files. Because device files have such a great chance of disrupting the entire system, you won't work with them now. You will perform only tasks that can be done without root access.

1. Create a new directory called ex92 with the mkdir command. Then cd into the directory. Run ls *-la* and check the number of links in the second column of the output for (.):

```
$ mkdir ex92
$ cd ex92
$ ls -la
total 2
drwxr-xr-x 2   spp  spp  512  May  3 13:04 .
drwxr-xr-x 3   spp  spp  512  May  3 13:04 ..
```

2. Why is the link count two for the directory? Whenever a directory is created, two links are always created, one for the filename in the parent directory and one for the special filename (.) inside the newly created directory.

3. Create another directory called newdir in this directory. Do another ls *-la* and check the link count for (.). The number of links changes from two to three, and the timestamp is updated:

```
$ mkdir newdir
$ ls -la
total 3
drwxr-xr-x 3    spp   spp   512   May   3 13:06 .
drwxr-xr-x 3    spp   spp   512   May   3 13:04 ..
drwxr-xr-x 2    spp   spp   512   May   3 13:06 newdir
```

4. Why did the changes occur? When newdir was created, the special link (..) was created inside newdir. That link points to the same inode as ex92 and (.). That is why there are now three links. Because the directory file was modified (to add the new directory), the timestamp changes.

5. Now, use

```
echo "This is a file" >> file92
```

to create a file called file92. Do an ls *-l* file92 to see the number of links it has. It has only one:

```
$ echo "This is a file" >> file92
$ ls -l file92
-rw-r-r-  1   spp   spp    15   May   3 13:15 file92
```

6. Use the ln command to create a new hard link to file92 called file92.link. Do an ls *-l* file92* to see the number of links each file reports:

```
$ ln file92 file92.link
$ ls -l file92*
-rw-r-r-  2   spp   spp    15   May   3 13:15 file92
-rw-r-r-  2   spp   spp    15   May   3 13:15 file92.link
```

7. Why did the link count change, but the timestamp didn't? The link count increased because these files point to the same inode. You can verify this with ls *-i* file92* to show the inode associated with each file. Because the file itself wasn't changed, this timestamp doesn't update:

```
$ ls -I file92*
 167211 file92    167211 file92.link
```

8. Now use ln *-s* to create a symbolic link to file92 called file92.soft. Again, do an ls *-l* file92* to see the number of links each file reports:

```
$ ln -s file92 file92.soft
$ ls -l file92*
-rw-r-r-  2    spp  spp    15   May  3 13:15 file92
-rw-r-r-  2    spp  spp    15   May  3 13:15 file92.link
lrwxrwxrwx 1   spp  spp     6   May  3 13:26 file92.soft ->> file92
```

9. Why do the files report the link counts they do, instead of three? The new soft link is a separate file. It has its own inode. If you want, do another ls *-i* file92* to verify that file92 and file92.soft have their own inodes.

10. In this final step, use cat file92.soft to see the contents of file92.soft. Then use rm file92 to delete file92. Finally, do another cat file92.soft to see the contents:

```
$ cat file92.soft
This is a file
$ rm file92
$ cat file92.soft
cat: cannot open file92.soft
```

11. What happens when you delete the file? File92.soft is an alias for the filename file92. Unlike file92.link, it points to a different inode as file92. When file92 is deleted, file92.soft no longer points to anything. However, file92.link is still associated with the same inode and data blocks, so the contents are still available through that name. Try cat file92.link to verify this statement.

Take a minute now to look at some scenarios of using a hard link and a symbolic (soft) link.

SCENARIO & SOLUTION

What if you want to access a file on one file system through a specific location on another file system?	You must use a symbolic link. Hard links cannot span file systems.
Two users need to collaborate on one file. They both want to access it from their own directory, and neither wants the other to be able to access their other files. What do you use?	If both users' directories are on the same file system, use a hard link. A soft link would require that one of the users allow the other user to have access to his or her directory.

CERTIFICATION SUMMARY

This chapter discussed two important concepts. The most important of this chapter—perhaps of the entire Solaris operating environment—is that everything is a file. The other concept discussed was managing the storage requirements of specific files. Proper management can allow a system to be useful for a long period of time and save much time, effort, and money in replacement.

Some of the more common commands for storage space management were discussed. They included tar, compress, pack, and zip. The tar command is a way of collecting files. The compress, uncompress, and zcat commands deal with an individual file and its size. The pack, unpack, and pcat commands are analogous commands to compress, uncompress, and zcat. The zip and unzip commands were covered as a way of compressing multiple files and then tying them together in a single command, much like compress and tar or pack and tar would do in multiple commands.

The types of files and the structure of a file comprised the second part of this chapter. The file types discussed were regular files, directories, links, and devices. The differences between the two types of regular files—text and binary—were explained and examples given. The differences between hard and soft (symbolic) links were explored and examples were shown. The use of character and block devices was also described.

Also, the last section of this chapter discussed how a file is stored on disk. The relationship among filenames, inodes, directory entries, and data blocks was explained. The contents of an inode were briefly touched on as well. The file system and directory structure was compared to that of a simple database.

TWO-MINUTE DRILL

Reducing the Size of Files and Directories for Tape Storage

❑ The tar command is useful to collect a number of files together into a single file.

❑ The compress command takes a single file and attempts to make it take less room using the Lempel-Ziv encoding format.

❑ The compress, uncompress, and zcat commands are hard links to each other. They are the same file, with multiple names.

❑ The pack command is a functional equivalent to compress.

❑ The pack and unpack commands are two different files. The pcat command is a symbolic link that points to unpack.

❑ The zip command implements the common PKZIP format often found on MS-DOS systems. It can be thought of as compressing each file and then making a tar archive of all the compressed files.

❑ The zip command is useful because the zip file can be added to, deleted from, and modified after it has been created, without intermediate steps.

Understanding Regular Files, Directories, Symbolic Links, Device Files, and Hard Links

❑ Everything is a file. A file is a related set of bits on a storage device.

❑ The Solaris file system can be thought of as a simple database. Each record (or file) contains an inode and zero or more data blocks.

❑ An inode contains information about a file, such as the owner, permissions, file type, timestamps, links, size, and physical location.

❑ A regular file is the most common type of file. It can be either text (legible), like a web page, a note, or a collection of recipes; or binary, such as a compiled program, a word processed document, or an image.

❑ A directory file contains information about other files. A directory does not actually contain files; it contains only the mapping of filenames to inodes.

❑ A symbolic or soft link is an alias to another file. It points to another filename, which could reside anywhere on the system.

❑ Device files provide a reference to a specific piece of hardware. They can either be character (raw, unbuffered) or block (cooked, buffered), depending on how data on them is accessed.

❑ A hard link is not a file itself. It is the directory entry that associates a filename with an inode.

SELF TEST

The following questions will help you measure your understanding of the material presented in this chapter. Read all the choices carefully because there might be more than one correct answer. Choose all correct answers for each question.

Reducing the Size of Files and Directories for Tape Storage

1. The tar command has five major modes. These modes can be described as which of the following?

   A. Add, subtract, multiply, divide, and modulus

   B. Create, extract, list, append, and update

   C. Create, copy, delete, compress, and move

   D. Pack, compress, zip, condense, and shrink

2. The four commands (tar, compress, pack, and zip) all have common filename extensions associated with them. Which of the following are the correct extensions?

   A. .arc for tar, .com for compress, .pc for pack, and .zip for zip

   B. .tar for tar, .gz for compress, .Z for pack, and .z for zip

   C. .tar for tar, .Z for compress, .z for pack, and .zip for zip

   D. .Z for tar, .z for compress, .pl for pack, and .gz for zip

3. Which of the following are reasons to worry about the storage requirements of files? (Choose all that apply.)

   A. Data will expand to fill the available storage space.

   B. Everything is a file.

   C. Limiting the size of files can reduce costs associated with backups (fewer tapes, smaller drives, and so on).

   D. Users are given disk quotas over which they can't go. The administrator must ensure they stay under their quotas.

4. Which of the following are advantages that zip provides over tar? (Choose all that apply.)

   A. The zip command is compatible with the PKZIP format commonly found on MS-DOS systems.

   B. zip files can be modified after they are created; files can be added, removed, or updated.

C. The zip command both collects files and compresses each file. The tar command only collects the files.

D. The zip command uses a highly optimized encoding algorithm. The tar command does no encoding; it simply slaps all the files together.

Understanding Regular Files, Directories, Symbolic Links, Device Files, and Hard Links

5. The Solaris operating environment defines a file as which of the following?

A. The smallest addressable area on a disk

B. A related set of bits on a storage device

C. A fixed size logical area of a disk

D. The space on a disk where the inode group lives

6. Which of the following is some information that can be found in an inode?

A. File type, owner, access time, permissions, and file size

B. File type, owner, creation time, number of links, and filename

C. Owner, access and modification times, size of file, and directory location

D. File type, access password, file permissions, and list of data blocks

7. Which of the following happens when you create a symbolic (soft) link?

A. The file system makes a copy of all the data blocks in the original file and associates them with the new file.

B. A new directory entry is created, the link count of the file is incremented, and both directory entries point to the same data blocks.

C. An alias to another file is created and an inode is used.

D. The original filename is deleted from the inode and the new filename is inserted.

8. Building on the discussion in this chapter, which of the following happens when a file system is created?

A. A character device is changed into a block device.

B. Inodes and data blocks are defined on a device.

C. The list of directories, files, and links is created.

    D. File systems can be neither created nor destroyed; they are a part of the disk drive when it comes from the manufacturer.

9. You do an ls *-l* on a file and see that the link count is 3. If you delete this file, which of the following happens?

    A. The directory entry is removed. The file contents can still be accessed through the other two filenames.

    B. All directory entries are removed. The file contents are no longer accessible.

    C. Nothing happens. The directory entry and the file will be deleted only if all links are deleted.

    D. The directory entry and the file are removed. The other links are now dangling and point to nothing.

LAB QUESTION

Given the information provided in this chapter, construct simple diagrams of the following items:

- The basic layout of a UFS file system
- The basic layout of a file on a file system
- The logical layout of a file within a directory

SELF TEST ANSWERS

Reducing the Size of Files and Directories for Tape Storage

1. ☑ **B.** The major modes of tar are *c* (create), *x* (extract), *t* (list), *r* (append), and *u* (update).
☒ **A** is incorrect because these are common arithmetic functions. **C** is incorrect because tar provides no compression functionality. It is used strictly to collect multiple files into a single file. In addition, once an archive is created, files cannot be deleted from it. **D** is incorrect because these are all terms to describe making something smaller. The pack, compress, and zip commands are all Solaris commands for that functionality.

2. ☑ **C.** These are the common extensions associated with each command.
☒ **A** is incorrect because, of these, only .zip is correct. **B** is incorrect because, of these, only .tar is correct. **D** is incorrect because none of these choices is correct.

3. ☑ **A and C. A** is correct because an old axiom states, "Data will expand to fill the available storage space." If files sizes are not monitored, space will fill more quickly and you'll need to purchase additional hardware more often. **C** is correct because smaller files mean smaller backups. This can be a considerable savings in tapes, drives, operator errors, and time.
☒ **B** is incorrect because the fact that everything is a file is not a reason for watching the size of files. **D** is incorrect because, although users may be given quotas on some systems, it is not the administrator's duty to manage their file use. It is the users' duty to manage their use.

4. ☑ **A, B, C, and D. A** is an advantage because PKZIP has been ported to many systems, not just Solaris and MS-DOS. This allows easy exchange of information across a wide variety of systems. **B** is an advantage because files inside a zip file can be added, replaced, or deleted. The tar command allows files to be added, and modified files are appended to the end of the archive (leaving the original file in the archive as well). There is no way to remove files from and archive without re-creating it. **C** and **D** are advantages because, to save space with tar, another command, like compress, must also be used.

Understanding Regular Files, Directories, Symbolic Links, Device Files, and Hard Links

5. ☑ **B.** A file is a related set of bits on a storage device.
☒ **A** is incorrect because the smallest addressable area on a disk is a sector. **C** is incorrect because a fixed-size logical area of a disk is a disk block. **D** is incorrect because the space on a disk where the inode group lives is the cylinder group.

6. ☑ A. Besides these items, it also contains the last modification time, the last time the inode was changed, the number of links to the file, and a list of data blocks.
   ☒ B is incorrect because neither the creation time nor the filename is kept in the inode. The creation time is not kept anywhere, and the filename is kept in the directory entry. C is incorrect because the directory location is not stored in the inode; it is contained in the directory file. D is incorrect because no access password is kept in the inode.

7. ☑ C. A soft link is essentially a regular file that points to another file. It takes up an inode and a small amount of disk space.
   ☒ A is incorrect because this is what happens when you copy a file using the cp command. B is incorrect because this is what happens when a hard link is created to an existing file. D is incorrect because the filename is not stored in the inode.

8. ☑ B. The inode groups (cylinder groups) and logical data blocks are defined. The superblock replicas, which maintain information about the file system, are also created.
   ☒ A is incorrect because both character and block devices normally exist for a disk drive. C is incorrect because no separate lists of files, directories, and links is maintained. D is incorrect because matter can be neither created nor destroyed, but file systems certainly can.

9. ☑ A. Removing a file simply deletes the directory entry. The actual data blocks (contents) are not freed until the link count goes to zero, signifying that there are no more links to the inode.
   ☒ B is incorrect because if you delete a file that has multiple links, only the directory entry you specified is removed. The other links, and the contents, are untouched. C is incorrect because you can delete any link you want; if there are other links, they will not be affected. D is incorrect because this happens if you have symbolic links pointing to a file you deleted. However, symbolic links are not registered in the inode link count.

LAB ANSWER

Basically, a UFS file system is composed of a number of cylinder groups spaced evenly across the disk, with areas of data blocks between the cylinder groups. This structure is shown here:

CG	Data blocks	CG	Data blocks	CG	Data blocks	CG	Data blocks

A file is an inode and some number of data blocks. Its structure looks similar to the following:

INODE → DATA BLOCKS

Within a directory, a file is a mapping of a name to an inode. A directory looks something like this:

Filename	Inode pointer	Data blocks, not actually in the directory itself
Filename 2	Inode2 pointer	Data blocks, not actually in the directory itself
Filename 3	Inode3 pointer	Data blocks, not actually in the directory itself

SUN® CERTIFIED SYSTEM ADMINISTRATOR

10

Understanding
the Boot Process

I have a recurring dream, in which I'm an actor with a leading role in a London West End play. I know my cue to enter is coming, but I don't know when. I don't know my lines, my character's name, or even the name of the play! I'm simply standing in the wings, trying to hear what the actors on stage are saying so that I can get some kind of clue as to what is expected of me.

I don't try to read too much into the significance of that dream. (After all, as Freud said, sometimes a cigar *is* just a cigar.) However, I think it's what a UNIX kernel must feel like when something has gone wrong and the system can't boot.

This chapter describes using the boot command, identifying the run state of the system, and using start and kill scripts. Understanding what to expect when a system is running as it should will help you locate the source of problems and fix it when it's not running properly.

CERTIFICATION OBJECTIVE 10.01

Understanding boot Command Functions

It's important to understand the boot command. If your system is in trouble, you could find yourself troubleshooting from the OpenBoot OK prompt. OpenBoot and the bootstrap process are covered in Chapter 2. The boot command is a programmable read-only memory (PROM) command that is run on a halted system from the OK prompt. Here, you learn about the boot command and how to use it to troubleshoot a system.

The boot command is a maintenance command that is used to modify the bootstrap process of the operating environment kernel. Before the kernel-loading process begins, you can use options to change how the bootstrap process happens.

The syntax of the boot command is

```
boot [device_name] [-options]
```

By default, the boot command simply boots the system:

```
ok boot
```

You can name another device from which to boot. For example, you could boot from the CD-ROM. You might have done this to install Solaris:

```
ok boot cdrom
```

The available options are the following:

- *-a* The "ask me" option. During the bootstrap process, this option prompts you for information on swap and root devices and for information regarding system files. This tool is handy to diagnose problems with the default configuration. Use this option if you need to boot from an alternate system file.

- *-r* The reconfigure option. This option looks for any new devices you have added to the system since the last time it was booted. This option causes the bootstrap process to probe all attached devices and update the entries in the /dev and /devices directories.

- *-s* The single-user option, also known as the "soup-for-one" option. This option brings the system to init *1* or init *s,* the single-user state. This state mounts the local file systems but doesn't allow user logins or network access.

- *-v* The verbose option. This option displays detailed startup messages.

exam
ⓦatch

As mentioned in Chapter 4, the -a, "ask me," and the -v, verbose, options are great learning tools. Use them to see which basic information the kernel requires during the bootstrapping process. In addition, keep in mind that these exams are based on the SPARC version of Solaris, not the Intel version. The best way to study for the exams and to prepare for a career as a Solaris sysadmin is to start using a SPARC system as soon as possible.

Now let's look at a couple of scenarios in which you might have to use the boot command.

SCENARIO & SOLUTION

You want to add an external SCSI tape device to your system. Which boot option should you use?	Add the new device using the boot *-r* command from the OpenBoot prompt.
The external tape device was working fine. Now it's not. How can you see if the device is loaded correctly during boot?	Use the verbose option, boot *-v.*

Mixing and Matching

It's possible to use the boot command to perform many useful troubleshooting functions. For example, let's look at the steps involved in booting from an alternative device. In this case, let's use the Installation CD-ROM.

1. Bring the system to PROM mode. Use either the STOP-A key combination or use the init command to halt the system.

2. At the OK prompt, type **n** for new command mode:

```
Type b (boot), c (continue), or n (new command mode)
>>n
Type  help  for more information
ok
```

3. Boot from the alternative device. Now you can make the system use the CD-ROM as the boot device:

```
ok boot cdrom
```

The system will boot from the Installation CD-ROM, and the installation process will begin. You can use this same process to boot from other bootable devices, such as a tape or an alternative hard disk.

CERTIFICATION OBJECTIVE 10.02

Reporting the Current Runlevel of a Solaris System

To see the runlevel your system is in, the easiest way is to use the who command, which shows who is currently logged in to your system, for example,

```
voyager:root # who
root          console      May 11 12:07     (:0)
tim           pts/2        May 11 11:40     (enterprise)
```

In this example, the root user on a system named *voyager* runs the who command with no options. It displays the user's login time, device logged in to, and from where. You can see that the root user is logged in on the system from the local console. You can also see that a remote user with the username *tim* has logged in recently from a system named *enterprise*.

The who command is also handy if you forget which account you've logged in on. Sometimes, as you log in on various accounts to set up environments or troubleshoot problems, you might forget who you are. This is when you use the who am i command, for example,

```
voyager % who am i
gibbst     pts/6          May 11 12:10     (borg)
```

The display tells you which account you're currently logged in on.

on the **Job** *Actually, if all you need to know is who you are logged in as, the id command is faster than who am i, and it gives you the same basic information. The need to use either command is usually a good indication that you need a break from your work.*

For the purposes of this chapter, let's look at one of the who command options: the *-r* option. The command who *-r* displays the system's current run state. Table 10-1 reviews the run states.

TABLE 10-1	Runlevel	Description
System Run States	Runlevel 0	The PROM monitor.
	Runlevel 1	The administrative or single-user state. This level mounts the local file systems, but all user logins are disabled.
	Runlevel 2	The first multiuser level where users can log in, but no resources are shared.
	Runlevel 3	The default runlevel. Users can log in and shared resources are available.
	Runlevel 4	Not currently used by Sun.
	Runlevel 5	Halts the system and, on some architectures, powers off the system.
	Runlevel 6	Reboots to the default init level.
	Runlevel *S* or *s*	Another way to get to the single-user mode.

The default runlevel on a Solaris system is runlevel 3. This runlevel is configured in the /etc/inittab file. For example, this is a portion of the default /etc/inittab file:

```
ap::sysinit:/sbin/autopush -f /etc/iu.ap
ap::sysinit:/sbin/soconfig -f /etc/sock2path
fs::sysinit:/sbin/rcS sysinit            >>/dev/msglog 2<>/dev/msglog </dev/console<R
is:3:initdefault:
p3:s1234:powerfail:/usr/sbin/shutdown -y -i5 -g0 >>/dev/msglog 2<>/dev/msglog
sS:s:wait:/sbin/rcS                      >>/dev/msglog 2<>/dev/msglog
</dev/console<Rs0:0:wait:/sbin/rc0                      >>/dev/msglog
2<>/dev/msglog </dev/console<Rs1:1:respawn:/sbin/rc1 >>/dev/msglog 2<>/dev/msglog
</dev/console<
```

The bolded line tells you the default init state for this system.

on the
ⓙob

When you're taking the Solaris exam, it's important to remember that the default init state on a Solaris system is 3. At some point in your career, you might want to change the default runlevel of a system, depending on how it's used and how you want it to respond to an unexpected power failure.

So if you need to see which runlevel you're in, use the who command with the -*r* option.

EXERCISE 10-2

What's Your Runlevel?

In this exercise, you use the who command to determine your current runlevel.

1. Once you've logged in to the system, use the who command with the -*r* option:

   ```
   sol:root #  who -r
   ```

2. Look at the display. It should look like the following example:

   ```
   .run-level 3  May 9 09:58     3      0  S
   ```

   This tells you that the system is currently at runlevel 3.

CERTIFICATION OBJECTIVE 10.03

Differentiating Between Basic *S* and *K* Script Activities

The boot process is covered in previous chapters. This section looks at the scripts that run at specific runlevels.

During the boot process, the system either comes to runlevel 3 (the default), or it boots to the runlevel specified. If you've used the init command to change the runlevel or have changed the /etc/inittab file's default runlevel, naturally, the system comes up in that runlevel. Each of the runlevels have separate directories that contain scripts the system runs as it enters that runlevel. These scripts follow a specific naming scheme.

Each runlevel has a script that governs the process of booting into that runlevel. They are located in the /sbin directory and are named after each runlevel. For example, when entering runlevel 3, the script called on by the init process is named /sbin/rc3. This run control script points the init process to another directory that contains individual scripts that start or stop processes, depending on whether the system is entering or leaving that runlevel.

EXERCISE 10-4

Using the stop and start Scripts

In this exercise, you'll look at the scripts that run for runlevel 3.

1. The stop and start scripts are located in the /etc directory and are named after each runlevel. After you've logged in to the system, change directories to /etc/rc3.d:

```
voyager:root # cd /etc/rc3.d
```

2. Using the ls command, look at the files contained in that directory:

```
voyager:root # ls
README        S15nfs.server   S50apache      S76snmpdx      S77dmi
```

3. Open the script that starts the NFS service:

```
voyager:root # more S15nfs.server
#!/sbin/sh
#
# Copyright (c) 1997-1999 by Sun Microsystems, Inc.
# All rights reserved.
#
#pragma ident   "@(#)nfs.server 1.30    99/06/10 SMI"

[ ! -d /usr/bin ] && exit

# Start/stop processes required for server NFS

case "$1" in
'start')
        # Clean up old /etc/dfs/sharetab - remove all nfs entries

        if [ -f /etc/dfs/sharetab ] ; then
                >>/tmp/sharetab.$$
                while read path res fstype opts desc; do
                        [ "x$fstype" != xnfs ] && \
                                echo "$path\t$res\t$fstype\t$opts\t$desc" \
                                >>>/tmp/sharetab.$$
                done </etc/dfs/sharetab<R
                # Retain the last modification time so that it can be truncated
                # by the share command when it is called first time after boot.

                /usr/bin/touch -r /etc/dfs/sharetab /tmp/sharetab.$$
                /usr/bin/mv -f /tmp/sharetab.$$ /etc/dfs/sharetab
        fi
```

This output is edited, but you'll see all the contents on your system. As you can see, this is a Bourne shell script that starts the NFS service.

The syntax of these scripts is very easy to follow. A capital *S* at the beginning indicates that it is a start script. The action a start script performs is to start a service. The number that follows the *S* indicates the order in which that script will run. So if the /etc/rc3.d directory contains the following,

```
README          S15nfs.server  S50apache      S76snmpdx      S77dmi
```

you can see that the NFS service will start before the Apache Web Server service. The NFS script, S15nfs.server, is a number 15; and the Apache script, S50apache, is a number 50.

Now let's take a look at the start script's evil twin, the kill script. kill scripts operate the same way as start scripts and use the same syntax, but the other way around: they stop, or kill, processes. Kill scripts use a capital *K,* as well as a number to indicate which runs before another.

The /etc/rc0.d directory is used as the system is being halted, because, as you remember, runlevel 0 is the halt state. So, it follows that the /etc/rc0.d directory would contain only *K,* or kill, scripts. For example, /etc/rc0.d/K28nfs.server is the script that stops the NFS service.

exam
ⓦatch

It's important to remember that **K** *scripts stop services and* **S** *scripts start them. Furthermore, carefully examine the formatting of any script used in exam questions. If a script is named s15nfs.server, for example, it won't be used by the init process because it doesn't follow the correct syntax.*

FROM THE CLASSROOM

Title UNIX Shell Scripts

At first glance, the shell scripting used in UNIX is pretty intimidating. The exams touch on the basics, but you'll find that you need a much deeper understanding of scripting as your sysadmin career progresses. Make sure you take every opportunity to practice writing and using scripts. Not only does this knowledge simplify your life, but it's an important skill for which prospective employers look. Some excellent web sites are dedicated to sharing and discussing shell scripts. Deciphering scripts

others have used is a great way to learn about scripting. In addition, you can find several excellent textbooks on shell scripting from your favorite online or bricks-and-mortar bookstore. However, the best way to learn is by doing. Take small steps, learn new syntax and commands to add a few at a time to your knowledge, and pretty soon, you'll wonder what was ever so confusing about them!

—Randy Cook, SCSA

CERTIFICATION SUMMARY

This chapter contains information that is covered in more detail in other chapters. The boot process is a separate objective on the exams, so it made sense to include some special tips as a separate chapter. It's important to keep in mind how the boot command is used to influence the boot process, how to tell which runlevel you're in, and what the start and kill scripts do. These three factors are not only important to passing the exams, but they can help you assist a confused Solaris kernel that, waiting just offstage, wants to go on but is not sure how. You're the director, saying, "It's *Macbeth*. You're Duncan. We're in Act I, Scene 6. Your first line is, 'This castle hath a pleasant seat . . .'"

✓ TWO-MINUTE DRILL

Understanding boot Command Functions

- ❏ The boot command is used to modify the bootstrap process from the OpenBoot OK prompt.
- ❏ You can boot from alternative devices such as a CD-ROM with the command boot cdrom.
- ❏ The *-a* option is the "ask me" option. You'll be prompted to either accept or change boot information.
- ❏ The *-r* option is used to add new devices.
- ❏ The *-s* option is used to boot into single-user mode.
- ❏ The *-v* option is used to see the boot messages as the system progresses into the proper runlevel.

Reporting the Current Runlevel of a Solaris System

- ❏ The command to see who is currently logged in to the system is the who command.
- ❏ The default runlevel is determined by an entry in the /etc/inittab file.
- ❏ To see at which runlevel the system is currently, use the command who -r.

Differentiating Between Basic *S* and *K* Script Activities

- ❏ The correct syntax for a start script includes a capital *S* and a sequence number.
- ❏ The correct syntax for a kill script includes a capital *K* and a sequence number.
- ❏ The sequence number determines the order in which the scripts will run.
- ❏ The scripts are located in /etc/rc#.d, with the pound sign (#) replaced by the runlevel with which they are associated.

SELF TEST

The following questions will help you measure your understanding of the material presented in this chapter. Read all the choices carefully because there might be more than one correct answer. Choose all correct answers for each question.

Understanding boot Command Functions

1. You've decided to load Solaris on your test workstation. You've loaded the installation media in the CD-ROM tray. Which command will you use to start the installation from the OK prompt?

   A. boot cdrom *-install*

   B. boot *-a* install

   C. install cdrom

   D. boot cdrom

2. If you run the command boot *-a*, which of the following will happen? (Choose all that apply.)

   A. The system will boot to the default runlevel.

   B. The system will display all the system startup messages.

   C. The system will prompt you for answers to default boot configuration settings.

   D. You will receive an error message.

3. What's the difference between the *-a* option of the boot command and the *-v* option?

   A. The *-a* option is the "ask me" option, which prompts for changes to boot settings. The *-v* option is similar but prompts for more detailed information.

   B. The *-a* option is the "ask me" option, which prompts for changes to boot settings. There is no *-v* setting.

   C. The *-a* option is the "ask me" option, which prompts for changes to boot settings. The *-v* option is the verbose setting, which displays the startup messages during the boot process.

   D. The *-a* option is the "ask me" option, which probes for new devices and asks if they should be installed. The *-v* option is the verbose setting, which displays the startup messages during the boot process.

Reporting the Current Runlevel of a Solaris System

4. Which command correctly tells you which user you are logged in as?

   A. whoami

   B. who *-i*

   C. id

   D. who *-r*

5. Which of the following is the output of the who *-r* command?

   A. `    .          run-level 3  May 11 09:58     3      0  S`

   B.
   ```
   root          console        May 11 12:07      (:0)
   gibbst        pts/2          May 11 17:01      (borg)
   root          pts/5          May 11 12:07      (:0.0)
   ```

   C. `    .          run-level 6  May 11 09:58     3      0  S`

   D. `Fri May 11 17:53:23 EDT 2001`

6. Which file determines the default init state?

   A. /etc/initstate

   B. etc/runlevel

   C. /sbin/rcd.d

   D. /etc/inittab

Differentiating Between Basic *S* and *K* Script Activities

7. Which of the following start scripts starts an application called submms?

   A. /etc/rc3.d/ S25submms

   B. /etc/rc3.d/ 525submms

   C. /etc/rc3.d/ K25submms

   D. None of the above

8. Which of the following uses the kill script syntax correctly?

A.   K36sendmail

B.   Ka.sendmail

C.   /etc/rc3.d

D.   S50apache

9. Why is there no directory named /etc/rc4.d?

A.   There is, although it's not used.

B.   Because there's no runlevel 4, there's no need for an /etc/rc4.d directory.

C.   It's a mistake—create one immediately!

D.   There is, and it's used to bring the system to runlevel 4.

LAB QUESTION

You have been asked to diagnose a boot problem with a Solaris server. You decide to watch the startup messages and see if you can determine the problem. What are the necessary steps?

SELF TEST ANSWERS

Understanding boot Command Functions

1. ☑ **D.** This command causes the system to boot from the CD-ROM and start the installation process.
☒ **A** is incorrect because the *-install* option is not needed. **B** is incorrect because the *-a* switch is not used to select a device. **C** is incorrect because there is no install command in OpenBoot.

2. ☑ **A and C.** The system will boot to the default runlevel, provided you don't make any changes in your answers that will cause it not to.
☒ **B** is incorrect because it is the result of using the *-v* option. **D** is incorrect because no error message will be displayed.

3. ☑ **C.** The difference is basically that the *-a* option prompts you for information and the *-v* option displays information.
☒ **A** is incorrect because the description for the *-a* option is right, but the *-v* option description isn't. **B** is incorrect because there is a *-v* option. **D** is incorrect because the description for the *-a* option describes the *-r* or reconfigure option.

Reporting the Current Runlevel of a Solaris System

4. ☑ **C.** The id command displays your login name as well as the who am i command.
☒ **A** is incorrect because /usr/ucb/whoami is available only if additional packages (SUNWscpu) are installed.
B is incorrect because there is no *-i* option with the who command. **D** is incorrect because the *-r* option displays the current runlevel.

5. ☑ **A.** This is the correct output of the who *-r* command.
☒ **B** is incorrect because this is the output of the who command with no options.
C is incorrect because runlevel 6 is the reboot state. **D** is the output of the date command.

6. ☑ **D.** This is the file that contains the default runlevel.
☒ **A, B,** and **C** are incorrect because they are filenames that don't exist.

Differentiating Between Basic *S* and *K* Script Activities

7. ☑   **D.** There is no way of knowing if the syntax contained in the script is correct. Just because the script is named correctly, using the correct syntax, doesn't mean the script is correctly written.
☒   **A** would be correct if you knew that the script was written correctly. **B** is incorrect because a *5* is used in place of an *S*. **C** is incorrect because the *K* indicates that the script is used to kill a process.

8. ☑   **A.** That is the correct syntax for a kill script.
☒   **B** is incorrect because it doesn't include a sequencing number after the *K*. **C** is incorrect because that is the directory that contains the scripts for runlevel 3. **D** is incorrect because it shows the correct syntax for a start script.

9. ☑   **B.** This runlevel can be used for customized runlevel needs, but it's not used by default.
☒   **A** is incorrect because there is no /etc/rc4.d directory. **C** is also incorrect because it is merely a joke. Don't create the directory unless you need to use a custom runlevel. **D** is incorrect because there is no runlevel 4.

LAB ANSWER

1. Use the who command to make sure no other users are currently logged in:

   ```
   voyager:root # who
   root        console      May 11 12:07     (:0)
   ```

2. Because all users are off the system, it's safe to boot the system to the PROM state:

   ```
   voyager:root # init 0
   ```

3. At the OK prompt, use the boot command with the *-v* option to watch the boot process and look for error messages:

   ```
   Type b (boot), c (continue), or n (new command mode)
   >>n
   Type  help  for more information
   ok boot -v
   ```

11

Configuring Disks

E very system you will touch as a system administrator will contain at least one hard disk. Some systems may have 2, 6, 20, or even more disks. Disks are essential to the operation of every system, and as the system administrator, you must understand exactly what hard disks are and how they work.

CERTIFICATION OBJECTIVE 11.01

Understanding Sun Hard Disks

Adding disks to a system can increase storage space, reliability, and, in some cases, the system's speed. How much of each of these results you achieve depends on many factors, including the size of the disk, its speed, and its type, as well as how the disk is configured within Solaris. Sometimes, you will need to remove disks from a system because of a disk failure, an upgrade, or to move data from one system to another. To succeed on the exam and also so that you can perform these tasks in the real world, you must know the steps involved in adding, removing, and configuring disks.

Hard Disk Mechanics

At a very simple level, a hard disk can be compared to a cassette tape. Both use magnetic fields to create magnetic patterns on a material, which can be read and recognized later. Cassette tapes use spools of a plastic-based material with metal particles embedded in it; hard disks use spinning *platters* or *disks* made of aluminum or glass, polished to mirror smoothness. A magnetic recording material is layered onto these platters; this material can be modified magnetically to represent data stored on the disk.

A typical disk has three to six platters, which rotate together at a high speed, usually 5600, 7200, or 10,000 revolutions per minute (RPM). In almost all cases, the faster the platters spin, the faster the disk can access the data stored on it.

Extending across the top and bottom of every platter is a small metallic arm with a magnetic head at its end. These arms move back and forth together across the platters, while the head reads and writes data on the platters. In a typical hard disk, these arms can move from the hub of the platter out to the edge and back, up to 50 times per second!

Each platter is divided into concentric circles, called *tracks.* Tracks are further broken down into *sectors,* which are the smallest addressable units in a track. There can be hundreds of sectors in a track, depending on the track's location on the disk. Inner tracks have fewer sectors than outer tracks.

Figure 11-1 shows a disk platter with one highlighted track and one highlighted sector. Although this illustration shows only a few tracks and sectors, a disk usually contains hundreds of tracks and thousands of sectors.

One more term you should be familiar with is *cylinder.* A cylinder is a bit more difficult to visualize than tracks and sectors. The platters in a hard disk are stacked up, and so are the heads that read the data from each platter. Because of this structure, all the heads move simultaneously so they can read separate tracks, but technically at the same physical location (only on a different platter). If you combine

FIGURE 11-1 Disk tracks and sectors

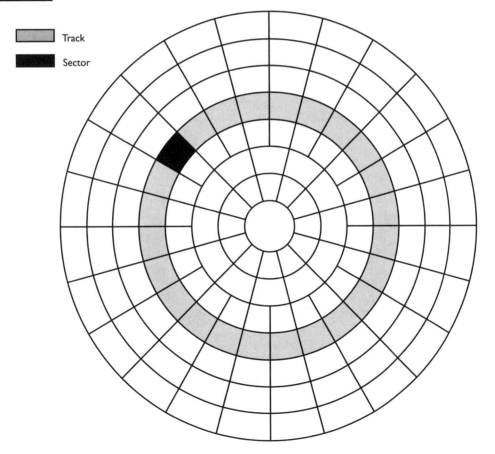

Track

Sector

the concentric circles on each platter that are accessed by the drive heads, you get a cylinder. In other words, the identically positioned tracks on each side of every platter together make up a cylinder. Figure 11-2 shows four disk platters, with one cylinder highlighted.

Storing Data

Before data can be written to a hard disk, the disk needs to be formatted and partitioned. Formatting and partitioning a disk involve three steps:

1. Physical formatting, also known as *low-level formatting* (LLF)

2. Partitioning

3. Logical formatting, also known as *high-level formatting* (HLF)

FIGURE 11-2   A disk cylinder

▨ Cylinder

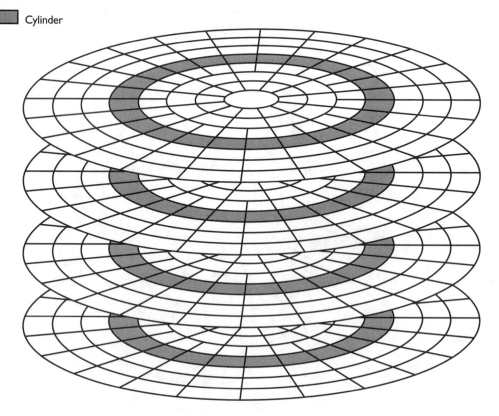

During a low-level format, the disk is divided into tracks, and these tracks are further divided into a specific number of sectors. Each sector is filled with random or test data. Almost all new disks have already been low-level formatted, so you need not worry about this step. Your disk is ready for the next step: partitioning.

Partitioning divides the disk into areas, called *partitions,* or *slices,* which will hold the file systems. Each partition is made up of disk cylinders. Most of the time, one disk partition corresponds to one file system in Solaris. To partition a disk in Solaris, use the format command, which is explained in depth in Chapter 12.

It's important to remember that a partition or slice refers to an area on a disk where a file system can be created. Once a slice is defined and a file system is created, the file system will be mounted by Solaris to a specific mount point within the file tree, such as /var, /usr, or /export/home.

When a high-level format is performed in Solaris, a disk slice is divided into cylinder groups, which contain several contiguous cylinders. The file system tries to spread its files and directories across the cylinder groups and to store data for a specific file within the same cylinder group. This arrangement minimizes the number of times the heads have to move, resulting in faster data transfers. Once the cylinders are put into cylinder groups, the slice is divided into *blocks,* which organize the structure of the files. In Solaris, the high-level formatting is done with the newfs command, explained in Chapter 20. On a Sun system, the default type of file system is the UNIX File System (UFS), which uses the following types of blocks, each of which stores specific bits of information:

- **Boot block**   Stores information used when the system is booted
- **Superblock**   Stores information about the file system
- **Inode**   Stores information about one file in the file system
- **Storage or data block**   Stores data for each file

The Boot Block

The *boot block* stores the instructions used when a system is booted. The boot block appears only in the first cylinder group on the disk and is the first 8KB in a slice.

The Superblock

The *superblock* includes the following information about the file system:

- Number of blocks in the file system (file system size)
- Number of data blocks in the file system

- Number of inodes
- Number of cylinder groups
- Block size
- Fragment size
- Free block count
- Free inode count

The superblock is so important to the file system that Solaris creates multiple backups of it for safekeeping. Occasionally, if the system is shut down incorrectly or if there is a disk problem, the primary superblock can become unreadable or out of sync with the backup superblocks. If this occurs, you need to restore the primary superblock, using one of the superblock backup copies in the file system. This issue will present itself when the disk is being checked with fsck, usually during a reboot. fsck tells you when the superblock is bad and cannot be repaired without your intervention.

EXERCISE 11-1

Restoring a Bad Superblock

This exercise shows how to choose an alternate superblock to restore the primary superblock.

1. Depending on the file system being repaired, you might have to boot into single-user mode so that the file system will not be in use. (This process is explained later in this chapter in the section "Removing Disks.")

2. Become superuser (root).

3. If the damaged file system is mounted, cd to a directory outside it and unmount the damaged file system:

```
# cd /
# umount /var
```

4. Display the superblock values with the newfs -N command. (*Caution:* It is important not to forget the -N option; otherwise, you will end up creating a new empty file system.) This command tells you where the alternate superblocks are placed in your file system:

```
# newfs -N /dev/dsk/c0t0d0s1
/dev/rdsk/c0t1d0s1:      8392072 sectors in 1781 cylinders of 19 tracks, 248 sectors
4097.7MB in 81 cyl groups (22 c/g, 50.62MB/g, 6208 i/g)
super-block backups (for fsck -F ufs -o b=#) at:
 32, 103952, 207872, 311792, 415712, 519632, 623552, 727472, 831392, 935312,
 1039232, 1143152, 1247072, 1350992, 1454912, 1558832, 1662752, 1766672,
 1870592, 1974512, 2078432, 2182352, 2286272, 2390192, 2494112, 2598032,
 2701952, 2805872, 2909792, 3013712, 3117632, 3221552, 3317280, 3421200,
 3525120, 3629040, 3732960, 3836880, 3940800, 4044720, 4148640, 4252560,
 4356480, 4460400, 4564320, 4668240, 4772160, 4876080, 4980000, 5083920,
 5187840, 5291760, 5395680, 5499600, 5603520, 5707440, 5811360, 5915280,
 6019200, 6123120, 6227040, 6330960, 6434880, 6538800, 6634528, 6738448,
 6842368, 6946288, 7050208, 7154128, 7258048, 7361968, 7465888, 7569808,
 7673728, 7777648, 7881568, 7985488, 8089408, 8193328, 8297248,
```

5. Choose an alternate superblock from the newfs –*N* command and specify it as an option to fsck:

```
# fsck -F ufs -o b=7361968 /dev/rdsk/c0t0d0s1
```

Inodes

An *inode* contains all the information about a particular file except its name. An inode takes 128 bytes of disk space and contains the following information about a file:

■ The file type (regular, directory, block special, character, link, and so on)

■ The file mode (the set of read/write/execute permissions)

■ The number of hard links to the file

■ The file owner's user ID

■ The group ID to which the file belongs

■ The number of bytes in the file

■ An array of 15 disk-block addresses

■ The date and time the file was last accessed

■ The date and time the file was last modified

■ The date and time the file was created

For every file on a disk, one inode is used to describe the file. When you create a file system, a fixed number of inodes are created in each cylinder group. Sometimes this number might not be enough. If you have an application that produces many small files, you might need to increase the number of inodes in your file system. Similarly, if you know your file system will be filled with only a few large files, you can decrease the number of inodes and save disk space, since each inode occupies 128 bytes. Use the *-i* option with newfs to increase or decrease the number of inodes when you create a file system. You can use the df command in the /usr/ucb directory to see how many inodes have been used and how many are free. Following is an example of how to run this command:

```
# /usr/ucb/df -i
Filesystem              iused     ifree    %iused   Mounted on
/dev/dsk/c0t0d0s0        1968     94864      2%     /
/dev/dsk/c0t0d0s6       41684    358700     10%     /usr
/dev/dsk/c0t0d0s1        2375     37497      6%     /var
/dev/dsk/c0t1d0s0       16131   1028605      2%     /export
```

Once you create your file system, there is no way to change the number of inodes! If you run out of inodes later, you must back up your data, make a new file system with more inodes, and then restore the data.

Storage or Data Blocks

Storage blocks, also called *data blocks,* occupy the rest of the space in the file system. These blocks contain the data files stored on the disk. The size of these storage blocks is determined at the time the file system is created. For a regular file, the storage blocks contain the contents of the file. For a directory, the storage blocks contain entries that give the inode number and the filenames of the files in the directory.

Disk Types

Two types of hard disks can be used in Sun systems: Integrated Device Electronics (IDE) and the Small Computer System Interface (SCSI—pronounced "scuzzy"). The choice of which disk to use in a system depends on two factors:

- The type (or types) of disks the system will support
- Your requirements for disk performance and configuration

Let's take a closer look at these two types of disks:

- SCSI disks are generally more expensive than IDE disks, and they require a SCSI disk controller that handles all the communication between the SCSI devices and the system. Because of this dedicated disk controller, accessing data on SCSI disks is often faster than on IDE disks. This performance difference is especially true when there are multiple disks in the system. Most Sun systems use SCSI disks.

- IDE disks are generally less expensive than SCSI disks. They have a small disk controller on each drive, which communicates directly with the system. One disadvantage of IDE disks is that you can install only two IDE disks for each IDE channel in your system, which is usually one or two channels. Another disadvantage is lower overall performance. Reading from and writing to IDE disks require the use of the system's processor, which can slow down other tasks running on the system. External IDE disks are not supported; only internal disks are supported. Only a few Sun systems use this type of disk. If your system supports only IDE disks, you can usually add a SCSI controller card to add SCSI disk support to the system.

FROM THE CLASSROOM

Why Sun Began Using IDE Disks in Some Systems

In the late 1990s, Sun began producing less expensive systems such as the Ultra 5 and Ultra 10 that use IDE disks instead of SCSI disks. These systems are intended for desktop and limited server applications that do not require heavy disk access or usage. A typical desktop workstation rarely contains more than one or two disks, and most users do not require super-fast access to those disks. With these limited requirements, IDE is an acceptable choice.

This move toward IDE was clearly a cost-saving measure that allowed Sun to produce and sell these systems at substantially less cost than previous models, which used SCSI disks.

—Bret Sanders, SCSA, MCSE

Disk Naming

When you refer to a disk in Solaris, you use its device name. Disk device names are a series of letters and numbers that take the form *cXtXdX*. The letters in the name are always the same (*c*, *t*, and *d*), but the *X*'s represent the numbers describing a particular disk on a particular system. Table 11-1 shows the components of a Solaris disk device name.

For example, the name *c0t0d0* refers to controller 0, target 0, LUN 0. Most likely, this is the name of the first disk in your system, and it is also most likely your boot disk.

Many times when you use the disk device name, you don't want to refer to the whole disk, but only to a partition or slice on the disk. In this case, the letter *s* and a number are added to the end of the name. In Solaris, you can have up to eight partitions on one disk, numbered 0 through 7. For example, the name *c1t5d0s6* refers to controller 1 (the second controller, because numbering starts at 0), disk target 5, LUN 0, partition 6 (the seventh partition).

| **TABLE 11-1** | Components of a Solaris Disk Device Name |

Identifier	Description
cX	*X* refers to the disk controller. When a Sun system gathers information about the disk controllers attached to the system, it assigns a number to each one, depending on the order in which the controller was discovered. The first controller discovered on the system is assigned the number 0. The second is assigned the number 1, and so on. On IDE systems, the first IDE channel is 0 and the second (if a second exists) is 1.
tX	*X* refers to the target number of the disk. This number is sometimes called the SCSI ID, and each disk on a controller must have a unique target number. The controller then uses this number to individually address each disk. On IDE disks, the primary disk's target ID is 0 and the secondary disk's ID is 1.
dX	*X* refers to the logical unit number (LUN) of the disk. In some disk arrays, the LUN is used to further break down the individual disks in the system. An array can use one target number for a group of disks, but then it uses this LUN to refer to individual disks within that group. This method is used extensively in SCSI disk arrays and CD changers, but for single disks, the number is always 0. For IDE disks, this number is always 0.
sX	*X* refers to the partition or slice number when you are referring to a particular partition on the disk.

on the **Job** *If you ever need help remembering the format of these names, you can execute a mount command without options. This command presents you with a list of mounted partitions with their corresponding disk device names.*

exam **Watch** *You should thoroughly understand disk names and what they mean. You should be able to name a disk, given its parameters. The exam might ask, for example, "Give the name for the disk on controller 1 with target 0, LUN 0."*

CERTIFICATION OBJECTIVE 11.02

Understanding the Uses of Character (Raw) Disks and Block Disks

When you use Solaris commands to perform operations on disks or file systems, you address them by specifying the full path to the device plus the device name. All disks on a system have a device entry in both the /dev/rdsk and the /dev/dsk directories. The /dev/rdsk entry refers to the *character* or *raw device,* and the /dev/dsk directory refers to the *block* or *buffered device.* Which of these paths you use depends on the action you want to perform. These two types of devices are not often interchangeable, and you must know when each is appropriate. When you're in doubt about which to use, refer to the man page for the utility you're running.

When you use the character device (/dev/rdsk), only small amounts of data are transferred, one character at a time. This data is written directly to the disk, bypassing system I/O buffers. Typically, printers, terminals, and some storage devices use the character device.

When you use the block device (/dev/dsk), the system is able to use its buffers to speed I/O transfers. Data is buffered or cached in memory until the buffer is full, and then the data is written to disk in larger "chunks." Typically, disks, tape drives, and CD-ROM drives use block devices.

Table 11-2 presents the general guidelines for using each type of device for disks.

exam **Watch** *Be sure you know the difference between raw and block device names and when to use each. You might want to memorize the type of name that some common commands use, such as mount, newfs, and df.*

TABLE 11-2	Using Device Types

Device Type	Description
Character (raw) disk device (/dev/rdsk)	Use this device name when you are referring to a physical disk or partition and not the file system on the disk. For instance, newfs creates a file system on a physical disk partition, so when you specify the physical location for newfs to create the file system, the raw device name is used.
Block disk device (/dev/dsk)	After a file system has been created on a partition, it can be referenced with its block device name. For example, the mount command uses the block device name because you're mounting a file system, not a physical disk partition.

Adding Disks

If your system does not have hot-pluggable disks, you'll need to shut it down before adding or removing disks.

on the

Job

It's always a good idea to completely shut down and power off the system before physically attaching any new devices, unless the system you're working on has hot-pluggable capabilities. Otherwise, adding a device to a powered-on system can damage the equipment.

Before you shut down, it's imperative that you make sure no one else is logged in to the system. Use the who command to verify that you are the only user logged in to the system. This command shows which users are logged in, when they logged in, and the IP address or hostname from which they are connected. Once you know who is logged in to the system, you can contact these users and warn them of the impending shutdown. Following is an example of using the who command:

```
# who
bret       pts/2        Apr  4 10:39    (hac2arpa.hac.com)
melissa    pts/4        Apr  4 14:33    (host44.exodus.net)
tony       pts/3        Apr  4 11:22    (usr06.primenet.com)
skip       pts/5        Apr  4 10:01    (classic.cybersand.com)
#
```

Once your system is shut down and powered off, it's safe to plug in the disk. You can make sure the disk will be recognized before booting the system, which will save you the time of booting up only to find that Solaris cannot recognize your new disk. Here's how: A few seconds after switching on the power, the system banner will appear. When it does, press STOP-A on the Sun keyboard, or, if you're connected to the system with a serial console, send a BREAK signal from your terminal. This action sends the system into the OpenBoot PROM (OBP). Some people call this the *OK prompt.* Older Sun systems use the double greater-than sign (>>) as the OBP, and newer Sun systems use OK as the prompt.

Once you see one of these prompts, type **probe-scsi** and wait for the results. This command queries the first disk controller in the system and returns a list of all recognized disks attached to that controller. If you have more than one disk controller, you might have to use the probe-scsi-all command instead. This command walks through all the controllers on the system and queries each one it finds. The following is an example of how to use the probe-scsi command:

```
{0} ok probe-scsi
Target 0
Unit 0    Disk        IBM DDRS39130SUN9.0GS98E9925477146
                          (C) Copyright IBM Corp
                          1997. All rights reserved
Target 1
  Unit 0    Disk        IBM DDRS39130SUN9.0GS98E5876546026
                          (C) Copyright IBM Corp
                          1997. All rights reserved
```

If you see your newly added disk in the output of these commands, chances are good that Solaris also will be able to recognize and use the disk. You now need to perform a reconfiguration boot so that Solaris will know to search for new devices attached to the system. This boot is done with a boot -*r* command at the OBP. If you like to plan ahead, you can create a file called reconfigure in the root directory that will tell the system to perform a reconfiguration boot the next time it boots up. Of course, you'd have to do this before shutting the system down to add the new disk.

One more way to make Solaris recognize the new disk is to use the devfsadm command once the system is up and running. This command is discussed in the following section.

on the job

Before shutting down a system to add disks or perform any other administrative task, be sure to find out if anyone is logged in to the system! Forgetting to check for other users can potentially be what is referred to as a CLM—a "career-limiting move."

CERTIFICATION OBJECTIVE 11.03

Adding New Device Configuration Information Without a Reboot of Solaris

In all previous versions of Solaris, you had to perform a reconfiguration boot to recognize new disks and other devices attached to the system. Solaris offers a tool that eliminates the need to reboot to discover new devices. This tool is the devfsadm command.

You can use the devfsadm command on a running system at any run level. When you run devfsadm with no options, your system tries to load every device driver in the system and then use each driver to attach to all possible devices. The system discovers any new disks or other devices attached since the last reboot or since the last time devfsadm was run. The /dev and /devices directories will be updated with the links and device paths appropriate for each device discovered.

Instead of running devfsadm without options (full discovery mode), it's a good idea to limit its search to the specific type of device you're adding. This will save time because the command will not explore all possible devices but only a subset of devices you specify. To specify this subset of devices, use the -c option. You must follow this option with the name of the device class (or classes) you'd like to search. Valid device classes are disk, tape, port, audio, or pseudo.

There are other options for the devfsadm command as well. Table 11-3 shows the options most commonly used.

TABLE 11-3 Command Options

Option	Description
-c device_class	Searches only for devices of the type you specify in device_class. Acceptable values for device_class are disk, tape, port, audio, and pseudo.
-C	Cleanup mode. Does extra cleanup to remove dangling logical links.
-s	Suppresses any changes to /dev or /devices. Use this option with -v for a dry run to see what the command will do when you run it.
-v	Prints changes to /dev and /devices in verbose mode. This option gives you much more information about what's happening, for troubleshooting purposes.
-i driver	Loads only a specific driver instance (sd for SCSI devicem, for instance).

EXERCISE 11-2

Using the devfsadm Command

This exercise shows you how to use the devfsadm command to make Solaris discover a new disk on a running system.

1. Use the devfsadm command to make the system recognize the new disk. Use the options to create verbose output and to look for only disk devices:

```
# devfsadm -v -c disk
devfsadm[324]: verbose: symlink /dev/dsk/c0t3d0s0 ->> ../../devices/sbus@1f,0/SUa
devfsadm[324]: verbose: symlink /dev/dsk/c0t3d0s1 ->> ../../devices/sbus@1f,0/SUb
devfsadm[324]: verbose: symlink /dev/dsk/c0t3d0s2 ->> ../../devices/sbus@1f,0/SUc
devfsadm[324]: verbose: symlink /dev/dsk/c0t3d0s3 ->> ../../devices/sbus@1f,0/SUd
devfsadm[324]: verbose: symlink /dev/dsk/c0t3d0s4 ->> ../../devices/sbus@1f,0/SUe
devfsadm[324]: verbose: symlink /dev/dsk/c0t3d0s5 ->> ../../devices/sbus@1f,0/SUf
devfsadm[324]: verbose: symlink /dev/dsk/c0t3d0s6 ->> ../../devices/sbus@1f,0/SUg
devfsadm[324]: verbose: symlink /dev/dsk/c0t3d0s7 ->> ../../devices/sbus@1f,0/SUh
devfsadm[324]: verbose: symlink /dev/rdsk/c0t3d0s0 ->> ../../devices/sbus@1f,0/Sw
devfsadm[324]: verbose: symlink /dev/rdsk/c0t3d0s1 ->> ../../devices/sbus@1f,0/Sw
devfsadm[324]: verbose: symlink /dev/rdsk/c0t3d0s2 ->> ../../devices/sbus@1f,0/Sw
devfsadm[324]: verbose: symlink /dev/rdsk/c0t3d0s3 ->> ../../devices/sbus@1f,0/Sw
devfsadm[324]: verbose: symlink /dev/rdsk/c0t3d0s4 ->> ../../devices/sbus@1f,0/Sw
devfsadm[324]: verbose: symlink /dev/rdsk/c0t3d0s5 ->> ../../devices/sbus@1f,0/Sw
devfsadm[324]: verbose: symlink /dev/rdsk/c0t3d0s6 ->> ../../devices/sbus@1f,0/Sw
devfsadm[324]: verbose: symlink /dev/rdsk/c0t3d0s7 ->> ../../devices/sbus@1f,0/Sw
```

e x a m

ⓦa t c h   *Make sure you know the command-line options for devfsadm and what they do!*

Removing Disks

When removing a disk from the system, you need to perform a reconfiguration boot. The devfsadm command works only when you are discovering new devices, not when you are removing devices. If you don't perform the reconfiguration boot, the system could still think the disk is attached and try to access it. A system that tries to access a nonexistent disk can slow considerably or even hang or crash.

Now that you have a better idea of how to add disks and how to use the devfsadm command, here are some possible scenario questions and their answers.

SCENARIO & SOLUTION

What if you've attached the disk, but Solaris does not recognize it?	Either perform a reconfiguration boot (boot -*r*) or use the devfsadm command to configure the system to see the disk.
What if you need to create a new partition or format a disk?	Use a raw device name (rdsk) because you'll refer to the physical disk location on which to create the partition.
What if you need to mount a disk partition?	Use a block device name (dsk) because you'll refer to a file system when you mount it.

The /etc/vfstab file is important to remember when removing a disk. This file tells the system where to find its partitions to mount while booting. If you forget to alter this file to remove any references to the disk being removed, your system might not be able to boot! During the boot process, the system tries to mount all the partitions listed in the /etc/vfstab file that have *Yes* in the Mount At Boot column. If one of these partitions no longer exists, the system will be unable to mount it, and this could halt the boot process. If this happens, you can enter single-user mode and edit the /etc/vfstab file to correct the problem. Here are the steps to do this:

1. At the obp, use the boot -*s* command to enter single-user mode. You will be asked for the root password to do system maintenance. The following shows an example of this process. In this example, the disk that contained the /var file system was removed:

```
{0} ok boot -s
Boot device: /sbus/SUNW,fas@e,8800000/sd@0,0  File and args: -s
SunOS Release 5.9 Version Generic_108528-06 64-bit
Copyright 1983-2000 Sun Microsystems, Inc.  All rights reserved.
configuring IPv4 interfaces: hme0.
Hostname: enterprise
mount: mount-point /var/run does not exist.
INIT: Cannot create /var/adm/
INIT: failed write of utmpx entry:"  "
```

```
INIT: failed write of utmpx entry:"   "

INIT: SINGLE USER MODE
Type control-d to proceed with normal startup,
(or give root password for system maintenance):
```

2. After entering the root password, you can use vi or another text editor to modify the /etc/vfstab file. Change or remove any lines in that file that reference the nonexistent disk. Instead of removing lines from a configuration file like this one, it's a good idea to comment it out by inserting a pound sign (#) at the beginning of the line. With this character at the beginning of the line, the system ignores the whole line. Then, in case you have to put the line back in later, you simply remove the pound sign. (Refer to Chapter 8 for more in-depth information on the /etc/vfstab file.)

3. Once the /etc/vfstab file is corrected, you can reboot the system normally, using the reboot or shutdown -r commands.

CERTIFICATION SUMMARY

All disks in a system have an entry in the /dev/rdsk and /dev/dsk directories. It is important to know which of these directories to use for the operation you're trying to perform. Use the character or raw device path (/dev/rdsk) when performing an operation on a disk or partition, such as creating a new file system. Use the block device path (/dev/dsk) when performing an operation on a file system, such as mounting a partition.

Solaris has a tool for adding devices to the system without rebooting: a command called devfsadm. It works by attempting to load every driver in the system and attach instances to all devices, eventually discovering any new devices added since the last reconfiguration boot or since the last time the devfsadm command was run. You can restrict the devfsadm command to search for only new devices of a certain type, such as a disk, by adding the -c option and specifying the type of device for which to search.

✓ TWO-MINUTE DRILL

Understanding the Uses of Character (Raw) Disks and Block Disks

❑ Use raw disk device names when referring to the physical disk or a physical disk slice.

❑ Use block device names when referring to a file system on a disk partition.

❑ Commands such as newfs and fsck use raw device names.

❑ Commands such as mount use block device names.

Adding New Device Configuration Information Without a Reboot of Solaris

❑ For Solaris to recognize a new disk attached to the system, use the devfsadm command.

❑ The devfsadm command runs faster if you use the -c option to specify devices it should look for.

SELF TEST

The following questions will help you measure your understanding of the material presented in this chapter. Read all the choices carefully because there might be more than one correct answer. Choose all correct answers for each question.

Understanding the Uses of Character (Raw) Disks and Block Disks

1. Which of the following describes an inode?

   A. It stores information about a file system.

   B. It stores information about the location of the superblocks.

   C. It stores information about a file.

   D. It stores information used to boot the system.

2. Which of the following would refer to the first partition on disk target 0, LUN 0, controller 3?

   A. /dev/rdsk/c3d0t0s1

   B. /dev/rdsk/c3d0t0s0

   C. /dev/rdsk/c3t0d0s1

   D. /dev/rdsk/c3t0d0s0

3. Which of the following is an example of a device name you would use when creating a new file system with the newfs command?

   A. /dev/dsk/c0t0d0s0

   B. /dev/rdsk/c0t0d0s0

   C. /dev/null

   D. /dev/disk/c0t0d0s0

4. You install an application that creates 200,000 small files in one file system. Now you're seeing messages in the system log that you've run out of inodes. How would you go about fixing this problem?

   A. Use the newfs –*i* command to create more inodes in the existing file system.

   B. Back up the data on the file system, use newfs –*i* to create a new file system with more inodes, and then restore the data.

   C. Move all the data to a tape device.

    D.   Use the tunefs command to increase the number of inodes available.

5.   When you reboot your mail server, you see the message "Bad superblock" while the disks are being checked. What must you do to correct this error?

    A.   Reboot again so fsck can fix the file system.

    B.   Run devfsadm *-s* to fix the superblocks.

    C.   It's not a serious problem and can be ignored.

    D.   Run fsck manually, specifying an alternate superblock.

Adding New Device Configuration Information Without a Reboot of Solaris

6.   You are running part of a web site with a Sun Enterprise 450 server with hot-pluggable disk capabilities, and it is running Solaris. You need to add another internal disk to the system. What is the quickest way to get the new disk online so that Solaris can use it?

    A.   Insert the new disk into an open drive bay, perform a reconfiguration boot, and then mount the disk.

    B.   Shut down the system, insert the disk, and perform a reconfiguration boot.

    C.   Insert the disk and immediately use the devfsadm command to recognize the disk.

    D.   Use the devfsadm command, insert the disk, and then mount the disk.

7.   Which of the following options will make the devfsadm command print more output to the screen?

    A.   *-v*

    B.   *-print*

    C.   *-C*

    D.   *-c*

8.   Your manager asks you to add a new disk to a Sun system that does not have hot-pluggable disk capability. What should you do to avoid potential damage to the system?

    A.   Insert the disk and use the devfsadm command to recognize it.

    B.   Insert the disk while in user level 1, then reboot.

    C.   Reboot the system with a reconfiguration boot, then insert the disk.

    D.   Shut down and remove power from the system, insert the disk, and then do a reconfiguration boot.

9. You need to add an external SCSI disk into an Ultra 10, a system that normally supports only IDE disks. How can you make this work?

   A. The disk is not compatible with the system and cannot be used.

   B. Attach the disk to another system first, format it, and then move it to the Ultra 10.

   C. Buy an IDE-to-SCSI converter and install it in the system.

   D. Buy a SCSI host adapter card for the system.

LAB QUESTION

You maintain the web and database servers at your company. The server responsible for logging all activity on the external web servers is an Enterprise 4500 and has hot-swappable disk capability. The system seems to have a bad disk. The disk still works for the most part, but in the system logs you can see disk media errors, and the disk seems slow to write data. Luckily, you have a spare disk identical to the original, ready to install. It already has been partitioned and formatted to be identical to the original.

The web logs are kept in /logs, and a partition made up of an entire disk is mounted there. The file system mounted on the /logs mount point is /dev/dsk/c1t0d0s6. This file system is a simple UFS partition, not part of a RAID array and not under volume management.

Demonstrate the steps and commands necessary to install your spare disk, which you will use for /logs, until the original disk can be replaced. The new disk will use the name c1t2d0.

SELF TEST ANSWERS

Understanding the Uses of Character (Raw) Disks and Block Disks

1. ☑ **C.** Inodes in a UFS file system describe the attributes of one file.
   ☒ **A** is incorrect because this describes a superblock. **B** is incorrect because this information is not stored in an inode. **D** is incorrect because this describes a boot block.

2. ☑ **D.** This path refers to controller 3, LUN 0, target 0, slice 0 (the first partition).
   ☒ **A** and **B** are incorrect because they are invalid device names. **C** is incorrect because it refers to the second partition (partition 1).

3. ☑ **B.** When referring to a location to create a file system, use the character (raw) device name.
   ☒ **A** is incorrect because it refers to the block device, which cannot be used with the newfs command. **C** is incorrect because the device name is not a disk. **D** is incorrect because this device name is fictitious.

4. ☑ **B.** Once you run out of inodes in a file system, there is no easy way to create more. This is the best option.
   ☒ **A** is incorrect because the newfs command can create only a new file system. It cannot create more inodes on an existing file system. **C** is incorrect because this will not solve the problem, and **D** is incorrect because the tunefs command cannot increase the number of inodes.

5. ☑ **D.** This is the only way to recover from a bad superblock. Specifying an alternate superblock restores the primary superblock.
   ☒ **A** is incorrect because fsck will not be able to check the file system without your intervention. **B** is incorrect because the devfsadm command does not fix superblocks. **C** is incorrect because the file system cannot be used until the superblock is repaired—quite a serious problem!

Adding New Device Configuration Information Without a Reboot of Solaris

6. ☑ **C.** This is the quickest way to accomplish the task.
   ☒ **A** is incorrect because you have to reboot the system, and this is not the quickest way to recognize a new disk. **B** is incorrect because it also requires a system reboot.

D is incorrect because the steps are out of order. The disk has to be attached before devfsadm will work.

7. ☑ **A.** The *-v* option creates verbose output from the devfsadm command.
    ☒ **B, C,** and **D** are incorrect because they do not specify verbose output.

8. ☑ **D.** On systems without hot-pluggable capability, you need to shut down the system entirely before adding new disks or other devices.
    ☒ **A** is incorrect because adding a disk to a running system could damage it. **B** is incorrect because the system is still running. **C** is incorrect because the steps are out of order, plus the system is not shut down when the disk is inserted.

9. ☑ **D.** Most Sun systems that use IDE disks can also use SCSI disks, if you install a SCSI host adapter card.
    ☒ **A** is incorrect because there is a way to make a SCSI disk work with the system. **B** is incorrect because formatting the disk doesn't solve the problem. The SCSI disk would still need some way to communicate with the Ultra 10. **C** is incorrect because there is no such thing as an IDE-to-SCSI converter.

LAB ANSWER

1. First, stop all processes that might be writing to the /logs partition. Because this partition was being used for web server logs, you'd need to stop your web server processes. You don't want any data being written when you are changing disks. Check to see that the mount point is no longer in use with the fuser command:

    ```
    # fuser -c /logs
    /logs:
    ```

2. Unmount the /logs partition:

    ```
    # umount /dev/dsk/c1t0d0s6
    ```

3. Insert the new disk. This is a hot-swappable disk system, so no rebooting or shutdown is necessary.

4. Run the devfsadm command to recognize the new disk:

    ```
    # devfsadm -c disk
    ```

5. Mount the new disk's file system onto the /logs mount point:

    ```
    # mount /dev/dsk/c1t2d0s6 /logs
    ```

6. Start up the web server processes that were writing to /logs.

7. Correct the /etc/vfstab file to reflect the change. If you forget this step, the previous (bad) partition will be mounted on /logs the next time you reboot. Here is the corrected line from that file:

```
/dev/dsk/c1t2d0s6  /dev/rdsk/c1t2d0s6  /logs  ufs  1  no  -
```

Solaris™

SUN® CERTIFIED SYSTEM ADMINISTRATOR

12

Working with the Format Command

CERTIFICATION OBJECTIVES

T he process of preparing a hard disk for storing data can be broken into three steps: low-level formatting, partitioning, and high-level formatting. *Low-level formatting* establishes the tracks and sectors on the disk; most of the time, this step is already done for you at the factory. *Partitioning* lays out where file systems will reside on your disk, dividing the disk into areas called *partitions* or *slices*. *High-level formatting* creates the file system in which the operating system will store data. In Solaris, the format command is used to do low-level formatting and partitioning.

CERTIFICATION OBJECTIVE 12.01

Using the format Command

You can use the format utility to perform low-level formatting, partitioning, and several other tasks. It allows you to label, repair, analyze, and scrub data from a disk. This utility works only on SCSI, IDE, and Fiber Channel disks that are directly seen by Solaris. It will not work on disk drives, CD-ROM drives, or tape drives, and it will not work with hardware RAID storage systems or with virtual disks managed by RAID software.

When invoking the format utility from the Solaris command line, you can use several options on the command line. Table 12-1 shows the more common options and what they do.

These options are specified on the command line, after the format command. Exercise 12-1 shows how to specify options to the format command.

exam
⏱atch

It's important to be familiar with the common options for the format utility and know what they do. Make sure you've practiced using the format command with the various options. Sometimes on the exam, you'll be given a command with a long string of options, and you'll be asked what it will do when it's run. Having hands-on experience with the options will help you answer these questions correctly.

TABLE 12-1	-d disk-name	Specifies which disk to work with. This disk name should be in the format *cXtXdX*. If you don't specify this option, a list of disks found in the system will be generated, and you can choose one by its number in the list.
Options for the format Command	-f command-file	To use this option, you must create a text file containing all the commands you want to run in the format utility. This is great if you are doing repetitive tasks on multiple disks, since you only have to do it once, create the command file, and then run with this option from then on.
	-l log-file	Creates a log of your entire session while you work in the format utility. You must specify the name of the log file to create.
	-m	Enables more detailed error messages within the program. Use this option if you're getting an error message and you need more information about what's going on.
	-M	Enables diagnostic messages in addition to more detailed error messages (such as the -m option).

EXERCISE 12-1

Using Options with the format Command

1. Run the format command to perform tasks on the disk c4t2d0. Use the options to specify the disk name and to create a log file called log.txt.

```
# format -d c4t2d0 -l log.txt
```

exam

Ⓦatch

Make sure you do not try to use the format command with disks that are under the control of RAID software such as Solstice DiskSuite or Veritas Volume Manager. These disks will be listed in the format utility, but changing the partitions or performing other tasks on these disks will give unpredictable results. Use the RAID software to change disk or slice parameters instead.

CERTIFICATION OBJECTIVE 12.02

Using the Menu Selections for the format Command

Once inside the format utility, you navigate through a series of menus and submenus to perform tasks on a disk. When typing a command, you can use abbreviations to speed the process. For example, to specify the partition command from the main menu, you can simply type **p** and press ENTER instead of spelling out the whole word. If more than one command starts with the same letter (such as disk and defect), you must spell out the command with enough letters to distinguish between them.

At any prompt, you may type a question-mark symbol (?) to get help. If you are at a menu prompt, this action displays a list of available menu commands. If you are at another type of prompt, it displays a brief description of the type of input that is appropriate.

Many prompts in the format utility have default answers, which show up in brackets at the end of a prompt. If the default answer is what you want, you can simply press ENTER without typing out the answer. The following is an example of a prompt with a default answer:

```
Enter partition id tag[root]:
```

Pressing ENTER at this prompt would be the same as typing **root** and pressing ENTER, because it's the default answer shown in the brackets.

In every menu, you'll see the option *!<cmd>*. This means that you can enter a Solaris shell command and immediately return to the format utility. To do this, enter the exclamation mark (!), then the command name. The following is an example of running an ls *-l* command from within the format utility:

```
format>> !ls -l
total 16
-rw-rw-r--   1 root      sys           5152 Apr 12 16:18 ps_data

[Hit Return to continue]
```

After entering the format command and choosing a disk to work with, the main menu appears, as shown next.

```
FORMAT MENU:
        disk       - select a disk
        type       - select (define) a disk type
        partition  - select (define) a partition table
        current    - describe the current disk
        format     - format and analyze the disk
        repair     - repair a defective sector
        label      - write label to the disk
        analyze    - surface analysis
        defect     - defect list management
        backup     - search for backup labels
        verify     - read and display labels
        save       - save new disk/partition definitions
        inquiry    - show vendor, product and revision
        volname    - set 8-character volume name
        !<cmd>     - execute <cmd>, then return
        quit
```

This menu displays all the major tasks you can perform with the format utility. Let's look at each of these in detail.

The disk Command

The Disk menu item allows you to switch the current disk, since you can perform tasks on only one disk at a time. It displays a list of disks on the system and prompts you to pick a disk to make current. This is the same list that is displayed when you start the format utility without the *-d* option. The list includes all the disks in your system that are seen by the operating system.

To select a disk, type the number in the list that appears next to the disk name you want to select. After you enter the number of the disk you want, the main menu reappears. Here is an example of the disk command:

```
format>> disk
AVAILABLE DISK SELECTIONS:
        0. c0t0d0 <N18G cyl 7506 alt 2 hd 19 sec 248>
           /sbus@1f,0/SUNW,fas@e,8800000/sd@0,0
        1. c0t1d0 <N9.0G cyl 4924 alt 2 hd 27 sec 133>
           /sbus@1f,0/SUNW,fas@e,8800000/sd@1,0
Specify disk (enter its number)[0]:
```

The type Command

Every disk must have a disk type that Solaris will know how to use. The disk type specifies the disk's interface type (SCSI or Fiber Channel), its geometry, and its speed. Most of the time, the type of disk is detected automatically. If it's not, or if you're using a nonstandard disk, you might have to specify the disk type using this command. To add a disk type to the list of known types, use the save command, discussed in the section "The save Command" later in this chapter. Invoking the type command displays a list of known disk types from which to choose. These disk types can be viewed and modified in the /etc/format.dat file.

The partition Command

This menu item brings up a submenu in which you can create or modify partitions or slices on your disk. This command is covered in more detail later in the chapter, in the section "The Numbers (0–7)."

The current Command

The current command displays the disk you've selected to work with, either on entering the format utility or with the disk command. The current command displays the disk device name, the disk geometry, and the pathname to the device. The following shows an example of the current command:

```
format>> current
Current Disk = c0t1d0
<N9.0G cyl 4924 alt 2 hd 27 sec 133>
/SBUS@1F,0/SUNW,FAS@E,8800000/SD@1,0
```

The format Command

The format command performs a low-level format of a disk. Disks rarely need this format because they come from the factory preformatted. One of the only reasons to run this command is if the disk is having problems and is in need of repair. Using this command to reformat your disk takes a considerable amount of time. Depending on the size of the disk, it could take anywhere from one to three hours, and this type of format can't be interrupted once it's started.

Once the format is complete, the format command automatically begins verifying your disk, checking the disk surface for defects. Any defects found on the disk will be added to the defect list and will not be used for storing data. The defect list is explained later in the chapter, in the section "The defect Command." Be warned: formatting destroys all data on the disk! An example using the format command is shown here:

```
format>> format
Ready to format.  Formatting cannot be interrupted
and takes 93 minutes (estimated). Continue? y
Beginning format. The current time is Fri Apr 13 14:25:38 2001

Formatting...
done

Verifying media…
        pass 0 - pattern = 0xc6dec6de
    4923/26/7

        pass 1 - pattern = 0x6db6db6d
    4923/26/7

Total of 0 defective blocks repaired.
```

The repair Command

The repair command repairs a specific sector on the disk. If you know that a particular sector on the disk is bad, you can repair it directly with this command. You might become aware of defective sectors when you run a surface analysis on the disk with the analyze command, or if you begin seeing error messages concerning a certain portion of the disk on a running system. The following output shows an example of such an error message. This particular example indicates that block 178 could be bad:

```
WARNING: /io-unit@f,e0200000/sbi@0,0/QLGC,isp@1,10000/sd@3,0 (sd33):
  Error for command 'read' Error Level: Retryable
  Requested Block 126, Error Block: 178
  Sense Key: Media Error
  Vendor 'SEAGATE':
  ASC = 0x11 (unrecovered read error), ASCQ = 0x0, FRU = 0x0
```

The label Command

Every disk has a special area set aside for storing information about the disk's controller, geometry, and slices. This information is called a *disk label* or a *volume table of contents (VTOC)*. After you're done making changes to a disk's partitions and other information, you must run the label command to write these changes to the disk. If you do not label the disk, your changes will not be saved.

Each of these commands, especially the label command, is important to know for the exam. Practice the commands to make sure you know exactly what they do and when to use them. The exam sometimes asks questions regarding which command to use to perform a particular task.

The analyze Command

The analyze command displays the Analyze submenu, from which you can perform a series of tests to check for bad areas of a disk. Some of the available tests destroy or corrupt a disk's current data; others leave the data intact. Here is the Analyze submenu:

```
format>> analyze

ANALYZE MENU:
        read      - read only test     (doesn't harm SunOS)
        refresh   - read then write    (doesn't harm data)
        test      - pattern testing    (doesn't harm data)
        write     - write then read        (corrupts data)
        compare   - write, read, compare (corrupts data)
        purge     - write, read, write    (corrupts data)
        verify    - write entire disk, then verify (corrupts data)
        print     - display data buffer
        setup     - set analysis parameters
        config    - show analysis parameters
        !<cmd>    - execute <cmd> , then return
        quit
```

The first seven commands (read, refresh, test, write, compare, purge, and verify) all run tests on the disk, reading and/or writing data to check the integrity of the disk's blocks. Sometimes, you might know which disk blocks are causing problems, or you want to test only a particular range of blocks. If this is the case, you can use the setup command to alter how each test will be performed.

When you run the setup command, you answer a series of questions, through which you can give a range of blocks to test (or test the entire disk), specify how many passes the test will run, specify whether defective blocks will be repaired, and specify other test parameters. At the end of each question is a pair of brackets with the default answer to the question. If the default answer is what you want, you simply press ENTER instead of typing the answer.

To view the current parameters for the tests, you can use the config command. The following output shows an example of the setup process. In this example, we want to test and repair only blocks 444431 through 444488:

```
analyze>> setup
Analyze entire disk[no]?
Enter starting block number[0, 0/0/0]: 444431
Enter ending block number[35368271, 7505/18/247]: 444488
Loop continuously[no]?
Enter number of passes[2]: 1
Repair defective blocks[yes]?
Stop after first error[no]?
Use random bit patterns[no]?
Enter number of blocks per transfer[58, 0/0/58]:
Verify media after formatting[yes]?
Enable extended messages[no]?
Restore defect list[yes]?
Restore disk label[yes]?
```

EXERCISE 12-2

Using the analyze/verify Command

The verify command in the Analyze submenu writes data in every sector on the disk and then verifies that data to check for bad sectors. This exercise walks you through this process.

 1. Become superuser and run the format utility, specifying a disk on the command line:

```
# format -d c0t1d0
```

 2. Type **analyze** to enter the Analyze submenu:

```
format>> analyze

ANALYZE MENU:
        read      - read only test    (doesn't harm SunOS)
        refresh   - read then write   (doesn't harm data)
        test      - pattern testing   (doesn't harm data)
        write     - write then read      (corrupts data)
```

```
compare  - write, read, compare (corrupts data)
purge    - write, read, write   (corrupts data)
verify   - write entire disk, then verify (corrupts data)
print    - display data buffer
setup    - set analysis parameters
config   - show analysis parameters
!<cmd>   - execute <cmd> , then return
quit
```

3. Choose the Verify option from the Analyze submenu, and type y to continue:

```
format>> verify
Ready to verify (will corrupt data). This takes a long time,
but is interruptible with CTRL-C. Continue? y
```

The defect Command

Every hard disk has a number of defective areas in which data cannot be reliably stored. At the factory, tests are performed on the disk, and a list of these defective areas is stored on the disk in the last two disk cylinders. This list is called a *defect list*. There can be hundreds or thousands of bad blocks on a disk; this is completely normal! As the disk is used, the disk controller might discover more bad blocks on the disk, in which case the controller can be told to add more defective blocks to the defect list. This list of newly discovered bad blocks is called the *grown defects list*.

The defect command brings up a submenu, through which you can view the details of the defects on a disk. Here is this submenu:

```
format>> defect

DEFECT MENU:
      primary  - extract manufacturer's defect list
      grown    - extract the grown defects list
      both     - extract both primary and grown defects lists
      print    - display defect list
      dump     - dump defect list to file
      !<cmd>   - execute <cmd>, then return
      quit
```

The first three commands (primary, grown, and both) select the defect list(s) you're interested in examining. The primary list is the list created by the manufacturer of the disk, and the grown list is the list of bad sectors found since the disk has been in operation. The both option selects both lists together. Once you've selected a list, you can use the print command to display it or the dump command to write the list to a file. Using the dump command prompts you for a filename to use for the list.

The backup Command

All disks have two copies of the disk label stored on them. If the primary label becomes corrupted, it can sometimes be restored with the backup label. You perform this task with the backup command.

The verify Command

The verify command displays the contents of the disk label or VTOC. The disk label includes the volume name (if your disk has one), the disk geometry, and the partition layout on the disk. The same information can be displayed with the prtvtoc command in Solaris. The following shows an example using the verify command:

```
format>> verify
Primary label contents:
Volume name = < <N        >>
ascii name  = <N18G cyl 7506 alt 2 hd 19 sec 248>
pcyl        = 7508
ncyl        = 7506
acyl        =    2
nhead       =   19
nsect       =  248
Part        Tag    Flag    Cylinders        Size          Blocks
  0        root    wm      0 -    86     200.17MB      (87/0/0)      409944
  1         var    wm     87 -   173     200.17MB      (87/0/0)      409944
  2      backup    wm      0 - 7505      16.86GB    (7506/0/0) 35368272
  3        swap    wu    174 -   507     768.46MB     (334/0/0)  1573808
  4 unassigned    wm      0                   0        (0/0/0)           0
  5 unassigned    wm      0                   0        (0/0/0)           0
  6         usr    wm    508 - 7505      15.72GB    (6998/0/0) 32974576
  7 unassigned    wm      0                   0        (0/0/0)           0
```

The save Command

The save command adds the current disk's specifications and partition table to the list of known disk types. It prompts you for a filename to add to, the default being format.dat in the current directory. If you want to add to the system's known disk types, specify the file /etc/format.dat.

The inquiry Command

The inquiry command shows information about the disk, such as the vendor, the product code, and the revision number. Here is an example:

```
format>> inquiry
Vendor:    IBM
Product:   DDRS39130SUN9.0G
Revision:  S98E
```

The volname Command

The volname command gives the disk a unique volume name. The volume name is written to the disk label with the disk's other information, such as its geometry and its partition information. Disks don't need volume names in Solaris, and disks don't have them by default. If you give your disks volume names, it can be easier to pick the correct disk out of a list because the disk will have a name that's meaningful to you. For example, *Disk8* might be easier to recognize than *c3t3d0*.

When entering a volume name with the volname command, remember to use double quotes ("") around the name. The following example shows a list of disks in the format command, when the disks have volume names. The names in the example are Int2G, Int9G, and Ext2G.

```
format>> disk

AVAILABLE DISK SELECTIONS:
       0. c0t0d0 <N2.1G cyl 2733 alt 2 hd 19 sec 80>   Int2G
          /sbus@1f,0/espdma@e,8400000/esp@e,8800000/sd@0,0
       1. c0t1d0 <N9.0G cyl 4924 alt 2 hd 27 sec 133>   Int9G
          /sbus@1f,0/espdma@e,8400000/esp@e,8800000/sd@1,0
       2. c0t2d0 <N2.1G cyl 2733 alt 2 hd 19 sec 80>   Ext2G
          /sbus@1f,0/espdma@e,8400000/esp@e,8800000/sd@2,0
```

The quit Command

The quit command quits the format utility and returns you to your Solaris command prompt.

FROM THE CLASSROOM

What's the Best Way to Completely Erase a Disk?

At times you might need to remove data from a disk, such as when the disk is being reused, sold, or decommissioned. One example is web site or application hosting, in which case a customer might decide to upgrade to a different machine or a newer type of storage. As the service provider, you would want to be able to reuse that disk for a new customer. However, it's important to make sure that the old customer's data is no longer on those disks! Another example is a department of a large company that wants to sell old disks to a different unit inside the company or to an outside party. This requires you to ensure that all the division's or company's data is completely removed from the disks.

The rm -*rf* or newfs commands are not sufficient for this task because they do not remove data from the disk. These commands make the data less easily accessible, but it is still physically there. The only way to completely erase data from a disk is to write data in its place on the disk. One of the best ways to do this is to use the verify command, in the analyze submenu, within the format utility. The verify command will write data into every disk sector twice and then restore the original disk label. Writing data into every sector on the disk ensures that no data remains accessible·on the disk if the disk should fall into the wrong hands. This process is commonly called *scrubbing* a disk.

—*Bret Sanders, SCSA, MCSE*

CERTIFICATION OBJECTIVE 12.03

Using the Menu Selections for the partition Subcommand Under the format Command

The most common use of the format utility is partitioning disks, and the Partition submenu is where you will probably spend most of your time while using the utility.

To review: Disks are divided into partitions, or slices, that contain file systems. Each slice is either used as *swap space* or mounted somewhere onto a *mount point* in the file tree, such as /var or /export/home. Figure 12-1 shows an example of slices on a disk.

It's up to you how many slices you create. In Solaris, you can create a minimum of one and a maximum of eight slices. Slice number two, however, is almost always reserved to include *all* the cylinders of a disk, so that all the cylinders can be referenced as one unit. This leaves slices 0, 1, and 3 through 7 to use for data partitions.

Opinions differ concerning the best partitioning scheme, but it depends on your system's intended purpose. Table 12-2 shows the common partitions and their typical uses.

FIGURE 12-1

Slices on a disk

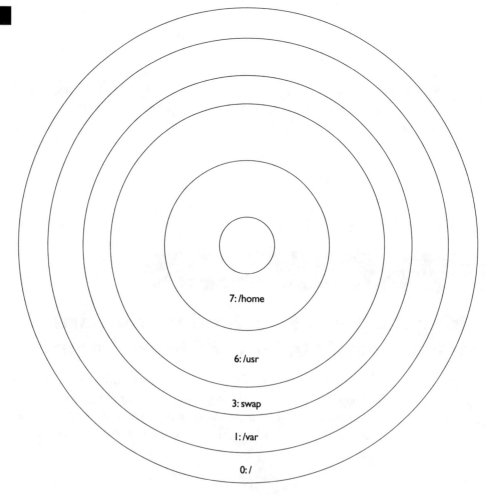

7: /home

6: /usr

3: swap

1: /var

0: /

TABLE 12-2	Common Disk Slices
/ (root)	Typically slice 0. This is the only required slice on a boot disk. It holds the crucial system files that boot and run the system.
/usr	Typically slice 6. Contains Solaris system files as well as other files specific to the system. If this is not made a separate slice, it will be a subdirectory in the root slice.
/opt	Typically slice 5. Many choose to install optional software for the system in this slice. If this is not made a separate slice, it will be a subdirectory in the root slice.
/var	Typically slice 1. Contains "varying" files—that is, active files that grow and shrink in size. Most of the system's log files are contained here, as well as users' incoming mail. If this is not made a separate slice, it will be a subdirectory in the root slice.
swap	Typically slice 3. The swap slice is for virtual memory. Historically, the swap slice was used when the system needed more RAM than was available. The system would use this disk slice for temporary memory until enough physical RAM was cleared. More recent versions of Solaris use swap space, even when it's not needed, to optimize memory usage.
/export/home	Typically slice 7. Where users' home directories are stored. Some people prefer home directories to be in /home or /usr/home, but in Solaris the default location is /export/home.

on the job

Sizing your slices when installing Solaris can be tricky, but the installer will recommend sizes for you if you choose Auto-Layout. Once you choose the partitions you want to create, the installer will create a recommended partition table with large enough slices to hold the data for your Solaris install. You can then customize this layout to change the names, sizes, or locations of your slices. Experience shows that having separate root, swap, /var, and /usr partitions works well. To avoid having separate /export/home and /opt partitions (which can run out of space), you can make /usr very large to hold home directories in /usr/home instead of /export/home, and software in /usr/local instead of /opt. I also like to have my log and mail files in a separate /var partition, separated from the root partition, so that logs and mail files cannot fill up the root partition. Other people prefer a single-slice disk layout, with the only partition being the root partition. With this layout, you'll never worry about running out of space on a particular partition, unless your disk is completely full. With experience, you'll develop your own method of creating and sizing your slices; there are many ways to handle these tasks.

When you enter the partition command from the main menu, you get the Partition submenu, shown in the following example. Each of these menu items is described in more detail in the following sections.

```
PARTITION MENU:
        0       - change `0' partition
        1       - change `1' partition
        2       - change `2' partition
        3       - change `3' partition
        4       - change `4' partition
        5       - change `5' partition
        6       - change `6' partition
        7       - change `7' partition
    select - select a predefined table
    modify - modify a predefined partition table
    name   - name the current table
    print  - display the current table
    label  - write partition map and label to the disk
    !<cmd> - execute <cmd>, then return
    quit
```

The Numbers (0–7)

The first eight items in this menu (the numbers 0–7) are for defining a particular slice. To define slice 0, you'd enter the number **0** and specify that slice's parameters. Once you've selected a number, you can enter the partition ID tag, its permission flags, its starting cylinder, and its size.

The Partition ID Tag

Partition IDs are no longer used by Solaris but are still included in the format utility for convention. The partition ID on a slice can be set to one of ten values: *unassigned, boot, backup, root, swap, usr, var, home, stand,* or *alternates.* Don't be confused about partition IDs; you can set them to whatever you want, and you can mount any partition anywhere you want. These IDs do *not* control where a partition is mounted in the file tree, even though they can be set to *root, usr,* or *var.* Even a partition that has the ID of *unassigned* can be used with no problem.

Permission Flags

Like partition IDs, permission flags on slices are included for historical reasons as well. Solaris does not use them. These are the valid permissions and their meanings:

- **wm**   Read/write, mountable
- **wu**   Read/write, unmountable
- **rm**   Read-only, mountable
- **ru**   Read-only, unmountable

Once again, these permission flags can be set to anything—it doesn't matter.

Starting Cylinder

This is the position of the starting point for the slice. Usually, the first partition starts at cylinder 0. Partitions should never overlap (except for slice 2), so it's very important to enter the numbers carefully! If you're creating a slice other than the first, the starting cylinder should be one cylinder higher than the ending cylinder of the previous slice. For example, if slice 0 used cylinders 0 to 57, slice 1 should start at cylinder 58.

Partition Size

The partition-size parameter sets the ending point on the disk where a slice stops, defining its size. When you're prompted for the size of the slice you're creating, you have several options of how to respond. You can give your answer in blocks, cylinders, megabytes, or gigabytes. Most of the time, it's convenient to respond in megabytes or gigabytes because these units are most likely what you've used to plan out your slices. Your response must consist of a number and a letter to specify which unit of measure you're using. For example, 100m means 100 megabytes, and 234498b means 234,498 disk blocks.

The select Command

The select command lets you choose a predefined partition table to apply to your disk. Sometimes, this can be faster than specifying parameters for each slice individually. Predefined partition tables are kept in the /etc/format.dat file. After selecting a predefined table, you must apply it to the disk with the label command.

The modify Command

The modify command displays a list of predefined partition tables, which you can use as templates to create a new partition table for your disk. The most common template, or *partition base,* is the all free hog template, which, when selected, creates one partition that occupies all disk space not used by other partitions. This free hog partition will grow and shrink as you change the sizes of the other partitions. When you choose All Free Hog, you start the partitioning session with a blank partition table. All partition values (except partition 2) will be set to 0. This way, no preexisting partition values will interfere with your new partition values.

Partition a Disk Using the All Free Hog Table

1. Become a superuser and run the format utility, specifying the disk on which you'd like to work:

   ```
   # format -d c0t1d0
   ```

2. Type the partition command at the format prompt:

   ```
   format>> partition
   PARTITION MENU:
               0        - change '0' partition
               1        - change '1' partition
               2        - change '2' partition
               3        - change '3' partition
               4        - change '4' partition
               5        - change '5' partition
               6        - change '6' partition
               7        - change '7' partition
           select - select a predefined table
           modify - modify a predefined partition table
           name   - name the current table
           print  - display the current table
           label  - write partition map and label to the disk
           !<cmd> - execute <cmd>, then return
           quit
   partition>>
   ```

3. Use the modify command to display the list of partition base tables:

   ```
   partition>> modify
   Select partitioning base:
           0. Current partition table (original)
           1. All Free Hog
   Choose base (enter number) [0]?
   ```

4. Choose the All Free Hog base and type **y** to continue:

```
Choose base (enter number) [0]? 1
Part       Tag     Flag   Cylinders     Size      Blocks
   0       root    wm     0             0         (0/0/0)              0
   1       swap    wu     0             0         (0/0/0)              0
   2       backup  wu     0 - 4923      8.43GB    (4924/0/0) 17682084
   3 unassigned    wm     0             0         (0/0/0)              0
   4 unassigned    wm     0             0         (0/0/0)              0
   5 unassigned    wm     0             0         (0/0/0)              0
   6       usr     wm     0             0         (0/0/0)              0
   7 unassigned    wm     0             0         (0/0/0)              0
Do you wish to continue creating a new partition
table based on above table[yes]? y
```

5. Select one partition to be the free hog partition:

```
Free Hog partition[6]? 6
```

6. Specify the size of each partition in megabytes, and make partition number five 2GB in size:

```
Enter size of partition '0' [0b, 0c, 0.00mb, 0.00gb]:
Enter size of partition '1' [0b, 0c, 0.00mb, 0.00gb]:
Enter size of partition '3' [0b, 0c, 0.00mb, 0.00gb]:
Enter size of partition '4' [0b, 0c, 0.00mb, 0.00gb]:
Enter size of partition '5' [0b, 0c, 0.00mb, 0.00gb]: 2gb
Enter size of partition '7' [0b, 0c, 0.00mb, 0.00gb]:

Part       Tag     Flag   Cylinders     Size      Blocks
   0       root    wm     0             0         (0/0/0)              0
   1       swap    wu     0             0         (0/0/0)              0
   2       backup  wu     0 - 4923      8.43GB    (4924/0/0) 17682084
   3 unassigned    wm     0             0         (0/0/0)              0
   4 unassigned    wm     0             0         (0/0/0)              0
   5 unassigned    wm     0 - 1168      2.00GB    (1169/0/0)  4197879
   6       usr     wm     1169 - 4923   6.43GB    (3755/0/0) 13484205
   7 unassigned    wm     0             0         (0/0/0)              0
```

7. Type **y** to confirm to make this the current partition table. Then type a name for the modified table:

```
Okay to make this the current partition table[yes]? y
Enter table name (remember quotes): "Big5Partition"
```

8. Type y to label the disk with the current partition table:

```
Ready to label disk, continue? y
```

The All Free Hog partition table could be referenced in the exam! Be sure to understand how to use it. Practice using the table to completely understand what it does and why it can save you time in partitioning your disks.

The name Command

Once you have modified your partition table, you can save it for future use on other disks. Before you save it with the save command, you must name it with the name command.

The print Command

The print command displays the current partition table. This is not necessarily the partition table stored on the disk, but the current table with which you are working. This partition table will not necessarily match the actual partition table on the disk until you use the label command to write it to the disk.

The label Command

The label command writes the current partition table to the disk. This information is stored in the disk label or VTOC.

SCENARIO & SOLUTION	
You see error messages in the log about a bad block. What should you do?	Run the repair command to repair or remap the bad block.
You need to create a partition that takes the remainder of the space on disk. How do you go about it?	Use the All Free Hog partition base table to create this partition.
You need to write the update VTOC on the disk. What do you do?	Use the label command.

CERTIFICATION SUMMARY

The format system administration tool prepares a disk for use in Solaris. The superuser runs the format command to divide the disk into slices, as well as to analyze and repair disks. Common options to invoke the format utility include *-d*, which specifies a disk to work with, and *-l*, to create a log file of all commands performed while in the utility.

Once slices have been defined for the disk with the partition command, the partition table must be written to the disk with the label command within the format utility. The label command stores the current partition table to the volume table of contents (VTOC), also called the disk label, which is stored on the first sector of the disk. The disk label can be read with the prtvtoc command at a Solaris command prompt or with the verify command within the format utility. The save command can be used to store partition layouts for use on other disks in the future. The partition layouts are stored in the /etc/format.dat file.

When in the Partition submenu, use the numbered menu items to alter partition specifications. The modify command prompts you to select a partition template or base to start with when creating a partition table. The most common partition base is the All Free Hog base, with which you specify the sizes of partitions, and the free hog partition will occupy the remaining space on the disk. You can use the select command to employ a predefined partition table, which you would apply to the disk with the label command.

✓ TWO-MINUTE DRILL

Using the format Command

❑ The format utility divides the disk into slices, or partitions.

❑ The format utility performs low-level formatting and repair operations on disks.

❑ The *-d* option specifies a disk with which to work.

Using the Menu Selections for the format Command

❑ The disk command specifies a new disk on which to work.

❑ The format command performs a low-level format of the disk.

❑ The analyze command performs tests on the disk.

❑ The partition command brings you to the Partition submenu, in which you can create or modify disk slices.

Using the Menu Selections for the partition Subcommand Under the format Command

❑ The numbered menu items specify that slice's size and position on the disk.

❑ The select command allows you to choose a predefined partition table to work with.

❑ The print command prints the current partition table to the screen.

❑ The label command writes the volume table of contents to the disk.

SELF TEST

The following questions will help you measure your understanding of the material presented in this chapter. Read all the choices carefully because there might be more than one correct answer. Choose all correct answers for each question.

Using the format Command

1. Which of the following commands starts the format utility, working on the disk c0t0d0?

    A. `format c0t0d0`

    B. `format -disk c0t0d0`

    C. `format /dev/dsk/c0t0d0`

    D. `format -d c0t0d0`

2. Which of the following commands starts the format utility while creating a log file called format.log?

    A. `format -log format.log`

    B. `format -l format.log`

    C. `format -m format.log`

    D. `format -x format.log`

3. You received 50 new disks that need to be formatted identically. What's the easiest way to perform this task with the format utility?

    A. Perform the task manually once, and create a command file. Use the *-f* option with the format utility to perform the same tasks on the other disks.

    B. Because it is an interactive tool, there is no way to automate tasks in the format utility.

    C. Use one of the predefined command files built into the format utility, and run format *-auto* to format the disks.

    D. Specify a master disk in the format utility and then use a partition base to automatically format the other disks.

Using the Menu Selections for the format Command

4. Your system has 45 disks installed in it, and the list of disks is several pages long. What can you do to make the correct disk easier to choose from the list?

   A. Use the flash command to blink the LED on the disk you want.

   B. Use the verify command to make sure you've selected the right disk.

   C. Give each disk a unique disk type in the format.dat file.

   D. Give each disk a meaningful name with the volname command.

5. What does the repair command do in the main menu of the format utility?

   A. Stops a disk completely for maintenance

   B. Displays several options for troubleshooting the SCSI device

   C. Repairs a specific block on the disk

   D. Automatically searches for and repairs bad sectors on the disk

6. You need to completely erase all confidential data from a disk before it's reused for another application. What is the best way to accomplish this task?

   A. Use the verify command within the Analyze submenu in the format utility.

   B. Use the newfs command.

   C. Use the fsck command

   D. Use the rm -rf command.

Using the Menu Selections for the partition
Subcommand Under the format Command

7. Which of these is not part of the disk label?

   A. The disk's volume name

   B. The disk's geometry

   C. The partition table for the disk

   D. The disk's defect list

8. Which slice is always used to reference all the cylinders on the disk?

   A. Slice 0

   B. Slice 1

   C. Slice 2

   D. Slice 8

9. When partitioning your disk, which partition ID do you need to assign to the swap partition?

   A. root

   B. unassigned

   C. swap

   D. None of the above

LAB QUESTION

On the console of your print server, you begin to see the following message, displayed multiple times:

```
WARNING: /io-unit@f,e0200000/sbi@0,0/QLGC,isp@1,10000/sd@4,0 (sd44):
Error for command 'read' Error Level: Retryable
Requested Block 1346, Error Block: 1399
Sense Key: Media Error
Vendor 'IBM':
ASC = 0x11 (unrecovered read error), ASCQ = 0x0, FRU = 0x0
```

The disk indicated in the error is your secondary data disk, not the root disk. The disk is made up of one partition, mounted on /usr/local/data, and its device name is c0t1d0.

Outline the steps necessary to repair this disk and restore service to your users.

SELF TEST ANSWERS

Using the format Command

1. ☑ D. This is the correct syntax for the command. The *-d* option is necessary to specify a disk, and it is followed by the disk name, in the form *c?t?d?*

   ☒ A, B, and C are incorrect because they are not in the proper form to start the format utility correctly.

2. ☑ B. The *-l* option specifies that all commands used while in the format utility should be logged to a file. Following the *-l* is the name of the log file, format.log.

   ☒ A, C, and D are incorrect because they will not specify the log file correctly.

3. ☑ A. This is the easiest way to accomplish this task. Formatting the first disk manually allows you to log the commands needed for a command file, which you'll use with the *-f* option to format the other disks.

   ☒ B is incorrect. The format utility can be used interactively or noninteractively. C is incorrect because there are no predefined command files and there is no *-auto* option. D is incorrect because there is no such thing as a master disk in the format utility, and partition bases do not help automate your task.

Using the Menu Selections for the format Command

4. ☑ D. This option is the only one that will help you pick out the correct disk from a list. Next to the disk's device name *(c?t?d?)* is its volume name, helping you determine which disk to choose.

   ☒ A is incorrect because there is no flash command (although such a thing would be handy!). B is incorrect because the verify command displays the disk label and does not give any new information in the disk list. C is incorrect because the disk type will not help you choose a disk.

5. ☑ C. The repair command prompts you for a specific block number to repair on the disk.

   ☒ A, B, and D are incorrect because there are no options that perform these functions.

6. ☑ A. The best option is to use the analyze/verify command within the format utility. This command writes data into every sector of the disk, making older data unrecoverable.

   ☒ B and D are incorrect because the newfs command creates a new file system on the disk but does not actually erase the data. C is incorrect because the fsck command does not erase data.

Using the Menu Selections for the partition Subcommand Under the format Command

7. ☑   **D.** The disk's VTOC contains the volume name, disk geometry, and partition map for the disk. The defect list is stored in a separate place on the disk.

   ☒   **A, B,** and **C** are incorrect because they are all included in the disk label.

8. ☑   **C.** Slice 2 always contains all the cylinders on the disk.

   ☒   **A, B,** and **D** are incorrect because these slices are not normally used for this purpose.

9. ☑   **D.** Partition IDs have no bearing on what the slices do in Solaris, so no partition ID *needs* to be assigned at all. Therefore, a swap partition can be assigned any partition ID.

   ☒   **A, B,** and **C** are incorrect because partition IDs are irrelevant in Solaris.

LAB ANSWER

The first step is to stop any processes using the /usr/local/data partition and notify any users on your system, if necessary. You can see what processes are using files and directories under a mount point with the fuser command, using the *-c* option. You will not be able to unmount the partition until all processes using it are stopped.

```
# fuser -c /usr/local/data
/usr/local/data:
```

1. Unmount the partition:

```
# umount /usr/local/data
```

2. Run the format command and select the disk from the list:

```
# format
Searching for disks...done
AVAILABLE DISK SELECTIONS:
       0. c0t0d0 <N18G cyl 7506 alt 2 hd 19 sec 248>
          /sbus@1f,0/SUNW,fas@e,8800000/sd@0,0
       1. c0t1d0 <N9.0G cyl 4924 alt 2 hd 27 sec 133>
          /sbus@1f,0/SUNW,fas@e,8800000/sd@1,0

Specify disk (enter its number): 1
```

3. Use the repair command to begin repairing the known bad block on the disk:

```
format>> repair
Enter absolute block number of defect: 1399
```

```
Ready to repair defect, continue? y
Repairing block 1399 (18/4/18)...ok.
```

You don't need to reformat the disk or restore data. When you run the repair command, the bad block is added to the growing defects list, and the disk will no longer use that block to store data. If this was the only bad sector on the disk, the problem is solved!

13

Performing Backup and Recovery

O ne of the most important jobs you perform as a system administrator is backing up your systems. If you fail to perform backups, you are relying on the chance that you won't lose any data. One of the most defining moments in the life of a system administrator is when you recover any data that is lost due to hardware failure or accidental deletion, and look like a hero or heroine in the face of management and users.

This chapter covers backup and recovery of Solaris UFS file systems. First, you'll learn about all the tools available to back up Solaris systems. For each one, you'll learn how to back up, list archived files, and restore files to their proper locations. You'll find out how to choose utilities that perform best for certain functions. Then you'll see how to back up and restore complete file systems, including how to restore the root file system in the event of a boot disk crash.

CERTIFICATION OBJECTIVE 13.01

Understanding the Functions of Backup, Archive, and Restore Utilities

This section describes all the commands you can use to back up and restore a system. You'll also learn about the options of each command and the kind of backup and restore for which they are commonly used.

The ufsdump Command

The ufsdump command, together with the ufsrestore command, is the most powerful of all backup options supplied by Sun for its Solaris operating environment. If you're not using any third-party utilities to back up your systems, chances are that you are using these commands to back up your system. These tools were written specifically to back up and restore UFS file systems.

Fortunately, ufsdump is easy to use and supports most tape drives automatically. The command can be included within scripts to back up file systems regularly. The command is also capable of performing full, incremental, and differential backups.

The ufsdump command works by running four passes against the raw file system. The first and second passes scan and estimate the file and directories that will be backed up. On the third and fourth passes, ufsdump goes through each of the files and directories and writes them to the backup media.

The command syntax of ufsdump and the major options and arguments are referenced in Table 13-1 and are as follows:

```
ufsdump <options> <arguments> <files/directories-to-backup>
```

A good example of ufsdump is backing up the /export/home file system that resides on the c0t0d0s6 disk:

```
# umount /export/home
# ufsdump 0uvf /dev/rmt/0 /dev/rdsk/c0t0d0s6
```

The ufsdump command operates on the information contained on the raw disk (for example, /dev/rdsk/c0t0d0s0) and writes it to the backup media. Files can change in memory and not be committed to disk when ufsdump comes along and writes the data. As a result, you might not have a complete backup of the file system.

TABLE 13-1 The ufsdump Command Options and Arguments

Option	Description
0–9	The backup level. Used to indicate either a full backup (0) or levels of incremental backups since the full backup (1–9).
-f dump-file	The dump filename. The device on which the backup will be stored. The default is the first tape drive /dev/rmt/0.
-S	Estimates the amount of space the backup would take on the backup media. Used to determine how many tapes you would need for the backup job. This option prints only the number of bytes the backup is estimated to consume.
-u	Updates the /etc/dumpdates file. This file contains a listing of successful backup jobs on file systems. Useful to determine when a file system has been backed up and the level at which the file system was backed up.
-v	Verify. This verifies the backup media against the original file system. The source file system must be unmounted.
-n	Notify. This option notifies all the operators in the sys group if the ufsdump process requires attention by sending a message to their terminals. Otherwise, warnings are displayed only on the terminal on which the user who invoked ufsdump is logged.

With a busy and rapidly changing file system, you will never have a complete backup. It is therefore wise to either boot the system in single-user mode or unmount the file system on which you are performing a backup. These methods ensure that you have a complete copy of the file system.

When dump level 0 is used in a backup command, it tells the ufsdump command to perform a full backup of the file system. Dump levels 1–9 refer to incremental backups of the file system. For example, you perform a level 0 backup on the first day and a level 1 backup on the second day. When you perform a level 2 backup, ufsdump copies only the files that have changed since the level 1 backup of the second day.

A typical ufsdump backup session looks like this:

```
# ufsdump 0uf /dev/rmt/0 /dev/rdsk/c0t0d0s0
DUMP: Writing 32 Kilobyte records
DUMP: Date of this level 0 dump: Sun May 27 09:54:06 2001
DUMP: Date of last level 0 dump: the epoch
DUMP: Dumping /dev/rdsk/c0t0d0s0 to /dev/rmt/0
DUMP: Mapping (Pass I) [regular files]
DUMP: Mapping (Pass II) [directories]
DUMP: Estimating 20453 blocks (610.56MB).
DUMP: Dumping (Phase III) [directories]
DUMP: Dumping (Phase IV [regular files]
DUMP: Tape rewinding
DUMP: 20451 blocks (610.42MB) on 1 volume at 64 KB/sec
DUMP: DUMP IS DONE
DUMP: Level 0 dump on Sun May 27 10:14:48 2001
#
```

Notice the four passes, the amount of data written, and the time it took to complete the backup.

It is always a good idea to make sure you have enough space on the device before you write to it. Use the ufsdump -S command to first make a dry run of the files you want to back up. If the device is too small to contain the backup, ufsdump takes the tape drive offline and prompts for a new tape. An example of the output of a size estimate looks like this:

```
# ufsdump -S /dev/rdsk/c0t0d0s0
651827200
#
```

The output of the ufsdump -S command is in bytes.

FROM THE CLASSROOM

Incremental vs. Differential Backups

Many people are confused when it comes to deciding whether to implement incremental or differential backup jobs between full backups. The terminology of incremental and differential backups differs among the various software products, so we need to establish what we mean when we talk about incremental and differential backups.

An *incremental backup* backs up only the changes from the last full or incremental backup. An example of this scenario is a Sunday full backup and a Monday incremental backup. On Tuesday, we would perform another incremental backup and back up only the changes that occurred between then and the incremental backup on Monday. The benefits of incremental backups are mostly space and time. Backing up only changes since the last incremental or full backup doesn't take up as much space and doesn't take as long as backing up data for the whole week or even a few days' worth. The disadvantage of incremental backups is that, in the event that you have to do a restore, you have to restore each incremental backup set since the last full backup. If you have a full backup one day and five incremental backups the following five days and, on the sixth day, the hard disk fails, you have to restore the full backup and five sets of incremental tapes.

A *differential backup* is similar to an incremental backup except that a differential backup backs up only the changes since the last full backup. An example of this scenario is a full backup on Sunday, a differential backup on Monday (really just an incremental), and a differential backup on Tuesday, that backs up Monday's changes and well as Tuesday's changes. Wednesday's differential backup captures the Monday, Tuesday, and Wednesday data, and so forth. The benefits of differential backups are that in the event of a restore, you have to restore only the full backup and the last differential backup. This saves time on a restore. The disadvantage of differential backups is that for every differential backup you do, you must back up the same data as the previous differential backup. For example, say that you do a full backup one day a week and six differentials for the rest of the week; on the sixth day, you are backing up six days' worth of changes. This takes up more and more space on the backup media every day and adds to the time of the backup.

The ufsdump implementation of incremental and differential backups is done with the dump-level options. With incremental backups, each backup job gets a higher dump-level number than the previous day's dump level. This ensures that we back up only the data since the last incremental.

(continued)

FROM THE CLASSROOM

	Monday	Tuesday	Wednesday	Thursday	Friday	Saturday	Sunday
Dump level	1	2	3	4	5	6	0

For differential backups, the dump-level number would not change for each differential backup. This ensures that for each differential backup, we copy all the data that is changed since the last full backup. We use 9s for the dump level, just to make sure we don't use a dump-level number that is higher and accidentally perform an incremental backup.

	Monday	Tuesday	Wednesday	Thursday	Friday	Saturday	Sunday
Dump level	9	9	9	9	9	9	0

—Rob Sletten, SCSA, MCSE, CCNA

on the
Job *The ufsdump command backs up file systems and has support for full and incremental backups.*

The ufsrestore Command

The ufsrestore command restores file systems that are backed up using the ufsdump command. One of the main advantages of ufsrestore is that it can be used in interactive mode, which lets a system administrator select files from an archive and extract them in a browser-like fashion in an almost shell-like environment. The syntax and major options for ufsrestore are given in Table 13-2 and shown here:

```
ufsrestore <options> <arguments> <files/directories-to-restore>
```

Listing Archives

You can use ufsrestore with the *-t* options to list the table of contents of an archive. This example lists the table of contents of a tape and the table of contents from an archive file:

```
# ufsrestore -t
```

| TABLE 13-2 | The ufsrestore Command Syntax and Major Options |

Option	Description
-i	Runs an interactive restore.
-x filename	Extracts the named file in a noninteractive restore.
-t	Table of contents; used to list files in a tape or archive file.
-r	Recursive extraction; used to restore file systems recursively. This option is used only when restoring a file system that has been newly created with the newfs command.
-v	Verbose. Prints the name of the file and its inode as it is extracted or listed.
-R	Resume. If you are restoring a file system that spans several tapes, this option allows ufsrestore to start from a checkpoint where it was interrupted.

Specifying just the -t option prints the table of contents from the /dev/rmt/0 tape drive. To print the table of contents from an archive file, use the -f archive-file options together with the list option of -t:

```
# ufsrestore -tf /dump.dmp
```

To list specific files from an archive, add an argument of the path of the file for which you are searching, and use the filename argument at the end of the command:

```
# ufsrestore -tf /dev/rmt/0 /usr/src/app/install
```

Because the archive stores pathname information in the table of contents, you need to specify the absolute pathname in the archive if you want to see only the specific file; otherwise, ufsrestore prints all matching filenames.

Using this additional file argument with ufsrestore in this way also tells you if a certain file you are looking for is located on an archive or tape, so you will be able to use ufsrestore in this way to determine the contents of your backup tapes.

Noninteractive Restores

The first way to perform restores is to specify either the entire archive for extraction or select various files from the ufsrestore command line. Use the -x parameter to extract the named files.

To perform a full extraction from a tape drive into the current working directory, use these options:

```
# ufsrestore -xvf /dev/rmt/0
```

The *-x* with no filename argument extracts the entire archive. The *-v* parameter prints a list of files to the console, and *-f /dev/rmt/0* specifies the tape drive. You will receive messages from ufsrestore similar to this:

```
# ufsrestore -xvf /dev/rmt/0
Verify volume and initialize maps
Media block size is 126
Dump    date: Wed April 18 16:04:21 2001
Dumped from: the epoch
Level 0 dump of an unlisted filesystem on server:/dev/rdsk/c0t0d0s0
Label: none
Extract directories from tape
Initialize symbol table.
Extract requested files
You have not read any volumes yet.
Unless you know which volumes your file(s) are on you should start
with the last volume and work towards the first.
Specify next volume #: 1
extract file ./files?.
Add links
Set directory mode, owner, and times.
set owner/mode for '.'? [yn] n
```

The ufsrestore command is very verbose in its action. During an extraction, ufsrestore prompts you to read in a volume. This is usually the first volume on the tape, which is designated by the number *1*. After the files are extracted, ufsrestore prompts you to set the owner and mode permissions on the directories. Respond with **y** or **n**.

To specify individual filenames from an archive file, use these parameters:

```
# ufsrestore -xvf /dump.dmp /usr/src/app/install
```

This command extracts the filename /usr/src/app/install into the current working directory. You need to specify the absolute pathname in the archive if you want to extract only the specific file; otherwise, ufsrestore extracts all matching filenames.

Interactive Restores

One of the most popular features of ufsrestore is the ability to perform *interactive restores*. With the ufsrestore *-i* option, you can enter a shell-like application in which you can do cd- and ls-type commands to move around the archive directory structure and tag and untag files for extraction. Once you have selected all the files for extraction, you can extract them all at once.

To perform an interactive restore, use the *-i* parameter together with the name of the archive device that contains the archive:

```
ufsrestore -if /dev/rmt/0
ufsrestore >>
```

This command gives you a prompt to continue entering commands.

All the commands and descriptions for an interactive ufsrestore session are given in Table 13-3.

TABLE 13-3	Command	Description
Interactive ufsresore Commands	ls [*directory*]	Lists directory.
	marked [*directory*]	Lists files marked for extraction.
	cd [*directory*]	Changes directory.
	pwd	Prints working directory.
	add [*file*]	Marks a file or directory for extraction.
	delete [*file*]	Unmarks a file or directory for extraction.
	extract	Extracts all marked files.
	setmodes	Sets modes on the directories.
	quit	Exits ufsrestore.
	what	Lists the header of the archive.
	verbose	Sets verbose mode to give additional details of files.
	paginate	Pauses after each screen load of information; useful for long ls lists.
	setpager	Sets pagination commands and options, such as *more*.
	help or ?	Prints a list of commands.

In this interactive ufsrestore session, the /usr/src/app/install file is extracted from the tape drive:

```
# ufsrestore -if /dev/rmt/0
ufsrestore >> ls
.:
 usr/
ufsrestore >> cd usr
ufsrestore >> ls
./usr:
 src/
ufsrestore >> cd src/app

ufsrestore >> ls

./usr/src/app:

 install
ufsrestore >> add install
ufsrestore >> extract
You have not read any volumes yet.
Unless you know which volume your file(s) are on you should start
with the last volume and work towards the first.
Specify next volume #: 1
Mount volume 1
then enter volume name (default: /dev/rmt/0) <enter>
set owner/mode for '.'? [y/n] n
ufsrestore >> quit
#
```

on the
job *The ufsrestore command can list files and directories in an archive, extract files and directories by the command line, and perform interactive restores.*

The tar Command

The tar command stands for *tape archiver* and is probably the most well-known UNIX backup and archiving command. Most software and source code that is written for UNIX systems is packed and distributed in TAR format because it is available on almost every UNIX system.

The tar command is quite easy to use and very similar to other backup commands. The syntax for tar is as follows; the description of the options appears in Table 13-4.

```
tar <options> <arguments> <files/directories-to-backup>
```

Some of the drawbacks of tar are that it cannot act upon raw disks the way ufsdump can. The tar command uses the logical file and directory names, like the ones you access on the system. Furthermore, tar does not have support for transporting user permissions and timestamps of the files. You need to use the chown and chmod commands to reset permissions when you restore files with the tar command.

Creating a tar Archive

Creating a tar archive is easy using the -c option. You copy the /export/home directory to the tape drive in this example:

```
# tar -cvf /dev/rmt/0 /export/home
```

This command uses the -c parameter to create the tar archive, and on the terminal of the user executing the command, it lists all files added to the archive and specifies to send the archive to the tape drive.

TABLE 13-4   The tar Command Options and Arguments

Option	Description
-c	Create. Indicates that you want to create an archive.
-v	Verbose. Prints the name of each file of the archive as it is created, listed, or extracted.
-f filename	The name of the tape device or filename of the backup media to which you want the archive to be written.
-t	Lists the files contained in the archive.
-x	Extracts the files from the archive.
-r	Replaces the named files in the archive.
-u	Update. The files are added if they don't exist already in the archive or if they have been modified since added to the archive.

If you simply want to create an archive file of a directory instead of sending it to the tape drive, you use the *-f <device-name>* parameter and specify a filename. This example tars up a user's home directory and stores it in /backup:

```
# tar -cvf /backup/fred.tar /export/home/fred
a /export/home/fred OK
a /export/home/fred/fred.txt
#
```

Be careful about how you specify the filenames and directories on the command line. If you use relative pathnames (such as export/home/fred/, home/fred, or just fred) instead of absolute pathnames, you will have problems when you extract these files because a relative pathname creates the directory structure from the directory from which you are currently running the extract. For example, if you are already in the /export directory and you extract a tar file that was built using the relative directory of fred, you create the directory structure /export/fred by mistake when you extract the tar file. If you were in the root directory /export/home, however, this would work correctly.

Listing a tar Archive

Use the *-t* option with tar to view a listing of the files in a tar archive. To view the files in the previous example's archive on your home directory, issue the following command:

```
# tar -tvf /backup/fred.tar
tar: blocksize = 4
drwxr-xr-x       0/1        0 April 19 22:25 2001 /export/home/fred
-rw-r--r--       0/1        0 April 27 05:43 2001 /export/home/fred/fred.txt
```

Extracting a tar Archive

Use the *-x* option to extract a tar archive:

```
# tar -xvf /backup/fred.tar
x /export/home/fred, 0 bytes, 0 tape blocks
x /export/home/fred/fred.txt, 10 bytes, 1 tape blocks
```

Be careful where you are in the directory structure when you are extracting a tar file. It is always a good idea to look at the tar file listing with the *-t* command before you extract the file to make sure the directory structure is compatible. tar files can contain relative pathnames of files, which might cause problems.

on the **Job** *The tar command does not support multivolumes on tape drives.*

The cpio Command

The cpio command stands for *copy in and out.* This command is useful for copying file systems from one disk to another. The cpio command is also more similar to ufsdump in that it supports detecting the end of media, such as the end of a tape, and prompts you to insert another tape. The cpio command is also the oldest backup command for UNIX, so most versions of UNIX have it. As the name implies, cpio has the most support for copying the standard output (stdout) to standard input (stdin).

There are some drawbacks to cpio. For example, although cpio is widely distributed on most versions of UNIX, the syntax between UNIX systems could be dissimilar. Command options can widely differ between systems, forcing you to learn the proper syntax for each UNIX system. Another drawback to cpio is that it does not support incremental backups without using additional commands such as find and searching for recently modified files. In addition, cpio is almost entirely driven by using pipes and redirects, thereby increasing the complexity of using the command.

The syntax of cpio and major options are given in Table 13-5 and shown here:

```
cpio <options> <command>
```

TABLE 13-5	Option	Description
The cpio Command Options and Descriptions	-c	Produces ASCII character output necessary for viewing filenames, ensuring cross-UNIX compatibility.
	-d	Creates directories as needed; used to create directories that do not already exist during an extraction.
	-i	Copy-in mode. This parameter causes listing or extraction of an archive.
	-o	Copy-out mode.
	-t	Lists the table of contents on the tape.
	-v	Produces output similar to the ls -l command.

There are two major modes of cpio: copy out and copy in. In copy-out mode, cpio writes something to either a file or a tape and is designated by the *-o* parameter. Copy-in mode is used on an archive file or tape to list or extract the archive's contents and is designated by the *-i* parameter.

Copying Files to Tape with cpio

The first command you need to use involves creating archives, whether on tape or as a disk file. The first example copies all files in a directory to a disk file using the cpio command:

```
# ls | cpio -oc >> /file.backup
```

Because cpio is unable to generate a list of files to back up on its own, you have to use the ls command and pipe the output to cpio. The cpio command then backs up those named files produced from the ls command and writes them to the backup file.

This example copies a directory and all subdirectories and files to tape:

```
# find . -print -depth | cpio -oc >> /dev/rmt/0
```

Again, cpio is unable to generate a list of files to back up on its own. You have to use the find command and pipe the output to cpio. Then cpio backs up each file and writes it to the tape device. You use the find command to list the current contents of the directory and all files and subdirectories underneath. The *-depth* parameter is used to tell find to list all the files first before the subdirectories.

Listing Files from Tape with cpio

As with any other backup command, you can use cpio to list the contents of a tape or archive file. This example uses the *-i* copy-in mode to tell cpio to accept the contents of the backup tape and process the output:

```
# cpio -ticv < /dev/rmt/0
```

This command redirects the contents of the tape drive into cpio with the options of *-t, -i, -c,* and *-v.* The important options here are *-i,* which tells cpio to operate in copy-in mode, and *-t,* which tells cpio to list the contents of the archive. The *-cv* option produces ASCII output and formats the listings to be similar to the ls *-l* command.

If you want to send a backup file to cpio for listing, you execute this command.

```
# cpio -ticv < /file/backup@Head
```

Extracting Files from Tape with cpio

To extract the contents of tapes and archive files, you use the copy-in mode of cpio again, just as you did in listing backups, except this time, you omit the *-t* parameter and use the *-d* option to tell cpio to create extracted directories if needed. You will also learn how to retrieve only certain files from an archive.

In the first example, let's extract an entire archive into the current directory:

```
# cpio -idvc < /dev/rmt/0
```

This command simply copies the entire contents of the cpio archive in the tape drive into the current directory. Remember how you build the cpio archive; this determines how the archive is extracted. If you use relative pathnames in your archive, the archive extracts and builds into the current directory. If you use absolute pathnames in the archive, they start from the root of the file system and extract there, possibly overwriting files and directories.

To extract only certain files from the archive, add a regular expression for cpio to search for in the archive:

```
# cpio -idvc "*.txt" << /dev/rmt/0
```

With the inclusion of the expression *.txt,* cpio searches the entire archive, looks for anything ending in *.txt,* and extracts it.

Keep in mind that cpio is searching the table of contents of the archive, and the files listed there are always full paths to the files. The cpio command might find a directory that matches and extract the entire directory and files contained in it, even if the files don't match the expression.

For example, if you are searching for the file install with the expression *install* and a directory called install matches it, the system extracts the entire directory and all files contained within it, even if the files do not match install. Consequently, if there are multiple files called install and you want to extract only the one you need, you have to use a regular expression that exactly matches the pathname/filename of the file you want, such as *usr/src/app/install.

The cpio command, along with ufsdump and unfsrestore, does have support for multivolume tapes, but cpio does not support incremental backups without using other programs such as find to search for files that have changed. In addition, cpio does not have the ability to create a list of files to back up on its own; it depends on other programs such as find and ls for that.

The dd Command

The dd command performs raw copies of media to media, such as cloning one hard disk to another. Another very popular use of dd is to copy a bootable floppy image file to a floppy disk.

The dd command works in block mode, copying raw blocks from one medium to another. By default, dd copies its standard into its standard out. This means that the input of dd is sent to its output, and the output is sent to the input. This might sound confusing, but it is by design. You can alter its standard in and out using particular options.

An example of dd copying standard in to standard out is when you simply type **dd** at the command line. The dd command gives no message back and appears to hang because null input is being sent to null output. If you were to halt the program using CTRL-C, you would get the following message:

```
# dd
^C
0+0 records in
0+0 records out
#
```

This means that zero records (blocks) were given to the input and zero blocks were written to the output.

To copy one medium to another, you need to replace the standard-in and the standard-out parameters. There are two ways of doing this: one with redirects, the other using the input file (*if=*) and output file (*of=*) parameters.

The following is an example of using redirects when an image file is copied to a floppy disk:

```
# dd < /floppy.img > /dev/fd0
```

This command copies the prepared floppy image into the dd command (standard in), and then dd writes it to the floppy drive (standard out).

You can use the same procedure with the more easily understood *if=* and *of=* parameters:

```
# dd if=/floppy.img of=/dev/fd0
```

To clone a hard disk to another one, simply substitute the raw disk devices, such as

```
# dd if=/dev/rdsk/c0t0d0s2 of=/dev/rdsk/c0t0d1s2
```

When cloning disk 0 to disk 1, notice that slice 2 is used. Because slice 2 on a Solaris UFS disk encompasses the entire drive, by specifying c0t0d0s2 and copying it to c0t0d1s2, you copy the entire disk to the clone disk.

After you clone a disk, it's always a good idea to check it for errors after using the dd command and then mount the new cloned drive to make sure everything is there:

```
# fsck /dev/rdsk/c0t0d1s2
# mount -F ufs /dev/rdsk/c0t0d1s0 /mnt
```

Which Command Is Best for Certain Tasks?

Now that you have an idea of the different types of backup and restore commands that are available to you, you can use the information in Table 13-6 to discover which command is best to use for certain tasks.

TABLE 13-6   Commands for Particular Tasks

Task	Command
Perform full and incremental backup and restores to tape	Use ufsdump and ufsrestore.
Clone entire disks	Use dd.
Copy file systems from one disk to another	Use cpio.
Package files and directories and transport them across UNIX systems	Use tar.

EXERCISE 13-1

Using tar

In this exercise, you learn how to use the tar command to back up directories and files to a disk file.

1. Use the tar command to back up the /var directory:

```
# cd/
# tar -cvf /varbackup.tar var
```

This command tars the /var directory into a tar file called varbackup.tar.

2. List the contents of the tar file:

```
# tar -tvf /varbackup.tar
```

This command prints the table of contents of the varbackup.tar file you created in Step 1.

3. Create a temporary directory and extract the contents of the tar file into the temporary directory:

```
# mkdir /temp
# cd /temp
# tar -xvf /varbackup.tar
```

4. Verify that the files were extracted successfully and that they match the contents of the /var directory. Finally, delete the temporary directory, along with the extracted files and the tar file:

```
# rm -rf /temp
# rm -f /varbackup.tar
```

In this certification exercise, you used the tar command to practice backing up the /var directory. You then listed the contents of the archive and extracted the files into a temporary directory to verify that the backup and restore were successful.

CERTIFICATION OBJECTIVE 13.02

Backing Up a File System to Tape

This certification objective outlines the steps necessary to back up a file system to a tape drive. The root file system located on the first disk of the system /dev/rdsk/ c0t0d0s0 is used as an example.

Boot to Single-User Mode

One of the key caveats of backing up file systems is that you cannot completely back up a file system that is busy. To have an accurate backup, you must boot to single-user mode, boot from the Solaris CD-ROM, or unmount the file system you are backing up. These practices ensure that no write operations are taking place on the disk at the time of backup.

If you do not follow this advice, you run the risk of making an incomplete copy of your data or of having the entire backup set be corrupted.

To boot to single-user mode, you can use the shutdown command:

```
# shutdown -y
```

This command brings the system down to single-user mode. Alternatively, you can boot from the Solaris CD-ROM from the openboot prompt with this boot command:

```
ok boot cdrom -s
```

When the Solaris CD-ROM boots, you can use the ufsdump command to back up the file system.

If you aren't backing up the root file system and it is not one of the core file systems such as /usr or /var, you can unmount the file system and back it up with ufsrestore. Next to booting off the CD-ROM, this option provides the best form of backup because no disks are mounted to the active root file system. An example of unmounting a nonroot or /usr file system is unmounting the /export file system:

```
# umount /export
```

Backing Up the File System

Let's back up the root file system with the ufsdump command:

```
# ufsdump 0uvf /dev/rmt/0 /dev/rdsk/c0t0d0s0
DUMP: Writing 32 Kilobyte records
DUMP: Date of this level 0 dump: Sun May 17 10:14:53 2001
DUMP: Date of last level 0 dump: the epoch
DUMP: Dumping /dev/rdsk/c0t0d0s0 to /dev/rmt/0
DUMP: Mapping (Pass I) [regular files]
DUMP: Mapping (Pass II) [directories]
DUMP: Estimating 20453 blocks (610.56MB).
DUMP: Dumping (Phase III) [directories]
DUMP: Dumping (Phase IV [regular files]
DUMP: Tape rewinding
DUMP: 20451 blocks (610.42MB) on 1 volume at 64 KB/sec
DUMP: DUMP IS DONE
DUMP: Level 0 dump on Sun May 27 10:14:48 2001
```

This command backs up the root file system with a dump level of 0, indicating a full backup.

on the
job

In looking at ufsdump output, you might notice that the date of the last level 0 dump is the epoch. Under most UNIX versions, the epoch is 00:00:00 GMT, January 1, 1970. UNIX keeps track of its time by the number of seconds that have passed since the epoch. Thus, the epoch is when the UNIX clock reads zero (0). Because most if not all files are younger than the epoch, ufsdump automatically backs up the file with any dump level if there hasn't yet been a level 0 backup of it.

exam
Watch

These are the steps necessary to back up a file system:
1. Boot to single-user mode.
2. Use the ufsdump 0uvf /dev/rmt/0 /dev/rdsk/device-name command to back up the file system.

Verifying the Backup

After the backup and before you put away the backup tape for safekeeping, you need to make sure that the backup was completed successfully and that the media is viable. There are several ways to verify that you have a good backup:

- Examine the /etc/dumpdates file.
- Use ufsrestore to examine the table of contents on the tape.
- Perform an extraction in a temporary directory.

Examining the /etc/dumpdates File

With the -*u* ufsdump option, ufsdump updates the /etc/dumpdates file. This file tracks full and incremental backups that are performed on the file system. When ufsdump successfully completes a backup of a file system, it updates this file. If ufsdump fails for some reason, ufsdump will not update /etc/dumpdates. Keep in mind that only raw disk backups update this file (for example, backing up /dev/rdsk/c0t0d0s0). This file will not be updated if you back up just a directory or files, even if you specify the -*u* option in ufsdump.

The /etc/dumpdates file has this format after you successfully back up your root file system:

```
# cat /etc/dumpdates
/dev/rdsk/c0t0d0s0 0 Wed May 3, 16:43:22 2001
/dev/rdsk/c0t0d0s0 1 Wed May 4, 15:45:32 2001
```

The /etc/dumpdates file lists two backups that have been performed: a level 0 full backup on May 3, and a level 1 incremental backup on May 4. These entries verify that the backup has succeeded.

Listing the Table of Contents on the Tape

Another option of verifying that the backup succeeded is to examine the tape with the list files option of ufsrestore. The -*t* parameter is used to list the files in this case:

```
# ufsrestore -tf /dev/rmt/0
```

This command prints the table of contents on the tape drive.

Extracting the Contents to a Temporary Directory

The best way to determine whether you have a good backup is to perform a restore into a temporary directory on the system or a separate system. Use the ufsrestore command with the -*x* parameter to extract the entire contents into a temporary directory.

Do not restore the file system to the /tmp directory because the /tmp directory uses the tmpfs file system type, which does not have support for ACLs and permissions:

```
# mkdir /restore
# cd /restore
# ufsrestore -xvf /dev/rmt/0
Verify volume and initialize maps
Media block size is 126
Dump   date: Wed May 3, 16:43:22 2001
Dumped from: the epoch
Level 0 dump of / on server:/dev/rdsk/c0t0d0s0
Label: none
Extract directories from tape
Initialize symbol table.
Extract requested files
You have not read any volumes yet.
Unless you know which volumes your file(s) are on you should start
with the last volume and work towards the first.
Specify next volume #: 1
extract file ./files?.
Add links
Set directory mode, owner, and times.
set owner/mode for '.'? [yn] n
```

After you restore the backup tape to the temporary directory, verify that all files and directories have been restored successfully.

EXERCISE 13-2

Using ufsdump

In this exercise, you learn to use the ufsdump command to back up a file system. You use the c0t0d0s1 slice of the first hard disk, which contains the /usr file system. Feel free to substitute your own file system. After you perform the backup, you will learn how to check to make sure it succeeded.

1. Boot the system to single-user mode:

   ```
   # shutdown -y
   ```

2. Perform a full backup of the /dev/rdsk/c0t0d0s1 file system:

   ```
   # ufsdump 0uf /dev/rdsk/c0t0d0s1
   ```

3. Verify that the ufsdump was successful by looking at the contents of the /etc/dumpdates file:

```
# cat /etc/dumpdates
```

4. Verify that the ufsdump was successful by using the ufsrestore -*t* command to view the table of contents:

```
# ufsrestore tf /dev/rmt/0
```

In this certification exercise, you learned how to back up a file system by booting the system into single-user mode and using the ufsdump command with a full backup to a tape drive. You also learned how to verify that the backup was successful by viewing the contents of the /etc/dumpdates file and using the ufsrestore command with the -*t* parameter to view the table of contents.

CERTIFICATION OBJECTIVE 13.03

Restoring a File System from Tape

Undoubtedly, disaster will strike and you will need to recover file systems from your backups. This certification objective covers how to restore your file systems from tape backup. In the previous certification objective, you backed up the root file system with the ufsdump command. Here, you will learn the steps necessary to restore this root file system. Recovering the root file system requires a few more steps than restoring a regular file system, so you can use these steps to restore a regular file system as well.

Booting from a CD-ROM and Preparing the New Disk Drive

The first step in recovering from a failed hard disk is to physically replace the disk and boot from the Solaris CD-ROM, then use the format command to configure the partitions for the file system to match the failed disk:

```
ok boot cdrom -s
```

This command boots the system from the CD-ROM without the interactive install and instead drops you into a shell prompt, from which you can type system commands. To format the new disk, use the format command and partition your disk according to the previous hard disk:

```
# format
```

Now that you have duplicated the failed hard disk's partition configuration, you need to create the UFS file system on the slice that will contain the root file system. Use the newfs command on the /dev/rdsk/c0t0d0s0 slice:

```
# newfs /dev/rdsk/c0t0d0s0
```

Now you are ready to mount the new disk and restore the root file system.

Mounting the Disk and Restoring from Backup

At this point, you have booted from the Solaris CD-ROM and used the format and newfs commands to set up the new hard disk. Now, while still booted off the CD-ROM, you will mount the drive to a temporary directory and finally start the restore of the root file system.

The first step is to create a temporary mount point to mount the new hard disk from the CD-ROM file system. Choose any mount point you want, but for these examples, the /mnt/restore mount point is used:

```
# mkdir /mnt/restore
```

After creating the mount directory, mount the file system in the mount directory and verify that it was mounted correctly using the mount command with no options:

```
# mount -F ufs /dev/dsk/c0t0d0s0 /mnt/restore
# mount
```

After the new file system is mounted, it is time to restore the file system. You first perform a cd (change directory) command into /mnt/restore and perform the restore there because /mnt/restore will become the root file system. Then you use the ufsrestore command to restore the root file system:

```
cd /mnt/restore
# ufsrestore -rvf /dev/rmt/0
```

The ufsrestore -*rvf* /dev/rmt/0 command recursively extracts the archive from the /dev/rmt/0 tape and restores it to the /mnt/restore directory, which eventually becomes the new root file system.

After the extraction, when you perform ls /mnt/restore, you will see a strange file called restoresymtable. This file is created by ufsrestore, which contains the information about full and incremental backups of this archive. Simply delete this file:

```
# ls -la /mnt/restore/restoresymtable
-rw-------   1 root   other   450856 May 30 20:25 restoresymtable
# rm -f /mnt/restore/restoresymtable
```

Now that you have restored the file system, unmount the disk from the temporary mount point and check the drive for errors with the fsck command:

```
# cd /
# umount /mnt/restore
# fsck /dev/rdsk/c0t0d0s0
```

Simply restoring the root file system on the new disk does not make this disk bootable; you need to copy a boot block to the drive so that the system can boot from the new disk. The installboot command creates a boot block. The syntax for creating a boot block for your specific architecture is

```
#installboot /usr/platform/'uname -i'/lib/fs/ufs/pboot
/usr/platform/'uname -i'/lib/fs/ufs/bootblk
/dev/rdsk/device-name
```

The use of the uname -*i* command within the directory path substitutes uname with the hardware architecture you are using. In this instance, you perform the installboot command using these parameters:

```
# installboot /usr/platform/'uname -i'/lib/fs/ufs/pboot
/usr/platform/'uname -i'/lib/fs/ufs/bootblk /dev/rdsk/c0t0d0s0
```

After the boot block has been installed, the root file system disk is completely restored. Repeat these procedures except for the installboot step, for each nonbootable file system on the system. For example, restore the /usr, /var, and /export file systems if you have them on separate slices.

After you completely restore all file systems, reboot the system and boot from the new disk:

```
# init 6
```

exam

ⓦatch

These steps are necessary to restore a file system:

```
#boot cdrom -s
#format
#newfs /dev/rdsk/device-name
#mount /dev/rdsk/device-name /mnt
#cd /mnt
#ufsrestore rvf /dev/rmt/0
#rm restoresymtable umount/mnt
#installboot /usr/platform/'uname -i'/lib/fs/ufs/pboot
/usr/platform/'uname -i'/lib/fs/ufs/bootblk
/dev/rdsk/device-name
#fsck /dev/rdsk/device-name
#reboot
```

EXERCISE 13-3

Using ufsrestore

In this exercise, you learn how to restore your previously created file system into a temporary directory.

1. Make a temporary directory in a file system that has enough space to contain the file system and change the directory to it:

   ```
   # mkdir /temp
   # cd /temp
   ```

2. Perform a complete restore of the file system into the temporary directory with the ufsrestore command:

   ```
   # ufsrestore rvf /dev/rmt/0
   ```

3. Verify that the files were extracted into the /temp directory:

   ```
   # ls -la /temp
   ```

4. Notice that the ufsrestore command created the restoresymtable file in the /temp directory. Delete the restoresymtable file:

```
# rm -f restoresymtable
```

In this certification exercise, you learned how to restore a complete file system into a temporary directory, verified that the files were created, and deleted the restoresymtable file, which is not needed after the restore.

CERTIFICATION SUMMARY

This chapter covered all the commands that are available to back up and restore a file system. It also discussed backing up complete file systems, restoring file systems—including the root file system, and restoring the boot block to make the new root disk bootable.

✓ TWO-MINUTE DRILL

Understanding the Functions of Backup, Archive, and Restore Utilities

❑ The ufsdump command does full and incremental restores of complete file systems or individual files and directories.

❑ The ufsdump command uses a 0 for a full backup or 1–9 for any level of incremental backups.

❑ The ufsrestore command lists or restores file systems or individual files and directories, either by extracting straight from the command line or interactively.

❑ The tar command does not have support for multiple tape volumes.

❑ The dd command copies raw blocks from its standard input (stdin) to its standard output (stdout).

Backing Up a File System to Tape

❑ Boot to single-user mode to make sure you create a complete backup.

❑ The /etc/dumpdates file is updated by ufsdump with the -u option.

❑ If you do not specify a device to back up to, the default is /dev/rmt/0.

❑ Specify the raw disk for ufsdump (/dev/rdsk/device-name), files, or directories for ufsdump to back up.

❑ Use the /etc/dumpdates file, ufsrestore with the -t option, or extract the contents of an archive into a temporary directory to verify a good backup.

Restoring a File System from Tape

❑ To restore the root file system, boot from CD-ROM with the -s option and prepare the new disk.

❑ Mount the new disk to a temporary directory and run the restore from there.

❑ The ufsrestore -r command recursively restores a file system.

❑ Delete the restoresymtable after restore.

❑ Use the installboot command to make the new root disk bootable.

SELF TEST

The following questions will help you measure your understanding of the material presented in this chapter. Read all the choices carefully because there might be more than one correct answer. Choose all correct answers for each question.

Understanding the Functions of Backup, Archive, and Restore Utilities

1. Which backup commands have the ability to support multiple tape volumes?

    A. tar

    B. ufsdump

    C. ufsrestore

    D. dd

    E. cpio

2. You want to clone a disk on the same system so that you can transfer the disk over to another system. Which command is best for this task?

    A. ufsdump

    B. cpio

    C. dd

    D. dump

    E. tar

3. What is the default tape device if you do not specify one with the *-f* option in ufsdump?

    A. /dev/mt/0

    B. /dev/tape

    C. /dev/rmt/1

    D. /dev/rmt/0

Backing Up a File System to Tape

4. What is the proper ufsdump syntax to perform a full backup of the root file system to a tape drive?

    A. ufsdump Sf /dev/rmt/0 /dev/

    B. ufsdump 0u /dev/rdsk/c0t0d0s0

    C. ufsdump 0uvf /dev/rmt/0 /dev/dsk/c0t0d0s0

    D. ufsdump 0if /dev/rmt/0 /dev/rdsk/c0t0d0s0

5. The ufsdump command has the ability to update which file?

    A. /etc/dumplog

    B. /etc/dumpdate

    C. /var/dumplog

    D. /etc/dumpdates

6. You examine the /etc/dumpdates file to find out if the system is being backed up. Strangely, the file is empty. What could be the possible reasons that this file is empty?

    A. Backups are not being performed.

    B. Backups are not being performed with the ufsdump -*u* option.

    C. Backups are being written to a disk file.

    D. Backups are not being written successfully.

Restoring a File System from Tape

7. What is one of the first steps to restoring the root file system?

    A. Boot the system from CD-ROM.

    B. Use the newfs command to make the file system on the new disk.

    C. Install the boot block.

    D. Format the new disk.

8. What is the proper syntax for extracting an entire archive with ufsrestore?

    A. ufsrestore

    B. ufsrestore -*t*

    C. ufsrestore -*x*

    D. ufsrestore -*I*

9. Which file does the ufsrestore command create during an extraction of a complete file system?

    A. restoresymtable

    B. dump.log

    C. /etc/dumpdates

    D. ufsrestore.log

LAB QUESTION

You are the system administrator for your company. One of your servers has recently had a root hard disk crash. All other file systems are located on other disks, which are fine. Outline the steps necessary to restore the tape backup of the root file system. You have replaced the failed hard disk with a new one.

SELF TEST ANSWERS

Understanding the Functions of Backup, Archive, and Restore Utilities

1. ☑ B, C, and E. The ufsdump, ufsrestore, and cpio commands all support multiple-volume tape drives.
   ☒ A is incorrect because tar does not support multiple tape volumes. D is incorrect because dd does not offer support for multiple tape volumes.

2. ☑ C. The best tool to clone disks is the dd command, which performs a low-level, raw-block copy of media.
   ☒ A is incorrect, although ufsdump could back up the files to tape and ufsrestore would restore them to the new drive, but this isn't the best way to clone a disk. B is incorrect because cpio is best suited to copying file systems. D is incorrect because the dump command does not exist. E is incorrect because tar is not the best way to clone hard disks.

3. ☑ D. If you do not specify another tape or device with the *-f* option of ufsdump, the default device will be /dev/rmt/0.
   ☒ A is incorrect because it is /dev/rmt/0, not /dev/mt/0. B is incorrect because there is no such device. C is incorrect because the first tape drive /dev/rmt/0 is the default tape device.

Backing Up a File System to Tape

4. ☑ B. The correct syntax to back up the root file system is ufsdump 0u /dev/rdsk/c0t0d0s0. The *0* parameter tells ufsdump to perform a full backup of the root file system. The absence of the *-f* parameter makes ufsdump write the backup to the /dev/rmt/0 tape drive.
   ☒ A is incorrect because the *-S* parameter estimates the ufsdump backup. C is incorrect because the root disk is specified as /dev/dsk/c0t0d0s0. The ufsdump command operates on the raw disk of /dev/rdsk/c0t0d0s0. D is incorrect because there is no such parameter as *-i*.

5. ☑ D. The ufsdump command updates the /etc/dumpdates file.
   ☒ A, B, and C are all incorrect because the files do not exist.

6. ☑ A, B, and D. It is possible that backups aren't being performed. This could cause the dumpdates file to be empty. You might not be using the *-u* option with ufsrestore, which would signal ufsrestore to update the /etc/dumpdates file. If backups are not completing successfully, ufsrestore does not update the /etc/dumpdates file.
   ☒ C is incorrect because writing backups to a disk file would not cause failure to update /etc/dumpdates.

Restoring a File System from Tape

7. ☑   **A.** The first step in this list is to boot the system from the Solaris CD-ROM.
   ☒   **B** is incorrect because you cannot use newfs without first booting from a CD-ROM. **C** is incorrect because installing the boot block is one of the last steps in restoring the root file system. **D** is incorrect because you cannot use newfs without first booting from CD-ROM.

8. ☑   **C.** The proper syntax to extract an entire archive is ufsrestore *-x*, which extracts the entire archive located in /dev/rmt/0.
   ☒   **A** is incorrect because it is missing the *-x* parameter. **B** is incorrect because the *-t* parameter lists the files in the archive. **D** is incorrect because, although you can extract an entire archive with an interactive ufsrestore, using the command line is preferred.

9. ☑   **A.** The file that the ufsrestore command creates during a recursive *-r* extraction is the restoresymtable file. This file contains full and incremental backup information about the volume. The file can safely be deleted.
   ☒   **B** is incorrect because the dump.log file does not exist. **C** is incorrect because ufsdump, not ufsrestore, updates this file. **D** is incorrect because the ufsrestore.log file does not exist.

LAB ANSWER

The steps you take to restore the root file system could vary, but they will be similar to the steps outlined here:

1. Boot from the Solaris CD-ROM:

```
ok boot cdrom -s
```

2. Format the new hard disk, duplicating the configuration of the old hard disk:

```
# format
```

3. Use newfs to make a new file system on the new hard disk:

```
# newfs /dev/rdsk/c0t0d0s0
```

4. Mount the new root file system in a temporary directory:

```
# mkdir /mnt/restore
# mount -F ufs /dev/dsk/c0t0d0s0 /mnt/restore
# cd /mnt/restore
```

5. Perform the restore:

```
# ufsrestore -rvf /dev/rmt/0
```

6. Delete the restoresymtable file:

```
# rm -f /mnt/restore/restoresymtable
```

7. Install the boot block:

```
# installboot /usr/platform/'uname -i'/lib/fs/ufs/pboot
/usr/platform/'uname -i'/lib/fs/ufs/bootblk /dev/rdsk/c0t0d0s0
```

8. Unmount the new file system

```
# umount/mnt/restore
```

9. Check the new file system for errors:

```
# fsck /dev/rdsk/c0t0d0s0
```

10. Reboot the system and boot from the new disk:

```
# reboot
```

SUN® CERTIFIED SYSTEM ADMINISTRATOR

14

Utilizing Basic Command Syntax

Computers today are the result of a long process directed at making them easier to use. The interface between the average user and the average computer has become an intuitive one, and by its very nature, this picture suggests to the user what to do. No one would argue against the benefits of being able to understand how to accomplish a task with little or no training, but it remains true that the graphical interface that is the modern method of computing is imprecise. The existence of a button to "click" on your screen implies that there could be other buttons with other functions that you do not have at your disposal. Therefore, the graphical interface, although intuitive and attractive, is also limiting.

The Solaris command-line interface is one of the reasons that many people avoid the whole world of UNIX. Solaris does have a graphical interface, but more frequently, the real work is done from the command line. The command line does not take excuses, and it does not offer hints. It does not give you a picture of a task with inviting buttons showing you how to do your job. If you do not know exactly what you want to do with the command-line interface, you will find yourself treated to a feeling of frustration unique to the computing world.

So why bother? Because although the command line is lacking in terms of aesthetics, it is beyond a doubt the most exact, concise, and perfect way to accomplish many tasks. The commands you will encounter are terse, unintuitive, and many times cryptic; but combined with other commands and with your knowledge of the underlying system, they become a beautiful and rich language—a language with which you can accomplish anything. With the command line, you are limited only by your knowledge and creativity.

You can certainly be a successful computer user without understanding the command line, yet a successful system administrator is somewhat defined by his or her ability to navigate this difficult terrain. A mastery of the commands cd, ls, mkdir, rmdir, file, cp, mv, rm, and touch will be at the cornerstone of any system administrator's knowledge. The concepts of absolute and relative pathnames and shell wildcards are fundamental to successful administration of any UNIX-based system. This chapter introduces you to these concepts in more detail.

CERTIFICATION OBJECTIVE 14.01

Moving Between Specified Points in a Directory Tree

The Solaris file system is made up of directories, subdirectories, and files that are all related to each other. This relationship is commonly called a *hierarchy* or *tree,* and the terms *hierarchical file system* or *tree file system* are frequently used and interchangeable. A hierarchical file system can be described with a few simple rules:

- A directory may contain zero or more files.
- A directory may contain zero or more subdirectories.
- A directory is always the subdirectory, or *child,* of only one *parent* directory.

You can see from these rules that a drawing of a directory can look like a tree (see Figure 14-1), with each directory having several subdirectories underneath it, like branches from a trunk. The only special case of this relationship is the first directory, called the *root* of the hierarchy.

exam
ⓦatch

Don't confuse the root of the file system with the root user. Although the same term is used for both purposes, they are two different concepts.

The root directory may contain zero or more files or subdirectories, but the special case is the parent directory of the root directory. To maintain the integrity of the file system rules, there must be a parent, but the root directory is the first directory. To overcome this inconsistency, the root directory is considered its own parent.

FIGURE 14-1

The hierarchical
file system as
a tree

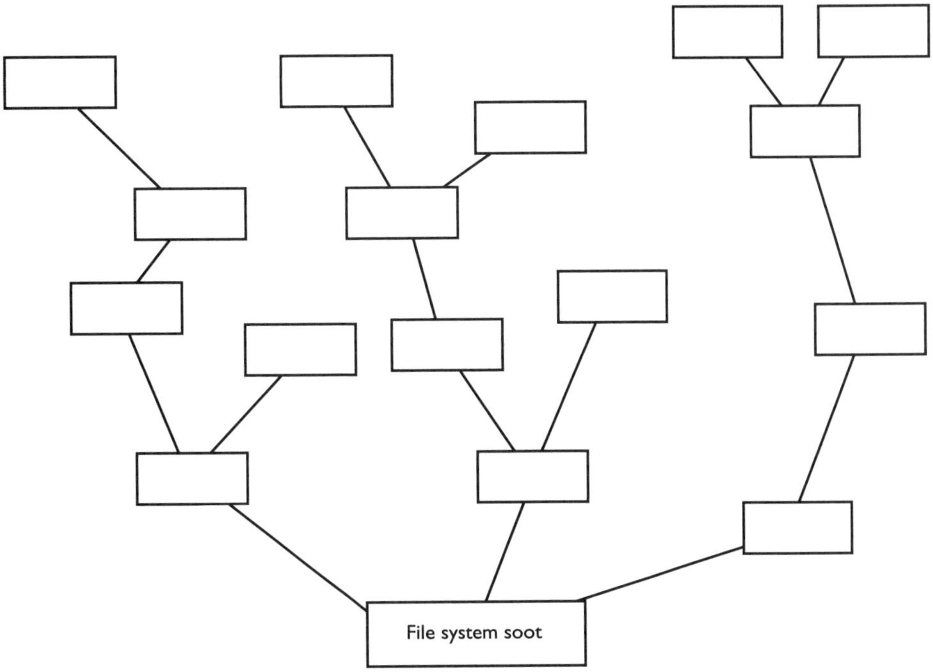

File system soot

Absolute Addressing of File System Objects

A fully qualified or absolute path always starts with the root directory. The UNIX nomenclature for the root directory is a single forward slash (/). If you were to create a picture of a file system tree and follow it to your objective from the root, you would see each subdirectory through which you would have to pass to get there. When addressing a file system object with a fully qualified name, you do the same thing.

For example, let's say you have a file named lettertomom.txt. This file is in a directory named letters, which is under a directory named text, which is under a directory named files, which is under the root directory /. You would give a fully qualified, absolute address to this file by starting with the root directory, and then listing each subdirectory until you get to the one containing the file. Finally, you list the filename itself:

```
/files/text/letters/lettertomom.txt
```

Note that the first slash (/) is the root directory, but afterward, the slash character serves only to separate each subdirectory from the next. An absolute address of a file system object always starts with a slash. If an address does not start with a slash, it is not an absolute address.

Relative Addressing of File System Objects

Every directory in a UNIX file system has two special subdirectories: *dot* (.) and *dot-dot* (..). These special subdirectories are a feature of the way the file system is actually implemented on the disk, and they can be quite useful to system administrators. For clarity, we refer to these directories as dot and dot-dot in discussion, but (.) and (..) in examples.

The dot directory is like the *You Are Here* spot on the map of the building where you were just hired as a Solaris administrator. More accurately, the dot directory is akin to you carrying around a spot of your own and putting it on the floor wherever you happen to be standing. It does not tell you where you are in relation to anything else, but it does tell you that where you are is right here, and right here is where you are. The dot directory essentially means the *current directory*. It is a legitimate subdirectory of the current directory, but it is also the same thing as the current directory.

The dot-dot directory is a reference to the parent of the current directory. If you were currently working in the directory /files/text/letters, for example, the dot-dot directory would be a reference to the /files/text directory.

FROM THE CLASSROOM

Understanding File Systems

A family tree is similar to a hierarchical file system. If you started your family tree from the time at which the first ancestor, John, stepped off the boat onto American soil in 1768, you would see a treelike structure where John is the root and his three children are subdirectories, and each of their children are subdirectories in the subdirectories. Now it is 2001, and you have just met a distant cousin. To establish your relationship, you can drag out the family tree and go all the way back to John to define your places in the family. John had a son who had a son who had a daughter who had a son who had a daughter who had you. Using the family tree, you have defined where you are in the family from the

root of the tree. This is, in UNIX terms, an *absolute address.*

A file system object may be considered a file or a directory that exists in your file system. Everything in the file system has a relationship to the top level of the file system due to the hierarchical nature of the system, much the way everyone in your family has a relationship to John because you are all children of his children. Just as you can define your place in the family by following the path of children from the root of the family tree, so too can you define the location of a file or directory in the Solaris file system by following the path of directories from the root of the file system.

—Andrew Seely, SCSA, LCP

Using these references, dot and dot-dot, helps determine where you are in the file system without saying anything about where you are in relation to the root of the file system. If your current directory is /files/text/letters, for example, you can address the lettertomom.txt file in a way that is relative to your current position, like this:

```
./lettertomom.txt
```

Note that this address has no reference whatsoever to your position in terms of the big picture of the file system hierarchy. If you had three files named lettertomom.txt in three different subdirectories, the preceding relative address would hold true for each one, provided you were in a directory that held it. This is because you are addressing the file from the point of view of where you are now, not where the file is compared to the start of the file system.

If your current working directory were /files/text/pictures, you could still address lettertomom.txt with a relative address by using the dot-dot notation. Remember that dot-dot means the parent directory; you can visualize this better by saying that dot-dot takes you *up* a directory. From /files/text/pictures, you can address your letter like this:

```
../letters/lettertomom.txt
```

Notice that you had to look to the parent of your current directory and then address a different child of that parent. You can address your sister in an absolute path by describing her lineage all the way from 1768, or you can simply say that she is another child of your parents. So it is that you can describe a file in absolute terms from root, or you can describe it in relative terms from where you are.

Commands for Navigating the File System

The number one command for navigating the file system is the change directory command, or cd. The cd command is a shell internal command, which means that the work that cd does occurs inside the code of your interactive shell instead of by a separate program file. The cd command takes a single argument, which is the address in the file system to which you want to move. This argument must be a directory; if it is not, the cd command will report an error and take no action. Using the cd command with no arguments invokes the default behavior of changing the current directory to your user home directory, which is found in the environment variable $HOME.

You may use the cd command with both absolute and relative addresses. From your current directory, you may move to the directory that holds your correspondence with an absolute address:

```
cd /files/text/letters
```

If you know where you are in the file system relative to your target, you can use cd with the dot and dot-dot directories. First, it is always important to know where you are; you can ascertain your location using the print working directory command, or pwd. This command does not take any arguments; it simply reports where you are in the file system hierarchy:

```
pwd
/files/text/pictures
```

Now, move to the letters directory using a relative path:

```
cd ../letters
```

If you are moving into a directory that is a subdirectory of your current directory, you can use relative addressing from your current directory:

```
pwd
/files/text
cd ./letters
```

In this situation, the dot-slash (./) part of the relative address is not required, so you can simply use this command:

```
cd letters
```

As you can see, navigation of the Solaris file system using relative and absolute addressing is easy, provided you have a good understanding of the hierarchical nature of the file system. The relative addressing provided by dot and dot-dot provides a powerful time-saver for the busy system administrator.

EXERCISE 14-1

Exploring the Solaris File System

This exercise gets you started by giving you a quick tour of the Solaris file system.

1. Determine your current directory:

   ```
   pwd
   ```

2. Change directory to root:

   ```
   cd /
   ```

3. Determine your current directory:

   ```
   pwd
   ```

4. Change directory back to your original directory using absolute addressing, for example,

   ```
   cd /export/home/john
   ```

5. Determine your current directory:

   ```
   pwd
   ```

6. Change directory up one in the file system using relative addressing:

   cd ..

7. Determine your current directory:

   pwd

8. Change directory back to your original directory, for example,

   cd john

9. Determine your current directory:

   pwd

10. Change directory up until you are at the root by repeating Steps 5 and 6.

11. Repeat Step 4.

12. Change directory up to the root with a single cd command using relative addressing by separating the dot-dot directory with slashes for each time you had to repeat Step 11, for example,

    cd ../../..

13. From the root directory, what happens when you do this?

    cd ..

14. From any directory, what happens when you do this?

    cd .

Using Metacharacter Combinations to Access Files and Directories Within the Directory Tree

A *metacharacter* is a character that has a value greater than itself when interpreted in the context of the UNIX shell environment. Most characters mean only what they say: an *A* is an *A*, nothing more. However, for a metacharacter, there is potential for that character to mean itself or perhaps many different things. Shell metacharacters provide a powerful tool when formulating UNIX commands because a metacharacter can say many potential things at one time, whereas the actual incarnation depends on the circumstance in which the metacharacter is deployed.

A certain set of metacharacters is dedicated to the idea of pattern matching. A *pattern match* is to text what a dress pattern is to finished dresses; the pattern is like an ideal of a section of text, and it is compared against actual text sections until a section is found that fits the pattern. This operation is similar to taking a dress pattern into a department store and looking at every dress until you find one that was made using your pattern. Although following this procedure in a dress shop would be tedious and not very useful, the UNIX shell provides the ability to do text pattern matches rapidly and efficiently, and you will find that the result is incredibly useful.

There are two distinctly different contexts for pattern-matching metacharacters in UNIX. Pattern matching for regular expressions and for file system wildcards both use metacharacters, but in subtly different ways. These differences are confusing enough to warrant spending time addressing them here, although a formal discussion of regular expressions is beyond the scope of this chapter.

A metacharacter, as you already know, is an idealized representation of text. This means the text being examined does not have to be literal; it can be a member of a class of possible alternatives. For example, imagine you are looking in your address book for the address of your brother in Somerset. If you find him listed under *Clutton, Somerset,* or *Clutton, BS18,* you stop looking because you know you found it. Both Somerset and BS18 are members of the class of appropriate things that could be. If you found an address that was *Coventry, CV1,* you would not have a match; CV1 is not in the range of potentials in your search.

Metacharacters operate the same way, but on a smaller scale. A metacharacter can define the possible values for a single character of text and can also define the possibilities for a string of characters. The metacharacters used in file system wildcards are the following:

- ? Any single character
- [ ] Any single character in a set
- * Any character in the quantity of zero to any number of contiguous characters

The importance of a metacharacter in a wildcard match is evident the first time you are doing something to a file and you do not know what it is named or where it is, or when you have a large number of files but you want to take action on only a subset of them.

Matching Any Single Character

The question mark (?) metacharacter can be used to describe an idealized text that includes a single character that can be anything. When creating the pattern, you use string literal characters where you want string literals to be matched, and you use the question mark (?) character where there must be a character, but you do not know what it is.

For example, say you are searching through text for the words *sandy* and *candy*. The *andy* portions of these two words are exactly the same, so you can represent those characters as themselves. However, the first character is potentially unknown to you: you know what you want it to be, but you do not know if you will find it or if it even exists in the list through which you are searching. You can define a pattern using the question-mark metacharacter to define the ideal text—some unknown single character followed by the characters *a, n, d,* and *y:*

```
?andy
```

This pattern, in the wildcard context, will match both *sandy* and *candy*. Perhaps, unfortunately for you, it will also match *randy* and *handy*. In a relatively small search list, this is OK, but in a very large list, it could become unwieldy to figure out the results. The pattern *?andy* would match, in a large list that contained them, all 26 words made by starting the word with each letter of the alphabet and ending it with *andy,* all 26 words made by starting the word with each capitalized letter of the alphabet, all 10 words made by starting the word with the numbers 0 through 9, and all the words that could be made by starting with the various punctuation marks. This seemingly simple pattern could return over 70 valid matches—probably not the exclusive list for which you had hoped!

Matching a Defined Set of Characters

The *character set* metacharacter allows you to define the characters that may be matched at any particular place. This is similar to the question-mark (?) metacharacter, but with a tighter focus. The question mark matches anything, whereas you can define a character set that matches only a few things for the position in your pattern.

In the preceding example, the pattern found the appropriate text, but it also found potentially a lot more. It would have benefited you if you could have said to look only for *s* or *c* followed immediately by *a, n, d, y.* You can do this with a character set:

```
[cs]andy
```

The brackets ([ ]) and anything in between define the set of possible matches for that single position in the searched text. In this case, the character set was defined to contain *c* and *s*. This pattern would not match something else, like *tandy*, because *t* is not in the character set that defines what the first character should be.

Character sets may have any number of values in them, and they may also contain ranges of values. A *range* is defined by the hyphen character (-); the beginning of the range comes immediately before the hyphen and the last character of the range comes immediately after. For example,

```
[F-H]eather
```

would match the text *Feather, Geather,* or *Heather.* The ordering of ranges in character sets is determined by the American Standard Code for Information Interchange (ASCII).

Other ranges and single-character members of the character set are placed immediately alongside each other in the set definition, which can make a character set a little hard to read, for example,

```
[f-hF-HlL]eather
```

This combination would potentially match *feather, geather, heather, Feather, Geather, Heather, leather,* or *Leather.* Notice that UNIX is sensitive to the case of text; *A* is not equal to *a* in UNIX, so a character set becomes very useful when dealing with text that might or might not be capitalized.

Matching Zero or More Contiguous Characters

The asterisk metacharacter (*) takes a shotgun approach to text matching. This metacharacter essentially says, "Match any number of anything." At first, this breadth seems so powerful as to almost be useless, but in fact, it can save a good deal of time and energy—especially when the task at hand might be uncertain.

The asterisk character matches any number of anything. This also means that it matches zero characters; a pattern can use an asterisk that does not correlate to anything in the matched text. This is different from the question mark (?) and brackets ([ ]), which must match a character of text.

For example, say that you have a large list of text that contains some very long words. You have never been able to spell *Withlacoochee,* but you need to find it in your list of text. You can dredge it up easily this way:

```
With*
```

This pattern will match a potentially large amount of text—in fact, everything that begins with *With*—but this might be an acceptable amount of imprecision for our task.

Mixing and Matching Metacharacters to Zero in the Perfect Match

You can combine any number of metacharacters in a pattern to achieve your pattern-matching goal. Although the result can become difficult to read, it provides an incredible amount of flexibility when dealing with the unknown.

For instance, patterns that would match *Withlacoochee* are

```
[Ww]ith*
[Ww]ithl??oochee
?ithl[ai][kc]oo*
```

The differences between using metacharacters with file system wildcards and regular expressions are subtle and will trip you up in practice. Table 14-1 provides a quick reference on the differences in the two contexts.

Applying Metacharacters to the UNIX File System

You have learned how to navigate the UNIX hierarchical file system with the cd and pwd commands. Except for the dot and dot-dot notations, you really had to know the directory and filenames that you wanted to address. This is no problem for small directory trees with a few files, but the Solaris operating environment is huge, with thousands of files across hundreds of directories. Knowledge of exactly where each file is located and how it is spelled is not a practical goal for even the most dedicated

TABLE 14-1   Metacharacters Combined with Wildcards and Regular Expressions

Metacharacter	Wildcard	Regular Expression
?	Matches any single character	Matches zero or one of the preceding characters
*	Matches zero or more of any combination of characters	Matches zero or more of the preceding characters
[ ]	Matches a single character position with any of the characters in the set	Matches a single character position with any of the characters in the set

system administrator. Luckily, with metacharacters, maybe you don't need to know everything, for instance,

```
pwd
/files/text/letters
cd ../graphics
pwd
/files/text/graphics
```

The cd command could have been shortened using a metacharacter—like this, for instance, if you had only one directory that started with *g:*

```
cd ../g*
```

If you wanted to find the letter to your mom, but you did not remember how you spelled the filename, you could use asterisks (*) in the fully qualified filename:

```
ls /files/text/letters/*mom*
```

This would, of course, get all the letters that had *mom* in the filename. If you also had a series of letters to your dad, but these were named dad1.txt, dad2.txt, and so on, you could address these using the question mark and brackets metacharacters. For example, this would address the first nine letters to your dad:

```
ls dad[1-9].txt
```

Because you know that the files in question conform to a certain format, you can address all nine files with a question-mark metacharacter:

```
ls dad?.txt
```

This works because you know that the filenames are *dad* followed by numbers, followed by *.txt*. You are free to use the shortest metacharacter available appropriate to the situation. If you wanted to view letters 23, 27, and 28, for example, you could do so like this:

```
more dad2[378].txt
```

The use of shell metacharacters in the file system wildcard context can be a powerful tool and a convenient time-saver for any system administrator. The metacharacters allow you to address files and directories that have difficult spellings; they also allow you to address ranges and groups of files and directories. This method of group addressing in the file system applies an economy of motion: operations that could take hundreds of steps, such as deleting select files from a list of hundreds or thousands, can potentially be done in a single step.

EXERCISE 14-2

Using Metacharacters to Navigate the File System

This exercise further demonstrates these concepts. You are at the root directory of the file system. Your directory tree includes these paths:

```
/export/home/john/files/text/letters
/usr/local/bin
/var/spool/cron/crontabs
```

1. Verify your current directory:

   ```
   pwd
   ```

2. Using a metacharacter for each directory, write a cd command that would shorten the amount of typing needed to get all the way into the /letters directory:

   ```
   cd /exp*/h*/joh?/fil*/t*/lett*
   ```

3. Using metacharacters, show the addressing that would match all the files that contain the word "perl" in /usr/local/bin:

   ```
   /usr/local/bin/*[Pp][Ee][Rr][Ll]*
   ```

4. Using a single metacharacter, show how to address every file in the /crontabs directory:

   ```
   /var/spool/cron/crontabs/*
   ```

CERTIFICATION OBJECTIVE 14.03

Listing Directory Contents and Determining the File Types Within a Directory

So far in this chapter, you learned about one of the most fundamental concepts in UNIX: the hierarchical file system. This representation of directories is the framework in which UNIX operates, and comfort in dealing with it will increase your ability to perform system administration tasks.

The next step in working with the file system is to be able to deal with the files that exist in it. On a superficial level, files in UNIX are very easy to work with. UNIX makes little distinction between file types; in fact, it even internally represents directories and system processes as files. So the file is really a basic data type for UNIX. Of course, at a deeper level, file issues can get very complex; but for our purposes, we will address looking at files, determining their attributes, and determining something about the contents of files without actually opening them.

Listing the Contents of a Directory

The command to list the contents of a directory is the list command, ls. The ls command is one of the Swiss Army knife–style UNIX commands: it tries to do a little bit of everything, so it can be tough to remember all the different ways that ls can be used. We limit our discussion to the most common options and uses, but keep in mind that there is more to the ls command.

The ls command with no arguments gives us the names of the files and directories that are contained in the current directory:

```
pwd
/export/home/john/letters
ls
lettertomom.txt    dad1.txt    dad2.txt    old_letters
```

Using ls this way tells us the names of the files and directories, but it does not tell us which is which, and it tells us nothing else about them.

The *-F* argument to ls tells us a little more. With *-F* the directory names are noted with a special flag in the listing:

```
ls -F
lettertomom.txt    dad1.txt    dad2.txt    old_letters/
```

The *-F* option also shows executable files with the asterisk (*) and symbolic links with the at sign (@) after the filenames, for example,

```
ls -F
normalfile    executablefile*    directory/    linkfile@
```

The *-a* option to ls shows UNIX hidden files. In UNIX, a hidden file is not hidden very well. In fact, the act of hiding files was never intended to truly hide them from users, but rather simply to keep certain configuration files from showing up in lists of files on the system. So it is not hard to see a hidden file, and it is also not hard to make one. The fact that a file is hidden has no bearing on its contents or potential use. Hidden files are defined simply by starting their filenames with a dot:

```
ls
file1    file2    file3
ls -a
.    ..    .hiddenfile1    .file1    file2    file3
```

Note that the dot and dot-dot directory references are treated as hidden files by the system.

The ls command has nearly two dozen different options, but the format of the command is always ls, followed by a dash and then multiple options put together, followed by a list of files and/or directories. Without the options, ls simply prints file and directory names. Without the list of files and/or directories, ls acts on the current directory. Don't be worried about the large number of options to ls; understanding the format of the command will help you through most questions.

The *-l* option might be the most used option for the ls command. The *-l* option shows not only the filename, but also the date of creation or last modification, the size of the file, the owner, the group owner, the link count, and the file permissions. In addition, certain special file characteristics are shown by the *-l* option:

```
ls -l
drwxr-xr-x    5 john    users       4096 Mar   3 10:27 Desktop
-rw-r--r--    1 john    users       1890 Feb  24 01:09 data
-rwxr-xr-x    1 john    users       145  Feb  22 19:45 middle
srwxrwxrwx    1 root    users       0    Apr   4 16:25 mysql.sock
```

In this example, four files are listed. The output of ls *-l* is given in columns. The first column identifies any system special file types and the general file permissions. This column is ten characters long. The first character shows special files; for instance, the file Desktop is a special file of type *d*, for directory. As far as we are concerned, Desktop is simply a directory; but from the internal representations of the UNIX file system, it is a special file type. The *s* shown for the file mysql.sock shows that this file is a file of type *socket*. A socket file is used for interprocess communications. Other file types you might encounter include *b* for block files, *c* for character files, and *l* for logically linked files. By far the most common character you will encounter in the first position is the hyphen (-). This character simply identifies the file as a regular file.

The next nine characters of the first column define the access permissions for the file. These nine characters are divided into three sets of three, defining the access permissions for the owner of the file, members of the file's group, and all other users. Each set of three characters is identical in function. The three characters represent the read, write, and execute permissions, respectively. A lack of a particular permission is indicated by a hyphen. The presence of the permission is indicated by an *r* for read, a *w* for write, and an *x* for execute.

The next column shows the link count for the file. This number represents the number of different filenames that share the same physical data comprising the file's contents. This number can be useful for very detailed file system analysis.

The next column shows the userid of the owner of the file. This is the user to whom the first three characters of the permission set apply.

The next column shows the UNIX group ownership that is associated with the file. By assigning a group ownership, it is possible to grant access to the file to a certain subset of users on the system. This group has access permissions as defined by the second set of three characters of the permission set.

The next column shows the file size in bytes. The column after that shows the date and time the file was created or last modified. Finally, the filename itself is displayed.

The various options to the ls command may be combined to gain further information about the files in your directory. For example, the command ls *-laF* would give the long listing as shown previously, but would include any hidden or dot files and would place a slash (/), asterisk (*), or at sign (@) after the filename, if appropriate.

The ls command also takes an optional list of arguments after its options. You can use ls to list the files in the current directory, but you can also give ls arguments of individual files and/or other directories, and these arguments can use the metacharacters discussed in the preceding section:

```
pwd
/usr/local
ls -aF /export/home
john/    sue/    ray/    heather/    userlist.txt@    hello*
```

Determining File Types

UNIX does not enforce a file type based on the filename, like some other operating systems do, but there is still a logical difference in the contents of different files. A text file is built differently than a binary file, and a shell script is functionally different from a letter to your mom. These different types of file contents can be ascertained in UNIX by using the file command.

The file command takes an argument of a list of files or wildcard filenames. The file command returns a list of the file types based on the contents of the first few bytes of the file, in correlation with a system configuration file called *magic*. The types of file contents that file is capable of understanding include these:

- ASCII text
- C program text
- Data
- Empty
- Directory
- Shell commands

The file command typically returns a file type of ASCII text if it is able to determine that the file's contents are textual and there are no other clues to the purpose of the file. Files that are not in a recognizable format are lumped into the data category. The file command is especially useful when you are trying to determine the purpose of files on your system.

EXERCISE 14-3

Assessing the Contents of Directories

The following exercise demonstrates the use of the ls and file commands. You are in a user directory of your file system, and you are trying to determine if the user is misusing the computer. (Your company has a policy against the use of corporate systems for programming by users, for example.) You can use the ls and file commands to determine if there is a breach of policy in progress.

1. Use the following command:

```
pwd
/export/home/cindy
```

2. Use the following command:

```
ls -laF
drwx------  8 cindy   users     4096 Apr 12 18:38 ./
drwxr-xr-x  7 root    root      4096 Jan  9 14:00 ../
-rw-r--r--  1 cindy   users      124 Jan  8 09:28 .bashrc
-rw-r--r--  1 cindy   users      688 Jan  8 09:28 .emacs
```

```
-rw-------  1 cindy  users      305 Jan 26 21:21 .mysql_history
-rw-r--r--  1 cindy  users     3710 Feb 24 01:11 data.out
-rw-r--r--  1 cindy  users     1898 Mar  4 01:09 h.txt
-rw-r--r--  1 cindy  users     2450 Mar  4 00:59 hther
-rw-r--r--  1 cindy  users       20 Apr 12 18:38 lettertomom.txt
-rwxr-xr-x  1 cindy  users      145 Feb 22 19:45 middle*
-rw-r--r--  1 cindy  users    39032 Apr  8 15:19 nova.lst
-rwxr-xr-x  1 cindy  users      356 Mar  7 00:25 timr*
```

3. Use the following command:

```
file *
data.out:          ASCII text
hther:             ASCII text
h.txt:             ASCII text
lettertomom.txt:   C program text
middle:            Bourne shell script text
nova.lst:          ASCII text
timr:              English text
```

From your analysis, it would appear that the user *cindy* is indeed writing a C program but hiding the contents in what appears to be a letter to her mom. Furthermore, it also appears that *cindy* has a Bourne shell script named *middle*. Although this is not incontrovertible evidence, it could show cause for a more detailed examination.

CERTIFICATION OBJECTIVE 14.04

Using Commands to Create or Remove Directories

The creation and deletion of directories in Solaris is a relatively simple process with a few simple rules and two basic commands: mkdir and rmdir.

Creating Directories with mkdir

To create a new directory, you can simply use this command:

```
mkdir newdirectoryname
```

You must have write permission to the current working directory, or this operation will fail. The *newdirectoryname* must not already exist as a directory or file, regardless of its permissions. If you are making a new directory, its parent must already exist. This situation could arise when you need to make a series of subdirectories:

```
pwd
/export/home/heather
mkdir files/text
```

The preceding command to make the new directory text will fail if the parent to text, files, does not exist. This operation can still be accomplished in a single step with the addition of the *-p* option to mkdir; this option creates all needed intermediate parent directories:

```
mkdir -p files/text
```

Removing Directories with rmdir

You can remove a directory in one of two ways: with the rmdir command or with the rm command. The rm command is covered in the next section; we address the rmdir command here.

To remove a directory, the rmdir command takes as an argument a list of one or more directories, either relative or absolutely addressed. A directory must be empty to be removed, and the user running the rmdir command must have write access to the parent directory to remove it:

```
ls -F
file1    file2*    file3    directory1/    directory2/
rmdir directory1
ls -F
file1    file2*    file3    directory2/
```

If the directory to be removed has subdirectories but no files, rmdir can be used with the *-p* option to remove the whole subtree:

```
ls -F
file1    file2*    file3    directory1/    directory2/
rmdir directory1
rmdir:  directory1:  Directory not empty
ls directory1
subdirectory1        subdirectory2
rmdir -p directory1
ls -F
file1    file2*    file3    directory2/
```

To remove a directory that has files in it, you must use the rm command.

EXERCISE 14-4

Adding and Removing Directories

The uses of the mkdir and rmdir commands are demonstrated in this exercise. You have several subdirectories under your home directory that need to be removed because they are from old projects. You have been given several new projects, some of which have subtasks, so you need to create new subdirectories to hold your works in progress.

1. Verify your current working directory:

   ```
   pwd:
   /export/home/Patrick
   ```

2. List the files in the current directory by type:

   ```
   ls -F
   Jan_project1/    Jan_project2/    Jan_project3/
   ```

3. Remove the three subdirectories using a wildcard:

   ```
   rmdir Jan*
   rmdir: Jan_project2: Directory not empty
   ```

   Notice that rmdir did not remove the nonempty directory.

4. List the files in the current directory by type again:

   ```
   ls -F
   Jan_project2/
   ```

5. Remove the remaining subdirectory and all its subdirectories:

   ```
   rmdir -p Jan_project2
   ```

6. Verify that the subdirectory is gone:

   ```
   ls -F
   ```

7. Make the new subdirectory:

   ```
   mkdir Feb_project1
   ```

8. Make subdirectories for Feb_project2:

   ```
   mkdir -p
   Feb_project2/subtask1
   ```

9. Make subdirectories for Feb_project2:

```
mkdir
Feb_project2/subtask2
```

10. Make the final subdirectory:

```
mkdir Feb_project3
```

Notice that Step 8 uses the *-p* option to create the tree, but in Step 9, *-p* is not needed because the parent was already created in the previous step.

Using Commands to Copy, Create, Rename, or Remove Files

Dealing with files, as you have seen throughout this chapter, is a common and essential part of Solaris system administration. The ability to actually manipulate the files themselves is a daily task. Copying and renaming files that need to be shared or are no longer used, creating new files for any number of purposes, removing temporary or outdated files that are using valuable storage space—these actions are the bread and butter of the system administrator.

Copying Files Using cp

The cp command is the basic tool used to make a copy of a file. In its simplest form, cp takes two arguments: the source filename and the destination or new filename. Provided that the user has read access to the source file and write access to the directory where the destination file will be created, cp creates an exact copy of the file:

```
cp oldfile newfile
```

The destination file need not be in the same directory. For that matter, neither does the source file. Both arguments can be addressed with relative or absolute pathnames, and wildcards may be used for the source file to copy multiple files:

```
cp /files/graphics/newcar.jpg /export/home/tim/car.jpg
cp /files/graphics/*.jpg ./mygraphics/
cp ../lettertomom.txt ../oldfiles/
```

Notice that the second two examples have directories as the target files. The cp command simply creates the copied file in the target directory, maintaining the original filename. The middle example shows the use of a wildcard with the copy command; in this case, all files that end in .jpg are copied to a subdirectory of the current working directory.

If the target file for cp is a file and the file already exists, the user must have write permission to the target file. The target will be overwritten and replaced by the source file.

You may also use the cp command to make a copy of a whole subdirectory tree and all the files it contains. The *-r* option to cp is the recursive option and causes cp to begin copying in the file tree from the point of the specified source through every subdirectory and file. The target is created as a new directory with the name specified, but all files and subdirectories from the original are copied to the new directory with their original names. For example,

```
Cp -r./files ./temporaryfiles
```

creates a new directory named temporaryfiles, into which are copied all the files and subdirectories that exist in the directory named files.

Creating Files Using touch and Output Redirection

The cp command creates a new file or files that are duplicates of the originals. At times, you might need to create a new file, but the contents of that file are not important. Or, you might need to run a Solaris command and capture the command's output to a file for later appraisal.

The touch command creates a file of zero length. The touch command takes as an argument a list of filenames; if the file does not exist and if the user has write access to the current directory or the directory where the file is to be created, the file is created with zero length. If the file already exists and the user has write permission to the file, the modification date and time are updated to the current date and time for the file:

```
# ls -l
-rw-r--r--    1 tomf  servicedeliv       1890 Feb 24 01:09 data
# touch data data1 data2
-rw-r--r--    1 tomf  servicedeliv       1890 Apr 12 20:03 data
-rw-r--r--    1 tomf  servicedeliv          0 Apr 12 20:03 data1
-rw-r--r--    1 tomf  servicedeliv          0 Apr 12 20:03 data2
```

A new file may be created by redirecting the output of a Solaris command. The cat command, for example, simply displays the contents of a file on the screen. This output may be captured by an output redirect and placed in a file. Redirection of regular output is accomplished with the double greater-than character (>>), placed between the command and the destination file. Either the destination file must not exist, or the user must have write permissions to the file to overwrite it. The directory in which the destination file exists must also allow write permissions for the user. Almost any Solaris command may have its output captured and redirected to a file in this way.

```
ls -l
-rw-r--r--     1 daveh   c2admin        1890 Feb 24 01:09 data
cat data >> moredata
ls -l
-rw-r--r--     1 daveh   c2admin        1890 Feb 24 01:09 data
-rw-r--r--     1 daveh   c2admin        1890 Feb 24 01:10 moredata
ls -l >> lsdata
ls -l
-rw-r--r--     1 daveh   c2admin        1890 Feb 24 01:09 data
-rw-r--r--     1 daveh   c2admin        1890 Feb 24 01:10 moredata
-rw-r--r--     1 daveh   c2admin         130 Feb 24 01:11 lsdata
```

on the **job**

The output redirection character (>>) is a useful tool for the system administrator. Several programs, such as system analysis tools or security log parsers, will run for a long time. Their output might take a while to create, and that output might be many pages long. So you have multiple programs to run, each taking a variable amount of time to produce a large quantity of data; if you use output redirection to capture this data to files, you will be able to run your analysis programs and do other tasks while they run, returning when they complete to analyze the saved output. A time-consuming and boring task can now be done when convenient, allowing other work to continue.

Renaming and Moving Files Using mv

You can use the move command, typed mv, to rename files or directories. You can also use it to move files from one directory to another and to move whole directories to be located under other directories. Relative and absolute file and directory addressing may both be used, and wildcards extend the power of this command.

The basic format of the mv command is

```
mv source target
```

where the source can be a file, directory, or wildcard, and the target can be a file or directory. The target may contain wildcards, provided that the wildcards reduce to a single target; mv is happy to move multiple source files identified by a wildcard, but it is unable to move them into multiple targets identified by wildcards, for example,

```
ls -l
-rw-r--r--      1 abshire  users          0 Apr 12 20:21 chrism
-rw-r--r--      1 abshire  users          0 Apr 12 20:21 donnah
-rw-r--r--      1 abshire  users          0 Apr 12 20:21 jasonp
-rw-r--r--      1 abshire  users          0 Apr 12 20:21 johnc
drwxr-xr-x  2 abshire  users       4096 Apr 12 20:23 special
#mv chrism chris_m
#mv  j* special
#mv donnah special/DonnaH
#ls -l
-rw-r--r--      1 abshire  users          0 Apr 12 20:21 chris_m
drwxr-xr-x  2 abshire  users       4096 Apr 12 20:25 special
#ls -l special
-rw-r--r--      1 abshire  users          0 Apr 12 20:21 DonnaH
-rw-r--r--      1 abshire  users          0 Apr 12 20:21 jasonp
-rw-r--r--      1 abshire  users          0 Apr 12 20:21 johnc
```

The most confusing aspect of the mv command is that it will do what you ask it to do, even if you did not formulate your command very well. The mv command moves your files into directories when you meant to say files, for example, and you might think you have lost them. The mv command is useful and powerful, but it demands some care when you use it.

Removing Files Using rm

The rm command is the basic tool for removing objects from your file system. Unfortunately, rm is also the basic tool new system administrators use to damage their systems, so exercise caution when you use it.

The rm command accepts as an argument a list of files, which may be relatively or absolutely addressed in the file system. If the user has write permissions to the file, or if the user is the owner of the file, the file is removed from the file system. Some special files, such as the sockets and block files discussed earlier in the section "Listing the Contents of a Directory," may not be removed quite as easily, and directories also require some extra work to delete:

```
rm file1
rm file[1-9]
rm file*
rm /export/home/andy/*
```

The asterisk metacharacter (*) is commonly used to remove all files. In practice, this command, as in the preceding example, removes all regular files to which the user has write access. Directories are not removed. Files that are owned by the user but for which the user does not have write access can be considered write-protected, and rm prompts for confirmation on each protected file.

The rm command has three important options to modify its behavior. The *-f* option is used when dealing with write-protected files. This option is commonly thought of as *force*, and indeed, it does force the removal of files for which the user has ownership but not permission. The *-f* option does not force the removal of directories or files for which the user does not have ownership:

```
rm file1
rm: remove write-protected file 'file1'? n
rm -f file1
```

The *-r* option makes rm perhaps the most dangerous command in Solaris. This option, commonly called *recursive*, removes files recursively. It also removes directories and their complete contents, including subdirectories. The same rules for rm apply; the user must have write permission or ownership of every file system object that is removed, or the operation will fail. The rm command is very thorough and continues to remove files and directories, even if it encounters objects that it must skip for lack of permission:

```
#ls -l
drwxr-xr-x    2 heather   hr_dept        4096 Apr 12 20:48 dir1
-rw-r--r--    1 heather   hr_dept           0 Apr 12 20:48 file1
#touch dir1/file2
#ls -l
drwxr-xr-x    2 heather   hr_dept        4096 Apr 12 20:48 dir1
-rw-r--r--    1 heather   hr_dept           0 Apr 12 20:48 file1
#ls -l dir1
-rw-r--r--    1 heather   hr_dept           0 Apr 12 20:48 file2
#rm *
#rm: 'dir1' is a directory
#ls -l
drwxr-xr-x    2 heather   hr_dept        4096 Apr 12 20:48 dir1
#touch file1
#ls -l
drwxr-xr-x    2 heather   hr_dept        4096 Apr 12 20:48 dir1
-rw-r--r--    1 heather   hr_dept           0 Apr 12 20:48 file1
#rm -r *
#ls -l
total 0
```

To protect yourself from the dangers of removing files by accident, you could employ the *-i* option to rm. This option means *interactive,* and it forces rm to ask you for confirmation before each file it deletes. The interactive option to rm is highly recommended for new users and system administrators, but it quickly becomes tedious when you are removing a large number of files.

on the **Job**

The rm command provides a common introduction to restoring a system from backups. Combined with the -r option, rm can open the door to catastrophic mistakes. For example, while doing an administrative task as the superuser, a new system administrator entered the command to remove a directory with an absolute pathname. Knowing that the directory was not empty, the administrator added the -r option but unintentionally added a space after the leading slash of the fully qualified directory name:

```
rm -r /(space)tmp/oldfilesdirectory
```

The rm command did what it was told and removed all files and directories, starting with the slash, the top of the file system. Given enough time, this command will remove almost every file from the file system.

EXERCISE 14-5

Copying, Renaming, Creating, and Deleting Files

The concepts of copying, renaming, creating, and deleting files can be demonstrated by following this exercise. Go through this sequence of commands, using the ls command at intervals to see the effects of your work. You will gain an appreciation for the way files are manipulated by the touch, mv, cp, and mkdir commands.

```
 1. touch file1
 2. mv file1 file2
 3. mv file2 file1
 4. cp file1 file2
 5. cp file2 file3
 6. mkdir directory1
 7. mv file? directory1
 8. mv directory1/* .
 9. mkdir directory2
10.  mv file? directory2
11.  mv directory2 directory1
12.  cp directory1/directory2/file* .
13.  cp directory1/directory2/file* directory1
14.  rm file1
```

```
15.   rm file2
16.   rm -r directory1/directory2
17.   rm -ri directory1
```

CERTIFICATION SUMMARY

This chapter discussed some of the details of interacting with the Solaris file system from the command-line interface. Although not as pretty or as popular as graphical interfaces, the command-line interface is the primary tool for many system administrators; comfort and skill in using it go a long way toward landing and enjoying any UNIX system administration job. Although the command-line interface offers power and flexibility, there is also room for obscure mistakes and hidden dangers, so you must exercise care at all times.

The Solaris file system is a hierarchical structure that operates based on basic rules. An understanding of these rules, combined with the knowledge of the basic commands covered in this chapter, is essential to Solaris system administration. Adding, copying, and deleting files and directories and navigating the file system are daily tasks, made easier with the addition of file system wildcard metacharacters. The metacharacters seem to provide a language all their own; they are cryptic and powerful, yet they also operate with the basic rules outlined in this chapter.

Understanding the basic concepts that drive the commands pwd, cd, mkdir, rmdir, cp, mv, ls, rm, touch, and file will take you a long way in your system administration career. The commands might change over time, but they will still rely on basic concepts; knowing these concepts will allow you to solve any system administration problem.

TWO-MINUTE DRILL

Moving Between Specified Points in a Directory Tree

❑ The print working directory (pwd) command identifies your current position in the file system hierarchy.

❑ File system objects are addressed using absolute pathnames or relative pathnames. Absolute paths always start with the root directory, written as a slash (/).

❑ The change directory (cd) command with relative or absolute pathnames is used to navigate the file system.

Using Metacharacter Combinations to Access Files and Directories Within the Directory Tree

❑ Metacharacters allow you to define a pattern of idealized text to use when addressing files or directories.

❑ There are two distinct contexts for using metacharacters in pattern matches, and these contexts have different syntaxes.

❑ Metacharacters can be used when you don't know the spelling of an object or when you want a single command to take action against a group of objects at one time.

Listing Directory Contents and Determining the File Types Within a Directory

❑ The file command is used to determine the type of a file in comparison to some basic file types based on the contents of the file.

❑ The ls command may be used to show detailed reports on the contents of directories.

❑ Hidden files are not normally shown by the ls command, but they can be seen with the *-a* option to ls.

Using Commands to Create or Remove Directories

❑ Directories are created using the make directory (mkdir) command. The user must have permission to write to the directory in which the new directory will be created, and the new directory must not already exist as a directory or file.

❑ Empty directories are removed using the remove directory (rmdir) command. To remove a directory, the user must have write permissions to the parent of the directory being removed.

❑ The *-p* option may be used with both mkdir and rmdir to add and delete, respectively, any parent directories involved in the adding or removing of a directory tree.

Using Commands to Copy, Create, Rename, or Remove Files

❑ The remove command (rm) is a powerful but dangerous tool; the *-i* option can save a user from careless mistakes.

❑ In Solaris, files are renamed by moving them to the new filename. Multiple files may be moved to a new directory as well. The move command (mv) can use wildcards to move multiple files to a new directory with one command.

❑ The touch command is used to create files of zero length.

SELF TEST

The following questions will help you measure your understanding of the material presented in this chapter. Read all the choices carefully because there might be more than one correct answer. Choose all correct answers for each question.

Moving Between Specified Points in a Directory Tree

1. Assume you are given the following sequence of commands:

```
#pwd
/home/users/john/files
#cd ../graphics
```

Which of the following is true? (Choose all that apply.)

A. The absolute pathname for the graphics directory is ../graphics.

B. Graphics and files are both subdirectories of the john directory.

C. john is the parent directory of users.

D. From graphics, the relative path to files is ../files.

Using Metacharacter Combinations to Access Files and Directories Within the Directory Tree

2. From among the following, choose all files that match this pattern:
/export/home/john/[a–z]123*.txt.

A. /export/home/john/a2stuff.txt

B. /export/home/john/a123.txt

C. /export/home/john/z3hidad.txt

D. /export/home/john/z123456.txt

3. The directory /export/home/john has these subdirectories: letters, games, graphics, and stuff. Which of the following commands will change directory from /export/home/john to /export/home/john/games?

A. cd g*

B. cd [lgs]*

C. cd ga*

D. cd

Listing Directory Contents and Determining the File Types Within a Directory

4. The ls *-F* command option places a special character at the end of the filename for which types of files?

A. Sockets, links, and directories

B. Directories, user files, and regular files

C. Executable files, link files, and directories

D. Block files, executable files, and character files

5. A hidden file is created by doing which of the following?

A. Using the attrib command

B. Adding a dot to the beginning of the filename

C. Using the hidefile command

D. Using the *-h* option with the createfil command

Using Commands to Create or Remove Directories

6. If you attempt to create a directory that already exists, but you do not have write permissions to that directory, what will happen?

A. The operation will fail. You must remove the original directory first.

B. The existing directory will be emptied of files.

C. The existing directory will be renamed to directory.bak.

D. The new directory will be created as a subdirectory of the original directory.

Using Commands to Copy, Create, Rename, or Remove Files

7. Which of the following is true of the rm *-r* command?

A. It removes files, directories, and the contents of directories, provided that the user has write permissions or ownership for all objects to be removed.

B. It removes everything in the user's home directory, to include dot files and hidden files, unless the *-h* option is used to save hidden files.

C. It removes all system and special files from the operating system.

D. It prompts you to remove hidden files.

8. The following command creates a new file:

```
ls -l >> newfile
```

Through what process is the new file created?

A. The double greater-than character (>>) represents output redirection.

B. The double greater-than character (>>) executes the creatfil program.

C. The double greater-than character (>>) implies that the ls -*l* is greater than newfile.

D. The double greater-than character (>>) executes the newfile command, which runs ls -*l*.

9. Which of the following is not handled by the mv command?

A. Makes a directory a subdirectory of another directory

B. Renames files

C. Makes multiple copies of files

D. Moves multiple files to a new directory

LAB QUESTION

You have just been hired as a new system administrator for a company whose computer infrastructure is almost entirely devoted to a desktop-oriented, graphically dependant operating system. They hired you because they just bought their first UNIX-based computer, which happens to be running Solaris.

You have been given a list of tasks to accomplish to make the system ready for the user community. These tasks include removing or saving some test files and directories and adding new user files and directories.

Here's your task list:

1. Locate any C program code files in the test user subdirectories under /usr/home.

2. If any such files were found, copy them to the repository directory (/usr/repository) under a subdirectory named with today's date.

3. Remove all files and subdirectories under /usr/home.

4. Three new users will be programming on this system: Andy, Patrick, and Cindy. For each user, create a directory using his or her name.

5. In each of these directories, create an empty file named ready_to_go.

6. For each directory, copy the file /etc/skel/profile to a file named .profile.

7. In the /usr/home directory, execute the command ls -*la* and capture its output to the file /usr/home/table_of_contents.

Show the sequence of commands, and what each does, that you would employ to accomplish this set of tasks.

SELF TEST ANSWERS

Moving Between Specified Points in a Directory Tree

1. ☑ **B and D.** Both the graphics and files subdirectories are contained within the john directory. A directory can have only one parent directory but can have zero or more subdirectories, so it follows that john is the parent of graphics because you used the dot-dot, or *up*, notation from files to get into john, from which you descended into graphics. The reverse relationship is true as well: from graphics, you need to go up a directory to john before you can access files.

   ☒ **A** is incorrect because an absolute pathname always starts with root (/). **C** is incorrect because users is above john in the hierarchy of the file system; users is the parent of john.

Using Metacharacter Combinations to Access Files and Directories Within the Directory Tree

2. ☑ **B and D. B** is correct because the first character, *a,* is matched by the character set [a–z]; 123 immediately follows as a string literal; and asterisk (*) matches zero or more characters, in this case, zero characters, followed by the string literal .txt. **D** is also correct because the first character, *z,* is matched by the character set [a–z]; 123 immediately follows as a string literal; and the asterisk (*) matches the next three characters, which happen to be 456. The string literal .txt follows to complete the pattern match.

   ☒ **A and C** are incorrect because both treat 123 as a character set. The 123 in the pattern is not enclosed in the character set metacharacters [ ], so it must be taken as a string literal—exactly 1 followed by 2 followed by 3.

3. ☑ **C.** By defining the pattern to start with the string literal *ga,* followed by any number of any characters, the ambiguity has been removed. Only one directory starts with the characters *g, a.*

   ☒ **A** is incorrect because cd must have a single directory as an argument. The pattern *g** will match two directories, games and graphics, which is an ambiguous cd command. **B** is incorrect because the pattern *[lgs]** matches all four subdirectories, creating an ambiguous cd command. **D** is incorrect because cd by itself will simply change directory to the user's home directory.

Listing Directory Contents and Determining the File Types Within a Directory

4. ☑ **C.** The *-F* option to ls identifies directories, links, and executables.

   ☒ **A, B, and D** are incorrect because these other types of files can be seen using the *-l* option tools.

5. ☑ B. Hidden files are defined as files that start with a dot.
   ☒ A, C, and D are incorrect because these commands do not exist in Solaris.

Using Commands to Create or Remove Directories

6. ☑ A. To create a new directory, no file system object by the same name can exist in the same place.
   ☒ B, C, and D are all incorrect because these actions are not part of the mkdir operation.

Using Commands to Copy, Create, Rename, or Remove Files

7. ☑ A. The user must have permission to write to any object that he or she attempts to remove, or the user must own it to delete it.
   ☒ B is incorrect because the *-h* option is not an option to the rm command. C is incorrect because rm does not distinguish between system files and regular user files. To rm, a file is a file. D is incorrect because rm only prompts to remove write-protected files, or all files if the *-i* option is used, regardless of whether these files are hidden or not.

8. ☑ A. The double greater-than character (>>) allows you to capture the output of a command and place it in a file.
   ☒ B and D are incorrect because the double greater-than character (>>) does not execute any commands; it simply creates a file. C is incorrect because the relationship between the ls command and the newfile file is not one of quantity.

9. ☑ C. The mv command does not make copies of files.
   ☒ A, B, and D are incorrect because they are all features of the mv command.

LAB ANSWER

First, log in to the computer and navigate the file system to the right directory:

```
cd /usr/home
```

Verify that you are in the right place, and see which files and directories are there:

```
pwd
/usr/home
ls -F
test_table_of_contents
test_user1/
test_user2/
```

Find any C program files in the test_user directories using the file command. Instead of entering each directory, you can do this with a single command and some metacharacters:

```
file test_user?/*
test_user1/program1.c: C program text
test_user1/data.dat: data
test_user2/testprog.c: C program text
test_user2/testprog_1Alpha.c: C program text
test_user2/testletter.txt: ASCII Text
```

You want to save the ones that are C program text. It turns out that they are all named with a .c file extension; otherwise, they all have unique filenames. This makes your saving job easy; you can simply copy them all to the repository with a single wildcard command. But first, you have to create the destination directory. Because repository is a subdirectory of /usr, just like home, you can use relative pathnames:

```
mkdir ../repository/Monday_backup
```

Then you can move the files:

```
mv test_user?/*.c ../repository/Monday_backup
```

Now you are ready to remove the test user directories and the existing table of contents. You know that the test user directories are not empty, but you want to accomplish the task with a minimum of typing and time spent. You can remove the directories and the table of contents with a single rm command:

```
rm -r *
```

This will remove the test_table_of_contents file and both test_user directories, including all files and subdirectories in them. There was no need to look any closer in these test directories; you already saved what you needed.

Next, you need to create your new user directories. The mkdir command will make multiple directories if they are provided as a list of arguments to this command:

```
mkdir andy patrick cindy
```

You need to create the ready_to_go file in each user directory to let the users know that their accounts are ready to use. This can be done with the touch command using relative paths:

```
touch andy/ready_to_go
touch patrick/ready_to_go
touch cindy/ready_to_go
```

Now you need to copy the /etc/skel/profile file to a file named .profile in each directory. For this, you can use the cp command and an absolute pathname for the source and a relative path for the destination:

```
cp /etc/skel/profile andy/.profile
cp /etc/skel/profile patrick/.profile
cp /etc/skel/profile cindy/.profile
```

Finally, you need to make the new table of contents in the /usr/home directory. First, make sure you are in the right place, and then use the ls command with output redirection to create the file:

```
pwd
/usr/home
ls -la >> table_of_contents
ls -F
andy/    cindy/    patrick/    table_of_contents
```

Task complete!

SUN® CERTIFIED SYSTEM ADMINISTRATOR

15

Working with the vi Editor

One of the main duties of a successful system administrator is editing files, whether configuration files for applications, system configuration files (such as /etc/hosts and /etc/inetd.conf), or shell scripts. On Solaris, and all other UNIX variants, the main system text editor is called *vi* or *vim (vi improved)*.

Short for *visual editor*, vi started as a line-based editor called *ex* but was modified in the late 1970s into the program we know today by Bill Joy, now chief scientist and corporate executive officer at Sun Microsystems. Originally released with the University of California at Berkeley (UCB) distribution of UNIX, vi became the official text editor for AT&T System V UNIX, Release 5, on which Solaris is based.

Solaris (and other UNIX variants) may have other text editors installed on a system for use. However, it is always a good idea to know the basic concepts of file editing using vi because it is almost guaranteed to be installed on any UNIX system an administrator might come across. In addition, in the event of a system crash or file system malfunction, if the system is bootable, vi will most likely be available, unlike other editors that might depend on a graphical user interface or extensive third-party system libraries.

One point to note about vi is that it is a text editor and not a "proper" word processor. Solaris provides many other tools (such as nroff/troff) for word processing. However, vi can be used for editing plain text, HTML code, or program source files. If the document you need to produce can be done with plain text, you can create it with vi. Many people write documents in vi, and then import the plain text into a What You See Is What You Get (WYSIWYG) word processor for final adjustments.

This chapter uses the system hosts-to-IP address table file, /etc/hosts, as an example of a system configuration file that would normally be edited by a typical system administrator.

CERTIFICATION OBJECTIVE 15.01

Switching Among the vi Editor's Three Modes of Operation

This chapter details ways to use the vi editor to create and modify text files—specifically, system configuration files needed for proper operation of a Solaris system. You will learn how to start the editor, move around in a document, edit text, and then use vi's search and search-and-replace functions to modify documents.

Starting the vi Editor

To edit or create system configuration files, you first need to be logged in to the system as the root user, or superuser. To edit files, you must either own the files or have write permission on them. Your command prompt will look a bit different as the superuser; it will be a hash mark or pound sign (#), whereas a normal user's prompt is the dollar sign ($). You start vi the same way, regardless of how you are logged in, by typing **vi** in lowercase letters at the command prompt:

```
# vi
```

Starting the editor without a filename will bring it up to edit a blank file. To edit a file that already exists, specify its name on the command line. To edit /etc/hosts, for example,

```
# vi /etc/hosts
```

To create a new file, do the same thing: specify its name on the command line. If the file does not already exist, it will be created. If you try to edit a file for which you do not have write permission or in a directory you do not own, vi will load the file and display it but will give an error if you try to save the file.

As an example, if you are logged in as a normal user and you try to edit the system /etc/hosts file,

```
$ vi /etc/hosts
```

vi loads the file and displays it. You are also allowed to make changes to the file *in memory*—but once you try to save it, an error message will appear at the bottom of your screen, in reverse video (black on white or white on black, depending on how your terminal or terminal emulator window is configured):

```
/etc/hosts: Permission Denied
```

This means that you do not have sufficient permission (no write access) to overwrite the original file. You can save the file under a different name, and then copy it over later as the root user. We walk through this process later in Exercise 15-2.

Editor Modes of vi Operation

The vi editor is "modal." As shown in Table 15-1, it has three distinct modes of operation: command, insert, and append.

Mode of Operation	Function
Command	Switches to insert mode and overtype mode; writes/saves files; handles search/replace operations
Insert	Inserts text when typed at the cursor position
Append	Appends text after the cursor

TABLE 15-1

Modes of vi Operation

Unlike most other editors, you cannot just start typing text after starting vi. You have to use command mode to tell the editor that you would like to start editing text. To switch into any of the editing modes, first make sure you are in command mode (by pressing ESC), and then type one of these letters:

- I   Switches to insert mode
- O   Switches to overtype mode
- A   Switches to append mode

Once in insert, overtype, or append mode, you may then start entering text. To switch between modes, go into command mode (again, by pressing ESC), and then press the key for the mode that you would like to activate. If your keyboard (or terminal) does not have an ESC or ESCAPE key, pressing the CTRL key and left-bracket ([ ) keys at the same time performs the same function as the ESC key.

on the **Job**

If you are not sure which editing mode you are in at any given time, press ESC to go into command mode. The ESC key always takes you into command mode, no matter what you are doing in the editor. Pressing it multiple times will do nothing bad or harmful to your document, although you need to press it only once. Once in command mode, you can then switch to an editing mode and be aware of what mode you are in.

Reading, Writing, and Saving Files

Before making any changes to critical system files, it is always a good idea to make a backup of the file(s) first. Use this command to make a backup of the /etc/hosts file:

```
# cp /etc/hosts /etc/hosts.backup
```

This way, if something goes wrong during editing—you delete too many lines, for example—you can simply copy the backup file over the original and not lose data:

```
# cp /etc/hosts.backup /etc/hosts
```

When creating or editing files with the vi editor, you will want to be able to save the file(s) once your work is done. To do so, first press ESC (to get into vi command mode), and then use one of the following commands:

- :q!   Quits without saving your file
- :w   Writes file without quitting (good for saving changes)
- :w <<*filename*>>   Writes file to <<*filename*>>
- :w! <<*filename*>>   Writes file to <<*filename*>> (forced overwrite of an existing file)
- :wq   Writes file, and then quits
- :wq!   Writes file, and then quits (forced overwrite of an existing file)
- ZZ   Writes file, and then quits (same as :wq)

You can also read files into the editor (to merge two documents, for example):

- :r <<*filename*>>   Inserts <*filename*> after current cursor position

FROM THE CLASSROOM

Editing System Config Files as a Nonroot User

A common occurrence (more common than you might think) among system administrators is mistakenly trying to edit a file when you do not have permissions to overwrite or modify that file.

Therefore, you might find yourself having done an hour's worth of changes to a program source code file, but when you try to save the file, you get a "Permission Denied" message, and you realize that you've just spent an hour editing a file but cannot save your changes!

Never fear—there is an easy way to avoid repeating the effort you've just expended. We'll use the vi command that lets you save your work to a temporary file with an alternative name, and then quite the editor. Say that the file you are editing is called *program.c*; let's write to a similar filename:

```
{ESC} :wq! program.c.tmp
```

(continued)

CERTIFICATION OBJECTIVE 15.02

Using the vi Editor Commands to Move the Cursor, and to Create, Delete, Copy, and Move Text

Now let's look at using keyboard commands and shortcuts to move around a document in vi while making changes. Because vi was first created and used before the GUI concept became popular, all the movement commands in vi use the keyboard. In most cases, they allow you to completely navigate around your document without having to reposition your hands from the home row on a normal QWERTY keyboard.

Editing Text with vi

One of the basic abilities that a screen-oriented text editor must have is the ability to reposition the cursor to add or edit text. The vi editor allows the cursor to move around by individual character(s), word(s), or line(s), or by entire screens of text. Unlike some text editors, vi does not use the arrow keys (if they are even present) on a keyboard or terminal to position the cursor when moving by character. Instead of arrow keys, vi uses some of the home row keys on the keyboard for cursor positioning.

You can move the cursor (again, you must be in command mode) up a line or down a line. Use the J key to move the cursor down one line and the K key to move up a line. To move left or right, use H to move left one character and L to move the cursor one character to the right. Here's a quick guide to keyboard movements:

- J   Moves the cursor down one line
- K   Moves the cursor up one line
- H   Moves the cursor left one character
- L   Moves the cursor right one character

To move more than one character up, down, left, or right, you can either press the movement key multiple times or, before pressing the movement key, type the number of characters that you would like to move. For example, to move the cursor up two lines, assuming that you are already in command mode (press ESC first if you're not sure), you would type this:

```
2k
```

To move the cursor right five characters, you'd do the same thing but with the different number key and movement key:

```
5l
```

To avoid having to count characters, vi allows movement by entire words (where a "word" is defined as a group of letters or numbers, separated on each end by a space). Here are the keystrokes for moving entire words at a time:

- W   Moves forward one word
- B   Moves backward one word
- E   Moves to the end of the current word

You can also move around by larger groups of words:

- 0   Moves to the beginning of the current line
- $ Moves to the end of the current line
- (Moves to the beginning of the current sentence

-) Moves to the beginning of the next sentence
- { Moves to the beginning of the current paragraph
- } Moves to the beginning of the next paragraph

We've already discussed repeating movement commands by prefacing them with numbers; this applies to the word, line, and sentence movement commands as well.

The vi editor does not limit cursor movement to characters, words, sentences, lines, or even whole paragraphs. You can also scroll up and down by entire screens or partial screens:

- CTRL-F   Scrolls forward (down) one screen
- CTRL-B   Scrolls back (up) one screen
- CTRL-D   Scrolls forward by half a screen
- CTRL-U   Scrolls back by half a screen

CTRL-D, for example, means to press the CTRL key and the D key at the same time. CTRL might also be labeled CONTROL on some keyboards.

In addition to moving back and forth by entire screens, you can also move around within the current screen:

- H   Moves to the first line on the screen
- L   Moves to the last line on the screen
- M   Moves to the middle line on the screen

For editing text, RETURN also works; it moves the cursor to the beginning of the next line on the screen, just like you would expect a typewriter to work.

EXERCISE 15-1

Adding a Line of Text to the Bottom of a Document

In this example, you add a host named *hera* with an IP address of 192.168.1.25 to the system hosts table.

1. Open the system hosts table in vi:

```
# vi /etc/hosts
```

2. Go to the bottom of the file:

```
[ESC]  G
```

3. Enter overwrite/append mode:

   o

4. Type the host and IP address info:

   `192.168.1.25` [TAB] `hera`

5. Change back to command mode:

   [ESC]

6. Write the file and exit:

   `:wq!`

If at any time while you are moving around in a document or editing text, your screen becomes garbled (as could occur while working on a Solaris system over a modem connection, for example), you can instruct vi to "redraw" your screen. First, enter command mode, and then press CTRL-L. Furthermore, to find out the total number of lines of text in your current document, press CTRL-G while in command mode. To jump to a specific line in your document, go to command mode, enter the number of the line to which you want to jump, and then type the capital letter G. For example, to jump to the twenty-third line of a document from anywhere in that document, type

`[ESC] 23G`

The vi editor also has commands that are useful for correcting typographical errors. Position the cursor at the beginning of the word or sentence that needs to be fixed, go into command mode, and then use one of the following:

- CW   Changes to the end of a word
- C$ Changes to the end of a line
- CC   Changes an entire line
- R   Replaces or changes a single character under the cursor

With the change commands, once issued, you are automatically put into insert mode, and your changes will take effect once you finish typing and press the ESC key.

Let's say you really mess up and would like to delete some text that you have edited. The vi editor makes that process easy as well, again starting from command mode:

- X   Deletes a current character
- DW   Deletes an entire word part of a word to the right of the cursor
- DD   Deletes an entire line

These delete commands can also be prefaced by a number to repeat them multiple times. If you mess up and mistakenly delete a character, word, sentence, or paragraph, you can easily get it back (as long as you haven't done any other editing in the meantime) by simply pressing ESC to get into command mode, and then pressing U to undo the edit. Pressing U multiple times will "undo the undo," or toggle back and forth.

e x a m
ⓦ a t c h
Most commands used in vi for moving around in a text file or deleting text can be repeated by prefacing them with the number of times to repeat the command (as numerals, not words—for example, 10 instead of ten).

Copying and Moving Text

Once you've written the perfect novel (or at least the perfect paragraph), you might want to move some text around. If you want to move just a line of text, move to the beginning of that line and use the dd command (the same command that deletes a line of text). When the line is deleted, it is saved in a *buffer* (a temporary storage space inside the editor). Before executing *any* other command, move the cursor to where you would like the line to be pasted, and then press P. The line will be pasted into the line below the cursor. If you delete a line of text with dd, you will lose it if you do not paste the line before editing, deleting, adding, appending, or inserting any other text.

To copy a line of text, move the cursor to the beginning of the line, and then press YY (which means *yank*) to copy the line of text into the buffer without deleting it. As with moving text, to paste a copy of the line, move the cursor to the line before where you want the text to go, and then press P to paste. You can copy multiple lines of text by prefacing *yy* with the number of lines to copy. For example, to copy eight lines of text,

8yy

Pasting multiple lines of text is identical to pasting single lines; just press P. *Do not* preface P with a number, unless you would like multiple copies of your group of lines to be inserted. You can undo pastes as well by pressing ESC, and then U for *undo.*

o n   t h e
ⓙ o b
If pasting a block of text multiple times, be sure to move the cursor to the end of the block before pasting the next one; otherwise, you'll end up with a lot of lines containing the first line of the block, then multiple copies of the rest of the block of text.

EXERCISE 15-2

Editing Text

As an exercise, pretend that a machine on your network is currently named *zeus* but is being renamed to *athena*. You have a record for zeus in your machine's /etc/hosts file, so you need to edit that file to reflect the hostname change.

1. Start vi and load the file (as the root user):

   ```
   # vi /etc/hosts
   ```

2. Search for the first occurrence of zeus. Enter command mode:

   ```
   [ESC]
   ```

   Search for zeus:

   ```
   /zeus
   ```

   Start the search:

   ```
   [ENTER]
   ```

3. The cursor should now be at the beginning of the word "zeus." Change the word "zeus" to the word "athena." Enter command mode:

   ```
   [ESC]
   ```

   Change word:

   ```
   cw athena
   ```

   Finish word change:

   ```
   [ESC]
   ```

4. Repeat the search for any other occurrences of zeus. Enter command mode:

   ```
   [ESC]
   ```

   Repeat the last search:

   ```
   /[ENTER]
   ```

5. Repeat Steps 3 and 4 as necessary.

6. Save the file. Enter command mode:

   ```
   [ESC]
   ```

   Write the file and quit:

   ```
   :wq
   ```

CERTIFICATION OBJECTIVE 15.03

Using vi Command Sequences to Search and Replace

The vi editor allows for easy semiautomated correction of errors in a document or replacement of one word or group of characters with another. This leads to easy maintenance of files such as host tables and is one of the features that makes it the most popular text editor in use among system administrators today.

Searching for Text

Let's say you just finished writing a shell script and need to change the name of a variable that was used in the script. However, you are at the top of the file and not sure of every place in the file where you used the variable. For this problem, you can use vi's search function to locate all the occurrences of a particular string of characters.

To use the search function, first enter command mode (by pressing ESC), then type a forward slash character (/), followed by the string that you would like to find in your document. Tell vi to start searching by pressing ENTER or RETURN. If the string is found, your cursor will be repositioned at the beginning of the first occurrence of that string. As an example, to search for the string *hosts*,

```
/hosts [ENTER]
```

If you have more than one occurrence of your search string in the file, to find the next instance, simply enter command mode (ESC), type a forward slash (/), and press ENTER. This sequence will automatically repeat your last search without requiring you to type the search string all over again. An ever-shorter keystroke sequence for repeating a search is simply pressing N, short for *next occurrence of <string>*. Again, your cursor will be positioned at the beginning of the string for which you are searching.

By default, vi searches for a string by going forward from the current cursor position. If you would like to search backward in the file, use the question-mark character (?) instead of the forward slash. As in a normal forward search, N repeats any backward searches as well.

Because the forward slash (/) is used as the search command, how do you search for a slash itself? To do this, you need to ESC the slash, or use another character before it in the search string to tell vi, "Search for this, don't interpret it."

The escape character used is the backslash (\). So, to search for the first occurrence of a forward slash in your document, use the following keystrokes:

```
[ESC] / \ / [ENTER]
```

This sequence finds the first occurrence of the forward slash in your document.

Other characters with special significance in a search string must be "escaped" as well; however, their use is beyond the scope of this book. These characters are the start-of-line indicator, a carat (^); the end-of-line indicator, a dollar sign ($); and a single character, the period (.). For more information on what these special characters do in search strings, read the appropriate vi manual page or search for information on regular expressions.

Searching and Replacing Text

If your document is very large, searching for each occurrence of a word or string and then manually retyping them can become tedious very quickly. Fortunately, vi provides a global search-and-replace function to automate such repetitive work. To search for the first occurrence of a string and replace it with another string, you first need to enter command mode, and then use the following syntax:

```
:s/<<string1>>/<<string2>>/ [ENTER]
```

This code replaces the first instance that vi finds of the entire string <<*string1*>> with <<*string2*>> in the current line. The *s* in the command stands for *substitute*.

To search for (or replace) a forward slash, escape it like you did with the search function. For example, to replace the string */bob* with */mary*, the search-and-replace command would look like this:

```
:s/\/bob/\/mary/ [ENTER]
```

To replace *all* occurrences of a string with another, preface the *s* in the command string with a percent sign (%):

```
:%s/<string1>/<string2>/ [ENTER]
```

This sequence replaces every occurrence of <<*string1*>> in the document with <<*string2*>>, without individual confirmation of each replaced string. Be very careful when replacing strings that can also be parts of words; if you're not careful, you could find that you unintentionally changed several other words throughout your document!

When searching for or globally replacing text in a document, don't forget to escape characters that can be interpreted, such as a forward slash, by preceding them with a backslash (\).Hopefully, by now you feel more comfortable using the vi editor to create and modify text files on your Solaris system. Next are some possible scenarios and solutions that you could run into as a systems administrator.

SCENARIO & SOLUTION

After editing a system configuration file and trying to save your changes, you get a message that says "File exists."	Instead of using :w or :wq, you'll need to force vi to save the file and overwrite the old one. (Most likely, the old file does not have write permission enabled.) To do this, use :w! or :wq!; the exclamation point signals vi to overwrite the old file no matter what the permissions on it might be.
Your company's Internet domain name has changed from company.com to megacorp.com, but you have hundreds of references to the old domain name in your /etc/hosts file.	Use global search and replace while editing /etc/hosts to replace the old domain name with the new one. To replace company.com with megacorp.com, for example, first enter command mode, and then use a global substitute command: `:%s/COMPANY.COM/MEGACORP.COM/g`
While editing a file, you realize that you don't want to overwrite the existing file, but you want to save the changes you've made anyway.	Write the file using a different filename: `:w <<new-filename>>`

CERTIFICATION SUMMARY

After learning the vi editor and the editing techniques described in this chapter, you should be able to accomplish most common Solaris system administration tasks regarding creating or editing system text and configuration files. You should also be able to deal with most basic system admin tasks regarding system text or configuration files after learning the editing techniques covered in this chapter. Once you are comfortable with the editor, you will be able to quickly and easily create new files or make changes to old ones.

✓ TWO-MINUTE DRILL

Switching Among the vi Editor's Three Modes of Operation

- ❑ ESC   Switches to command mode from any edit mode
- ❑ I   Switches to insert mode from command mode
- ❑ O   Switches to overtype mode from command mode
- ❑ A   Switches to append mode from command mode

Using the vi Editor Commands to Move the Cursor, and to Create, Delete, Copy, and Move Text

- ❑ K or J   Moves the cursor up or down a line
- ❑ H or L   Moves the cursor left or right one character
- ❑ W   Moves to the beginning of the next word
- ❑ 0 or $ Moves to the beginning or end of the current line
- ❑ (or)   Moves to the beginning or end of the current sentence
- ❑ { or }   Moves to the beginning or end of the current paragraph
- ❑ X   Deletes the current character
- ❑ DW   Deletes the entire current word
- ❑ DD   Deletes the entire current line
- ❑ YY   Yanks a line of text into the buffer
- ❑ <<*x*>>YY   Yanks <<*x*>> number of lines of text into the buffer
- ❑ P   Pastes the buffer below the line the cursor is on
- ❑ <<*x*>>P   Repeats the paste <<*x*>> number of times

Using vi Command Sequences to Search and Replace

- ❑ /<<*string*>>   Searches forward for the first occurrence of <<*string*>>
- ❑ /[ENTER] or N   Repeats a search
- ❑ ?*string*   Searches backward for the first occurrence of <<*string*>>
- ❑ :s/<<*x*>>/<<*y*>>/g   Replaces the first occurrence of <<*x*>> with <<*y*>>
- ❑ :%s/<<*x*>>/<<*y*>>   Replaces all occurrences of <<*x*>> with <<*y*>>

SELF TEST

The following questions will help you measure your understanding of the material presented in this chapter. Read all the choices carefully because there might be more than one correct answer. Choose all correct answers for each question.

Switching Among the vi Editor's Three Modes of Operation

1. Which key do you press to change into command mode while using vi?

    A. CONTROL

    B. ENTER

    C. COMMAND

    D. ESC

2. What should you do first before entering text into a file using vi?

    A. Nothing; just start typing.

    B. Change to insert or overtype mode.

    C. Enter command mode by pressing ESC.

    D. Press the HELP key on your Sun keyboard.

Using the vi Editor Commands to Move the Cursor, and to Create, Delete, Copy, and Move Text

3. Which command sequence should be used to copy eight lines of text into a buffer?

    A. Press YY eight times.

    B. Press the numeral 8 and then YY.

    C. Press the numeral 8 and then C.

    D. :copy8.

4. After copying those eight lines of text, you want to paste multiple copies of those lines into your document. How would you go about doing so?

    A. Position the cursor where you want the text to go, and press P eight times.

    B. Press [ESC] 8P.

    C. Paste the text, move the cursor to the bottom of the text, and then paste again. Repeat as many times as necessary.

    D. Use the mouse and the Cut and Paste commands.

5. You are in the middle of a document and want to go back to the very first line (top). To do this, you would do which of the following?

    A. Press 1G in command mode to jump to the first line of text.

    B. Press PGUP repeatedly until you reach the top.

    C. Hold down K until you scroll to the top of the document.

    D. Use the arrow keys.

6. You've used the word "dictionary" in a document when you meant to use "thesaurus." After placing your cursor at the beginning of the word, you do which of the following?

    A. Press *x* ten times to delete the word, go into insert mode, and type **thesaurus.**

    B. Go into command mode, press CW, type **thesaurus**, and go back into command mode.

    C. Highlight and delete the word with your mouse.

    D. Delete the entire document and start over. The vi editor doesn't allow for corrections.

7. Which four keys move the cursor left, down, up, and right?

    A. The arrow keys

    B. A, S, D, and F

    C. H, J, K, and L

    D. PGUP, PGDN, INSERT, and HOME

Using vi Command Sequences to Search and Replace

8. Which character is used to start a string search in vi?

    A. =

    B. |

    C. *s*

    D. /

9. What is it called when you use a backslash before a forward slash in a search string to indicate that you are actually searching for a forward-slash character?

    A. Slashing the forward slash

    B. Escaping the forward slash

    C. Separating the forward slash

    D. Hashing the forward slash

10. What would a search-and-replace string look like to replace the first instance of *dog* with *cat* in a document?

A. `/s/cat/dog/`

B. `:s/dog/cat/`

C. `replace/dog/cat/`

D. `.cat\dog`

LAB QUESTION

Your company is renumbering (changing the IP addresses) of its internal network from 192.168.1.*x* to 192.168.10.*x*. You would like to avoid having to retype the /etc/hosts file on every machine. How would you use vi to automate this task, and what would the syntax look like?

SELF TEST ANSWERS

Switching Among the vi Editor's Three Modes of Operation

1. ☑ D. CONTROL-[also works as a substitute for ESC.
   ☒ A is incorrect because the CONTROL key by itself does nothing. B is incorrect because ENTER is used only to edit text and signify the end of a search or command string. C is incorrect because there is no COMMAND key on a Sun system.

2. ☑ B. You must be in an editing mode before you can enter text with vi.
   ☒ A is incorrect because vi is a modal editor. C is incorrect because you cannot enter text into a document in command mode. D is incorrect because this key will do nothing while you're running vi.

Using the vi Editor Commands to Move the Cursor, and to Create, Delete, Copy, and Move Text

3. ☑ B. This *yanks* the eight lines of text following the cursor into the buffer.
   ☒ A is incorrect because this would simply copy a single line of text into the buffer eight times in a row. C is incorrect because *c* does not copy lines of text into the buffer. D is incorrect because this command does not exist.

4. ☑ C is the correct answer.
   ☒ A is incorrect because you can't simply repeat a paste command with a numeral, since the first line will get overwritten. B is incorrect because the same single line will get pasted on top of itself. D is incorrect because the version of vi shipped with Solaris does not support a GUI.

5. ☑ A and C. Both will work.
   ☒ B and D are incorrect because PGUP, PGDN, and the arrow keys are not supported in vi.

6. ☑ A and B. B is more efficient.
   ☒ C is incorrect because vi does not support a graphical user interface. D is incorrect because, even though it *would* work, it would be the hard way of doing things.

7. ☑ C. h, j, k, and l move the cursor left, down, up, and right.
   ☒ A is incorrect because vi does not officially support arrow keys. B and D are incorrect because vi does not support these keys for cursor movement.

Using vi Command Sequences to Search and Replace

8. ☑ D. The forward slash (/) is used to start a string search in vi.
   ☒ A, B, and C are incorrect because you must use the forward slash (/) to start a string search in vi.

9. ☑ B. Using a backslash before a forward slash in a search string to indicate that you are actually searching for a forward-slash character is called "escaping the forward slash."
   ☒ A, C, and D are incorrect.

10. ☑ B. :s/dog/cat/
    ☒ A, C, and D are incorrect because to replace the first instance of *dog* with *cat*, the search-and-replace string must look like :s/dog/cat/.

LAB ANSWER

You would use vi's built-in search-and-replace function to change all instances of 192.168.1. to 192.168.10. The syntax would look like this, once the file is loaded and you are in command mode:

```
:%s/192.168.1./192.168.10./g
```

Note: Do not simply search and replace using this string:

```
:%s/.1/.10/g
```

This is incorrect because if a system has the IP address of 192.168.1.1, its entry would then be changed to 192.1068.10.10. Always try to be as specific as possible when doing global searches and replaces to avoid changing data that doesn't need to be modified.

SUN® CERTIFIED SYSTEM ADMINISTRATOR

16

Working with a Remote Connection

CERTIFICATION OBJECTIVES

V arious tools, including rlogin, rsh, rcp, and ftp, are available in Solaris to make managing and administering remote systems easier. These tools are very flexible and allow the administrator to complete many tasks easily. Some of the most common tasks, such as logging in to remote systems, executing commands remotely, and transferring files between systems, are discussed in this chapter.

CERTIFICATION OBJECTIVE 16.01

Performing Remote System Operations

The first half of this chapter introduces remote login, remote copy, and remote shell commands, collectively referred to as the *R services*. Remote login (rlogin) allows a user to conduct a remote session. Remote shell (rsh) adds flexibility to rlogin, allowing for ease and unattended scripting. Finally, remote copy (rcp) provides for file copying between systems.

Using rlogin

The rlogin command initiates a login session with a remote system. The connection to the remote machine is transparent and provides many of the advantages of a local terminal. The rlogin command possesses advantages over existing remote programs such as Telnet because it is more versatile and, in some circumstances, easier to use. Some of the benefits of rlogin are enhanced authentication, additional command-line options, suspend, and the passing of environment variables.

When running rlogin, you must specify the hostname of the remote system you want to log in to. If no username is specified in the rlogin command line, the default local username is used to log in to the remote system. For instance, if you would like to log in to the system earth.foo.com with the same username as on the local account, you could do the following:

```
[kev@sun.foo.com]$ rlogin earth.foo.com
Password:

Welcome to earth.foo.com!!
[kev@earth.foo.com]$
```

This user successfully logged in to the host earth.foo.com.

Because users move from system to system, figuring out which host a user is logged in to can be a confusing proposition. To clarify which system you are on, you can set the PS1 (prompt) variable to display the user ID and hostname. This process is described further in Chapter 4.

Besides the required remote hostname, rlogin also supports options in the following syntax:

```
rlogin [ -8EL ]  [ -ec ]  [ -l username ]  hostname
```

In this syntax, the *username* is the user ID requested on the remote host. Table 16-1 describes these options further.

The *-l username* option is used frequently because users on one system might not have the same username on another. To specify a different username, you can run the following command:

```
[sarah@sun.foo.com]$

[sarah@sun.foo.com]$ rlogin -l snewhall earth.foo.com
Password:

Welcome to earth.foo.com
[snewhall@earth.foo.com]$
```

This code shows that the username, displayed in the user prompt, has changed from *sarah* to *snewhall* when the user logs on to earth.foo.com.

The rlogin command also supports an escape sequence. When sent, this character causes the terminal to disconnect from the remote system and return to the local

TABLE 16-1	Option	Description
The login Options	*-l*	Specifies username on the destination machine
	-ec	Specifies escape character *c*
	-E	Stops any character from being accepted as an escape sequence
	-8	Passes 8-bit data across the network instead of 7-bit data
	-L	Specifies that the session may be run in litout mode

shell. With this escape sequence, you can switch between local and remote systems. The following demonstrates the use of the escape sequence:

```
[kev@sun.foo.com]$
$ ~^Z
[1]+  Stopped                    rlogin sun.foo.com
[kev@earth.foo.com]$
```

The escape sequence shown here (~^Z) is the key sequence tilde (~) directly followed by CTRL-Z. Notice that the terminal session was suspended and the user then had access to the local terminal. Even though it seems like quite a lot of trouble, this sequence can save you a great deal of time. In the following example, the user employs an escape sequence to avoid logging out of the remote system and closing his applications:

```
[kev@sun.foo.com]$ ~^Z
[1]+  Stopped                    rlogin sun.foo.com
[kev@earth.foo.com]$ ls
logrotate-3.3.tar.gz
[kev@earth.foo.com]$ fg
rlogin sun.foo.com

[kev@sun.foo.com]$
```

Notice the use of the fg command, which will foreground your remote session and return you to the remote terminal. This command allows you to toggle between systems.

When you rlogin to a host, the system checks for the /etc/nologin file. If this file exists, all users are denied access to the system. This can be very helpful for administrators, as in the following example:

```
$ rlogin sunserver.foo.com
System is going down in 10 minutes - Please login at a later time
```

The administrator is able to inform its users that the system will be rebooted, and it can limit other users from accessing the system. Keep in mind that the existence of /etc/nologin does not affect users currently logged in to the system.

The rlogin command also passes the local terminal information to the remote session in the form of the environment variable. Specifically, the terminal, or TERM, variable, which defines how your screen interprets input and output, is propagated to the remote session. The following shows the terminal variable before and after the rlogin process:

```
[kev@earth.foo.com]$ TERM=vt50
[kev@earth.foo.com]$ export TERM
[kev@earth.foo.com]$ rlogin sun.foo.com

Welcome to sun.foo.com
!![kev@sun.foo.com]$ echo $TERM
vt50
```

Notice that the *vt50* value is still set after the user logs in to the remote system sun.foo.com.

Authentication

The rlogin feature, along with rsh and rcp, has several different methods of authentication, including system-to-system and user-to-user authentication. *System-to-system authentication* is used when an administrator decides that two systems are equal or have almost equal user base and organizational needs. An example of this situation occurs when members of an accounting department use a business LAN. In this situation, system-to-system authentication allows all users of the accounting department to move between hosts effortlessly.

System-to-system authentication is accomplished through the use of the /etc/hosts.equiv file. Once a client connects to the server, the server checks to see if the client system is a trusted host. The trusted hosts are listed in the /etc/hosts.equiv file and controlled by the local system administrator. A typical hosts.equiv file is shown here:

```
earth.foo.com
sun.foo.com
-mars.foo.com
```

Each entry can be prefaced by a plus sign (+) or minus sign (−) to signify trusted or not trusted, respectively. If neither plus nor minus is specified, hosts are assumed to be trusted. If the remote system is listed without a minus entry, the user is granted access locally without being prompted for a password, as shown in the following example:

```
[kev@sun.foo.com]$ rlogin earth.foo.com

Welcome to earth.foo.com
!![kev@earth.foo.com]$
```

Local user *kev* is able to access the account *kev* on the remote system without being prompted for a password. Unlike Telnet, rlogin with host authentication, the user's ASCII password is never sent over the network to the remote system. Although the password is never sent across the network, host security now depends on all trusted systems. Consequently, if one trusted system's security is compromised, all hosts that trust that system also have their security compromised.

Understand and test hosts.equiv files. You should also understand the security risk involved in "trusting" another remote system. The exam is sure to mention the security risks inherent in use of the /etc/hosts.equiv file.

If system-to-system authentication fails, rlogin then goes to *user-to-user authentication.* In this type of authentication, the user is able to configure remote systems to trust a specified list of systems. To accomplish this task, the user places in the root of his or her home directory the file .rhosts, in the format

```
earth.foo.com kevin
sun.foo.com
```

If in the .rhosts file only a hostname is specified, the same login name is assumed. An example follows:

```
[kevin@sun.foo.com]$ rlogin earth.foo.com
 Welcome to earth.foo.com!!

[kevin@earth.foo.com]$ cat .rhosts
sun.foo.com
```

Notice that the .rhosts file contains an entry for sun.foo.com. In the previous example, the user *kevin* would be able to log in to earth.foo.com from the system named sun.foo.com, but any other user logging in from sun.foo.com would not be trusted and therefore would not be able to access the system without password authentication. This is different from the /etc/hosts.equiv file, because all users from the system are allowed access under that method.

e x a m
Ⓦa t c h

On the exam, you might be asked how to log in to a remote server without being prompted for a password. This question screams /$HOME/.rhosts file, and just knowing the format and location of the .rhosts file will be an easy source of points on the exam.

Keep in mind that for both the /etc/hosts.equiv file and the $HOME/.rhosts file, the hostname is the official name and not a nickname. By default, neither of these files exists; they must be created and modified for system-to-system or user-to user authentication to operate.

o n   t h e
Ⓙo b

A plus entry (+) in the /etc/hosts.equiv file causes the service to trust all systems. The same is true with .rhost and double plus entries (+ +), which will cause all users to be trusted from all systems. This is undoubtedly a security problem and should be avoided.

Remote Shell (rsh)

The rsh command is used to execute a command on a remote system. This command must be configured with system-to-system (/etc/hosts.equiv) and/or user-to-user ($HOME/.rhosts) authentication. If an authentication method is not configured, rsh returns an error message because it is not prompted for a password during execution.

You can use rsh only to execute a command that does not require user interaction. Any command with prompts or that requires user input will hang, causing an error and program termination. The format for the rsh command is as follows:

```
rsh -n -l username hostname command
```

Table 16-2 describes the rsh command options.

TABLE 16-2	Option	Description
The sh Options	*-l*	Specifies the username
	-n	Redirects output from the command to /dev/null

The -*l* option is the same as the -*l* option for the rlogin command; it allows you to specify a different username on the remote system. The rsh -*n* option is most frequently used in unattended scripting because the output is not necessary.

A standard use of rsh is to execute a command remotely, as shown in this example:

```
[kevin@sun.foo.com]$ rsh -l kev earth.foo.com /usr/sbin/prtconf

System Configuration:  Sun Microsystems   sun4u
Memory size: 128 Megabytes
System Peripherals (Software Nodes):

SUNW,Ultra-5_10
    packages (driver not attached)
        terminal-emulator (driver not attached)

(remainder not shown)
```

This example runs the prtconf command on the remote host and displays the output of the command on the local terminal.

The following is an advanced example of the use of the rsh command from an unattended backup script:

```
[kev@sun.foo.com]$tar cf - . | rsh earth.foo.com dd of=/dev/rmt0
```

Notice how the tar stream of data is sent over rsh to the remote machine's backup tape drive. The rsh command takes the input stream of data and passes it to the remote command dd, which stores it in the tape device (/dev/rmt0). The command seems complex, but it displays one of the best features of rsh: trouble-free remote command execution.

Remote Copy (rcp)

The rcp command is used to copy files to and from remote systems. It augments rlogin and rsh by adding the ability to access remote files easily and quickly. The rcp command can be used only with system-to-system (/etc/hosts.equiv) and user-to-user ($HOME/.rhosts) authentication, as described in the previous section. If these authentication methods are not configured, rcp, like rsh, is not able to prompt for a password and will return an error message.

The format for the rcp command is illustrated here:

```
rcp [-p] filename1 filename2
rcp [-pr] filename..directory
```

A filename may be a standard local file or a remote file. One of the parameters must be a local directory or file; otherwise, rsh returns the error message "Permission denied." The remote file must be specified in the following format:

```
hostname:path
username@hostname:filename
```

You use *username@hostname* to specify a username different from that of the local user. The following example displays a simple remote copy performed with rcp:

```
[kev@earth.foo.com]$rcp sun.foo.com:/tmp/test.bin /home/kev
```

The file /tmp/test.bin on the remote machine sun.foo.com is copied to the local machine and placed in the /home/kev directory. Table 16-3 describes additional rcp command options.

The *-p* option tries to keep extended file access control list permissions if the file system on the remote system allows this procedure. The *-r* option is used to specify a directory. This option copies the directory and all its files, including any subdirectories and their files, to the target. Using the *-r* option with rcp is one of the most common uses for rcp. The *-r* option allows a user to move directory trees to and from remote systems, as shown in the following example:

```
[kev@sun.foo.com]$rcp -r earth.foo.com:/tmp /tmp
```

This command copies the contents of /tmp and its subdirectories to the local directory /tmp. The directory could contain both ASCII and binary files, because rcp copies both file types correctly.

TABLE 16-3	Parameter	Meaning
The rcp Optional Parameters	*-p*	Tries to retain the access control list, modification time, access time, and modes of the original files and directories
	-r	Recursive copy

SCENARIO & SOLUTION

How do you log in to a server without being prompted for a password?	On the remote server, add an entry in your .rhosts file with the system from which you would like to log in.
How do you execute a remote command in a script?	Use the rsh *-l username hostname* command.
How can you easily copy a directory from a remote system to the local system?	Use rcp *-r hostname:/ directory / destination/*dir.

on the
Job

Solaris rcp supports files of a size greater than 2GB (largefiles). Keep in mind, however, that although Solaris supports largefiles, the target system must also be able to support these files: in other words, Solaris (8 or 9) <–> Solaris (8 or 9), Solaris (8 or 9) <–> any UNIX system with largefiles support.

EXERCISE 16-1

Remotely Executing Commands

1. rlogin to a system on your local network:

   ```
   rlogin host
   ```

2. Add your local system to the .rhost file:

   ```
   echo "<myhost> username" >>>> .rhosts
   ```

3. Log off from the remote system:

   ```
   logout
   ```

4. Execute the command uptime on the remote system:

   ```
   rsh remotehost uptime
   ```

CERTIFICATION OBJECTIVE 16.02

Transferring Files Between a Local System and a Remote System

File Transfer Protocol (ftp) is an Internet standard that was created to facilitate the management of files between remote systems. A user connects to a remote computer and, after a login process, that prompts for a username and password, the user is able to create, rename, and delete files and directories on the remote system.

The ftp standard uses a simpler authentication scheme than the rlogin, rsh, and rcp services: ftp checks the local /etc/passwd and /etc/shadow files for the user and password authentication, respectively. If the username/password combination is valid, it then checks the /etc/ftpd/ftpusers file for the login name. If the login name matches one found in the ftpusers file, the server rejects the session and sends an error message of "Login incorrect" and "Login failed." This process seems counterintuitive, but keep in mind that users in the ftpusers file are *not* allowed access to the system.

e x a m
ⓦ a t c h

Remember, ftp does not use the same authentication methods as rcp, rsh, and rlogin. The .rhosts and hosts.equiv files have no significance to ftp.

The format for the ftp command is as follows:

```
ftp [-dginvt] [-T timeout] hostname
```

The ftp command is very versatile and supports several command options, which are described in Table 16-4.

The Solaris 9 ftp client has been enhanced to allow the use of passive mode (-p). This supports connecting to a remote host from behind a firewall.

Once login to the remote system is complete, ftp prompts the user with a command-line interface (CLI). The ftp CLI provides commands that allow the user to mancuver through the remote file system and transfer, delete, and create files and directories. Table 16-5 shows an abbreviated list of ftp CLI commands.

TABLE 16-4   The ftp Command Options

Command Option	Meaning
-d	Enables debugging
-g	Disables filename regular expressions
-I	Turns off interactive prompting during multiple file transfers
-n	Does not auto-login, ignoring the .netric file
-T timeout	Specifies the timeout value in seconds
-v	Shows all responses from the server
-t	Enables packet tracing (unimplemented)

TABLE 16-5   The ftp CLI Commands

Command	Meaning
delete remote-file	Deletes a remote file.
get remote-file [local-file]	Transfers a remote file local system.
mget remote-files	Transfers multiple remote files to the local system.
lcd [directory]	Changes the target directory on the local system.
ls [remote-directory	-al] [local-file]	Displays a list of contents of a directory on the remote system.
put local-file[remote-file]	Stores a local file on the remote machine.
mput local-files	Expands a wildcard list of files and transfers them to the remote system.
mkdir	Creates a directory on the remote system.
prompt	Toggles interactive prompting.
pwd	Displays current directory.
hash	Toggles hash-sign (#) printing for each data block transferred. The size of a data block is 8192 bytes.
quit or bye	Disconnects from the remote system.

In the following example, a user *kamorin* logs in to the server, sets the transfer type to binary, requests files, and logs off of the system. Retrieving files stored on a remote system is a common use of ftp.

```
$ ftp earth.foo.com
Connected to earth.foo.com.
220 logger FTP server (SunOS 5.9) ready.
Name (earth.foo.com:kamorin): kamorin
331 Password required for kamorin.
Password:
230 User kamorin logged in.
ftp>> bin
200 Type set to I.
ftp>> get fc100_man.ps
200 PORT command successful.
150 Binary data connection for fc100_man.ps (xxx.xxx.xxx.xxx,34059).
226 Transfer complete.
ftp>> bye
221 Goodbye.
$
```

Notice that at the CLI prompt, the user sets the type to binary (ftp>> bin). This is necessary because the file the user plans to transfer is a postscript (fc100_man.ps) binary file. If sent in ASCII mode, the file would be corrupted. Always set transfer mode to binary, unless you are transferring text-only files between operating systems.

on the
() o b

File permission can sometimes change when a file is transferred through ftp. This is due to the system saving files with local default permissions. Be sure to double-check your local file permissions after file transfer is complete.

On occasion, the ftp client interface can be uninformative. To improve the amount of information, you can turn on hashing. Hashing displays a hash, or pound sign (#) once a specified amount of data has passed to or from the remote server, usually 8KB. This procedure can also help determine if an ftp transfer has hung, since in that situation, pound signs will stop appearing on the screen. The following example uses the hash command to display transfer progress:

```
ftp sun.foo.com
Connected to sun.foo.com.
220 sun FTP server (SunOS 5.9) ready.
```

```
Name (sun.foo.com:kev): kev
331 Password required for kev.
Password:
230 User kev logged in.
ftp>> bin
200 Type set to I.
ftp>> cd /tmp
250 CWD command successful.
ftp>> hash
Hash mark printing on (8192 bytes/hash mark).
ftp>> get file.bin
200 PORT command successful.
150 Binary data connection for file.bin (xxx.x.x.x,61183) (5456344 bytes).
#####################################################################
#####################################################################
#####################################################################
#####################################################################
########################
226 Binary Transfer complete.
local: file.bin remote: file.bin
5456344 bytes received in 0.61 seconds (8699.53 Kbytes/s)
ftp>> bye
221 Goodbye.
```

Notice how the pound sign is displayed in the output. Over slower connections such as modems, this feature is extremely helpful; otherwise, the user is left guessing the file transfer status.

Another helpful CLI command is the prompt command. The user can access the prompt CLI command to turn off query-interactive prompting. This command is especially helpful when you are downloading multiple files, because the ftp client will no longer prompt you for confirmation on each individual file. An example of interactive prompting, as opposed to noninteractive prompting, is demonstrated by the following:

```
$ ftp sun.foo.com
Connected to sun.foo.com.
220 sun FTP server (SunOS 5.9) ready.
Name (earth.foo.com:kev): kev
331 Password required for kev.
Password:
230 User kev logged in.
```

```
ftp>> cd /home/kev/public_html
250 CWD command successful.
ftp>> bin
200 Type set to I.
ftp>> mget *
```
mget basic.css? y

```
200 PORT command successful.
150 Binary data connection for basic.css (xxx.x.x.x,61223) (902 bytes).
226 Binary Transfer complete.
local: basic.css remote: basic.css
902 bytes received in 0.00082 seconds (1069.00 Kbytes/s)
```
mget career.html? y

```
200 PORT command successful.
150 Binary data connection for career.html (xxx.x.x.x,61224) (2747 bytes).
226 Binary Transfer complete.
local: career.html remote: career.html
2747 bytes received in 0.00059 seconds (4562.27 Kbytes/s)
```

The user is prompted *y* (yes) or *n* (no) for each individual file, as opposed to the following scenario, in which all files are transferred with a single command:

```
ftp>> prompt
Interactive mode off.
ftp>> mget *
200 PORT command successful.
150 Binary data connection for basic.css (xxx.x.x.x,61232) (902 bytes).
226 Binary Transfer complete.
local: basic.css remote: basic.css
902 bytes received in 0.00057 seconds (1534.60 Kbytes/s)
200 PORT command successful.
150 Binary data connection for career.html (xxx.x.x.x,61233) (2747 bytes).
226 Binary Transfer complete.
local: career.html remote: career.html
2747 bytes received in 0.00058 seconds (4601.40 Kbytes/s)
ftp>>
```

In both preceding examples, the user transfers were completed successfully, but the second user was able to leave the session and continue with other work while ftp continued until completion.

EXERCISE 16-2

Transferring and Receiving Files Using ftp

1. Start a terminal session on a local system. ftp to a remote system in your environment. When prompted, enter your username and password:

   ```
   ftp hostname
   ```

2. Toggle interactive prompting off:

   ```
   ftp>>prompt
   ```

3. Transfer file(s) from your local directory to the remote system:

   ```
   ftp>> mput *
   ```

4. Receive file(s) from the remote system:

   ```
   ftp>> mget *
   ```

5. Close the remote ftp session:

   ```
   ftp>> bye
   ```

FROM THE CLASSROOM

UNIX-to-Windows File Transfers

Remember to turn on ASCII mode (ftp>>ascii) when transferring ASCII files to or from a UNIX system. ASCII mode adds or strips the carriage return/line feed to or from your files, depending on the destination systems, and saves you major headaches later. For instance, when you are transferring an ASCII file from a Windows system to a UNIX system and binary mode is on, the file will contain both carriage returns and line feeds. This is not the desired effect, because the file will now have

^M at the end of every line when viewed in an editor such as vi in UNIX. If the file you transferred was a configuration file, the daemon might fail to load and you'll wonder why. Use ASCII mode in ftp to avoid this situation; otherwise, you might also be able to use

```
tr -d '\015' < filename > filename.new
```

to remove the extra character after the fact.

—*Kevin Amorin, SCSA, SCNA, CCNA, MCSE*

CERTIFICATION SUMMARY

In this chapter, you learned about remote services that allow users greater control of and access to remote files and systems. Administering remote systems in Solaris is made manageable because of the unique properties of each of these remote services. Specifically, rlogin allows for easy access and authentication between configured systems. The rsh and rcp commands supplement rlogin to make the *R* services more complete by adding the versatility of transferring files and remote command execution.

Finally, ftp is a powerful and flexible tool for remote file manipulation. Some of the functions ftp allows for are creating, renaming, and deleting files and directories; maneuvering through remote file systems; expediting file transfer and retrieval; providing file type options such as binary or ASCII; and monitoring the progress of file transfers. When used to their fullest extent, ftp and the other remote services allow a user to accomplish most necessary tasks quickly and easily without needing to physically access the remote machine.

✓ TWO-MINUTE DRILL

Performing Remote System Operations

❑ The $USER/.rhosts file contains the hostname/username pair used for user-to-user authentication.

❑ The /etc/hosts.equiv file is used with the remote services to allow all users on trusted systems to log in to the local system without being prompted for password authentication.

❑ The /etc/nologin file can be used by the administrator to limit user access.

❑ The rlogin command should be executed in the following format:

```
rlogin -l username hostname
```

❑ The rlogin command passes the local environment variables, including TERM, to the remote system during login.

❑ The format for the rsh command is as follows:

```
rsh [-1 username] hostname [command]
```

❑ The format for the rcp command is as follows:

```
rcp file username@hostname:filename
```

Transferring Files Between a Local System and a Remote System

❑ The common format for ftp is as follows:

```
ftp hostname
```

❑ The ftp CLI command mget retrieves every file matching a regular expression in the current directory.

❑ The prompt CLI command toggles interactive prompting, allowing for easy multiple-file transfers.

❑ The /etc/ftpd/ftpusers file lists the usernames that are *not* able to log in to the local system through ftp.

❑ The ftp CLI command hash provides you with status information during ftp file transfers.

❑ When transferring files across different architectures, remember to set ASCII or binary mode, depending on file type.

SELF TEST

The following questions will help you measure your understanding of the material presented in this chapter. Read all the choices carefully because there might be more than one correct answer. Choose all correct answers for each question.

Performing Remote System Operations

1. A user would like to copy the /data directory and its contents from the local machine sun.foo.com to a remote system venus.foo.com /tmp directory. Which of the following options will accomplish this task most effectively, assuming that venus.foo.com has an entry in the /etc/hosts.equiv file for sun.foo.com?

   A. `rcp sun.foo.com:/data /tmp`

   B. `rcp venus.foo.com:/data sun.foo.com:/tmp`

   C. `rcp -r /data venus.foo.com:/tmp`

   D. `rcp -r /tmp sun.foo.com:/data`

2. A user is known as *sarah* on earth.foo.com and as *snewhall* on mars.foo.com. This user would like to occasionally display all the processes running on the system mars.foo.com from the system earth.foo.com. Neither earth.foo.com nor mars.foo.com has any entries in the /etc/ hosts.equiv file. In her home directory on mars.foo.com, the user has placed an entry *earth.foo.com sarah* in the .rhosts file. Which of the following will, from the local system earth.foo.com, run the ps command on the remote system mars.foo.com as the user *snewhall*?

   A. `rsh mars.foo.com ps -ef -l snewhall`

   B. `rsh ps -ef -l snewhall`

   C. `rsh ps -ef mars.foo.com -l snewhall`

   D. `rsh -l snewhall mars.foo.com ps -ef`

3. Your web server logs need to be analyzed on a daily basis. Your web server, www.foo.com, stores its logs in the /www directory. The system that does the analysis is logger.foo.com. The logs will be placed in the /log/www directory on *logger*. Which of the following options from the system logger.foo.com would best accomplish this task?

   A. `rcp -r logger.foo.com:/www /var/log/www`

   B. `rcp -r www.foo.com:/www /log/www`

   C. `rcp -r /var/log/www www.foo.com:/www`

   D. `rcp -r /www www.foo.com:/var/log/www`

4. Your company would like an inventory of all its systems, including CPU type, model, RAM, and architecture. You can retrieve this information using the prtconf command on a local system. You currently have an .rhosts file on all systems trusting the computer earth.foo.com and the user *kamorin*. The user plans to execute a command from a script and substitute the $HOSTNAME variable for one of any of the systems on the corporate network. Logged in as the user *kamorin* on earth.foo.com, how would you best retrieve the data requested?

A. `rlogin -l kamorin $hostname /usr/bin/prtconf`

B. `rlogin $hostname -l kamorin /usr/bin/prtconf`

C. `rsh $hostname -l kamorin /usr/bin/prtconf`

D. `rsh $hostname /usr/bin/prtconf -l kamorin`

Transferring Files Between a Local System and a Remote System

5. How would a user display the status of files being transferred in the ftp CLI?

A. prompt

B. hash

C. mprompt

D. status

6. What are two ways of turning off interactive prompting with ftp? (Choose two.)

A. `prompt`

B. `ftp -i`

C. `ftp -T`

D. `ftp -v`

7. A user on your server ftps to a remote host and constantly gets the response, "Connection timeout." You are sure the problem isn't on your server. Which of the following can the user try to rectify the problem?

A. `ftp -t 10000 hostname`

B. `ftp -v 10000 hostname`

C. `ftp -i 10000 hostname`

D. `ftp -T 10000 hostname`

8. You receive a "Login incorrect" error when trying to ftp to a remote server. However, you are able to log in with the same username and password through rlogin. What is most likely the problem on the remote server?

A. The username is not listed in the /etc/.rhosts file.

B. The username is listed in the /etc/ftpd/ftpusers file.

C. The username is listed in the /etc/hosts.equiv file.

D. The user's password is incorrect.

9. A user has been transferring HTML files to the UNIX web server. She has just called you, the system administrator, with a problem. It seems that when that user logs in to the web server to make a quick change, she sees an extra character on every line. What is the most likely fix for the problem?

A. Resend the HTML files and set the ftp mode to binary.

B. Resend the HTML files and set the ftp mode to ASCII.

C. Use the ftp prompt CLI command to avoid the extra characters.

D. Tell the user there is no character and go on about your business.

LAB QUESTION

You, the user *sue,* would like to run a script that pulls information from hostB to hostC. The script requires the rcp command and must have user-to-user authentication enabled. You are logged in to your local system, hostA. You would also like to be able to rlogin to hostB from hostA without being prompted for a password. You plan to execute this script from hostB. Using the following list, correctly number the sequence of events that will accomplish this task (some items will not be used):

_____ rlogin to hostB without being prompted for a password.

_____ Execute the script.

_____ Create an .rhosts file with this entry:

```
hostB sue
hostA sue
```

_____ ftp the .rhosts file to hostB and hostC.

_____ rlogin to hostB.

_____ ftp the .rhosts file to hostA and hostB.

_____ rlogin to hostA without being prompted for a password.

_____ Create an .rhosts file with this entry:

```
hostA sue
hostC sue
```

SELF TEST ANSWERS

Performing Remote System Operations

1. ☑ C. This command copies the /data directory from the local machine to the remote machine venus.foo.com /tmp directory.
   ☒ A and B are incorrect because they do not specify an *-r* recursive directory copy. D is incorrect because it does not specify the remote system venus.foo.com in the command line.

2. ☑ D. This command executes the command ps *-ef* on the remote system mars.foo.com as the user *snewhall*.
   ☒ A, B, and C are incorrect because they do not follow the rsh command syntax; the *-l* option must precede the remote hostname.

3. ☑ B. This command will handle the task best.
   ☒ A, C, and D are incorrect because they do not have the correctly ordered syntax.

4. ☑ C. This command executes the prtconf command on any remote system specified by the hostname.
   ☒ A and B are incorrect because they start a terminal session rlogin instead of executing a command. D is incorrect because the *-l* option cannot follow the command.

Transferring Files Between a Local System and a Remote System

5. ☑ B. Using hash displays the status of files.
   ☒ A is incorrect because prompt toggles interactive prompting for multiple-file transfers. C is incorrect because the CLI command mprompt does not exist. D is incorrect because the status command displays the current status settings variables of ftp, including the hash setting *on* versus *off*.

6. ☑ A and B. These are the two ways to turn off interactive prompting.
   ☒ C. This command changes the default timeout value for a session. D is incorrect because it shows all responses from the server.

7. ☑ D. This command increases the timeout value to 10000.
   ☒ A is incorrect because it will not return an error but is not implemented. B is incorrect because it displays all server responses. C is incorrect because it turns off interactive prompting.

8. ☑ **B.** Most likely, the username is listed in the /etc/ftpd/ftpusers file.
☒ **A** and **C** are incorrect because ftp does not use .rhosts or hosts.equiv files. **D** is incorrect because the user's password is correct since he is able to log in with his name and password.

9. ☑ **B.** Although the other answers might be technically possible, the most likely answer is that the Windows carriage-return/line-feed characters are corrupting the file.
☒ **A, C,** and **D** are incorrect because **B** is the most likely fix.

LAB ANSWER

The proper order is as follows:

1. Create an .rhosts file with the entry

```
hostB sue
hostA sue
```

2. ftp the .rhosts file to hostB and hostC.

3. rlogin to hostB without being prompted for a password.

4. Execute the script.

These steps, in this order, will accomplish the goals set out in the lab exercise.

Part II

Sun Certified Administrator Examination for Solaris 9 Study Guide, Exam 310-012

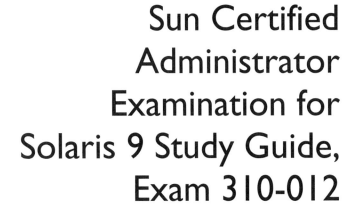

CHAPTERS

SUN® CERTIFIED SYSTEM ADMINISTRATOR

17

Understanding the Client/Server Relationship

CERTIFICATION OBJECTIVES

The computing architecture evolution began with the mainframe configuration. In this system, referred to as *centralized computing,* a single server with multiple remote dumb terminals accessed the system. Essentially, a *dumb terminal* is a monitor and keyboard with serial connectivity to the server. These terminals were an inexpensive way to allow multiple users to simultaneously access a server.

Eventually, the advancement in technology and reduction in computer prices made it possible to extend this environment to everyone's desks. The idea of having a "personal" computer on the desktop became popular. More and more networks turned to this *distributed computing* model. This model essentially decentralized the computing environment and spread it around among workers within a company site and around the world.

In the 1980s, the term *client/server* was introduced as a new way of looking at the computing environment. In a client/server computing environment, a host is designated as the server and is connected to other hosts designated as clients for access, similar to the mainframe environment. In today's client/server environment, the application has a significant role in communication between the server and the clients.

The Sun Open Network Computing (ONC+) architecture features applications that provide services; these applications include Network File System (NFS), Federated Naming Service (FNS), Network Information Service (NIS), Network Information Service Plus (NIS+), and Domain Name System (DNS). These applications use the client/server model and are accessible over a network.

The client/server model describes the relationship between two networked hosts in which one of the hosts, the client, makes a request for a service, and the server host responds to that request. The term *server* is used to describe a host or an application that is designed to provide one or more services. The server runs processes or services that answer requests from the clients. A server can also be a client that requires services from another server. The term *client* is used to describe a host or an application that uses the services provided by other hosts or applications. Some clients rely exclusively on the server to function correctly. Others are capable of functioning independent of the server.

The communication process starts when the client application makes a request to the server application. The client application then waits for a reply from the server application before proceeding with the next routine or request.

The following are some additional terms and definitions that will help you better understand the Solaris computing environment:

- **Host**   Any system that is connected to a network.
- **Hostname**   A unique name assigned to a host to identify it on a network.
- **Network**   A collection of computing resources, such as hosts, printers, and routers, that are physically connected to allow communication among them.
- **Internet Protocol (IP) address**   A system of identifying hosts and their locations on TCP/IP networks. An IP address is a 32-bit number split up into four 8-bit octets. The addresses are split into three classes: A, B, and C. Even though this system allows for a huge number of possible unique addresses, they are very close to running out. The current version of IP is version 4; version 6, usually referred to as IPv6, is currently in the final stages of development. IPv6 allows for 128-bit addressing, as well as other much-needed improvements such as better security and autoconfiguration. Solaris is capable of using both the current IPv4 and the new IPv6.
- **Multiuser**   A host that is capable of allowing more than one user to access the system's resources.
- **Multitasking**   The capability to manage resources for multiple processes at the same time, as in the Solaris kernel. This allows the OS to run multiple programs and tools at the same time.
- **Distributed processing**   A type of processing that enables resources to be shared across the network.

on the job   *Note the difference between multiuser and multitasking.*

CERTIFICATION OBJECTIVE 17.01

Understanding the Servers Used in the Solaris 9 Network Environment

Servers are systems that rely on no other hosts for their resources. They function independently on the network. To function in a standalone configuration, the system is required to have an internal disk and hardware such as keyboards, monitor, CPU, memory, and a network interface card. The standalone host's file system consists of the following:

- A root (/) file system, which contains the system files
- A local swap to store programs and data once the physical memory is filled
- /usr, which contains the executables and libraries to support the system
- /opt, which contains third-party software, or software that was not included in the Solaris 9 operating system bundle

To provide support for the clients, the server must have the following file systems:

- /export, which contains shared data
- /export/home, which contains home directory data
- /export/swap, which contains the swap space for the clients

You can choose from among a wide variety of server software for web servers, name servers, and NFS servers, but there are only seven basic types of servers, as defined by Sun:

- Action servers
- Application servers
- Caching-only servers
- Communications servers
- Print servers
- Session servers
- X-servers

Let's take a quick look at each type.

Action Servers

An *action server* is a computer that provides access to a variety of actions. For example, a Solaris server can be configured to be a JumpStart Automatic Installation server. This type of server is covered in much more detail in Chapter 29. Basically, it is a server that uses preconfigured data and files to automatically install Solaris on a client system over the network. A dedicated backup server is a type of action server. By configuring the backup client software to interact with the backup server software, your backups will be performed routinely and recoveries will always be available.

Application Servers

An *application server* is a computer that provides access to software for client systems. For example, a database client application relies on the server side of the application to return information from database searches. Another use of this type of server is Sun's Star Office Server application. The idea is that the application's main executable files reside on a central server, and the user can access them from anywhere.

Caching-Only Servers

A *caching-only server* is a domain name server that has no authoritative control over its domain. This server queries other DNS servers that have authority for the information needed and caches that data locally. Often, network traffic or the load on your name server itself could slow down name resolution. One way to speed up the service for users is to provide a caching-only server, which returns information it has received from previous requests or from other Domain Name System servers.

Communications Servers

A *communications server* is basically a gateway or a router. It provides address translation, name resolution, and protocol conversion, and it can authenticate a user's right to access resources. It's not difficult to configure a Solaris server to act as a router. The software needed is installed by default. In this role, your server routes requests from your local area network, either internally or externally to other networks. Although it doesn't provide all the functionality of a router, it can be a very handy extra bit of security.

Print Servers

A *print server* can be either a system that has one or more printers connected or the internal process that manages print requests. For the purposes of this chapter, the former definition applies.

As much as you might be hearing about the coming "paperless society," you'll find that one of the most important services your network provides to users is access to printers. This access can be configured in a number of ways. Most networks have installed printers at convenient locations, and the users send their print jobs to the closest one or to the one that provides the needed printing services (color, collation, and so on). A print server is the central server that manages the print resources. It translates the print request and data from the user's system and passes it to the correct printer. This process frees up resources on the user's system. The print server also manages access permissions and gives the sysadmin administrative power to delete stuck jobs or to prioritize one print job over another.

Session Servers

A *session server* is a system that provides centralized access to session files. A *session file* is a file that resides on the session server and is used whenever you log in to a system on the network.

For example, you might have users who log in to multiple workstations but want the same environmental settings and access to files in their home directories. Rather than update their profile files every time you needed to make a change and then "ftp-ing" those files to all the workstations, you can create the users' home directories on a central session server and export the directories to the remote workstations. That way, no matter which workstation the users log in from, their own profiles are run and they have access to their home directory files. This type of client is referred to as a *dataless client,* which is discussed in the "Dataless Clients" section, later in this chapter.

X-Servers

The X Windows system is designed to send its output somewhere else. It was designed to push display data from one system to another. It can, of course, send the data to itself, which is what you see if you use a GUI at the local console on the system.

Basically, the visual display of an X Windows system has two parts: the X-server and the GUI. The GUI, such as CDE, can be located on the X-server or on a remote client. As a type of server, an *X-server* provides the means of seeing graphics remotely. The following exercise shows how to use the Netscape browser from an X-server on a remote system.

EXERCISE 17-1

Remote Browsing

In this exercise, you'll see the display from a remote system on your local system. This can be helpful if, for example, the remote system is connected only to a terminal console and you want to access GUI-based applications.

1. Log in to your X-server system. For the purposes of this exercise, the server system is called *luna*:

```
login: root
password: ********
Welcome to Luna!
Last login: Fri May 11 23:20:10 from uruk
<<<root@luna>>> #
```

2. To allow a remote system to have access to your display, set permissions with the xhost command. This example uses the remote system named *sol,* so you need to give sol permission to access the X-server resources of luna. To do that, you can use the xhost command to add sol to the list of systems that have that access:

```
<<<root@luna>>> #    xhost + sol
sol being added to access control list
<<<root@luna>>> #
```

Notice that sol has been added to the list of systems that can access the X-server.

3. Telnet to the remote system:

```
<<<root@luna>>> #    telnet sol
Trying 192.168.1.1...
Connected to sol.
Escape character is '^]'.
SunOS 5.9
login: ra
Password: ********
Welcome to SOL!!
Last login: Sun May 13 16:35:16 from luna
```

```
Sun Microsystems Inc.   SunOS 5.9        Generic February 2000
[[ra:sol]] $
```

Now that you're logged in to the remote system, you can send the output of the Netscape application to your local system. Remember, you're sitting at luna, reaching out over the network to sol. Now you'll start the Netscape web browser on sol and see it on luna.

4. Start Netscape and, using the *-display* option, send the output to your local system:

```
[[ra:sol]] $netscape -display luna:0.0
```

5. Using the *-display* option and putting in the hostname of where you want the display to go, send the Netscape application output to luna. Then you will see the Netscape browser window open on your X-client luna.

---

on the
job

Make sure you understand the use of xhost. The man page is the best resource. It's a very easy, quick way to make your server a huge security risk if you're not careful!

Now take a look at some scenarios and solutions that will help you determine the kind of server you need in various situations.

SCENARIO & SOLUTION

Which server do you set up if you have users who are at different locations all day?	Set up a session server.
What if your users complain of slow name resolution?	Set up a caching-only server.
What if you need to run Admintool on a system with a busted monitor?	Use your local system as an X-server.

Make sure you understand the difference between a type of server and a client and the various kinds of server and client applications that exist. For the purpose of studying for the exam, this section listed and discussed the types of servers and clients as defined by Sun. For example, a JumpStart Install server or a web server are kinds of action servers.

CERTIFICATION OBJECTIVE 17.02

Understanding the Clients Used in the Solaris 9 Network Environment

A *client* is a host that accesses the resources of a remote server. As you've seen, these resources can be processing power, file space, or applications.

There are three basic types of clients in a Sun environment:

- Dataless clients
- Diskful clients
- Diskless clients

Let's take a quick look at each one.

Dataless Clients

A *dataless client* is a client system that relies on a server system, such as the session server described in the "Session Servers" section earlier, for its home directory. A dataless client uses its own local disk for its root directory and swap space. This type of client is great for client systems that have little available storage space or for users who need access from multiple workstations. In addition, by doing its own swapping, this type of client doesn't demand as many resources from the server.

Diskful Clients

A *diskful client* is the opposite of a dataless client. It relies on a server for system resources but has local space available for file storage.

There are or soon will be several brands of diskful clients on the market. The advantage of using this type of client is mainly price and ease of administration.

Diskless Clients

A *diskless client* relies on an OS server for all its disk storage and resources. This type of configuration is no longer officially supported by Sun, but you could run into some legacy use of it in your travels. This type of client makes big demands on the server and on the network. It's a return to the early days of computing, before everyone needed his or her own personal computer. There have been several false starts to marketing new versions of this type of client. The next wave of networked PCs will offer a very low price and fast GUI-based access and will still likely be ignored by most corporate users.

CERTIFICATION SUMMARY

This chapter briefly covered the types of servers and clients found in a Solaris computing environment. It discussed the client/server relationship as being a result of increased need for more resources at the desktop. The client is the host that uses the resources of a remote system. The server is the remote system that provides those resources.

✓ TWO-MINUTE DRILL

Understanding the Servers Used in the Solaris 9 Network Environment

❑ An action server provides actions or services to clients.

❑ An application server does the majority of processing of a client's application.

❑ A caching-only server queries DNS servers for client requests.

❑ A communications server acts as a gateway.

❑ A print server manages print services.

❑ A session server stores environmental and login files locally for client systems.

❑ An X-server allows a remote system to use its X Windows display.

Understanding the Clients Used in the Solaris 9 Network Environment

❑ A dataless client stores user files remotely.

❑ A diskful client has local storage for user files.

❑ A diskless client uses no local storage of user or system files.

SELF TEST

The following questions will help you measure your understanding of the material presented in this chapter. Read all the choices carefully because there might be more than one correct answer. Choose all correct answers for each question.

Understanding the Servers Used in the Solaris 9 Network Environment

1. Which of the following describes a server?

   A. Any system that accesses the resources of another.

   B. A system that allows another system to display its X Windows display.

   C. A system that is configured to provide resources to other systems.

   D. All Solaris systems are servers.

2. Which of the following best describes the client/server relationship?

   A. The client/server relationship is a myth; there's no such thing.

   B. It's the relationship between the host system, which requires the resources of another system, and the system that provides those resources.

   C. It's a system in which both partners give equally to the relationship, with neither more important than the other.

   D. It's a server that provides management of print services on a network.

3. Which of the following is an action server?

   A. A server configured to route HTTP requests

   B. A backup server

   C. A web server

   D. A DNS server

Understanding the Clients Used in the Solaris 9 Network Environment

4. Which of the following best describes a client?

   A. A selfish system that always takes and never gives anything back

   B. Any system that provides services to other systems

    C. Any system with the word "client" in its hostname

    D. A system that is configured not to need the services of any other system

5. Which of the following best describes a dataless client?

    A. A system that has no local storage.

    B. A client that has no data at all of any kind.

    C. There is no such thing.

    D. A client that has its user's home directories on a remote server.

6. Which of the following best describes a diskful client?

    A. A client with no more available space on the file system

    B. A client that has space available for local storage but relies on a remote server for swapping and system files

    C. A client that doesn't need the services of any other system; a fully independent system

    D. A client that is completely dependent on another system to operate

7. Which of the following best describes a diskless client?

    A. A disk with no space for local storage and that relies on the services of an OS server.

    B. A client with no space available for any local storage.

    C. A client that relies on the services of another for all its storage and system files.

    D. Sun no longer supports diskless clients.

LAB QUESTION

You have a number of database contractors who will be coming onsite and working for the next few months. While they're in your office, they'll be moving between two departments, using several different workstations every day. Because most of their project will involve collecting data, they will need access to the databases they're building each day. In addition, to avoid confusion, their desktop and environmental settings should follow them as they move from machine to machine. Your boss has asked you to configure a system that will allow the contractors to complete the project but that doesn't require them to manually transfer files around every day. What's the best solution?

SELF TEST ANSWERS

Understanding the Servers Used in the Solaris 9 Network Environment

1. ☑ C. A server is a standalone system that doesn't require the services of another to function, but is configured to provide resources to others.
   ☒ A is incorrect because it describes the function of a client. B is incorrect because it describes a type of server known as an X-server. D is incorrect because a Solaris system can be configured as a client.

2. ☑ B. The client takes what the server offers.
   ☒ A is incorrect because it's no myth. C is incorrect in terms of servers but sounds like something from nearly every wedding ceremony you've ever heard. D is incorrect because it describes a type of server known as a print server.

3. ☑ B, C, and D. All are examples of servers that provide services or actions to clients.
   ☒ A is incorrect because it describes a communications server.

Understanding the Clients Used in the Solaris 9 Network Environment

4. ☑ A. A client system is designed to take resources from another.
   ☒ B is incorrect because it describes the actions of a server, not a client. C is incorrect because the hostname is not a factor. D describes a standalone system.

5. ☑ D. A dataless client keeps all the user's data on a remote system.
   ☒ A is incorrect because a dataless client uses its local disk for swapping and for the root file systems. B is incorrect because it does keep system data locally. C is incorrect because they do exist.

6. ☑ B. A diskful client has space available for local storage but relies on a remote server for swapping and system files.
   ☒ D is also correct but better describes a diskless client. A is incorrect because this is not what determines a diskful client. C is incorrect because it describes a standalone system.

7. ☑ C. A diskless client relies on another server for applications, system files, and storage.
   ☒ A is incorrect because it uses the word "disk." Make sure you read each answer carefully on the actual exams! B is incorrect because a system that has space available can still be configured as a diskless client. Just because it has the space doesn't mean it uses it. D is a true statement but does not answer the question.

LAB ANSWER

The first step in a situation like this is to contact the users—in this case, the contractors. Find out as much about their needs as you can. How much data will they be adding each day? Which applications will they need access to? What is their skill level? Which level of security and permissions will they require to complete their project? How many different workstations will they be accessing?

In this particular situation, it would appear that configuring a session server would be the best way to provide the users with the resources they need. By making sure that the session server has adequate available space, and then exporting the users' home directories and mounting them to the various remote workstations, each user will have all of his or her files, and their environmental variables will follow them from machine to machine.

This solution requires you to create user accounts on each of the separate workstations and define their home directories as the mounted directory from the session server, unless your environment uses NIS/NIS+ to manage user accounts across systems. Then only a single central account entry is necessary. You will also want to make sure your new session server directories are part of your backup routine and that the files are backed up as often as needed by the users.

Solaris™

SUN® CERTIFIED SYSTEM ADMINISTRATOR

18

Understanding the Solaris Network Environment

T his chapter focuses on the Solaris network environment. To administer a network consisting of Solaris systems, it is important to understand the network concepts, as well as commands that are available in Solaris for network administration.

The chapter begins with an introduction to the layered architecture of network protocols, including the seven-layer OSI model and the five-layer TCP/IP model. This is followed by a discussion of Ethernet, and then an explanation of ARP is provided for a better understanding of how TCP/IP and Ethernet work with each other. These discussions provide details on the commands provided in Solaris to administer these technologies and lead directly into an outline of network interface commands. The next part of the chapter provides insight into the remote procedure call (RPC) service and its specifics. Finally, the chapter finishes with a discussion of commands that start and stop network services.

Recognizing the Function of Each Layer of OSI Model

The *Open Systems Interconnection (OSI) model* is a framework that divides network protocol functions into seven separate layers. The OSI was a working group within the International Standards Organization (ISO), and therefore some people refer to the model as the *ISO seven-layer model.* The OSI model is very generic and can be used to explain virtually any network protocol. A solid understanding of the OSI model is necessary to master the areas of computer networking and data communications. However, it is important to remember that the OSI model is just a model, and very few actual protocols possess all seven layers outlined in this model.

One of the purposes of the OSI model is to facilitate communications between systems, making networking possible between heterogeneous hardware and software architectures. Each layer is defined with its own services or functions to ensure that data can be successfully transmitted between devices. Each layer relies on the layer below it to provide a service. Generally, the model is diagrammed with Layer 1 at the bottom and Layer 7 at the top. (See Figure 18-1.)

FIGURE 18-1

The seven layers
of the OSI model

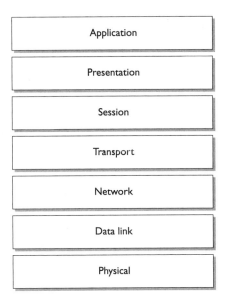

There are numerous advantages to using the OSI model. The model breaks down network protocols into specific functions. This provides software developers the ability to change features of one layer without changing the code for the other layers. The model also simplifies troubleshooting by allowing network administrators to follow the methodology of testing functionality at a lower layer before looking at the layer above it.

Encapsulation

Encapsulation is the process by which information from an upper layer of the model is inserted into the data field of a lower layer. Data created by an application is passed down from the application layer to the presentation layer. The presentation layer adds its own header and footer to the data from the application layer and passes it on to the session layer. The session layer adds its header and footer to the data and passes it on to the transport layer. This process repeats itself until the data reaches the physical layer. The physical layer does not care about the meaning of the data. It simply converts the data into bits and places it on the transmission medium.

When the data arrives at its destination, the receiving station's physical layer picks up the data and performs the reverse process (known as *de-encapsulation*). The physical layer converts the data into frames, which are passed on to the data link layer. The data link layer removes its header and footer and passes the data on to the network layer. Once again, the process repeats itself until the data reaches all the way up to the application layer.

Data communications in the OSI model is *peer-to-peer communication.* This means that the physical layer of the transmitting station communicates directly with the physical layer of the receiving station. The application layer on the transmitting station communicates directly with the application layer on the receiving station. The same concept applies to all seven layers. Each layer of the OSI model is discussed in detail in the sections that follow.

e x a m
ⓦ a t c h

You will be expected to identify the functions of each layer of the OSI model as well as be able to classify at which layer an application or protocol falls.

Application Layer

The *application layer* is the topmost layer of the OSI model. It represents the software programs and network services accessed by the user. These services include web browsing, file transfer, electronic mail, and network management. Examples of application layer protocols include File Transfer Protocol (FTP), HyperText Transfer Protocol (HTTP), Network File System (NFS), and Telnet.

Presentation Layer

The *presentation layer* ensures that information exchanged between machines is in a syntax that can be understood by both the sending and receiving host. This layer is responsible for providing the following services:

- **Translation** Information exchanged between two application programs is usually encoded in a particular format, whether character strings, numeric values, or other defined data structures. Before transmission, this data needs to be converted into a stream of bits. At the receiving end, the bit stream needs to be converted back to its receiver-dependent format. The presentation layer is responsible for interoperability between the sender's and receiver's message formats.

- **Encryption** To ensure that data is securely transmitted across the network, data can be encrypted. *Encryption* is the process of converting data into a secret code. *Decryption* reverses the original process to transform the secret coded message back into its original form. The presentation layer is responsible for performing encryption at the transmitting station and decryption at the receiving station.

- **Compression** Data compression can reduce the amount of data that is carried through the network and can therefore improve network performance. If compression is implemented, the presentation layer is responsible for both the compression and the decompression of the data.

Examples at the presentation layer include data representation standards (ASCII, JPEG, GIF), data encryption standards (MD5, RC4), and compression standards.

Session Layer

The *session layer* is responsible for maintaining dialogs. It establishes, maintains, and ends sessions across the network. It allows for systems to enter into a dialog and allows communication between two processes. The session layer manages data streams and determines who can transmit data at what time and for how long. Examples at the session layer include named pipes, mail slots, and RPC, which is used by applications such as NFS and Network Information Service (NIS).

Transport Layer

The *transport layer* handles source-to-destination delivery of messages. It oversees the segmentation and reassembly of network layer packets and ensures that data arrives at its destination in an orderly fashion. (A unit of information at the transport layer is referred to as a *segment*.) In the case of a connection-oriented protocol, the transport layer is responsible for making a connection from the source to the destination; maintaining the connection during packet delivery; and, finally, terminating the connection at the end of data delivery. In contrast, a connectionless transport protocol delivers packets without establishing any connections.

Network Layer

The *network layer* breaks up data from the transport layer into fragments known as *datagrams* (or packets). This layer then delivers these datagrams from a source to a destination. At the network layer, logical addressing is assigned to systems. Routers and routing protocols run at this layer.

Data Link Layer

The *data link layer* is responsible for specifying physical addressing and protocol characteristics. This layer converts network layer data into data units known as *frames*. Ethernet and Token Ring are examples of data link layer protocols. Devices that operate at the data link layer include bridges and switches.

Physical Layer

The *physical layer* of the OSI model defines the electrical, mechanical, procedural, and functional specifications for activating, maintaining, and deactivating the physical link between communications systems. At this layer, physical characteristics such as media type, voltage levels, data speeds, and physical connectors are defined. It is the responsibility of the physical layer to carry a stream of *bits* from one station to another. Devices that operate at the physical layer include hubs and repeaters.

EXERCISE 18-1

Identifying the Function of Each OSI Layer

This exercise tests your knowledge of the OSI model. The users of the network report that they can't reach systems on the other side of a new switch. Which layer is the likely place where communication is failing?

Assuming that the cabling infrastructure, end-user systems, and network interface cards (NICs) have not been changed, the failure is probably occurring at Layer 2 of the OSI model, the data link. Switches and bridges are examples of devices that operate at the data link layer.

CERTIFICATION OBJECTIVE 18.02

Defining the Function of Each Layer in the TCP/IP Model

Transmission Control Protocol/Internet Protocol (TCP/IP) was developed prior to the OSI model, so layers in the TCP/IP model do not exactly match those in the OSI model. The TCP/IP model consists of five layers:

- Application
- Transport

- Internet
- Network interface
- Hardware

Figure 18-2 provides a comparison between the TCP/IP model and the OSI reference model. The functions of the TCP/IP layers are described in the sections that follow.

Application Layer

The *application layer* of the TCP/IP protocol maps to functions of the application, presentation, and session layers of the OSI model. Many application protocols exist,

FIGURE 18-2

Comparison of the TCP/IP and OSI models

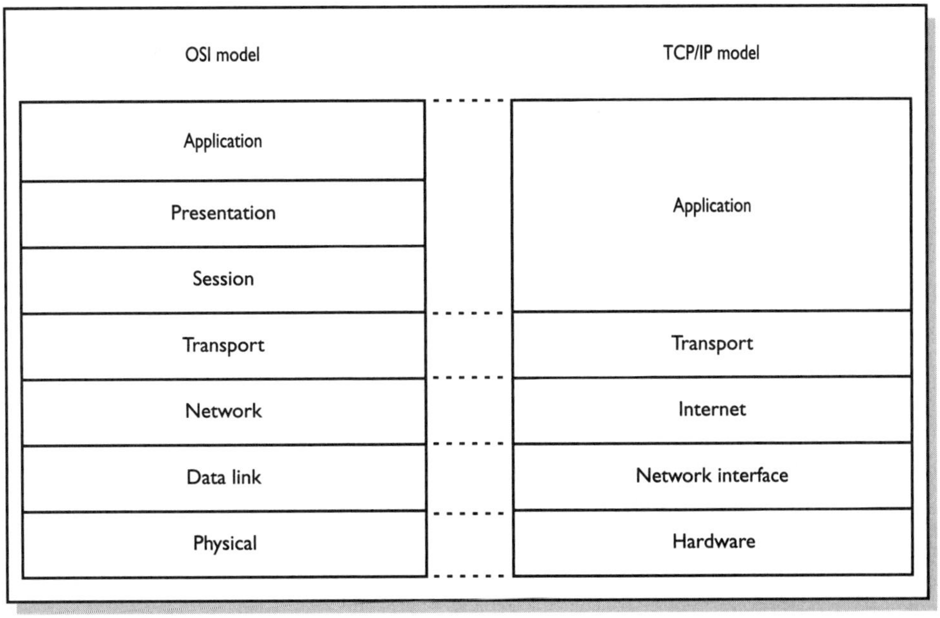

OSI model	TCP/IP model
Application	Application
Presentation	
Session	
Transport	Transport
Network	Internet
Data link	Network interface
Physical	Hardware

and new applications are constantly added at this layer. Some common examples of TCP/IP application protocols include the following:

- **Telnet**   This protocol provides a means to log in to a system remotely through a network.

- **File Transfer Protocol (FTP)**   This protocol is used to transfer data files from one system to another.

- **HyperText Transfer Protocol (HTTP)**   This protocol is used by web browsers to retrieve HTML pages from a web server.

- **Simple Mail Transfer Protocol (SMTP)**   This protocol is used to deliver e-mail.

Transport Layer

Two commonly used protocols at the *transport layer* of the TCP/IP protocol stack are Transmission Control Protocol (TCP) and User Datagram Protocol (UDP). Both protocols are available as a part of the Solaris kernel. The transport layer header includes a source and a destination port number, which are used to determine the application program from which the TCP or UDP segment is sourced, as well as the application for which the segment is destined.

Transmission Control Protocol (TCP)

TCP provides reliable service using connection-oriented delivery. Before a TCP-based application can begin sending data to another TCP-based application, the two processes must first establish a connection with each other. Once the connection is established, data can be exchanged. To ensure that data is delivered reliably, TCP uses sequence numbers in every segment, and every transmission must be acknowledged by the receiving station. Examples of services that use TCP as their transport mechanism include FTP, Telnet, NFS, SMTP, HTTP, and NNTP (Network News Transfer Protocol).

User Datagram Protocol (UDP)

Unlike TCP, UDP is a lightweight protocol that provides connectionless best-effort delivery of data. Data is transferred one segment at a time, and no reliability mechanisms are used. This is why UDP is sometimes known as a *stateless* protocol—because the stations running UDP do not have confirmation that a segment was delivered. Because there is no overhead to set up a connection, UDP is a more efficient protocol than TCP. Examples of services that use UDP as their transport mechanism include DNS, RIP (Raster Image Processor), NFS, SNMP, and DHCP/BOOTP.

Internet Layer

Below the transport layer in the TCP/IP protocol stack exists the *Internet layer*. As defined in RFC 791, IP is the heart of TCP/IP and is the most important protocol at the Internet layer. IP is an unreliable and connectionless protocol used to deliver datagrams.

Because it is a connectionless protocol, IP does not establish an end-to-end connection before transmitting data. Instead, it relies on upper-layer protocols to establish connections if they require connection-oriented service. In addition, IP provides best-effort service because it provides no error detection or recovery. Once again, IP relies on upper-layer protocols to perform these functions if required.

The Internet layer is also responsible for routing datagrams across the network to their final destinations. Systems that belong to the same network do not need a router placed between them. However, if multiple IP networks are being used, a router must be placed between the networks so that IP datagrams can be routed from one network to the other.

The Internet Control Message Protocol (ICMP) is another example of a protocol at the Internet layer. ICMP is responsible for error detection and sending messages that are intended for TCP/IP itself. ICMP is used by applications such as ping and traceroute.

FROM THE CLASSROOM

IP Addresses

In IP addressing, the TCP/IP protocol suite routes datagrams at the network layer based on IP addresses. An *IP address* is a 32-bit numeric address generally written as four decimal numbers separated by periods. Each number can be between 0 and 255. For example, 10.4.23.254 is an IP address. To connect a private network to the Internet, an IP address needs to be registered with the Internet Assigned Numbers Authority (IANA). Every IP address consists of two parts—one identifying the network, the other identifying the node. The IP subnet mask determines which part of the IP address belongs to the network address and which part belongs to the

node address. If you perform a bitwise logical AND of an IP address and its subnet mask, you are left with the network portion of the IP address.

Although the IANA is responsible for the assignment of unique IP addressing for systems connected to the Internet, RFC 1918 specifies ranges of IP addresses that are set aside for private home or corporate networks that are not connected to the Internet. According to the RFC, these networks are 10.*x.x.x*, 172.16.*x.x*-172.31.*x.x*, and 192.168.*x.x*.

—Umer Khan, SCSA, SCNA, CCIE, MCSE, CNX, CCA

Hardware and Network Interface Layers

Similar to the OSI model, the TCP/IP model also defines *physical* and *data link layers*. However, the TCP/IP protocol stack does not define any standards for these layers. It provides support for all standard and proprietary protocols. This is why it is possible to run TCP/IP over a variety of transmission mediums in both LAN and WAN environments. As implemented in Solaris, protocols at network interface and hardware layers appear as device drivers.

EXERCISE 18-2

TCP/IP Addressing

This exercise examines some of the files and commands necessary to configure TCP/IP addressing on a Solaris system.

1. Log in to your Solaris system as a superuser (i.e., root).

2. The hostname command can be used to determine the name of a system:

```
# hostname
jaguar
```

3. When a system initially boots, it uses the /etc/hostname.*xxx* file (where *xxx* is the name of the network interface) to determine the hostname assigned to the network interface. It then uses the /etc/hosts file to match the hostname against an IP address. To determine the IP address that will be assigned to your machine, take a look at the /etc/hostname.*xxx* and /etc/hosts files:

```
# cat /etc/hostname.hme0
jaguar
# cat /etc/hosts
127.0.0.1    localhost
192.168.2.2    jaguar
```

4. Solaris stores IP subnet mask information in the /etc/netmasks file. To determine the network mask that is being used by your system, take a look at the /etc/netmasks file:

```
# cat /etc/netmasks
192.168.2.0    255.255.255.0
```

5. The default router through which the system communicates is stored in the /etc/defaultrouter file. On bootup, this file is used to add a static default route into the routing table. View this file to determine the static default route that is configured on your system:

```
# cat /etc/defaultrouter
192.168.2.1
```

This exercise covered the files that the system uses to determine TCP/IP addressing information. The parameters that are generally configured on each TCP/IP host include the IP address, subnet mask, and the default router. In Solaris, all of these are configured in text files that exist in the /etc directory.

Understanding the Features and Functions of the Ethernet

Ethernet is the most popular LAN technology in use today. Other LAN types include Token Ring, Fiber Distributed Data Interface (FDDI), and LocalTalk. Ethernet was developed by a joint venture among Digital Equipment Corporation, Intel Corporation, and Xerox. Ethernet is a data link layer technology that was designed as a broadcast bus technology, meaning that every Ethernet system on a wire sees every frame that is transmitted. The access mechanism used by Ethernet is *carrier-sense multiple access with collision detection* (CSMA/CD).

Ethernet was invented in 1972 by Robert Metcalf and David Boggs while they were working at the Xerox Palo Alto Research Center. Digital, Intel, and Xerox continued development through version 2.0, which was released in 1982. Then the Institute of Electrical and Electronics Engineers (IEEE) 802 project redesigned the frame format and is now referred to as the 802.3 frame. The IEEE 802 project redesigned and standardized many communication protocols used today, such as wireless Ethernet (802.11) and Token Ring (802.5). The project was named *802* upon its formation in February 1980.

CSMA/CD

Ethernet is a shared medium, making it possible for two nodes to attempt to send data at the same time. If two Ethernet hosts try to transmit a frame at the same time, a collision occurs (and the result is garbage data). This is why the Ethernet standard calls for *carrier sensing,* meaning that before a station transmits on an Ethernet segment, it listens for the carrier that is present when another station is talking. If another station is transmitting, this station waits until no carrier is present.

The phrase *multiple access* refers to the fact that when a station has completed transmission, it immediately allows another station to gain access to the medium, therefore allowing multiple stations access. This is unlike Token Ring, where a station has to wait for a token frame before it is allowed to transmit.

The term *collision detection* represents another very important feature of Ethernet. In an Ethernet network, sometimes two stations simultaneously detect no carrier and transmit at the same time, resulting in a collision. In case this happens, when the collision occurs, all stations are able to detect this collision and ignore the data that is received. The transmitting station waits a period of time before retransmitting the frame. The duration of the wait time is determined randomly to reduce the chances of a second collision.

e x a m
ⓦ a t c h

As you read the following section, pay close attention to each field of the Ethernet frame, including its placement and size. It is a good idea to memorize the format of the frame before you take the exam.

The Ethernet Frame

Ethernet traffic is transported in units of frames, where each frame has a definite beginning and end. Sun Solaris uses the Ethernet II frame format by default. The frame consists of a set of bits organized into several fields. (See Figure 18-3.)

An Ethernet frame is defined as having six fields:

- **Preamble (8 bytes)**   The preamble is a synchronization sequence consisting of 0's and 1's. The preamble helps a NIC determine the beginning of an Ethernet frame.

- **Destination address (6 bytes)**   The first field followed by the preamble is the destination address, which specifies the data link address of the next station to which this frame is being transmitted. A destination address of all 1's specifies that this is a broadcast frame.

- **Source address (6 bytes)**   The next 6 bytes contain the data link address of the previous station that transmitted this frame.

- **Type (2 bytes)**   This field is used to identify the type of data that is encapsulated in the frame. Examples include IP, Internet Control Message Protocol (ICMP), Address Resolution Protocol (ARP), and Reverse Address Resolution Protocol (RARP).

- **Data (46–1500 bytes)**   This field contains data from an upper layer. The length of the data must be between 46 and 1500 bytes. If the data generated

---

FIGURE 18-3   The Ethernet frame format

Preamble	Destination address	Source address	Type	Data	CRC
8 bytes	6 bytes	6 bytes	2 bytes	46–1500 bytes	4 bytes

by the upper layer is less than 46 bytes, padding is added to make the data 46 bytes long. If it is greater than 1500 bytes, the upper layer needs to transmit the data in multiple frames. The maximum amount of data that Ethernet can transfer is 1500 bytes; this is also known as the *maximum transfer unit* (MTU).

■ **CRC (4 bytes)** The last 4 bytes are the *cyclical redundancy check* (CRC), also known as the *frame check sequence* (FCS). This value is calculated from all the bits of the Ethernet frame and its contents but ignoring the preamble and the CRC itself. The receiving host performs the same calculation and compares the calculated *checksum* to the frame *checksum*. If the values do not match, the frame is determined to be corrupt and is discarded.

Ethernet Addressing

Each Ethernet card in the world has a unique hardware address assigned to it. The address is also known as the medium access control (MAC) address, the burned-in address (BIA), or simply the Ethernet address. This address is a 48-bit binary number generally represented as 12 hexadecimal digits (six groups of two digits) separated by a dash or a colon. The address is set at the time of the NIC's manufacture, although it can usually be changed through software. Figure 18-4 provides an example of a MAC address.

MAC addresses are designed to be unique so that each NIC can pick up only frames that are addressed to it. Without MAC addresses, there would be no way

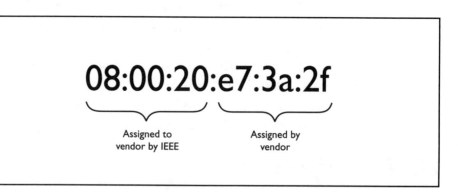

to distinguish between NICs. This raises an important question: how are MAC addresses ensured to be unique? Unique Ethernet addresses are administered by the IEEE. The IEEE assigns the first three octets of the MAC address, also known as the *organizational unit identifier (OUI)*, to NIC vendors. It is then the responsibility of each vendor to ensure that the last three octets of the MAC address are unique on each NIC that the vendor manufactures. The OUI assigned to Sun Microsystems is 08:00:20.

On Sun systems, the Ethernet address is read from the IDPROM on the system board. By default, all network interfaces on a system have the same MAC address assigned to them.

Three types of MAC addresses are used for communication on a network:

- **Unicast**   A unicast frame is destined to a unique host on the network and is identified by an individual MAC address of a network interface.

- **Multicast**   Multicast frames are addressed to a group of hosts on a network. A single frame sent to a multicast address is received by all the hosts in that particular multicast group and ignored by hosts that do not belong to the group.

- **Broadcast**   A broadcast frame is addressed to all hosts on an Ethernet segment and is passed on to the upper layers on all hosts. The destination MAC address of all 1's is reserved for broadcasts and is represented by *ff:ff:ff:ff:ff:ff* in hexadecimal format.

EXERCISE 18-3

Identifying a System's Ethernet Address

Each Ethernet station possesses a unique MAC address. In this exercise, you will identify the unique MAC address configured on your system.

1. Power on your Solaris system.

2. Bring your system to the PROM level by pressing STOP-A.

3. Identify the Ethernet address of your system by typing **banner** and pressing ENTER. You should see the MAC address of your system.

CERTIFICATION OBJECTIVE 18.04

Understanding the Characteristics of RARP and ARP

In an Ethernet or Token Ring network, machines communicate using data link layer addresses. Any higher-layer protocols must find a means to relate their network layer addresses to actual data link addresses. In the case of the TCP/IP protocol stack, this task is accomplished using the *Address Resolution Protocol* (ARP), which is defined in RFC 826.

Before entering a detailed discussion of ARP, it is important to understand the difference between network layer addresses and data link layer addresses. A *data link layer address* refers to the actual burned-in hardware address on a network card. A *network layer address* (e.g., an IP address) is a logical address generally configured in software by a network administrator. Network layer addresses are used to provide end-to-end communication and generally do not change as a datagram passes through the network.

Any time a TCP/IP host has an IP datagram to send to another host on the same network, it has the logical (IP) address of the destination. However, the IP datagram is encapsulated within a frame (at the data link layer), which allows it to pass through the physical network. For the source host to create this frame, it needs to know the data link layer address of the destination. This mapping of network layer addresses to data link layer addresses can be accomplished either statically or dynamically.

ARP is responsible for maintaining this table of mappings. When ARP receives a request to translate an IP address to a hardware address, it checks for the address in its table. If a mapping is not found, the following steps are followed:

1. The sender creates an ARP query packet, which is broadcast throughout the network. This packet contains the IP address of the destination host, with the question, "Which host has this IP address assigned, and what is your hardware address?" Each host on the local network receives the broadcast.

2. All machines except the target drop the packet, since it is the only machine that recognizes its IP address.

3. The target machine responds with an ARP response. In this response, it includes its MAC address.

4. The original sender receives the ARP response, and it now creates an ARP mapping for the target host.

Figure 18-5 provides an example of an ARP query.
Figure 18-6 shows the response generated by the target host.

FIGURE 18-5   An ARP query

```
# snoop -v arp
Using device /dev/hme (promiscuous mode)
ETHER:   ----- Ether Header -----
ETHER:
ETHER:   Packet 1 arrived at 19:25:19.05
ETHER:   Packet size = 42 bytes
ETHER:   Destination = ff:ff:ff:ff:ff:ff, (broadcast)
ETHER:   Source      = 8:0:20:cf:76:e8, Sun
ETHER:   Ethertype = 0806 (ARP)
ETHER:
ARP:   ----- ARP/RARP Frame -----
ARP:
ARP:   Hardware type = 1
ARP:   Protocol type = 0800 (IP)
ARP:   Length of hardware address = 6 bytes
ARP:   Length of protocol address = 4 bytes
ARP:   Opcode 1 (ARP Request)
ARP:   Sender's hardware address = 8:0:20:cf:76:e8
ARP:   Sender's protocol address = 192.168.222.4
ARP:   Target hardware address = ?
ARP:   Target protocol address = 192.168.222.1
```

FIGURE 18-6   An ARP response

```
# snoop -v arp
Using device /dev/hme (promiscuous mode)
ETHER:   ----- Ether Header -----
ETHER:
ETHER:   Packet 2 arrived at 19:25:19.05
ETHER:   Packet size = 60 bytes
ETHER:   Destination = 8:0:20:cf:76:e8, Sun
ETHER:   Source      = 0:2:fd:65:5c:a7,
ETHER:   Ethertype = 0806 (ARP)
ETHER:
ARP:     ----- ARP/RARP Frame -----
ARP:
ARP:     Hardware type = 1
ARP:     Protocol type = 0800 (IP)
ARP:     Length of hardware address = 6 bytes
ARP:     Length of protocol address = 4 bytes
ARP:     Opcode 2 (ARP Reply)
ARP:     Sender's hardware address = 0:2:fd:65:5c:a7
ARP:     Sender's protocol address = 192.168.222.1
ARP:     Target hardware address = 8:0:20:cf:76:e8
ARP:     Target protocol address = 192.168.222.4
```

on the
Ö o b   *If two machines on the same network are unable to communicate with one*
               another, be sure to check the ARP table to ensure that the IP addresses are
               being correctly mapped to MAC addresses.

ARP maintains a table of mappings between IP addresses and Ethernet addresses.
The ARP table is generally built dynamically, although static ARP entries can also be
populated. The /usr/sbin/arp command is used to display and modify contents of
the ARP table. Examples of the arp command are as follows. To list all ARP entries:

```
# arp -a
Net to Media Table: IPv4
Device   IP Address            Mask            Flags  Phys Addr
------   --------------------  --------------- -----  ---------------
hme0     192.168.2.2           255.255.255.255        00:60:73:81:17:fa
```

```
hme0   192.168.2.1           255.255.255.255         00:02:fd:65:5c:a7
hme0   jaguar                255.255.255.255 SP      08:00:20:cf:76:e8
hme0   BASE-ADDRESS.MCAST.NET 240.0.0.0       SM      01:00:5e:00:00:00
```

To find the ARP entry for a machine with the IP address 192.168.2.1:

```
# arp 192.168.2.1
      192.168.2.1 (192.168.2.1) at 0:2:fd:65:5c:a7
```

To delete an ARP entry for the IP address 192.168.2.1:

```
# arp -d 192.168.2.1
```

To add a permanent entry to the ARP table:

```
# arp -s 192.168.2.4 08:00:20:35:f3:4a
```

A permanent entry stays in the ARP table until the system is rebooted. To create a temporary ARP entry (which expires in 3 to 4 minutes):

```
# arp -s 192.168.2.5 08:00:20:35:f3:4a temp
```

To create a published ARP entry (which allows a host to answer ARP requests for another host):

```
# arp -s 192.168.2.3 08:00:20:35:f3:4a pub
```

To load ARP entries from a file:

```
# arp -f filename
```

exam
Ⓦatch   *Be sure to read the man pages for all commands mentioned in this chapter. Understanding the capabilities and parameters for each of these commands will help you answer the practical questions in the certification exam.*

Now that you have a good understanding of ARP, some possible scenario questions and their answers are next.

SCENARIO & SOLUTION	
How would you find the MAC address of a remote machine?	Ping the remote machine's IP, and then execute ARP *ip_address.*
When would you use a published ARP entry?	A published ARP entry is useful if you are running systems that do not understand the ARP protocol. In this case, a Solaris system can provide the ARP responses for these hosts.

Reverse Address Resolution Protocol (RARP) is used by diskless systems to determine their own IP addresses. Remember that ARP begins with the knowledge of an IP address and an unknown Ethernet address. ARP resolves the IP address into an Ethernet address. RARP is the exact reverse of this process.

When a diskless client boots up, it knows its Ethernet address but does not know its IP address. To obtain its IP address, it sends an RARP request on the network, advertising its MAC address and requesting an IP.

The RARP request is broadcast throughout the network. If this RARP request is received by an RARP server and an entry for the diskless client's MAC address exists in the *Ethers* table, the server responds with an RARP reply. The diskless client then learns its own IP address through the RARP reply and continues the bootup process.

To start the RARP server process on a system, log in to the system as root, and execute the following command:

```
# /usr/sbin/in.rarpd
```

This command will start the rarp daemon, which uses the /etc/ethers file to map Ethernet addresses to IP addresses. Before starting the daemon, you must add entries into the /etc/ethers and /etc/hosts files. Entries in the /etc/ethers file are in the following format:

```
ether-address hostname # comment
```

Here is an example:

```
8:0:20:3:a8:9d:e7 jaguar # This is a comment
```

Entries in the /etc/inet/hosts file are in the following format:

```
ip-address hostname # comment
```

Here is an example:

```
192.168.2.2 jaguar # This is a comment
```

The aliases portion of a host entry is often used to specify the fully qualified domain name (FQDN) of a system, for example,

```
192.168.2.2 jaguar jaguar.zoo.org # This is a comment
```

When an RARP server receives an RARP request, it first compares the source Ethernet address in the RARP request frame to entries in the /etc/ethers file. If a match is found, it takes the hostname in the /etc/ethers file and compares it to the /etc/hosts file. If a match is found, it returns the IP address in an RARP reply packet.

EXERCISE 18-4

Understanding arp Commands

The ARP table maintains IP-address-to-MAC-address mappings in a table. The arp command can be used to view and modify contents of this table. In this exercise, you will become familiar with the use of this command.

1. Log in to your Solaris system as a superuser.

2. View the contents of the ARP cache table:

```
arp -a
```

3. Ping a host on your network that is not already in the ARP cache:

```
ping 192.168.1.10
```

4. View the contents of the ARP cache table again:

```
arp -a
```

You should see an ARP entry for the host you just pinged.

5. Delete the ARP entry:

```
arp -d 192.168.1.10
```

6. View the contents of the ARP cache table:

```
arp -a
```

The ARP entry for 192.168.10 should be gone.

This exercise analyzed the contents of the ARP table. You dynamically created an ARP entry by pinging a host, which triggered the ARP process and created an entry in the ARP table. You then deleted this entry using the arp *-d* command.

CERTIFICATION OBJECTIVE 18.05

Using Commands to Display Information About the Local Network Interface

Solaris provides a variety of commands for monitoring and configuring local network interfaces. Two commonly used commands include ifconfig and netstat.

The ifconfig Command

You can use the ifconfig command to view a network interface and its parameters. It is used by the system at boot time to set up the network interfaces. The command is invoked by the /etc/rcS.d/S30network.sh script. It is also used later during the bootup process by the /etc/rc2.d/S72inetsvc script to reset the network interface parameters, if necessary, based on information learned from NIS/NIS+.

To get information on an interface, the syntax of the ifconfig command is

```
ifconfig { interface | -a }
```

The first argument to the ifconfig command is generally the name of an interface. The interface name is a driver name followed by a number—for example, *hme0* for the first Fast Ethernet interface. To view information on all interfaces, the single *-a* argument can be used.

Let's look at some examples. To view the status of all interfaces, you would use the following:

```
# ifconfig -a
lo0: flags=1000849<P,PCK,RNNNG,TCT,Pv4> mtu 8232
        inet 127.0.0.1 netmask ff000000
hme0: flags=1000843<P,RCT,RNNNG,TCT,Pv4> mtu 1500
        inet 192.168.1.3 netmask ffffff00 broadcast 192.168.1.255
        ether 8:0:20:fd:c7:4f
```

To view the status of a specific interface, use this:

```
# ifconfig hme0
hme0: flags=1000843<P,RCT,RNNNG,TCT,Pv4> mtu 1500
        inet 192.168.1.3 netmask ffffff00 broadcast 192.168.1.255
        ether 8:0:20:fd:c7:4f
```

The first item in the output of this command is the device name—in this case, *hme0*. The flags provide information on the status of the interface. The MTU represents the size of the largest frame that can be transmitted through this interface. *inet* specifies the Internet address used on the interface. This is followed by the IP netmask and the broadcast address. The last line displays the Ethernet address of the interface.

The following flags might appear in the output of an ifconfig command:

- **Up**   Indicates that the interface is up and running and that the system can send and receive frames through this interface.

- **Down**   Indicates that the interface is in a down state and is not being used by the system to pass any data.

- **Running**   Indicates that the interface is recognized by the kernel.

- **Multicast**   Indicates that the interface supports a multicast address.

- **Broadcast**   Indicates that the interface supports broadcasts.

- **Notrailers**   Indicates that trailers are not included at the end of Ethernet frames. This flag is ignored by Solaris and is provided only for compatibility with previous releases of UNIX.

A network administrator may also use the ifconfig command to modify the parameters for an interface, as shown next.

```
ifconfig interface [ address ] [ netmask { mask | + } ] [ broadcast
{ broadcast_addr | + } ] [ up | down ] [ plumb | unplumb ]
```

The IP address that is to be assigned to this interface is *address*. The IP network mask for this interface is *mask*. The *broadcast* parameter can be used to specify a nondefault broadcast IP address for this network. The + parameter, when used with either the netmask or the broadcast parameters, selects the default value for that parameter. The *up* and *down* parameters are used to toggle the state of the interface. In the *up* state, an interface is fully operational. If an interface is marked as *down*, the system does not attempt to transmit any data through that interface. The *plumb* and *unplumb* options can be used to open the device associated with the physical interface name and set up the necessary streams needed for IP to function.

on the

Job

The ifconfig command is a great way to make changes to network interfaces without downing the whole system. However, be very careful when you use this command. If not used properly, it can result in the loss of network connectivity. Make sure no users are using the network capabilities of a given interface before you take the interface offline.

Let's look at some examples. To enable an interface:

```
# ifconfig hme0 up
# ifconfig hme0
hme0: flags=1000863<P,RCT,RNNNG,TCT,Pv4> mtu 1500
        inet 192.168.1.3 netmask ffffff00 broadcast 192.168.1.255
        ether 8:0:20:fd:c7:4f
```

To disable an interface:

```
# ifconfig hme0 down
# ifconfig hme0
hme0: flags=1000862<RCT,RNNNG,TCT,Pv4> mtu 1500
        inet 192.168.1.3 netmask ffffff00 broadcast 192.168.1.255
        ether 8:0:20:fd:c7:4f
```

To assign an IP address to an interface and bring it up:

```
# ifconfig hme0 10.1.1.2 netmask 255.255.0.0 broadcast 10.1.255.255 up
# ifconfig hme0
```

```
hme0: flags=1000863<P,RCT,RNNNG,TCT,Pv4> mtu 1500
        inet 10.1.1.2 netmask ffff0000 broadcast 10.1.255.255
        ether 8:0:20:fd:c7:4f
```

The netstat Command

You can use the netstat command to obtain statistical information on an interface, for example,

```
# netstat -i
Name  Mtu  Net/Dest     Address     Ipkts    Ierrs Opkts   Oerrs Collis Queue
lo0   8232 loopback     localhost   472      0     472     0     0      0
hme0  1500 192.168.1.3  jaguar      1167872  0     29145   0     19     0
```

EXERCISE 18-5

Using Network Interface Management Commands

In this exercise, you will practice some of the commands you learned to manage network interfaces in a Solaris environment.

1. Log in to your Solaris system as a superuser.

2. Issue the following command to check the status of your network interfaces:

```
# ifconfig -a
lo0: flags=1000849<P,PCK,RNNNG,TCT,Pv4> mtu 8232
        inet 127.0.0.1 netmask ff00000
hme0: flags=1000843<P,RCT,RNNNG,TCT,Pv4> mtu 1500
        inet 192.168.2.2 netmask ffffff00 broadcast 192.168.2.255
        ether 8:0:20:cf:76:e8
```

3. You will now take down the *hme0* network interface. Before doing so, you should ensure that no users are logged in to the system through this interface. Enter the following command:

```
# ifconfig hme0 down
```

4. The *hme0* network interface should now be down. To verify that it is down, enter the following command:

```
# ifconfig -a
lo0: flags=1000849<P,PCK,RNNNG,TCT,Pv4> mtu 8232
```

```
                         inet 127.0.0.1 netmask ff00000
          hme0: flags=1000842< RCT,RNNNG,TCT,Pv4> mtu 1500
                         inet 192.168.2.2 netmask ffffff00 broadcast 192.168.2.255
                         ether 8:0:20:cf:76:e8
```

5. Notice that the *up* flag no longer shows up for the *hme0* interface, indicating that the interface is down. Bring the interface back up:

   ```
   # ifconfig hme0 up
   ```

6. You now want to check the statistics for your interface. Identify the number of collisions on your interface by entering the following command, and then look at the Collis column:

```
# netstat -i
Name  Mtu   Net/Dest     Address        Ipkts   Ierrs Opkts   Oerrs Collis Queue
lo0   8232  loopback     localhost      6450    0     6450    0     0      0
hme0  1500  dmz          dmz            1091139 0     400183  2     11565  0
```

In this exercise, you used interface configuration commands to look at interface parameters as well as bring an interface down and back up. You then viewed the statistics for the interface to determine how many collisions had occurred on it.

CERTIFICATION OBJECTIVE 18.06

Understanding the Relationship Between the RPC Service and the rpcbind Process

Network services operate using an agreed-upon port number. To eliminate the problem of configuring too many services on too many hosts, Sun extended the client/server model by introducing remote procedure calls (RPCs). A client, using RPC, can connect to a server process, rpcbind, which is a special registered service. The rpcbind process listens on TCP port 111 for connections for all RPC-based applications and binds a client request to the appropriate port number for the server process.

RPC uses *program numbers* to uniquely identify applications. Program numbers are centrally administered by Sun. Program-name-to-program-number mappings are maintained in the /etc/rpc file. If a service is not registered with RPC and a client tries to reach the service, rpcbind will return an error message: "RPC TIME OUT, PROGRAM NOT FOUND." The rpcbind process is automatically started during the bootup process by the /etc/rc2.d/S71rpc script.

Some RPC-based services are started at boot time. Others are started on demand by /usr/sbin/inetd. A list of these on-demand services can be viewed by looking at the /etc/inetd.conf file. Each RPC program is identified using a unique program number. It is the network administrator's responsibility to ensure that the /etc/rpc file is always kept up to date with the services that are referenced in /etc/inetd.conf.

The syntax for entries in the /etc/rpc file is as follows:

```
name-of-RPC-program    RPC-program-number    aliases    # Comments
```

Here are examples of entries in an RPC database (/etc/rpc):

```
rpcbind    100000    portmap sunrpc portmapper
nfs        100003    nfsprog
mountd     100005    mount showmount
```

EXERCISE 18-6

Examining RPC Services

In this exercise, you will take a look at the RPC services that are running on your system.

1. Log in to your Solaris system as a superuser.

2. The rpcbind server converts RPC program numbers into universal addresses. It must be running on a host to make RPC calls to a server running on that machine. Check to see if the rpcbind process is running by entering the following command:

```
# ps -eaf | grep rpcbind
root    123    1  0    Mar 12 ?           0:00 /usr/sbin/rpcbind
```

3. View the RPC database on your system by looking at the /etc/rpc file:

```
# more /etc/rpc
rpcbind           100000   portmap sunrpc rpcbind
rstatd            100001   rstat rup perfmeter
rusersd           100002   rusers
nfs               100003   nfsprog
ypserv            100004   ypprog
mountd            100005   mount showmount
```

4. Also, take a look at the RPC services that are being spawned by inetd:

```
# grep rpc /etc/inetd.conf
100232/10       tli      rpc/udp wait root /usr/sbin/sadmind        sadmind
rquotad/1       tli      rpc/datagram_v  wait root /usr/lib/nfs/rquotad  rquotad
```

CERTIFICATION OBJECTIVE 18.07

Listing Registered RPC Services

You can use the /usr/sbin/rpcinfo command to obtain information on RPC services. To identify all RPC services registered on a host, use the following command:

```
# rpcinfo -p [hostname]
   program vers proto   port   service
   100000    4   tcp     111   rpcbind
   100024    1   udp   32772   status
   100232   10   udp   32773   sadmind
   100011    1   udp   32774   rquotad
   100002    2   udp   32775   rusersd
```

To identify a particular service that is running on a server:

```
# rpcinfo -u [hostname] sadmind
program 100232 version 10 ready and waiting
```

To make an RPC broadcast to all hosts and check who responds:

```
# rpcinfo -b sadmind 10
10.1.3.100.128.4 netserver
```

EXERCISE 18-7

Examining RPC Commands

In this exercise, you will use the rpcinfo command to view the list of services registered on your system.

1. Log in to your Solaris system as a superuser.

2. Display the RPC information for the system by entering the following command:

```
# rpcinfo
```

3. Identify all the RPC services registered on another host on the network by entering the following command:

```
# rpcinfo -p hostname
```

CERTIFICATION OBJECTIVE 18.08

Starting and Stopping Network Services via the Command Line

Network services are either RPC based or non-RPC based. Furthermore, network services are started either on bootup or dynamically. If they are started dynamically, the inetd process takes care of the startup process. Configuration for the inetd process is stored in the /etc/inetd.conf file.

To stop a non-RPC-based service that is started at bootup, simply kill the daemon that is responsible for that service by using the pkill command. If it is a service spawned by inetd, remove the entry for that service from the /etc/inetd.conf file and restart inetd (pkill -HUP inetd).

To unregister an RPC-based program, you need to use the rpcinfo command to delete the service:

```
# rpcinfo -d sadmind 10
```

To reregister services that were stopped, simply restart inetd:

```
# pkill -HUP inetd
```

CERTIFICATION SUMMARY

Networking protocols are often described with reference to the seven-layer OSI model. The TCP/IP model is divided into five layers. As data is passed down the layers, it is encapsulated. For both of these protocol models, it is important for a Solaris network administrator to be able to identify at which layer a particular application works. This knowledge aids in configuration as well as troubleshooting.

Ethernet has become one of the most prevalent data link layer technologies in the market. It uses the CSMA/CD mechanism to provide multiple systems access to a single transmission medium.

The Solaris operating system was designed to operate in a network environment. On the certification exam, not only will you find questions that test your theoretical knowledge of the networking technologies that Solaris uses, but you will also be asked to provide command syntaxes. To prepare for this situation, read the man pages for the important commands and practice them on an actual Solaris system.

TWO-MINUTE DRILL

Recognizing the Function of Each Layer of the OSI Model

❑ The OSI model consists of seven layers: application, presentation, session, transport, network, data link, and physical. Each layer represents a unique function and relies on the layer below it to provide a service.

❑ Encapsulation is the method by which upper-layer information is placed inside the data field of a lower layer in a network protocol. At a transmitting station, data is encapsulated as it passes from the application layer down to the physical layer. At the receiving station, the data goes through a de-encapsulation process as it travels from the physical layer back up to the application layer.

Defining the Function of Each Layer in the TCP/IP Model

❑ The TCP/IP model consists of five layers: application, transport, Internet, network interface, and hardware. These layers can be mapped against those of the OSI model.

❑ Two commonly used protocols at the transport layer of the TCP/IP protocol stack are Transmission Control Protocol (TCP) and User Datagram Protocol (UDP). TCP provides connection-oriented reliable data delivery service, whereas UDP provides connectionless, unreliable data delivery.

Understanding the Features and Functions of the Ethernet

❑ Ethernet is a data link layer protocol that uses the carrier-sense multiple access with collision detection (CSMA/CD) mechanism to allow multiple stations to share a single medium of transmission.

❑ The Ethernet frame consists of a preamble, start frame delimiter, destination MAC address, source MAC address, a data field, and a CRC. The destination MAC address can be unicast, multicast, or broadcast.

Understanding the Characteristics of RARP and ARP

❑ Address Resolution Protocol (ARP) is used by systems to map Layer 3 addresses to Layer 2 MAC addresses. ARP entries are cached and maintained in an ARP table. The arp command can be used to view and modify entries in this table.

❑ Systems use Reverse Address Resolution Protocol (RARP) to determine their IP addresses. For RARP to function, an RARP server must be configured with IP-address-to-MAC-address mappings.

Using Commands to Display Information About the Local Network Interface

❑ The /usr/sbin/ifconfig command can be used to view and set parameters for network interfaces. It is used by the system on bootup to bring up a network interface, but it can also be used by a network administrator to manually change interface parameters.

❑ The /usr/bin/netstat -i command can be used to obtain statistics on a local network interface. It provides counters for the number of input packets, output packets, input errors, output errors, and collisions.

Understanding the Relationship Between the RPC Service and the rpcbind Process

❑ To alleviate the problem of configuring too many services on a system, Sun created an RPC service that does not require port numbers to be defined at boot time.

❑ The rpcbind process is responsible for interpreting incoming requests and passing them on to the appropriate server process. RPC services register themselves with rpcbind when they start, and they are assigned a port number at that time.

Listing Registered RPC Services

❑ RPC database entries are listed in the /etc/rpc file.

❑ The rpcinfo command can be used to view a list of RPC services that are currently running.

Starting and Stopping Network Services via the Command Line

❑ To stop an RPC-based network service from the command line, use the rpcinfo -d command. This command will unregister the service from RPC.

❑ To reregister RPC services, restart the inetd daemon with an -HUP signal.

SELF TEST

The following questions will help you measure your understanding of the material presented in this chapter. Read all the choices carefully because there might be more than one correct answer. Choose all correct answers for each question.

Recognizing the Function of Each Layer of the OSI Model

1. Which of the following are *not* layers of the OSI model? (Choose all that apply.)

   A. Transport

   B. Encryption

   C. Network

   D. Data link

   E. TCP

   F. Session

Defining the Function of Each Layer in the TCP/IP Model

2. Which of the following are characteristics of UDP? (Choose all that apply.)

   A. Connection oriented

   B. Reliable

   C. Connectionless

   D. Unreliable

3. Which layer of the TCP/IP model is responsible for logical addressing of end systems?

   A. Hardware

   B. Transport

   C. Internet

   D. Application

Understanding the Features and Functions of the Ethernet

4. You attach a network analyzer to monitor Ethernet frames. Which of the following would you *not* see as a part of an Ethernet frame?

   A. Source MAC address

   B. Destination MAC address

C. Type code

D. CSMA/CD

Understanding the Characteristics of RARP and ARP

5. Which of the following commands displays the contents of the ARP table?

A. /usr/sbin/ifconfig -a

B. /usr/sbin/arp -a

C. /usr/sbin/ifconfig -s

D. /usr/sbin/arp -s

6. A diskless client on your network uses RARP to obtain its IP address when it boots up. You notice that the diskless client is sending an RARP request but is not receiving a response from the RARP server. Which of the following files should you check on the RARP server? (Choose all that apply.)

A. /etc/hosts

B. /etc/rarp.conf

C. /etc/ethers

D. /etc/hostname.hme0

Using Commands to Display Information About the Local Network Interface

7. You install a new network card in your Solaris system and boot it up. However, the output of ifconfig -a does not show the newly installed network interface card. What is wrong?

A. You need to reboot the system twice for the network card to function.

B. You need to run the ifconfig *interface-name* enable command to enable the network interface.

C. You need to run the ifconfig *interface-name* plumb command to enable the network interface.

D. The ifconfig -a command does not show all network interface cards.

Understanding the Relationship Between the RPC Service and the rpcbind Process

8. On which port does the RPC service operate?

   A. 111

   B. 21

   C. 23

   D. 101

9. On your Solaris system, you run the spray program, which uses RPC. The spray program is not one of the services started on bootup. Which daemon takes care of starting this service on demand?

   A. nfsd

   B. inetd

   C. rpcd

   D. sprayd

Listing Registered RPC Services

10. You are on a Solaris system and would like to view a list of all the RPC program numbers and names. What do you type?

    A. cat/etc/rpcinfo

    B. cat/etc/rpc

    C. cat/etc/rpcinfo.conf

    D. cat/etc/rpc.conf

Starting and Stopping Network Services via the Command Line

11. Which of the following would you use to delete a registered RPC service?

    A. rpcremove *servicename*

    B. rpcdelete *servicename*

    C. rpcinfo *-d servicename*

    D. rpc *-d servicename*

12. You are working on a production Solaris service, and you accidentally deregister an RPC service. How would you restart this service?

A. rpcinfo *-s servicename*

B. rpcstart *servicename*

C. pkill -HUP rpc

D. pkill -HUP inetd

LAB QUESTION

There are two hosts on a network, Host A and Host B. (See Figure 18-7.) Assume that both hosts were recently booted up, and neither one of them has an ARP cache populated. The user on Host A types

```
ping 192.168.1.3
```

Describe the sequence of packets that are exchanged between the two hosts.

FIGURE 18-7	
Host A and Host B	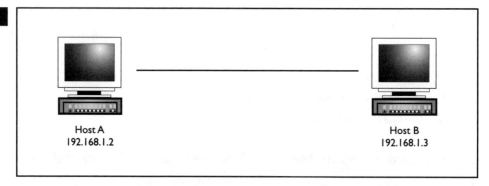

Host A
192.168.1.2

Host B
192.168.1.3

SELF TEST ANSWERS

Recognizing the Function of Each Layer of the OSI Model

1. ☑ B and E. Encryption and TCP are not layers in the OSI model. The seven layers of the OSI model are application, presentation, session, transport, network, data link, and physical.
   ☒ A, C, D, and F are incorrect because they are all part of the seven-layer OSI model.

Defining the Function of Each Layer in the TCP/IP Model

2. ☑ C and D. UDP provides connectionless, unreliable datagram delivery.
   ☒ A and B are incorrect because UDP provides no reliability, nor does it establish connections.

3. ☑ C. IP addresses are a form of logical addressing used at the Internet layer.
   ☒ A, B, and D are incorrect because although these are layers of the TCP/IP model, they are not responsible for IP addressing.

Understanding the Features and Functions of the Ethernet

4. ☑ D. CSMA/CD describes the concept behind how Ethernet functions. It is not a part of the Ethernet frame.
   ☒ A, B, and C are incorrect. These are all fields that are a part of the Ethernet frame.

Understanding the Characteristics of RARP and ARP

5. ☑ B. arp -*a* displays the contents of the ARP table.
   ☒ A, C, and D are incorrect because these commands do not display the contents of the ARP table.

6. ☑ A and C. The server /etc/hosts and /etc/ethers file must have entries for the diskless client. In addition, the in.rarpd process must be running on the server.
   ☒ B is incorrect because no such file exists. D is incorrect because this file is not related to RARP functionality.

Using Commands to Display Information About the Local Network Interface

7. ☑ C. This command associates a physical device and sets up the streams necessary for IP to use that device.

☒ A is incorrect because rebooting will have no effect. B is incorrect because there is no such command. D is incorrect because this command does show all plumbed interfaces.

Understanding the Relationship Between the RPC Service and the rpcbind Process

8. ☑ A. The rpcbind service operates on TCP port 111.

☒ B, C, and D are incorrect ports for rpcbind.

9. ☑ B. inetd is responsible for spawning on-demand services, both for RPC- and non-RPC-based applications.

☒ A is incorrect because it does not dynamically spawn network services. C and D are incorrect because these daemons do not exist.

Listing Registered RPC Services

10. ☑ B. The /etc/rpc file contains mappings of program names and numbers.

☒ A, C, and D are incorrect because these files don't exist.

Starting and Stopping Network Services via the Command Line

11. ☑ C. This command allows a service to be deregistered from RPC.

☒ A, B, and D are incorrect because they are invalid commands.

12. ☑ D. Restarting the inetd process will reinitialize RPC and reregister all the services that were deleted.

☒ A, B, and C are incorrect because they are invalid commands.

LAB ANSWER

1. Host A needs to obtain the MAC address of Host B. It sends out a broadcast ARP request to determine the MAC address of the host with IP address 192.168.1.3.

2. Host B, upon receiving the ARP request from Host A, responds with an ARP response.

3. Host A receives the ARP response and populates its ARP table with the IP address and MAC address of Host B.

4. Host A sends a ping (an ICMP echo) packet toward Host B.

5. Host B responds with a ping reply (an ICMP echo reply) packet.

SUN® CERTIFIED SYSTEM ADMINISTRATOR

19

Utilizing Solaris syslogc

I mportant to any operating system is the ability to capture system and application errors and exceptions. Without such functionality and the ability to report events as they occur, system downtime can be excessive. Every UNIX administrator should learn not only which logging tools are available, but how best to use them. Perhaps one of the most underused tools is also one of the most powerful logging mechanisms: syslog. This chapter examines the use of syslog; how to configure it to more fully trap system messages; and how to route the messages to various points, including a central logging area, specific users, and multiple log files based on error type.

CERTIFICATION OBJECTIVE 19.01

Understanding the Functions of syslog

The syslog facility is the general-purpose logging facility native to all UNIX systems, including Solaris. It consists of an application programming interface (API), syslog( ); logger, which is a UNIX command used to write single-line messages to the syslog log file from either a script or from the command line; /etc/syslog.conf, which is the configuration file controlling syslog daemon behavior; and syslogd, the syslog daemon, which receives and routes system log events from syslog( ) calls and logger.

By default, messages logged by syslog are written to /var/adm/messages. Additionally, the dmesg command scans the messages file for recently occurring errors and outputs the information to the standard output. If you use the hyphen (-) option with dmesg (dmesg -), you will see which messages have occurred since you last ran dmesg.

The syslog facilities and alert levels give a system administrator the ability to greatly customize messages based on message type and priority, giving special handling to the various message types as appropriate for your site. The section "Deducing syslog Behavior from Its Configuration File," later in this chapter, explores in detail the various facilities, alert levels, and actions.

In my experience, one of the best methods to use for real-time error checking is to open a terminal session on the system, and then run this command:

```
tail -f /var/adm/messages
```

Using the -f option with tail allows you to watch each message written to the file as it occurs, which can be a great proactive monitoring tool. I have also used dmesg with the hyphen (-) option (dmesg -), redirecting it to a log file with datestamps to get a point-in-time type of output of dmesg. I've done this in shell scripts when syslog capabilities were not being used and corporate management did not want to use syslog. A simple script like this can be most helpful:

```
#!/usr/bin/ksh
date +%m%d%y-%H:%M:%S >>>> /home/jdennis/dmesg.log
dmesg - >>>> /home/jdennis/dmesg.log
```

CERTIFICATION OBJECTIVE 19.02

Understanding the Syntax of the syslog Configuration File

To understand and use syslog, your first step is to understand the syslog configuration file, /etc/syslog.conf. It is important to understand this file, its syntax, and the various options available if you plan to use the syslog facility.

The syntax of /etc/syslog.conf is a topic that is likely to be covered on the exam. Pay close attention to the following descriptions of the syntax of the facilities, levels, and actions.

The file /etc/syslog.conf contains information used by the system log daemon, syslogd, to forward a system message to appropriate log files and/or users. To better understand the syslog.conf file, let's break down one of the file's entries and examine its components:

```
*.err;kern.debug;daemon.notice;mail.crit          /var/adm/messages
```

This entry has a SELECTOR field, followed by an ACTION field. These are tab-separated fields. The SELECTOR field in this case consists of four separate facility/level combinations. They are

- *.err
- kern.debug
- daemon.notice
- mail.crit

Note that SELECTOR field entries are separated by a semicolon. All of these selectors have the action of being written to the log file /var/adm/messages.

Let's break this down even further. The *.err line indicates that *all* messages from all facilities (excluding the mark facility; see Figure 19-1) with a severity level of err (see Table 19-2) will be written to the specified logfile—in this case, /var/adm/messages. In the case of the kern.debug entry, all messages generated by the kernel with a severity level of *debug* will be written to the logfile.

You probably get the picture now. Tables 19-1 and 19-2 present more information on the facilities and levels.

As mentioned in the preceding example, the ACTION field indicates where the message is to be forwarded. There are four basic options for action:

- An absolute filename indicates that messages specified by the selector are to be written to the specified file.

- The name of a remote host, prefixed with an at sign (@), such as @uxssa01, indicates that messages specified by the selector are to be forwarded to syslogd on the named host. The hostname *loghost* is the symbolic hostname given to the machine that will log syslogd messages. Every machine is loghost by default.

- A comma-separated list of usernames indicates that messages specified by the selector will be written to the users if they are logged in.

- An asterisk indicates that messages specified by the selector are to be written to all logged-in users.

FIGURE 19-1

A sample
syslog.conf file

```
#ident  "@(#)syslog.conf    1.4     96/10/11 SMI" /* SunOS 5.0 */
#
# Copyright (c) 1991-1993, by Sun Microsystems, Inc.
#
# syslog configuration file.
#
# This file is processed by m4 so be careful to quote (`') names
# that match m4 reserved words.  Also, within ifdef's, arguments
# containing commas must be quoted.
#
*.err;kern.notice;auth.notice                   /dev/console
*.err;kern.debug;daemon.notice;mail.crit        /var/adm/messages
*.alert;kern.err;daemon.err                      operator
*.alert                                          root
*.emerg                                          *
# if a non-loghost machine chooses to have authentication messages
# sent to the loghost machine, un-comment out the following line:
#auth.notice                   ifdef(`LOGHOST', /var/log/authlog, @loghost)
mail.debug                     ifdef(`LOGHOST', /var/log/syslog, @loghost)
#
# non-loghost machines will use the following lines to cause "user"
# log messages to be logged locally.
#
ifdef(`LOGHOST', ,
user.err                                         /dev/console
user.err                                         /var/adm/messages
user.alert                                       `root, operator'
user.emerg                                       *
)
*.info                         /cauni2/opr/config/uxhrdev/pipe/oprpipe0002
```

TABLE 19-1 Recognized Values for Facilities

Value	Description
user	Messages generated by user processes. This is the default priority for messages from programs or facilities not listed in this file.
kern	Messages generated by the kernel.
mail	The mail system.
daemon	System daemons, such as in.ftpd and in.Telnetd.
auth	The authorization system: login, su, and getty, among others.
lpr	The line printer spooling system (lpr, lpc).
news	Reserved for the USENET network news system.
uucp	Reserved for the UUCP system. Currently, UUCP does not use the syslog mechanism.

TABLE 19-1   Recognized Values for Facilities *(continued)*

Value	Description
cron	The cron/at facility; crontab, at, cron.
local0-7	Reserved for local use.
mark	Used internally for timestamp messages produced by syslogd.
*	An asterisk indicates all facilities except the mark facility.

Blank lines in the syslog.conf file are ignored. Lines beginning with a pound sign (#) are treated as comment lines.

exam
⩍atch   *For the exam, be prepared to identify the facilities that are available, their severity levels, and the actions that can be performed. These are common areas that trip people up on exams.*

TABLE 19-2   Recognized Values for Level (in Descending Order of Severity)

Value	Description
emerg	For panic conditions that would normally be broadcast to all users.
alert	For conditions that should be corrected immediately, such as a corrupted system database.
crit	For warnings about critical conditions, such as hard device errors.
err	For other errors.
warning	For warning messages.
notice	For conditions that are not error conditions but might require special handling. A configuration entry with a level value of notice must appear on a separate line.
info	Informational messages.
debug	For messages that are normally used only when debugging a program.
none	Do not send messages from the indicated facility to the selected file. For example, a selector of *.debug;mail.none sends all messages except mail messages to the selected file.

on the **Job**

In the environments in which I have worked, I found syslog to be one of the most underused (and in some cases, completely unused) functions of the system. Given syslog's power, it is amazing how few people really understand and appreciate its capabilities. One of the first things I generally do is designate a single server, usually my sysadmin server, as the loghost for all other servers. To do this, I specify in the host tables of each server that uxdssa01 is the loghost. This gives me the ability to easily track down error messages from any given server from one central point of administration.

CERTIFICATION OBJECTIVE 19.03

Deducing syslog Behavior from Its Configuration File

As shown in the preceding examples, once you understand the syntax of the syslog configuration file, it is much easier to customize syslog for your environment. The following configuration file will help you understand what syslog is doing:

```
*.notice                    /var/log/notice
mail.info                   /var/log/info
 *.crit                      /var/log/critical
 kern;mark.debug          /dev/console
 kern.err                    @uxdssa01
 *.emerg                     *
 *.alert                     root,operator
 *.alert       /var/log/alert
 auth.warning      /var/log/auth
```

In this example, syslogd logs all notice messages to /var/log/notice. All mail system info messages are logged to a file named /var/log/info. All critical messages are logged to /var/log/critical, and all kernel messages and 20-minute marks are written to the system console.

Kernel messages of err (error) severity or higher are forwarded to the machine named *uxdssa01*. Emergency messages are forwarded to all users. The users *root* and *operator* are informed of any alert messages, and the alerts are also written to the

/var/log/alert file. All messages from the authorization system of warning level or higher are logged in the file /var/log/auth.

It is also important to note that, when you make changes to the syslog.conf file, these changes are not dynamic. You must either restart the daemon or cause it to reread its configuration file by sending a -SIGHUP signal to its process ID. This can be accomplished as follows:

```
ps -aef | grep syslog
```

Look for the PID of the syslogd daemon, and then run this command:

```
kill -HUP {syslogd-PID}
```

Given this snippet of a syslog.conf file, consider the following scenarios and solutions:

```
*.err;kern.notice;auth.notice                  /dev/console
*.err;kern.debug;daemon.notice;mail.crit       /var/adm/messages
*.alert;kern.err;daemon.err                     operator
*.alert                                         root
*.emerg                                         *
*.alert;kern.err,daemon.err                     operator
```

SCENARIO & SOLUTION

To where would you expect kernel notice messages to be sent?	The system console, /dev/console.
Who would receive all the emergency notices?	All logged-in users. The *.emerg line, with the trailing wildcard, sends all emergency notifications to all logged-in users.
What is wrong with the syntax of the last line of the file?	There is a comma separating kern.err and daemon.err. The delimiter must be a semicolon.

Configuring syslog Messages to Increase the Logging Level for login and Telnet

In today's Internet world, with a large percentage of the population online, it becomes important not only to have good security in place, but to be able to track security information, such as connections to a server. The syslog.conf file does not enable higher-level security; rather, it tracks it at various severity levels, based on your needs. This section explores how you can increase the logging severity level for login and Telnet.

login logging is not normally enabled when a system is installed. To enable this logging, you may modify the file /etc/default/login, uncommenting the SYSLOG line and editing the lines as appropriate. SYSLOG determines whether the syslog LOG_AUTH facility should be used to log all root logins at level LOG_NOTICE and multiple failed login attempts at LOG_CRIT level. Here is an example of the /etc/default/login file with these parameters set:

```
# SYSLOG determines whether the syslog(3) LOG_AUTH facility should be used
# to log all root logins at level LOG_NOTICE and multiple failed login
# attempts at LOG_CRIT.
#
SYSLOG=YES
```

When these parameters are set, you will be able to track login activity using syslog. For example, let's say you have SYSLOG=YES in /etc/default/login, and in your /etc/syslog.conf, you have auth.notice going to /var/adm/auth.messages. When someone logs in as root, you get the following message:

```
$ tail -f auth.messages
May  2 12:16:39 simba login: ROOT LOGIN /dev/pts/1 FROM tarzan.jungle.com
```

When someone repeatedly fails to log in correctly, you get this message:

```
May  2 12:17:44 simba login: REPEATED LOGIN FAILURES ON /dev/pts/3 FROM
tarzan.jungle.com
```

To show more clearly how to use the different severity levels of syslog, imagine you create the directory /var/adm/auth and modify /etc/syslog.conf as follows:

```
auth.notice                                /var/adm/auth/messages
auth.err                                   /var/adm/auth/errors
auth.crit                                  /var/adm/auth/critical
auth.debug                                 /var/adm/auth/debug
daemon.notice;daemon.debug;daemon.crit     /var/adm/daemon/messages
```

This will enable you to see what each of these severity levels will track. First, let's look at /var/adm/auth/messages. As shown in syslog.conf, this file contains all auth.notice messages:

```
simba# more messages
May  2 12:54:07 simba login: REPEATED LOGIN FAILURES ON /dev/pts/3 FROM
tarzan.jungle.com
```

Now, look at /var/adm/auth/errors:

```
simba# more errors
May  2 12:54:07 simba login: REPEATED LOGIN FAILURES ON /dev/pts/3 FROM
tarzan.jungle.com
```

And here is /var/adm/auth/critical:

```
simba# more critical
May  2 12:54:07 simba login: REPEATED LOGIN FAILURES ON /dev/pts/3 FROM
tarzan.jungle.com
```

And finally, here is /var/adm/auth/debug:

```
simba# more debug
May  2 12:53:32 simba login: pam_authenticate: error Authentication failed
May  2 12:54:03 simba last message repeated 4 times
May  2 12:54:07 simba login: REPEATED LOGIN FAILURES ON /dev/pts/3 FROM
tarzan.jungle.com
```

As you can see, the various severity levels of syslog are not greatly used for Telnet sessions. What you can see in the debug log file, however, is the pam_authenticate error. Any time a user fails to log in, you can see these errors if you are tracking them through syslog.

One, additional file that is useful is /var/adm/loginlog. This file is not created by default, so if you want to use it, you must create it. It needs to be owned by root, with a group of sys, and read/write permissions only for the owner. This file tracks *all* failed login attempts, whether singular failures (such as mistyping) or multiple failures. (*Note:* This is not a syslog function but a function of the login process.)

Telnet access is not logged by default. To collect data about incoming TCP connections, the inetd daemon must be started with the *-t* flag. This flag tells inetd to trace all incoming TCP connections. It logs the client's IP address and TCP port number and the name of the service using syslog. When you have tracing enabled, inetd uses the daemon facility code and priority-level notice. Messages like the one shown here are logged:

```
Apr 17 15:17:05 simba inetd[481]: Telnet[7592] from 192.168.0.3 4636
```

CERTIFICATION OBJECTIVE 19.05

Using the Command Line to Update the System Log

The logger function of syslog allows a system administrator to customize logging capabilities outside of syslog. For example, in shell scripts, you could trap such things as when a file system reaches a certain threshold of space use—maybe 90 percent full. In your shell script, you can use logger to write the message to one of the syslog files, in addition to the other processing you might be doing in the script. The syntax for logger is as follows:

```
logger [-i] [-f file] [-p priority] [-t tag] [message] ...
```

Supported options for logger are

- *-f (file)* Uses the contents from *file* as input for the message to log.
- *-i* Logs the process ID (PID) of the logger process with each line.
- *-p (priority)* Logs the message with the specified priority. The message priority can be specified numerically or as a facility.level pair. For example,

```
-p local3.info
```

assigns the message priority to the info level in the local3 facility. The default priority is user.notice.

- ■ *-t(tag)* Marks each line added to the log with the specified tag.

Here's an example of a logger message embedded in a shell script:

```
logger -p local3.info -t JSWNOTICE -f /home/sysadm/msgtags/jsw
```

In this case, the shell script tries a function, and if it fails, it instructs logger to send a message with the tag (*-t*) JSWNOTICE, using the file (*-f*)/home/sysadm/msgtags/jsw as the input file for the message information. Because local3.info in syslog.conf identifies that these messages are to be sent to /home/sysadm/logs/jsw.notices, you can look there for the line written by logger.

on the job

My co-workers and I use logger rather extensively on the job. The syslog loghost is centralized to one server and multiple shell scripts are used on other servers to track key information about the systems, including performance data, login attempts, and so on. All this information is sent via logger to the syslog daemon for routing to the loghost. The following command lives in /etc/profile:

```
logger -p local0.notice -t LOGIN "User $LOGNAME has logged in"
```

And the /etc/syslog.conf file contains this line to route the information:

```
local0.notice                    @loghost
```

As mentioned earlier, loghost is defined in the /etc/hosts table as follows:

```
192.168.0.14  mastadon   loghost
```

EXERCISE 19-1

Using logger to Enhance System-Logging Capabilities

This exercise explores the use of logger to enhance system error reporting. In your environment, say you have a window up for your operators that tails the /var/adm/messages file. You run shell scripts to check for various conditions, such as file systems running out of space or processes that are dying. You write a simple shell script that reads an error file and shows how logger can help you in this process.

First, your messages file will be called fs.msg, so create that in your home directory:

```
90:local1.warning:FS90THRESH:Filesystem at 90% threshold
95:local1.alert:FS95THRESH:Filesystem at 95% threshold
100:local1.emerg:FSFULL:Filesystem 100% FULL
```

Then your shell script will look like this:

```
#!/usr/bin/ksh
for filesystem in `df -k | awk '{print $6}' | sed '1d'`
do
SPACEAVAIL=`df -k $filesystem | sed '1d' | awk '{print $5}' | sed 's/%//'`
if [[ $SPACEAVAIL -gt "89" ]]; then
        PRIORITY=`grep $SPACEAVAIL /home/jdennis/fs.msgs | awk -F":" '{print $2}'`
        TAG=`grep $SPACEAVAIL /home/jdennis/fs.msgs | awk -F":" '{print $3}'`
        MSG=`grep $SPACEAVAIL /home/jdennis/fs.msgs | awk -F":" '{print $4}'`
        logger -p $PRIORITY -t $TAG $filesystem:$MSG
else
        echo "No message logged"
fi
done
```

Create that file in your home directory as well, being sure to make it executable, and then modify your /etc/syslog.conf file to indicate where your local3 messages will be sent:

```
local3.*     /var/adm/messages
```

Refresh the syslogd daemon by doing a kill -HUP on the PID of the syslogd process; then run the script.

In this example, you are looking for a file system with greater than 89 percent usage. When you find that information, you will grab from the fs.msgs file the message that is appropriate to the space usage of that file system and write that message to the log file.

Output from this script would be sent to /var/adm/messages and be formatted as follows:

```
May  2 16:48:39 simba FS95THRESH: /usr:Filesystem at 90% threshold
May  2 16:48:40 simba FS95THRESH: /vol03:Filesystem at 90% threshold
```

```
May  2 16:48:40 simba FS95THRESH: /vol04:Filesystem at 90% threshold
May  2 16:48:40 simba FS95THRESH: /vol05:Filesystem at 90% threshold
```

You now have a real-life example of how to use logger to enhance your logging capabilities.

CERTIFICATION SUMMARY

This chapter discussed how to use syslog to enhance your system-reporting capabilities. When you understand and use system functions such as syslog, you will have far greater capability to monitor your systems without having to do a lot of shell scripting and custom programming.

✓ TWO-MINUTE DRILL

Understanding the Functions of syslog

❑ The configuration file that controls syslog daemon behavior is /etc/syslog.conf.

❑ The syslog daemon is syslogd.

❑ The UNIX command that allows a user to write single-line messages to the syslog log file is logger.

Understanding the Syntax of the syslog Configuration File

In the syslog configuration file, three distinct fields control the actions of any system event:

❑ The facility is where the event originated: user, kernel, mail, daemons, auth, lpr, news, uucp, cron, mark, *, and local0-7.

❑ The severity refers to levels of severity of the event: emerg(ency), alert, crit(ical), err(or), warning, notice, info, debug, and none.

❑ The action indicates the disposal of the event: an absolute filename, a remote host, a list of users, or all users.

Deducing syslog Behavior from Its Configuration File

The behavior of syslog is controlled by the various actions available. They are

❑ A filename (absolute path, such as /var/adm/messages)

❑ A remote host (loghost, for example, or the name of the host)

❑ A list of users, comma separated

❑ All users (indicated by an asterisk (*) in the ACTION field)

Configuring syslog Messages to Increase the Logging Level for login and Telnet

❑ You can increase the logging level of Telnet, login, and FTP daemons by changing options in various locations in the system.

❑ For the ftpd daemon, you can change the debug and logging levels with flags in the /etc/inet.conf.

❑ For Telnet, you can trace incoming Telnet (and TCP/IP) connections by starting inetd with the *-t* flag.

❑ For login, you can trace login information by modifying /etc/default/login and changing/uncommenting the SYLOG line.

Using the Command Line to Update the System Log

❑ logger allows a system administrator to write single-line messages to the syslog log file. This can be done via shell scripts or the command line. The logger function has three options:

❑ *-i* logs the PID of the process with each line written.

❑ *-p* identifies the priority of the message logged, such as local0.notice; user.notice is the default.

❑ *-t* allows you to mark each line written with a specific tag, such as an identifier that indicates by which program or shell script the message was generated.

SELF TEST

The following questions will help you measure your understanding of the material presented in this chapter. Read all the choices carefully because there might be more than one correct answer. Choose all correct answers for each question.

Understanding the Functions of syslog

1. Which of the following statements is true about syslog?

    A. It is the syslog daemon.

    B. It is a function designed to trap syslog messages from within a Korn shell script.

    C. It is an application programming interface used by syslog.

    D. It is a command-line logging function of syslog.

2. Which of the following statements is true about syslog.conf?

    A. It resides in the /etc/syslog/conf directory.

    B. It is the configuration file that controls the behavior of the syslog daemon.

    C. It does not exist on UNIX systems by default; it must be created by the system administrator.

    D. It contains user IDs for those users who are permitted to use syslog.

Understanding the Syntax of the syslog Configuration File

3. What is wrong with the following line of the syslog.conf file?

    ```
    *.err;kern.notice,auth.notice    /dev/console
    ```

    A. You cannot direct errors and notice messages to /dev/console on the same line of the configuration file.

    B. Each line for a facility notice message must be on a separate line in the configuration file.

    C. The facility.severity entries must be separated by a semicolon, not a comma.

    D. /dev/console is not a valid destination for notice messages.

4. Which of the following lines is correct for an action that sends messages to users?

    A. ```*.alert;kern.err;daemon.err   root,sysop,sysadmin```

    B. ```*.alert;kern.err;daemon.err   root:sysop:sysadmin```

```
C. *.alert;kern.err;daemon.err        root;sysop;sysadmin
D. *.alert;kern.err;daemon.err        (root, sysop, sysadmin)
```

Deducing syslog Behavior from Its Configuration File

5. How would a blank line in the configuration file affect the functionality of syslog?

A. A blank line would cause syslog to not process the next line in the file.

B. A blank line would cause syslog to not function at all.

C. A blank line would have no effect; it would be skipped over and would not affect the functionality of syslog.

D. A blank line is considered a continuation of the previous line.

6. Where would you expect messages to be delivered, given the following line?

```
*.emerg        *
```

A. All emergency messages would be sent to the console, the log file, and all users.

B. All emergency messages would be sent to the console, the log file, the loghost, and all users.

C. All emergency messages would be sent to the console and the loghost.

D. All emergency messages would be sent to all logged-in users.

Configuring syslog Messages to Increase the Logging Level for login and Telnet

7. What is the effect of having SYSLOG=YES in the /etc/default/login file?

A. This will cause all root-level login authentication messages to be directed to the syslog log file.

B. This will cause all root logins to be logged at LOG_NOTICE level and multiple failed login attempts to be logged at the LOG_CRIT level.

C. This simply means that you want to run syslog on the system.

D. This has no effect on the system or on syslog.

Using the Command Line to Update the System Log

8. Where are messages generated by logger logged by default?

    A. The messages file in /var/adm

    B. /var/log/logger.log

    C. /var/log/syslog.log

    D. The syslog log file as defined in /etc/syslog.conf

LAB QUESTION

Show the steps necessary to implement a custom logging message in a shell script (using logger) using a priority of local0.notice, using a tag HDWERR to identify the message, and identifying a log file named /var/log/local.notices to store the messages.

SELF TEST ANSWERS

Understanding the Functions of syslog

1. ☑ C. syslog( ) is an API used by syslog.
   ☒ A is incorrect because syslogd is the daemon. B is incorrect because syslog( ) is not a Korn shell function. D is incorrect because logger is the UNIX command-line function designed to write to the syslog log files.

2. ☑ B. syslog.conf is the configuration file that controls the behavior of syslog.
   ☒ A is incorrect because the full path to the configuration file is /etc/syslog.conf. C is incorrect because the syslog.conf file does exist by default; its usage is defined by the system administrator. D is just plain incorrect. No user IDs are associated with syslog.conf, save for users whose messages might be routed to as an action.

Understanding the Syntax of the syslog Configuration File

3. ☑ C. The facility.severity entries must be separated by a semicolon.
   ☒ A is incorrect because you can send the errors and notices to /dev/console on the same line. B is incorrect; you can put multiple notice messages on the same line. D is incorrect because you can send notice messages to /dev/console.

4. ☑ A. Actions that send messages to users are defined with a comma-separated list of users.
   ☒ B is incorrect because a colon is not a valid separator for a user list. C is incorrect because a semicolon is not a valid separator for a user list. D is incorrect because the names should not be in parentheses.

Deducing syslog Behavior from Its Configuration File

5. ☑ C. Blank lines are ignored.
   ☒ A is incorrect because a blank line has no effect on the processing of any line in the syslog.conf file. B is incorrect because blank lines do not cause syslog to stop functioning. D is incorrect because blank lines serve no purpose; they are ignored.

6. ☑ D. An asterisk (*) indicates that the message is to be sent to all logged-in users.
   ☒ A, B, and C are all incorrect because there is no wildcard to send messages to any destination except to all logged-in users.

Configuring syslog Messages to Increase the Logging Level for login and Telnet

7. ☑   B. It will cause all root logins to be logged at LOG_NOTICE level and multiple failed login attempts to be logged at the LOG_CRIT level.

☒   A is incorrect because this controls more than just root-level login information to be logged. C is incorrect because SYSLOG=YES has no effect on whether syslog runs or not. D is incorrect because it does have an effect on the system or syslog.

Using the Command Line to Update the System Log

8. ☑   A. By default, syslog messages are sent to the /var/adm/messages file.

☒   B, C, and D are incorrect because the default location is /var/adm/messages.

LAB ANSWER

1. Insert the line

```
logger -p local0.notice -t HDWERR
```

into the shell script.

2. Insert the line

```
local0.notice   /var/logs/local.notice
```

into the syslog.conf file.

3. Restart the syslog daemon or cause it to reread the configuration file by sending a SIGHUP to the PID of the syslogd daemon.

SUN® CERTIFIED SYSTEM ADMINISTRATOR

20

Disk
Management

CERTIFICATION OBJECTIVES

20.01   Using Utilities to Create, Check, and Mount File Systems

20.02   Understanding the Logical Pathname Differences Between Physical Disks and Virtual Disks

20.03   Knowing the Advantages of a Virtual Disk Management Application

20.04   Understanding the Characteristics and Functions of DiskSuite and Sun StorEdge VM

✓   Two-Minute Drill

Q&A   Self Test

D*isk management* is one of the most important system administration functions in most companies. It is unusual to have a wealth of unused disk space just lying around waiting to be used. Therefore, dividing up disk space when needed and assuring that each application and user has the appropriate resources is very critical and, in some cases, constitutes a full-time job. Increasing numbers of companies are advertising for sysadmins with capacity-planning skills.

This chapter explores the standard Solaris utilities to create, check, and mount file systems, as well as exploring Sun StorEdge Volume Manager (SEVM) and Solstice DiskSuite. (Solstice DiskSuite is now called Solaris Volume Manager and has been enhanced to include a number of new options; these will be covered later in this chapter and briefly in Appendix A.)

CERTIFICATION OBJECTIVE 20.01

Using Utilities to Create, Check, and Mount File Systems

Various utilities in the Solaris operating environment allow creation and manipulation of file systems. To create a file system, you need newfs. Once it is created and you've created your mount point, you need mount to provide user access to it. Furthermore, if you have difficulty, fsck is your most valuable tool. This chapter covers these topics in detail.

Creating File Systems

To create a file system in the Solaris operating system, you must decide first which disk to use, how large a file system you want, which characteristics you want the file system to have, what you are going to name it, and who is going to access it.

Once you have determined which disk to use, you use the format command to partition the disk:

```
simba# format
Searching for disks...done
AVAILABLE DISK SELECTIONS:
```

```
      0. c0t0d0 <N9.0G cyl 4924 alt 2 hd 27 sec 133>
         /pci@1f,4000/scsi@3/sd@0,0
      1. c0t1d0 <N9.0G cyl 4924 alt 2 hd 27 sec 133>
         /pci@1f,4000/scsi@3/sd@1,0
      <cut>
     16. c5t0d0 <N9.0G cyl 4924 alt 2 hd 27 sec 133>
         /pci@6,4000/scsi@4,1/sd@0,0

Specify disk (enter its number): 16
selecting c5t0d0
[disk formatted]

FORMAT MENU:
        disk       - select a disk
        type       - select (define) a disk type
        partition  - select (define) a partition table
        current    - describe the current disk
        format     - format and analyze the disk
        repair     - repair a defective sector
        label      - write label to the disk
        analyze    - surface analysis
        defect     - defect list management
        backup     - search for backup labels
        verify     - read and display labels
        save       - save new disk/partition definitions
        inquiry    - show vendor, product and revision
        volname    - set 8-character volume name
        !<cmd>     - execute <cmd>, then return
        quit
format>> partition
PARTITION MENU:
        0         - change '0' partition
        1         - change '1' partition
        2         - change '2' partition
        3         - change '3' partition
        4         - change '4' partition
        5         - change '5' partition
        6         - change '6' partition
        7         - change '7' partition
        select - select a predefined table
        modify - modify a predefined partition table
        name   - name the current table
        print  - display the current table
        label  - write partition map and label to the disk
        !<cmd> - execute <cmd>, then return
        quit
partition>> print
Current partition table (original):
Total disk cylinders available: 4924 + 2 (reserved cylinders)
```

```
Part      Tag    Flag    Cylinders        Size            Blocks
  0 unassigned    wm    0                0         (0/0/0)              0
  1 unassigned    wm    0                0         (0/0/0)              0
  2    backup     wu    0 - 4923         8.43GB    (4924/0/0)  17682084
  3       -       wu    0 -    0         1.75MB    (1/0/0)           3591
  4       -       wu    1 - 4923         8.43GB    (4923/0/0)  17678493
  5 unassigned    wm    0                0         (0/0/0)              0
  6 unassigned    wm    0                0         (0/0/0)              0
  7 unassigned    wm    0                0         (0/0/0)              0

partition>>
```

You can see from the output of the format command that disk c5t0d0 has a large amount of unused space (the entire disk), so it makes sense to use this disk to create the file system(s). Let's use newfs to create the file systems on slice /dev/rdsk/c5t0d0s4.

At this point, you need to understand the Solaris disk-naming convention. As shown in the preceding code, the disk selected is c5t0d0, and the file system was created on slice 4. What exactly does this mean? Let's break it down:

c5 = controller 5
t0 = target 0
d0 = disk 0
s4 = slice 4

Additionally, you need to understand the logical pathnames of the disks. The /dev directory contains logical pathnames for disk devices, which are links to the physical pathnames in the /devices directory. Each disk device has a /dev/rdsk entry and a /dev/dsk entry.

/dev/dsk/c0t0d0 identifies the block device for a particular disk, whereas /dev/rdsk/c5t0d0 identifies the raw device for that disk. When you create or check a file system, you use the raw device as the pathname, whereas when you mount or check space on a file system, you use the block device.

Using the newfs Command

Use of newfs is as follows:

```
newfs [-Nv] [mkfs-options] raw-device
```

Or, in our example:

```
newfs [-Nv] [mkfs-options] /dev/rdsk/c5t0d0s4
```

The newfs command has two options, and multiple mkfs options can be used with newfs. Options to newfs are the following:

- *-N*   Do not create the file system, but print the parameters that would be used to create the file system.

- *-v*   Be verbose; reveal everything that is happening with this process, including the mkfs options.

In addition, several mkfs options are called by newfs. These options can be used to override the default parameters of mkfs. These options are the following:

- *-a apc*   The number of alternate blocks per cylinder (SCSI devices only) to reserve for bad block replacement. The default is 0.

- *-b bsize*   The logical block size of the file system in bytes (either 4096 or 8192). The default is 8192. The sun4u architecture does not support the 4096 block size.

- *-c cgsize*   The number of cylinders per cylinder group.

- *-d gap*   Rotational delay. The expected time (in milliseconds) to service a transfer completion interrupt and initiate a new transfer on the same disk. It is used to decide how much rotational spacing to place between successive blocks in a file. This parameter can be changed using the tunefs command. The default is disk-type dependent.

- *-f fragsize*   The smallest amount of disk space in bytes to allocate to a file. The acceptable values must be a power of 2 and can range from 512 up to the logical block size, which by default is 8192. For example, if the logical block size of the file system is 8192, the acceptable values for fragsize are 512, 1024, 4096, and 8192. The default fragsize is 1024.

- *-i nbpi*   Number of bytes per inode. This figure specifies how many inodes will be created in the file system. The number is divided into the total size of the file system to determine how many inodes to create. It should be set according to the expected average size of files in the file system. If fewer inodes are desired (larger files to be created), a larger number should be used, effectively creating fewer inodes. If smaller files are to be created, a smaller number need to be used, effectively creating more inodes. Table 20-1 shows the default for nbpi.

Disk Size	Density
< 1GB	2048
1–2GB	4096
2–3GB	6144
3GB+	8192

TABLE 20-1

nbpi Disk Sizes and Densities

- **-m free**   Also known as *minfree,* this option sets the minimum percentage of free space to maintain in a file system. Once a file system reaches the minfree threshold (100%–minfree%=available%), a normal user cannot continue to write to the file system. This space can be accessed only by the superuser. This is one of several parameters that can later be changed by the superuser using the tunefs command.

- **-n nrpos**   The number of different rotational positions in which to divide a cylinder group. The default is 8.

- **-o (space or time)**   When creating the file system, you can choose whether it will try to minimize the time spent allocating blocks or minimize the fragmentation of the file system on the disk. The default is time.

- **-r rpm**   The disk speed in revolutions per minute. The default is 3600.

- **-s size**   The file system size in sectors. The default is to use the entire partition.

- **-t ntrack**   The tracks per cylinder on the disk. The default is taken from the disk label.

- **-C maxcontig**   The maximum number of blocks belonging to one file, which will be contiguously allocated before inserting a rotational delay. The default is determined from the maximum transfer rate of the disk. UFS supports up to 1,048,576.

Of all the available mkfs options, the most commonly used are the *-b, -f, -i, -m, -n,* and *-o* options.

Now, to create your file system, use the following command:

```
newfs -v -m 5 /dev/rdsk/c5t0d0s4
```

This command creates the file system using the mkfs defaults, except that you want to set minfree to 5 percent, thereby allowing the users to use up to 95 percent of the file system.

As mentioned, newfs can also be run in dry-run format, allowing you to see how the command will execute before the live run. The following is the output of newfs *-Nv* on one system:

```
# newfs -Nv /dev/rdsk/c5t1d0s4
mkfs -F ufs -o N /dev/rdsk/c5t1d0s4 17678493 133 27 8192 1024 256 1 120 8192 t 0 -1 8 12 8
Warning: 1 sector(s) in last cylinder unallocated
/dev/rdsk/c5t1d0s4:     17678492 sectors in 4923 cylinders of 27 tracks, 133 sectors
        8632.1MB in 308 cyl groups (16 c/g, 28.05MB/g, 3392 i/g)
super-block backups (for fsck -F ufs -o b=#) at:
 32, 57632, 115232, 172832, 230432, 288032, 345632, 403232, 460832, 518432,
 576032, 633632, 691232, 748832, 806432, 864032, 921632, 979232, 1036832
(output cut off here)
```

Mounting File Systems

Once you have created your file system, you need to make it available for use. To do that, use the mount command. To mount a file system, you must first have an empty directory to use as the mount point. Actually, the directory doesn't have to be empty, but once you mount the file system on it, you will not be able to access any files that were in the directory prior to the mount. Once the file system is unmounted, you will be able to access those files again.

There are several options to the mount command, explored here. Many of these options are the same for both the mount and umount commands. Usage is as follows:

```
mount [ -p| -v]
mount [-F FSType] [generic_options] [-o specific_options] [-O] special| mount_point
mount [-F FSType] [generic_options] [-o specific_options] [-O] special mount_point
mount -a [-F FSType] [-V] [current_options] [-o specific_options] [mount_point]
```

The umount command unmounts a currently mounted file system. Syntax for umount is

```
umount [-f] [-V] [-0 specific_options]special|mount_point
umount -a [-f] [-V] [-o specific_options] [mount_point]...
```

The /etc/mnttab file contains information about mounted file systems. Mounting a file system adds an entry to the mount table; umount removes an entry from the table.

Only a superuser can mount or unmount file systems using mount and umount. The mount command can also be used to see which file systems are mounted. Any user can use mount to list mounted file systems.

Options for mount and umount are as follows:

- *-F FSType* This option is used to specify the FileSystemType (FSType) that will have the mount/umount command performed against it. The FSType must either be specified or be able to be determined from /etc/vfstab, /etc/default/fs, or /etc/dfs/fstypes. This option is more commonly used for file systems that might not already have entries in /etc/vfstab, such as a CD-ROM file system. For example, the command

```
mount -F hsfs -o ro /dev/dsk/c6t0d0s0 /cdrom
```

  would allow you to mount a CD-ROM to the mount point /cdrom in read-only mode.

- *-a [mount_points . . .]* This option performs mount or umount operations in parallel, when possible:

  - If mount points are not specified, mount attempts to mount all file systems that have the Mount at Boot field in /etc/vfstab set to *yes*. If you specify the mount point(s), the Mount at Boot field is ignored.

  - In the case of umount, if you specify the mount point(s), umount will unmount only those mount points. If you do not specify a mount point, umount will attempt to unmount *all* file systems in /etc/mnttab, except the system-required file systems (/, /usr, /var, /var/adm, /var/run, /proc, /dev/fd, and /tmp).

- *-f* This option forcibly unmounts a file system. Take care when you use this option because it can cause data loss if a file is open. Without this option, umount will not allow a file system to be unmounted if a file on the file system is busy. Programs that attempt to access files after the file system has been unmounted will get an EIO error message.

- *-p* This option prints the list of mounted file systems in the /etc/vfstab format. For this option to be used, it must be the only option specified.

- *-v* This option prints the list of mounted file systems in verbose format. It must be the only option specified.

■ *-V* This option echoes the complete command line but does not execute the command. The umount command generates a command line using the options and arguments provided by the user and adding to them information derived from /etc/mnttab. This option should be used to verify and validate the command line.

Options that are commonly supported by most FSType-specific command modules are generic_options. The following are available:

■ *-m* This option mounts the file system without making an entry in /etc/mnttab.

■ *-g* Used on clustered systems, this option globally mounts the file system on all nodes of the cluster. On a nonclustered system, this option has no effect.

■ *-o* This option specifies FSType-specific options in a comma-separated (without spaces) list of suboptions and keyword-attribute pairs for interpretation by the FSType-specific module of the command.

■ *-O* This option, the overlay mount, allows the file system to be mounted over an existing mount point, making the underlying file system inaccessible. If this is attempted on a preexisting mount point without setting this flag, the mount will fail, producing the error message "Device busy."

■ *-r* This option mounts the file system as read-only.

Checking File Systems

Once you have created your file systems, you might occasionally need to perform corrective action on them. The fsck command checks and optionally repairs file system inconsistencies. By default, if fsck detects a problem, the user will be prompted as to the disposition of the problem, and fsck waits for a *yes* or *no* response. If the user does not have write permission on the file system being checked, fsck defaults to no action.

Use of fsck is as follows:

```
fsck [-F FSType] [-m] [-V] [special]...
fsck [-F FSType] [ -n| N| y| Y] [-V] [-o FSType-specific-options] [special]...
```

for example,

```
fsck -F ufs -n -V /dev/rdsk/c5t0d0
```

Options to fsck are the following:

- *-F FSType*   This option specifies the file system type on which to operate, such as ufs.

- *-m*   This option checks but does not repair. This option checks that the file system is suitable for mounting and returns the appropriate exit status, for example,

```
# fsck -m /dev/rdsk/c7t5d3s4
vxfs fsck: /dev/rdsk/c7t5d3s4 already mounted
vxfs fsck: sanity check: /dev/rdsk/c7t5d3s4 already mounted
```

- *-n | -N*   This option assumes a *no* response to all questions asked by fsck; it does not open the file system for writing.

- *-V*   This option echoes the expanded command line but does not execute the command. The option might be used to verify and validate the command line, for example,

```
# fsck -V /dev/rdsk/c7t5d3s4
fsck -F vxfs /dev/rdsk/c7t5d3s4
```

This code snippet shows that the actual command that would be run is fsck *-F vxfs* on this device, even though the file system type was not specified. That is because the file system type was derived from the entry in /etc/vfstab for this particular device.

- *-y | -Y*   This option assumes a *yes* response to all questions asked by fsck.

- *-o*   The specific options can be any combination of the following options, comma separated, with no spaces between characters:

  - *b=n*   Use alternate superblock *n* as the superblock for the file system to be checked. Block 32 is always one of the alternate superblocks. You can determine the location of the other superblocks by running newfs with the *-Nv* options. For example, if you run fsck on a file system like the following,

```
# fsck /dev/rdsk/c5t1d0s4
** /dev/rdsk/c5t1d0s4
BAD SUPER BLOCK: MAGIC NUMBER WRONG
USE AN ALTERNATE SUPER-BLOCK TO SUPPLY NEEDED INFORMATION;
eg. fsck [-F ufs] -o b=# [special ...]
where # is the alternate super block. SEE fsck_ufs(1M).
```

you can then run fsck -b=32 /dev/rdsk/c5t1d0s4 in an effort to fix the problem. This is not always successful.

- ■ *f* This option forces checking of the file systems regardless of the state of their superblock clean flag.

- ■ *p* This option checks and fixes ("preens") the file system noninteractively. Exit immediately if there is a problem requiring intervention. This option is required to enable parallel file system checking.

- ■ *w* This option checks only writable file systems.

exam
Watch

You should learn the options available for mount, newfs, and fsck in preparation for the exam. It is common for exam questions to cover options that might not be a command's most common options but that do provide enhanced functionality.

on the
Job

Some corrective actions performed by fsck could result in loss of data. It is advisable to run in interactive mode (not using the -y or -n options) so that you can see which actions will be taken prior to fsck executing the attempt to correct the problem. It is also not recommended to run fsck on a mounted file system; doing so can result in data inconsistency. The operating system buffers file system data. Running fsck on a mounted file system can potentially cause the operating system's buffers to become out of date with respect to the disk. If you cannot unmount the file system to run fsck, you should try to ensure that the system is quiescent and reboot immediately after fsck is run. This might not be sufficient and could cause a system panic if fsck modifies the file system.

Table 20-2 identifies exit codes that will be returned from fsck.

TABLE 20-2	Code	Description
Exit Status Codes Returned from fsck	0	File system OK, does not need checking.
	1	Erroneous parameters were specified for the command.
	3	File system is unmounted and needs checking (fsck -*m* only).
	33	File system is already mounted.
	34	Cannot stat device.
	36	Uncorrectable errors detected; terminate normally.
	37	A signal was caught during processing.
	39	Uncorrectable errors detected; terminate immediately.
	40	For root, same as 0.

EXERCISE 20-1

Creating and Manipulating a File System

In this exercise, you'll do the following:

- Create a file system.
- Make a mount point.
- Mount the file system.
- Unmount the file system.
- Check the file system.

On your system, identify a disk that you can use for this purpose. (Hopefully, you have a test system on which to perform this exercise!) Now run the following commands. On my system, I use disk /dev/dsk/c5t0d0 and slice 0 of that disk. Here are the commands to run:

```
newfs -v -m 5 /dev/rdsk/c5t0d0s0
mkdir /testdir
mount /dev/dsk/c5t0d0s0 /testdir
umount /testdir
fsck /dev/rdsk/c5t0d0s0
```

There, that wasn't difficult, was it? Now let's go on to more fun stuff.

Understanding the Logical Pathname Differences Between Physical Disks and Virtual Disks

To properly manage the disks in your environment, it is important that you understand the difference between the logical pathname to a physical disk and the pathname to a virtual disk. A *virtual disk,* or logical disk, is a disk that could be an accumulation (or concatenation) of several disks and, as such, gives more flexibility in use than physical disks. You are not limited by the size of the physical disk when you use a virtual disk.

Looking at the output from the following df -*k,* you can see that there are both physical and virtual disk–based file systems:

```
# df -k
Filesystem              kbytes     used    avail capacity  Mounted on
/dev/vx/dsk/rootvol      77464    68150     9237      89%  /
/dev/vx/dsk/usr         490097   476992    12615      98%  /usr
/proc                        0        0        0       0%  /proc
fd                           0        0        0       0%  /dev/fd
/dev/vx/dsk/var         963869   614486   347777      64%  /var
/dev/vx/dsk/opt         482824   269359   212983      56%  /opt
swap                   3108216      400  3107816       1%  /tmp
/dev/vx/dsk/rootdg/vol01        17678336 16250388 1410716      93%    /vol01
/dev/vx/dsk/rootdg/vol02        17678336 11487924 6095764      66%    /vol02
/dev/vx/dsk/rootdg/vol03        17678336 16665188  998236      95%    /vol03
/dev/vx/dsk/rootdg/vol04        17678336 16802216  865224      96%    /vol04
/dev/dsk/c4t0d0s0      8880128  8124480   750468      92%   /vol05
```

The file system, /vol01, is a virtual disk–based one, whereas the file system /vol05 is a physical disk–based one.

The pathname /dev/vx/dsk/[*volumegroup*]/[*volumename*] identifies that vol01 is a virtual disk under control of the Sun StorEdge Manager software. If a disk is not under control of volume management software, it has a pathname of /dev/dsk/ *cXtXdXsX*, where *c* = controller, *t* = target, *d* = disk, and *s* = slice.

With some of the more cryptic parts of the operating system, it is very useful to come up with a catchphrase by which to remember important information. A teacher friend came up with the phrase "Catch that darned squid" to remember the cXtXdXsX syntax. This approach to remembering concepts might not be for everyone, but it is a commonly used mnemonic device. Find one that works for you; it will help you remember not only this syntax, but many more details in your personal and professional life.

EXERCISE 20-2

Fun with Virtual Disk Management Software

On one of your Solaris systems that has a virtual disk management application installed, do the following:

1. Execute the df *-k* command:

```
# df -k
Filesystem               kbytes     used    avail capacity  Mounted on
/dev/vx/dsk/rootvol       77464    68372     9015     89%    /
/dev/vx/dsk/usr          490097   476992    12615     98%    /usr
/proc                         0        0        0      0%    /proc
fd                            0        0        0      0%    /dev/fd
/dev/vx/dsk/var          963869   614491   347772     64%    /var
/dev/vx/dsk/opt          482824   269359   212983     56%    /opt
swap                    3108720      400  3108320      1%    /tmp
/dev/vx/dsk/rootdg/vol01 17678336 16250392 1410712    93%    /vol01
/dev/vx/dsk/rootdg/vol02 17678336 11487924 6095764    66%    /vol02
/dev/vx/dsk/rootdg/vol03 17678336 16665188  998236    95%    /vol03
/dev/vx/dsk/rootdg/vol04 17678336 16802216  865224    96%    /vol04
```

2. Execute view /etc/vfstab:

```
device            device           mount      FS     fsck    mount     mount
#to mount         to fsck          point      type   pass    at boot options
#
#/dev/dsk/c1d0s2 /dev/rdsk/c1d0s2 /usr         ufs    1       yes       -
fd          -         /dev/fd fd      -     no      -
/proc       -         /proc   proc    -     no      -
/dev/vx/dsk/swapvol    -         -         swap   -     no      -
/dev/vx/dsk/rootvol     /dev/vx/rdsk/rootvol  /      ufs    1       no        -
/dev/vx/dsk/usr /dev/vx/rdsk/usr        /usr   ufs    1       no        -
/dev/vx/dsk/var /dev/vx/rdsk/var        /var   ufs    1       no        -
/dev/vx/dsk/opt /dev/vx/rdsk/opt        /opt   ufs    2       yes       -
swap        -         /tmp    tmpfs   -     yes    nosuid
#NOTE: volume rootvol (/) encapsulated partition c0t0d0s0
#NOTE: volume usr (/usr) encapsulated partition c0t0d0s1
```

TABLE 20-3	Virtual	Physical
Virtual to Physical Disk Translation	/dev/vx/dsk/rootvol	/dev/dsk/c0t0d0s0
	/dev/vx/dsk/usr	/dev/dsk/c0t0d0s1
	/dev/vx/dsk/var	/dev/dsk/c0t0d0s3
	/dev/vx/dsk/opt	/dev/dsk/c0t0d0s4

```
#NOTE: volume var (/var) encapsulated partition c0t0d0s3
#NOTE: volume opt (/opt) encapsulated partition c0t0d0s4
#NOTE: volume swapvol (swap) encapsulated partition c0t0d0s5
/dev/vx/dsk/rootdg/vol01        /dev/vx/rdsk/rootdg/vol01        /vol01   vxfs   3      yes      -
/dev/vx/dsk/rootdg/vol02        /dev/vx/rdsk/rootdg/vol02        /vol02   vxfs   3      yes      -
/dev/vx/dsk/rootdg/vol03        /dev/vx/rdsk/rootdg/vol03        /vol03   vxfs   3      yes      -
/dev/vx/dsk/rootdg/vol04        /dev/vx/rdsk/rootdg/vol04        /vol04   vxfs   3      yes      -
```

3. Correlate the virtual disk name to the physical disk name. In this case, the volumes match up, as shown in Table 20-3.

This exercise should give you an idea of how to determine the virtual to physical mapping.

CERTIFICATION OBJECTIVE 20.03

Knowing the Advantages of a Virtual Disk Management Application

In most storage environments, it is common to need such capabilities as disk mirroring, disk striping, and disk concatenation. Most UNIX environments either have or make available a *virtual disk management package* (which we'll abbreviate as *VDM* for simplicity's sake). Such a package is also commonly called *logical volume management software.* These packages make possible the previously mentioned capabilities.

With a VDM, a system administrator can define the disks to be controlled and the way they are to be used. The primary advantages of VDM applications are ease of administration, abilities such as mirroring of volumes, concatenation and striping of disks, and greater data availability. Here's what those terms mean:

- **Concatenation**   Allows you to create a larger file system than could be created on one single disk by combining multiple physical disks into one logical/virtual volume.

- **Striping**   Allows you to stripe a file system across multiple physical disks. This method is traditionally used to enhance performance. (The more spindles that are running, the faster are throughput and access to data.)

- **Mirroring**   Allows you to protect data by having two or more copies of the data, usually on separate disks.

- **RAID configurations**   Allows you to create a software-based redundant array of independent disks (RAID) solution using a VDM application.

As a refresher on RAID, the most commonly used RAID levels are the following:

- **RAID 0**   Striping, or concatenation, of disks. This option provides the lowest amount of data integrity because there is no redundancy.

- **RAID 1: mirroring**   Provides probably the greatest level of data integrity but at greater expense because double the number of disks are required.

- **RAID 0+1**   Striping plus mirroring.

- **RAID 5**   A series of disks built in to an array, whereby data is written to portions of the array, and parity information is written to other portions of the array. In the event of disk failure, the data can be rebuilt using the remaining data and parity information.

Additionally, there are RAID levels 2, 3, and 4, which are not commonly used. Drawbacks to RAID 3 and RAID 4 are their use of a single parity disk, whereas RAID 2 provides error detection but not error correction.

exam
ⓦatch

Concepts such as the meanings and characteristics of the various RAID levels are commonly covered on exams. To do well on the exam and also as a means of professional growth, read up on the RAID levels and which levels are supported in both Solaris Volume Manager and Sun StorEdge Volume Manager.

CERTIFICATION OBJECTIVE 20.04

Understanding the Characteristics and Functions of DiskSuite and Sun StorEdge VM

As mentioned in the previous section, two of the more commonly used VDM applications in Solaris are Solaris Volume Manager (formerly Solstice DiskSuite) and Sun StorEdge Manager. Each has its own merits, as explored in this section. Solaris Volume Manager has been enhanced with the following options:

- **Soft partitions** Allows numerous partitions on a single drive, thus breaking the eight-slice barrier.

- **Device ID support** Preserves Solaris Volume Manager configuration even if disks are moved or rearranged.

- **Active monitoring of disks** Detects silent failures.

- **Solaris Management Console–based interface** Enables you to manage the enhanced storage devices through the same management interface that is used for other Solaris management tasks.

- **Solaris Volume Manager WBEM application programming interface (API)** Enables standards-based management of Solaris Volume Manager from any compliant tool.

- **Solaris 9** Seamlessly supports upgrading existing systems that run Solaris DiskSuite (SDS) to the Solaris Volume Manager without disturbing or changing the configuration. Upgrades of mirrored root file systems are fully and automatically supported.

Appendix A provides more details about Solaris Volume Manager.

Solstice DiskSuite

SDS, as is true of most VDM applications, uses virtual disks to manage physical disks. In SDS, these devices are known as *metadevices*.

The applications on the system use the metadevice, just as they would a physical device. All I/O requests are sent through the metadevice to the underlying physical device.

SDS has the capability of concatenating disks into a larger metadevice, mirroring metadevices, and creating a RAID 5 configuration. Hot-spare capabilities are also included in SDS.

Solaris Volume Manager Objects

SDS contains three basic objects:

- **Metadevices**   These can be simple, mirrored, RAID 5, or trans. Metadevices are basically a collection of disk slices, or disks, that SDS combines and that appear to the system as a single device.

- **Metadevices state database (and state database replicas)**   The metadevices state database contains information on disk about the state of your DiskSuite configuration. Without this database, DiskSuite cannot operate.

- **Hot-spare pool**   As the name indicates, this is a pool (collection) of slices reserved for use in the event of a slice failure on a submirror or RAID 5 metadevice. The hot-spare pool is automatically used in the event of a failure.

Solaris Volume Manager Configuration Files

Device files created by Solaris Volume Manager are of the format /dev/md/dsk/dnn or /dev/md/dsk/d1. Two files contain information critical to the operation of SDS:

- **/etc/lvm/mddb.cf**   This file records the locations of state database replicas. When state database replica locations change, an entry will be made by SDS in this file. Similar information is entered into the /etc/system file.

- **/etc/lvm/md.tab**   This file can be used as input to the command-line utilities metainit, metadb, and metahs to create metadevices, state database replicas, or hot spares. A metadevice, a group of state database replicas, or a hot spare may have an entry in this file.

The following is a sample md.tab file, complete with some example configuration data and a brief description of each example:

```
#1 - (state database and replicas)
mddb01 -c 3 c0t1d0s0 c0t2d0s0 c0t3d0s0
#
# 2 - (stripe consisting of two disks)
d15 1 2 c0t1d0s2 c0t2d0s2 -i 32k

# 3 - (concatenation of four disks)
d7 4 1 c0t1d0s0 1 c0t2d0s0 1 c0t3d0s0 1 c0t4d0s0
# 4 - (mirror)
d50 -m d51
d51 1 1 c0t1d0s2
```

Let's look at this material in more detail:

- This entry creates three state database replicas on each of the three slices indicated. The metadevice state database is named mddb01. The *-c 3* option specifies that three state database replicas be placed on each slice. You activate this entry using the metadb command.

- The number 1 specifies to create a metadevice consisting of one stripe. The number 2 specifies how many slices will be used to create the stripe and which devices they are on (c0t1d0s2 and c0t2d0s2). The *-i 32k* option indicates that a 32KB interlace value will be used. (The default is 16KB.)

- The number 4 specifies to create a metadevice of four stripe slices in the concatenated metadevice. Each stripe is made of one slice; therefore, you specify the number 1 for each slice.

- This example shows a one-way mirror, /dev/md/dsk/d50. The *-m* creates a one-way mirror consisting of submirror d51.

Generally, you do not have to maintain mddb.cf, because SDS updates it automatically. The configuration information in md.tab might be different from the current metadevices, hot spares, and state database replicas. It is used only at creation of the metadevices, not to recapture the configuration at boot time.

Additional files used by SDS are these:

- **/etc/lvm/md.cf** This is a backup copy of a local disk set's configuration. SDS provides this file for recovery purposes. If (maybe *when* is more appropriate) you change the SDS configuration, SDS automatically provides this backup copy, with the exception of hot sparing.

on the job

You should never directly edit either the mddb.cf file or the md.cf file. SDS writes to these files automatically, and editing them could potentially render them unusable. At a minimum, when SDS does its automatic write, your modifications to the file could be overwritten. This same philosophy holds true for many dynamic configuration files, including /etc/mnttab. In prior releases of Solaris, /etc/mnttab was a text file. In Solaris 8, it is a file system of the type MNTFS and is mounted as read-only. No administration is needed, nor should any be done, on this file.

- ■ **/kernel/drv/md.conf**   SDS reads this configuration file at startup. The file contains two editable fields: nmd, which defines how many metadevices the configuration can support, and md_nsets, which is the number of disk sets. The default value for nmd is 128, which can be increased to a maximum of 1024. The default value for md_nsets is 4, which can be increased to a maximum of 32.

- ■ **/etc/lvm/mdlodg.cf**   This file controls the behavior of DiskSuite's mdlogd SNMP trap-generating daemon. This file is a text file and can be edited to specify where the SNMP trap data should be sent when the SDS driver detects a specified condition.

- ■ **/etc/rcS.d/S35lvm.init**   This is the SDS startup file for reloading metadevice configuration information at system boot time.

- ■ **/etc/rc2.d/S95lvm.sync**   This is the SDS startup file for resyncing metadevices at system boot time.

The DiskSuite Tool

Once you have configured your system to use SDS, you can use the DiskSuite tool to get information. The very useful DiskSuite tool is a GUI to SDS, but it is limited in its capabilities. Some commands still must be performed from the command line. Table 20-4 compares the DiskSuite tool with the command line.

SNMP Capabilities

Additional SNMP capabilities are built into SDS, so you can send error messages to a central console or to a log file. As mentioned previously, the file /etc/opt/SUNWmd/ mdlodg.cf controls how SNMP traps are sent.

TABLE 20-4	Function	Command-Line Utility	DiskSuite Tool GUI
The DiskSuite Tool and the Command-Line Utility	Addition of/removal of disks in disk set	Yes	No
	Addition of/removal of hosts in disk set	Yes	No
	Creation of/removal of disk sets	Yes	No
	Switching metadevice names	Yes	No
	Renaming metadevices	Yes	Yes
	Monitoring metadevice performance	No; iostat could be used to monitor the metadevices	Yes
	Maintenance of SparcStorage Arrays	No; you would need to use ssaadm instead	Yes

Sun StorEdge Volume Manager

Sun StorEdge Volume Manager (SEVM) is, in my experience, the more commonly used virtual disk management application.

SEVM uses virtual disk devices, called *volumes,* which consist of physical disks that have been placed under SEVM control. Applications access these volumes in the same manner as they would access a physical disk. These volumes and their components are called *volume manager objects*. As in SDS, SEVM allows for concatenation of disks, mirroring, RAID configurations, and striped configurations.

Unlike SDS, the commands are less cryptic and the GUI is much more powerful. Almost all SEVM commands can be executed from the GUI; the exception is when the product is first installed. At that time, the initial configuration must be handled from the command line by running vxinstall to create the rootdg disk group and initialize at least one disk. Once this task is accomplished, you can use the GUI for all other functions.

SEVM Objects

You must become familiar with several objects in SEVM to fully understand the functionality of the product:

- **VM disks**   The virtual representation of a physical disk or, at minimum, a disk partition. VM disks consist of a public region, to which data can be written, and a private region, where configuration data is kept.

- **Disk groups**   A logical grouping of one to many disks sharing a common set of characteristics. Generally, it's a good idea to create a datadg in which to store user data and a dbvg to store database applications. rootdg is created by default when vxinstall is run and is required for SEVM to function.

- **Volumes**   What the applications, database, and file systems "see"; they appear as a physical disk partition but have far greater flexibility than a disk partition, because they are not limited to a single disk.

- **Subdisks**   Subsets of a VM disk and the base units via which SEVM allocates space. Whenever you create a volume on a VM disk, a subdisk is also created.

- **Plexes**   Also referred to as *mirrors,* the containers that hold subdisks in the SEVM configuration.

StorEdge Volume Manager Files

Device files created by SEVM are of the format

```
/dev/vx/dsk/[volume group]/[volume name]
```

or, for example,

```
/dev/vx/dsk/rootdg/usr
```

The main files that contain configuration information for SEVM are the following:

- **volboot**   The volboot file is the bootstrap file for the root disk group and defines a system's host ID. This file is usually located in /etc/vx/volboot. This file also contains disk access records and is scanned on system startup to find a disk belonging to the rootdg disk group and containing this system's host ID. When a suitable disk is located, its configuration is read to obtain a more complete list of disk access records that are used as the second-stage bootstrap of rootdg and to locate all other disk groups.

■ **/etc/rcS.d/S25vmvx-sysboot**   This is the first startup script for SEVM and sets up the root (/) and /usr volumes as needed.

■ **/etc/rcS.d/S35vxvm-startup1**   This script runs after S25vxvm-sysboot and requires the root (/) and /usr to be available. The script configures other volumes needed early in the Solaris boot sequence.

■ **/etc/rcS.d/S85vxvm-startup2**   This startup script must be run *after* the root (/), /usr, and /var are mounted. This script starts some I/O daemons, rebuilds the /dev/vx/dsk and /dev/vx/rdsk directories, imports all disk groups, and starts all volumes that were not started earlier in the boot sequence.

Notification of Events with SEVM

Unlike SDS, SEVM does not have built-in SNMP trap capabilities. However, with a little scripting knowledge and use of the logger function of syslog (as shown in

SCENARIO & SOLUTION

Given the pathname /dev/md/dsk/d51, which virtual disk management application would you expect is in use?	Solstice DiskSuite.

If you ran fsck on a file system and got a message like this,
`# fsck /dev/rdsk/c5t1d0s4`
`** /dev/rdsk/c5t1d0s4`
`BAD SUPER BLOCK: MAGIC NUMBER WRONG`
`USE AN ALTERNATE SUPER-BLOCK TO`
`SUPPLY NEEDED INFORMATION;`
what could you do to try to recover from this error?
	If you actually got this error, fsck would tell you what to do in the last part of the message, which was cut from the scenario
	`eg. fsck [-F ufs] -o b=# [special ...]`
	where the pound sign (#) is the alternate superblock. So you could start by running this:
	`fsck -b=32 /dev/rdsk/c5t1d0s4`

How could you determine where alternate superblocks are on the file system?	Execute this command: `newfs -Nv /dev/rdsk/c5t1d0s4` (Don't forget the *-N* or you'll need more than an alternate superblock to fix this problem!)

Chapter 19), you can use the vxprint utility of SEVM to generate syslog messages or you can use vxprint to generate an e-mail to notify the administrator of such events.

CERTIFICATION SUMMARY

In this chapter, you learned how to create file systems, check them, and mount and unmount them. Now you should also be able to determine whether a disk is a virtual disk or a physical disk. You have also been briefly introduced to virtual disk management applications such as Solaris Volume Manager and Sun StorEdge Volume Manager. It behooves you to become very familiar with all the concepts contained in this chapter, because disk management is a very critical function in a system administrator's job and is no doubt likely to figure heavily in the exam.

TWO-MINUTE DRILL

Using Utilities to Create, Check, and Mount File Systems

❏ The newfs command is used to create new file systems.

❏ The mount command is used to allow access to file systems.

❏ The umount command is used to take a file system offline.

❏ The fsck command is used to check and repair file systems.

Understanding the Logical Pathname Differences Between Physical Disks and Virtual Disks

❏ Physical disk pathnames are generally of the form /dev/dsk/*cXtXdX* or /dev/rdsk/*cXtXdX*.

❏ Virtual disk pathnames are generally of the form /dev/*[VDM]*/dsk.

Knowing the Advantages of a Virtual Disk Management Application

❏ Virtual disk applications offer the following advantages over physical disks:

❏ Concatenation of disks into one volume or metadisk

❏ Striping of file systems over multiple volumes

❏ Mirroring of volumes for higher data availability

❏ Software-based RAID configurations

Understanding the Characteristics and Functions of DiskSuite and Sun StorEdge VM

❏ Solaris Volume Manager uses metadevices for virtual disk management.

❏ Sun StorEdge Manager uses volumes for virtual disk management.

❏ Both Solaris Volume Manager and Sun StorEdge Volume Manager allow for all the advantages of a virtual disk management application.

SELF TEST

The following questions will help you measure your understanding of the material presented in this chapter. Read all the choices carefully because there might be more than one correct answer. Choose all correct answers for each question.

Using Utilities to Create, Check, and Mount File Systems

1. You've been asked to create a 2GB file system on disk /dev/dsk/c2t0d0s0. Which of the following commands would be the most appropriate to use?

   A. newfs -*Nv* /dev/dsk/c2t0d0s0

   B. newfs -*v* /dev/dsk/c2t0d0s0

   C. newfs -*v* /dev/rdsk/c2t0d0s0

   D. newfs -*Rv* /dev/rdsk/c2t0d0s0

2. Which of the following commands would mount a vxfs file system?

   A. mount -*type* vxfs /dev/vx/dsk/vol01 /vol01

   B. mount -*F* vxfs /dev/vx/dsk/vol01 /vol01

   C. mount -*a* vxfs /dev/vx/dsk/vol01 /vol01

   D. mount -*fstype* vxfs /dev/vx/dsk/vol01 /vol01

Understanding the Logical Pathname Differences Between Physical Disks and Virtual Disks

3. Which of the following pathnames points to a physical disk?

   A. /dev/vx/dsk/rootdg/usr

   B. /dev/dsk/c0t0d0s0

   C. /dev/rdsk/c0d0s0

   D. /dev/md/dsk/d0

4. Which is one of the advantages of a virtual (logical) disk over a physical disk?

    A. You don't have to be concerned with the /dev/*xxx*/*xxx* syntax of the disk path.

    B. You can write Windows-based files to a virtual disk.

    C. Logical disks are generally more flexible to use than physical disks.

    D. Logical disks come with a free pass to Mr. Spock's speech at the Star Trek convention.

Knowing the Advantages of a Virtual Disk Management Application

5. Given the following output of df -*k*, what assumption can you make about these file systems?

```
/dev/vx/dsk/rootdg/vol01    17678336 16250391 1410712    93%    /vol01
/dev/dsk/c5t2d0s4           17678336 11487924 6095764    66%    /vol02
```

    A. All file systems are under the control of Sun StorEdge Volume Manager.

    B. All file systems have been created using a volume management application.

    C. /vol02 is not under the control of Sun StorEdge Volume Manager.

    D. None of the above.

6. Given the context of this chapter, to what does the term *striping* refer?

    A. The markings on a Bengal tiger

    B. The lines on a highway

    C. The ability to lay out your data across multiple devices

    D. The new markings for Sun's latest line of servers

Understanding the Characteristics and Functions of DiskSuite and Sun StorEdge VM

7. In Solstice DiskSuite, which of these files contains backup copies of configuration information?

    A. /etc/lvm/md.conf.bak

    B. /etc/lvm/md.cf

    C. /etc/lvm/mddb.cf

    D. /etc/lvm/md/md.cf

8. Sun StorEdge Volume Manager refers to the logical devices as what?

A. ldisks

B. pdisks

C. volumes

D. metadevices

LAB QUESTION

Match the following numbered RAID levels with the appropriate items in the list that follows. (There will be one unused item.)

1. Provides error detection but not error correction

2. Writes parity information across all disks in the array

3. Handles stripes and mirrors

4. Handles only mirrors

Matching list:

A. RAID 0

B. RAID 0+1

C. RAID 2

D. RAID 5

E. RAID 1

SELF TEST ANSWERS

Using Utilities to Create, Check, and Mount File Systems

1. ☑ **C.** When creating a file system using newfs, you must supply the raw device name.
 ☒ **A, B,** and **D** are all incorrect because none of them uses the raw device name. Additionally, **D** is incorrect because there is no *R* option to newfs, and **A** is incorrect because the *-N* option tells newfs to not do the action but to echo the commands and output that would be generated.

2. ☑ **B.** The correct option to mount to specify a file system type is *-F [fstype]*.
 ☒ **A** is incorrect because *-fstype* is not a valid option for mount. **C** is incorrect because *-a* would try to mount all file system types, and vxfs is not a parameter to that option. **D** is incorrect because *-fstype* is not a valid option for mount.

Understanding the Logical Pathname Differences Between Physical Disks and Virtual Disks

3. ☑ **B** and **C.** These pathnames represent a physical disk in Solaris. Even though the pathname starts out as a proper physical disk path, the last part (c0d0s0) does not include the controller information. If it were c0t0d0s0, it would also be correct.
 ☒ **A** is incorrect because this pathname would be representative of a disk under control of Sun StorEdge Volume Manager. **D** is incorrect because this pathname is representative of a disk under the control of Solstice DiskSuite.

4. ☑ **C.** Logical disks give more flexibility because you are not limited to the physical size and characteristics of the physical disk.
 ☒ **A** is incorrect because, even with a logical disk, you still have the standard naming conventions of /dev/*something*/*something* and even another /*something*. **B** is incorrect because, even though it's not a common practice, you can save Windows-based files on either a virtual or a physical disk. **D** is incorrect because, even though maybe it's a nice idea, no free Star Trek convention passes are given with a virtual disk.

Knowing the Advantages of a Virtual Disk Management Application

5. ☑ **C.** If /vol02 were under the control of Sun StorEdge Volume Manager, its pathname should be /dev/vx/dsk/ *[volumegroup]* /vol02.
   ☒ **A** is incorrect because /vol02 has a physical disk pathname. **B** is incorrect because, if /vol02 were created using a volume management application, its pathname would not be /dev/dsk/ *[diskname]*, it would show a volume or metadevice pathname. **D** is incorrect because there is a correct answer.

6. ☑ **C.** Striping is used to lay out data across multiple devices, usually for performance reasons.
   ☒ **A** and **B** are incorrect because, although those are fun definitions, they have nothing to do with the contents of this chapter. **D** is incorrect, although if it helps Sun more effectively market their servers, it might be worth a try.

Understanding the Characteristics and Functions of DiskSuite and Sun StorEdge VM

7. ☑ **B.** A backup copy of the local disk set configuration is automatically created in /etc/opt/ SUNWmd/md.cf whenever a change is made to the configuration.
   ☒ **A** is incorrect because it is a made-up name. **C** is incorrect because the mddb.cf file contains state database replica information. **D** is incorrect because the pathname should be /etc/opt/ SUNWmd/md.cf.

8. ☑ **C.** SEVM calls the logical devices volumes.
   ☒ **A** and **B** are incorrect because neither SEVM nor SDS refers to the devices as ldisks or pdisks. **D** is incorrect because SDS calls the devices metadevices.

LAB ANSWER

The answers are 1-C, 2-D, 3-B, and 4-E.

21

Solaris Pseudo File Systems and Swap Space

In the mid 1980s, along with the introduction of the Network File System (NFS) in SunOS 2.0, Sun introduced a new framework called the *Virtual File System* (VFS) to support kernel file systems. VFS changed the way the SunOS kernel handled file systems. Instead of building support for a single class of physical storage into the kernel, as was done previously, VFS allowed the kernel to modularly support different file system types. This capability broadened the definition of what constitutes a file and made possible advanced file systems like NFS, in which the file might not be in physical storage attached to the local machine. The VFS framework added a great deal of flexibility to SunOS 2.0. This flexibility was also later incorporated by AT&T into its UNIX System V release 4 (SVR4) and by Sun into all later versions of the SunOS operating system.

Solaris pseudo file systems are built on top of the functionality provided by the VFS and present nonregular file objects as files. Solaris pseudo file systems include autofs, cachefs, fdfs, fifofs, nfs, procfs, sockfs, and tmpfs. This chapter illustrates how to understand Solaris pseudo file systems and focuses on using commands to manipulate procfs, the process file system.

Loosely related to the idea of pseudo file systems is the Solaris Virtual Memory System. Virtual memory allows the operating system to make more memory available to a process than is really on the system. Solaris accomplishes this goal by using a special file called a *swap file* as though it were memory. The concepts behind the swap file and the related tmpfs file system are connected to pseudo file systems. This chapter covers specifics on Solaris swap implementation and how to add swap space.

CERTIFICATION OBJECTIVE 21.01

Understanding the Characteristics of Solaris Pseudo File System Types

In Solaris, under the VFS, all file system functionality is provided by *kernel modules*. File system kernel modules are loaded when the system boots and must be in place before the kernel can mount each file system. Kernel modules enable the kernel to independently and dynamically load the functions that it needs to implement each file system at run time. Developers no longer need to compile a new version of the kernel for each system on which multiple file systems must be supported. When the kernel calls a file system function, the module for that file system answers the call, executes the function, and returns control to the kernel.

Pseudo file systems are simply file systems that represent objects instead of regular files. Pseudo file system functionality is also implemented by kernel modules, and function requests are translated by the module into operations that make sense for the objects managed. Output from the modinfo command shows which file system modules are loaded by your kernel and which file systems your system currently supports, as shown here:

```
# modinfo|grep fs
  6 10138000    431b    1    1  specfs (filesystem for specfs)
 10 10140858   27453    2    1  ufs (filesystem for ufs)
 25 101eafee    1b0f2    5    1  procfs (filesystem for proc)
 29 102153d7    dfc0    8    1  sockfs (filesystem for sockfs)
 53 102645e9    3420    3    1  fifofs (filesystem for fifo)
 73 102bc172    709f    -    1  ufs_log (Logging UFS Module)
 74 102c2f91     fd0   12    1  fdfs (filesystem for fd)
 75 102c3af9    42d9  201    1  doorfs (doors)
 75 102c3af9    42d9  201    1  doorfs (32-bit door syscalls)
 76 102c7acd    1538    4    1  namefs (filesystem for namefs)
 77 102c8d77    1594   15    1  mntfs (mount information file system)
 78 102ca097    1592a   11    1  tmpfs (filesystem for tmpfs)
 81 102d073a   29b54  106    1  nfs (NFS syscall, client, and common)
 81 102d073a   29b54  106    1  nfs (NFS syscall, client, and common)
 81 102d073a   29b54   16    1  nfs (network filesystem)
 81 102d073a   29b54    7    1  nfs (network filesystem version 2)
 81 102d073a   29b54   17    1  nfs (network filesystem version 3)
 85 10305a57    65b3   18    1  autofs (filesystem for autofs)
102 1027fb36    7247    9    1  hsfs (filesystem for HSFS)
```

Kernel modules must be loaded before a mount command is issued to attempt to mount a pseudo file system, or the mount command will simply fail.

Characteristics of procfs

The process file system, procfs, is a pseudo file system that presents the kernel process tree as a directory structure located under /proc. Each running process is displayed as a directory named the same as its process identifier (PID) number. Each of these process directories contains a set of files that are mapped to the kernel data and control structures for the corresponding process. Modifying these control files modifies the running process.

procfs is implemented by the module /kernel/fs/procfs and is loaded automatically by the kernel during the system boot. The procfs file system is mounted by the standardmounts script, using its entry in /etc/vfstab. It is very important that the /proc entry in vfstab not be removed for any reason because other system functions rely on /proc being mounted. Removing /proc from vfstab can result in a broken Solaris installation.

Once mounted, process files are presented dynamically by the procfs module. These files are created by the procfs module as the /proc is accessed. These files always represent the exact state of the corresponding process at that time.

The /proc Directory Tree

Files in the /proc directory are either read-only files that provide access to process memory and data or write-only files that can control process behavior. The most important areas of the /proc directory structure are the following:

- **/proc** This is the root of the process directory tree and the mount point.
- **/proc/***pid* Each process running on the system has a subdirectory under /proc that is named the same as the PID. This is the top-level directory for that process.
- **/proc/***pid***/ctl** This is a write-only file that programmers can use to control the behavior of the process. Signal data written to this file is sent to the process.
- **/proc/***pid***/status** Programmers can use this file to determine the general state and status of a process, whether it is stopped or started.
- **/proc/***pid***/map** This file presents information on the process address space map.
- **/proc/***pid/psinfo* This file contains the same information on the process displayed by the /usr/bin/ps command.
- **/proc/***pid/cred* This file returns the system credentials being used by the process.

Each file and directory under /proc/pid is owned by the owner of the process. Not all file operations are valid on these files. You cannot change the owner of a process file, delete it, or change its permissions. You can only read and write them.

It is important to note that the files contained in /proc are all binary files, and their contents cannot be directly viewed. However, Solaris provides several tools to read and display the information that these files contain. The next section looks at these tools in detail.

Characteristics of the Virtual Memory System

The Solaris virtual memory system is a core part of the Solaris operating environment. Virtual memory allows running processes to use more memory than is physically available on the system. Solaris accomplishes this goal by periodically moving sections of memory that haven't been accessed recently off to disk storage.

Solaris memory is divided into sections called *pages*. On UltraSPARC architectures, each page of memory is 8KB and represents the minimum amount of memory that a process can allocate for its use. Each page of memory has a corresponding 8KB section in a special file called a *swap file*. Solaris uses the swap file to store memory pages that haven't been accessed in a long time.

Solaris uses a special process called the *page scanner* that constantly checks the last access time for each page of memory and moves old pages out of physical RAM and into the swap file. This process is called *paging* or *swapping out memory*. When a process attempts to access a page of its memory that has been paged to the swap file, the system generates a special error called a *page fault* and moves that page back into memory so that the process can access it. The effect of this design is that heavily accessed pages are kept in memory, where they can be read quickly, and rarely accessed pages are moved to disk.

Not all pages of memory can be paged by the page scanner. Some areas of memory, such as those used by the kernel, are off limits and are referred to as *nonpagable* or *locked* areas of memory. Every page of memory, except for the nonpagable areas, is backed by a swap location in swapfs.

How Solaris Allocates Virtual Memory

Each Solaris process has the ability to allocate pages of additional memory for its use. When a process requests additional memory, pages of memory are assigned from available physical RAM. Because each page of memory must also be backed by disk storage, a corresponding amount of space is also reserved in the swap file. This space is only reserved and is not really used unless the page scanner needs to swap the page to disk.

Swap space allocation goes through three stages. When a process first requests additional memory, an equal amount of swap space is *reserved* to back the file. When swap space is reserved, the system doesn't actually do anything except keep track of how much swap space has been spoken for. The page of memory has not yet been assigned a location in the swap file. This isn't a problem because nothing has been written to the page of memory yet. There is nothing there for the page scanner to swap to disk.

When the amount of reserved space is greater than the virtual swap space, the system decides that it is out of memory and throws an out-of-swap-space error if processes try to reserve additional memory. With swapfs, the amount of virtual swap space available is equal to the amount of pagable physical memory plus the amount of available physical space in the swap file.

When a process actually begins writing data to a reserved page of memory, the system assigns the page to a physical location in the swap file. This is now referred to as *allocated* swap space. If the page scanner needs to swap out the page to disk, it writes it to the assigned location in the swap file. With this method, only pages of memory that actually contain data allocate space in the swap file. This system enables Solaris to very efficiently manage its swap file usage. Even if a process reserves a large amount of memory, Solaris is intelligent enough to allocate only the minimum amount of physical swap space needed to back it.

You use the swap command to manage the physical swap space on a Solaris system. In the section "Creating and Adding a Swap File to the System Swap Space," later in this chapter, you will use the swap command to add swap devices. You can use the swap command to view a summary of your current swap allocation, as shown here:

```
# swap -s
total: 29976k bytes allocated + 5712k reserved = 35688k used,
207536k available
```

Reading the output of the swap -s command is often confusing because the command mixes up the terms *reserved* and *allocated*. On the system just shown, 29,976KB of memory have been reserved for processes and have not yet been touched; 5712KB are allocated and contain actual data. These allocated pages have been assigned a physical location in the swap file. These figures add up to 35,688KB of swap space that has been used, with 207,536KB still available in the physical swap file.

Because Solaris makes very efficient use of swap space, normal Solaris systems can run with smaller swap files. Typically, swap file size should be 0.5 to 1.5 times physical memory. On most other UNIX-based systems, swap file size must be a minimum of

2 times physical memory; and on Windows NT, it can be up to 3 times physical memory. Swap requirements can vary, however, even on Solaris. You should always contact the vendor of any application that will run on your system to find out the recommended amount of swap space for that application.

EXERCISE 21-1

Determining Available Swap Space

This exercise demonstrates how to determine the size of available swap space on your system.

1. Log in to the system as any user.

2. Type **swap -s** at the command prompt.

3. Add together the used and available numbers to determine the total amount of swap space.

CERTIFICATION OBJECTIVE 21.02

Using Commands to Extract Information from Entries in the /proc Directory

Solaris provides several useful commands for extracting information from the /proc directory. These utilities read from the /proc files and display process statistics in a friendly format. Most of them take a list of PID numbers as input and also accept /proc/*pid* or the shell expansion /proc/*. In the case of /proc/*, they return information for all running processes on the system.

Each of the process information commands can also be used to analyze a core file instead of a running process. The kernel creates a core file for a process right before it kills it with a signal. These core files are usually named *core* and contain a snapshot of the process state just before it is terminated. To analyze a core file, substitute the path to the filename for the PID number. Core files can also be created by the gcore command.

You should be aware that each of these commands actually stops its target process to gather information. Running these commands on processes such as an X-server can cause the screen to freeze while the process is stopped.

All these utilities are located in /usr/bin, so you might need to add /usr/bin to your path if it's not already there. Table 21-1 provides a quick reference to the commands and describes their purposes.

You should work with each of the process information commands listed in Table 21-1 before taking the exam. Pay careful attention to the options supported by each command listed in Table 21-2.

Table 21-2 describes the options that each process information command supports. One option (-F) is common to all the commands. Other options are command specific.

TABLE 21-1	Process Information Command	Description
Quick Reference to the Process Information Commands	pflags	Prints the /proc tracing flags
	pcred	Reads the /proc/pid/cred file and displays the process credentials
	pmap	Reads the /proc/pid/map file and prints the address space map
	pldd	Prints the dynamic libraries to which the process is currently linked
	psig	Prints the signal actions of each process
	pstack	Prints a stack trace for each lwp in the process
	pfiles	Reports fstat and fcntl information for files that the process currently has open
	pwdx	Reports the process' current working directory
	pstop	Writes to /proc/pid/cntl and stops the process
	prun	Reverse of pstop; writes to /proc/pid/cntl and sets the process running
	pwait	Returns when the specified process has terminated
	ptree	Prints the process tree, indenting each child process below its parent
	ptime	Uses microstate accounting to time the command with increased precision

TABLE 21-2	Option	Description
Process Information Command Options (from the Man Page)	-r	If the process is stopped, displays its machine registers (pflags only)
	-r	Prints the process' reserved addresses (pmap only)
	-x	Prints resident/shared/private mapping details (pmap only)
	-l	Prints unresolved dynamic linker map names (pmap only)
	-a	All; includes children of process 0 (ptree only)
	-v	Verbose; reports terminations to standard output (pwait only)
	-F	Force; grabs the target process even if another process has control

Use the -F option with caution. If there is already a process trying to control the process you are examining, using -F to forcibly take control away is asking for trouble.

Process Information Command Examples

The process information commands can be extremely helpful for system administration. Each command gives you an "under the hood" view of what a specific process is doing. The output from three of the most commonly used commands in this section is examined next.

The ptree Command: Displaying Parent and Child Process Relationships

Understanding output of the ptree command can make system administration easier. The ptree command shows a visual representation of the relationship between parent and child processes. If you run ptree with the PID of the Korn shell process (ksh) from a graphical desktop, you will get output similar to that shown next, which shows that ksh (430 -ksh) is a child process of the graphical terminal program (428 /usr/dt/bin/dtterm -C -ls). The following also shows that ksh has a child process of its own—in this case, the running ptree command (526 ptree 430):

```
# ptree 430
258   /usr/dt/bin/dtlogin -daemon
  273   /usr/dt/bin/dtlogin -daemon
    333   /bin/ksh /usr/dt/bin/Xsession
      378   /usr/dt/bin/sdt_shell -c    unset DT;   DISPLAY=:0;    /u
        381   -ksh -c    unset DT;   DISPLAY=:0;    /usr/dt/bin/dtses
          395   /usr/dt/bin/dtsession
            402   dtwm
```

```
427    /usr/dt/bin/dtexec -open 0 -ttprocid 2.wyEMt 01 394~
  428   /usr/dt/bin/dtterm -C -ls
    430   -ksh
      526   ptree 430
```

Unless you run ptree with the *-a* option, it shows only the parents and children of the process that you specify on the command line. Running ptree with the *-a* option shows the parent/child relationships for all the processes currently running on the system. Output from ptree with the *-a* option will be lengthy and should probably be piped or directed into a file.

The pldd Command: Displaying Process Libraries

Most applications use *dynamic link libraries* (DLLs). DLLs are implemented as files and provide reusable functions that programmers can call from their code. DLLs serve the very useful purpose of providing prewritten functionality that programmers can use in their applications, with very few strings attached. Most library files are located in /usr/lib and are shared by all the applications that run on the system. *Dynamic linking* is the process whereby an application uses a function provided by a library file at run time.

There are a few potential problems with libraries, however. One such problem is that installing a new application on the system can overwrite a library in /usr/lib with an older version. This can interfere with applications that expect to use the newer version. Another common problem is that a process can have linked to a library file when you want to replace or delete it.

FROM THE CLASSROOM

Using Wildcards

When practicing the process information commands, many students try using the commands only with the PID number of a process. Although this works, using PID numbers ignores the true power of the process file system. Because each process exists as a directory in the process file system, you can issue commands against multiple processes using wildcard characters. Try it out. Type **pldd /proc/***, and Solaris will list every library in use in every process on the system. This can be particularly useful in scripts.

—*Brian Albrecht, SCSA, MCSE, TCEC, CCNA*

The pldd command is an easy way to determine which libraries a process is currently using. A sample output from a pldd command is shown next. Each line of output lists a library containing functions to which the ksh process has currently linked.

```
# pldd 430
430:    -ksh
/usr/lib/libsocket.so.1
/usr/lib/libnsl.so.1
/usr/lib/libc.so.1
/usr/lib/libdl.so.1
/usr/lib/libmp.so.2
/usr/platform/sun4u/lib/libc_psr.so.1
/usr/lib/locale/en_US.ISO8859-1/en_US.ISO8859-1.so.2
```

The pldd command is simple to use and takes no options other than the standard *-F* (force). The force option forces pldd to acquire the target process, even if another process is already reading its statistics.

The pmap Command: Showing the Process' Address Space

The pmap command displays the ranges of memory that are being used by the process. This is called the *process address map*. A sample output from the pmap command is shown next. This figure shows the address map of the Korn shell process (ksh).

```
# pmap 430
430:    -ksh
00010000  192K read/exec           /usr/bin/ksh
00040000    8K read/write/exec     /usr/bin/ksh
00042000   40K read/write/exec      [ heap ]
FF180000  664K read/exec           /usr/lib/libc.so.1
FF236000   24K read/write/exec     /usr/lib/libc.so.1
FF23C000    8K read/write/exec     /usr/lib/libc.so.1
FF260000   16K read/exec           /usr/lib/locale/en_US.ISO8859-1/en_US.ISO8859-1.so.2
FF272000   16K read/write/exec     /usr/lib/locale/en_US.ISO8859-1/en_US.ISO8859-1.so.2
FF280000  552K read/exec           /usr/lib/libnsl.so.1
FF31A000   32K read/write/exec     /usr/lib/libnsl.so.1
FF322000   32K read/write/exec     /usr/lib/libnsl.so.1
FF340000   16K read/exec           /usr/platform/sun4u/lib/libc_psr.so.1
FF350000   16K read/exec           /usr/lib/libmp.so.2
FF364000    8K read/write/exec     /usr/lib/libmp.so.2
FF380000    8K read/write/exec      [ anon ]
```

```
FF390000    40K read/exec          /usr/lib/libsocket.so.1
FF3AA000     8K read/write/exec    /usr/lib/libsocket.so.1
FF3B0000     8K read/exec          /usr/lib/libdl.so.1
FF3C0000   128K read/exec          /usr/lib/ld.so.1
FF3E0000     8K read/write/exec    /usr/lib/ld.so.1
FFBEC000    16K read/write/exec       [ stack ]
```

The first column of the output displays the starting address of the range of memory. The second column shows the length of the range of memory. This number is always divisible by 8KB, since Solaris allocates memory in 8KB pages. The third column indicates the kind of permissions the process has into this range of memory. The final column is a description of the contents of the range of memory. If the memory contains a memory-mapped file, pmap displays the name of the file.

You have now seen some examples of using the process information commands to analyze running processes. The following exercise introduces you to using the commands to analyze a core file.

EXERCISE 21-2

Analyzing a Core File with pwdx

In this exercise, you will determine the working directory of the shell process from its core file. For the purposes of this exercise, you will use the gcore tool to generate a core file. In a production environment, you would probably be analyzing the core file of a process that terminated abnormally.

1. Determine the PID of the shell by typing **ps**.

2. Create a core file from the shell process by typing **gcore -o corefile <pid>**.

3. Now analyze the core file by typing **pwdx ./corefile**.

When you analyze the core file with pwdx, it should return the current working directory. This is correct because the shell was using that directory when you generated the core file.

Now that you understand more about the process information commands, some possible scenario questions and their answers are next.

SCENARIO & SOLUTION

What if you need to find the current working directory of a script that you just started?	Use pwdx on the process ID of the script.
What if you need to wait for another process to finish before your script goes on?	Call the pwait command from your script with the PID of the process to wait on.
What if you need to stop a process?	Use pstop.
What if your program just core dumped and complained about access denial?	Use pcred on the core file to see which credentials the process was using.
What if you need to know how long a command takes to run?	Use ptime to time it.

CERTIFICATION OBJECTIVE 21.03

Creating and Adding a Swap File to the System Swap Space

Solaris supports the use of almost any type of file as a swap area. Solaris can use an NFS-mounted file, a regular file, or a disk slice. Solaris also has the ability to use multiple files as swap areas. This section illustrates how to view existing swap files, create a swap file, and add a new swap area to the system, and how Solaris remounts system swap files when it boots.

Listing Existing Swap Areas

You use the swap command to administer swap space. To list all swap areas on the system, type **swap -l**. The output of this command has five columns, as described in Table 21-3.

Each line listed by swap -*l* is a different swap file that the system is using to provide swap space. These files can be local or NFS-mounted.

TABLE 21-3	Column	Description
	Path	The pathname for the swap area
Output Format of the swap -l Command (from the Man Page)	dev	The major/minor device number in decimal if it is a block special device; zeros otherwise
	Swaplo	The swaplow value for the area in 512-byte blocks
	Blocks	The swaplen value for the area in 512-byte blocks
	Free	The number of 512-byte blocks in this area that are not currently allocated

Creating and Adding a New Local Swap File

The first step in adding a new local swap file is to create the actual file you will use as the swap. You can create this file with the mkfile command. The mkfile command takes two arguments: a size and a filename. The size argument defaults to bytes but can be changed to kilobytes, blocks, or megabytes using the *k, b,* or *m* suffixes. Once mkfile is run, the file can be added to system swap space using the swap *-a* command. You must be the superuser to use swap *-a.* This process is shown here:

```
# mkfile 250m /usr/newswapfile
# swap -a /usr/newswapfile
```

Once the file is added using the swap *-a* command, it is available for use as swap space and shows up in the output of swap *-l.* It is no longer available, however, if you reboot at this point. To make this assignment permanent, you must modify vfstab. You will learn about this in the section "Modifying vfstab to Make It Stick," later in the chapter.

on the job

Swap files are read from and written to very frequently. When creating a local swap file, you should be very aware of the disk and controller on which it resides. Do not put a swap file on a disk that is already heavily used, because system performance will suffer as a result.

Creating and Adding an NFS-Mounted Swap File

Adding an NFS-mounted swap file is exactly the same as adding a locally mounted swap file, with one extra consideration. To add an NFS-mounted swap file, the NFS server must first export the file. Here's the process:

1. Create the file on the NFS server using the mkfile command exactly as described in the preceding section.

2. Add the following line to /etc/dfs/dfstab on the NFS server to export the file:

```
share -F nfs -o rw=clientname,root=clientname path-to-swap-file
```

3. Run the shareall command on the NFS server.

4. On the client, add the following line to /etc/vfstab to mount the exported file system:

```
server:path-to-swap-file - local-path-to-swap-file nfs - - -
```

5. On the client, run mount:

```
mount local-path-to-swap-file
```

6. Add the file to swap space using the command:

```
swap -a local-path-to-swap-file
```

Once these steps are complete, you should see the swap file listed as available swap space with the swap *-l* command. You will lose this swap file on reboot unless you complete the steps in the next section.

on the **job** *NFS-mounted file systems are typically slower and have inherently more latency than local disks. A slow swap file often equals a slow system; for this reason, it is best to use locally mounted swap files wherever possible.*

Modifying vfstab to Make It Stick

Once you have created and added swap files to the system using the swap *-a* command, you must add them to /etc/vfstab so that the system recognizes them the next time it boots. During a system boot, the system runs the /sbin/swapadd script to add swap files to the system. The swapadd script parses vfstab, looking for swap entries, and adds them with the swap *-a* command. Swap file entries in vfstab should take the form described in Table 21-4.

TABLE 21-4	Device to Mount	Device to fsck	Mount Point	FSType	fsck Pass	Mount at Boot	Mount Options
Adding a Swap File Entry to vfstab	path-to-swap-file	-	-	swap	-	-	-

Because you are not using the mount *-a* command to mount this file system, the mount point and mount at boot options must always be set to a hyphen (-). The swapadd script runs before the system issues the mount *-a* command. If the mount at boot option is set, mount *-a* attempts (and fails) to mount the swap file after swapadd already adds into swap space.

In the case of an NFS-mounted swap file, this entry in vfstab should come after the NFS entry. The swapadd script is intelligent enough to recognize that the swap file depends on the NFS mount being in place. The swapadd script always mounts the NFS file system automatically before it attempts to add the swap file into swap space.

Now that you understand all the steps involved in adding a swap file, you can try it yourself.

EXERCISE 21-3

Adding a Local File to System Swap Space

In this exercise, you add a 250MB swap file into the system swap space.

1. Create a 250MB local file under /opt using mkfile. (You can make the file smaller if your /opt is not large enough to handle 250MB.)

2. Add the local file to system swap space using the swap *-a* command.

3. Verify that the local file is a usable part of system swap space using the swap *-l* command.

4. Modify /etc/vfstab and add an entry for the swap file so that /sbin/swapadd adds the swap file into the system swap space for you each time you reboot.

5. If you want to make the addition of this swap file persistent across system boots, add the following line to /etc/vfstab:

```
/opt/swapfile- -      swap   -       -    -
```

CERTIFICATION SUMMARY

In this chapter, you learned that Solaris pseudo file systems represent objects instead of regular files. Solaris pseudo file systems include procfs and swapfs, and are implemented as kernel modules. The procfs system is mounted on /proc, and the process files have the same file ownership as the running processes. Solaris provides a set process information commands that allow you to read process information from /proc. These commands gather information by stopping the running process.

The swapfs pseudo file system is implemented on top of the Solaris virtual memory. Virtual memory allows the system to use more memory than is physically available. Solaris accomplishes this goal by transferring sections of memory called pages to disk. The disk area where these pages are stored is called the swap file. Solaris supports using local and network-mounted files as swap files. New swap files can be added using the swap *-a* command but must also be added to /etc/vfstab only if you want the swap file to be persistent across boots.

✓ TWO-MINUTE DRILL

Understanding the Characteristics of Solaris Pseudo File System Types

❑ Solaris pseudo file systems represent objects instead of regular files.

❑ Solaris pseudo file systems are implemented as kernel modules.

❑ The procfs process file system is mounted on /proc at system boot.

❑ Each directory in /proc represents a running process.

❑ Directories and files in /proc have the same ownership as their corresponding processes.

Using Commands to Extract Information from Entries in the /proc Directory

❑ The process information commands are used to extract statistics from the /proc directory.

❑ Each command actually stops the process that it is examining.

❑ The process information commands can also be used to examine core files.

❑ The ptree command displays only child/parent relationships for the specified process unless the -*a* option is used.

❑ The pldd command can be used to view the library files a process is using.

Creating and Adding a Swap File to the System Swap Space

❑ The swap command is used to administer swap files.

❑ Swap files can be local or NFS-mounted.

❑ The swap -*a* command is used to add a swap file to swap space.

❑ The /sbin/swapadd script parses /etc/vfstab and adds the swap file back into swap space each time the system boots.

❑ Swap files must be added to /etc/vfstab with the mount at boot option set to - (a hyphen).

SELF TEST

The following questions will help you measure your understanding of the material presented in this chapter. Read all the choices carefully because there might be more than one correct answer. Choose all correct answers for each question.

Understanding the Characteristics of Solaris Pseudo File System Types

1. How are pseudo file systems implemented in Solaris?

    A. As dynamic link library files

    B. As kernel modules

    C. As executable files

    D. As shell scripts that run when the system boots

2. Which UID must you have to check the statistics of a process using the process information commands?

    A. root

    B. system

    C. The same as the owner of the process

    D. procctl

3. If a system has 512MB of physical memory, how large should its swap space be?

    A. Between 768 and 1280MB

    B. Between 51 and 256MB

    C. 512GB

    D. Between 256 and 768MB

Using Commands to Extract Information from Entries in the /proc Directory

4. You are using the pldd command to verify the library files that are being used on a large production server to prepare for an upcoming application upgrade. Suddenly, the help desk calls you and says that a large number of trouble tickets have opened complaining of X Windows sessions freezing on the same machine on which you are working. What should you do to troubleshoot the problem?

A. Use the ptree command to find the parent process of each X-server and increase the nice value.

B. Use the pstop and prun commands to stop and restart each X-server process.

C. Stop using the pldd command because it stops the X-server to check statistics and can cause X Windows sessions to freeze.

D. Immediately proceed with the application upgrade because these types of problems are often caused by older software.

5. You are writing a shell script that needs to stop a web server process, wait for it to shut down, and then delete several temporary files and restart the web server. Which process commands could you use to wait for the web server process to stop?

A. ptime

B. pwait

C. pwaiton

D. pstop

Creating and Adding a Swap File to the System Swap Space

6. Which command is used to list the current swap files in the system swap space?

A. swap -*s*

B. swap -*l*

C. swap -*a*

D. swap -*d*

7. Which file must you modify to make an added swap file permanent?

A. /etc/vfstab

B. /sbin/swapadd

C. /etc/dfs/dfstab

D. /etc/swaptab

LAB QUESTION

You have recently moved your data center to a new facility and reconstructed your entire environment from the ground up on leased hardware. Lately, you have experienced a number of unscheduled server outages on the new equipment. These outages are occurring during peak usage times, and your company's management is stressing the importance of availability. You suspect that some junior administrators might not have created sufficient swap space or added swap to the vfstab correctly.

Identify the correct actions to take to verify your swap space on each server from the following list; then place a number to the left of each step, indicating the correct order of completing the step:

__ Add additional swap files to /etc/vfstab to make it stick during a reboot.

__ Check the amount of physical memory available using the prtconf command.

__ Verify that swap space is 0.5 to 1.5 times physical memory using the swap -l command.

__ Add the new swap file to swap space using swap -a.

__ Create an additional swap file if needed.

__ Verify that the new swap is listed in swap space with the swap -l command.

SELF TEST ANSWERS

Understanding the Characteristics of Solaris Pseudo File System Types

1. ☑ **B.** Solaris pseudo file systems are implemented as kernel modules.
   ☒ **A, C,** and **D** are incorrect. These are all executable file types, but Solaris uses kernel modules to extend kernel functionality.

2. ☑ **C.** The process information commands read statistics from the process files in the /proc file system. These files are owned by the owner of the process.
   ☒ **A, B,** and **D** are incorrect. Most files in /proc are not world-readable, so you must be the owner of the process.

3. ☑ **D.** System swap space should be between 0.5 and 1.5 times physical memory.
   ☒ **A, B,** and **C** are incorrect. All these swap values are either too high or too low.

Using Commands to Extract Information from Entries in the /proc Directory

4. ☑ **C.** The pldd command does stop each process when it checks its statistics. In this case, your activities were the cause of the performance issues.
   ☒ **A** is incorrect because all process information commands stop their processes to check statistics. The ptree command only makes the situation worse. **B** is incorrect because the pstop and prun commands simply pause and resume the X-server process without accomplishing anything. **D** is incorrect because you should never install an application onto a production server without ample testing first.

5. ☑ **B.** The only correct answer is pwait. The pwait command allows a script to wait until another process has stopped.
   ☒ **A** is incorrect because ptime times the elapsed time that it takes a process to execute. **C** is incorrect because there is no pwaiton command. **D** is incorrect because pstop stops the process, not waits for it.

Creating and Adding a Swap File to the System Swap Space

6. ☑ **B.** The swap -l command lists all available swap areas.
   ☒ **A** is incorrect because swap -s only summarizes how much swap space is available. **C** is incorrect because swap -a adds a new swap file to swap space. **D** is incorrect because swap -d deletes a swap file from swap space.

7.   ☑   **A.** The swapadd script reads from /etc/vfstab and adds the listed swap files into the system each time it boots using the swap -*a* command.
    ☒   **B, C,** and **D** are incorrect because modifying these files will have no effect on persistent swap space.

LAB ANSWER

The use of virtual memory in Solaris is very efficient, but even the most efficient memory manager can run into problems if there is simply not enough space available for a swap file. Many administrators remember to create a swap file and add it in using the swap -*a* command, but they forget to add it to /etc/vfstab. The next time the system reboots, the swap file just disappears. This can cause some very hard-to-detect problems.

   The correct order to verify swap space is as follows:

1. Check the amount of physical memory available using the prtconf command.

2. Verify that swap space is 0.5 to 1.5 times physical memory using the swap -*l* command.

3. Create an additional swap file if needed.

4. Add the new swap file to swap space using swap -*a.*

5. Verify that the new swap is listed in swap space with the swap -*l* command.

6. Add additional swap files to /etc/vfstab to make it stick during a reboot.

Solaris™

SUN® CERTIFIED SYSTEM ADMINISTRATOR

22

Working with NFS

CERTIFICATION OBJECTIVES

The Network File System (NFS) has become a standard of resource sharing. It is a Sun Microsystems product built to use the Transmission Control Protocol/Internet Protocol (TCP/IP) and Sun's Remote Procedure Call (RPC) and External Data Representation (XDR) specifications. NFS is easy to use, reliable, and has the ability to share files among different operating systems.

NFS gives the system administrator several means of quickly and easily distributing resources. It gives users a fast way of accessing needed resources, as well as a means to expand a crowded local hard disk, and it is easier than using the FTP command every time you need a file from another machine.

CERTIFICATION OBJECTIVE 22.01

Understanding the Functions of NFS Servers and Clients

The *NFS server* can be any machine that uses NFS to share its local resources with remote machines. You designate a machine as an NFS server using the share command or by editing its /etc/dfs/dfstab file and starting the two NFS server daemons, mountd and nfsd. The *NFS client* is the machine that accesses the shared resources from an NFS server. The NFS client "mounts," or adds, the remote files to its local hierarchy. Then, depending on the permissions placed on the resources by the NFS server, the NFS client can use those shared resources as though they were stored on the client's local hard disk. (See Figure 22-1.)

Now that you know the difference between the NFS server and the NFS client, don't get them confused! This brief summary of the two NFS devices will help you distinguish between them in your mind:

- **NFS server**   A host that allows its resources to be accessed by other hosts
- **NFS client**   A host that accesses the resources of other hosts

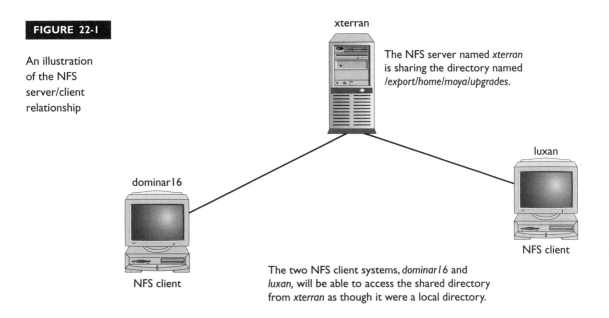

FIGURE 22-1

An illustration of the NFS server/client relationship

xterran

The NFS server named *xterran* is sharing the directory named */export/home/moya/upgrades.*

luxan

NFS client

dominar16

NFS client

The two NFS client systems, *dominar16* and *luxan,* will be able to access the shared directory from *xterran* as though it were a local directory.

CERTIFICATION OBJECTIVE 22.02

Making Resources Available and Unavailable for Mounting as Shared Resources

Solaris uses *distributed file system* (DFS) commands to share and mount file resources. Several files are used to set up shares to be mounted and shared automatically. The root user can edit these files to share and mount remote resources.

On the NFS server, the daemons that will run are mountd and nfsd. The files used are as follows:

- /etc/dfs/dfstab
- /etc/dfs/sharetab
- /etc/rmtab

The commands used on the NFS server are share, unshared, shareall, and unshareall.

On the NFS client, the daemons that will run are statd and lockd. The files used are as follows:

- /etc/vfstab
- /etc/mnttab

The commands used by the NFS client are mount, umount, mountall, and umountall.

The NFS Server Daemons

NFS needs daemons running to operate. The two daemons on the NFS server are mountd and nfsd. When the NFS client tries to access a shared remote resource, a mount request contacts the NFS server's mount daemon, mountd. The client's mount process gets the file handle of the requested remote resource and writes the information locally to /etc/mnttab. The file handle is a unique designation assigned by the NFS server for each shared file or directory. It is an encoding of information unique to that resource, including disk device number, inode generation number, and inode number.

on the
job

The NFS client takes the information as it is sent by the server. It has no way of knowing whether the information is still valid or what other factors could be affecting the requested resource. For example, the inode generation number is generated each time a new inode is used or an old one reused. If you restore a shared file system without unmounting the shares, the NFS clients will not be able to access the shared resources.

Once the client gets the requested file handle, the mountd daemon on the NFS server makes an entry in the /etc/rmtab file. This is where the server keeps track of the files that are currently mounted on remote clients. The file contains an entry for each mounted resource. The format of the entry is as follows:

```
remote hostname : local filesystem name
```

The mountd daemon also clears out all old entries in /etc/rmtab every time it starts and when a client sends an unmount request.

The other daemon used by the NFS server is nfsd. When an NFS client requests a shared resource from an NFS server, the nfsd daemon gets the request and passes the requested information on the shared resource back to the client process.

The NFS Client Daemons

On the NFS client side, there are two daemons, statd and lockd. They work together to provide locking functions and recovery of shared files if a crash occurs. These two daemons start automatically and rarely require any intervention by the user or administrator.

The share Command

The NFS server uses the /usr/sbin/share command to make local resources available to remote clients, or if run with no options, to display all the file resources that are currently shared.

exam
Ⓦatch

The share command displays all the resources that are available to be mounted, whether they are currently mounted or not.

The share command writes information about all the shared resources to the file /etc/dfs/sharetab.

The format of the share command is as follows:

```
share [ -F file system type ] [ -o options ] [ -d description ]
pathname-to-resource
```

- *-F file system type*   This specifies the type of file system the shared resource is on.

- *-o options*   This specifies the type of access the clients have to the resource.

- *-d description*   This is a short description of the resource. It is displayed if the share command is run with no options. Make sure you enclose the message within quotes.

- *pathname-to-resource*   This names the resource on the server to be shared.

The type of access (specified by *-o* options) gives the NFS server administrator several ways of allowing users access to the shared resource and how much access users can have. The choices are as follows:

- *rw*   This stands for *read/write,* which means that all clients will be able to read and write to the shared resource. This is the default and is used if no option is specified.

- *rw=client:client*   This specifies that the named clients have read/write access to the resource. You can add as many hostnames, separated by colons, as needed.

- *ro*   This stands for *read-only*, which means the server allows clients to only read the shared resource, not make any changes to it.
- *ro=client:client*   This specifies that the named hosts have only read access to the shared resource.
- *root=client:client*   The root account on the named hosts has superuser access to the shared resource.

Multiple options can be used, as long as they are separated by commas. NFS share permissions affect the resource, not the files contained in the resource. If an attempt is made to write to a read-only (ro) file system, the NFS client refuses to pass the request back to the server. On a read/write (rw) file system, the NFS client will pass the request to the server. At that point, the individual file permissions take effect. So even though a file system may be mounted read/write, if you don't have the proper file permissions to modify a file, the modification will fail.

EXERCISE 22-1

Using the share Command

Use the share command to make a resource available to another user. For example, the user named *jcrichton* has a directory named /export/home/moya/ upgrades. He wants to share the directory so that other users can access it on their local systems. He would run the share command with the following options:

```
# share -F nfs -o rw=luxan:pleisar, ro=dominar16:nebari,
root=moya -d  "Keep Rygel from messing with these files!"
/export/home/moya/upgrades
```

The result of running this command is that the hosts named *luxan* and *pleisar* have read/write access to the shared directory. The hosts named *dominar16* and *nebari* are able to mount the shared resource, but only with read permissions. The root user on the host named *moya* has full superuser access to the resource. However, if *jcrichton* had previously set read-only permissions on the directory locally, only read-only access would be allowed, despite the settings added to the share command.

The unshare Command

To make the resource unavailable for mounting by a remote system, you use the unshare command. The format of the unshare command is similar to that of the share command:

```
unshare [ -F nfs ] path-to-resource
```

- *-F nfs*   This specifies the file system type. This option is not really necessary, because NFS is the default choice.
- *path-to-resource*   This specifies the path used to share the resource.

EXERCISE 22-2

Using the unshare Command

Use the unshare command to make a shared resource unavailable. For example, if *jcrichton* decides to stop sharing his upgrades directory, he will run

```
# unshare /export/home/moya/upgrades
```

Now all the clients who try to access the resource will find it unavailable.

CERTIFICATION OBJECTIVE 22.03

Using the /etc/dfs/dfstab File on an NFS Server to Enable Automatic Sharing of Resources

Running the share command does not make the resource permanently available for mounting by remote clients. To set up an NFS file server, you must edit the /etc/dfs/dfstab file. This will automatically share the resource whenever the host enters runlevel 3. To edit the file, simply add the share command as though you were running it from the command line.

EXERCISE 22-3

Editing the /etc/dfstab File

Edit your /etc/dfstab file to make a resource always available. For example, if *jcrichton* wanted to make available the resource /export/home/moya/upgrades—a regular NFS shared resource—while the system is in runlevel 3, he would edit the /etc/dfs/dfstab file by adding this line:

```
share -F nfs    /export/home/moya/upgrades
```

Because he added no options, all clients will have read/write access.

Next, start the NFS server daemons, mountd and nfsd, by running the script called /etc/init.d/nfs.server and add the start switch. The full command is

```
/etc/init.d/nfs.server start
```

Now the specified resources will be available for mounting.

Displaying a Server's Available Resources for Mounting

To make sure the specified resource is available, use the dfshares command.

For example, if *jcrichton* ran this command on his machine named *xterran,* he would see this output displayed:

```
xterran # dfshares
RESOURCE                                    SERVER ACCESS     TRANSPORT
xterran:/export/home/moya/upgrades  xterran -  -
```

- **RESOURCE** This is the resource that is available to be mounted remotely. Notice the name of the host preceding the resource pathname.

- **SERVER** This specifies the name of the system that is making the resource available.

- **ACCESS** This displays the access permissions assigned to the resource by the NFS server. If the permissions can't be determined or if they were left at the default (*rw* for read/write), a hyphen (-) is displayed.

- **TRANSPORT** This is the transport provider over which the resource is shared.

From the NFS client, use the showmount command to see which resources are available on an NFS server. The showmount command has several useful options. The format is

```
showmount   [-ade]   <hostname>
```

- **-a**   This displays the resources that have been locally mounted and from which remote system.

- **-d**   This displays the local resources that have been remotely mounted.

- **-e**   This displays the resources available to be mounted.

EXERCISE 22-4

Using the showmount Command

Use the showmount command to see which resources a remote NFS server is sharing. Using the *-e* switch and naming the host, you can see the files that are available to be mounted from a remote system.

For example, if the user *jcrichton* wanted to see the resources that were shared on the NFS server named *moya,* he would run this command:

```
xterran # showmount -e moya
export list for moya:
/export/home/moya/upgrades (everyone)
```

This display tells him that the only directory currently being shared on *moya* is the upgrades directory and that everyone has access to it.

Mounting a Resource from Another System

The NFS client uses the mount command to mount shared resources locally. The mount command format is similar to that of the share command used by the NFS server:

```
mount [ -F nfs ] [ -o options ] path-to-resource path-to-local-mount-point
```

- **-F nfs**   This specifies NFS as the file system type. This is not required because if it is not specified, the default is NFS.

- **-o options**   This specifies options such as access permissions to the resource locally. The option *rw* (read/write) is the default. The option *ro* (read-only) can also be specified.

- *path-to-resource* This specifies the NFS server hostname and the path to the shared resource on the server. The server name and the path are separated by a colon.

- *path-to-local-mount-point* This specifies the location on the NFS client to which the shared resource will be mounted. This mount point must have been created prior to running the mount command.

For example, now that *jcrichton* has shared the /export/home/moya/upgrades directory on his machine named *xterran,* the user *kdargo* has decided to mount it locally. To mount the directory on *kdargo's* machine, *luxan,* she would run the mount command like this:

```
kdargo # mount xterran:/export/home/moya/upgrades /etc/moya/upgrades
```

Because *kdargo* didn't specify the file system type, her machine, *luxan,* defaults to NFS, which is correct. Because she didn't specify any options, the mount point is *rw* (read/write) on her machine. She specified that the remote resource be mounted to the local directory she created, /etc/moya/upgrades.

Multiple options can be used. Each one must be separated by a comma. Some of the most frequently used options are these:

- *rw* or *ro* These stand for *read/write* or *read-only.* The default is read/write.

- *bg* or *fg* These stand for *background* or *foreground.* If the mount command fails, the process tries again, either in the background or in the foreground. The default is to retry in the foreground.

- *soft* or *hard* *soft* returns an error if the NFS server doesn't respond; *hard* continues to try until the server does respond. The default is *hard.*

- *intr* or *nointr* These stand for *interrupt* or *no interrupt.* If *intr* is specified, the keyboard commands can be used to kill a hung hard-mounting process. The *nointr* option disables the ability to stop the mounting process with the keyboard. The default is *intr.*

- *suid* or *nosuid* This enables or disables the setuid execution. The default is *suid.*

- *timeo=n* This allows you to set the timeout to *n* tenths of a second. The default is eleven-tenths, or 1.1 seconds.

- *retry=n* This sets *n,* or the number of times the mount process retries the mount operation. The default is 10,000.

Even though you might never use any of the options other than rw and ro, make sure you know them. You can expect the exam to ask about the result of using the mount command with any of these options.

The command to unmount a mounted resource is umount. The umount command is used to break the connection to a local or remote resource. The command's format is

```
# umount [ -F nfs ] path-to-resource path-to-local-mount-point
```

- *-F nfs*   This specifies NFS as the file system type. This option is not required because if it is not specified, the default is NFS.
- *path-to-resource*   This specifies the NFS server hostname and the path to the shared resource on the server. The server name and the path are separated by a colon.
- *path-to-local-mount-point*   This specifies the location on the NFS client to which the shared resource was mounted.

For example, once the user named *kdargo* was finished with the resource mounted from the server named *xterran,* she used this command to unmount it from her local NFS client machine named *kdargo,* as follows:

```
kdargo # umount xterran:/export/home/moya/upgrades /etc/moya/
upgrades.
```

Be very careful that you don't confuse the umount command with the word "unmount." Although it would seem logical to have named the unmounting command unmount, the command is spelled with only one n.

CERTIFICATION OBJECTIVE 22.04

Using the /etc/vfstab File to Enable Persistent Mounting of Resources on an NFS Client

Just like the share command, the mount command doesn't make a permanent mount point connection. To do that, you must edit the /etc/vfstab file. That way, needed NFS resources will be mounted when the client machine is booted.

The fields in the /etc/vfstab file are as follows:

- **device to mount**   This specifies the name of the server and the pathname of the remote resource. The server name and path are separated by a colon.

- **device to fsck**   This field is always null. The file system is never checked from the client.

- **mount point**   This field specifies the default mount point for the file resource on the local client. This local mount point must already exist on the client.

- **FSType**   This field is always NFS, for NFS system resources.

- **fsck pass**   This field is always null. The file system is never checked from the client.

- **mount at boot**   This field is either yes or no and specifies whether the resource should be mounted automatically during the booting of the client.

- **mount options**   This field is a comma-separated list of the mount command options.

For example, the user *zhaan* on the machine named *delvian* wants to mount *jchrichton*'s /export/home/moya/upgrades directory from the NFS server named *xterran*. The user *zhaan* would edit the /etc/vfstab by adding a line, as shown in Figure 22-2.

With this entry in the /etc/vfstab file, the user *zhaan* is mounting the remote directory from the machine named *xterran* to the local directory /home/upgrades. It will be mounted at boot. The option *soft* means that if the directory can't be mounted after the first attempt, an error message will be generated. The option *bg*, for *background*, means that the mount attempt will be made in the background during the boot process.

exam
ⓦatch

The /etc/vfstab file controls the mounting of local mounts as well as resources from an NFS server.

Manually Mounting and Unmounting with mountall, umountall, shareall, and unshareall

Let's look at several commands you can use to save time when dealing with NFS resources.

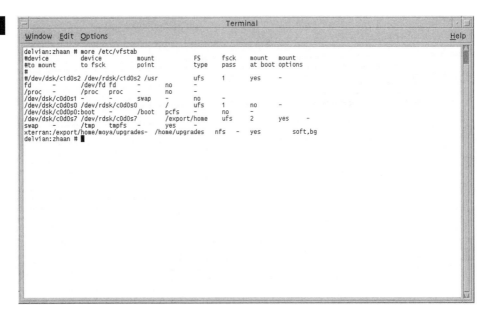

FIGURE 22-2

The user
zhaan edits the
/etc/vfstab file

The mountall and umountall Commands

The mountall and umountall commands are used on an NFS client to mount or unmount multiple local or remote mount points.

The mountall Command   With no arguments, the mountall command mounts all the resources listed in the /etc/vfstab file, with *yes* under Mount at boot. The format of the command is as follows:

```
# mountall -r [ -F nfs ]
```

If you add the *-r* option, only remote file resources are affected. If you use *-l* instead of *-r*, only local files are affected.

The umountall Command   With no arguments, all mounted resources will be unmounted. This command will not unmount root, /proc, /var, or /usr. Furthermore, if a file system is busy, it might not unmount. The format of umountall is similar to that of the mountall command:

```
# umountall -r [ -F nfs ]
```

If you add the *-r* option, only remote file resources are affected. If you use *-l* instead of *-r*, only local files are affected.

The shareall and unshareall Commands

The shareall and unshareall commands are used on an NFS server to share and unshare multiple resources.

The shareall Command This command is used to share multiple resources. With no arguments, it shares all the resources listed in the /etc/dfs/dfstab file. The format is as follows:

```
# shareall [ -F nfs ]
```

The *-F nfs* option is used if different file types are being shared. The default is nfs.

The unshareall Command This command is used to unshare multiple resources. With no arguments, it unshares all the currently shared files listed in the /etc/dfs/sharetab file. The format is as follows:

```
# unshareall [ -F nfs ]
```

The *-F nfs* option is used if different file types are being shared. The default is NFS.

Now that you understand the concept of mounting resources, here are two common problems and their possible solutions:

SCENARIO & SOLUTION	
You can't mount a resource from the NFS server. When you run the mount command, you get a message: "NFS server not responding." What's the solution?	Make sure that nfsd and mountd are running on the server and that the resource is properly shared with the share command.
When you try to mount a file to your local drive, the error message says, "Mount: /temp_mount not found." What should you do?	Make sure you create the local mount point prior to running the mount command. The mount command won't create the local mount point for you.

FROM THE CLASSROOM

It's All About Communicating

An old Scottish legend is reminiscent of NFS.

After years of warring among the Scottish clans, the leaders agreed to a truce. They would all meet to discuss their grievances and decide once and for all on the disputed boundaries. It was bound to be a heated debate at best, and few people, including most of the leaders, had any hope that the fighting would stop.

Despite their lack of enthusiasm, the head of each clan traveled to the meeting place. Sure enough, on the morning of the first day, it looked like the negotiations were doomed. They couldn't even decide who was to sit at the head of the table during the talks! After hours of arguing and just when it looked like half the room was about to attack the other half, the oldest clan leader, the eldest of the MacGregor Clan, hobbled over to the middle of the table and sat down in the chair nearest him. As the rest of the clan leaders watched, he slammed his fist on the tabletop and announced, "Wherever the MacGregor sits *is* the head of the table!" The rest of the leaders followed his example, sat down, and got to work.

NFS is the "MacGregor" you will use to bring everyone to your table.

Using NFS, you have the opportunity to make your life as a Solaris system administrator much easier. Furthermore, like most things that make your life easier, NFS can also make your life much more complicated. Make sure you plan carefully before implementing an NFS scheme, and monitor its use regularly.

When I work with future gurus, one thing indicates to me that they have reached a milestone in their Solaris education: they start using NFS.

At some point in every student's learning process, he or she realizes that using NFS will be easier than FTP-ing all over the network. This realization is usually a good indication to me that the student has begun to think in terms of the network instead of the workstation and has begun to look for ways to work smarter, not harder.

The network communications capabilities of Solaris are impressive. At first, all the available tools can be overwhelming. The best way to prepare for the exam is to use a Solaris network every chance you get.

I always recommend that, to prepare for these exams, students set up a lab to practice the various elements of the tests on a working Solaris system. Now is the time to take it a

(continued)

FROM THE CLASSROOM

step further. Work as hard as you can to get your Solaris machines out of a test lab environment and into a working network as soon as possible. The test lab is a great way to safely practice using Solaris. You can install, configure, and run commands as much as you want, without inconveniencing other users. That is still an important aspect of your training for this exam. However, now you need to start working on Solaris as much as possible to incorporate the knowledge you are acquiring into your everyday computing routine.

When I was preparing for this exam, I set a goal for myself. By a set date, I wanted to have replaced my home network with Solaris machines everywhere possible. I researched, planned, and then gradually migrated my file and print servers, my primary workstation—even my laptop—to the Solaris platform. I noticed a huge jump in my knowledge and confidence as I began to use Solaris all the time instead of during only study-lab sessions.

However, I still need to keep other operating systems around. For all its strengths,

Solaris is not the first choice for computer game developers. Furthermore, I work with a variety of audio, visual, and networking applications that run on other platforms. Mainly, I want to keep my skills sharp on other platforms because so many networks in the IT world are of the mixed-breed variety. That is where NFS is a tremendously valuable tool. Using NFS, I am able to share resources and access them from anywhere on my network.

If you haven't already done so, you are bound to run into what I call "platform zealots." They will take every opportunity to tell you why their chosen OS is the best, all others are a waste of time, blah, blah, blah. Personally, I like diversity. My first choice is Solaris—but rather than get into the OS Holy Wars, I have learned to use a variety of systems and learned how to make them work together on a network.

Because, as we all know now, where NFS sits *is* the head of the table!

—Randy Cook, MCSE, SCSA

CERTIFICATION SUMMARY

NFS is fairly straightforward. Your server is an NFS server if you are allowing others to mount your resources. Your client is an NFS client if you mount the remote resources of others. Your server is both if you do both.

An NFS server uses the share and unshare commands to administer the resources. The server also uses the /etc/dfs/dfstab file to allow resources to be shared. An NFS client uses the mount and umount commands to mount and unmount a resource locally. An NFS client also uses the /etc/vfstab file.

Once you get your mind wrapped around these commands, you should have no trouble using NFS.

✓ TWO-MINUTE DRILL

Understanding the Functions of NFS Servers and Clients

❏ NFS stands for Network File System; DFS stands for distributed file system.

❏ An NFS server makes local file systems available across a network to other systems.

❏ The NFS client mounts the remote resources shared by the NFS server.

❏ On the NFS server, the daemons that will run are mountd and nfsd.

❏ The files used on the NFS server are /etc/dfs/dfstab, /etc/dfs/sharetab, and /etc/rmtab.

❏ On the NFS client, the daemons that will run are statd and lockd.

❏ On the NFS client, the files used are /etc/vfstab and /etc/mnttab.

Making Resources Available and Unavailable for Mounting as Shared Resources

❏ The share command is used to make local resources available to be mounted remotely.

❏ *rw* stands for *read/write*.

❏ *ro* stands for *read-only*.

Using the /etc/dfs/dfstab File on an NFS Server to Enable Automatic Sharing of Resources

❏ The /etc/dfs/dfstab file can be edited to make resources available to remote clients, even after the server is booted.

❏ The NFS server daemons, mountd and nfsd, are started by running the /etc/init.d/nfs.server start script.

❏ Use the dfshares command to make sure the specified resource is available for mounting.

❏ The showmount *-e <hostname>* command displays all the available resources on the named NFS server.

❏ The NFS client uses the mount command to mount remotely shared resources locally.

❏ The umount command unmounts locally mounted files.

Using the /etc/vfstab File to Enable Persistent Mounting of Resources on an NFS Client

❏ The /etc/vfstab file is used to persistently mount local and remote resources.

❏ The mountall command with no arguments mounts all the resources listed in the /etc/vfstab file that have *yes* under Mount at boot.

❏ With the umountall command and no arguments, all mounted resources except root, /proc, /var, and /usr will be unmounted.

❏ The shareall command is used to share multiple resources.

❏ The unshareall command is used to unshare multiple resources.

SELF TEST

The following questions will help you measure your understanding of the material presented in this chapter. Read all the choices carefully because there might be more than one correct answer. Choose all correct answers for each question.

Understanding the Functions of NFS Servers and Clients

1. A machine that allows other machines to mount its file systems is serving which function?

   A. An NFS client

   B. An NFS server

   C. A share server

   D. An install server

2. Which of the following is not a daemon used by the NFS service?

   A. statd

   B. mountd

   C. nfsd

   D. smtpd

3. An administrator of an NFS client decides to start the NFS client daemons statd and lockd to mount a directory from an NFS server. What should the administrator do first?

   A. Run the /etc/nfs.client script with the *start* option.

   B. Nothing; the daemons will start automatically once the mount command is executed.

   C. Run the shareall command.

   D. Reboot the machine.

Making Resources Available and Unavailable for Mounting as Shared Resources

4. Which command is used to make resources available for mounting from an NFS server?

   A. The share command

   B. The mount command

   C. The permissions on the resources to be shared

   D. A directory under the root directory named netshare

5. How do you stop a resource from being shared?

   A. ushare

   B. unshare

   C. unshareall

   D. share *-stop*

Using the /etc/dfs/dfstab File on an NFS Server to Enable Automatic Sharing of Resources

6. Which file would a user edit to make a resource available for mounting by remote clients?

   A. The /etc/dfs/dfstab file

   B. The .dfstab file in the user's home directory

   C. The /etc/vfstab file

   D. The hidden /etc/.share file

7. A user has forgotten the resources that have been made available for mounting. Which command will show this information?

   A. echo $DISPLAY

   B. dfshares

   C. dfs *-local*

   D. more /etc/vfstab

8. A user wants to mount all the available resources on the network on his local machine. Which command will do this?

   A. mountall

   B. mount *-net*

   C. mount *-all*

   D. mount

Using the /etc/vfstab File to Enable Persistent Mounting of Resources on an NFS Client

9. A user has decided to mount a resource permanently. Which file needs to be edited?

   A. The /etc/dfs/dfstab file on the NFS server

   B. The /etc/vfstab file on the NFS client

    C. The /usr/vfstab file on the NFS client

    D. The /etc/rmtab file on the NFS server

10. Which option will a user add to the /etc/vfstab file to stop a mount process from continuously trying to mount a resource until the server responds?

    A. *hard*

    B. *yes*

    C. *soft*

    D. *bg*

11. If a user runs the umountall command at the command prompt, what will be the result?

    A. All files local and remote will be unmounted.

    B. All remote and local directories except root, /proc, /var, and /usr will be unmounted.

    C. Nothing; the command must specify local or remote directories.

    D. The system will reboot and ask which files to mount.

12. What is the command shareall used for?

    A. To share all the directories on a local machine to make backing up easier

    B. To share multiple resources as listed in /etc/dfstab

    C. To share one directory

    D. To share more than one directory

13. If a directory has read-only permissions set on it and the share command adds the *rw* option, which setting will be available to remote NFS clients?

    A. Read-only.

    B. Read/write.

    C. The user attempting to access the resource will be asked for a password.

    D. None; the conflicting settings will stop the resource from being mounted.

14. What is the best way for a user to remind himself or herself what a share is going to be used for?

    A. Mount the resource. A message will be displayed once the resource is mounted.

    B. Run the share command with the *-d* switch when creating the share and add a message.

    C. Run the dfshares command with the *-d* switch when creating the share and add a message.

    D. Keep a running text file containing a running list of all the shares and the reasons they were made available for mounting by NFS clients.

15. How would a user see a list of the resources available from an NFS server?

    A. Use the showmount command with the *-e* switch and the NFS server name.

    B. Use the showmount command with the *-a* switch.

    C. Use the showmountall command.

    D. Use the mount command and the NFS server's name.

LAB QUESTION

You are the system administrator of a new Solaris system. You have been asked to make a directory available for others to store and retrieve files. Only the users from the system *sgcommand* need read and write access to the files. The users from *sg2, sg3,* and *sg4* need only read access. The name of the server with the resource to be shared is *sg1*. The name of the directory to be shared is /export/home/survey. What are the steps necessary to complete this assignment?

SELF TEST ANSWERS

Understanding the Functions of NFS Servers and Clients

1. ☑ **B.** His machine will be an NFS server.

   ☒ A is incorrect because the machine sharing the resource is the server and the machine accessing the shared resource is the NFS client. C is incorrect because there is no such term as *share server*. D is incorrect because an install server is used during automated installation over a network.

2. ☑ **D.** smtpd is not a daemon used by the NFS service.

   ☒ A, B, and C are incorrect. Only smtp is not a daemon used by the NFS service.

3. ☑ **B.** There is no need to start the daemons manually.

   ☒ A is incorrect because there is no script called /etc/nfs.client. The NFS server daemons are started by running a script called /etc/init.d/nfs.server with the start command. C is incorrect because the shareall command refers to files listed in the /etc/dfs/dfstab file on the NFS server. D is an unnecessary step.

Making Resources Available and Unavailable for Mounting as Shared Resources

4. ☑ **A.** Using the share command, a user can make files available to be mounted remotely on other machines.

   ☒ B is incorrect because the mount command is used to mount files, not make them available for mounting. C is incorrect because the access permissions set on a file will not make them available to be mounted, and there is no shared permission. D is incorrect because the name of the file or its location has no bearing on its status as a shared resource.

5. ☑ **B.** The unshare command will stop sharing a resource.

   ☒ A is incorrect because there is no command called ushare. The command umount unmounts a resource that has been mounted locally by an NFS client. C is incorrect because the unshareall command makes all resources unavailable to NFS clients. D is incorrect because the share command is used to share resources, and there is no option in that command to stop sharing a resource.

Using the /etc/dfs/dfstab File on an NFS Server to Enable Automatic Sharing of Resources

6. ☑ **A.** This is the file that will make a resource available for mounting by remote clients. It has an advantage over simply using the share command in that the resources named in this file will remain available for mounting every time the system is booted.

☒   **B** is incorrect because there is no .dfstab file located in any home directory. **C** is incorrect because the /etc/vfstab file is used on an NFS client to mount resources automatically. **D** is incorrect because there is no hidden .share file.

7.   ☑   **B.** The dfshares command displays the local resources that are available for remote mounting.
☒   **A** is incorrect because it will show the environmental setting for the display variable and has nothing to do with the NFS resources. **C** is incorrect because there is no DFS command; DFS stands for *distributed file system* and refers to the commands available in sharing and mounting resources. **D** is incorrect because the contents of /etc/vfstab list the resources, local and remote, to be mounted at boot.

8.   ☑   **D.** However, each resource must be named individually, and the user must have created local mount points for each resource to be mounted locally. In addition, just because a resource is shared on a network, that doesn't mean every user has full access to it. The access permissions can be set to read-only.
☒   **A** is incorrect because mountall mounts all the contents already listed in the /etc/vfstab file; it does not search the network for available resources. **B** and **C** are incorrect because there is no *-all* or *-net* option on the mount command.

Using the /etc/vfstab File to Enable Persistent Mounting of Resources on an NFS Client

9.   ☑   **B.** Once the file /etc/vfstab is edited correctly, the named remote resource will be mounted to the local NFS client each time the client is booted.
☒   **A** is incorrect because the /etc/dfs/dfstab file is used by the server to make resources available. **C** is incorrect because the vfstab file is not located in the /usr directory. **D** is incorrect because the /etc/rmtab file is used by the mountd daemon on the NFS server to keep track of mounted resources.

10.   ☑   **C.** When *soft* is added under *options,* the client tries to mount the resource once. If the attempt fails, an error message is displayed.
☒   **B** is incorrect because the answer *yes* is available only under Mount at boot. If *yes* is added, the resource is available when the machine is booted. If *no* is listed, the resource won't be mounted at boot. **A** is incorrect because the specification *hard* causes the mount process to keep trying to access the named resource until the server responds. **D** is incorrect because *bg* is an option that tells the process to continue trying to mount a remote file in the background instead of doing it in the foreground, the default.

11.   ☑   **B.** The command umountall with no options will attempt to unmount all mounted resources except for the root, /proc, /var, and /usr directories.

☒ **A** is incorrect because not all the local directories will be unmounted. **C** is incorrect because the command runs with no options. **D** is incorrect because the umountall command does not change the system's run state.

12. ☑ **D**. The shareall command makes all the resources listed in the /etc/dfs/dfstab file available to be shared by remote NFS clients.
☒ **A** is incorrect because it reads the contents of only the /etc/dfs/dfstab file, not the entire file structure hierarchy. **B** is incorrect because the correct location of the file is /etc/dfs/dfstab, not /etc/dfstab. **C** is incorrect because the shareall command is used on multiple directories.

13. ☑ **A**. The access permissions set on the file locally take precedence over the permissions set by the share command.
☒ **B** is incorrect because the access options set by the share command can't change the directory permissions. **C** is incorrect because the NFS server validates the user by his or her username. **D** is incorrect because the resource will be shared but with the permissions set on the directory by the local file system.

14. ☑ **B**. When creating the share, add the -*d* option with a text message in quotation marks. This message is available when using the share command with no options.
☒ **A** is incorrect because mounting the resource will give the NFS client no option to create a message, and therefore no message will be displayed. **C** is incorrect because the dfshares command is used to see which resources are shared locally. Although **D** does provide a way to track the reasons for making a resource available, it is not the best way.

15. ☑ **A**. The showmount -e *<hostname>* command displays all the available resources on the named NFS server.
☒ **B** is incorrect because the showmount command with the -*a* switch displays the resources that are currently mounted and the hostname of each NFS client that has mounted the resources. **C** is incorrect because there is no showmountall command. **D** is incorrect because you must know the name of the shared resource to mount it.

LAB ANSWER

1. Edit the file /etc/dfs/dfstab on *sg1* by adding the following line:

```
share -F nfs -o rw=sgcommand, ro=sg2,sg3,sg4 /export/home/survey
```

Make sure the NFS servers and clients can resolve each other's names. Depending on how name resolution is handled on your network, this could mean editing the /etc/hosts files or adding the information to your DNS servers.

2. If this is the first time a resource has been shared on this system or if the NFS daemons aren't running, run this command:

```
# /etc/init.d/nfs.server start
```

By default, once a Solaris system enters runlevel 3, the NFS service will start. This is a configurable option, of course, but most admins would rather it started at boot time. Occasionally, due to network problems, CPU usage, or just cosmic rays, the NFS service could hang or crash. You can see if the NFS server daemons are running by using the commands

```
# ps -ef | grep mountd
```

and

```
# ps -ef | grep nfsd
```

Each command should show you that the NFS server process is running. If it is not, run the command

```
# /etc/init.d/nfs.server start
```

If you want to stop and start the services, use the *stop* option, then the *start* option, for example,

```
# /etc/init.d/nfs.server stop
# /etc/init.d/nfs.server start
```

3. Make sure the resource is available by running the dfshares command on the NFS server. You should be able to see the resource.

Solaris™
SUN® CERTIFIED SYSTEM ADMINISTRATOR

23
Using AutoFS

In today's complex internetworking world, all the resources a user might need are not typically stored on one fileserver. Resources that one user might need could be on a server on the local LAN, whereas another user's resources could be located on a server on a different continent. With resources being so widely geographically distributed, we need a way for users to get the resources they need, without having to manage the resources for them.

AutoFS is a client-side service that automatically mounts and unmounts network resources on demand, without the need for system administrator intervention. The AutoFS service, together with the automountd daemon, intercepts a user's request for a resource, searches the network for the location of the resource, and automatically mounts it. This whole process is transparent to the user. When the user is finished with the resource, the AutoFS service automatically dismounts the resource after a period of inactivity.

This chapter thoroughly covers the AutoFS service, the automount command, the automountd daemon, the map files that list all the network resources, and how AutoFS integrates with directory services such as Network Information Service (NIS) and Network Information Service Plus (NIS+). First, you'll learn about the benefits of using AutoFS. Then you'll be introduced to the various types of map files, which are read by the automountd daemon, and learn how to write your own automount maps. Finally, you'll learn about the timing of stopping and restarting the AutoFS services.

CERTIFICATION OBJECTIVE 23.01

Understanding the Benefits of Using the Automount Utility

AutoFS offers users many benefits. For instance, it mounts file systems automatically, without user or system administrator intervention, as well as automatically unmounting them after the user is finished. Another benefit is that the system automatically uses your network naming server environment so you can distribute file systems across your corporate network. Another benefit is that AutoFS can use *failover,* so a failed file system will not interrupt your users' work. Let's look at each benefit individually.

Automatic File System Mounting

One of the benefits of AutoFS is that file system mounting is done automatically, with no user or system administrator intervention.

When a user makes a request to an AutoFS file system (for example, when a user issues a cd, or change directory, command to an AutoFS directory), AutoFS intercepts this call and forwards it to the automountd daemon. The automountd daemon then mounts the resource and sends a reply back to AutoFS. AutoFS then allows the waiting user command to execute. This process is transparent to the user.

For example, you use the mount command to see the currently mounted file systems:

```
$ mount

/ on /dev/dsk/c0t3d0s0 read/write/setuid/largefiles on Mon Apr 23 13:16:34
2001
/proc on /proc read/write/setuid on Mon Apr 23 13:16:34 2001
/dev/fd on fd read/write/setuid on Mon Apr 23 13:16:34 2001
/tmp on swap read/write on Mon Apr 23 13:16:35 2001
```

Then you use the list directory command to see which directories are available in the /opt directory:

```
$ ls -la /opt

total 8
drwxrwxr-x    4 root        sys              512 Mar 22 21:38 .
drwxr-xr-x   27 root        root            1024 Apr 25 12:03 ..
drwxrwxr-x    4 root        sys              512 Mar 22 21:38 SUNWebnfs
drwxrwxr-x    3 root        sys              512 Mar 22 21:34 SUNWits
```

Even though /opt/bin does not exist when you do a directory listing on /opt, you issue a cd command into /opt/bin to invoke AutoFS and mount the directory automatically:

```
$ cd /opt/bin
```

You then issue a list directory command again on /opt and see which directories are available in /opt:

```
$ ls -la /opt

total 24
drwxrwxr-x    5 root        sys              512 Apr 29 12:53 .
```

```
drwxr-xr-x   27 root      root        1024 Apr 25 12:03 ..
drwxrwxr-x    3 root      bin         7680 Apr 21 19:07 bin
drwxrwxr-x    4 root      sys          512 Mar 22 21:38 SUNWebnfs
drwxrwxr-x    3 root      sys          512 Mar 22 21:34 SUNWits
```

The directory /opt/bin has been mounted automatically! To verify that the mount actually exists, you issue the mount command again:

```
$ mount
/ on /dev/dsk/c0t3d0s0 read/write/setuid/ on Mon Apr 23 13:16:34 2001
/proc on /proc read/write/setuid on Mon Apr 23 13:16:34 2001
/dev/fd on fd read/write/setuid on Mon Apr 23 13:16:34 2001
/tmp on swap read/write on Mon Apr 23 13:16:35 2001
/opt/bin on server1:/opt/bin read/write/remote on Sun Apr 29 12:54:06 2001
$
```

Simply issuing a cd command into an AutoFS file system causes the AutoFS file system to automatically mount the requested resource and allows the command to take place without any user intervention or knowledge of the mount.

Unmounting File Systems

Another benefit of AutoFS is that file systems unmount themselves automatically after a period of inactivity. This feature saves network bandwidth because you don't have NFS resources mounted all the time. It also saves CPU power on the NFS file server. This assures that resources are mounted only as needed and unmounted when no longer used.

Using Centralized Naming Services for Manageability

You can set up AutoFS to use network-naming services on your network (such as NIS/NIS+) and include the network maps. This is a great benefit because you can define resources across your whole network and not have to visit each machine to update the local maps.

Using Redundancy to Make File Systems Highly Available

You can configure AutoFS to use multiple servers for redundancy to provide failover for file systems. The failure of one individual file system will not prevent your users from accessing replicated information on another server, because AutoFS automatically uses another server if the first server does not respond.

exam
ⓦatch

There are four benefits to using AutoFS:

- File systems are mounted automatically.
- File systems are unmounted automatically after a period of inactivity.
- AutoFS uses centralized naming services for manageability.
- Redundancy can be used to make file systems highly available.

EXERCISE 23-1

Knowing the Layout of File Systems on Your System

The first step in configuring AutoFS is to discover the mount point structure of your system. This exercise takes you through the steps of finding out what is mounted on your system and which file systems are remote. This information will guide you to determine what you are sharing via NFS and what is already mounted both locally and remotely.

1. View the contents of your /etc/vfstab for the list of mounts that are mounted at boot:

```
# cat /etc/vfstab
```

Any remote NFS file system that is mounted automatically during bootup will be referenced here. Look for the NFS mount syntax of

```
server1:/usr/local        -        /usr/local      nfs      -        yes
rw,bg,hard,intr,timeo=15,retrans=10
```

2. See if you are automatically sharing any file systems through NFS. The /etc/dfs/dfstab file automatically shares any entry listed in this file:

```
# cat /etc/dfs/dfstab
```

If you are sharing any file systems, the syntax will be similar to this:

```
share -F nfs -o ro -d "/usr/local" /usr/local
```

You can also use the share command with no options to print the current shares on the system,

```
# share
```

which will produce output similar to this:

```
-      /usr/local    ro "/usr/local share"
-      /export/home  rw  "Home Directories"
```

3. Finally, view your currently mounted file system with the mount command:

```
# mount
```

This command outputs your currently mounted file systems. If any are remote, they will look similar to this:

```
/opt/bin on server1:/opt/bin read/write/remote
on Sun Apr 29 12:54:06 2001
```

The important things to look at are the *server:/pathname* entry and the keyword *remote,* which signifies that the mount is a remotely located resource.

This exercise covered ways to discover whether you are mounting any remote file systems automatically, any file systems that you are sharing to the network, and your currently local and remotely mounted file systems. This exercise helps you in configuring AutoFS by knowing the layout of the file systems on your system.

CERTIFICATION OBJECTIVE 23.02

Defining the Types of Automount Maps

AutoFS uses text files called *maps* that are stored as both local files on the system and networkwide; such is the case with NIS and NIS+. These text files contain mounting information that the AutoFS service uses to mount resources automatically. There are four kinds of maps: master, direct, indirect, and special.

The Components of AutoFS

AutoFS has three components: the automount command, which runs at system startup and creates the initial set of mounts; the AutoFS kernel file system, which listens for mount requests; and the automountd daemon, which mounts and unmounts file systems. Let's examine each portion of the AutoFS system.

The automount Command

The automount command first runs at system startup, reads the master map, and creates the initial set of mounts. At system startup, the automount command first runs from the /etc/init.d/autofs script. This script also starts the automountd daemon. The automount command is independent of the automountd daemon, which makes it possible to directly modify maps without restarting the automountd daemon.

The AutoFS File System

The AutoFS file system is a kernel file system that listens for requests for mounts. The AutoFS file system then invokes the automountd daemon to handle the mount if it receives a request for a mount.

The automountd Daemon

The daemon handles the mounting and unmounting of file systems. This daemon is started from the /etc/init.d/autofs script along with the automount command. The AutoFS file system notifies the automountd daemon when it needs to perform a mount or an unmount. The automountd daemon then mounts or unmounts the resource and sends a message back notifying the AutoFS kernel file system.

How AutoFS Works

It is important to understand how AutoFS functions. AutoFS compares the information contained within maps to the information stored in the mount table /etc/mnttab:

1. At system boot time, the /etc/init.d/autofs script starts the automountd daemon and calls the automount command.

2. The automount command reads the master maps and creates the initial set of mount points. For example, automount creates the mount point /home, defined in auto_master. The automount command also compares the information in the maps with the information contained in the system mount table /etc/mnttab and updates it as necessary.

3. The AutoFS file system listens for requests on these initial mount points. On receiving a request, AutoFS holds the request and calls the automountd daemon to mount the resource.

4. The automountd daemon searches all the maps for the mount point location and mounts the remote resource specified in the map.

5. The automountd daemon then sends a message back to AutoFS, and AutoFS allows the waiting command to execute.

6. The AutoFS file system calls the automountd daemon to unmount the file system after a period of inactivity.

Master Maps

The auto_master *master map* contains a listing of all direct, indirect, and special maps, and is the first map read by the automount command and the automountd daemon when the system starts up. This map contains all the references to direct and indirect maps, as well as a few built-in special maps.

The master map has the following syntax, as defined in Table 23-1:

```
mount-point    map-name  [mount-options]
```

TABLE 23-1	Command	Description
Syntax of Master Maps	*mount-point*	The full absolute pathname of a directory.
	map-name	The filename of the map. Local files are also assumed to be in the /etc directory if the map name is not preceded by a slash (/).
	mount-options	An optional comma-separated list of mounting options. Any NFS option can be used as an option in AutoFS.

The following shows a typical auto_master map file:

```
# Master map for automounter
#
+auto_master
/net       -hosts       -nosuid,nobrowse
/home         auto_home       -nobrowse
/xfn       -xfn
/-      auto-direct
```

Any line starting with a pound sign (#) is a comment and is ignored by AutoFS. The +auto_master statement includes the name service auto_master file, such as the one exported by NIS or NIS+. Without the plus sign (+) in front of a filename, the statement refers to a local file. For example, if you wanted to include another local file in the master map configuration, you would add the path to the file, such as /path/ to/filename. The rest of the master map contains all the direct, indirect, and special maps.

Direct Maps

A *direct map* contains both the client mount point (the local mount point) and the remote file system to be mounted. This structure differs from that of an indirect map, which contains the absolute mount point in the master map file (/etc/auto_master) and the relative mount point in the indirect map file.

Direct maps have the following syntax, as defined in Table 23-2.

```
key   [mount-options]   location
```

The following is an example of a direct map:

TABLE 23-2	Command	Description
Syntax of Direct Maps	*key*	The pathname of the mount point on the local system. This is where the resources will be mounted.
	mount-options	The options you want to apply to the mount. An example is read-only. This field is optional. Any NFS option can be used as an option in AutoFS.
	location	The location of the remote resource. The field follows the *servername:/ path/ to/ resource* format.

```
# /etc/auto_direct direct map
#
/usr/local    -ro    blue:/export/usr/local
/opt                 red:/export/opt
```

This map specifies that, whenever a request is made to access /usr/local on the local system, the AutoFS file system notifies the automountd daemon, and the automountd daemon automatically mounts the file system /export/usr/local on the server *blue*. The file system /export/opt is mounted automatically from the server *red*.

exam
Ⓦⓐⓣⓒⓗ
Remember that a direct map contains both the absolute pathname of the local mount point and the remote server and pathname.

Indirect Maps

Indirect maps are referenced in the master map. An indirect map contains the beginning absolute pathname of the mount point in auto_master and contains the relative pathname of the mount point in the indirect map. For example, auto_master contains the /home absolute path, and the indirect map auto_home contains the user directory *george*, thereby creating the path /home/george for the user.

Indirect maps have the following syntax, as defined in Table 23-3.

```
key  [mount-options]  location
```

TABLE 23-3	Command	Description
Syntax of Indirect Maps	*key*	A simple directory name (no slashes). This name is added to the mountpoint defined in the master map.
	mount-options	The options you want to apply to the mount—for example, read-only. This field is optional. Any NFS options can be used as an option in AutoFS.
	location	The location of the remote resource. The field follows the servername:/path/to/resource format.

An example of an indirect map is /etc/auto_home. Look at how this map is defined in the /etc/auto_master master map here:

```
# Master map for automounter
#
+auto_master
/net        -hosts         -nosuid,nobrowse
/home       auto_home          -nobrowse
/xfn        -xfn
/-          auto_direct    -ro
```

Here, /home is the beginning mount point defined in /etc/auto_master. All relative directories contained in /etc/auto_home mount from below this directory. Because all files not prepended with a slash (/) are assumed to be in the /etc directory, the statement auto_home refers to the /etc/auto_home file.

The following is a typical indirect /etc/auto_home file:

```
# Home directory map for the automounter
#
george      server1:/export/home/george
sherry      server2:/export/home/sherry
+auto_home
```

In this example, /etc/auto_master defines the initial mount point as /home, so George's home directory is mounted as /home/george, because an indirect map's mount point is always defined as relative from the mount point defined in /etc/auto_master.

exam
Watch

Indirect maps contain only the local mount point relative to the absolute pathname contained in master maps.

on the
Job

Home directories are the most common AutoFS resource to mount. However, each user's workstation auto_home file needs to be edited to add the user's home directory and every other home directory for every other user.

A better way would be to edit and include the NIS or NIS+ auto_home map, which is disseminated throughout the network. Then you only have to edit the NIS/NIS+ auto_home file for every user you have on the network.

An even better way to handle this task is through string substitutions in the NIS/NIS+ auto_home file. You can use the asterisk (*) and the ampersand (&) to substitute keys. The following code shows an example of using asterisks and ampersands as substitution characters.

```
# Home directory map for the automounter
#
*        server1:/export/home/&
```

The asterisk (*) says that, for any directory underneath /home (remember, because this is an indirect map, /home is defined in the auto_master file), mount the corresponding remote resource. The ampersand (&) says that, for any key, substitute its value for the ampersand.

For example, if the user george logged in to his workstation, his home directory /home/george would automatically be mounted from server1:/export/home/george.

Using this method, you will never have to edit auto_home maps when you add users (providing that the remote server never changes).

Special Maps

Special maps are stored in the /etc/auto_master master map file. Some typical special map files are the /net map, which maps the hosts database to the /net directory, and the /xfn map, which maps a Federated Naming Service (FNS) namespace to the /xfn directory.

The /net Map

The special /net map statement includes the local hosts database in the AutoFS configuration. Systems defined in the hosts databases that have exported file systems are accessible under the /net directory.

The /xfn Map

The special /xfn map provides the inclusion of resources from the FNS namespace.

FROM THE CLASSROOM

Default Directory for Home Directories

Many people ask me why the default location for home directories in Solaris is /export/home instead of simply /home, as in other UNIX systems. They also note that /home exists, but nothing is inside it, nor can they delete it. This is because /home is a directory created by AutoFS and defined in /etc/auto_master. AutoFS creates the master mount point if it doesn't exist, and it won't allow it to be deleted. Solaris assumes that you want to mount home directories in /home from /export/ home using AutoFS, so that is why the default directory for home directories is /export/home.

—*Rob Sletten, SCSA, MCSE, CCNA*

EXERCISE 23-2

Creating a User and a Home Directory

The most common use of AutoFS is to transparently mount user home directories across a network. This exercise shows you how to configure the auto_home indirect map to automatically mount a user's home directory upon logging in to the system.

1. Create a new user on the system. The user's home directory should be set to /home/user1. Create the user's home directory in /export/home:

```
# adduser -d /home/user1 user1
# mkdir /export/home/user1
```

2. The indirect map /etc/auto_home is already set up in /etc/auto_master, so all you need to do is edit the /etc/auto_home file and set up the home directory entries. Using an editor, add the following to /etc/auto_home:

```
user1    -rw  localhost:/export/home/user1
```

3. Remember that, because indirect maps are read every time a mount occurs, you do not need to restart AutoFS after you edit the /etc/auto_home file. Log in as this new user using the substitute user command as root:

```
# su - user1
```

4. Now that you are logged in as user1, verify that your home directory is /home/user1:

```
$ pwd
/home/user1
$
```

5. Run the mount command to see that the /export/home/user1 directory is mounted as /home/user1:

```
$ /sbin/mount
(output omitted)
/home/user1 on /export/home/user1 read/write/setuid/dev=1980000
   on Fri May  4 10:40:08 2001
```

This exercise showed you how to create a user and a home directory in /export/ home and how to automatically mount that home directory using AutoFS under the mount point /home whenever the user logs in.

CERTIFICATION OBJECTIVE 23.03

Setting Up Automount to Read a Direct Map

This section teaches you how to set up AutoFS to read a direct map. The first step in this process is modifying the master map /etc/auto_master to add the direct map. The second step is creating and populating the new direct map; finally, the third step is restarting the AutoFS service.

Editing the /etc/auto_master Master Map

First, you need to add the direct map statement to the master map file /etc/ auto_master. You do so by adding the direct map statement to the existing /etc/auto_master map file, as shown here:

```
# Master map for automounter
#
+auto_master
```

```
/net      -hosts        -nosuid,nobrowse
/home      auto_home        -nobrowse
/xfn      -xfn
/-        auto_direct       -ro
```

The /- statement says not to associate any mount point in /etc/auto_master with the direct map. This means both the local mount point and the remote directory are specified solely in the direct map.

The auto_direct statement refers to the /etc/auto_direct file that must be created. Because there is no slash (/) in front of the filename, the file is assumed to be in the /etc directory. The filename auto_direct is used by convention and is only a guideline.

Creating and Editing /etc/auto_direct Direct Map

Now you need to create the direct map /etc/auto_direct and populate the map with mount points and remote resources. The following is a typical auto_direct file:

```
/usr/local/bin       -ro: green:/export/usr/local/bin
/usr/local/share     -ro: blue:/export/usr/local/share
/usr/local    -ro   \
  /bin          green:/export/usr/local/bin
  /share        blue:/export/usr/local/share
/opt/bin    -ro    red:/export/opt/bin \
          black:/export/opt/bin
```

Notice that, in the first statement, you mount /usr/local/bin from the server *green* and /usr/local/share from the server *blue*. Use the backslash (\) to separate long lines.

The second statement mounts the /opt/bin directory to the server *red*, and if it is unavailable, mounts it from the server *black*. You could also state the mount this way if the two servers, red and black, have the same exported path:

```
/opt/bin  -ro  red,black:/export/opt/bin
```

on the job

You probably do not want to list multiple remote servers for resources that are read/write because it allows the files to be edited and thus not be consistent across the mirrors. It's best to configure replica servers as read-only.

on the job

Specifying multiple servers—for example, server1:/pathname server2:/ pathname—is a way to introduce failover in AutoFS. AutoFS automatically uses another remote server if one becomes unavailable or doesn't respond to the NFS mount.

You can influence the order of selection of these servers by using the concept of weighting, which tells AutoFS in what order to try different servers.

You specify weighting by enclosing a number in parenthesis after the server name, for example,

```
/opt/bin  -ro  red(1):/export/opt/bin black(2):/export/opt/bin \
               yellow(3):/export/opt/bin
```

This tells AutoFS to use the server red *first, and if it's unavailable, to use the server* black *and finally the server* yellow.

Restarting the AutoFS Service

Because you have modified the master and direct maps, you need to restart the AutoFS service. You can do this several ways. One way is to issue the command

```
# automount
```

This command tells the automount command to scan the master and direct maps for new mounts or to remove old mounts that no longer exist. The next section, "Determining When the Automount Daemon Should Be Restarted," goes into further detail on the various options of restarting the AutoFS service.

on the Job

You can use variables in your maps to provide client-specific mount points. A variable defined in a map is prepended with a dollar sign ($) in front of the variable name. The variable names are listed in Table 23-4.

TABLE 23-4	Variable	Description	Derived From
Variable Names and Descriptions	ARCH	Architecture type	/usr/kvm/arch
	CPU	Processor type	uname *-p*
	HOST	Hostname	uname *-n*
	OSNAME	Operating system name	uname *-s*
	OSREL	Operating system release	uname *-r*
	OSVERS	Operating system version	uname *-v*

The following is an example of an auto_direct map using variables.

```
# /etc/auto_direct direct map
#
/var/spool/pkg  -ro  patchserver1:/export/patches/$CPU/$OSREL
```

In this example, a Solaris SPARC client substitutes the variables $CPU and $OSREL for sparc and 5.9, respectively. The system is using the processor type and operating system release variables to determine the remote mount pathname of the location of Solaris patches. The system automatically mounts the directory containing the patches for the processor architecture and operating system release.

Variables are most effective using AutoFS maps that are distributed over NIS/NIS+, because you can write a single entry for a mount point that can be used by many systems with differing architectures.

EXERCISE 23-3

Setting Up Direct Maps

In this exercise, you add a direct map entry to your auto_master map, share your /tmp directory, and create a direct map to mount your /tmp directory to an AutoFS mount point of /temp. This exercise allows you to practice setting up direct maps as part of your certification process.

1. Edit your auto_master file and include the auto_direct file by adding this line:

    ```
    /-  auto_direct      -ro
    ```

2. Allow your /tmp directory to be mounted via NFS with the command share /tmp, and verify that the directory is shared with the share command, again with no arguments:

    ```
    #share /tmp
    # share
    ```

3. Create the auto_direct file and add the direct map /temp -ro localhost:/tmp:

    ```
    # echo "/temp  -ro  localhost:/tmp" >>>> /etc/auto_direct
    ```

4. Restart AutoFS using the automount -v command or with the start/stop script:

    ```
    # automount -v
    # /etc/init.d/autofs stop ; /etc/init.d/autofs start
    ```

5. Notice that you did not create the AutoFS mount point /temp. AutoFS creates the directory if it doesn't exist when the auto_master file is reread by Step 4. Verify that the mount point /temp exists by doing a directory listing on the root file system (/):

```
# ls -la /
```

6. Issue the mount command to see currently mounted file systems:

```
# mount
```

7. Change directory into the AutoFS mount point /temp using the cd command:

```
# cd /temp
```

8. Issue the mount command again to see the currently mounted file systems. /temp should be mounted now:

```
#mount
(output omitted)
/temp on /tmp read only/setuid/dev=2 on Fri May 4 09:24:33 2001
```

This exercise showed you how to edit your auto_master master map to include the auto_direct direct map, share your /tmp directory, and write the auto_direct map to configure a mount point called /temp. By accessing the mount point /temp, the temporary directory /tmp was automatically mounted by AutoFS.

CERTIFICATION OBJECTIVE 23.04

Determining When the Automount Daemon Should Be Restarted

Because the master and direct maps are read when the AutoFS service starts, modifying these files requires the service to be restarted.

Modifying indirect maps does not require the service to be restarted because the indirect map is read-only when a mount occurs in the key directory specified in the master map /etc/auto_master—for example, /home/username.

There are several ways to restart AutoFS. These include using the automount command and using the startup/shutdown script /etc/init.d/autofs. In addition, this section discusses modifying the default timeout for unmounting of directories.

Restarting via the automount Command

After a master or direct map is modified, you can issue the automount command to force AutoFS to reread the master and direct maps and compare them to what is already mounted. The automount command compares the mounts in the maps with the information contained in the system mount table /etc/mnttab and updates it as necessary.

Table 23-5 provides details of the syntax of the automount command, which is as follows:

```
automount   [-t duration] [-v]
```

Restarting via the /etc/init.d/autofs Startup Script

The /etc/init.d/autofs script is called during system startup and shutdown. This script can take two parameters, *start* and *stop*. To start the AutoFS service:

```
# /etc/init.d/autofs start
```

To stop the AutoFS service:

```
# /etc/init.d/autofs stop
```

TABLE 23-5	Option	Description
Syntax of the automount Command	*-t duration*	Duration (in seconds) that a file system is mounted as idle before it is automatically unmounted. The default is 600 seconds (10 minutes).
	-v	Verbose. Reports on all new mounts and unmounts.

This script also exists as /etc/rc2.d/S74autofs and /etc/rc0.d/K41autofs. When the system enters runlevel 2, the /etc/rc2.d/S74autofs script is run with the start parameter to start the AutoFS service, and when the system enters runlevel 0, the /etc/rc0.d/K41autofs script is run with the stop parameter to stop the AutoFS service. Let's take a look at the script:

```
#!/sbin/sh
#
# Copyright (c) 1993-1998 by Sun Microsystems, Inc.
# All rights reserved.
#
#ident   "@(#)autofs     1.6     98/12/14 SMI"
case "$1" in
'start')
        /usr/lib/autofs/automountd </dev/null >/dev/msglog 2>>&1
        /usr/sbin/automount &
        ;;

'stop')
        /sbin/umountall -F autofs
        /usr/bin/pkill -x -u 0 automountd
        ;;
*)
        echo "Usage: $0 { start | stop }"
        ;;
esac
exit 0
```

Note that the script contains a start section and a stop section and executes the corresponding section depending on the parameter passed to the script manually or at system startup or shutdown.

exam
ⓦatch

AutoFS must be restarted using the automount command or executing the startup script after modifying any master or direct map. Indirect maps are read only when the automountd daemon needs to read the map to perform a mount, so modification of an indirect map does not require a restart.

Modifying the Default Idle Timeout Value

The default time that resources will be automatically dismounted after being idle is 600 seconds (10 minutes). Sometimes, you might need to modify this time according to the needs of your users and network.

Issuing the automount command with the *-t* duration parameter changes the default timeout value. For example,

```
$ automount -t 300
```

changes the default timeout value to 300 seconds (5 minutes).

To permanently change this variable after the system restarts, you need to modify the startup script /etc/rc2.d/S74autofs and change the /usr/sbin/automount & statement in the start portion of the script to /usr/sbin/automount *-t* 300 &:

```
(beginning omitted)

'start')
        /usr/lib/autofs/automountd </dev/null >/dev/msglog 2>>&1
        /usr/sbin/automount -t 300 &
        ;;

(end omitted)
```

Troubleshooting

Problems can occur when you are using AutoFS. The following shows some tips you might need when you're troubleshooting AutoFS.

SCENARIO & SOLUTION	
What if AutoFS is not including the NIS auto_master and auto_home maps?	1. Make sure +auto_master and +auto_home are included in your local maps. 2. Make sure the NIS maps have been updated on the NIS master server (cd /var/yp ; make all). 3. Make sure /etc/nsswitch.conf includes NIS on your files name server switch.

What if AutoFS is not automatically mounting your home directory?	Make sure your home directory appears in the /etc/auto_home map. For example,
	
	`username`
	`servername:/export/home/username`

What if AutoFS does not provide feedback when you restart it using the automount command?	Use the *-v* (verbose) switch and automount will report all mounts and unmounts.

SCENARIO & SOLUTION

What if when you try to stop the AutoFS service using the /etc/init.d/autofs script, you get an error message that says a mount is busy?	Make sure no processes or users are using the mount point.
What if AutoFS will not work?	Verify that the automountd daemon is running by executing this command: `ps -ef	grep automountd.`  Stop and start the AutoFS service by executing this command: `/etc/init.d/autofs start.`
What if when you cd to an AutoFS mount point, the system gives you a "Not found" error?	1. Make sure your syntax is correct in your maps. 2. Restart AutoFS.

EXERCISE 23-4

Stopping and Restarting the AutoFS Service

In this exercise, you restart the AutoFS service and change the idle timeout so you will be able to see automatic dismounting of the file systems. Then you start and stop the AutoFS service using the startup script /etc/init.d/autofs.

1. On your system, verify that AutoFS is running with this command:

   ```
   # ps -ef | grep automountd
   ```

2. Restart AutoFS using the automount -v command and change the timeout parameter to 10 seconds:

   ```
   # automount -t 10 -v
   ```

3. From the previous exercise, mount the AutoFS mount point /temp by issuing the cd command into the /temp directory:

   ```
   # cd /temp
   ```

4. Verify that the mount has occurred using the mount command:

   ```
   # mount
   (output omitted)
   /temp on /tmp read only/setuid/dev=2 on Fri May 4 09:50:33 2001
   ```

5. Leave the /temp file system by using the cd command to your home directory:

```
# cd /
```

6. After a period of inactivity, the /temp file system automatically dismounts itself. The period of time could vary from 10 seconds upward, depending on your system. Practice starting and stopping the AutoFS service using the /etc/init.d/autofs script:

```
#/etc/init.d/autofs stop
# /etc/init.d autofs start
```

This exercise showed you how to stop and restart the AutoFS service with the automount command and the /etc/init.d/autofs script, and you learned how changing the mount idle timeout affects the unmounting of shares by AutoFS.

CERTIFICATION SUMMARY

In this chapter, you learned that AutoFS is a client-side service that has the ability to mount and unmount file systems on demand, use network-naming services, and provide redundancy and failover for file systems.

You also learned about the three components of AutoFS—the automount command, the AutoFS kernel file system, and the automountd daemon—and how AutoFS performs its functions. You also learned how to configure AutoFS through indirect and direct maps and how to restart the AutoFS service.

TWO-MINUTE DRILL

Understanding the Benefits of Using the Automount Utility

❏ One of the benefits of AutoFS is that file systems are mounted on demand.

❏ File systems are automatically unmounted after an idle timeout.

❏ Name servers such as NIS and NIS+ can be used with AutoFS to include network resources automatically.

❏ Redundancy can be used to make file systems highly available.

Defining the Types of Automount Maps

❏ There are four types of maps: master, direct, indirect, and special.

❏ Master maps are the first maps that are read by the automounter.

❏ Direct maps always contain both the local mount point and the remote resource.

❏ Indirect maps always contain the local mount point relative to the mount point contained in the master map.

❏ Special maps point to the hosts database or to FNS.

Setting Up Automount to Read a Direct Map

❏ The /- entry in the auto_master file states that the local mount points are stored in the direct map rather than the master map.

❏ Editing a direct map requires restarting AutoFS.

❏ Multiple remote servers can be specified by implementing failover.

Determining When the Automount Daemon Should Be Restarted

❏ AutoFS can be restarted using the automount command.

❏ The /etc/init.d/autofs script can be used to start AutoFS.

❏ Editing a master map requires restarting AutoFS.

❏ Editing a direct map requires restarting AutoFS.

❏ Editing an indirect map does not require restarting AutoFS.

SELF TEST

The following questions will help you measure your understanding of the material presented in this chapter. Read all the choices carefully because there might be more than one correct answer. Choose all correct answers for each question.

Understanding the Benefits of Using the Automount Utility

1. AutoFS is which kind of service?

    A. A service that runs over NIS/NIS+

    B. A client-side service

    C. A server-side service

    D. A type of name resolution

2. While explaining to your managers why your company should implement AutoFS, which valid reasons would you give them? (Choose all that apply.)

    A. AutoFS conserves network bandwidth.

    B. User home directories can be consolidated onto home directory servers that are easier for system administrators to back up.

    C. AutoFS needs to be configured only on the server for it to work.

    D. You can use your existing NIS+ name service to distribute file systems throughout your network.

    E. Users will be able to pick and choose the file systems to which they want to connect.

Defining the Types of Automount Maps

3. Which type of map is auto_home?

    A. Master

    B. Special

    C. Direct

    D. Indirect

4. A user calls you to complain that she receives a "No directory" error message when she logs in to her computer. She also cannot find any of her files. You know that her home directory is

located on a home directory server, not her local workstation. When you log in to her workstation, which of the following map files do you see or check?

A. The direct map auto_home

B. The indirect map auto_direct

C. The /etc/hosts file

D. The /etc/passwd file

E. The indirect map auto_home

Setting Up Automount to Read a Direct Map

5. Which are the correct entries in a direct map? (Choose all that apply.)

A. share -ro server1:/export/share

B. /usr/share -rw server1,server2:/export/share

C. /- -ro server1:/export/home

D. /share server1:/export/share server2:/export/share

6. A user calls you and says that he cannot access the man pages on his system. You have a man page server located in your network. Which of the following is the best way to give him access to the man page server?

A. Tell him to Telnet to the man page server and access the man pages from there.

B. Configure his workstation to automatically mount the man page server using NIS.

C. Configure his workstation to automatically mount the man page server using a direct map.

D. Configure his workstation to automatically mount the man page server using a special map.

7. Which of the following are components of the AutoFS service? (Choose all the apply.)

A. automountd

B. /etc/hosts

C. NIS

D. automount

E. NFS

F. The AutoFS kernel file system

8. Which of the following maps contains all the direct and indirect map names?

   A. auto_home

   B. auto_master

   C. auto_direct

   D. auto_share

   E. autofs

Determining When the Automount Daemon Should Be Restarted

9. Under which of the following circumstances would you need to run the automount command to restart AutoFS?

   A. Deletion to the /etc/auto_home file

   B. Addition to the /etc/hosts file

   C. Addition to the /etc/auto_master file

   D. All of the above

10. A junior system administrator calls you and states that he cannot get a resource, located on a different server, to mount. He states he has edited the /etc/auto_direct file located on the system he is working on to include the local mount point and the remote server and pathname. What should he do to troubleshoot the problem? (Choose all that apply.)

   A. Run the automount -v command.

   B. Reboot the system.

   C. Make sure the remote server is actually sharing the resource.

   D. Edit /etc/auto_direct on the remote server.

   E. Issue the /etc/init.d/autofs restart command.

LAB QUESTION

You are a UNIX system administrator for an architectural firm. The firm needs to distribute an NFS shared directory of files containing client diagrams located on a file server called *archserver1* to approximate a client UNIX workstation. You currently need to mount the shared directory /export/share/archfiles to the client mount point of /usr/share/archfiles. Outline the steps necessary to perform this action.

SELF TEST ANSWERS

Understanding the Benefits of Using the Automount Utility

1. ☑ **B.** AutoFS is a client-side service that runs on the local system and mounts remote file systems.
   ☒ **A** is incorrect because AutoFS does not exclusively run over NIS/NIS+. **C** is incorrect because AutoFS is not a server-side service. **D** is incorrect because AutoFS is not a type of name resolution.

2. ☑ **A, B, and D.** AutoFS conserves network bandwidth by unmounting file systems when they're not needed. User home directories can be consolidated on file servers and mounted automatically by AutoFS when a user logs in, instead of having the user's home directory stored on the user's workstation and having to back up each workstation. You can use AutoFS over your existing network naming service.
   ☒ **C** is incorrect because AutoFS is a client-side service, not a server-side service. **E** is incorrect because the user does not choose which server to connect to; mounting of file systems is transparent to the user.

Defining the Types of Automount Maps

3. ☑ **D.** The /etc/auto_home map is an indirect map.
   ☒ **A** is incorrect because auto_home is not a master map. **B** is incorrect because auto_home is not a special map. **C** is incorrect because auto_home is not a direct map.

4. ☑ **E.** The auto_home indirect map contains a listing of her home directory.
   ☒ **A** is incorrect because auto_home is an indirect map, not a direct map. **B** is incorrect because auto_direct is a direct map. **C** is incorrect because /etc/hosts contains a list of hostnames and IP addresses of other systems on the network. **D** is incorrect because, although the /etc/passwd file does contain the pathname of her home directory, it does not tell you why her directory isn't being mounted when she logs in.

Setting Up Automount to Read a Direct Map

5. ☑ **B and D.** Direct maps have the syntax of the absolute pathname, mount-options, and location.
   ☒ **A** is incorrect because *share* is a relative mount point. **C** is incorrect because /- is used only in master maps.

6. ☑ C. Man pages are best mounted using a direct map.
   ☒ A would work, but it is incorrect because it's not the *best* way to access man pages. **B** is incorrect because AutoFS is used to mount remote directories. **D** is incorrect because special maps are not commonly used to mount man page directories.

7. ☑ **A, D,** and **F.** The AutoFS service has three parts: the automountd daemon, the AutoFS kernel file system, and the automount command.
   ☒ **B, C,** and **E** are incorrect because they are not part of the AutoFS service.

8. ☑ **B.** The master map auto_master contains a listing of all direct and indirect maps.
   ☒ **A** is incorrect because auto_home is an indirect map. **C** is incorrect because it is a direct map. **D** is incorrect because auto_share does not exist. **E** is incorrect because AutoFS is a kernel file system.

Determining When the Automount Daemon Should Be Restarted

9. ☑ **C.** Addition to the /etc/auto_master file. The master map is read only during startup of the AutoFS service, thereby necessitating a restart of the service to reread this file.
   ☒ **A** is incorrect because /etc/auto_home is an indirect map. **B** is incorrect because the /etc/hosts database is a special map. **D** is incorrect because not all of the answers are correct.

10. ☑ **A, B,** and **C.** Issuing the automount *-v* command restarts the AutoFS service. Rebooting the system also restarts the AutoFS service, and the remote system does actually have to share the resource via NFS before another system can mount it via AutoFS.
    ☒ **D** is incorrect because AutoFS is a client-side service, not a server-side service, so nothing has to be done on the remote system besides sharing the resource. **E** is incorrect because the /etc/init.d/autofs script takes only *start* and *stop* as parameters.

LAB ANSWER

There are many ways to give users access to NFS shared directories. The best way is to use AutoFS and tell your users to access that directory. The steps to accomplish this task may include the following:

1. Make sure the directory on the server *archserver1* is shared out by NFS:

   ```
   # share
   ```

2. Edit the auto_master master map on the client workstation and add the following auto_direct map statement to auto_master:

   ```
   /-    auto_direct    -ro
   ```

3. Create the /etc/auto_direct file on the client workstation and add the following contents:

   ```
   /usr/share/archfiles  -ro  archserver1:/export/share/archfiles
   ```

4. Restart AutoFS on the client workstation by issuing the automount command, restarting via the /etc/init.d/autofs script, or rebooting the system:

   ```
   # automount
   ```

5. Issue a cd command into /usr/share/archfiles on the client workstation and verify that the mount occurred:

   ```
   # cd /usr/share/archfiles
   ```

6. Verify the mount using the mount command:

   ```
   # mount
   ```

Solaris™
SUN® CERTIFIED SYSTEM ADMINISTRATOR

24

Working with the Cache File System

CERTIFICATION OBJECTIVES

One of the drawbacks of network storage is that gaining access to resources that are stored across the network increases the load that your network has to carry. Every day, the network is forced to carry more and more traffic, applications, voice, and video. Performance suffers when the network cannot keep up with the increasing amount of traffic required to travel over it. As a result, users complain about how long it takes to get their data and run their applications. There must be a simple way to improve their data access time.

CacheFS is a client-side service that caches network stored files and directories locally on your system and improves the access times of slow CD-ROM devices. Using CacheFS, you can decrease the load on the network, improve the response time of your file servers, and improve the server's scalability. Your users will see a dramatic speed increase in terms of accessing their frequently used files and applications, as well as the additional ability to access them across slow links such as dialup lines.

This chapter discusses the CacheFS file system in detail and shows you how to set up a cache file system, check the status and perform consistency checking of CacheFS, set up logging of CacheFS, do integrity checking, and tear down and delete a CacheFS file system.

CERTIFICATION OBJECTIVE 24.01

Configuring the Cache File System in an Existing Client/Server Environment

The CacheFS system is a client-side service. It works by caching to a local cache directory the user's frequently used files and applications that are stored on a Network File System (NFS) file server or local CD-ROM. Once these files and applications are loaded in the cache directory, any subsequent access to the data will result in very fast access times as the CacheFS file system uses the cached data.

The CacheFS works like this:

1. The cache directory is created on the local system using the cfsadmin *-c* command. This directory holds all the cached data.

2. The remote NFS directory or local CD-ROM is mounted to the mount point of the cached file system. This is the mount point at which the user will access the data.

3. The user accesses the data in the mount point of the cache.

4. CacheFS retrieves the data for the user and copies the data to the cache directory.

5. Any subsequent requests for the data will come directly from the data stored in the cache directory.

Before you learn about the configuration of CacheFS, you need to know a few terms:

- **Back file system**   The real file system that is being cached. For example, the NFS system server1:/usr/local.

- **Back file system type**   The file system type that is being cached. The possible types are NFS or High Sierra System (HSFS) for CD-ROMs.

- **Front file system**   The local file system where the cache will live.

- **Cache file system**   The local mount point of the resource to be cached. For example, the back file system server1:/usr/local is mounted to the cache file system /usr/local.

- **Cache directory**   The directory in which the cache data will be stored. For example, /var/cache contains all the data that is cached from the cache file system /usr/local.

It is important to understand these terms because they are used extensively throughout this chapter in text and command syntax, as well as on the exam and on the job.

Creating the Initial Cache Directory

The first step in configuring a cache file system is creating the directory in which all the cached data will be stored. This point is where the frequently accessed data will be stored. This directory can hold multiple cache file systems. Users normally don't directly access this directory, although as a system administrator, you need to access this directory to perform consistency checking, statistical analysis, and maintenance.

You use the cfsadmin command to create the cache directory and set up the file structure. Table 24-1 defines the syntax for creating a cache directory, which is as follows:

```
cfsadmin  -c  [ -o cache-options]  cache-directory
```

This directory need not exist because it is created by the cfsadmin command. You will receive an error message from cfsadmin if you attempt to create a cache directory on an existing directory.

For example, to create a cache directory called /cache, perform these commands as root:

```
# cfsadmin -c /cache
```

After you create a cache directory, you should check to make sure that it was created successfully. You can use the cfsadmin -l command to check on the cache directory. You will see this command later in the chapter, in the section "Verifying That Mounting Was Successful," but for now, you can issue this command:

```
cfsadmin -l <cache-directory>
```

You will see the configuration of the cache directory, as in the previous examples:

```
# cfsadmin -l /cache
cfsadmin: list cache FS information
      maxblocks       90%
      minblocks        0%
      threshblocks    85%
      maxfiles        90%
      minfiles         0%
      threshfiles     85%
      maxfilesize      3MB
```

TABLE 24-1	Option	Description
Creation of Cache Directories Options	*-c*	Creates a cache in the specified directory.
	-o cache-options	Optional CacheFS parameters separated by commas.
	cache-directory	The name of the directory where the cache will reside. This directory should not exist.

The preceding code verifies that the cache directory exists and is properly configured. Once this cache directory is created and verified, you can start mounting file systems in the cache.

e x a m
ⓦ a t c h

To create a cache directory, you use the cfsadmin -c <cache-directory> command.

Mounting Remote File Systems Within the Cache

After the initial cache directory is created, you can now start mounting file systems in the cache. There are three ways of handling this task. The first way is using the mount command manually. The second way is to automatically mount it at bootup using the /etc/vfstab file. The third way is to use the AutoFS file system so that the file system will be automounted only when the user first accesses the file system. Let's look at these three methods in more detail.

Using the mount Command to Mount Cache File Systems

Using the mount command is a manual process and needs to be used again whenever the cached file system is unmounted or after system reboots. You should use the mount command first for the initial setup of a cached file system and to test before you automatically mount it at system boot using /etc/vfstab or autofs.

The use of the mount command is as follows; common syntax descriptions are shown in Table 24-2:

```
mount -F cachefs -o backfstype=fstype,cachedir=cache-directory,[ options]\
back-filesystem mount-point
```

Keep in mind that the backslash (\) in the command syntax signals that you want to continue the command on another line.

For example, to mount the remote file system server1:/usr/local to the /usr/local file system on the client and cache the data into /cache, you would use this syntax:

```
# mount -F nfs -o backfstype=nfs,cachedir=/cache server1:/usr/local /usr/local
```

After the mount command is issued, the remote directory is mounted to the local cache directory. Any access to the data stored in /usr/local results in the data being brought over from the network and stored in the local cache directory. Any subsequent access to the data is made from the cache directory.

TABLE 24-2   CacheFS Mount Options

Option	Description
-F cachefs	The type of the file system being mounted—in this case, cachefs.
-o	File-system–specific options separated by commas.
backfstype=fstype	The back file system type. For CacheFS, this will be either nfs or hsfs.
cachedir=cache-directory	The pathname of the local cache directory where the back file system will be cached.
cacheid=ID	A name for the back file system that will be stored in the cache directory. You refer to these cache IDs when doing maintenance of the cache. If you do not specify a cache ID, CacheFS automatically constructs one.
backpath=/path	Specifies where the back file system is already mounted locally. Must be read-only.
back-filesystem	The path of the back file system. For NFS, this path is in the *server:/path* format. For HSFS, this path is /dev/cdrom.
mount-point	The local mount point of the cached file system. This is where the user will access the data.

on the Job

To mount CD-ROMs, use the HSFS as the back file system type. You also need to specify the mount option of backpath=/path to tell CacheFS that the CD-ROM is also mounted locally in another location—for example, backpath=/cdrom/cdrom0. In addition, you need to mount the CD-ROM as read-only for this command to work. The entire mount command syntax will be similar to this:

```
# mount -F cachefs -o \
  backfstype=hsfs,cachedir=/cache,backpath=/cdrom/cdrom0,ro \
  /dev/cdrom0 /localcdrom
```

exam
Watch

The minimum mount command syntax to mount a cached file system is

```
mount -F cachefs -o backfstype=fstype,cachedir=cache-directory \
back-filesystem mount-point
```

Remember that the backfstype is the type of file system that will be mounted (e.g., NFS or HSFS).

Automatically Mounting Cache File Systems Using /etc/vfstab

You can configure cached file systems to automatically mount during system boots, similar to how NFS mounts are mounted, by editing the /etc/vfstab table. To automatically mount the file system at boot, edit /etc/vfstab and add the new entry to the bottom of the file.

After you create a mount directory, you are encouraged to use the mount command first to mount a new cached file system before you modify the /etc/vfstab file to mount it automatically.

In the previous section, you learned how to mount the resource server1:/usr/local using the mount command. You now add this resource to automatically mount during system startup. Add the following to the /etc/vfstab file:

```
#device          device    mount    FS       fsck  mount     mount
#to mount        to fsck   point     type     pass  at boot   options
#
server1:/usr/local  /cache  /usr/local  cachefs  2     yes   backfstype=nfs
```

This entry in the /etc/vfstab file automatically mounts the server1:/usr/local resource in the cached directory on system startup. Because the mount and umount commands read the /etc/vfstab file, you can now unmount and mount the cached directory using the shortcut method:

```
# umount /usr/local
# mount /usr/local
```

Automatically Mounting Cache File Systems Using AutoFS

You can also use AutoFS to mount cached file systems automatically. AutoFS differs from other methods of mounting by mounting the resource automatically only when the data is accessed or requested.

For example, when a user issues a change directory (cd) command into a cached file system, AutoFS mounts the cached directory in the background, but it appears to the user that the file system has always been mounted. Later, after the user has not accessed the resource, AutoFS unmounts the cached directory after a period of idle time.

Chapter 23 discusses complete configuration of AutoFS. This chapter discusses how to add the CacheFS parameters to the AutoFS maps.

In the previous examples, you mounted the resource server1:/usr/local using the mount command and adding it to the /etc/vfstab file. Let's now configure it so that AutoFS mounts the cached directory.

Add the following to the /etc/auto_direct file:

```
/usr/local  -fstype=cachefs,backfstype=nfs,cachedir=/cache server1:/usr/local
```

This entry assumes that you have configured the direct map /etc/auto_direct to the master /etc/auto_master map. After the entry is added to the auto_direct map, AutoFS needs to be restarted so that it rereads the new entry in the direct map.

exam
ⓦatch

There are three ways to mount cached file systems: using the mount command, editing the /etc/vfstab file, and using AutoFS.

Verifying That Mounting Was Successful

After you create the cache directory and mount cached file systems into it, you should verify that the mounts took place successfully. The best way to verify proper mounting is to use the mount command to view the currently mounted file systems, as in the following example:

```
# mount
(output omitted)
/usr/local on /cache/.cfs_mnt_points/server1:_usr_local
remote/read/write/setuid/backfstype=nfs/cachedir=/cache/dev=2ec0009 on Thu May 10
18:56:15 2001
```

From this output, you can see that the remote server /usr/local is mounted to the local mount point of /usr/local using CacheFS.

EXERCISE 24-1

CacheFS Setup and Mounting

In this certification exercise, you will set up CacheFS to cache a directory locally on your own system.

1. Share out your /tmp directory:

   ```
   # share /tmp
   ```

2. Create a cache directory on your system:

   ```
   # cfsadmin -c /cache
   ```

3. Execute the cfsadmin -*l* command to see whether the cache was created successfully. The system will print the cache configuration if the cache was created:

   ```
   # cfsadmin -l /cache
   ```

4. Create a front file system mount point called /temp into which to mount the /tmp directory:

   ```
   # mkdir /temp
   ```

5. Mount the remote /tmp directory into the cache:

   ```
   # mount -F cachefs -o backfstype=nfs,cachedir=/cache localhost:/tmp /temp
   ```

6. Use the mount command to make sure the mount was successful. You should see the new cache mount at the bottom of the list:

   ```
   # mount
   ```

7. Use the cachefsstat command on the new cached file system and observe the output:

   ```
   # cachefsstat /temp
   ```

8. Perform a directory listing on the /temp directory and compare it to the /tmp directory. They will be the same:

   ```
   # ls -la /temp
   # ls -la /tmp
   ```

This certification exercise took you through the steps for creating a cache directory and a cached file system using your own system as both a caching client and a back file system NFS server. This exercise also showed you how to verify that the cache directory was created and the mounting of the cached file system in the cache was successful.

CERTIFICATION OBJECTIVE 24.02

Using Appropriate Commands to Check the Status and Consistency of the Cache File System

Under normal circumstances, once CacheFS is set up on the system, user or system administrator maintenance is not required. The cache normally runs itself without user interaction. Occasionally, though, it might be necessary to monitor the status of the cache file system. In addition, it is necessary to make sure that the front and back file systems are synchronized to ensure that CacheFS has the latest data in the cache from the remote file system.

This section discusses how to check the status of the cache and make sure the cache is consistent with the remote file systems. First, it is important to define the term *consistency*: the synchronization between the front file system (the cache) and the back file system (the remote file system being cached).

Checking the Status of CacheFS

For many reasons, you will want to check the status of CacheFS. One reason is if you deploy a new application to your users, you might want to monitor how this application works with the CacheFS settings on the caching systems. Another reason is if your users report problems accessing files and directories; in that case, you might want to monitor their cache to see how it is performing for them. Let's examine a few commands you can use to check the CacheFS status.

The cachefsstat Command

You use the cachefsstat command to view statistics about your cache file system. The syntax of the cachefsstat command, described in Table 24-3, is as follows:

```
cachefsstat [-z] mount-point
```

TABLE 24-3	Option	Description
The cachefsstat Command Options	*-z*	Resets the counters so that subsequent executions of the cachefsstat command occur from statistics after resetting the counter
	mount-point	The mount point of the cache file system

The cachefsstat command reports on four statistics: cache hit rate, consistency checks, modifies, and garbage collection. For example, running cachefsstat on your /usr/local cache file system produces this result:

```
# cachefsstat /usr/local
/usr/local
    cache-hit-rate:  88%   (33 hits, 6 misses)
    consistency checks:    3  (2 pass, 1 fail)
      modifies:    0
#
```

These terms are defined as follows:

- **cache hit rate**   The percentage of hits versus total attempts to access the data in the cache. This statistic also reports on the number of hits (cache data returned to the user) and misses (data that was not in the cache and had to be retrieved from the back file system).

- **consistency checks**   The number of consistency checks CacheFS has performed on the cache directory. Also, the number of passing checks that have verified that the data has not changed on the back file system and the number of failed checks that the data has changed.

- **modifies**   The number of writes or creates the cache has accepted.

exam
ⓦatch

Use the cachefsstat command to view the cache hit rate, consistency checks, and modifies of the cached file system.

The cfsadmin -*l* Command

You have already used the cfsadmin -*l cache-directory* command to verify that you have successfully created a cache directory. This section explores what you can glean from the output of this command:

```
cfsadmin -l cache-directory
```

This command produces this typical output:

```
# cfsadmin -l /cache
cfsadmin: list cache FS information
     maxblocks      90%
     minblocks       0%
     threshblocks   85%
     maxfiles       90%
```

```
minfiles        0%
threshfiles    85%
maxfilesize     3MB
server1:_usr_local:_usr_local
server1:_opt:_opt
```

This command prints the current configuration of your cache directory—in this example, the /cache directory. The last two lines of the example are the cache IDs of all the file systems mounted in the cache. You will use the cache ID names later in this chapter, in the section "Deleting Cache File Systems from the Cache Directory," to delete file systems from the cache directory.

The cache ID of each file system is automatically determined by the system when the file system is first mounted to the cache. You can override the cache ID by using the cacheid=cacheid-name in the options section of the mount command, the /etc/vfstab file, or AutoFS maps. Table 24-4 describes the rest of the parameters.

You almost never have to modify the cache directory settings. These settings are designed for maximum cache efficiency. However, be aware that the cache uses up to 90 percent of the front file system for caching; you might want to restrict the cache from taking up so much space.

| **TABLE 24-4** | The cachefsstat Command Options |

Options	Description
maxblocks	The percentage of the maximum space a cache can use based on the front file system. Default is 90 percent.
minblocks	The percentage of the minimum space a cache can use based on the front file system. Default is 0 percent.
threshblocks	The percentage of the total blocks that a cache can use once it has reached the *minblocks* parameter. Default is 85 percent.
maxfiles	The percentage of the maximum number of files a cache can use based on the front file system. Default is 90 percent.
minfiles	The percentage of the minimum number of files a cache can use based on the front file system. Default is 0 percent.
threshfiles	The percentage of the total files that a cache can use once it has reached the *minfiles* parameter. Default is 85 percent.
maxfilesize	The largest file size based on megabytes that a cache can store.

exam
⓪atch

Use the cfsadmin -l command to view the configuration of the cache directory and view the cache IDs on any cache file system that has been or was mounted in the cache.

Checking the Consistency of CacheFS

Consistency refers to the synchronization of the files and directories between the remote file system (the back file system) and the cache. By default, CacheFS performs consistency checking on the cache file systems automatically, without user involvement.

Using the cachefsstat command, you can see consistency checking:

```
# cachefsstat /usr/local
/usr/local
    cache-hit-rate:  82%   (29 hits, 6 misses)
    consistency checks:    21   (20 pass, 1 fail)
      modifies:    0
#
```

In this case, CacheFS has performed 21 consistency checks since the file system was mounted in the cache. Passing a consistency check means that CacheFS has compared what is stored in the cache with what is stored on the remote back file system and found them to be synchronized. If a consistency check fails, the caches were not synchronized, and CacheFS has performed synchronization to keep the cache and the back file system current.

Using Consistency Checking on Demand

Sometimes, it's not necessary to have CacheFS automatically perform consistency checks. If you have data that you know will never change or be modified, you can reduce system and network load even further by preventing CacheFS from performing automatic consistency checks on that data. An example of data that will never change is CD-ROMs that are mounted as read-only.

You can use the *demandconst* option to prevent CacheFS from performing automatic consistency checks. You can still manually perform consistency checks using the cfsadmin *-s mount-point* command on the cache file system mount point. If you try to perform a manual consistency check when CacheFS is performing automatic consistency checks, you receive this error message:

```
# cfsadmin -s /usr/local
cfsadmin: CacheFS file system /usr/local is not mounted demandconst.
```

To enable on-demand consistency checking, you add the *demandconst* option to your mount command, /etc/vfstab file, or AutoFS map. For example, this mount command mounts the remote /usr/local file system to the local /usr/local mount point with the *demandconst* option:

```
# mount -F cachefs -o backfstype=nfs,cachedir=/cache,demandconst \
server1:/usr/local /usr/local
```

After the cache file system is mounted as *demandconst*, the cachefsstat consistency check statistic never automatically increments; it increments only as you manually perform consistency checks using the cfsadmin *-s mount-point* command.

exam
ⓌatcH

CacheFS automatically performs consistency checking. You cannot force a manual consistency check unless the cache file system is mounted with the demandconst option.

<hr>

EXERCISE 24-2

<hr>

Checking Status and Consistency

In this certification exercise, you use the example from Exercise 24-1 to perform some commands to check the status of the cache and perform consistency checking on the cache file system.

1. Execute the cachefsstat command on the /temp cache file system and examine the output:

   ```
   # cachefsstat /temp
   ```

   Notice that the consistency check counter is incrementing. With this mount, consistency checking is performed by CacheFS automatically.

2. Use the cfsadmin *-l* command to look at the cache configuration. Notice that the cached file system /temp has an entry in the output as a cache ID similar to localhost:_tmp:_temp:

   ```
   # cfsadmin -l /cache
   ```

3. Try to perform a consistency check on the cache file system using the cfsadmin *-s* command:

   ```
   # cfsadmin -s /temp
   ```

4. Notice that you are unable to perform the consistency check because the cache file system is not mounted with the *demandconst* option. Unmount the cached file system from the cache:

```
# umount /temp
```

5. Remount the cache file system to the cache with the *demandconst* option:

```
# mount -F cachefs -o ackfstype=nfs,cachedir=/cache,demandconst\
localhost:/tmp /temp
```

6. Make sure the mount was successful using the mount command:

```
# mount
```

7. Perform the cachefsstat command on the /temp cache file system. Wait for 1 minute, and perform the command again. Notice that the consistency check counter is not incrementing:

```
# cachefsstat /temp
```

8. Create a temporary file in the back file system /tmp:

```
# touch /tmp/cachetest
```

9. Perform a directory listing on the cache file system /temp. Notice that everything is there except for the new file you just created in /tmp:

```
# ls -la /temp
```

10. Perform a consistency check on the cache file system /temp:

```
# cfsadmin -s /temp
```

11. Perform a directory listing on the cache file system /temp. Notice that now the new file /temp/cachetest file is present!

```
# ls -la /temp
```

In this certification exercise, you checked the configuration of the cache directory and the status of the cache file system. You also remounted a cache file system using the *demandconst* option and saw the effects of creating files on the back file system when the system is not automatically performing consistency checks. This exercise also covered manually performing consistency checks.

CERTIFICATION OBJECTIVE 24.03

Setting Up Cache File System Logging

In addition to monitoring the status and consistency of CacheFS, you might want to actively monitor CacheFS by setting up logging of the activity. This way, you can tune the cache to your systems and applications, as well as troubleshoot advanced problems.

To set up logging of CacheFS, you first use the cachefslog command to set up the log. After some time elapses, you can analyze the CacheFS data with the cachefswssize command and determine if your caches are running efficiently. Finally, with the cachefsstat command, you can tune the cache using information obtained from logging of CacheFS.

Configuring Logging Using cachefslog

You use the cachefslog command to create the log file for cache file systems. The syntax for creating a log file is defined in Table 24-5 and appears here:

```
cachefslog -f log-file-path mount-point
```

For example, to configure logging in the previous examples, you would use the following syntax:

```
# cachefslog -f /var/log/cachefs.log /usr/local
/var/log/cachefs.log: /usr/local
```

The response shown from CacheFS indicates that it is now logging CacheFS statistics on the /usr/local cache file system. To see which cache file systems are being logged, execute the cachefslog *mount-point* command again:

```
# cachefslog /usr/local
/var/log/cachefs.log: /usr/local
#
```

TABLE 24-5	Option	Description
The cachefslog Command Options	*-f*	Indicates the setup of a log file
	log-file-path	Specifies the pathname and name of the logfile
	mount-point	Specifies the mount point of the cache file system

It is important that you determine where your log file should be placed. Log files can get fairly large on active systems, so you need to place the log file in a directory that contains enough space for it to grow. These files do not trim themselves and grow until logging is turned back off.

To configure logging of cached file systems, use the cachefslog -f log-file-path mount-point command to create a log file and configure CacheFS to log the cache file system.

Viewing the CacheFS Log File

To view the CacheFS log file, you use the cachefswssize command. This command shows you the CacheFS working set size, which prints the amount of space the cache is using. The cachefswssize command takes only the name of the log file created with the cachefslog command as an argument:

```
cachefswssize log-file-path
```

For example, to view the results of the /usr/local log file, you issue this command:

```
# cachefswssize /var/log/cachefs.log
  /usr/local
          end size:        464k
    high water size:       464k

  total for cache
        initial size:    11632k
            end size:      464k
    high water size:       464k
```

The cachefswssize command prints statistics on the mounted cache file system and then prints statistics for the entire cache. Because you have configured only the /usr/local file system in the log, you see only that entry. If you had other cache file systems configured for logging, you would see each one and then the total summary statistics for the cache. Table 24-6 contains the definitions of the size parameters for the cachefswssize command.

With the information contained in these log files, you can tune your cache for your network and application environment.

Use the cachefswssize log-file-path command to view the current contents of the log file and report the sizes of each cache file system, as well as the sizes of the total cache directory.

TABLE 24-6	Option	Description
The cachefswssize Command Options	*end size*	The current size of the cache or cache file system in kilobytes at the time the cachefswssize command is executed
	high water size	The largest size in kilobytes the cache or cache file system has been during logging
	initial size	The initial size of the cache in kilobytes

Modifying the Cache

There are two ways to modify cache parameters. One way is to delete and re-create the cache directory from scratch. The other way is to use the cfsadmin -*u* command to modify the cache on-the-fly. However, not all parameters can be modified with the cfsadmin -*u* command.

Modifying the Cache by Re-creating the Cache Directory

Refer to the first section of this chapter, "Creating the Initial Cache Directory," which describes how to create the cache directory. You modify the default cache parameters by adding options to cfsadmin -*c*. For example,

```
# cfsadmin -c -o maxblocks=50 /cache
```

creates the /cache cache directory with the *maxfiles* setting changed from the default percentage of 90 percent to 50 percent. Refer to the cfsadmin -*c* -*o* options earlier in this chapter (in the section "Creating the Initial Cache Directory") for a list and description of all the options you can change.

Modifying the Cache by Using the cfsadmin -*u* Command

You can use the cfsadmin -*u* command to alter the cache directory on-the-fly. Values can only be increased, never decreased. If you want to decrease the parameters, you have to delete the cache and re-create it using the previously described method. All file systems must be unmounted from the cache before you can issue these commands.

The syntax of the cfsadmin -*u* command is thus:

```
cfsadmin -u [ -o cachefs-parameters ] cache-directory
```

For example, for the /usr/local example, you want to change the *maxfiles* setting from its default of 90 percent to 95 percent. You issue these commands:

```
# umount /usr/local
# cfsadmin -u -o maxfiles=95 /cache
#
```

on the **Job**

The most likely reason you would alter the cache directory is so that the cache will not take up most of the disk space on the front file system. Sun states that, for optimum caching, CacheFS uses 90 percent of the front file system by default.

Stopping CacheFS Logging

After you have completed CacheFS log analysis, you should turn off logging to prevent the file systems from filling up with large log files. You use the cachefslog *-h* command to turn off logging. The syntax of the command is

```
cachefslog -h mount-point
```

In these examples, you turn off logging on /usr/local using this command:

```
# cachefslog -h /usr/local
not logged: /usr/local
```

The "not logged:" output from the command signifies that logging is turned off for that cache file system mount point.

EXERCISE 24-3

CacheFS Logging Setup and Analysis

This certification exercise covers creating a log file on a cache file system, analyzing the data contained within the log file, and causing logging to stop, using the CacheFS setup outlined in Exercise 24-1.

1. Configure logging on the /temp cache file system using the log file of /cache.log. Notice that the system's response indicates that the cache file system is not being logged:

```
# cachefslog -f /cache.log /temp
/cache.log: /temp
```

2. Access some files and directories in the /temp directory to force caching of data within the cache.

3. Analyze the log file using the cachefswssize command and note the output:

```
# cachefswssize /cache.log
```

4. Notice that the cache file system /temp has end and high water size entries. In addition, the total for the cache will have initial, end, and high water sizes. Now turn off logging on the /temp cache file system and delete the log file you created:

```
# cachefslog -h /temp
not logged: /temp
# rm /cache.log
```

In this certification exercise, you learned how to configure logging on an existing cache file system using the cfsadmin -f command. You also used the cachefswssize command to view and analyze the data contained within the log file after you forced the cache to cache some data. Finally, you stopped logging the cached file system and deleted the log file.

Performing a Check of the Cache File System

Whenever you modify the cache or a cache file system, you might need to perform an integrity check on the cache directory. An example of a cache modification is when you delete a cache file system from the cache directory. An example of a cache file system modification is if the back file system structure is modified.

You will be notified when you must verify the integrity of the cache directory when you try to mount cache file systems in the cache and receive messages similar to this:

```
# mount -F cachefs -o backfstype=nfs,cachedir=/cache server1:/usr/local
/usr/local
May 10 19:35:00 unknown cachefs: WARNING: cachefs: cache not clean. Run fsck
mount -F cachefs: mount failed No space left on device
#
```

The CacheFS version of the fsck command is provided to verify the integrity of your cache directories. All cache file systems need to be unmounted from the cache directory before you can modify the cache directory.

The syntax of the CacheFS version of fsck follows; the descriptions of the syntax appear in Table 24-7:

```
fsck -F cachefs [ -m -o noclean ] cache-directory
```

In the example of /usr/local, you can force an integrity check of the cache directory by issuing these commands:

```
# umount /usr/local
# fsck -F cachefs /cache
# mount /usr/local
```

Sometimes, for certain cache file systems and cache directories, you might need to bring the system down to single-user mode to make effective changes and repairs to cache directories and cache file systems.

exam
ⓦatch

You cannot perform an integrity check on a cache directory that has mounted cache file systems. Use the fsck -F cachefs cache-directory command to perform an integrity check.

TABLE 24-7	Option	Description
The fsck Command Options	*-F cachefs*	Specifies that the CacheFS version of fsck is used
	-m	Checks the file system but makes no repairs
	-o noclean	Forces a check on the file system but makes no repairs
	cache-directory	The location of the cache directory

CacheFS Integrity Checking

In this exercise, you perform a manual check of the file system. Use Exercise 24-1 as your initial setup for the cache.

1. Unmount the /temp cache file system from the cache:

   ```
   # umount /temp
   ```

2. Perform a fsck file system integrity check on the cache directory:

   ```
   # fsck -F cachefs /cache
   ```

3. Remount the cache file system in the cache:

   ```
   # mount -F cachefs -o backfstype=nfs,cachedir=/cache,demandconst\
   localhost:/tmp /temp
   ```

In this certification exercise, you learned how to unmount the cache file system from the cache, performed a manual fsck file system integrity check on the cache directory to make sure there are no errors in the cache, and remounted the cache file system in the cache.

CERTIFICATION OBJECTIVE 24.05

Identifying the Steps to Dismantle and Delete a Cache File System

During your maintenance of CacheFS, you sometimes need to dismantle and delete cache file systems and cache directories. This section covers the commands that you use to dismantle and delete CacheFS systems.

Deleting Cache File Systems from the Cache Directory

The first step in dismantling a CacheFS system is to delete all the cache file systems from the cache directory. You use the cfsadmin *-d* command for this task. The syntax to delete cache directories is as follows, and Table 24-8 describes the syntax:

```
cfsadmin -d [ all ] cacheid-name cache-directory
```

Before you are allowed to delete any cache file systems from the cache directory or delete the cache itself, you must unmount all cache file systems from the cache directory. Otherwise, you will get a "Cache in use" error message.

The cfsadmin *-d* command takes the cacheid parameter of the cached file system to delete or the parameter of *all,* which deletes all cache file systems and removes the cache directory. The cache ID can be found using the cfsadmin *-l cache-directory* command, which you have used before. Take another look at the output of this command using the examples:

```
# cfsadmin -l /cache
cfsadmin: list cache FS information
    maxblocks      90%
    minblocks       0%
    threshblocks   85%
    maxfiles       90%
    minfiles        0%
    threshfiles    85%
    maxfilesize     3MB
      server1:_usr_local:_usr_local
      server1:_opt:_opt
```

TABLE 24-8	Option	Description
The cfsadmin Delete Command Options	*-d [all]*	Deletes a cache file system specified by the *cacheid-name* parameter, or *all* deletes all cache file systems and removes the cache directory
	cacheid-name	The cache ID of the cache file system to delete
	cache-directory	The pathname of the cache directory

The last two lines of this command's output state that two cache file systems are contained in this cache directory. The first cache ID is server1:_usr_local:_usr_local; the second is server1:_opt:_opt. CacheFS automatically names the cache IDs when you first mount the cache file system. With this naming convention, it is easy to distinguish the remote server and pathname that are mounted to the pathname locally. You can change the automatic naming using the cacheid= option during the mounting of the cache file system.

To delete the /usr/local/ cache file system from the cache directory, issue the following command:

```
# umount /usr/local
# umount /opt
# cfsadmin -d server1:_usr_local:_usr_local /cache
```

This command produces no output. If you want to verify that the cache file system was deleted, you use the cfsadmin -l /cache command again:

```
# cfsadmin -1 /cache
cfsadmin: list cache FS information
    maxblocks        90%
    minblocks         0%
    threshblocks     85%
    maxfiles         90%
    minfiles          0%
    threshfiles      85%
    maxfilesize       3MB
      server1:_opt:_opt
```

As you can see, after deletion of the server1:_usr_local:_usr_local cache ID, the cache ID no longer appears in the output of the cfsadmin -l command.

Deleting the Cache Directory

When you use the cfsadmin -d all *cache-directory* command, the command removes all remaining cache file systems and finally deletes the cache directory itself. After this command, you need to re-create the cache directory using the cfsadmin -c command.

In the example, you can delete all the cache file systems and remove the cache directory by specifying this command:

```
# cfsadmin -d all /cache
```

exam

Watch

Use the cfsadmin -l cache-directory command to determine the cache ID of the cache file system you want to delete. Use the cfsadmin -d cacheid cache-directory command to delete the named cache ID. Removing the last cache ID from the cache directory deletes the cached directory.

EXERCISE 24-5

Deleting CacheFS

In this exercise, you will learn how to find the cache ID of a cache file system and delete the cache file system from the cache. Use Exercise 24-1 as your initial setup for the cache.

1. Unmount the cache file system from the cache:

   ```
   # umount /temp
   ```

2. Use the cfsadmin *-l* command to find the cache ID of the cache file system you unmounted. The cache ID is localhost:_tmp:_temp:

   ```
   # cfsadmin -l /cache
   ```

3. Delete the cache ID from the cache using the cfsadmin *-d* command:

   ```
   # cfsadmin -d localhost:_tmp:_temp /cache
   ```

4. Execute the cfsadmin *-l* command on the cache again:

   ```
   # cfsadmin -l /cache
   ```

Notice that you will get an error message because when you delete the last cache ID, the cache directory will be deleted as well. You could also have used the command cfsadmin *-d* all to delete all the caches at once and remove the cache directory.

In this exercise, you unmounted the cache file system from the cache, used the cfsadmin *-l* command to find the cache ID of the cache file system, deleted the cache file system, and removed the cache directory.

CERTIFICATION SUMMARY

In this chapter, you learned about the CacheFS file system and the benefits of using CacheFS in your network environment. CacheFS is useful to your network to reduce network traffic between file servers and clients and gives the users better response times for files and applications.

You also learned how to set up and configure CacheFS, how to monitor the status of your caches, how to configure the login process for your caches to find out if your cache is tuned correctly; how to verify the integrity of your caches; and, finally, how to delete your caches.

✓ TWO-MINUTE DRILL

Configuring the Cache File System in an Existing Client/Server Environment

❑ The cfsadmin *-c cache-directory* command is used to create a cache directory.

❑ There are three ways to mount a cache directory: using the mount command, adding the cache directory to the /etc/vfstab file, and using AutoFS.

❑ The minimum syntax for using the mount command is mount *-F* cachefs *-o* backfstype=fstype,cachedir=*cache-directory server:pathname mount-point.*

❑ Types of file systems you can mount in the cache are NFS and HSFS.

Using Appropriate Commands to Check the Status and Consistency of the Cache File System

❑ Consistency refers to the synchronization between the front file system (the cache) and the back file system (the remote file system being cached).

❑ The cachefsstat *mount-point* command prints the cache hits and misses, performs consistency checks, and reads from the cache file system.

❑ The cfsadmin *-l cache-directory* command prints the cache configuration parameters and cache IDs of all the cache file systems.

❑ The demandconst mount option disables automatic consistency checking.

❑ The cfsadmin *-s mount-point* command forces a consistency check on a cache file system mounted as *demandconst.*

Setting Up Cache File System Logging

❑ The cachefslog *-f log-file-path mount-point* command creates a log file and configures the cache file system for logging.

❑ The cachefslog *mount-point* command prints the name of the log file for the given mount point.

❑ The cachefswssize *log-file-path* command analyzes the log file and reports the sizes of the cache file systems and total sizes of the cache.

❑ The cachefslog *-h mount-point* command stops logging on the cache file system.

Performing a Check of the Cache File System

❑ Modification or deletion of cache file systems requires an integrity check of the cache directory.

❑ Use the fsck *-F* cachefs *cache-directory* command to verify the integrity of the cache directory.

❑ All cache file systems must be unmounted before you implement integrity checking.

Identifying the Steps to Dismantle and Delete a Cache File System

❑ All cache file systems must be unmounted before you delete them.

❑ Use the cfsadmin *-l cache-directory* command to list all the cache IDs in the cache directory.

❑ Use the cfsadmin *-d cacheid cache-directory* command to delete cache IDs from the cache.

❑ Using the cfsadmin *-d* all *cache-directory* command or deleting the last cache ID from the cache directory removes the cache directory.

SELF TEST

The following questions will help you measure your understanding of the material presented in this chapter. Read all the choices carefully because there might be more than one correct answer. Choose all correct answers for each question.

Configuring the Cache File System in an Existing Client/Server Environment

1. You are trying to decide the best way to automatically mount a new cache file system on system boot. Which of the following are ways of automatically mounting a cache file system? (Choose all that apply.)

   A. Add the new mount to the dfstab file.

   B. Add the mount to the AutoFS map.

   C. Add the mount to the vfstab file.

   D. Use the mount command.

2. Which of the following are types of file systems that are available to be mounted in the cache? (Choose all that apply.)

   A. HSFS

   B. CDFS

   C. UFS

   D. NFS

Using Appropriate Commands to Check the Status and Consistency of the Cache File System

3. Which of the following commands prints the configuration of the cache directory?

   A. cfsadmin *cache-directory*

   B. cachefsstat *-l cache-directory*

   C. cachefsadmin *-l cache-directory*

   D. cfsadmin *-l cache-directory*

4. Which of the following statistics does the cachefsstat command *not* report on?

   A. Cache modifies

   B. Cache size

   C. Consistency checks

   D. Cache hit rate

Setting Up Cache File System Logging

5. Which command reports on the logs of cache file systems?

   A. cachefslogsize

   B. cachelogsize

   C. cfsadmin

   D. cachefslog

   E. cachefswssize

6. You use the cachefswssize command to look at a cache file system's statistics. What does the high water size statistic mean?

   A. The *high water size* reflects the maximum size the cache will ever be.

   B. The *high water size* reflects the highest size the cache has ever been.

   C. The *high water size* reflects the maximum size the cache file system will ever be.

   D. The *high water size* reflects the end size of the cache.

Performing a Check of the Cache File System

7. A user receives a "Cache not clean" error message when her system boots and she accesses her files in the cache file system /files. When you log in to her machine, which command would you run to perform an integrity check of the file system?

   A. fsck -F nfs /cache

   B. fsck -F cachefs /files

   C. cfsadmin -s /files

   D. cachefs -F cachefs /cache

   E. fsck -F cachefs /cache

Identifying the Steps to Dismantle and Delete a Cache File System

8. Which of the following commands retrieves the cache IDs of cache file systems?

   A. cfsadmin

   B. cachefsstat

   C. cacheid

   D. cachefslog

9. You want to delete all cache file systems from the cache and remove the cache directory. Which command would you use?

   A. cfsadmin *-d* all /cache

   B. cachefs *-d* all /cache

   C. cfsadmin *-d* all

   D. cfsadmin *-d* /cache

LAB QUESTION

You are in charge of distributing a new version of Netscape Navigator to all your workstations. This is the primary tool that your users work with on a daily basis, so application speed is very important. You decide to configure each workstation to cache the application from the NFS remote server navserver:/opt/netscape.

Outline the steps necessary to configure one workstation to cache this application. Then configure logging on this cache file system. Because the application will not change or be updated frequently, mount with the options to prevent consistency checking and mount it as read-only. The local cache directory will be /var/cache and the log filename should be /var/log/cache.log. The cache file system should be mounted as /netscape. As you are performing the steps necessary to accomplish this task, also verify each step as necessary.

SELF TEST ANSWERS

Configuring the Cache File System in an Existing Client/Server Environment

1. ☑ B and C. AutoFS maps and the /etc/vfstab are ways to automatically mount cache file systems.
   ☒ A is incorrect because /etc/dfs/dfstab is the file to configure automatic sharing of NFS resources. D is incorrect because mount is a manual way of mounting cache file systems.

2. ☑ A and D. The High Sierra File System (HSFS) and the Network File System (NFS) are both valid file system types to mount in a cache.
   ☒ B is incorrect because CDFS does not exist. C is incorrect because UFS is used on local hard disks.

Using Appropriate Commands to Check the Status and Consistency of the Cache File System

3. ☑ D. The cfsadmin -l *cache-directory* command prints the current cache parameters along with the cache IDs of all cache file systems.
   ☒ A is incorrect because the -l parameter is missing. B is incorrect because cachefsstat gives you statistics on a cache file system. C is incorrect because there is no such command as cachefsadmin.

4. ☑ B. The cachefsstat command does not report on the size statistic. Only CacheFS logging reports the sizes of the cache file systems.
   ☒ A, D, and C are all incorrect because cachefsstat does report on *modifies, consistency checks,* and *hit rates.*

Setting Up Cache File System Logging

5. ☑ E. The command cachefswssize reports on the sizes of the cache file systems by analyzing the log files.
   ☒ A and B are incorrect because there are no such commands. C is incorrect because the cfsadmin command does not report on the sizes of the cache file systems. D is incorrect because the cachefslog command only configures logging; it does not report on the log file.

6. ☑ B. The *high water size* reflects the highest the cache or cache file system has ever been during the logging period.

☒ **A** is incorrect because CacheFS logging does not report on maximum sizes for the cache. **C** is incorrect because CacheFS logging does not report on maximum sizes for the cache file system. **D** is incorrect because the *high water size* does not refer to the current size of the cache or the cache file system.

Performing a Check of the Cache File System

7. ☑ **E.** The command fsck *-F* cachefs /cache performs an integrity check on the cache directory.
☒ **A** is incorrect because you use cachefs as the file system type, not nfs. **B** is incorrect because you perform the integrity check on the cache directory, not the cache file system. **C** is incorrect because the cfsadmin *-s* command performs a consistency check. **D** is incorrect because there is no such command as cachefs.

Identifying the Steps to Dismantle and Delete a Cache File System

8. ☑ **A.** The command cfsadmin *-l* retrieves the configuration of the cache and a listing of all cache IDs of the cache file systems.
☒ **B** is incorrect because cachefsstat only retrieves statistical information for cache file systems. **C** is incorrect because there is no such command. **D** is incorrect because cachefslog does not report cache IDs; it only configures logging.

9. ☑ **A.** The correct command syntax for deleting all cache file systems and removing the cache directory is cfsadmin *-d* all /cache.
☒ **B** is incorrect because there is no such command as cachefs. **C** is incorrect because the *cache-directory* name is missing from the end of the command. **D** is incorrect because the *-d all* command is missing from the command to tell the system to delete all cache file systems.

LAB ANSWER

The exact steps you will take to cache this application can vary, but they will be similar to the following:

1. Create the cache directory /var/cache on the local workstation:

   ```
   # cfsadmin -c /var/cache
   ```

2. Verify that the cache directory was created using cfsadmin:

   ```
   # cfsadmin -l /var/cache
   ```

3. Use the mount command to mount the cache file system into the cache:

```
# mount -F cachefs -o backfstype=nfs,cachedir=/var/cache,demandconst, ro\
navserver:/opt/netscape /netscape
```

4. Make sure the cache directory was mounted successfully:

```
# mount
```

5. Create and configure logging on the new cache file system:

```
# cachefslog -f /var/log/cache.log /netscape
```

These are the basic commands to accomplish these tasks. You could include other testing commands as well. You might also want to include commands to check the statistics of the cache file system and analyze the log data.

25

Understanding Naming Services

T his chapter discusses naming services as they relate to Solaris 9. *Naming services* provide resources for users and systems to communicate over the network. They provide processes to manage and access the information. This information is usually referred to as a *namespace*.

The naming services mentioned in this chapter follow the client/server model. Clients request information from the server; the server responds by interpreting the request from a database of information.

CERTIFICATION OBJECTIVE 25.01

Understanding the Purpose of a Naming Service

Naming services can serve many purposes. They are usually used to centralize administration, reduce administration redundancy, provide features to prevent a single point of failure, and ensure consistent and timely updates of information.

Centralized Administration

With the use of naming services, system administrators can centralize their information on one server. This server is usually called the *master server*. The master server maintains information that used to be maintained on each individual host, such as the usernames and passwords for user accounts, hostnames, and automount maps. Because the information is maintained on one server, there is no need to keep a copy on all the individual computers. For this reason, naming services also allow for easier information management. When the information changes, you need to make only one change on the master server—which expedites the propagation of the new information and reduces the amount of work you must perform.

Consistency

Because all the changes are made on the master server, the information that the clients receive is the most current, eliminating the possibility of a client missing any updated information. Once a change is made, the information is updated immediately on the master server, allowing the client to receive the new information as soon as possible. If a host goes down while the information is being updated, that host will receive the new information as soon as it comes back online.

Preventing a Single Point of Failure

Even though naming services require only one master server, they allow for multiple secondary servers (often referred to as *slave servers* or *replica servers*). These secondary servers store copies of the information databases that are on the master server. When changes occur to the master server, the server sends updates to the secondary servers to make sure they get the changes. This system eliminates a single point of failure. Clients can also make requests for information from the secondary servers. This takes some of the network load off the master server. Network performance is improved by the secondary servers handling some of the requests.

on the **Job**

A good system administrator is always looking for a way to eliminate redundant work and automate tasks. Furthermore, it is important for system administrators to look for ways to improve network performance and plan for disaster recovery by eliminating single points of failure.

CERTIFICATION OBJECTIVE 25.02

Defining the Various Naming Services and Comparing Their Functionality

Solaris supports a variety of naming services. Some of them are very similar to each other. Some can even be used in combination with others to provide an ideal environment. The naming services that Solaris supports and that will be covered on the exam are the following:

- Domain Name service (DNS)
- Network Information Service (NIS)
- Network Information Service Plus (NIS+)
- Lightweight Directory Access Protocol (LDAP)

exam **Watch**

Be sure to remember the supported naming services for Solaris 8 and 9. These services have changed from Solaris 7, which had Federated Naming Service (FNS) instead of LDAP.

Domain Name Service

DNS is the naming service of choice for the Internet. It is used to translate hostnames to IP addresses and IP addresses to hostnames. The software commonly used for DNS is the Berkeley Internet Name Domain (BIND) software. In Solaris, when DNS is chosen during installation, the BIND software is installed.

History

Before DNS in the mid 1980s, when the Internet was young, applications had to perform hostname-to-IP-address and IP-address-to-hostname lookups via local file lookups. The file used was /etc/hosts. Administrators populated this file with the information from a master file. This file, maintained by the SRI's Network Information Center, was named hosts.txt. SRI kept a copy of the hosts.txt file on a single host machine, SRI-NIC.

When new hosts were added to the ARPANET (the early name for the Internet), administrators had to download the hosts.txt file. Furthermore, names could not be duplicated, so if there was a host under the name of *company,* no one else could use that name. This was a major drawback to the naming scheme.

As the Internet grew, it became harder for one entity to maintain the one hosts.txt file. By the time one updated hosts.txt file could reach everyone, it was already obsolete. DNS was designed to address the drawbacks of the hosts.txt file. DNS allowed distributed administration, consistency, and duplicate naming. Now two companies could have the same name, such as sales.company.com and sales.organization.com, for hosts in their domains.

Namespace

The DNS namespace is referred to as a *domain:* usually a collection of hosts grouped together because of ownership or physical location. These domains can be divided into *subdomains.*

Domain names are presented in a hierarchical format. The hierarchy begins with the root (.). Next is a top-level domain; then comes the individual's or company's domain. Last comes the hostname or any subdomains. For example, in the domain sales.company.com, *sales* is the host, *company* is the domain, and *com* is the top-level domain.

DNS Files

When you type the address **www.company.com** into your web browser and press ENTER, your computer goes through a series of steps. The following is a list of files that the computer consults during these steps.

- **/etc/nsswitch.conf** This file tells the system the service to use to resolve queries for information. This file should have DNS for the keyword linked with hostnames:

```
# You must also set up the /etc/resolv.conf file for DNS name
# server lookup.  See resolv.conf(4).
hosts:      files dns
```

- **/etc/resolv.conf** This file specifies the DNS servers that should be used to resolve hostnames to IP addresses or IP addresses to hostnames. The following is a sample of what the file might contain:

```
search company.com
nameserver 192.168.1.2
nameserver 192.168.1.3
```

Once the requests reach their server, the server uses a set of files to resolve the hostname. The following files are the ones that the server uses to translate the name www.company.com into an IP address:

- **/etc/named.conf** This is the BIND configuration file that is used by the DNS server to specify authoritative zones and data files. The file contents are

```
options {
  DIRECTORY "/var/named";
};
zone "." in {
  type hint;
  file "named.root";
};
zone "company.com" in {
  type master;
  file "company.com";
};
```

- **named.ca** This file is used to reference the IP address of the Internet root DNS servers.

- **named.local** This file contains the DNS records for the loopback address referred to as the *localhost*.

- *domainname* This file contains the DNS records that map the hostnames to the IP address (A-type records). The actual name and location of this file can vary and are specified in the /etc/named.conf file. The name is usually the same as the domain name. In this case, it would be company.com.

```
@@   IN SOA nameserver.company.com.  hostmaster.company.com. (
1        ; Serial number
43200    ; Refresh timer - 12 hours
3600     ; Retry timer - 1 hour
604800   ; Expire timer - 1 week
86400    ; Time to live - 1 day
)
www.company.com.    IN  A  192.168.1.10
```

- *domainname.rev* This file contains the DNS records that map the IP addresses to the hostnames (PTR-type records). The actual name and location of this file can vary and are specified in the /etc/named.conf file.

Network Information Service

NIS focuses on making network administration more manageable by providing centralized control over a variety of network and system information. With NIS, you can control hostnames, users, groups, IP addresses, and network services. NIS also provides a platform-independent solution for administration.

NIS uses information in databases called *maps* to distribute information among a variety of servers. All the updates are performed from one centralized location automatically and reliably. This system ensures that all clients share the same information in a consistent manner.

Parts

The information that NIS stores is organized in a namespace referred to as a *domain*. Within this domain, the information is stored in NIS maps. The server uses these maps to translate requests from the client. For example, most people use NIS to centralize authentication. When a user attempts to log in from a workstation, NIS sends a request to the master server for the domain in which NIS resides. The master server then consults its map for usernames and passwords and compares this information to the information that was sent with the request. If the information matches the contents of the map, the user is granted access to the network.

NIS Domains

NIS domains are a type of *flat namespace*. This means that an NIS domain does not use a hierarchy for organization. NIS domains are used to arrange hosts, users, and networks. If your organization is connected to the Internet, you can use NIS in combination with DNS to resolve hostnames to IP addresses and IP addresses to hostnames, allowing NIS to handle the local information and DNS to handle the Internet lookups.

NIS Maps

NIS maps are stored on the master server. These maps were designed to serve the same purpose as many of the configuration files found under the /etc directory. These files are used as the source for NIS maps and can create a large set of maps. Custom maps can also be created for specific network environment needs. NIS domain maps typically include the passwd, group, hosts, ethers, netgroup, auto_home, auto_master, bootparams, aliases, netmasks, networks, protocols, rpc, services, timezone, and IP nodes.

Network Information Service Plus

NIS+ is very similar to NIS except it has more features. NIS+, like NIS, supports redundant servers, which it calls *replicas*. NIS+ was designed from scratch to replace NIS. The features that were added were expanded to meet today's intranet needs. Some additional information that NIS+ stores relates to security, mail, printers, and other network services.

NIS+ Namespace

NIS+ uses a dynamic namespace that can be changed at any time by an authorized user. The NIS+ namespace uses a hierarchical structure similar to that of DNS. This structure allows it to conform to the logical hierarchy of an organization. This layout also allows it to be unrelated to the physical layout of the organization. In addition, you can divide the namespace into multiple domains. Clients can access information from other domains in addition to their own.

The NIS+ namespace allows for distributed administration due to its built-in security authentication. Each user has a login password and a network password. NIS+ uses the network password to authenticate users who want to make modifications. Users must have certain permissions to make a change. Authorized users can make changes and propagate updates immediately instead of doing batch updates, as with NIS.

FROM THE CLASSROOM

NIS+ vs. NIS

Most people have the misconception that NIS+ is simply an upgraded version of NIS with a few improvements. This assumption is incorrect. NIS+ was designed from scratch as an alternative to NIS. It has no relationship to NIS beyond the fact that they serve the same purpose. NIS+ uses a completely different architecture and set of commands. For NIS, the commands start with *yp,* like the ypstart command that starts the NIS services.

NIS+ commands start with *nis,* like the nistbladm command that is used to administer NIS+ table objects. NIS+ does allow NIS compatibility for clients with a YP-compatibility mode. This feature allows the NIS+ server to respond to NIS client requests as well as NIS+ client requests.

—Fedil Grogan

on the **Job** *In today's network environment, security is a major concern, so anything that will tighten security is a plus. That's where the security authentication features of NIS+ come in.*

NIS+ Objects

NIS+ has five basic types of objects: directory objects, table objects, entry objects, group objects, and link objects. When these objects are addressed, they are always separated by a dot. This type of addressing closely resembles the way DNS addresses are laid out. An example of an NIS+ directory object is groups_dir.company.com.

Directory Objects

Directory objects are used to divide the NIS+ namespace into multiple parts. These objects can contain one or more other types of objects. The main directory object of each domain contains the org_dir and the group_dir. The org_dir contains the table objects for that domain. The group_dir contains the information for the NIS+ administrative group objects.

Table Objects

Table objects serve the same function as NIS maps: they provide network information. NIS+ uses table objects to store the information that is used to resolve client requests. NIS+ has 17 predefined table objects. Zero or more entry objects are contained in the table objects. The nistbladm or nisaddent commands are used to administer table objects. Some NIS+ table objects are

- **auto_home**   Stores the location of users' home directories
- **auto_master**   Stores the AutoFS map information
- **bootparams**   Stores the location of the root, swap, and dump partitions to be used by diskless workstations
- **cred**   Stores the credentials for NIS+ principals
- **group**   Stores the group name, GID, and member information
- **ethers**   Stores the Ethernet addresses of systems
- **hosts**   Stores the hostnames and IP addresses of computers in your network
- **mail_aliases**   Stores mail addresses and aliases
- **netgroup**   Stores network members and groups defined in the NIS+ domain
- **netmasks**   Stores netmasks for known networks
- **networks**   Stores networks and names given to those networks
- **passwd**   Stores password information about user accounts
- **protocols**   Stores IP protocols used within the NIS+ domain
- **rpc**   Stores RPC program numbers for RPC services
- **services**   Stores IP services and their port numbers
- **timezone**   Stores time zones of workstations in the NIS+ domain

exam
Ⓦatch

NIS+ table objects are the only type of NIS+ objects covered in the Solaris System Administration II (SA-288) class. Therefore, the exam will probably test your understanding of only these objects.

Group Objects

For the NIS+ administration groups, NIS+ uses group objects. These groups are used to control the access rights for modification to the NIS+ domain on a group basis rather than an individual basis. The command used to administer the group objects is nisgrpadm.

Link Objects

Link objects are simply pointers to other objects. Link objects usually point to table object entries. They are basically the same as symbolic links in UNIX or shortcuts in Windows operating systems. They can be administered with the nisln command.

e x a m
ⓦa t c h

NIS and NIS+ are the naming services that the exam covers in detail.

Lightweight Directory Access Protocol

LDAP is usually used with another naming service to provide a standardized set of rules for hierarchical naming structures, authorization practices, and configuration attributes. LDAP is ideally suited for read-intensive environments, not environments that need frequent updates. Many people use LDAP for e-mail address books, as resource locators for online phone directories, to centralize network management, and to tighten security.

CERTIFICATION OBJECTIVE 25.03

Identifying the Right Naming Service to Use for Your Network

When deciding which type of naming service to use for you network, you must consider many factors. One of the first things to look at is the size of your network. You also need to evaluate your network needs. Here are some reasons to use certain naming services over others:

- **Files** Usually used for small LANs; uses /etc/nsswitch.files as a template.
- **DNS** Primarily used for the Internet but also best suited for large LANs or WANs; uses /etc/nsswitch.dns as a template.
- **NIS** Used for LANs; uses /etc/nsswitch.nis as a template.
- **NIS+** Used for organizations with multiple LANs; uses /etc/nsswitch.nisplus as a template.
- **LDAP** Used for LANs and WANs; uses /etc/nsswitch.ldap as a template.

Assume that your company has a fairly large LAN under one organization but also has a connection to the Internet. For this setup, you decide to use NIS to centralize the administration of network information, accounts, and DNS for hostnames on the Internet. To set up these configurations, you need to look at the naming service switch file.

Naming Service Switch File

The *naming service switch file* you use to set up a naming service is the /etc/nsswitch.conf file. It stores the information the computer needs to determine the naming service to use. By default, Solaris has some template files that you can use as a starting point. To use these templates, you need to simply copy them as /etc/nsswitch.conf. The template files are as follows:

- **/etc/nsswitch.files**   Specifies only local /etc files to be consulted.
- **/etc/nsswitch.dns**   Specifies local /etc files to be consulted for everything but host entries. Host entry lookups are resolved with DNS.
- **/etc/nsswitch.nis**   Specifies the NIS database as the primary source of information except for the passwd, group, automount, and aliases maps. These templates consult the local /etc/files first and then the NIS database.
- **/etc/nsswitch.nisplus**   Specifies the NIS+ database as the primary source of information except for the passwd, group, automount, and aliases maps. These templates consult the local /etc/files first and then the NIS+ database.
- **/etc/nsswitch.ldap**   Specifies the LDAP database as the primary source of information except for the passwd, group, automount, and aliases maps. These templates consult the local /etc/files first and then the LDAP database.

Because you are primarily using NIS, you would need to copy the /etc/nsswitch.nis file by using this command:

```
hostname# cp /etc/nsswitch.nis /etc/nsswitch.conf.
```

/etc/nsswitch.conf
After you have copied the template file to /etc/nsswitch.conf, you can modify it to meet your needs. The file contains a list of 19 databases, the naming service that will be used for resolution, naming service status codes and actions, and the order in which the naming services are consulted. Here's an example:

```
hosts:    files [NOTFOUND=return]   dns
```

There are seven choices of databases that you can use:

- **files**   Refers to the local /etc/files
- **dns**   Refers to the host's entry to use only DNS
- **nis**   Refers to an NIS map
- **nis+**   Refers to an NIS+ table
- **ldap**   Refers to using LDAP
- **user**   Refers to only the printers entry
- **compat**   Used to specify an old-style plus sign (+) syntax for the passwd and group information

e x a m

ⓌＷ**a t c h**   *Be familiar with the /etc/nsswitch.conf file, including the syntax of the entries. The following is what your /etc/nsswitch.conf file would look like because you used /etc/nsswitch.nis as the template:*

```
#
# /etc/nsswitch.nis:
#
# An example file that could be copied over to /etc/nsswitch.conf; it
# uses NIS (YP) in conjunction with files.
#
# "hosts:" and "services:" in this file are used only if the
# /etc/netconfig file has a "-" for nametoaddr_libs of "inet" transports.

# the following two lines obviate the "+" entry in /etc/passwd and /etc/group.
passwd:     files nis
group:      files nis

# consult /etc "files" only if nis is down.
hosts:      nis [NOTFOUND=return] files
ipnodes:    files
# Uncomment the following line and comment out the above to resolve
# both IPv4 and IPv6 addresses from the ipnodes databases. Note that
# IPv4 addresses are searched in all of the ipnodes databases before
# searching the hosts databases. Before turning this option on, consult
# the Network Administration Guide for more details on using IPv6.
#ipnodes:    nis [NOTFOUND=return] files

networks:   nis [NOTFOUND=return] files
protocols:  nis [NOTFOUND=return] files
rpc:        nis [NOTFOUND=return] files
ethers:     nis [NOTFOUND=return] files
```

```
netmasks:    nis [NOTFOUND=return] files
bootparams:  nis [NOTFOUND=return] files
publickey:   nis [NOTFOUND=return] files

netgroup:    nis

automount:   files nis
aliases:     files nis

# for efficient getservbyname() avoid nis
services:    files nis
sendmailvars:    files
printers:        user files nis

auth_attr:   files nis
prof_attr:   files nis
project:     files nis
```

Status Codes and Status Code Actions

Status codes are returned from the database source that was consulted for resolution. Two actions can be specified for each status code: continue and return. *Continue* tells the naming service switch to try the next source. *Return* tells the naming service switch to stop looking for the entry. The status codes that can be returned are SUCCESS, UNAVAIL, NOTFOUND, and TRYAGAIN. The meanings of these codes are indicated by their names.

on the job

The return status code action is the default action for the SUCCESS status code, and the continue status code is the default for the rest of the status codes.

exam Watch

Be sure you know the status codes and the meanings of the actions.

Because you need DNS for your Internet connection, you need to make a change in the /etc/nsswitch.conf file listed in the preceding discussion. You need to change the hosts entry from

```
hosts:       nis [NOTFOUND=return] files
```

to

```
hosts:       dns  nis [NOTFOUND=return] files
```

This change tells your machine to use DNS to look up hostnames and to use NIS for everything else.

SCENARIO & SOLUTION	
You want to use NIS as your naming service. Which file would you use to configure nsswitch.conf?	/etc/nsswitch.nis.
Your computer is connected to the Internet, and you need a naming service to resolve hostnames to IP addresses and IP addresses to hostnames. Which service should you use?	DNS.
What if you want the naming service to cease after getting a status code of NOTFOUND when doing host lookups?	Add [**NOTFOUND=return**] after the naming service source at which you want it to cease.

CERTIFICATION SUMMARY

Naming services are a very important topic for Part II of the Solaris Administration Exam. This chapter provided an overview of the various naming services and how they work. You should now understand the concepts of naming services and how to implement them in your network. You should also understand how naming services can apply in real-world situations. And you should be able to assess a situation and determine information about the naming services involved.

TWO-MINUTE DRILL

Understanding the Purpose of a Naming Service

❑ Naming services can ease management with centralized file administration.

❑ Naming services can reduce redundant information by allowing changes to be made on one server.

❑ With naming services, clients will receive consistent information.

❑ When changes are made, the updates are performed immediately.

❑ Naming services can reduce single point of failure.

Defining the Various Naming Services and Comparing Their Functionality

❑ Naming services provide a solution that addresses specific needs or architectures.

❑ DNS resolves IP addresses to hostnames and hostnames to IP addresses.

❑ NIS centralizes information for LAN resources, which may include user accounts, hostnames, services, and other configuration files that would normally be on each host.

❑ NIS+ centralizes information for LAN resources. It is similar to NIS but has expanded abilities such as built-in authentication and cross-domain lookups.

❑ LDAP combines naming services with directory services. It allows objects to have attributes.

Identifying the Right Naming Service to Use for Your Network

❑ Files are usually used for small LANs and use /etc/nsswitch.files as a template.

❑ DNS is primarily used for the Internet but is also best suited for large LANs or WANs. It uses /etc/nsswitch.dns as a template.

❑ NIS is used for LANs and uses /etc/nsswitch.nis as a template.

❑ NIS+ is used for organizations with multiple LANs and uses /etc/nsswitch.nisplus as a template.

❑ LDAP is used for LANs and WANs and uses /etc/nsswitch.ldap as a template.

SELF TEST

The following questions will help you measure your understanding of the material presented in this chapter. Read all the choices carefully because there might be more than one correct answer. Choose all correct answers for each question.

Understanding the Purpose of a Naming Service

1. Which of the following are reasons to use a naming service? (Choose all that apply.)

    A. For consistency

    B. To reduce the risk of single point of failure

    C. To increase workstation performance

    D. To centralize administration

2. Which files do naming services usually take the place of?

    A. /etc/init.d files

    B. /etc files

    C. /var/yp/*domainname* files

    D. /usr/bin files

3. Naming services maintain information from which of the following files?

    A. /etc/passwd

    B. /etc/hosts

    C. /etc/groups

    D. /etc/group

Defining the Various Naming Services and Comparing Their Functionality

4. Your company is looking to implement a naming service but is very concerned about the security of using one. The company is thinking about going with NIS or NIS+. Which suggestion should you give the decision makers?

    A. Implement NIS+ because of its built-in authentication.

    B. Implement NIS because it has a hierarchical namespace.

    C. Discourage them from using a naming service.

    D. Implement NIS because it supports multiple domain lookups.

5. Where does NIS+ store its information that it uses to resolve client requests?

   A. Maps

   B. Table objects

   C. Group objects

   D. Zones

6. Your company is organized into multiple departments and is using NIS+. Why is using NIS+ the best solution over other naming services? (Choose all that apply.)

   A. NIS+ has a hierarchical namespace.

   B. NIS+ has a flat namespace.

   C. NIS+ is an upgrade of NIS.

   D. NIS+ allows cross-domain lookups.

Identifying the Right Naming Service to Use for Your Network

7. Your company has a small LAN with five computers. Which naming service would be best suited to your network?

   A. NIS, because it centralizes administration of user accounts

   B. Local files, because the overhead of maintaining a naming service is not beneficial for small LANs

   C. DNS, because it allows one server to maintain the hostnames and IP addresses

   D. NIS+, because it has built-in authentication

8. Which of the following actions is used in the /etc/nsswitch.conf file to tell the naming service to try the next source?

   A. Continue

   B. Return

   C. Success

   D. Next

9. Your company is using NIS for its primary naming service and the employees want to connect to the Internet. What is the best way for the company to integrate this change into its network?

   A. Change the primary naming service to DNS.

   B. Change the hosts entry in the nsswitch.conf file to read

   ```
   hosts:     dns  nis [NOTFOUND=return]  files
   ```

C. Delete the hosts entry in the nsswitch.conf file.

D. Add the DNS servers to the /etc/resolv.conf file.

10. Return is the default status code action for which status code(s)?

A. TRYAGAIN

B. UNAVAIL

C. SUCCESS

D. NOTFOUND

LAB QUESTION

Your company has been thinking about setting up a naming service. The decision makers are not that concerned about security but do want to be on the Internet. They have decided to use NIS and DNS. List the steps you would take to set up and implement a server for your company.

SELF TEST ANSWERS

Understanding the Purpose of a Naming Service

1. ☑ **A, B, and D.** All are benefits of using naming services.
   ☒ C is incorrect because using a naming service does not increase workstation performance.

2. ☑ **B.** Naming services usually take the place of local /etc files such as /etc/hosts, /etc/passwd, and /etc/group.
   ☒ A is incorrect because the /etc/init.d files are used by the system at system startup. C is incorrect because the files in /var/yp/*domainname* are the files used by NIS to resolve client queries. D is incorrect because the /usr/bin files are the executable binary files that users are allowed to use.

3. ☑ **A, B, and D.** When you use a naming service, the information that is in these files is maintained by the naming service.
   ☒ C is incorrect because a file named /etc/groups does not exist.

Defining the Various Naming Services and Comparing Their Functionality

4. ☑ **A.** One of the biggest differences between NIS and NIS+ is security. NIS+ was developed with security in mind and offers a built-in authentication method.
   ☒ B and D are incorrect because they describe features of NIS+, not NIS. C is incorrect because there is no reason to discourage anyone from using a naming service.

5. ☑ **B.** NIS+ stores its information in table objects.
   ☒ A is incorrect because maps are used by NIS. C is incorrect because NIS+ uses group objects to control the access rights for modification to the NIS+ domain. D is incorrect because it is used by DNS.

6. ☑ **A and D.** Having a hierarchical namespace allows NIS+ to share a layout similar to that of the company, and because NIS+ allows cross-domain lookups, you can look up information in other domains.
   ☒ B is incorrect because NIS+ has a hierarchical namespace. C is incorrect because NIS+ is not an upgrade of NIS. It was completely rewritten from scratch.

Identifying the Right Naming Service to Use for Your Network

7. ☑ **B.** Due to the small size of the network, you can easily maintain the local files on the computers.
   ☒ A, C, and D are incorrect because the benefits mentioned would have no sizable impact.

8. ☑ **A.** If the naming service request returns the specified status code, it will try the next source.

☒ **B** is incorrect because return tells the naming service to stop if it returns the specified status code. **C** is incorrect because SUCCESS is a status code. **D** is incorrect because next is not a valid status code action.

9. ☑ **B.** Adding DNS to the front of the source list tells the workstation to consult DNS first to resolve hostnames.

☒ **A** is incorrect because if you switch to DNS, you lose the ability to administer user authentication and other administration services. **C** is incorrect because you still need the hosts entry in the /etc/nsswitch.conf file. **D** is incorrect because you still need an entry in the /etc/nsswitch.conf to redirect requests to DNS.

10. ☑ **C.** Return is the default status code action for TRYAGAIN.

☒ **A**, **B**, and **D** are incorrect because the default for these status codes is continue.

LAB ANSWER

On the server:

1. Install Solaris on a server that will be the master server for the naming services.

2. Configure NIS on the master server.

3. You can also configure DNS on the master server.

On the clients:

1. Copy /etc/nsswitch.nis to /etc/nsswitch.conf.

2. Change the hosts entry to read

```
hosts:   dns   nis [NOTFOUND=return]   files
```

3. Add the DNS servers to the /etc/resolv.conf file.

![Solaris™ SUN® CERTIFIED SYSTEM ADMINISTRATOR]

26

Using Network Information Service (NIS)

Part of the system administrator's job is to maintain the database of information that is required to operate on the network. These files, also collectively referred to as a *namespace,* are used to keep track of the system's users, groups, permission, services, and hosts. On a small network, this can be done by modifying the data on each host or copying the data from host to host. On a medium-sized to large network, this process can be cumbersome or even unmanageable. Network Information Service (NIS) was designed to assist the administrator in the task of maintaining the system. The information is maintained on the master host, and, once modified, it is distributed to the rest of the domain automatically. This scheme provides a reliable process to distribute the network information files; it ensures consistency among all the hosts in the domain. NIS was designed to function in a LAN environment.

Originally released by Sun as Yellow Pages (YP), NIS was renamed because Yellow Pages is a registered trademark of the United Kingdom of British Telecommunications plc. NIS is now licensed and supported by multiple vendors.

on the
()ob

Most NIS commands and processes still contain YP in their names, making them easy to identify. If you are looking for NIS-related processes that are running on your system, try executing this command:

```
/usr/bin/ps -ef | grep yp
```

NIS uses the client/server model. NIS servers provide information files via services to the clients. These hosts communicate using remote procedure calls (RPCs). The communication data is encapsulated in the User Datagram Protocol (UDP) and transferred between the client and the server.

on the
()ob

NIS+ is somewhat similar to NIS but adds some features. The NIS+ domain supports a hierarchy—that is, a subdomain within the domain. NIS+ also has additional security features that require the clients to authenticate into the domain before they are allowed to access the information in the namespace. NIS+ is gradually being replaced by LDAP and support may be dropped in future versions of Solaris.

Understanding the Processes and Components of the NIS Domain: Master, Slave, and Client

An NIS domain is a group of hosts. Each host is configured to participate and share information within the domain. An NIS domain contains no hierarchy. There are no subdomains within the NIS domain. The NIS domain name can be up to 256 characters long and is case sensitive.

on the Job

For better security, it is recommended that your NIS domain be configured with a different name from that of your DNS domain. If you simply change the domain name to the same name as your NIS domain name, a host can participate in your domain and potentially act as an NIS server.

EXERCISE 26-1

Configuring a Name Service Domain

This exercise describes the steps to configure a name service domain for a host.

1. Execute the *domainname* command to set the domain name:

   ```
   # domainname corporate
   ```

2. Create a /etc/defaultdomain file and enter the domain name in the file. This step ensures that on the next reboot, the domain will be configured with the same name.

3. To verify the domain name, execute

   ```
   # domainname
   ```

   The /etc/defaultdomain file contains simply the name of the domain, for example,

   ```
   # cat /etc/defaultdomain
   corporate
   ```

A host can be easily configured to be in an NIS domain using the command *domainname*. On each reboot process, the /etc/defaultdomain file is used to determine the domain name of the default name service; therefore, you must also create this file with the name of the domain listed inside.

To control the way the client host looks up name service information, Sun provided the name switch file /etc/nsswitch.conf. Sun provides four templates of the /etc/nsswitch.conf file based on name service configured on the host:

- **/etc/nsswitch.file**   Uses the local /etc directory to look up services (or no name service is configured)
- **/etc/nsswitch.nis**   Uses NIS as the primary name service
- **/etc/nsswitch.nisplus**   Uses NIS+ as the primary name service
- **/etc/nsswitch.ldap**   Uses LDAP as the primary name service

Each line of the /etc/nsswitch.conf file lists the type of information, the source to reference, and a status condition. The status condition specifies the next action based on the status message of the search. There are four status messages:

- **SUCCESS**   The information was found using the specified source.
- **NOTFOUND**   The file or map did not contain the information that the client is looking for.
- **UNAVAIL**   There is no response from the source or the source was not found.
- **TRYAGAIN**   The source was found but did not respond to the query.

Based on the status message, a client can potentially take one of two actions:

- **Return**   Stop searching.
- **Continue**   Continue with the search using the next source defined.

The condition in which the client searches for the information is based on a combination of the status message and the action. The default status conditions that follow apply to all services specified in the /etc/nsswitch.conf:

- **SUCCESS=return**   The information was found. Stop and return the value.

- **NOTFOUND=continue**   The information could not be located; continue searching using the next source. If this is the last source specified, return a NOTFOUND message.

- **UNAVAIL=continue**   There is no response from the source or the source is not found. Continue searching using the next source. If this is the last source specified, return a NOTFOUND message.

- **TRYAGAIN=continue**   The source was found but did not respond to the query. Continue searching using the next source. If this is the last source specified, return a NOTFOUND message.

The default status conditions do not have to be specified in the switch file. Nondefault status conditions must be enclosed by square brackets. The following example displays the default configuration line in /etc/nsswitch.nis for host lookup with a nondefault condition:

```
hosts:  nis [NOTFOUND=return] files
```

In this example, the following can occur:

- The information is located in the NIS hosts map. A SUCCESS status message is returned.

- The information is not located in the NIS map. The application stops searching for the information and returns a NOTFOUND message.

- The NIS hosts map is unavailable. Continues to search for the information in the /etc/hosts file.

- The NIS hosts map is busy. The application returns a TRYAGAIN message and continues to search in the /etc/hosts file.

on the
(j)o b   *Be sure you fully understand the function of /etc/nsswitch.conf and the templates that have been provided by Sun. Programs that use getXXbyYY functions look up the information using the order of the name service listed in this file.*

To configure the /etc/nsswitch.conf file, you simply copy to the file one of the templates that Sun has provided and make any changes to the file that relate to your environment.

EXERCISE 26-2

Configuring the /etc/nsswitch.conf File for the NIS Environment

This exercise covers the steps to configure the /etc/nsswitch.conf file for the NIS environment.

1. Copy the /etc/nsswitch.nis template to /etc/nsswitch.conf:

   ```
   # cp /etc/nsswitch.nis /etc/nsswitch.conf
   ```

   The default configuration for the hosts lookup is

   ```
   hosts:  nis [NOTFOUND=return] files
   ```

2. Modify this line to allow searching to also use DNS and the local hosts table by specifying

   ```
   hosts:  files nis dns [NOTFOUND=return]
   ```

   The following is an example of an /etc/nsswitch.conf file:

```
#
# /etc/nsswitch.nis:
#
# An example file that could be copied over to /etc/nsswitch.conf; it
# uses NIS (YP) in conjunction with files.
#
# "hosts:" and "services:" in this file are used only if the
# /etc/netconfig file has a "-" for nametoaddr_libs of "inet"
transports.

# the following two lines obviate the "+" entry in /etc/passwd and /etc/group.
passwd:     files nis
group:      files nis

# consult /etc "files" only if nis is down.
hosts:      files nis dns [NOTFOUND=return]
ipnodes:    files
# Uncomment the following line and comment out the above to resolve
# both IPv4 and IPv6 addresses from the ipnodes databases. Note that
# IPv4 addresses are searched in all of the ipnodes databases before
# searching the hosts databases. Before turning this option on, consult
# the Network Administration Guide for more details on using IPv6.
#ipnodes:    nis [NOTFOUND=return] files
networks:    nis [NOTFOUND=return] files|
```

```
protocols:   nis [NOTFOUND=return] files
rpc:         nis [NOTFOUND=return] files
ethers:      nis [NOTFOUND=return] files
netmasks:    nis [NOTFOUND=return] files
bootparams:  nis [NOTFOUND=return] files
publickey:   nis [NOTFOUND=return] files

netgroup:    nis

automount:   files nis
aliases:     files nis

# for efficient getservbyname() avoid nis
services:    files nis
sendmailvars:   files
printers:       user files nis

auth_attr:   files nis
prof_attr:   files nis
project:     files nis
```

exam
ⓦatch   *When configuring an NIS master server, do not modify the default*
/etc/nsswitch.conf file until after the domain is configured. (See
Exercise 26-4 for more information on this topic.)

NIS stores the information in databases called *maps* located in the /var/yp/ *domainname* directory. For example, the maps for the corporate domain reside in the /var/yp/corporate directory. The maps are converted from the ASCII or text version into ndbm format at the initial setup of the NIS master server. Once updated, the maps are re-created by the make process.

The maps are in two-column configuration, where one column is the key and the other is the value. Each map consists of two files: a .pag and a .dir file. The naming conventions for these files are *map.sortkey.pag* and *map.sortkey.dir,* where *map* is the name of the map, *sortkey* is the lookup key for the file, *pag* is the map's data file, and *dir* is the index to the .pag file. Thus, some network information data is organized into two or more maps. For example, the host map is stored in four separate files: hosts.byaddr.dir, hosts.byaddr.pag, hosts.byname.dir, and hosts.byname.pag. The map host.byname.pag contains the hostname as the key, and host.byaddr.pag contains the IP address of the hosts as the key. Table 26-1 describes the default NIS maps.

| TABLE 26-1 | Default NIS Maps |

Nickname	Maps	Description
aliases	mail.aliases, mail.byaddr	Mail addresses and aliases
bootparams	bootparams	Pathname for partitions required by boot clients
ethers	ethers.byname, ethers.byaddr	Hosts' Ethernet addresses
group	group.byaddr, group.bygid	Groups information
hosts	hosts.byaddr, hosts.byname	Hosts' information
ipnodes	ipnodes.byaddr, ipnodes.byname	IPv4 and IPv6 addresses
netgroup	netgroup, netgroup.byhost, netgroup.byuser	Network group information
netmasks	netmask.byaddr	Network masks
networks	networks.byaddr, networks.byname	Network names and IP addresses
passwd	passwd.byname, passwd.byuid, passwd.adjunct.byname, netid.byname	User accounts and password information associated with accounts
protocols	protocols.byname, protocols.bynumber	Registered network protocols
rpc	rpc.bynumber	Registered RPC programs
services	services.byname, services.byservice	Registered services and their associated numbers
none	ypservers	List of NIS servers

e x a m
Ⓦatch

The Solaris NIS environment contains the map ipnodes to support IPv6. Also included are maps to support Role-Based Access Control (RBAC) such as auth_attr and prof_attr.

There are three types of hosts in the NIS domain:

- The master server
- Slave servers
- Clients

Now that you have an idea of how the maps are configured, here are some quick scenarios and solutions related to the commands to work with maps.

SCENARIO & SOLUTION

Which command do you use if you want to view the data in the maps?	/usr/bin/ypcat *mapname* Example: /usr/bin/ypcat passwd
Which command do you use to view the key value of the maps along with the information within the map? Use this command to view the ypservers map.	/usr/bin/ypcat -k *mapname* Example: /usr/bin/ypcat -k ypservers
Which command do you use to view a single entry in the table using a key?	/usr/bin/ypmatch -k *keyname mapname* Example: /usr/sbin/ypmatch -k sysadmin group
Which command do you use to view an entry in the table without using the key?	/usr/bin/ypcat *mapname* | grep *item* Example: /usr/sbin/ypcat passwd | grep sysadmin
Which command do you use to verify the /etc/nsswitch.conf configuration with NIS service?	/usr/bin/getent *service item* Example: /usr/bin/getent passwd sysadmin
Which command do you use to display the map's nickname?	/usr/bin/ypcat -x
Which command do you use to determine which server is the master of a map?	/usr/bin/ypwhich *mapname* Example: /usr/bin/ypwhich aliases

e x a m
ⓦatch *Pay close attention to the process that runs on each type of NIS host.*

The NIS Master Server

The domain must be configured with one master server. The master server contains the centralized copy of the maps. Once the data files are updated, the NIS master server pushes a copy of its maps to the slave servers. Table 26-2 describes the processes that run on the NIS master server.

TABLE 26-2	Process	Description
NIS Master Server Processes	ypbind	Name service binding process
	ypserv	Server process used to look up information in the maps
	ypxfer	Transfers the maps to the slave server
	rpc.yppasswdd	Handles password-changing requests
	rpc.ypupdated	Updates information for NIS according to the /var/yp/updaters configuration file

Experience shows that it makes sense to configure a single host as the NIS master server and DNS primary name server. This practice simplifies the task of maintaining the hosts table for NIS and DNS because the data is located locally. The administrator can create a script to update the DNS table when the data in the NIS hosts table is updated. It is also recommended that you set up NIS slaves and DNS secondary servers in the same domain for redundancy.

The NIS Slave Server

NIS slaves function as backups for the master server. Each time the data on the master server is modified, a copy of the map is sent to the slaves. If configured in broadcast mode, NIS clients search for the NIS server using an RPC broadcast. The router cannot forward broadcast packets from one subnet to another. Thus, RPC packets cannot reach a server if the server is on a different subnet from the client. Therefore, an NIS slave must be set up on each subnet that has an NIS client. Table 26-3 describes the processes that run on the NIS slave server.

The NIS Client

The NIS client runs a process called *ypbind.* The function of ypbind is to locate an NIS server on the network. There are two ways to configure the client: using broadcast or directly connecting using a server list. If configured to run the broadcast mode, ypbind sends a broadcast on the network to find the NIS server. It connects to the first NIS server the response to the request regardless of whether the server is the master or one of the slaves. This process is called *binding.* If configured using a server list, the ypbind process sources the /var/yp/binding/*domainname*/ypservers list for the names of all the NIS servers to which it can bind. Table 26-4 describes the processes that run on the NIS client.

	Process	Description
TABLE 26-3		
NIS Slave Server Processes	ypbind	Name service binding process
	ypserv	Server process used to look up information in the maps

TABLE 26-4	Process	Description
The NIS Client Process	ypbind	Name service binding process

Configuring an NIS Master, Slave, and Client

To configure NIS, you must first plan your domain carefully. You should have knowledge of your network layout; such knowledge will help determine the configuration of your clients and how many slave servers you must have. The order to setting up an NIS domain is as follows: initialize the NIS master server, then the NIS slave server(s), and, finally, all clients. The following sections describe the steps to configure an NIS master, slave, and client. Before executing the steps, ensure that your network is functional.

Configuring an NIS Master Server

Before initializing the NIS master server, you must first determine the directory in which to store the text version of the maps, prepare the files for the conversion process, and configure the Makefile.

EXERCISE 26-3

Preparing the NIS Master Server

This exercise describes the steps to prepare the NIS master server.

1. The default directory for the text version of the map files is /etc. Because this is also where the local information files are stored, it is recommended that you choose a different location. Create this directory on the server. Make sure you pay attention to the permission setting on this directory. You must determine the user, group, and world access to protect the data in this area from unauthorized modification.

2. Copy the files from the local /etc directory into the source directory. Copy both the /etc/passwd and the /etc/shadow files into the source directory. Edit these files and remove root and all Admin-related accounts such as daemon, bin, sys, adm, lp, uucp, nuucp, listen, nobody, noaccess, and nobody4. The final passwd and shadow file should contain only user-related accounts.

3. Copy the /etc/mail/aliases to the source directory.

4. Modify the /var/yp/Makefile and change the value of the DIR, PWDIR, and ALIASES. Add a section for any custom maps that you want to add to the domain. (See Exercise 26-7 for more information on this topic.)

5. Determine the hostnames and IPs of all NIS slave servers.

Once you have prepared the information to set up the NIS master server, you can then initialize the server. The maps are automatically converted from the text source.

<hr/>

EXERCISE 26-4

<hr/>

Configuring the NIS Master Server

This exercise describes the steps for configuring the NIS master server.

1. Log in to root on the master server.

2. Make sure the /etc/nsswitch.conf file is configured to use the local file as the source:

   ```
   # cp /etc/nsswitch.files /etc/nsswitch.conf
   ```

3. Edit the /etc/hosts or /etc/inet/ipnodes file and add an entry for all NIS slave servers.

4. Initialize the server and build the maps:

   ```
   # cd /var/yp
   # /usr/sbin/ypinit -m
   ```

5. When prompted by ypinit, enter the name of the slave servers. The ypinit program will continue to prompt you for the name of the servers, so if you have no more slave servers, press ENTER to continue. This step is necessary to initialize NIS slave servers.

6. ypinit will prompt you to answer *Y* or *N* to verify the list of slave servers. Answer *Y.*

   The ypinit program will launch a make process that runs the makedbm command to convert the text source file into the maps and associate the master server to each map.

7. Prepare the /etc/nsswitch.conf file. Refer to Exercise 26-2 for more information.

8. Start the NIS service on the master server:

   ```
   # /usr/lib/netsvc/yp/ypstart
   ```

Although it is not necessary, it is recommended that you reboot the server to ensure that the NIS service will start up correctly.

Configuring the NIS Slave Server

To initialize the NIS slave server, you must first convert the host into an NIS client so that it can obtain the initial NIS maps from an NIS server. You can repeat these steps for all the NIS slave servers in your domain.

EXERCISE 26-5

Configuring the NIS Master Server

This exercise describes the steps to configure an NIS slave server.

1. Log in to root on the slave server.

2. Configure the domain for the host by executing the *domainname* command.

3. Prepare the /etc/nsswitch.conf file. Refer to Exercise 26-2 for more information.

4. Modify /etc/inet/hosts or /etc/inet/ipnodes and add the information for all NIS servers.

5. Convert the hosts into an NIS client so the maps can be transferred to the system first:

   ```
   # /usr/sbin/ypinit -broadcast
   ```

6. Initialize the host as an NIS slave, where the *master_server* is the name of the NIS master server:

```
# /usr/sbin/ypinit -s master_server
```

Although it is not necessary, it is recommended that you reboot the server to ensure that the NIS service will start up correctly.

Configuring the NIS Client

An NIS client can be initialized using one of two options: a broadcast or server list method. The method in which the NIS client is initialized is based on the network configuration and the design of the NIS domain.

EXERCISE 26-6

Configuring the NIS Client

This exercise describes the steps to configure an NIS client.

1. Log in to root on the client.

2. Configure the domain for the host by executing the *domainname* command.

3. Prepare the /etc/nsswitch.conf file. Refer to Exercise 26-2 for more information.

4. Execute the /usr/sbin/ypinit command to initialize the NIS service on the client.

5. To use the broadcast method, use this command:

```
# mkdir /var/yp/binding/domainname
# usr/lib/netsvc/yp/ypbind -broadcast
```

6. To use the server list method, use this command:

```
#/usr/sbin/ypinit -c
```

7. Enter the list of NIS servers.

Once the system is initialized, it is suggested that you reboot the client to ensure that the NIS service is working correctly. You can also verify the service by executing a /usr/bin/ypcat command and retrieve an NIS map.

FROM THE CLASSROOM

Broadcast vs. Server List

When configuring an NIS client, you must determine when to use the broadcast method and when to use the server list method. Each method has its drawback. NIS clients using the broadcast method cannot send the broadcast packets across routers. Therefore, you are required to set up an NIS slave server within the client's local subnet. NIS clients using the server list method are capable of binding directly to the NIS server, but are limited to the list of servers in their databases. If these servers are not functional, the system will not switch to broadcast mode to attempt to bind to an NIS server.

The server list method is sometimes preferred over the broadcast method because the server list method gives the administrator control over which server the client can bind to. In a controlled environment (for example, an engineering laboratory), the administrator can ensure that the clients can bind to only a specific server. If this environment is secure, the administrator also has the option of providing partial information from the NIS maps in the production environment, thus controlling access to information such as the passwd, group, and hosts maps.

—*Ray Tran*

CERTIFICATION OBJECTIVE 26.03

Adding a New NIS Map to an Existing Network

Not all network information is available in the default configuration of the NIS environment. Sometimes, it is necessary for the administrator to add custom maps. The most common custom maps are automount maps such as auto_direct.

EXERCISE 26-7

Adding a New NIS Map to an Existing Domain

This exercise describes the steps to add a new map to the existing NIS domain. The example uses the following configuration for the NIS domain:

- The domain name is corporate.
- The source directory is located in /etc/yp.
- The new map is auto_direct.

These are the steps:

1. Log in to the NIS master server as root.

2. Change directory to the NIS source and create the text file version of the new map:

```
# cd /etc/yp
vi auto_direct
```

3. Convert the text file into a map using the /usr/sbin/makedbm command:

```
# /us/sbin/makedbm auto_direct /var/yp/corporate/auto_direct
```

4. Transfer the new map to the slave servers using the yppush command:

```
# /usr/lib/netsvc/yp/yppush auto_direct
```

To ensure that the new map is rebuilt each time you modify the source data, modify the /var/yp/Makefile and add the information for the new map into the file. This is shown next.

EXERCISE 26-8

Adding a New NIS Map to the Makefile

This exercise describes the steps to add a new map to the Makefile. It uses the configuration in the previous exercise as an example.

1. Log in to the NIS master server as root and edit the /var/yp/Makefile.

2. Add an entry for the new auto_direct map to the *all* line:

```
all: passwd group hosts ethers networks rpc services protocols \
     netgroup bootparams aliases publickey netid netmasks c2secure \
     timezone auto_master auto_home auto_direct
```

3. Press TAB to specify the blank space at the beginning of the line.

4. Create an auto_direct.time entry in the middle of the file:

```
auto_direct.time:  $(MAPDIR)/auto_direct
     -@if [ -f $(MAPDIR)/auto_direct ]; then \
          sed -e "/^#/d" -e s/#.*$$// $(MAPDIR)/auto_direct \
          | $(MAKEDBM) - $(YPDBDIR)/$(DOM)/auto_direct; \
          touch auto_direct.time; \
          echo "updated auto_direct"; \
          if [ ! $(NOPUSH) ]; then \
               $(YPPUSH) auto_direct; \
               echo "pushed auto_direct"; \
     else \
          : ; \
          fi \
     else \
          echo "couldn't find $(MAPDIR)/auto_direct"; \
     fi
```

5. Add an entry at the end of the file as follows:

```
auto_direct: auto_direct.time
```

Updating and Propagating an NIS Map in an Existing Network

To update the NIS maps, you simply edit the source text file of the map, and then convert and push the map using the /usr/ccs/bin/make program. These steps must be performed on the NIS master server.

on the
job *You should use a source code control process similar to RCS or SCCS for data protection. Such a process ensures that only one person can modify the source file at a time, thus preventing the data from being corrupted.*

EXERCISE 26-9

Updating and Propagating Existing Maps

This exercise describes the steps to update and propagate existing maps.

1. Log in to the NIS master server as root.

2. Change directory to the NIS source and create the text file version of the new map:

   ```
   # cd /etc/yp
   ```

3. Modify the source text file.

4. Change to the /var/yp directory and execute the /usr/ccs/bin/make command to convert the maps and push the information to the NIS slave servers:

   ```
   # cd /var/yp
   # /usr/ccs/bin/make map
   ```

5. Verify that your changes appear in the map, where *map* is the name of the map you modified:

   ```
   # /usr/bin/ypcat map
   ```

on the
job *Some maps are modified more frequently than others. For example, you are more likely to modify the passwd map than the services map. Each time you execute the /usr/ccs/bin/make command, update the NIS maps. All maps are converted and pushed to the slave servers. In a large NIS environment with a large number of NIS slave servers, this process can take up bandwidth on the LAN. Sun provides three scripts to use with cron for periodic transfer of the maps: ypxfr_1perday, ypxfr_1perhour, and ypxfr_2perday. By combining two processes, you can reduce the list of maps that are transferred during the make process and, creating cron jobs using the ypxfr shell script, you can reduce the network traffic to support the NIS environment.*

CERTIFICATION OBJECTIVE 26.05

Adding and Removing NIS Slave Servers in the Existing NIS Environment

After the NIS environment is configured, you might need to add or remove an NIS slave server. Adding a slave server to the existing NIS environment is required if you are setting up a new network subnet and your NIS clients are initialized using the broadcast method. Removing a slave server is necessary if you are taking an old server offline.

EXERCISE 26-10

Adding or Removing an NIS Slave Server from the Domain

This exercise describes the steps to add or remove a slave server.

1. Log in to the NIS master server as root.

2. Change to the NIS domain directory, where *domainname* is the name of your NIS domain:

   ```
   # cd /var/yp/domainname
   ```

3. Convert the ypservers map into an ASCII or text file using the /usr/sbin/makedbm command:

   ```
   # /usr/sbin/makedbm -u ypservers >> /etc/yp/ypservers
   ```

on the *Job* *For ease of editing this information in the future, you should place the aforementioned file in the source data location.*

4. Edit the /etc/yp/ypservers file and add or remove the name of the slave server. Save and exit the editor.

5. Convert the text version back to database format using the /usr/sbin/makedbm command:

   ```
   # /usr/sbin/makedbm /etc/yp/ypservers ypservers
   ```

6. Verify the ypservers map to make sure the NIS master is aware of the changes:

```
# /usr/sbin/makedbm -u ypservers
```

7. See Exercise 26-5 to configure the NIS slave server. If you are removing the server, please ignore this step.

exam
ⓦatch

NIS clients will not bind to the new NIS slave server until the NIS service is stopped and restarted (or the client is rebooted). To stop and start the NIS service, complete Exercise 26-11.

EXERCISE 26-11

Stopping and Starting the NIS Service

1. Execute the following command:

```
/usr/lib/netsvc/yp/ypstop
```

2. Now execute this command:

```
/usr/lib/netsvc/yp/ypstart
```

CERTIFICATION SUMMARY

NIS enables the administrator to maintain the information files that are required to operate a network in a central location. This process also provides a reliable and consistent distribution of this information to the hosts within the NIS domain.

From the NIS master server, the administrator can make changes to the services files. The files are then converted into their database format, called *maps*. The maps are then populated to all other NIS slave servers. The client's application makes the appropriate call to look up the information in these maps.

✓ TWO-MINUTE DRILL

Understanding the Processes and Components of the NIS Domain: Master, Slave, and Client

❑ The /etc/defaultdomain contains the name of the name service domain.

❑ The /etc/nsswitch.conf file controls the way the client's application searches for information in the name services.

❑ Maps are databases containing the information for NIS services. Maps are stored in ndbm format using a two-column configuration. One column contains the key; the other contains the value associated with that key.

❑ The NIS master server contains the central repository of the maps. NIS slave servers are used as backups for the NIS master server. An NIS slave server must be configured on each network subnet if the NIS clients are configured using the broadcast method.

❑ The NIS client runs a process called ypbind, which searches and connects to an NIS server using a method called *binding*.

Configuring an NIS Master, Slave, and Client

❑ The /usr/sbin/ypinit *-m* command configures the master server.

❑ The /usr/sbin/ypinit *-s* command configures the slave server.

❑ The /usr/sbin/ypinit *-broadcast* command configures the NIS client using broadcast mode.

❑ The /usr/sbin/ypinit *-c* command configures the NIS client to use the server list method.

Adding a New NIS Map to an Existing Network

❑ To add a map, you must first convert the text file into database format using the /usr/sbin/makedbm command. Then push the map to the slave servers using the /usr/lib/netsvc/yp/yppush command.

❑ You add an entry in the /var/yp/Makefile to ensure that the new map is automatically converted and pushed to the slave servers along with the other maps.

Updating and Propagating an NIS Map in an Existing Network

❑ After you modify the information file, you execute the /usr/ccs/bin/make command from the /var/yp directory (on the NIS master server) to convert and push the maps to the slave servers.

Adding and Removing NIS Slave Servers in the Existing NIS Environment

❑ The ypservers map contains the list of NIS slave servers.

❑ To edit the ypservers map, you must first convert the map into a text file using the /usr/sbin/makedbm command.

SELF TEST

The following questions will help you measure your understanding of the material presented in this chapter. Read all the choices carefully because there might be more than one correct answer. Choose all correct answers for each question.

Understanding the Processes and Components of the NIS Domain: Master, Slave, and Client

1. What is the function of the /etc/nsswitch.conf file?

   A. To configure which name service the host will be using

   B. To control how the client searches for data in the name services

   C. To allow the client system to search for NIS information on a specified server

   D. To configure the message that is returned to the client's application when the application searches for information in the name service

2. Which statements are true about maps? (Choose all that apply.)

   A. Maps are in binary ndbm format.

   B. Maps store their actual location on the NIS server in its registry.

   C. The information in the map files is organized in a two-column format, where one column is the key and the other the value.

   D. The map files are located on the NIS servers in the /var/yp/*domainname* directory.

   E. The location of the map files is configurable. All you need to do is change the value of the PWDIR variable in the /var/yp/Makefile before you create the maps.

3. What is the role of the NIS master server? (Choose all that apply.)

   A. It contains the repository for the text version of the maps. Administrators modify these text files to update the maps.

   B. It is used to propagate the maps to NIS slave servers.

   C. It is used to poll the NIS clients to ensure that the NIS services are running on them.

   D. It is used to pull the updated maps from NIS slave servers.

Configuring an NIS Master, Slave, and Client

4. Your company relies solely on the NIS passwd map for all user logins. You have just finished configuring an NIS client on a workstation. You execute the /usr/sbin/ypcat command to test the accessibility of your maps, and everything is working correctly. You want to verify that you are able to log in to your NIS client system, so you execute the command /usr/sbin/ypcat passwd | grep *testuser*. The command executes successfully and returns the passwd entry for *testuser*. You Telnet into the new workstation as *testuser* and receive a "Login incorrect" message. Assuming that you spelled the login name correctly and have entered the correct password, what is a possible problem?

   A. The passwd map is corrupted; therefore, when you logged in, the workstation was unable to locate the login information for *testuser*.

   B. You have forgotten to copy the /etc/nsswitch.nis to /etc/nsswitch.conf; therefore, when you logged in as *testuser,* the client was looking for the login information only in the /etc/passwd and /etc/shadow files. Because the entry for *testuser* does not exist in the local file, you received a "Login incorrect" message.

   C. You forgot to run a make the last time you edited the passwd map.

   D. *testuser* does not belong to the sysadmin group; therefore, it is not authorized to log in to this workstation.

Adding a New NIS Map to an Existing Network

5. You would like to add a custom map to your NIS domain and make it available as soon as possible. This custom map will contain the password entries of all employees who no longer work at your company. What is the order of the steps you need to follow to accomplish this task?

   A. Create the text file containing the password entries of the X-employees. Execute the yppush command to push the map to the slave servers. Modify /var/yp/Makefile to include the new map.

   B. Create the text file containing the password entries of the X-employees. Execute the makedbm command to convert the text file into the map. Execute a make command to convert and push the maps.

   C. Create the file containing the password entries of the X-employees. Modify the /var/yp/Makefile to include the new map.

   D. Create the text file containing the password entries of the X-employees. Execute the makedbm command to convert the text file into the map. Execute the yppush command to push the map to the slave servers. Modify the /var/yp/Makefile to include the new map.

6. Which file is used to set up automatic map rebuild and propagating?

    A. /var/yp/Makefile

    B. /usr/ccs/Makefile

    C. /var/yp/binding/domain/ypservers

    D. ypxfrd

Updating and Propagating an NIS Map in an Existing Network

7. You must add an entry in the NIS passwd map. What is the order of operation to accomplish this task?

    A. Modify the source file for the passwd map. Change directory to /var/yp and execute the /usr/ccs/bin/make command.

    B. Modify the map files passwd.byname.pag and passwd.byname.pag in the /var/yp/domain directory. Execute the /usr/ccs/bin/make command.

    C. Edit the /etc/passwd and /etc/shadow files. Change directory to /var/yp and execute the /usr/ccs/bin/make command.

    D. Execute the makedbm command to convert the passwd map to text files in the /tmp directory. Add an entry to the text file and execute the /usr/ccs/bin/make command.

Adding and Removing NIS Slave Servers in the Existing NIS Environment

8. Which NIS map contains the list of NIS slave servers in the domain?

    A. hosts

    B. ypserver

    C. ypservers

    D. nisservers

LAB QUESTION

Your company has grown in the last four months, and managing the growing number of systems in your environment has become an impossible task. Your company has modified the computing environment model from individually owned workstations to shared access. Everyone should be able to access any workstation in the company. You decide it is time to implement NIS in your environment. Because your company is still small enough, the admin in charge of the network has implemented only two subnets with one router as the gateway. One subnet is dedicated to the engineering department; the other is for all the other departments in the company.

Everyone in the engineering department has a UNIX workstation with the individual login information in the local /etc/passwd and /etc/shadow files. In other words, the /etc/passwd and /etc/shadow files contain the login information for the person who uses the workstation. Each workstation has different entries in its /etc/hosts table. There is no consistent configuration for the /etc/hosts tables. The other departments have a total of eight UNIX workstations, also with their individual login and hosts tables.

Your department policy has always been that the engineering department has priority over all the other departments in your company. The engineers must have 24/7 access with 99.99 percent uptime. (The 1 percent downtime is allowed for system maintenance.) The budget for your NIS project allows for only two servers. Describe the strategy for setting up your NIS domain and list the steps that you must execute to set up the domain.

SELF TEST ANSWERS

Understanding the Processes and Components
of the NIS Domain: Master, Slave, and Client

1. ☑ **B.** The /etc/nsswitch.conf file is used to control search order in which the client's application accesses the information in the name services.

☒ **A, C,** and **D** are incorrect because they do not define any functions of the /etc/nsswitch.conf file.

2. ☑ **A, C,** and **D.**

☒ **B** is incorrect because the maps do not store information about their location and there is no registry in the maps. **E** is incorrect because you cannot change the location of the map files.

3. ☑ **A** and **B.** The administrator must edit the text version of the maps on the NIS master server, and then run a make process to convert the files to maps. The master server pushes the maps to the NIS slave servers.

☒ **C** is incorrect because the NIS master server does not verify the services on the NIS clients. **D** is incorrect because, by default, the NIS master server pushes the information to NIS slave servers.

Configuring an NIS Master, Slave, and Client

4. ☑ **B.** When you attempted to log in to the workstation, the program made a system call to attempt to confirm the *testuser* login. It was unable to retrieve the information because the passwd service in the /etc/nsswitch.conf allows searches only in the local file. To confirm this problem, you can run the command /usr/bin/getent passwd *testuser*.

☒ **A** and **C** are incorrect because you already verified the map entry for *testuser*. **D** is incorrect because there is no special group configured on the workstation.

Adding a New NIS Map to an Existing Network

5. ☑ **D** is correct.

☒ **A** is incorrect because the text file was not converted to a map. **B** is incorrect because the make command will not transfer the map until the new map is added to the /var/yp/Makefile. **C** is incorrect because the maps needed to be converted and pushed to the slave servers.

6. ☑ A is correct.

☒ B is incorrect because /usr/ccs/Makefile does not exist. C is incorrect because /var/yp/binding/domain/ypservers is an NIS map containing a list of slave servers. D is incorrect because the ypxfrd deamon runs on the NIS master server.

Updating and Propagating an NIS Map in an Existing Network

7. ☑ A is correct.

☒ B is incorrect because the maps are in binary format and cannot be easily edited. C is incorrect because you are editing only the local copy of the passwd table, which will not affect the NIS map. D is incorrect because the make command will convert only the files that are located in the existing network environment in the designated source directory.

Adding and Removing NIS Slave Servers in the Existing NIS Environment

8. ☑ C is correct.

☒ A is incorrect because the hosts map contains hostname and IP reference. B and D are incorrect because ypserver and nisservers are incorrect map names.

LAB ANSWER

Because the engineering department has priority and requires the most uptime, you should assign the two servers on the engineering subnet. One of the servers will be configured as the NIS master and the other as the NIS slave. If the NIS server is unavailable, the NIS slave server will answer the client's requests. To configure the clients on the engineering subnet, you can use the broadcast method. The eight UNIX workstations in the other subnet should be configured using the server list method. This will cause the clients to directly bind to the servers in the engineering subnet. Your steps should be as follows:

1. Collect the login information from each UNIX workstation and create a file to contain the entries.

2. Collect the hosts table entries from all the workstations and combine them into a text file for the hosts map.

3. Prepare the NIS master server and the text source files.

4. Initialize the NIS master server on the engineering subnet.

5. Initialize the NIS slave server on the engineering subnet.

6. Initialize the NIS clients on the engineering subnet using

   # /usr/sbin/ypinit -broadcast

7. Verify that workstations in the other subnet can communicate with the NIS master and the slave servers.

8. Add the hostname and IP of the NIS master and slave servers to the local /etc/hosts table.

9. Initialize the NIS clients on the other subnet using

   # /usr/sbin/ypinit –c

10. Enter the name of the NIS master server and NIS slave server.

11. Verify the maps on the workstations.

12. Clean up the local passwd, shadow, and hosts files.

Solaris™
SUN® CERTIFIED SYSTEM ADMINISTRATOR

27

Utilizing
Role-Based
Access Control

N ew in Solaris 8 and enhanced in Solaris 9, *role-based access control* (RBAC) provides a flexible alternative to the traditional UNIX security model. Previous versions of the Solaris operating environment were limited to an all-or-nothing, superuser-based security system in which individual users were either extremely powerful or very limited. With RBAC, you, as a system administrator, are able to bundle up the access privileges needed to accomplish a certain task and assign only those privileges to an individual user or a group of users. This flexibility empowers you to dispense to a user the needed amount of system access—no more, no less.

Solaris implements RBAC in four text-based database files. This chapter prepares you for the exam by introducing you to the concepts of the traditional UNIX execution security model and how it compares with RBAC. You will explore RBAC in depth and discover how it can be controlled directly (by manipulating the information in the four data files) or indirectly (using a new set of Solaris commands).

CERTIFICATION OBJECTIVE 27.01

Relating Role-Based Access Control to Solaris Security

The addition of RBAC to the Solaris operating environment addresses the flexibility of the traditional UNIX execution security model. Traditional UNIX security is implemented through two mechanisms: file permissions and execution security. This section examines the traditional UNIX security model and compares it with the RBAC security model.

A Look at the Traditional Solaris Security Model

In 1969, two AT&T researchers, Ken Thompson and Dennis Ritchie, began work on a new operating system for a Digital PDP-7 computer. Their research was an offshoot of their work on the U.S. Department of Defense funded MULTICS project and would eventually be called UNIX, as a parody of that earlier system. MULTICS was developed with security very much in mind and was intended to allow different classes of secret government information to exist on the same machine, with strict access controls.

In contrast to the large Defense Department roots of MULTICS, UNIX was created by two guys in a research lab and further developed by thousands of computer science students at universities across the world. In most early UNIX implementations, security was, at best, a secondary consideration. Many early systems did not even implement root passwords, since everyone who had a key to the computer room was supposed to have superuser access anyway.

The growing popularity of UNIX and the rising number of users connected to UNIX machines via networks necessitated the enforcement and evolution of the UNIX security model. UNIX security grants system access to each user based on the user's account. Accounts are identified by *username* and authenticated through a shared secret called a *password*. UNIX accounts can be members of one or more groups.

Traditional UNIX security takes two forms: file access security and file execution security. Both types of traditional UNIX security permissions are stored on a per-file basis in a file index called an *inode*. Each file is associated with an account that owns it and a group of accounts that have access to it. Access and execution permissions are granted in three classes of granularity: the permissions granted to the file owner, the permissions granted to the file group, and the permissions granted to everyone else.

Traditional UNIX File Access Permissions

This section touches only briefly on traditional UNIX file access permissions because they are the focus of earlier chapters. UNIX file access permissions control which user accounts are able to read and execute each individual file. Like all UNIX permissions, different sets of permissions can be granted to three different entities: the file owner, the file group, and everyone else. Each set of permissions is stored in the file's inode (index node) and can be viewed using the ls -*l* command. The following is a sample output of an ls -*l* command:

```
$ ls -l
total 1
-rw-rw-r--   1 root     sys          728 Jan  5  2000 file_one
-rw-r-----   1 root     sys          149 Jan  5  2000 file_two
```

The first set of text at the beginning of each line shows the file permissions for each class of access, beginning with a single character that denotes the file type, followed by three groups of three characters each. Each three-character group denotes the file permissions for a different class of access. The first three-character group displays permissions for the file's owner. The second group displays permissions for members of the file's group. The third set displays permissions for everyone else on the system. Each three-character group displays read permissions as an *r* and write permissions as a *w*. In the preceding example, file_one is readable (r) and writable (w) by its owner (root). It can be read from and written to by members of its group (sys), and it can only be read by everyone else on the system.

The traditional UNIX security model can grant only these three classes of access. It is not possible to implement security that is more granular than owner, group, and everyone. It is not possible to, for instance, grant different file access permissions to each user on the system.

Solaris addresses the inflexibility of the traditional UNIX security model with access control lists (ACLs). ACLs permit an administrator to grant different access permissions on a per-user basis. ACLs are covered in detail in Chapter 6.

Traditional UNIX File Execution Permissions

Related to the idea of UNIX file access permissions are file *execution permissions.* Execution permissions pertain only to executable files and scripts. Execution permissions control which accounts or groups of accounts can execute a given file and the access permissions the shell has as it executes the file. UNIX execution permissions are also maintained on a per-file basis and stored in each file's inode. These permissions can be displayed using the ls *-l* command in the same way as UNIX file access permissions. Each of the three-character permission groups discussed in the previous section also denotes execution permission. If the third character of the three-character set is an *x,* that class of account is allowed to execute the file. The following is a sample output from the ls *-l* command showing files with the execute permission set:

```
$ ls -1
total 175
---s--x--x   1 uucp     uucp        19568 Jan  5  2000 uuname
-r-xr-xr-x   1 root     uucp         3536 Jan  5  2000 uupick
---s--x--x   1 uucp     uucp        61832 Jan  5  2000 uustat
-r-xr-xr-x   1 root     uucp         1927 Jan  5  2000 uuto
---s--x--x   1 uucp     uucp        70852 Jan  5  2000 uux
-r-xr-xr--   1 root     bin         17360 Jan  5  2000 vacation
```

In the example output, the root user is allowed to execute the vacation file because the *x* bit is set in the first three-character group. Because this group pertains to the file owner and because root owns the file, root is allowed to execute the file. In contrast, an account with username *brian* that is not a member of the bin group will not be allowed to execute the vacation file. Because *brian* is not the file owner and not a member of the file group, he falls under the *everyone else* category. The *everyone else* three-character group does not have an *x,* and thus *brian* is not allowed to execute the file. Like file access permissions, execution permissions revolve around the three-class model of file owner, file group, and everyone else. Execution permissions can be granted only granularly to these three entities. You cannot assign a different set of execution permissions to each account on the system using the traditional UNIX model.

When an account executes a file, the resulting process runs with the access permissions of that account. The new process can only read and write files that the calling account can read or write—that is, unless the SUID or SGID bits are set. Similarly to the execution bit, the SUID and SGID bits are stored in the file's inode and displayed by ls -*l.* The preceding sample output shows the SUID bit set for the uuname file. This bit, displayed as an *s* character in the execution slot of the file owner group, does not signify permissions granted to the owner of the file. Rather, it denotes that when the file is executed, the resulting process runs with the permissions of the file owner rather than the account that executed it. So, for instance, if you logged in with your *brian* account and executed the uuname file, the resulting process would run with the access permissions of the root user instead of with *brian*'s permissions. The SGID bit works the same way, but the resulting process runs with the access permissions of the file's group.

Like access permissions, traditional UNIX execution permissions are limited because they can be assigned only to the file owner, the file group, or everyone else. If you need a certain user to be able to perform some administration functions as root, you must either give that user the root password or set the owner and SUID bit on the administration executables so that they execute as root. If you go the root password route, the user has much more power than he or she actually needs. If you choose to set the SUID bit, everyone who runs the tools that you change will be running them as root. Both solutions have severe limitations.

on the
Job

You could consider creating a shell script and setting the SUID bit so that the script executes as root. This seems like a good idea because it would allow you to run certain tools as root without modifying the SUID bit on the programs themselves. In reality, however, this practice can open up an enormous security hole. Because shell scripts are interpreted by the shell, when you run a SUID shell script, Solaris starts up a root version of the shell to interpret the script. If the user can find a way to interrupt the script, the user will find himself or herself unchecked, running a working root shell. This is not a good idea.

Solaris RBAC provides a safe way to run scripts as root. Using execution attributes, you can assign the root user (or any user) as the UID to run the script. Unlike traditional SUID, however, RBAC has a special shell called a profile shell. RBAC has one of these shell executables for each of the traditional UNIX shells: pfsh for Borne, pfksh for Korn, and pfcsh for the C shell. These shells execute the SUID script or executable. They are designed to remove security risks by minimizing the superuser environment.

The RBAC Security Model

In contrast to the owner-group-everyone traditional Solaris security model is the new RBAC. RBAC enables the administrator to finely control execution permissions by sorting user capabilities into two concepts: authorizations and executions. These capabilities can then be grouped together to form profiles, and these profiles are assigned to a user or role. This model provides a much more flexible environment because the same command can be designated to execute with different UIDs in each profile. Using RBAC, a user's security environment is determined by the construction of the profile that is assigned to the user's account, not by setting immutable security attributes in each command's inode. RBAC thus extends the security model to enable the administrator to seamlessly create a security context for one user without affecting the security context for others.

Authorization Attributes

Authorization attributes are a new concept in Solaris security. Authorizations are defined in the /etc/security/auth_attr database and are checked by certain privileged applications to verify whether they should be able to use restricted functionality. Authorizations can be assigned to a profile or directly to a user. When a user attempts to use an "authorization-aware" privileged application, the application searches the /etc/security/auth_attr file to make sure the user is assigned the appropriate authorization before it executes the command. These authorizations are application specific, and the application must be designed to take advantage of this new Solaris feature. Several of the core operating system utilities have already been rewritten with authorization awareness, but many GNU or third-party utilities have yet to adopt this model.

Execution Attributes

If the application or command that you need to use is not authorization aware, RBAC still enables you refined control over its operation through execution attributes. Defined in /etc/security/exec_attr, execution attributes identify the path to a command and set the UID under which the command executes. This command/UID pair is assigned to a profile, and that profile is assigned to a user or role. Each profile can define command execution UIDs differently in the exec_attr database. Thus, a user with the printer management profile could be set up to execute the lpadmin command as the lp user, whereas a user with the system administrator profile would run the same command as root. Both of these executions are defined without setting the SUID bit of the file or affecting how any other user executes the command. Execution attributes are a very flexible way of controlling execution permissions on a per-user rather than per-file basis.

Profiles

Solaris RBAC profiles group together authorization and execution attributes into a security group that can be assigned to one or more users or roles. Profiles are defined in the /etc/security/prof_attr database. Profiles provide the means by which action authorizations are assigned.

Users and Roles

RBAC defines additional attributes for Solaris user accounts. The /etc/user_attr database tracks the profiles assigned to a user and the authorizations that are directly assigned. Additionally, the user attribute database defines a new type of user called a *role*. Role accounts can be assigned authorizations and profiles, but users cannot log in directly as role accounts. Users must use the su utility to change to a role. Assigning profiles to a role does not have as great a potential to compromise security as assigning them directly to user accounts because they are protected by both the user's password and the role account's password.

EXERCISE 27-1

Traditional Solaris Security: Setting the SUID Bit

Now that you have some background information on Solaris security, in this exercise, you will practice setting an SUID bit using the chmod command.

1. You must be logged in as root to complete this exercise. Create a directory called *test* and change into it:

```
mkdir test
cd test
```

2. Copy the cp command into the directory:

```
cp /bin/cp ./
```

3. Make sure it is owned by root:

```
chown root cp
```

4. Set the SUID bit on the command:

```
chmod 4755 cp
```

5. Now, anyone who runs this file will run it as root. To verify that the SUID bit has been set, use the ls *–l* command and compare the output with the example before this exercise:

```
ls -l
```

6. Don't forget to delete this superuser version of cp once you have finished with it!

```
rm ./cp
```

CERTIFICATION OBJECTIVE 27.02

Understanding the Role-Based Access Control Database Features

Solaris RBAC is supported by four databases. Each of the pieces of RBAC, as described in the preceding section, has its own database. Table 27-1 describes the locations of these databases.

This section describes the format of each database in detail. It also explores some new tools and new options in some old tools for managing the RBAC databases. Finally, it also looks at some common exam questions on creating and assigning RBAC profiles.

RBAC Database Format

Each of the database files described in Table 27-1 uses a format similar to that of the /etc/password and /etc/shadow databases. RBAC attributes are stored in a colon-separated list. Each of the database files can be written to only by root. Any program that intends to directly manipulate these databases must either be run by the root user or have the traditional SUID bit set and be owned by the root user.

The Authorization Attributes Database

All authorizations are stored in /etc/security/auth_attr. Authorizations can be assigned directly to a user or role. They can also be assigned indirectly by assigning them first to a profile, and then assigning the profile to a user or role. Authorizations are added to the database by directly editing the auth_attr database file. The following code describes the format of the auth_attr database file. This file uses a colon-delimited format similar to /etc/passwd.

```
authname:res1:res2:short_desc:long_desc:attr
```

TABLE 27-1	RBAC Component	Database File Path
RBAC Component Databases	Authorization attributes	/etc/security/auth_attr
	Execution attributes	/etc/security/exec_attr
	Profiles	/etc/security/prof_attr
	Users and roles	/etc/user_attr

Table 27-2 describes each of the fields in the auth_attr database.

The following example shows an excerpt from the auth_attr file, displaying several of the default Solaris operating environment authorizations:

```
#
solaris.*:::Primary Administrator::help=PriAdmin.html
solaris.grant:::Grant All Rights::help=PriAdmin.html
#

solaris.audit.:::Audit Management::help=AuditHeader.html
solaris.audit.config:::Configure Auditing::help=AuditConfig.html
solaris.audit.read:::Read Audit Trail::help=AuditRead.html
#
solaris.device.:::Device Allocation::help=DevAllocHeader.html
solaris.device.allocate:::Allocate Device::help=DevAllocate.html
solaris.device.config:::Configure Device Attributes::help=DevConfig.html
solaris.device.grant:::Delegate Device Administration::help=DevGrant.html
solaris.device.revoke:::Revoke or Reclaim Device::help=DevRevoke.html
#
solaris.jobs.:::Cron and At Jobs::help=JobHeader.html
solaris.jobs.admin:::Cron & At Administrator::help=JobsAdmin.html
solaris.jobs.grant:::Delegate Cron & At
Administration::help=JobsGrant.html
solaris.jobs.user:::Create at or cron jobs::help=JobsUser.html
```

Notice the special .grant and .revoke authorizations. Any authorization that ends in the suffix .grant or .revoke is a special authorization giving the user, role, or profile the ability to grant or revoke the base authorization. Returning to the earlier example, a user with the solaris.jobs.grant has the ability to assign the solaris.jobs.* series of authorizations to another user, role, or profile.

The Execution Attributes Database

Execution attributes are stored in the /etc/security/exec_attr database, the format of which is shown next. Unlike authorizations, execution attributes cannot be assigned directly to a user or role. Execution attributes are properties of a profile, and that corresponding profile must be assigned to a user or role. Execution attributes define a command and attributes for how the command is going to run, such as UID, GID, EUID, and EGID. The exec_attr database uses a colon-delimited format similar to /etc/passwd.

```
Name:policy:type:res1:res2:id:attr
```

TABLE 27-2	The auth_attr Database Fields

Field Name	Description
authname	A character string that identifies the authorization. Each authname must be unique. They are hierarchical and similar in construction to Internet domain names. Authorizations for Solaris operating environment privileges begin with *solaris*. Custom authorizations in your environment should begin with the reverse of your Internet domain: for example, com.corporationname. Authname suffixes describe the functionality being authorized. For example, a user with the solaris.jobs.admin authorization has the security privileges to modify cron jobs.
res1	Not used; reserved field for future use by Sun.
res2	Not used; reserved field for future use by Sun.
short_desc	A short human-readable name to describe the authorization. Typically displayed in application GUI drop-down lists.
long_desc	A long human-readable description of the authorization. Typically displayed by application help files.
attr	Optional. A list of semicolon-separated key-value pairs. These pairs describe optional attributes of the authorization. The only widely used key at this time is help, which identifies an HTML help file for the authorization.
attr	Optional. A list of semicolon-separated key-value pairs. These pairs describe optional attributes of the authorization. The only widely used key at this time is help, which identifies an HTML help file for the authorization.

Table 27-3 describes each of the fields in the exec_attr database.

TABLE 27-3	The exec_attr Database Fields

Field Name	Description
Name	The name of the profile that contains the execution attributes. Profile names are case sensitive.
Policy	The security policy of this attribute. Currently, suser is the only valid value.
Type	The type of attribute. Currently, cmd is the only valid value.
res1	Not used; reserved field for future use by Sun.
res2	Not used; reserved field for future use by Sun.

TABLE 27-3	The exec_attr Database Fields (continued)

Field Name	Description
id	The full path to the command. Wildcards can be used, but arguments cannot be passed to the command. To pass arguments, you must include them in a script, and then specify the path to the script in this field.
attr	Optional; a list of semicolon-separated key-value pairs. These pairs describe optional attributes of the execution attribute. There are four valid keys: UID, GID, EUID, and EGID. Each UID key is set to either a userid number or name. GID keys are set to either a group ID number or name. These keys specify the real or effective user and group that the command will execute.

The following is an excerpt from the exec_attr file, displaying several of the default Solaris execution attributes:

```
All:suser:cmd:::*:
Audit Control:suser:cmd:::/etc/init.d/audit:euid=0;egid=3
Audit Control:suser:cmd:::/etc/security/bsmconv:uid=0
Audit Control:suser:cmd:::/etc/security/bsmunconv:uid=0
Audit Control:suser:cmd:::/usr/sbin/audit:euid=0
Audit Control:suser:cmd:::/usr/sbin/auditconfig:euid=0
Audit Control:suser:cmd:::/usr/sbin/auditd:uid=0
Audit Review:suser:cmd:::/usr/sbin/auditreduce:euid=0
Audit Review:suser:cmd:::/usr/sbin/praudit:euid=0
Audit Review:suser:cmd:::/usr/sbin/auditstat:euid=0
Printer Management:suser:cmd:::/etc/init.d/lp:euid=0
Printer Management:suser:cmd:::/usr/bin/cancel:euid=0
Printer Management:suser:cmd:::/usr/bin/lpset:egid=14
Printer Management:suser:cmd:::/usr/bin/enable:euid=lp
Printer Management:suser:cmd:::/usr/bin/disable:euid=lp
Printer Management:suser:cmd:::/usr/sbin/accept:euid=lp
Printer Management:suser:cmd:::/usr/sbin/reject:euid=lp
Printer Management:suser:cmd:::/usr/sbin/lpadmin:egid=14
Printer Management:suser:cmd:::/usr/sbin/lpfilter:euid=lp
Printer Management:suser:cmd:::/usr/sbin/lpforms:euid=lp
Printer Management:suser:cmd:::/usr/sbin/lpmove:euid=lp
Printer Management:suser:cmd:::/usr/sbin/lpshut:euid=lp
Printer Management:suser:cmd:::/usr/sbin/lpusers:euid=lp
```

Notice the special All profile. This profile grants all execution attributes and is typically assigned only to the superuser.

FROM THE CLASSROOM

UIDs vs. EUIDs

It is easy to become confused about the difference between a UID and an EUID. UIDs are real user IDs, and EUIDs are effective user IDs. Every Solaris process has two identities: its real ID and its effective ID. Normally, these two are the same. When you log in, both identities are set to your login identity.

Occasionally, you might want to change your UID. You can assume the root user ID to create a user or change to the print administrator to delete a print job. When you use the su command to change your identity, you log in and obtain a new shell. This shell has the real user ID (UID) of the new user.

Occasionally, though, you need to run a single command as a different user using an SUID command. When you execute an SUID command, your UID stays the same, but your effective user ID (EUID) changes to the owner of the file for the duration of the SUID command. This grants you the *effective* privileges of that user for a short duration.

RBAC execution attributes allow you fine-grained control over whether your commands run with the real or effective permissions. RBAC even allows you to specify real or effective group permissions or any combination thereof.

—*Brian Albrecht, SCSA, MCSE, TCEC, CCNA*

The Execution Profile Attributes Database

An execution profile is a way to bundle authorizations and execution attributes. Execution profiles can be assigned to users or roles and grant all the profile authorizations and execution attributes to that user or role. Profile definitions are stored in the /etc/security/prof_attr database. The following describes the format of the prof_attr database. This database uses a colon-delimited format similar to /etc/passwd.

```
profname:res1:res2:desc:attr
```

Table 27-4 describes each of the fields in the prof_attr database.

TABLE 27-4	The prof_attr Database Fields

Field Name	Description
profname	The name of the profile. This name must match character for character the corresponding profile name in exec_attr, or the system will not associate any execution attributes with this profile. Profile names are case sensitive.
res1	Not used; reserved field for future use by Sun.
res2	Not used; reserved field for future use by Sun.
desc	A human-readable long description of the profile. This text should accurately describe the profile and explain its purpose
attr	Optional; a list of semicolon-separated key-value pairs. These pairs describe optional attributes of the authorization. One widely used key at this time is help, which identifies an HTML help file for the profile. A second possible key is auths. This key specifies a comma-separated list of authorization assigned to the profile. Authorization names can also be specified using the wildcard character. For example, auths=solaris.jobs.* assigns the profile all the solaris.jobs authorization.

The following is an excerpt from the prof_attr file, displaying several of the default Solaris execution attributes:

```
All:::Standard Solaris user:help=All.html
Audit Control:::Administer the audit
subsystem:auths=solaris.audit.config,solaris.jobs.admin;help=AuditControl.html
Audit Review:::View the audit trail:auths=solaris.audit.read;help=AuditReview.html

Device Management:::Control Access to Removable
Media:auths=solaris.device.*;help=DevMgmt.html
Printer Management:::Control Access to Printer:help=PrinterMgmt.html
```

Notice again the special All profile. This profile assigns *all* other profiles to a user or role. This essentially makes a user account or role into superuser. This profile should be assigned with great care because it automatically assigns the ability to grant or revoke other profiles.

The User Attributes Database

The user attributes database extends the /etc/passwd and /etc/shadow databases. The user attributes database defines extended security attributes and ties the Solaris user account to RBAC. This database also introduces the concept of a *role:* an account for which the type in the user_attr database is set to role. Role accounts must exist in /etc/passwd and /etc/shadow as well as /etc/user_attr. They cannot log in to the system, however. Authorizations and profiles can be assigned to a role account. A user can then gain access to those authorizations and profiles using the su command to change to the role user. Role accounts are intended to be used only to perform administration tasks.

The following shows the colon-separated format used in the user_attr database. This format is similar to that used in /etc/passwd. Table 27-5 describes each field in the user_attr database.

```
user:qualifier:res1:res2:attr
```

Of the fields listed in Table 27-5, the attr field has the most significance in determining a user's or role's security environment. Options that can be placed in the attr field are the following:

- **Auths**   A comma-separated list of authorizations from the auth_attr database that will be directly assigned to the user or role. Wildcards can be used to designate more than one suffix.

- **Profiles**   A comma-separated list of profiles from the prof_attr database that are assigned to the user or role. The listed user has all the privileges for each authorization or execution attribute assigned each of his or her profiles.

- **Roles**   A comma-separated list of roles to which the user can switch using the su command. Each role assigned in this manner must also be defined in

TABLE 27-5   The user_attr Database Fields

Field Name	Description
User	The account username. This must be the same as what is recorded in the /etc/passwd and /etc/shadow databases.
qualifier	Not used; reserved field for future use by Sun.
res1	Not used; reserved field for future use by Sun.
res2	Not used; reserved field for future use by Sun.
Attr	Optional; a list of semicolon-separated key-value pairs. These pairs describe optional security attributes of the user or role. Valid values are auths, profiles, roles, and type.

/etc/user_attr, as well as in /etc/passwd and /etc/shadow. Roles cannot be assigned to another role, only to users.

■ **Type** An attribute that signifies whether the entry is a user or a role. In either case, there must be a corresponding entry in /etc/passwd and /etc/shadow.

The following code shows an excerpt from the Solaris default /etc/user_attr database:

```
root::::type=normal;auths=solaris.*,solaris.grant;profiles=All
```

Be careful to separate the auths with commas. The auth= section is one attr key-value pair, and must be separated from additional key-value pairs with a semicolon. The individual authorizations themselves, however, should be separated with commas.

RBAC Tools

Solaris 8 added several new commands for managing RBAC. Several other tools have gained new options to allow you to manage RBAC alongside traditional Solaris security. This section examines some of those tools and how they relate to the RBAC databases and each other. Table 27-6 briefly describes each RBAC command.

TABLE 27-6   Quick Reference to the RBAC Tools

RBAC Command	Description
profiles	Lists the profiles assigned to the specified user
roles	Lists the roles assigned to the specified user
roleadd	Adds a role to the /etc/user_attr, /etc/passwd, and /etc/shadow files
rolemod	Modifies an existing role by modifying its entry in /etc/user_attr, /etc/passwd, and /etc/shadow files
roledel	Deletes an existing role from /etc/user_attr, /etc/passwd, and /etc/shadow files
useradd	Adds a user to the /etc/user_attr, /etc/passwd, and /etc/shadow files
usermod	Modifies an existing user by modifying its entry in /etc/user_attr, /etc/passwd, and /etc/shadow files
userdel	Deletes an existing user from /etc/user_attr, /etc/passwd, and /etc/shadow files

Many RBAC tools take different command-line options. Each tool has a different purpose and use.

The Profiles and Roles Commands: Displaying User Properties

The profiles and roles commands are used to display RBAC information for a user. Roles displays the roles that are currently assigned to the user in the /etc/user_attr database. You can specify one or more usernames on the command line. If you don't specify a username on the command line, roles display information for the current user. The following is an output from the roles command:

```
# roles john
role1,super
```

The profiles command is similar to the roles command except that it displays the profiles that are assigned to the current user in the /etc/user_attr database. The profiles command is also able to take multiple usernames on the command line and returns information on the current user if none is specified. Unlike roles, however, profiles also take the *-l* option, which instructs the profiles command to also list the execution attributes for each profile. The following is a sample output from the profiles command:

```
# profiles root
All
```

The roles and profiles commands are straightforward. They are very useful in determining exactly which attributes have been assigned to a particular user without parsing through the entire set of RBAC databases.

The roleadd, rolemod, and roledel Commands: Managing Roles

You use the role* commands to manage role accounts in the RBAC databases. You should use these commands to add, modify, and remove role entries rather than modifying the text file directly. The roleadd and rolemod commands take a similar set of command-line options. The only difference between the two is that roleadd supports an additional option *-D* for viewing and setting system default properties for roles. Other than *-D,* the rolemod uses a subset of the command options used by roleadd. Table 27-7 lists and describes these options.

Calling roleadd without the *-D* option adds a role to the RBAC databases. Calling rolemod with the same set of options modifies an existing role entry within

| TABLE 27-7 | Command-Line Options for roleadd and rolemod (from the Man Page) |

Option	Description
-b base_dir	The default base directory for the system if *-d* dir is not specified. base_dir is concatenated with the account name to define the home directory. If the *-m* option is not used, base_dir must exist.
-c comment	Any text string. It is generally a short description of the role. This information is stored in the role's /etc/passwd entry.
-d dir	The home directory of the new role. It defaults to *base_dir/ account_name*, where *base_dir* is the base directory for new login home directories and *account_name* is the new role name.
-D	Displays the default values for *group, base_dir, skel_dir, shell, inactive,* and *expire.* When used with the *-g, -b,* or *-f* options, the *-D* option sets the default values for the specified fields. The default values are as follows: group: other (GID of 1) *base_dir:* /home *skel_dir:* /etc/skel *shell:* /bin/sh *inactive:* 0 *expire:* Null *auths:* Null *profiles:* Null
-e expire	Specifies the expiration date for a role. After this date, no user is able to access this role. The expire option argument is a date entered using one of the date formats included in the template file /etc/datemsk. If the date format that you choose includes spaces, it must be quoted. For example, you can enter 10/6/90 or October 6, 1990. A null value (" ") defeats the status of the expired date. This option is useful for creating temporary roles.
-f inactive	The maximum number of days allowed between uses of a role ID before that ID is declared invalid. Normal values are positive integers. A value of 0 defeats the status.
-g group	An existing group's integer ID or character-string name. Without the *-D* option, it defines the new role's primary group membership and defaults to the default group. You can reset this default value by invoking *roleadd -D -g group.*
-G group	An existing group's integer ID or character-string name. It defines the new role's supplementary group membership. Duplicates between group with the *-g* and *-G* options are ignored. No more than NGROUPS_MAX groups can be specified.
-k skel_dir	A directory that contains skeleton information (such as .profile) that can be copied into a new role's home directory. This directory must already exist. The system provides the /etc/skel directory that can be used for this purpose.

TABLE 27-7	Command-Line Options for roleadd and rolemod (from the Man Page) *(continued)*

Option	Description
-m	Creates the new role's home directory if it does not already exist. If the directory already exists, it must have read, write, and execute permissions by group, where *group* is the role's primary group.
-o	Allows a UID to be duplicated (nonunique).
-s shell	The full pathname of the program used as the user's shell on login. It defaults to an empty field, causing the system to use /bin/sh as the default. The value of *shell* must be a valid executable file.
-u uid	The UID of the new role. This UID must be a nonnegative decimal integer below MAXUID as defined in <sys/param.h>. The UID defaults to the next available (unique) number above the highest number currently assigned. For example, if UIDs 100, 105, and 200 are assigned, the next default UID number will be 201. (UIDs from 0–99 are reserved for possible use in future applications.)

those databases. Calling the roleadd command with the *-D* option displays or changes the defaults used when adding a new role. The following is an example of using the roleadd command with the *-D* option to show system defaults:

```
# roleadd -D
group=other,1  project=,3  basedir=/home
skel=/etc/skel  shell=/bin/pfsh  inactive=0
expire=  auths=  profiles=All
```

A related but simpler command is roledel. This command deletes a role entry from the RBAC databases. This command takes only one option, *-r,* to remove the role's home directory, in addition to deleting the role entry.

It is essential to remember that all three role commands modify the /etc/user_attr, /etc/passwd, and /etc/shadow databases. A role entry must exist in all three databases to be valid, and it must be deleted from all three databases when removed from the system.

The useradd, usermod, and userdel Commands: Managing Users

The user* commands are used to manage user accounts in the RBAC databases. These commands are very similar in function to the role commands. The useradd command also supports the *-D* option for setting default user properties. (For a complete set of command-line options for useradd or usermod, refer to Table 27-7.) The following shows sample output from a useradd -D command. This output is similar in structure to using roleadd -D.

```
# useradd -D
group=other,1  project=,3  basedir=/home
skel=/etc/skel  shell=/bin/sh  inactive=0
expire=  auths=  profiles=  roles=
```

The usermod command is used to modify an existing user, just as rolemod is used to modify an existing role. In addition, like rolemod, usermod does not support the -D option.

The command used to delete user entries, userdel, is identical in usage to roledel. The userdel command also supports the -r option to delete a user's home directory.

It is important to remember that the user commands also modify all three RBAC databases: /etc/user_attr, /etc/passwd, and /etc/shadow.

exam
Ⓦⓐⓣⓒⓗ

It is important to understand that the command-line options for useradd and roleadd are virtually identical. Practice adding some users and roles before taking the exam.

Now that you have a better understanding of the RBAC commands, here are some possible command scenarios and their solutions.

SCENARIO & SOLUTION

How do you add a user to RBAC?	Use the useradd command.
How do you modify the defaults for roles, then add five new roles using those defaults?	Use the roleadd command with -D to set the defaults, then use roleadd to add the roles not specifying values for the properties that should be set to the defaults.
How do you view the default user options for a security audit?	Use the useradd -D command.
How do you view profiles that have been assigned to a user?	Use the profiles command.
How do you assign the prt_mgr profile to user *john*?	Type **usermod -P prt_mgr john.**

Adding a New Role to the System

In this exercise, you add a role to the system called jr_admin that has the print_admin and solaris.device.* authorizations. Then you assign this role to user *john*.

1. Use roleadd to add the role. Type this command:

   ```
   roleadd -A solaris.device.* -P print_admin jr_admin
   ```

2. Set a password for the new role using the passwd command:

   ```
   passwd jr_admin
   ```

3. Assign the role to user *john* with the usermod command:

   ```
   usermod -R jr_admin john
   ```

CERTIFICATION SUMMARY

In this chapter, you learned about role-based access control, or RBAC. RBAC provides a flexible execution security system to replace the all-or-nothing, SUID-based traditional UNIX security model. RBAC attributes are stored in four databases: user_attr, auth_attr, exec_attr, and prof_attr.

RBAC functionality can be controlled using a special set of commands, whose profiles and roles display the profiles and roles assigned to existing users. The roleadd, rolemod, roledel, useradd, usermod, and userdel commands are used to add new roles and new users. These commands use similar syntax and command options.

✓ TWO-MINUTE DRILL

Relating Role-Based Access Control to Solaris Security

❑ The traditional Solaris/UNIX security model is based on assigning file access permissions to users, groups, and everyone.

❑ Every user who can run a file with the SUID bit set will run it as the SUID user; this is an all-or-nothing approach.

❑ The /etc/user_attr database is a text file that stores extended user information and role definitions.

❑ The /etc/security/auth_attr database stores system authorizations that can be assigned to users or profiles.

❑ The /etc/security/exec_attr database stores profile execution attributes that define commands—UID pairs.

❑ The /etc/security/prof_attr database stores profile definitions.

❑ To assume a role, you must su to that role.

Understanding Role-Based Access Control Database Features

❑ The profiles command shows the profiles assigned to a user.

❑ The roles command shows the roles assigned to a user.

❑ The roleadd command adds a new role to the /etc/user_attr, /etc/passwd, and /etc/shadow databases.

❑ The roleadd -D command views and sets role property defaults for all subsequent commands.

❑ The useradd command adds a new user to the /etc/user_attr, /etc/passwd, and /etc/shadow databases.

❑ The useradd -D command views and sets user property defaults for all subsequent commands.

❑ The usermod command modifies an existing user.

❑ The useradd and roleadd commands use virtually identical syntax and options.

SELF TEST

The following questions will help you measure your understanding of the material presented in this chapter. Read all the choices carefully because there might be more than one correct answer. Choose all correct answers for each question.

Relating Role-Based Access Control to Solaris Security

1. Given the following output, which user has read/write/execute permissions to file_one?

```
total 1
-rwxrw-r--   1 root      sys        728 Jan  5  2000 file_one
-rw-r-----   1 root      sys        149 Jan  5  2000 file_two
```

   A. root

   B. sys

   C. Jan

   D. No one

2. Which database(s) store(s) RBAC profile execution attributes?

   A. /etc/init.d

   B. /etc/security/exec_attr

   C. /etc/exec_attr

   D. /etc/passwd

   E. All of the above

3. Which database(s) store(s) RBAC authorization attributes?

   A. /etc/init.d

   B. /etc/security/auth_attr

   C. /etc/security/exec_attr

   D. /etc/passwd

   E. All of the above

4. Which database(s) store(s) RBAC role information?

   A. /etc/passwd

   B. /etc/user_attr

    C. /etc/shadow

    D. All of the above

    E. None of the above

Understanding Role-Based Access Control Database Features

5. Which command shows the profiles assigned to the current user?

    A. profiles

    B. profile *-u*

    C. usershow

    D. userprop

6. Which command changes the defaults for system user properties?

    A. usermod *-D*

    B. useradd *-D*

    C. rolemod *-D*

    D. roleadd *-D*

    E. vi /etc/defaults

7. Which command assigns a role to a user?

    A. rolemod *-u*

    B. usermod *-r*

    C. usermod *-R*

    D. admintool

    E. All of the above

8. Which command do you use to assign a role password?

    A. passwd

    B. rolemod *-p*

    C. rolemod

    D. usermod *-p*

LAB QUESTION

Your company's finance department has created a new group to perform internal audits on a custom accounting application. Part of the audit application runs several Sun servers, and you have been asked to give several auditors extended permissions on those machines. Because the accounting application server was installed as the root user (against your objections), auditors need to run commands in the /usr/local/bin/audit directory as the root user. They also need to be assigned the com.mycompany.accounting.audit authorization attribute.

Explain how to add the various authorizations, execution attributes, profiles, and users onto a system to support your accounting auditors.

SELF TEST ANSWERS

Relating Role-Based Access Control to Solaris Security

1. ☑ **A.** The owner of file_one is the only one with read/write/execute permissions. The output lists the file owner as root.
   ☒ **B, C,** and **D** are all incorrect because none of them owns the file.

2. ☑ **B.** Profile execution attributes are stored in /etc/security/exec_attr.
   ☒ **A, C, D,** and **E** are all incorrect because these are not RBAC databases.

3. ☑ **B.** Authorization attributes are stored in /etc/security/auth_attr.
   ☒ **A, C, D,** and **E** are all incorrect because these are not RBAC databases.

4. ☑ **D.** Role information must also be entered in /etc/passwd, /etc/user_attr, and /etc/shadow before the role is active on the system.
   ☒ **A, B,** and **C** are all only partially correct, and **E** is incorrect because there is a correct answer.

Understanding Role-Based Access Control Database Features

5. ☑ **A.** The profiles command with no options lists the profiles assigned to the current user.
   ☒ **B, C,** and **D** are all incorrect because these commands or options do not exist.

6. ☑ **B.** The usermod command with the -D option modifies user property defaults for any subsequent user created on the system.
   ☒ **A, C, D,** and **E** are all incorrect. The usermod and rolemod commands do not use the -D option. The roleadd command modifies the system defaults for subsequent roles, not users. The vi command is used for editing text files.

7. ☑ **C.** The usermod command with the -R option assigns a role to a user account.
   ☒ **A, B, D,** and **E** are all incorrect because these commands do not assign roles to a user account.

8. ☑ **A.** Role passwords are assigned just like user account passwords, using the passwd utility.
   ☒ **B, C,** and **D** are all incorrect because the passwd command is the only way to assign a password to a role.

LAB ANSWER

Let's add the accounting users and profiles into the system from the top down, starting with the user accounts.

1. Add each user to the system using the useradd command. If the users are already on the system (perhaps they are members of the finance group who already had accounts), you can skip this step.

2. You must create a profile to support your accounting auditors. You need to add the following line to the /etc/security/prof_attr database:

```
Accounting Audit:::accounting:auths=com.mycompany.accounting.audit
```

3. Now assign this profile to each of your users using the usermod command:

```
usermod -P "Accounting Audit" username
```

4. Next, create the application-specific authorization attribute by adding the following line to your /etc/security/auth_attr database:

```
com.mycompany.accounting.audit:::Accounting Audit::
```

5. Finally, you must give your accounting profile users access to their auditing commands and allow them to run as the root UID. In this case, the effective root user ID (EUID) should be sufficient for your purposes. Add the following line to the /etc/security/exec_attr database:

```
Accounting Audit:suser:cmd:::/usr/local/bin/audit/*:euid=0
```

That's all there is to it! Your accounting users are now ready to audit their application. They can run their commands with root privileges, and you need not stay up at night worrying that one of them is going to destroy your system.

Solaris

SUN™ CERTIFIED SYSTEM ADMINISTRATOR

28

Solaris Management Console and Solstice Admin Suite

R eleased as part of the Web-Based Enterprise Management (WBEM) initiative, Solaris Management Console (SMC) 2.1 and Solaris AdminSuite 3.0 (AdminSuite is no longer supported in Solaris 9, but the references are kept in the book for users of previous versions of Solaris) are Java-based applications designed to assist you in the task of managing the Solaris environment. This chapter provides an overview of the two applications.

SMC 2.1 is available as an option when installing the Solaris operating system. AdminSuite is part of the Solaris Admin Pack release. Previous versions of AdminSuite were released in the Solaris Easy Access Server (SEAS) bundle. SEAS is no longer available because most of the applications in this bundle are now included in the Solaris operating system.

The Solaris Management Console

The Solaris Management Console (SMC) is a GUI application that provides a central location to access a set of administrative tools. The SMC has three major parts:

- The console or the client provides access to the tools from anywhere within the network. The client system can access multiple consoles, which connect to multiple servers.

- The server process allows the consoles to connect to the server and access the SMC tools. The default port for the SMC server is 898.

- The SMC tools are grouped in a hierarchical configuration called the *toolbox*. The administrator can configure the toolbox using the SMC *toolbox editor*.

AdminSuite

Similar to SMC, AdminSuite allows you to maintain the database of users, groups, and hosts locally or over the network. These databases can exist on the local host or in an NIS or NIS+ domain. AdminSuite contains wizards that walk you through tasks.

Understanding the Configuration of the Solaris Management Console

The SMC interface provides a common GUI for system administration tools and utilities. It allows the use of these administration tools and utilities both locally and remotely.

To start the SMC, type the following command:

```
/usr/sadm/bin/smc
```

To set the preferences for the SMC, select Console | Preferences. Preferences can be configured for the following items:

- **Console**   Configures how the console should start, as well as the location of the home toolbox

- **Appearance**   Defines the console layout and allows the user to select interaction style

- **Toolbar**   Defines the appearance of the toolbar

- **Fonts**   Specifies the fonts, font sizes, styles, and colors used in the SMC

- **Tool Loading**   Defines how the toolboxes will be loaded

- **Authentication**   Selects how SMC authentication is handled when loading tools from multiple servers

The SMC toolbox is an organized view of the applications or tools that are available. The toolbox presents the data in a hierarchical tree for accessibility. Each SMC server is configured with a default toolbox named *this_computer*. The actual toolbox file is named with a .tbx extension. The default location of the *this_computer* toolbox is /var/sadm/smc/toolboxes/*this_computer*/*this_computer*.tbx. The toolbox is made up of the following components:

- **Management Tools**   At the topmost level of the tools tree, the Management Tools contain the toolbox. Multiple toolboxes from different servers can be added to the management tools. The default toolbox file for the Management Tool is /var/sadm/smc/toolboxes/smc/smc.tbx.

■ **Folders**   These contain groups of tools.

■ **Tools**   These are applications that are compatible with SMC applets.

■ **Links**   These link to other toolboxes.

■ **Applications that are not SMC tools**   Also referred to as *legacy applications,* these can be a script or a command-line interface (CLI), an X Windows application, or a Uniform Resource Locator (URL).

An example of the standard tree in the navigation pane of the toolbox is shown here:

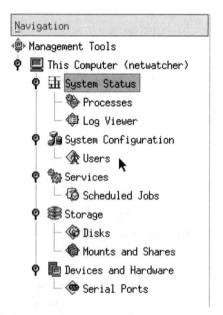

You can configure the toolbox using the toolbox editor. The toolbox editor allows you to make modifications including these:

■ Create links to other toolboxes from the Management Tools level or from the toolbox level.

■ Create a local or server toolbox.

■ Add folders to the toolbox.

■ Add tools to the toolbox.

- Modify the toolbox items properties.
- Add a legacy application to the toolbox.

You can configure the toolbox in two ways: using the GUI or executing the smcconf command. Let's take a look at each method.

Configuring the Toolbox Using the GUI

The recommended way to configure the toolbox is to run the toolbox editor in GUI mode. Although any account can modify the toolbox in SMC, only the root account is allowed to save modifications. To enter the toolbox editor, execute the following command:

```
# /usr/sadm/bin/smc edit &
```

By default, Management Tools automatically loads the SMC toolbox. You can create links to toolboxes that are on the current server or located on other servers.

EXERCISE 28-1

Adding Links to Other Toolboxes

In this exercise, you will add links to other toolboxes under Management Tools.

1. Log in as root and start the toolbox editor:

   ```
   # /usr/sadm/bin/smc edit &
   ```

2. Select Management Tools in the navigation pane. First, open the toolbox by selecting Toolbox | Open, as shown in the next illustration, or select the Open Toolbox icon. Select the top level of the toolbox instead of Management Tools.

3. Select Action | Add Toolbox URL to launch the wizard, as shown here:

4. Select either Server Toolbox or Local Toolbox to add one or the other, as shown next. Then click the Next button to continue. If this is a local toolbox, the wizard displays a file browser for locating the toolbox file.

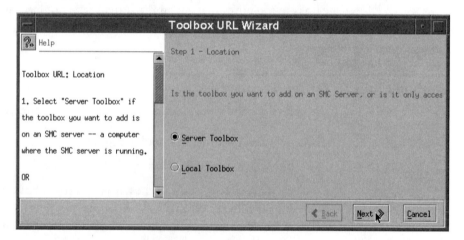

5. Remove the current server's name and enter the new server's name, as shown next. Click Next to continue.

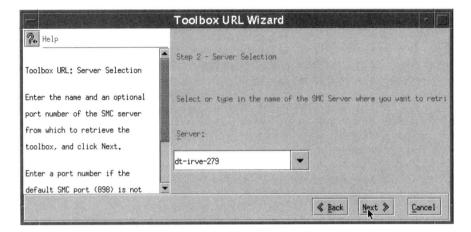

6. If SMC is running correctly on the target server, the wizard automatically displays the available toolboxes on the server, as shown next. Select the This Computer toolbox from the Toolboxes selection window. Then click Next.

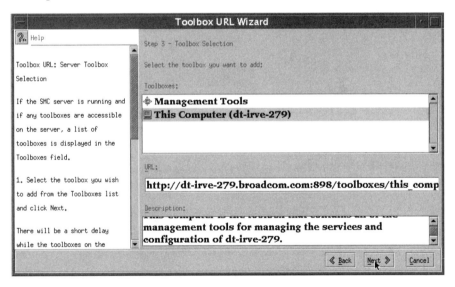

7. For the name and description of the toolbox, use the default setting of Use Toolbox Defaults, and click Next.

8. Select the Use Toolbox Defaults setting for the icons option (shown next). Click Next.

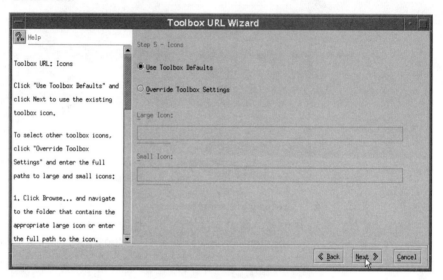

9. Select the management scope for this toolbox, as shown next. This option allows for selection of the type of name service that this toolbox will manage. The default option is Override, where you can choose to specify a name service such as LDAP, NIS+, NIS, or local files. Click Finish to continue. The wizard completes the process by adding the new toolbox under the Management Tools level or the This Computer level, based on your earlier toolbox selection.

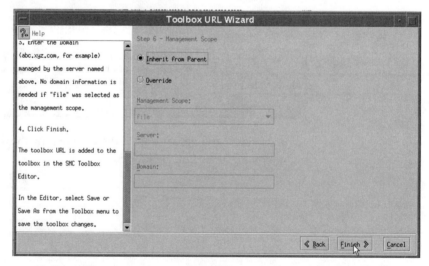

10. Save the Management Tools toolbox by selecting File | Save As, or click the Save As icon.

11. Transverse the directory selection box to locate the file /var/sadm/smc/toolboxes/smc/smc.tbx for the Management Tools and the file /var/sadm/smc/toolboxes/ *this_computer/ this_computer*.tbx for the This Computer toolbox. Select the file and then click the Save button to continue (shown next).

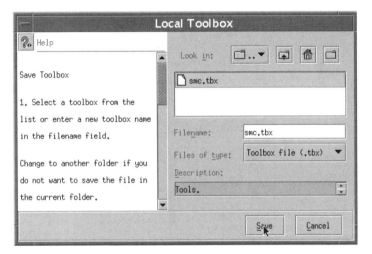

12. To access the new toolbox, run SMC and select the new toolbox link under Management Tools.

You can create additional toolboxes that can be accessed via the SMC. The toolbox can be located on the local disk or configured as the server toolbox.

EXERCISE 28-2

Creating a Local or Server Toolbox

In this exercise, you will create a new toolbox.

A server toolbox must be located in the default toolbox directory /var/sadm/smc/toolboxes. To initialize a server toolbox, first create a directory under /var/sadm/smc/toolboxes to store the toolbox files. Then copy any custom icon files into this directory.

1. Select Toolbox | New, as shown next, to launch the New Toolbox Wizard.

2. Enter the name of the toolbox in the Full Name text box. Then enter the description for the toolbox in the Description text box. Click the Next button to continue (shown next).

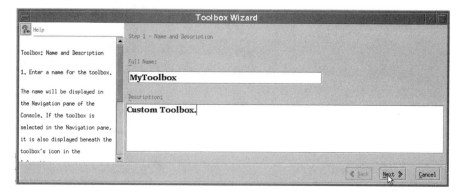

3. Select the icon file to represent the toolbox, as shown next. The default icon file is automatically loaded. If you want custom icons, click the Browse button and locate the new icon file using the file browser. Click the Next button to continue.

4. This option can be a name service, such as LDAP, DNS, NIS+, NIS, or local files.

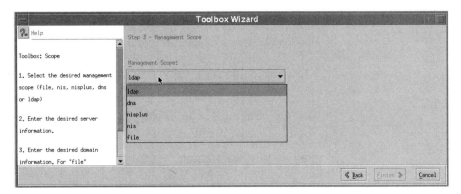

5. Enter the name of the server, as shown next. The default server name is the current server. Click the Finish button to complete the steps.

6. Save the toolbox. (Refer back to Exercise 28-1, Steps 10 and 11, for more details.) If this is a server toolbox, be sure to select the directory located under /var/sadm/smc/toolboxes. If this is a local toolbox, select any directory you want.

If the new toolbox is configured as a server toolbox, it will be displayed when you browse the server's toolboxes. Local toolboxes can be accessed using only the file browser.

To organize the tools within the toolbox, you can create folders to separate the tools into their functions.

Adding Folders to the Toolbox

In this exercise, you will add a folder to the toolbox.

1. Open the toolbox to modify. Select Actions | Add Folders to launch the wizard.

2. Enter the name of the folder and the description, as shown next. The description should be an instruction to click the item with the message indicating what the items will be under this folder. Click Next to continue.

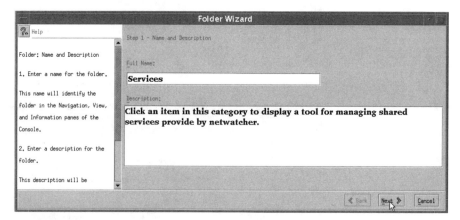

3. The wizard displays the default icons to be used for this folder. If you want custom icons, click the Browse button to launch a file browser to select the appropriate files. Click Next.

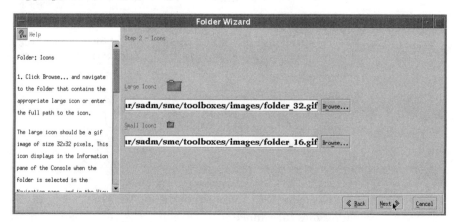

4. Select the management scope. The default is Inherit From Parent. Click the Finish button to complete the task.

5. Save the toolbox. (Refer to Exercise 28-1, Steps 10 and 11, for more details.)

The folder will be added and displayed under the toolbox you previously selected.

The applications or tools located under the folders of the toolboxes are standard SMC Java applications. You can add additional tools to the folders by using the Add Tool Wizard.

EXERCISE 28-4

Adding Tools to the Toolbox

In this exercise, you will use the Add Tool Wizard to add more tools.

1. Open the toolbox to modify it. Select Action | Add Tool.

2. Enter the name of the server on which the tools are located in the Server text box, and then click the Next button to continue, shown next.

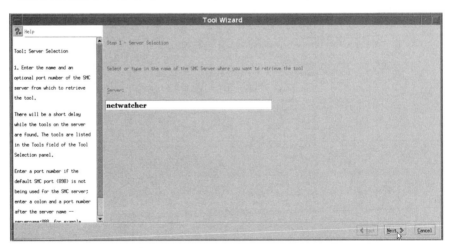

3. The wizard displays the list of tools that are available in the next window. Select the tool from the Tools list. Then click Next, as shown next.

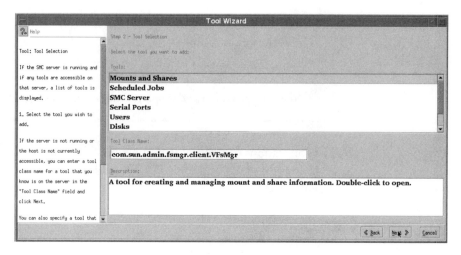

4. To specify a custom name and description for this tool, select the Override Tool Settings option, and then enter the new name and description. The default setting is Use Tool Defaults. Click Next.

5. The wizard displays the default icons to be used for this tool (shown next) If you want custom icons, click the Browse button to launch a file browser to select the appropriate files. Click Next.

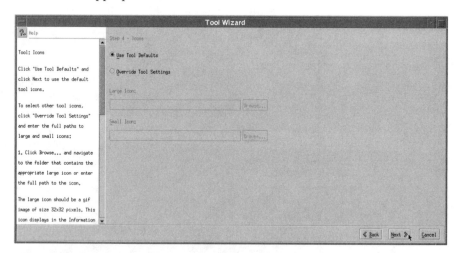

6. On this screen, you select the management scope. The default is Inherit From Parent. Click Next.

7. A tool can be loaded in two ways: when it is selected inside the console or when the console is loaded. If you choose the second option, the console will take longer to load on the screen because it also has to load the tools. The default selection is Load Tool When Selected (shown next). Select the option to load this tool, and then click the Finish button to complete the process.

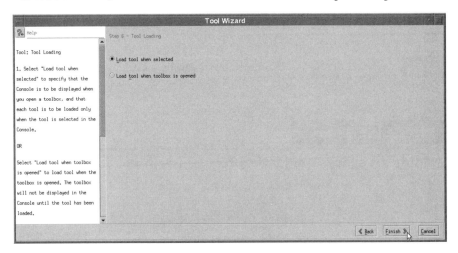

8. Save the toolbox. (Refer to Exercise 28-1, Steps 10 and 11, for more details.)

The new tool will be added to the selected folder.

Once configured, the information for the toolbox, folders, and tools can be modified easily.

EXERCISE 28-5

Modifying the Toolbox Item Properties

In this exercise, you will modify the properties of an item in the toolbox.

1. Open the toolbox to modify. Select the toolbox, folder, or tool to modify.

2. Select Action | Properties to launch the proper wizard.

3. Depending on the item selected in the navigation pane, the wizard prompts for the information that can be modified. The information can be name,

description, icons, or management scope. Follow the instructions in the wizard and enter the new information.

4. Once it is completed, save the toolbox.

The new information is registered with the toolbox and is used the next time you access SMC.

A non-SMC application can be a CLI, an X Windows application, or a URL. To access these applications using SMC, you must add them to the toolbox.

EXERCISE 28-6

Adding a Legacy Application to the Toolbox

In this exercise, you will add a legacy application to the toolbox.

1. Open the toolbox to modify it. Select the folder under which to file the application, and then select Action | Add Legacy Application to launch the wizard.

2. Select the type of application to be added. This can be a CLI, an X Windows application, or a URL. Enter a descriptive name for the application, and then enter the path to the application. Click Next to continue, as shown next.

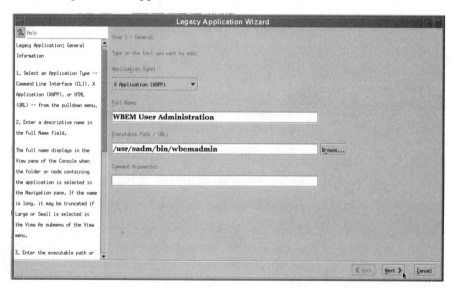

FROM THE CLASSROOM

Understanding Tools

As UNIX system administrators, we often make fun of our Windows NT counterparts for heavy reliance on GUIs. However, to completely understand Solaris, we need to understand all the tools, both GUI and non-GUI, that it makes available. The availability of a single console to centrally manage a collection of Solaris systems can reduce total cost of ownership by reducing the amount of time it takes to administer individual systems. The integration of all GUI-based administrative tools into a single console with a consistent interface also makes it very easy to learn. To be a good systems administrator, it is important to know how to perform a task multiple ways, both through the command line and through the GUI interface.

—*Umer Khan, SCSA, SCNA, CCIE, MCSE, CNX, CCA*

3. Choose the custom icons or use the default settings. Click Finish to complete the task.

4. Once it is completed, save the toolbox.

The application will be added to the folder and can be accessed using the SMC.

CERTIFICATION OBJECTIVE 28.02

Understanding the Features of the Solaris Management Console

exam
ⓦatch
It is more important to understand SMC's features than to know exactly which menus to use to perform a certain task.

The standard set of tools in the SMC includes the following:

■ User administration, including user account maintenance, group maintenance, and role-based access control (RBAC) setup and maintenance

- Process control
- Cron job control
- Disk management, including the ability to create and view disk partitioning information
- UFS mounts and NFS shares management
- Serial port management
- Log maintenance
- Performance
- Patches
- Projects

on the ***job***

Although you can use GUI tools to perform system administration, it is sometimes a better choice to use the command line. The decision to go with GUI versus the command line depends on the complexity of the task that needs to be performed.

User Administration

You can use SMC to administer user accounts. Select Users under System Configuration. The options shown here are available:

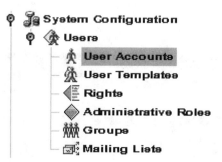

You can add a user or multiple users through SMC. Using user templates, you can create named sets of properties that users have in common and use those sets as a starting point to create new users. The User Rights section of SMC allows for administration of RBAC. (For more information, refer to Chapter 27 on role-based access control.) As the name suggests, the Administrative Roles section of SMC allows you to assign administrative roles to users. Group management is also possible with SMC, allowing you to add, modify, or delete user groups. Finally, you can add, remove, and modify mailing lists (aliases) through SMC.

Process Control

Process administration is also possible through SMC. Under System Status, select Processes, as shown here:

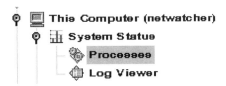

This choice should display a list of currently active processes. (See Figure 28-1.)

Clicking a process brings up details on that process. You can also right-click a process and select Delete to kill that particular process.

Cron Job Control

You can use SMC to control cron jobs. Under Services, select Scheduled Jobs. To modify an existing cron job, click it once. To create a new cron job, select Action | Add Scheduled Job.

FIGURE 28-1   Currently active processes

Name	PID	Owner	PPID	CPU%	Size (...	State	Command
⚙ init	1	root	0	0.0	784	Sleeping	/etc/init -
⚙ pageout	2	root	0	0.0	0	Sleeping	pageout
⚙ fsflush	3	root	0	0.4	0	Sleeping	fsflush
⚙ sac	281	root	1	0.0	1752	Sleeping	/usr/lib/saf/sac -t 300
⚙ utmpd	215	root	1	0.0	1016	Sleeping	/usr/lib/utmpd
⚙ syslogd	167	root	1	0.0	3672	Sleeping	/usr/sbin/syslogd
⚙ sysevent	49	root	1	0.0	1392	Sleeping	/usr/lib/sysevent/syseventd
⚙ picld	60	root	1	0.0	1896	Sleeping	/usr/lib/picl/picld

Disk Management

To administer disks from SMC, select Disks under Storage. Select the disk you want to administer. A list of partitions should appear. Clicking a partition allows you to view or modify its properties.

UFS Mounts and NFS Shares Management

To administer mounts and shares from SMC, select Mounts And Shares under Storage. This feature allows you to add and remove mounts and shares, as well as view disk space usage statistics.

Serial Port Management

To administer serial ports from SMC, select Serial Ports under Devices And Hardware. Click the serial port you want to modify.

Log Maintenance

To perform log file maintenance, select Log Viewer under System Status. Click a log entry to view its details. You can also modify log file settings by selecting Action | Log File Settings.

exam
ⓦatch

Learn to navigate through SMC quickly so that you can respond to scenario-based questions that require you to perform a certain task in SMC.

CERTIFICATION OBJECTIVE 28.03

Understanding the Features of the Solaris AdminSuite

The Solaris Admin Pack includes AdminSuite. You can also download it from the Sun Microsystems web site. AdminSuite provides much of the same functionality as SMC. AdminSuite allows administrators to modify users, hosts, groups, netgroups, serial ports, mounts, shares, logs, and more for a local machine, a remote machine, or an NIS or NIS+ domain. AdminSuite is a Java-based application that can be installed on UNIX as well as on a Microsoft Windows PC.

Installation on a Solaris System

Insert the Solaris Admin Pack CD-ROM into your Solaris system. Run /cdrom/s9ap/installer. The screen shown in Figure 28-2 should appear.

1. Click Next to continue. Select Custom Install, and click Next. (See Figure 28-3.)

2. If you are installing AdminSuite 3.0.1, select Default Install; for all other products, choose No Install, as shown in Figure 28-4. Click Next.

3. Click Install Now, as shown in Figure 28-5. Wait while the installation completes.

4. Click Next to continue. (See Figure 28-6.)

5. Click Exit, as shown in Figure 28-7. The installation of AdminSuite 3.0.1 is complete.

FIGURE 28-2

Installing the Solaris 8 Admin Pack

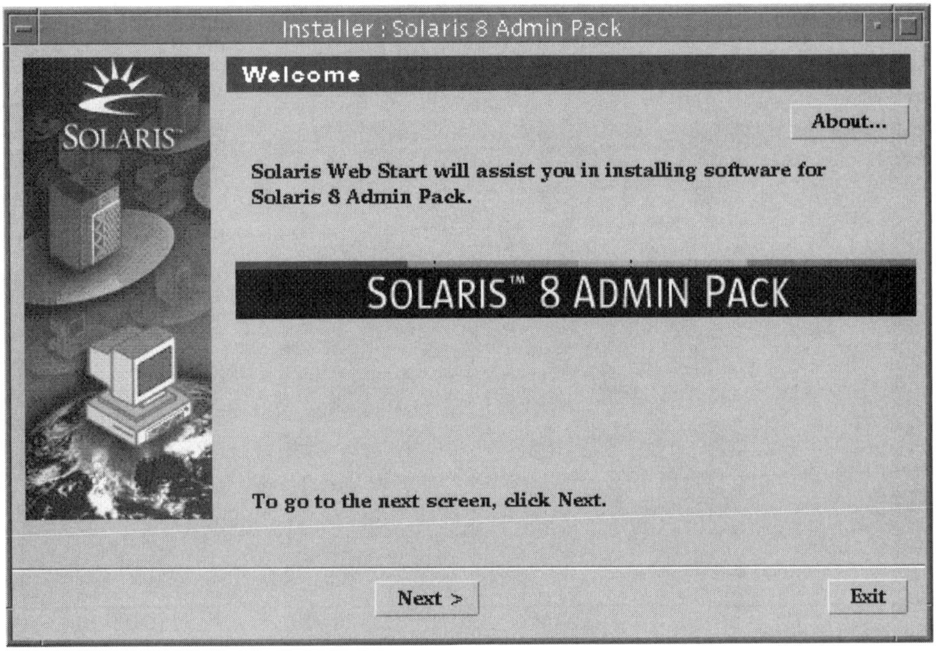

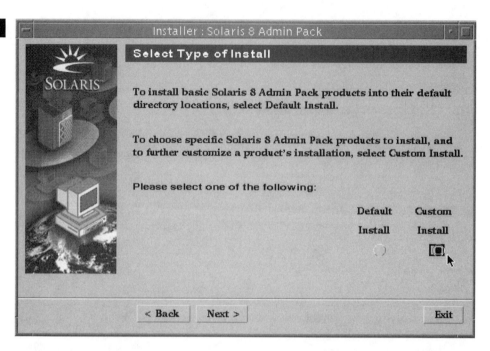

FIGURE 28-3

Selecting the custom installation

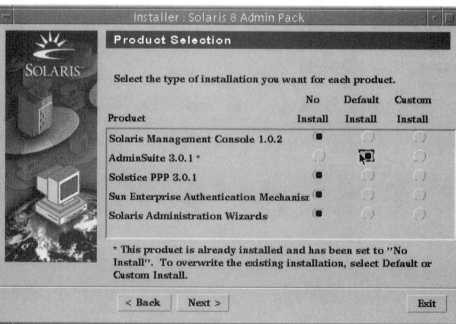

FIGURE 28-4

Selecting the default installation for AdminSuite 3.0.1

FIGURE 28-5

Install Now

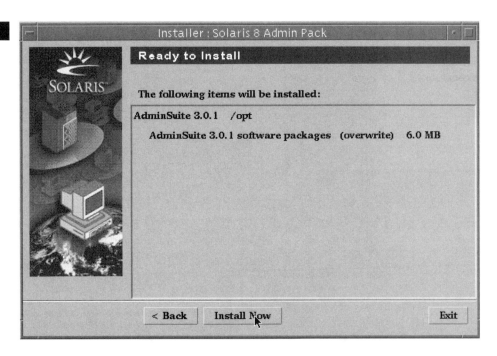

FIGURE 28-6

Click Next
after Installation
Summary

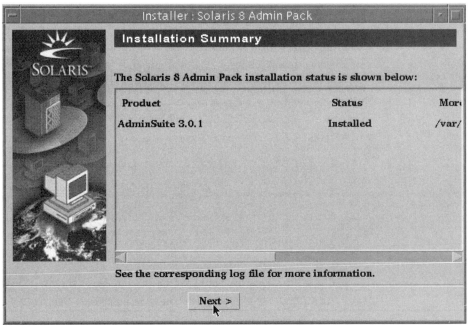

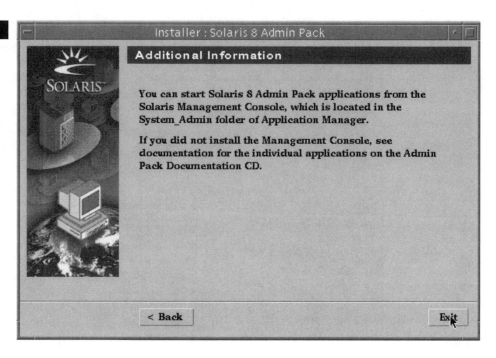

FIGURE 28-7

Installation
is complete

Installation on a Windows System

Insert the Solaris Admin Pack CD-ROM into your Microsoft Windows system. The screen shown in Figure 28-8 will appear.

AdminSuite requires the Sun Java Development Kit. If you don't already have that kit installed on your system, install it first. Otherwise, begin the AdminSuite installation process by clicking Install AdminSuite. The installation program will start.

1. Select the language, as shown in Figure 28-9, and click OK.

2. Click Next to continue in the Welcome screen. (See Figure 28-10.)

3. Select the destination folder, and click Next (Figure 28-11).

4. Enter a server name or IP address, and click Next (Figure 28-12). Wait while the program installation completes.

5. Click Finish on the Setup Complete screen, as shown in Figure 28-13. AdminSuite is now installed on your Microsoft Windows system.

FIGURE 28-8

The Solaris 8
Admin Pack
Start screen

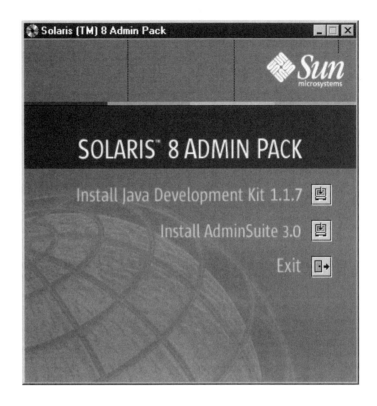

FIGURE 28-9

Selecting the
language

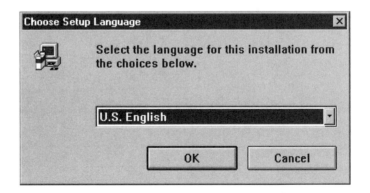

FIGURE 28-10

Click Next on
the Welcome
screen

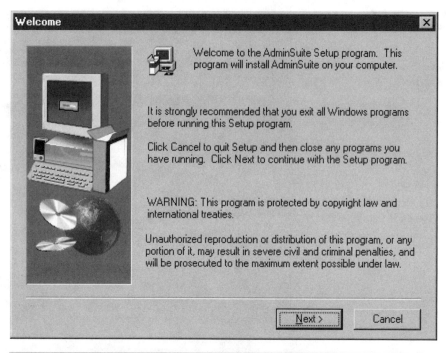

FIGURE 28-11

The Choose
Destination
Location screen

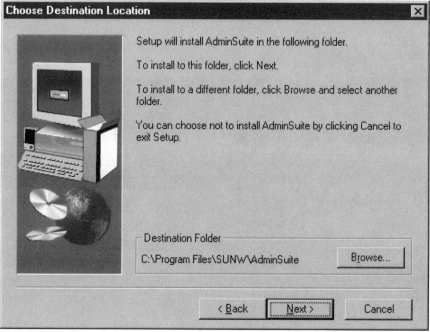

FIGURE 28-12

The Enter
Information
screen

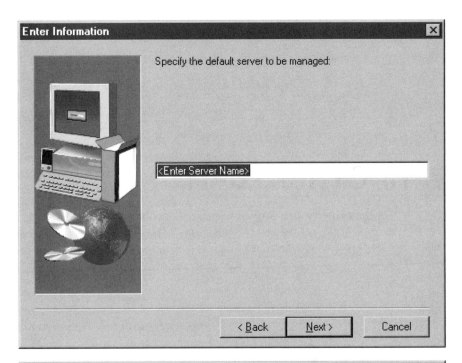

FIGURE 28-13

The Setup
Complete screen

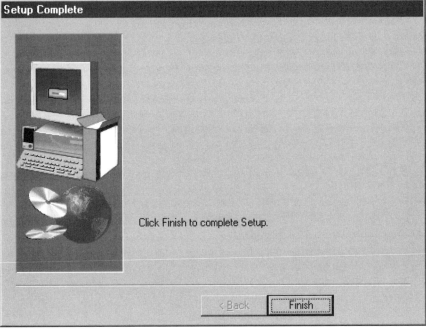

Running AdminSuite

To run AdminSuite on a Solaris system, execute the following command:

```
# /opt/SUNWseam/3_0/bin/admapp
```

To run AdminSuite on a Microsoft Windows system, select AdminSuite Client under Start | Programs | Sun | AdminSuite.

CERTIFICATION SUMMARY

Although Solaris provides a variety of command-line tools for administering systems, it also makes GUI administration tools available. In this chapter, you learned about two of these enterprisewide management tools: Solaris Management Console (SMC) and Solaris AdminSuite. Both SMC and AdminSuite are Java-based GUI applications used to administer a local computer, remote computer, or NIS/NIS+ domains.

✓ TWO-MINUTE DRILL

Understanding the Configuration of the Solaris Management Console

❏ You can adjust SMC preferences by selecting Console | Preferences. You can modify settings for the following categories: console, appearance, toolbar, fonts, tool loading, and authentication.

❏ You can configure SMC toolboxes by running the SMC toolbox editor. This allows you to create custom toolboxes or modify existing toolboxes.

Understanding the Features of the Solaris Management Console

❏ SMC provides the ability to administer systems across the enterprise.

❏ SMC can be used to administer user accounts, groups, cron jobs, disks, mounts and shares, serial ports, processes, and log files.

Understanding the Features of the Solaris AdminSuite

❏ Solaris AdminSuite is a Java-based GUI application that comes with the Solaris Admin Pack or can be downloaded from the Sun Microsystems web site. AdminSuite can run on a Solaris machine or a Microsoft Windows system.

❏ AdminSuite can be used to administer a local system, a remote system, or an NIS or NIS+ domain.

SELF TEST

The following questions will help you measure your understanding of the material presented in this chapter. Read all the choices carefully because there might be more than one correct answer. Choose all correct answers for each question.

Understanding the Configuration of the Solaris Management Console

1. What is the default port for the SMC server?

A. 788

B. 137

C. 898

D. 888

2. What is a requirement for being able to save toolboxes in the SMC toolbox editor?

A. Having save privileges

B. Membership in the editors group

C. Being the root account

Understanding the Features of the Solaris Management Console

3. Which of the following can you *not* administer with the SMC?

A. User accounts

B. Mail aliases

C. Cron jobs

D. Logging

E. Printers

Understanding the Features of the Solaris AdminSuite

4. How can the Solaris AdminSuite installation files be obtained? (Choose all that apply.)

A. By default as a part of a full Solaris install

B. From the Solaris Admin Pack CD-ROM

C. Downloaded from sunfreeware.com

D. Downloaded from the Sun Microsystems web site

5. Which of the following is a requirement for installing Solaris AdminSuite on Microsoft Windows?

   A. Perl

   B. X Windows emulation software

   C. The Java Development Kit

   D. None of the above

LAB QUESTION

You would like to create a customized toolbox for a junior system administrator that allows her to administer the machine named *netwatcher* with the following settings:

- Ability to administer NIS domain *domain*
- The custom application /home/admin/legacy.pl

List the steps you would follow to customize the toolbox.

SELF TEST ANSWERS

Understanding the Configuration of the Solaris Management Console

1. ☑ C. The default port for the SMC server is 898.
   ☒ A, B, and D are incorrect because these are not the default ports for the SMC server.

2. ☑ C. The root account has the ability to save toolboxes.
   ☒ A and B are incorrect. Although any user is allowed to modify toolboxes, only the root account can save them.

Understanding the Features of the Solaris Management Console

3. ☑ E. Printers cannot be administered from the Solaris Management Console.
   ☒ A, B, C, and D are incorrect because user accounts, mail aliases, cron jobs, and logging can all be administered from the SMC.

Understanding the Features of the Solaris AdminSuite

4. ☑ B and D. Solaris AdminSuite is available on the Solaris Admin Pack CD-ROM. It can also be downloaded from www.sun.com.
   ☒ A and C are incorrect because Solaris AdminSuite is not a part of the Solaris install, and AdminSuite is not available as a download from sunfreeware.com.

5. ☑ C. The Java Development Kit is required for Solaris AdminSuite to run in a Windows environment.
   ☒ A and B are incorrect because Solaris AdminSuite does not require Perl or X Windows emulation. D is incorrect because there is a correct answer.

LAB ANSWER

1. Launch the SMC toolbox editor:

   ```
   # /usr/sadm/bin/smc edit &
   ```

2. Select Toolbox | New.

3. Under Full Name, type **Junior Administrator**. Under Description, type **Toolbox for Junior Administrator**. Click Next to continue.

4. Select the default icons by clicking Next to continue (shown next).

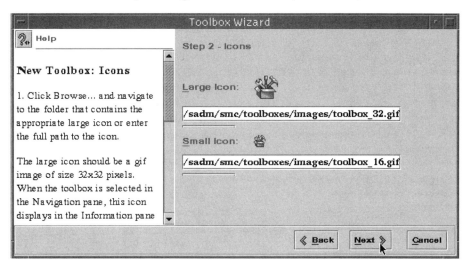

5. Under Management Scope, select Nis. For server, enter **netwatcher**. For Domain, enter **domain**. Click Finish.

6. Select the toolbox. Then select Action | Add Legacy Application.

7. Under Application Type, select Command Line Interface (CLI). Under Full Name, type **Custom App**. Under Executable Path/URL, type **/home/admin/legacy.pl**. Leave the Command Arguments field blank. Click Next to continue (shown next).

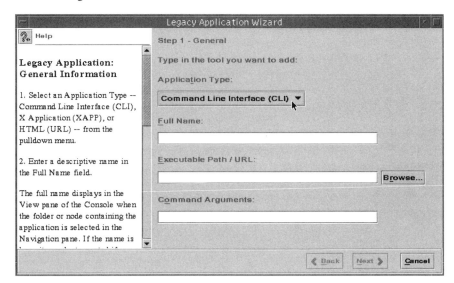

8. Leave the default description and icons as they are, and click Finish (shown next).

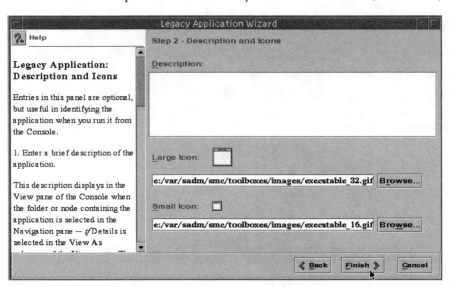

9. Close the toolbox editor. You will be asked if you want to save the toolbox. Click Yes.

29

JumpStart Automatic Installation

How much of your time do you think you've spent watching the progress bar of an installation creep across the screen? Probably too much! The first time you successfully install Solaris on a machine, you'll be in for a treat. Installing a new OS for the first time is like your tenth Christmas morning: you're old enough to know what is going on and young enough to still feel the magic. When the machine reboots and you get that login screen for the first time signaling a successful installation, it's a great feeling.

But as you're installing your twentieth machine in one evening with a missed deadline, a curious user, and a nervous boss behind you, somehow the magic disappears. That's when JumpStart Automatic Installation server becomes your new best friend.

To prepare for this exam, you should plan to do the manual installation several times. You should install using different default settings, different custom package installs, and different network and hardware settings. You should become familiar with the interactive installation and the web-based install. You also need to do a custom JumpStart automatic install.

This chapter guides you through the proper planning, configuration, and execution of a successful custom JumpStart installation.

JumpStart was first included with the release of SunOS 4.1.1 Revision B. It was designed to make the installation of SunOS easier and faster. JumpStart has not changed much since its introduction. Using JumpStart is a great way to free your time from tedious installation procedures and standardize the machines on your network. You can use it to perform these tasks:

- Set up brand new systems
- Upgrade current systems to a new Solaris release
- Move existing systems to the Solaris platform

CERTIFICATION OBJECTIVE 29.01

Defining the Main Components of a JumpStart Server

There are three main components to consider when you are setting up a network to use automatic installation.

The first two are Solaris' capabilities for network booting and automatic system configuration. The third component is the configuration files JumpStart uses to customize the installation process. You must have a good understanding of all three elements to perform a successful JumpStart installation.

First, let's talk about *network booting*: the term usually refers to a dumb terminal running everything it needs over a network connection from a server. These terminals are also called *diskless clients* for the same reason they are called *dumb*. Basically, there is no hard disk, so no local storage. A dumb terminal is simply a means of accessing the processing power and resources of a server over a network connection. This is very different from the client/server design found on many networks today.

When discussing network booting in terms of a custom JumpStart installation, we're referring to an install client's ability to reach out across the network and get the information it needs to begin the installation process. A host machine, also referred to as an *install client,* using a JumpStart automatic installation follows similar procedures as one of those terminals.

To use the network booting capabilities of Solaris for a JumpStart installation, you need several services set up on the network:

- **Install server** A host with the Solaris installation files stored locally, ready to be used by the install client.

- **Boot server** A host that allows an install client on the same subnet to boot and access the network. This way, the boot server can access the installation files stored on the install server.

- **Configuration server** The server that contains the customized files used to set up each install client. These files automate the process by recognizing the client, answering the installation questions, and loading specific software based on predefined parameters.

In most cases, all three of these services can be provided by the same machine. However, if the install client is on a different subnet, a boot server will have to be configured on the install client's subnet.

These three server configurations are discussed in much more detail later in this chapter.

The next component you need to set up a network for an automatic JumpStart installation is Solaris's ability to *automate system configuration.* It wouldn't be very automatic if someone had to sit there and answer such questions as, "What IP address should this host have?" or "What hostname do you want assigned?" For that reason, if you are running NIS, NIS+ or LDAP, you can configure the name service to provide the information needed during installation. The boot server's /etc/host file contains the IP address and hostname of the install client; the name service provides everything else. If you aren't running NIS or NIS+, you can configure a file called sysidcfg.

The third main component needed in a JumpStart automatic installation is the *configuration files* used to customize the installation on each install client. These files will be loaded on the profile server or can be loaded on from a disk. The JumpStart directory on the profile server contains the following:

- **A rules file** This file defines how the install clients will be split up into groups called *classes* for installation. Each class has a different way of being installed. The rules file defines the characteristics for each class and names the class file used for each separate class. The install clients fall into one of these defined classes.

- **A class file** Each class has a file that defines how the installation is done for that class. The class file can be named anything. The rules file designates the class file that is used for each class.

- **The rules.ok file** The rules file is not actually used during automatic installation; the rules.ok is used instead. Once the rules file and class files are created, you run a script called *check* that checks the syntax of the rules and class files. If they are OK, the check script creates the file called rules.ok. This is the file that is actually used to define the class to which each install client will belong and the class file used for each class' installation.

on the job   *A couple of optional scripts, called begin and finish scripts, run pre- and post-installation instructions. The creation and use of these scripts are not part of the Solaris 9 exam. They're considered an advanced feature of the JumpStart installation process, so you should prepare to use them at some later point in your career.*

CERTIFICATION OBJECTIVE 29.02

Using the add_install_client Script Syntax

To add clients to your install and boot servers, you use the add_install_client script that comes with the Solaris Installation CD-ROM. This script has several options and variables you can use to add information about the install clients to the install and boot servers. The available options for this script are

- *-e* Specifies the Ethernet address of the install client. This option must be used if no sysidcfg or name service is running on the network.
- *-f* Specifies the boot_file_name of the client to be installed.
- *-i* Specifies the IP address of the install client. This option must be used if no sysidcfg or name service is running on the network.
- *-s* Specifies the name of the install server and the pathname to the installation image.
- *-c* Specifies the name of the configuration server and the pathname to the configuration directory.
- *-p* Specifies the name of the profile or configuration server and the pathname to the sysidcfg file.
- *-n* Specifies the name service to be used for this installation.
- *host_name* Defines the hostname of the install client.
- *platform_group* Defines the platform of the system to be installed. This platform can be determined either by the use of the uname *-m* command or by consulting the hardware manual that came with the system.

If the install client is on a different subnet from the install server, a boot server must be configured on the install client's subnet. Once that is done, run the add_install_client script on the install client's boot server. The script will allow the install client to boot using the boot server on its subnet and reach the install server on the other subnet to complete the installation.

The add_install_client script updates the /etc/bootparams file on the install and boot servers. If you are using NIS as a name service, copy the updated /etc/ bootparams information to the NIS /etc/bootparams file. Then update the bootparams NIS map by running this command:

```
# cd /var/yp; /usr/ccs/bin/make
```

CERTIFICATION OBJECTIVE 29.03

Using the Boot Service Function on a Subnet

Most often, the install server and the boot server are configured on the same machine. However, you might need to install clients that are on a different subnet from your install server. In that case, you need to install a boot server on the same subnet as the install clients.

EXERCISE 29-1

Creating a Boot Server

Follow these steps to build your boot server:

1.. First, create a directory to house the boot image files, for example,

```
# mkdir /export/boot_me
```

2. Next, insert the Solaris Installation CD-ROM into the CD-ROM drive and mount the drive on the machine that you will make the boot server.

3. Now change to the Tools directory on the CD-ROM .

4. Run the script called setup_install_server with the *-b* switch, and add the pathname on the boot server to the directory into which the files will be loaded. The *-b* option tells the install script that you are setting up a boot server. The command should look like this:

```
#   ./setup_install_server  -b /export/boot_me
```

5. After the configuration directory is set up, you will run the add_install
   _client script.

on the **Job**   *Make sure you have enough space on the boot server. The boot image is*
approximately 115MB. The setup_install_server script won't start copying
files if it determines that there is insufficient space. Run the command df -kl
to see whether there is enough available space.

CERTIFICATION OBJECTIVE 29.04

Understanding the Events That Occur During the JumpStart Client Boot Sequence

You've researched the needs of the install clients, you've edited the necessary files
and run the tests, and now you are ready to go. This section describes how to start
the installation process on the install clients and what happens when you do.

On newer Sun machines, for an initial install, all you have to do is power on
the machines. For older machines or upgrades, from the PROM ok prompt, use
this command:

```
ok boot net - install
```

Once that is done, here is what happens next:

1. The install client issues a Reverse Address Resolution Protocol (RARP)
   request. It is used to determine the install client's IP address.

2. The boot server's in.rarpd daemon uses its ethers and hosts databases to map
   the install client's Ethernet address to an IP address and responds to the
   install client's RARP request with the appropriate IP address.

3. The install client, giddy with its newly discovered identity, uses Trivial File
   Transfer Program (TFTP) to get the JumpStart boot image from the boot
   server. TFTP is used to transfer small files. No login authentication is used.

4. The install client issues a hostconfig request.

5. The name server returns the information contained in the /etc/bootparams database.

6. Now the install client uses the bootparams information to mount the root partition and the /kernel/unix from the boot server. At this point, the INIT program starts. Once the boot server has finished booting the install client, it hands the process off to the configuration server.

7. The install client mounts the configuration directory, and the sysidtool runs. The sysidtool uses the sysidcfg file of the name service to set up the initial configurations.

8. The install client determines which class it is in from the information in the rules.ok file on the profile server.

9. If a begin script is specified, it is run at this point.

10. The install client mounts the installation image file from the install server and begins the installation of the Solaris OS.

11. After the installation process completes as specified in the class file, the install client is rebooted. If a finish script is named in the rules.ok file, it is run before the install client is rebooted.

12. Once the install client has rebooted, the JumpStart automatic installation is complete.

CERTIFICATION OBJECTIVE 29.05

Using the Necessary Files to Support the JumpStart Boot Operation

The sysidcfg file is used in the absence of NIS or NIS+, or in place of them. When an install client does a network installation boot, it first tries to find basic configuration information about itself, such as its root password or domain name, from a sysidcfg file. If such a file isn't available, the client looks for the information from NIS or

NIS+. If the install client still can't find the information, it prompts the user for the necessary information. You can configure the name service, either NIS or NIS+, or the sysidcfg file to create a completely "hands-free" installation.

Understanding the sysidcfg File With and Without Name Service Support

When an install client boots up for the first time, it looks for a sysidcfg file first. The client needs to have some basic information to reach across the network to the install server. At first, an install client is pretty dumb by any standard. It doesn't even know its own name or address. Because the sysidcfg file is used before any other database, you can use it even if you are currently using NIS or NIS+ on your network. If you aren't running NIS or NIS+, you must have the sysidcfg file configured to automate the installation process. With no NIS or NIS+ servers and no sysidcfg file, somebody has to manually enter the information when requested by the installation process.

The sysidcfg file's location is determined by the information in the script called add_install_client. The add_install_script is discussed in the next section, "Setting Up a JumpStart Install Server System."

The keywords used in the sysidcfg file are

- **name_service [domain_name]** Can contain NIS, NIS+, OTHER, NONE [domain_name=*domainname*].

- **network_interface [hostname IP address netmask]** Can contain *interface name* [hostname=*hostname* ip_address=*ip address* netmask=*netmask*].

- **root_password** Contains the encrypted password from /etc/shadow.

- **system_local** Contains the information from /usr/lib/locale file and designates the language to use during installation.

- **terminal** Contains an entry from the /usr/share/lib/terminfo file.

- **timezone** Contains an entry from the /usr/share/lib/zoneinfo/ file and designates the time zone for the install client's location.

■ **timeserver** Can be localhost, an IP address, or hostname of the machine to be used as a time server. If you use the value localhost, the time currently set on the install client is used. If another machine is specified, that time is used to configure the install client.

on the
job

It is also possible to use a sysidcfg file from a disk on a local drive. On x86 systems, for example, the file should be on the device configuration disk.

There are a couple of points to keep in mind about the information contained in the sysidcfg file:

■ The keywords can be in any order.

■ The keywords aren't case sensitive.

■ A keyword can be repeated with different values, but only the first instance of the keyword's value is used. For example, in a sysidcfg file, the following information is entered:

```
timezone=US/Eastern
timeserver=badabing
timeserver=localhost
name_service=none
root_password=p4ASqD0PLKz
system_locale=US_eng
terminal=dtterm
```

Even though the keyword timeserver is entered twice, the only one with a value that will be used is the first entry. So, the install clients that use this sysidcfg script will all be configured to use the machine named *badabing* to set their local time.

The information contained on the sysidcfg file is pretty basic and is designed to be a generic starting point for all the install clients. If you need different values for different machines, you can create multiple sysidcfg files. However, the sysidcfg files must be in different directories. Then different add_install_client scripts need to be configured to match the locations of the appropriate sysidcfg files.

exam
Watch

Other keywords are available, such as monitor, display, and pointer, but they are specific to Solaris installs on x86 systems. The Solaris exam will test your knowledge of the custom JumpStart installation process on SPARC systems. However, you might find it useful to be familiar with the x86 keywords if you are setting up a home lab.

If no sysidcfg file is found, you can configure the network's name service to provide the initial configuration information.

CERTIFICATION OBJECTIVE 29.07

Setting Up a JumpStart Install Server System

The install server is the host machine that stores the Solaris installation files from the Solaris CD-ROM and makes them available to the install clients. The use of an install server in automatic installations means you don't need CD-ROM drives installed on each install client. Furthermore, once the files are installed on the install server, you generally won't need to make any changes to them. Unless you're upgrading by adding new patches, the files can stay where they are, as they are, for any install client's automatic installation.

on the job

The install files can be installed on the install server in several ways. They can be run from the CD-ROM drive, from an NFS mount, or by loading the files to the local drive. The recommended way of setting up an install server is to load the needed installation files from the Solaris installation CD-ROM to the local drive of the install server. This is the fastest and most reliable way to configure an install server.

EXERCISE 29-2

Creating an Install Server

To build your install server, follow these steps:

1. First, create a directory to house the installation files, for example,

   ```
   # mkdir /export/install
   ```

2. Next, insert the Solaris Installation CD-ROM and mount the drive on the machine you will make the install server.

3. Now change to the Tools directory on the CD-ROM.

4. Run the script called setup_install_server and add the pathname on the install server to the directory where the files will be loaded. The command should look like this:

   ```
   # ./setup_install_server /export/install
   ```

   This command will copy the installation files to the specified directory on the install server, creating an install image.

5. Update the installation image with the latest patches. Use this command:

```
# patchadd -C /export/install patch_number
```

6. After the configuration directory is set up, run the add_install_client script. This script adds the patch named to the install image. Run this command for all the patches you want to install. Now when your install clients are installed with JumpStart from this install server, they will be installed with the latest patched version of Solaris.

---

on the
Job *The installation image can be 400MB or more. The setup_install_server script will let you know if you don't have enough space on the named directory. If you want to check before running the script, run the command df -kl. This command shows you the amount of space used and space available for each partition on your local disk.*

CERTIFICATION OBJECTIVE 29.08

Using the add_to_install_server, modify_install_server, and add_install_client Scripts

One of the advantages of the custom JumpStart process is that you can make changes to it after configuration. This means you don't have to re-create all the components of your JumpStart servers every time you need to change your installation.

The add_to_install_server Script

The add_to_install_server script is used to add other Solaris Installation CD-ROMs to your install server. For example, if you were to add support for another language to your JumpStart process, you'd run the add_to_install_server script found on the Language CD-ROM . This script will be found on the CD-ROM you plan to add and can't be used to add applications or other third-party CD-ROMs for which the script wasn't designed.

Two options are available for this script:

- **-p** Specifies the path to the CD-ROM to be added
- **-s** Allows users to select from the available products

The modify_install_server Script

After you've run the setup_install_server script, what if you want to change the installation image? The modify_install_server script can be used to replace the install image on an installation server.

There is only one option for this script:

- **-p** Keeps the original install image by renaming it Boot.orig

The add_install_client Script

You use the add_install_client script to add clients to your install server. You must run this script from your installation image, which, as you recall, can be either a mounted Installation CD-ROM or an Installation CD-ROM that has been copied to disk or from the boot server's boot directory.

The add_install_client script has several options, as discussed previously in the section "Using the add_install_client Script Syntax." The big advantage of this script is that you can use it to update your client list as your network grows.

CERTIFICATION OBJECTIVE 29.09

Creating a Configuration Server with a Customized Rules File and Class Files

The configuration server contains the configuration directory. This directory contains the customized configuration files used by install clients during an automatic installation. Most often, you will combine the configuration server, boot server, and install server on one machine.

EXERCISE 29-3

Creating the Configuration Server

Now provide the specific customization files your installations will need by following these steps:

1. Create the directory that will be the configuration directory, for example,

   ```
   # mkdir /export/config
   ```

2. Copy the contents of the directory named jumpstart_sample from the Solaris Installation CD-ROM to your newly created configuration directory. This directory contains some files that will make your setup much easier. There are samples of rules and class files and a finish script. This directory also contains the check script, which is needed to build the rules.ok file.

3. Group each machine to be installed into classes, and create the rules file. As discussed earlier in the chapter, each machine must fall into a category or group of predefined parameters. These groups are called *classes*. The rules file defines the parameters for each class. Each class has a class file, which defines how to install the install clients that are members of that class. The process of creating rules and class files is described later in this chapter.

4. If needed, create the begin and finish scripts. This step is optional. You don't need begin and finish scripts to perform an automatic installation. They are used to do advanced customization during installation. Begin and finish scripts are very handy. You can use them for a number of functions:

   - Adding files to install client's local directories
   - Setting up printers
   - Setting environmental variables
   - Editing system files such as the /etc/motd file
   - Adding packages not included in the installation

5. The begin script is run before the class file, which is run before the installation actually starts. The finish script runs after the class file but before the system is rebooted.

exam
Ⓦatch

For the Solaris Certification Tests, you won't be required to know all the available parameters for begin and finish scripts. Mainly, you need to know when they run, what they are used for, and that they are an optional part of an automatic installation. However, you should get in the habit of using them; they will save you time in configuring all the little details that are part of setting up a network client.

6. Finally, run the check script. This script checks the rules and class files for syntax errors and provides basic preemptive troubleshooting. As long as the check script finds no errors, it creates a file called rules.ok. This file is placed in your configuration directory. The rules.ok file, not the file called rules, is the one that is actually used during installation.

7. An optional step at this point is to run the pfinstall command. This command does a dry run of the installation process using your class files, but it doesn't actually install or change anything. The command is located in /usr/sbin/ install.d, and the class file to be tested must be named, as well as the location of the installation image. For example, to run the command on a class file named soprano_crew with the installation image on the install server located on /export/install, you would run the following:

```
# /usr/sbin/install.d/pfinstall -D -c /export/install  soprano_crew
```

8. The *-D* option will start a simulated installation without making any changes. The *-c* option points the command to the location of the installation image.

Now that you know the steps for creating a configuration directory, let's create your rules and class files to use during installation.

You use the rules file to classify machines by predefined characteristics, such as hostname, memory size, domain name, or model. Each line in the rules file has a keyword and a value, followed by the name of the class file to be used by machines matching this definition. The names of the begin and finish scripts are defined here if they are used. The format is

```
keyword  keyword_value  [&& [!]] keyword  keyword_value   begin_script_name
class_file_name    finish_script_name
```

The valid keywords are

- **any**   Used for the install clients that don't fall into any other predefined class. Always make sure this keyword is used last! The JumpStart installation process reads the rules from the top down and uses the first match!

- **hostname**   Defines a specific rule for a named host.

- **model**   Allows you to define a rule for all machines of the same model.

- **arch**   Allows you to create rules specifically for install clients on either the SPARC or *x*86 hardware architecture.

- **installed**   Used for upgrading clients with operating systems currently installed. You can define a rule based on the system currently running on the client. The valid keyword_values are

  - **Solaris_2.x**   Matches a named version of Solaris. The *x* must be replaced by the version number for which you want the rules file to look.

  - **SunOS4.x**   Matches the older SunOS 4.*x* operating system.

  - **any**   Matches any version of Solaris.

- **karch**   Matches the install client's kernel architecture. The valid keyword values are sun4u, sun4e, sun4c, sun4m, or i86pc. If you have a similar system already installed or will be upgrading this install client, you can see which type of kernel architecture is present by using the command uname -*m*. If it is a brand new system with no operating system installed, check the hardware documentation.

- **totaldisk**   Matches the total amount of disk space on the install client.

- **disksize**   Allows you to name a disk device, such as *c0t1d0* and a size range.

- **memsize**   Matches the amount of memory loaded on the install client. You can also use a range of memory. For example, memsize 128–256 would match any install client with between 128MB and 256MB of RAM.

- **network**   Matches an install client's network number.

You can use two symbols in conjunction with these keywords and values:

- **!**   Specifies that the next keyword and value are not to be used

- **&&**   Allows you to join several keywords and values

on the
ⓙob

***When you create the configuration directory, you will have copied a sample
rules file over to the configuration server. Use that file as a template for your
first couple of attempts at creating your rules file.***

Here is an example of a rules file:

```
#This rules file was created by cmoltisanti on 2/00 for the soprano.crew.org installation
domainname soprano.crew.org && memsize 128-256 ! arch x86 - sparc_class printer_setup
domainname soprano.crew.org && installed Solaris_2.6 && arch x86  x86_after  x86_class -
any          ! hostname  pwalnuts                        -  anybody_class -
```

In this rules file, the pound sign (#)is used to place a comment in the file.

The first rule states that all install clients from the soprano.crew.org with between
128MB and 256MB of RAM that are not *x*86 machines will use the class file named
sparc_class and the finish script named printer_setup.

The second rule states that any install client from the soprano.crew.org that has
Solaris 2.6 currently installed and is on the *x*86 architecture will use the class file
named *x*86_class and the begin script called *x*86_before.

The last rule is used for any install client that doesn't fall into either of the first
two categories. Any install client except the machine with the hostname pwalnuts
will use the class file named anybody_class.

exam
ⓦatch

***Don't forget that the rules file is read by the install process from the top
down! The first line that matches the install client is the one used. If you use
the any keyword, make sure it is placed last!***

Now that you know how to create a rules file that points the install client to a
class file, let's take a look at how to create class files.

The class file determines how the install client is installed and which software gets
installed. Just like the rules file, the class file uses specific keywords and values. The
valid keywords for the class file are the following:

- **install_type**   The value must be either initial_install or upgrade. This
  keyword must be in every class file; otherwise, the check script will fail and
  not create the rules.ok file.
- **system_type**   This can have a value of *standalone, dataless,* or *server.* If the
  system_type keyword is not used, the default *standalone* is used.

■ **partitioning** The valid values are *default, existing,* or *explicit.* Logically enough, the default is *default* and is used if this value is not specified. *default* tells the installation process to partition the disk based on the software selected.

■ **package** The value is the package name and whether the package name is to be installed or deleted.

■ **locale** The valid values are the locale names for the available languages on the installation image, for example,

```
locale de
```

This keyword and value would install the German language version (*de* for *Deutsche*) of Solaris.

■ **num_clients** The valid value is the number of diskless clients this server supports. This keyword is valid only if *server* is specified as the system_type. The default number is 5.

■ **client_swap** The value is the size of the swap file for each diskless client. This keyword is valid only if *server* is specified as the system_type. The default is 24MB each.

■ **filesys** This value can be used for automatically mounting NFS resources, for example,

```
filesys baddabing:/export/employee/stats - /business/baddabing/employee/stats  ro
```

This keyword and value mount the /export/employee/stats file from the host named *baddabing* as read-only on the local directory of the install client named /business/ baddabing/employee/stats. The hyphen (-) specifies that a name server is running on the network; otherwise, the IP address of the NFS server must replace the hyphen.

Here's an example of a class file:

```
# This class file created by cmoltisanti on 2/00 for the soprano.crew.org installation and
#should only be associated with SPARC machines.
install_type  initial_install
system_type server
num_clients 2
client_swap 50
package SUNWciu8  delete
package SUNWadmap add
```

The first two lines are commented out by the pound sign (#).

This class file is used for initial installations to install servers. Each install client using this class file will have support for two diskless clients, and each diskless client will get 50MB of swap space. This class file will also delete the package named SUNWciu8 and add the package named SUNWadmap.

CERTIFICATION OBJECTIVE 29.10

Configuring NIS Name Service Support for JumpStart

If no sysidcfg file is found, the network's name service can be configured to provide the initial configuration information. Let's take a look at configuring the name service to get install clients ready for a JumpStart installation.

To use the NIS name service for an automatic installation, you must configure the following information:

- **Time zone**   The time zone in which the install client is located
- **Netmasks**   The network mask assigned to this install client
- **Locale**   The language used during installation
- **IP address**   The IP address the install client will be assigned during installation
- **Host name**   The name assigned to this install client
- **Bootparams**   The location of the swap, dump, and root partitions for diskless clients

To update the time zone, create or update the time zone database on the name server. Add the time zone information and the domain that will use the information. An entry in /etc/timezone might look like this:

```
US/Eastern      soprano.crew.net
```

Update the netmasks database with the network mask information. For example, add a line in /etc/netmasks like this:

```
145.172.10.0      255.255.255.0
```

Then update the NIS maps on the NIS master by running this command:

```
# cd /var/yp; make
```

To add the information for IP address, hostname, and Ethernet address, you must edit the /etc/ethers and /etc/hosts databases on the NIS master.

First, add the Ethernet and hostname of the install client to the /etc/ethers file. Then add the IP address and hostname to the /etc/hosts file. Each install client needs an entry so that each is assigned an IP address and hostname and to make sure that their hostnames are associated with the correct Ethernet addresses.

You also need to designate one existing machine on your network as the time host. Do this by adding the alias *timehost* to one of the hostnames in the /etc/hosts file. Now all the install clients will get their settings for time and date from this machine.

Next, rebuild the NIS maps on the NIS master by running this command:

```
# cd /var/yp; make
```

If the installation media from which you are installing contains multiple languages, you need to specify the language used for the install clients. To do this in NIS, you must first edit the file named /var/yp/Makefile.

The first entry you make is to add the word *locale* to the end of the line that begins with *add:*. When you are finished, the line should look like this:

```
all: passwd  group  hosts  ethers   networks   rpc  services  protocols  netgroup
bootparams \   aliases  timezone   locale
```

Next, add the following code after the last *.time entry:

```
locale.time:  $(DIR) /locale
        -@if  [  -f  $ (DIR) /locale ]; then  \
              sed -e "/^#/d"  -e s/#.*$$// $(DIR)/locale \
              | awk ' [ for (i = 2; i<NF; <Ni++) print $$i,  $$0]' \
              | $(MAKEDBM) - $(YPDBDIR)/$(DOM)/locale.byname;  \
              touch locale.time; \
              echo "updated locale"; \
              if [  !  $(NOPUSH)  ];  then \
                      $(YPPUSH)  locale.byname;  \
                      echo "pushed locale";  \
              else  \
              :  ;  \|
              fi  \
```

```
else  \
            echo  "couldn't find $(DIR) /locale"; \
fi
```

At the end of the /var/yp/Makefile file, add the line *locale: locale.time* after the *timezone : timezone.time* entry. It should look like this:

```
timezone: timezone.time
locale: locale.time
```

Next, edit the /etc/locale file. If the file doesn't exist, create it. Here you specify the domain name or the name of the install client that will be configured.

The file should be in this format:

```
domain_name (or host_name)  locale_value
```

The valid values are

- English: C
- French: fr
- German: de
- Italian: it
- Spanish: es
- Swedish: sv

So, if you are installing install clients in the fictitious domain named soprano .crew.org and all the install clients will be using the English-language version of Solaris, the entry in /etc/locale on the NIS master would look like this:

```
soprano.crew.org    C
```

If the install client machine named *walnuts* were to be installed with the Italian language, the entry in the /etc/locale file on the NIS master would look like this:

```
walnuts      it
```

Once you have edited the files, run the following command to update the maps:

```
# cd /var/yp;make
```

on the
Job

You can check to see if the NIS master has been updated correctly by running the command ypcat locale.

The procedure for setting the default language in NIS+ is different from the NIS procedure.

First, use the following command on the NIS+ name server to build the table named locale.org_dir:

```
#  nistbladm -D access=og=rmcd, nw=r -c locale_tbl name=SI, nogw=locale=,nogw=
comment=,nogw= locale.org_dir. 'nisdefaults -d'
```

Now you can add the information by running this command:

```
#  nistbladm -a name=domain_name( or host_name) locale=locale
comment=comment locale.org_dir. 'nisdefaults -d'
```

The *domain_name* (or *host_name*) value is where you add the name of the domain whose members will be installed with these default language settings. You can also list a specific single *host_name* of a single install client.

The *locale* value contains the language the install clients will use. The available choices are the same as what is available in NIS:

- English: C
- French: fr
- German: de
- Italian: it
- Spanish: es
- Swedish: sv

The *comment* field, again quite logically, is used for comments. Make sure you surround any comment of more than one word with quotation marks.

For example, if the install clients in the soprano.crew.org domain were all going to be installed with the English-language version of Solaris, the command would look like this:

```
# nistbladm -a  name=soprano.crew.org  locale=C  comment="Default Install with
English" locale.org_dir.  'nisdefaults -d'
```

Now let's take a look at a few scenario questions and their answers.

SCENARIO & SOLUTION

You're setting up a series of clients that are on a different subnet from your install server. Do you have to create a new Jumpstart installation server?	No. All you need is a boot server on your client's subnet.
What if you need to add some new clients that don't fall into any rules you've created before?	Add a new rule, run the check program to update the rules.ok file, and then run the add_install_client script.

on the job

If you want to make sure the NIS+ information has been updated correctly, run the niscat locale.org_dir command.

If you don't configure a sysidcfg file, the NIS, or the NIS+ name service, the installation will stop while the process prompts the user for the initial configuration information.

FROM THE CLASSROOM

The Importance of Hands-On Experience

Before you take the exam, you might have had a chance to experience the process of setting up a custom JumpStart installation. Sun Microsystems takes these certifications very seriously, and the last thing you want to see happen is that an SCSA or SCNA certification is not respected. To that end, they have designed the tests to be more than a "memorize-and-forget" experience. The Solaris Certification Exams test not only your ability to retain the information covered in this book, but also your real-world experience with Solaris. It is very important that, as you prepare for the exam, you make every attempt to use Solaris in as many situations as possible. This is not only important to successfully pass the Solaris Certification Tests, but it's important in terms of your career in the IT field. No matter how many acronyms you can put after your name, you'll have no credibility if you can't do the work.

(continued)

FROM THE CLASSROOM

Many people preparing for this exam tend to blow off the JumpStart feature. The excuse is that it requires too many resources to set up in a home lab. Don't you believe it!

The built-in testing capability with the check script and pfinstall command are perfect for anyone who wants to practice the JumpStart feature. You can set everything up and test it without actually installing a machine.

However, if you have the resources, you should try doing it for real. All it takes is one machine to be the boot/configuration/install server and one to be the install client. Remember, these exams are a test of your ability to perform, not memorize! The more hands-on preparation you do, the better you'll do on the exam.

—*Randy Cook, MCSE, SCSA*

CERTIFICATION SUMMARY

JumpStart is a very popular feature of Solaris, especially on large networks. One of the best features about JumpStart is that the install, boot, and configuration servers can all be located on the same machine. This setup makes the whole process very easy to configure.

When taking the exam, separate the functions of each server in your mind, but remember that they can physically all be in one place. In addition, remember that the boot server must be on the same subnet as the install client. This point is easy to forget if you have not had the chance to perform a large-scale JumpStart installation.

✓ TWO-MINUTE DRILL

Defining the Main Components of a JumpStart Server

❑ The three main servers are the boot, install, and configuration servers.

❑ There are many files available for a custom JumpStart installation.

❑ The rules.ok file defines groups or classes to which install clients can belong.

Using the add_install_client Script Syntax

❑ There are three different versions of this command. It is used to add a client to the install server.

Using the Boot Service Function on a Subnet

❑ A common problem when designing a custom JumpStart installation is forgetting that a boot server is needed across subnets.

Understanding the Events That Occur During the JumpStart Client Boot Sequence

❑ Make sure you not only understand the process of configuring the installation, but also the behind-the-scenes actions that are taking place.

Using the Necessary Files to Support the JumpStart Boot Operation

❑ The sysidcfg file is a handy tool. Make sure you understand how it's created and what it's used for. Remember, it's used in place of a name service server.

Understanding the sysidcfg File With and Without Name Service Support

❑ The sysidcfg file can be used if a name service exists or in place of it. Without either, the install process will stop and wait for the information to be entered manually.

Setting Up a JumpStart Install Server System

❑ The setup_install_server can be used to either create the install server or, if the *-b* switch is used, a boot server. Make sure you have allowed adequate space for the install server installation files. The setup-install_server script tells you if you don't have enough space before it starts copying files.

Using the add_to_install_server, modify_install_server, and add_install_client Scripts

❑ These three scripts are used to make changes or additions to a configured JumpStart server.

Creating a Configuration Server with a Customized Rules File and Class Files

❑ The rules.ok file is the actual file used to split the install clients into groups, which are called *classes*. The rules.ok file is created after you've built the rules file by running the check script.

Configuring NIS Name Service Support for JumpStart

❑ A properly configured name service server can replace a sysidcfg file.

SELF TEST

The following questions will help you measure your understanding of the material presented in this chapter. Read all the choices carefully because there might be more than one correct answer. Choose all correct answers for each question.

Defining the Main Components of a JumpStart Server

1. Which of the following best describes an install server?

   A. A server on which you will install Solaris

   B. The system administrator who will be responsible for the JumpStart installation setup

   C. The system on which the Solaris installation files will be stored to be used by the clients

   D. CD 1 of the Solaris Installation media

Using the add_install_client Script Syntax

2. Which option would you use to specify the name of the install server?

   A. The -e option

   B. The -i option

   C. The -installserver option

   D. The -s option

Using the Boot Service Function on a Subnet

3. After creating the boot directory on a system you want to create as a boot server, you run the following script:

   ```
   ./setup_install_server /boot
   ```

   What happens?

   A. The script adds the pathname of the boot server's boot image files.

   B. The script fails because the -s option is missing.

   C. The script fails because you should be running the setup_boot_server script.

   D. The script fails because the -b option is missing.

Understanding the Events That Occur During the JumpStart Client Boot Sequence

4. You are installing Solaris on a new Sun workstation that has no operating system installed. Which of the following options will you use to begin the installation process?

   A. Boot the system to single-user state. Use the command boot -install.

   B. Using the STOP-A keyboard combo, get to the PROM ok prompt and use the command boot -install.

   C. Boot the system using the device configuration disk provided with the Solaris Installation Media Kit.

   D. Power on the system.

Using the Necessary Files to Support the JumpStart Boot Operation

5. Which of the following best describes the sysidcfg file?

   A. The file used by a name service server to configure an install client

   B. The file used by the system administrator to review the results of the installation process

   C. A configuration file used to provide basic installation information to the install client

   D. A file that provides the install client with its hostname

Understanding the sysidcfg File With and Without Name Service Support

6. Which information is not provided to the install client by the sysidcfg file?

   A. The name and contact information of the system administrator in case of any problems during installation

   B. The time zone to use

   C. The type of name service to use

   D. The time server to use

Setting Up a JumpStart Install Server System

7. Which statement best describes the setup_install_server script?

   A. It is an optional step.

   B. It is a required step to set up an install server.

C. It doesn't actually copy any files; it only points out the location of the shared Installation CD-ROM.

D. It can copy files only to an install server.

Using the add_to_install_server, modify_install_server, and add_install_client Scripts

8. Which command would you use to remove an install client named raprile?

A. add_install_client -x raprile.

B. add_install_client -r raprile.

C. There is no way to remove a client once it's been added to the install server.

D. None of the above.

Creating a Configuration Server with a Customized Rules File and Class Files

9. Which file is used to define the groups or classes of install clients?

A. The rules file

B. The rules.ok file

C. The classes.ok file

D. The pfinstall file

Configuring NIS Name Service Support for JumpStart

10. Which of the following is not configurable information used by the NIS name service for a JumpStart installation?

A. Netmasks

B. Bootparams

C. Hostname

D. Username

LAB QUESTION

As the system administrator of a LAN, you have been asked to add a client named *furio* to the JumpStart installation process. The configuration, install, and boot servers are all on a system named *tsoprano*. The installation directory is /jumpstart. The system to be installed is a SPARCstation 5. How will the add_install_client script syntax look?

SELF TEST ANSWERS

Defining the Main Components of a JumpStart Server

1. ☑ C. The install server is where the installation files are stored so that the clients to be installed can access them.

☒ A is incorrect because Solaris must already be installed before you can create a system and install server. B is incorrect because no specific title is required by the person doing the configuration. D is also incorrect because it refers to the media, not a server.

Using the add_install_client Script Syntax

2. ☑ D. The -s option specifies both the name and the pathname to the installation image.

☒ A is incorrect because this will specify the Ethernet address of the install client. B is incorrect because it will specify the IP address of the client. C is incorrect because there is no installserver option.

Using the Boot Service Function on a Subnet

3. ☑ D is correct because the -b option is required to create the boot server.

☒ A is incorrect because the script will fail without the -b switch. B is incorrect because there is no -s option available with this script. C is incorrect because there is no setup_boot_server script provided with the installation media.

Understanding the Events That Occur During the JumpStart Client Boot Sequence

4. ☑ D. Provided that there is no other previous Solaris installation, the host will attempt to find a boot server.

☒ B is incorrect because this is the procedure you would follow to reinstall or upgrade a system that already has Solaris installed. C is incorrect because this is the method for installing Solaris on an x86 system.

Using the Necessary Files to Support the JumpStart Boot Operation

5. ☑ C. This is the file used to provide the client with the information it needs to begin the installation process.

☒ **A** is incorrect because a sysidcfg file is used in place of configuring a name service server to provide this information. **B** is incorrect because it's used before the installation process actually begins, not after. **D** is incorrect because this information is provided by the rules.ok file.

Understanding the sysidcfg File With and Without Name Service Support

6. ☑ **A.** If there's a problem with the installation and the system administrator doesn't catch it, don't worry, the users will find you.

☒ **B, C,** and **D** are all information that can be provided by the sysidcfg file.

Setting Up a JumpStart Install Server System

7. ☑ **B.** This script is used to define the location of the files that the installation clients will use to install Solaris.

☒ **A** is incorrect because it is a required step. **C** is incorrect because it copies the files to the install server. **D** is incorrect because it can be used to create a boot server if the *-b* option is used.

Using the add_to_install_server, modify_install_server, and add_install_client Scripts

8. ☑ **D.** The correct script to remove an install client from the JumpStart install server is rm_install_client, with the hostname of the client to be removed.

☒ **A, B,** and **C** are incorrect because there is no *-x* switch provided with the add_install_client script and, although it's not often used, there is a way to remove a client.

Creating a Configuration Server with a Customized Rules File and Class Files

9. ☑ **B.** Although **A** could be your first choice, remember that the check script reads the rules file you created and creates the rules.ok file. The rules.ok file is what the installation process uses.

☒ **A** is incorrect because the installation process uses rules.ok. **C** is incorrect because there's no classes.ok file. **D** is incorrect because the pfinstall file is an optional, but smart, step to use to test your class files.

Configuring NIS Name Service Support for JumpStart

10. ☑ D. A root account is created as part of the installation process, but the NIS name service server won't create other usernames.

☒ A, B, and C are incorrect because this is all information NIS can provide.

LAB ANSWER

The script will look like this:

```
# add_install_client -c tsoprano:/jumpstart furio sun4m
```

There are actually three versions of the add_install_client script. The *-d* option is used if the client is a DHCP client, which naturally requires that a DHCP server be configured on the network. The example shows the basic use of the script. The platform group was determined using the uname *-m* command on another SPARCstation 5 system.

Part

III

Appendixes

A

What's New in Solaris 9

"Solaris has a long and proud history at the forefront of open systems technology. As the best-selling UNIX system, Solaris is pervasive in the enterprise, and its legendary reputation for reliability and scalability is well deserved. The current release of Solaris—Solaris 9—represents both an incremental improvement and a major change in direction for the operating environment. Existing innovations and strengths are built upon in the core operating system, including support for IPv6, IPSec, new networking standards, improved threading, and volume management. However, Solaris is much more than yet another operating system—it is the foundation for Sun ONE, the new platform for enterprise applications. Sun ONE provides support for directory services, enterprise Java applications, firewall security, Kerberos, and interoperability tools."

—Dr Paul Watters

The following are the new and enhanced key features from the Solaris 9 release:

- **Solaris 9 Resource Manager** The Solaris 9 Resource Manager improves functionality for allocating, monitoring, and controlling system resources.

- **Linux Compatibility** Many Linux applications run virtually unchanged in the Solaris operating environment.

- **Increased Security** Solaris 9 includes significant security enhancements, such as the following features:

- **Internet Key Exchange** Internet Key Exchange (IKE) enables administrators to manage larger numbers of secure networks.

- **Solaris Secure Shell** Secure shell allows a user to securely access a remote host over an unsecured network.

- **Secure LDAP Client** A new Lightweight Directory Access Protocol (LDAP) library provides for SSL (TLS) and CRAM-MD5 encryption mechanisms.

- **Strong Encryption** Strong encryption with a maximum size of 128 bits is available as a default for certain functionality.

- **iPlanet Directory Server 5.1** iPlanet™ Directory Server 5.1 is now an integrated part of Solaris 9.

- **Solaris Volume Manager** The Solaris Volume Manager provides storage management tools that enable you to create and manage RAID volumes, as well as transactional (logging) devices and soft partitions.

- **File System Enhancements** Solaris 9 contains several file system enhancements.

- **Solaris Live Upgrade 2.0**   Solaris Live Upgrade provides a method of upgrading that substantially reduces downtime.

- **Web Start Flash**   You can now create a reference installation of the Solaris operating environment and replicate that installation on many other machines.

- **Minimal Installation**   You can now install a minimal set of packages with Solaris 9, then add only the packages you need.

- **Multiple Page Size Support**   Multiple Page Size Support (MPSS) allows a program to use any hardware-supported page size to access portions of virtual memory.

- **Improved Multithreading Library**   Solaris 9 now contains an improved and faster multithreading library.

B

About the CD

The CD-ROM included with this book comes complete with MasterExam and the electronic version of the book. The software is easy to install on any Windows 98/NT/2000/XP computer and must be installed to access the MasterExam feature. You may, however, browse the electronic book directly from the CD-ROM without installation. To register for a second bonus MasterExam, simply click the Additional Training link on the CD Main Page and follow the directions to the free online registration. You can access the additional chapter material on the Solaris 9 Upgrade Exam using the same Additional Training link. You must register and log in to access this material.

System Requirements

Software requires Windows 98 or higher, Internet Explorer 5.0 or above, and 20 MB of hard disk space for full installation. The Electronic book requires Adobe Acrobat Reader. To access Online Training from LearnKey you must have RealPlayer Basic 8 or Real1 Plugin, which will be installed automatically when you launch the on-line training.

Installing and Running MasterExam

If your computer CD-ROM drive is configured to auto run, the CD-ROM will automatically start up upon inserting the disk. From the opening screen you may install MasterExam by pressing the MasterExam button. This will begin the installation process and create a program group named "LearnKey." To run MasterExam use Start | Programs | LearnKey. If the auto run feature did not launch your CD-ROM, browse to the CD-ROM and click the RunInstall icon.

MasterExam

MasterExam provides you with a simulation of the actual exam. The number of questions, type of questions, and the time allowed are intended to be an accurate representation of the exam environment. You have the option to take an open-book exam, including hints, references, and answers; a closed-book exam; or the timed MasterExam simulation.

When you launch MasterExam, a digital clock display will appear in the upper-left corner of your screen. The clock will continue to count down to zero unless you choose to end the exam before the time expires.

Electronic Book

The entire contents of the Study Guide are provided in PDF format. Adobe's Acrobat Reader has been included on the CD-ROM.

LearnKey Online Training

The Additional Training link will also allow you to access online training from Osborne.Onlineexpert.com. Course sessions may be purchased directly from www.LearnKey.com or by calling (800) 865-0165.

The first time you run Training, you will be required to register with the online product. Follow the instructions for a first-time user. Please make sure to use a valid e-mail address.

Prior to running Online Training you will need to add the Real Plugin and the RealCBT plugin to your system. This will automatically be facilitated to your system when you run the training the first time.

Help

A help file is provided through the help button on the main page in the lower-left corner. Individual help features are also available through MasterExam and LearnKey's Online Training.

Removing Installation(s)

MasterExam is installed to your hard drive. For best results for removal of programs use the Start | Programs | LearnKey | Uninstall option to remove MasterExam.

If you want to remove the Real Player use the Add/Remove Programs Icon from your Control Panel. You may also remove the LearnKey training program from this location.

Technical Support

For questions regarding the technical content of the electronic book or MasterExam please visit www.osborne.com or e-mail customer.service@mcgraw-hill.com. For customers outside the 50 United States, e-mail international_cs@mcgraw-hill.com.

LearnKey Technical Support

For technical problems with the software (installation, operation, removing installations) and for questions regarding LearnKey Online Training content, please visit www.learnkey.com or e-mail techsupport@learnkey.com.

Glossary

ACL   *See* Access Control Lists

Access Control List (ACL)   Used in the Solaris environment to provide granular control of file permissions.

Action server   This is a server that provides actions or services to clients.

add_install_client   Used with the Jumpstart automatic installation method, this script adds clients to your Install and Boot Servers.

Address Resolution Protocol (ARP)   Used by systems to map layer-3 addresses to layer-2 MAC addresses. ARP entries are cached and maintained in an ARP table.

application server   This is a server that does the majority of processing of an application for a client.

ARP   *See* Address Resolution Protocol

ASCII   Stands for American Standard Code for Information Interchange and defines the way a system reads basic text.

AutoFS   This service can also be used to mount cached file systems automatically.

banner   The banner command is used to create a display in large letters or to display system information during the bootstrapping process.

boot   The process of loading and executing the operating system, also referred to as "bootstrapping."

boot block   A boot block stores the instructions used when booting the system, and it is necessary for the system to boot. The boot block appears only in the first cylinder group on the disk and is the first 8KB in a slice.

Boot Server   Used with the Jumpstart automatic installation method, the Boot Server is a host that allows an install client on the same subnet to boot and access the network. This way it can get the installation files stored on the Install Server.

bootstrap   From the phrase "pull itself up by its own bootstraps," this refers to the power-up sequence of a system. *See* boot.

Bourne Shell   Written by SR Bourne and found on nearly all versions of UNIX.

C-Shell   A UNIX shell written to resemble the C programming language.

cachefs   (Cache File System) file system type is used as a disk cache area in order to speed access to slower file systems such as CD-ROMS (hsfs) or network-based file systems (NFS).

caching-only server   This is a server that queries DNS servers for client requests.

CDE   *See* Common Desktop Environment

chmod   This command is used to modify permissions of existing files and directories.

cluster   A cluster is a logical collection of several packages.

CLI   *See* Command Line Interface

client   A term used to describe a host or an application that uses the services provided by other hosts or applications.

client-server   This is a networking model that describes the relationship between two networked hosts in which one of the hosts, the client, makes a request for a service and the server host response to that request.

Command Line Interface (CLI)   Refers to a console or terminal session where commands are entered at the system prompt.

Common Desktop Environment (CDE)   One of the two GUIs included with Solaris.

Communications server   A server that acts as a gateway.

Compress   This command takes a single file and attempts to make it take less room by utilizing the Lempel-Ziv encoding format.

Concatenation   A method of combining data disks that allows a system administrator to create a larger file system than could be created on one single disk by combining multiple physical disks into one logical/virtual volume.

Configuration Server   Used with the Jumpstart automatic installation method, the Configuration Server is the server that contains the customized files used to setup each install client.

core files   When a process terminates unexpectedly it may dump its unwritten data to a core file named "core" and contain a snapshot of the process state just before it is terminated.

Core Operating Environment   This software group, referred to as *SUNWCreq*, is the minimum required software for a system to run.

cp   A command used to make a copy of a file.

cpio   This command stands for "copy in and out" and is useful for copying file systems from one disk to another.

Cylinder group   The space on a data disk where the inode group lives.

daemon   A program that runs in the background to manage system functions.

Dataless client   This is a client that stores user files remotely.

dd   This command is used to perform raw copies of media to media such as cloning one hard disk to another.

devalias   An OpenBoot command that allows you to create a device alias, just as nvalias does. However, devalias creates a temporary alias (until the next reset), while nvalias creates a permanent alias.

Developer Operating Environment   This package, *SUNWCprog*, includes everything from the End User Operating Environment, plus the software required for a developer.

Device files   Device files are a symbolic way to reference a specific hardware device.

df   This command is used to display disk space usage by a file system. If used with no options, it is used to get output with size information in blocks and number of files.

Differential   A type of backup that is similar to an incremental backup (except a differential backup only backs up the changes since the last full backup).

Directory   A file that contains information about other files.

Diskfull client   This is a type of client installation that provides local storage for user files.

Diskless client   This is a type of client installation that uses no local storage of user or system files.

DNS   *See* Domain Name Service

Domain Name Service (DNS)   Used to resolve ip addresses to hostnames and hostnames to ip addresses. It is the name service of choice for the Internet.

du   This command is used to display disk space usage by directory.

eeprom   Short for "electrically erasable programmable read only memory," this is the command used to change or display the values of the firmware.

Eject   This command is used to eject a floppy diskette or CD-ROM.

Encapsulation   Encapsulation is the method by which upper layer information is placed inside the data field of a lower layer in a network protocol.

End User Operating Environment   This software group, referred to as SUNWCuser, is the software group that would generally be used on a desktop workstation.

Ethernet   A type of network that utilizes the Carrier Sense Multiple Access with Collision Detection (CSMA/CD) mechanism to allow multiple stations to share a single medium of transmission.

fdformat   This command is used to format floppy diskettes.

File system   A file system is a collection of files and directories organized in a hierarchical structure.

File Transfer Protocol (ftp)   An application used to transfer files from one system to another.

Finger   The finger command will show Login account, name, and GECOS field from the password file /etc/passwd.

fsck   This stands for File System Check. It's a standard UNIX utility used to check and if it's necessary to repair the integrity of file systems before they are mounted.

ftp   *See* File Transfer Protocol

fuser   This command is used to display and/or kill the processes of users currently accessing a file system.

grep   A command used to search files for a specified pattern.

groupadd   The command that adds a new group definition to the system and modifies the /etc/group file as appropriate.

groupdel   Deletes a group from the system.

groupmod   Used to modify information pertinent to a given group in the system.

halt   The halt command can be thought of the opposite complement to the shutdown command. It will immediately transition the system to the PROM mode without running the *sbin/rc0* script. Instead of stopping the processes through the run control scripts, it will signal init to send a termination signal to all processes.

Hard link   This is a directory entry to reference a specific file.

Host   A host is any system connected to a network.

Hostname   A command used to assign a new name or display the name of a host on a network. It must be a unique name to distinguish this machine from other machines.

hsfs   (High Sierra and ISO or International Standards Organization 9660 File System Standard) file system type is used for mounting media with read-only data such as CD-ROMs.

HTTP   *See* HyperText Transfer Protocol

HyperText Transfer Protocol (HTTP)   This protocol (HTTP) is used by web browsers to retrieve pages from a web server.

IDE   *See* Integrated Device Electronics

Incremental A type of backup that is defined as backing up only the changes from the last full or incremental backup.

init The "ancestor" of all processes that run on the Solaris 9 Operating Environment, this command is responsible for starting all the processes that prepare the system for use.

inittab A file located at /etc/inittab, this file is used to describe the run levels and set the default run level.

inode An inode contains information about a file: the type of file, the owner, the access and modification times, the access permissions, the number of links to the file, the size of the file, and the physical location of the data blocks.

Install Server Used with the Jumpstart automatic installation method, the Install Server is a host with the Solaris installation files stored locally, ready to be used by the install client.

Integrated Device Electronics (IDE) These disks are generally less expensive than SCSI disks. They have a small disk controller on each drive, which communicates directly with the system.

IP address An Internet Protocol address is a 4-octet, 32-bit number used to uniquely identify systems and resources on a network and the Internet.

IPv6 The latest version of the Internet Protocol that allows for better security and increased available addresses.

Jumpstart A method of preconfiguring an installation of Solaris so that the install process requires little or no input.

Kernel The kernel is the very heart of the operating system. It communicates instructions to the hardware, and schedules and executes all of the system commands. It manages all of the daemons, devices, and the system resources such as memory, swap space, and file systems. When you are running a shell program, such as the Bourne shell, you are using that program to communicate with the kernel.

kill This command provides an administrator with a mechanism to send a signal to a running process.

Korn Shell An expanded version of the Bourne shell.

LDAP *See* Lightweight Directory Access Protocol

Lightweight Directory Access Protocol (LDAP) Usually used with another naming service to provide a standardized set of rules for hierarchical naming structures, authorization practices, and configuration attributes.

ls This command lists the contents of a directory.

man The man command, short for "manual," is the way we access information about the commands and configuration files on our system. It's not a difficult command to learn or use.

manpath An environment variable used to describe the location of the man pages.

Metacharacter A character that has a value greater than itself when interpreted in the context of the UNIX shell environment.

Mount point A mount point is the location of a partition on the hard drive that has been segregated from other partitions.

Mirroring This is a type of RAID configuration that allows a system administrator to protect data by having two or more copies of the data, usually on separate spindles.

mkdir This command is used to create a directory.

mount   Adds access to remote systems or to provide access to local file systems.

mountall   Without any arguments, this command mounts all of the resources listed in the **/etc/vfstab** file, with **yes** under "mount at boot."

mv   Used to move files or directories from one location to another.

Network   A collection of computing resources, such as hosts, printers, routers, and so on, physically connected to allow communication.

Network Information Services (NIS)   Focuses on making network administration more manageable by providing centralized control over a variety of network and system information.

Network Information Services Plus (NIS+)   Very similar to NIS but with more features such as built-in authentication and cross-domain lookups.

newfs   Creates a new ufs file system.

NIS   *See* Network Information Services

NIS+   *See* Network Information Services Plus

Nonvolatile Random Access Memory (NVRAM)   Often used instead of OpenBoot, NVRAM actually refers to the chip on which OpenBoot system configuration variables are stored.

NVRAM   *See* nonvolatile random access memory

OpenBoot   Firmware that controls the boot process of a Sun workstation and provides useful diagnostic capabilities.

Operating environment   An operating environment is a term used by Sun Microsystems to describe the complete installation media, including third-party software and the core operating system, which comes with the Solaris 9 Installation Kit.

Operating system   An operating system is a set of programs that manages all system operations and provides a means of communication between the user and the resources available to that user.

pack   This command takes individual files and attempts to store them in a more compact fashion.

passwd   The /etc/passwd file is the central file containing all the user account information. It is also the command that is used to change a user's password.

pkgadd   A command used to unpack a software package and install it on the system.

pkgchk   A command used to verify the installation of a package and to check files for correctness based on the information of the package to which they belong.

pkginfo   Used to gain information about a package.

pkgrm   Removes a previously installed package.

patchadd   Used to install a patch or patches on the system and check on the currently installed patches.

patchrm   Removes, or backs out, a patch from a system.

Path   A term used to describe a file's location.

pcat   Pcat is like *zcat*—it uncompacts the file in memory, sends the output to *standard output*, and leaves the original file untouched.

pcfs   *See* Personal Computer File System

Personal Computer File System (pcfs)   Used for reading and writing DOS (Disk Operating System) formatted floppy diskettes.

pgrep   Allows you to quickly retrieve the PID of a process based on a substring of the process name.

pldd   An easy way to determine which libraries a process is currently using.

pkill   Very similar to pgrep, except that it eliminates the *-l* option and replaces it with an option to specify a signal to pass.

pmap   Displays the ranges of memory being used by the process.

POST   *See* Power On Self Test

Power On Self Test (POST)   Part of the bootstrapping process, which tests all of the installed hardware to ensure it is working properly.

Poweroff   The poweroff command is used to immediately shutdown the system and turn off the power, if the hardware supports it.

Print server   A server that manages print services.

Programmable Read Only Memory (PROM)   The portion of memory reserved for bootstrap information.

PROM   *See* Programmable Read Only Memory

prstat   This command provides process information at a configured interval. The output provided is similar to ps, although its dynamic nature is a valuable added benefit.

ps   A command used to display a listing of processes running on the system.

psig   Takes one or more PIDs as parameters and prints out a list of each signal, and the process's response to it.

ptree   Shows a visual representation of the relationship between parent and child processes.

quot   This command is used to display disk space usage by user name.

RAID   *See* Redundant Arrays of Inexpensive Disks

RARP   *See* Reverse Address Resolution Protocol

RBAC   *See* Role-Based Access Control

rcp   This command is used to copy files to and from remote systems.

Reboot   The command used to restart the operating system.

Redundant Arrays of Inexpensive Disks (RAID)   A term that refers to the method of writing the same data to several disks at the same time to prevent data loss.

Reverse Address Resolution Protocol (RARP)   Used by systems to determine their IP address.

rlogin   Used to establish a remote login session on a local console.

rm   This command is the basic tool for removing objects from your file system.

rmdir   Deletes a directory.

rsh   Used to execute a command on a remote system.

Role-Based Access Control (RBAC)   Enables the administrator to finely control execution permissions by sorting user capabilities into two concepts: authorizations and executions.

Run level   A named operating state that defines the available resources and services.

Scalable Processor Architecture (SPARC)   The term used to describe the Sun Microsystems proprietary processor design.

SCSI   *See* Small Computer Systems Interface

sdtprocess   This command provides methods for sending signals and killing processes via its GUI (graphical user interface).

Server   A term used to describe a host or an application that is designed to provide one or more services.

Session server   A server that stores environmental and login files locally for client systems.

SGML   *See* Standard Generalized Markup Language

Share   This command is used to make local resources available to remote clients or, if run with no options, to display all the file resources that are currently shared.

Shareall   Used to share multiple resources.

Shell   The interface between you and the kernel.

Showrev   This command will print out information about the currently running system including hostname, hosted, operating system version, platform and architecture, hardware provider, network domain name, and kernel version. The *-p* option is used to show information on the installed patches.

Shutdown   Used to transition a running system to another run level cleanly, using the *init* process.

Signal   This is a message sent to a process in order to affect its operation.

Simple Mail Transfer Protocol (SMTP)   The protocol used to deliver electronic mail.

Small Computer Systems Interface (SCSI)   Pronounced "scuzzy." These disks are generally more expensive than IDE disks, and they require a SCSI disk controller, which handles all the communication between the SCSI devices and the system

SMTP   *See* Simple Mail Transfer Protocol

Software group   A collection of software used during installation to determine how a particular system will be used.

Solaris Management Console (SMC)   A Graphical User Interface (see GUI) application that provides a central location to access a set of administrative tools.

SPARC   *See* Scalable Processor Architecture

Standard Generalized Markup Language (SGML)   A method used to mark a document, such as man pages, with tags to describe how to read the text.

Stop-A   The keyboard combination used to bring a system to the console monitor, also known as the "ok" prompt.

Striping   A type of RAID configuration that allows a system administrator to stripe a file system across multiple physical disks, this is traditionally used to enhance performance (more spindles running = faster throughput and access to data).

Subnet mask   Also known as a netmask, this is used to determine what network a particular system is on. The netmask details how to break the IP address into the network address and the host address.

Superblock   The area of a disk that is used to store file system information.

swap   Used to administer swap space.

swapfs   (Swap File System) file system type is used to provide swap space to the system.

sync   Flushes all previously unwritten system buffers out to the hard drives in order to make sure that no data is lost.

Symbolic link   This is a special kind of file that is an alias to another file.

syslog   Syslog refers to the general purpose logging facility native to all UNIX systems.

tar   This command, short for *Tape AR*chive, is used to collect all the files together in a single file.

TCP   *See* Transmission Control Protocol

TCP/IP   *See* Transmission Control Protocol/Internet Protocol

Telnet   This protocol provides a means to login remotely into a system through a network.

Terminal   Also be referred to as a "console," it is a serial port device attached to a UNIX system that gives a basic command-line interface connection.

tmpfs (Temporary File System) file system type is used by the /tmp file system and utilizes local memory for file system operations, which is much faster than a disk-based file system.

Touch This command creates a file of zero length.

Transmission Control Protocol (TCP) One of the two commonly used protocols at the transport layer of the TCP/IP protocol stack. The other is User Datagran Protocol (UDP). TCP provides connection-oriented reliable data delivery service.

Transmission Control Protocol/Internet Protocol (TCP/IP) A suite of network communications protocols that consists of five layers: Application, Transport, Internet, Network Interface, and Hardware. These layers can be mapped against those of the OSI model.

udf *See* Universal Disk Format

UDP *See* User Datagram Protocol

UFS *See* Unix File System

ufsdump Used to backup files.

ufsrestore Restores files systems that are backed up using the ufsdump command.

Unix File System (UFS) The type of file system recognized by the UNIX Operating System.

umask Defines the permissions on newly created files.

umount Used to stop access to remote systems or local file systems.

umountall   Without any arguments, all mounted resources will be unmounted.

uncompress   Performs the opposite function of compress—it takes a compressed file (named with a .Z extension) and uncompresses it, saving it without the extension.

Universal Disk Format (udf)   UDF, which was new in Solaris 8, is the industry standard format used to store information on optical media technology. This udf file system type is used for reading information mainly from DVDs, but can also be used for CD-ROMs and floppy diskettes that contain UDF file systems.

unshare   Makes the resource unavailable for mounting by a remote system.

unshareall   Used to unshare multiple resources.

unpack   This command, like *uncompress*, restores a file to its original size and saves it as its original name.

unzip   Unzip can be used to extract file from a zip file, list the files in a zip file, or check a zip file for errors.

uptime   Displays the length of time since the system was last rebooted.

useradd   Used to create a new user account, adding information as appropriate to the /etc/passwd, /etc/group, and /etc/shadow files, and creating the user home directory if requested.

User Datagram Protocol (UDP)   Provides connectionless, unreliable data delivery and is one of the two commonly used protocols at the transport layer of the TCP/IP protocol stack. The other is TCP.

userdel   Deletes a user's login from the system and makes the appropriate modifications to the /etc/passwd, /etc/group, and /etc/shadow files, as well as deleting the users home directory, if requested.

usermod   Used to modify existing user accounts.

vi   This term stands for "visual editor" and is a command-line text editor.

volcheck   This command will verify that you have a properly formatted floppy diskette inserted into the disk drive.

volrmmount   Used to mount or unmount removable media such as floppy disks.

Web Start   A type of installation that provides a Java-powered GUI to the Solaris Operating Environment installation process.

who   Displays the users currently logged into a system.

whoami   This command will display the username of the current terminal.

X server   A server that allows a remote system to use its X Windows display.

zcat   This command is exactly the same as calling *uncompress* with the *-c* option: it uncompresses the file in memory, sending the output to *standard output* and leaving the original file untouched.

zip   A recent addition to the Solaris Operating Environment, zip implements the common PKZIP format often found on MS/DOS-based systems.

INDEX

Page numbers in *italics* refer to illustrations or charts.

NUMBERS & SYMBOLS

32-bit support, system installation, 61–62
64-bit support, system installation, 61–62
(hash mark/pound sign)
    /etc/syslog.conf file, 532
    ftp command, 457–458
    vi editor, 427
$ (dollar sign), regular expressions for searching file content, 147
* (asterisk)
    indirect maps, 642
    regular expressions for searching file content, 146
    rm command, 412
    searching for files and directories within directory tree, 395, 397–398
>> (redirection character), output redirection, 410
[...] (brackets)
    accessing files and directories within directory tree, 395, 396–397, *398*
    regular expressions for searching file content, 147
^ (carat), regular expressions for searching file content, 146
. (period), regular expressions for searching file content, 146
. (dot) directory
    See also period (.)
    relative addressing of file system objects, 390, 391
.. (dot-dot) directory
    See also period (.)
    relative addressing of file system objects, 390–392
! (exclamation mark), format command menu selections, 328
? (question mark)
    regular expressions for searching file content, 146
    searching for files and directories within directory tree, 395, 396, *398*
/ (slash), file systems and root directories, 8

A

absolute addressing of file system objects, moving between points in directory tree, 390, *391*
absolute mode, chmod command, 157, *158*
access control, role-based. *See* RBAC
ACL entry, getfacl command, 164
ACLs (access control lists), 163–170
    See also file security
    file system (FACLs), 163
    getfacl command, 163–166
    overview, 163
    scenarios and solutions, *170*
    self test, 174–175
    self test answers, 177
    setfacl command, 166–169
    two-minute drill, 171

ACTION field, INITTAB file, 96
action servers, 475
    See also servers
actions, rebooting, *30*
adding disks, character devices and block devices, 312–313
adding folders to SMC toolbox, 784–785
adding groups, groupadd command, 130
adding legacy applications to SMC toolbox, 788–789
adding roles. *See* roleadd command
adding tools to SMC toolbox, 785–787
adding users. *See* useradd command
add_install_client script, JumpStart Automatic Installation server, 811–812, 819
Address Resolution Protocol. *See* ARP
addresses
    absolute. *See* absolute addressing of file system objects
    data link layer versus network layer, 502
    Ethernet, 500–501
    IP. *See* IP addresses
    relative. *See* relative addressing of file system objects
add_to_install_server script, install server and JumpStart Automatic Installation server, 818–819
administration commands, package, 66–72
administration terminology, 4–11
    See also exam 310-011; system concepts
    daemons, 4–6
    file systems, 8–9
    kernels, 9–10
    operating systems, 10–11
    processes, 4–6
    self test, 18–19
    self test answers, 20
    shells, 6–8
    two-minute drill, 17
administrative tasks, file system. *See* file system administrative tasks
AdminSuite. *See* Solaris AdminSuite
admintool graphical interface, package administration commands, 66
alert messages, syslog facility, 533–534
aliases, device. *See* device aliases
All Free Hog table, Partition submenu of format command, 342–344
allocated versus reserved memory, virtual memory system, 584
allocating memory, virtual memory system, 583–585
analyze command, 332–334
    See also format command menu selections
    exercise, 333–334
answers
    lab. *See* lab answers
    self test. *See* self test answers
application layer
    OSI model, 490
    TCP/IP, 493–494
application servers, 475
    See also servers
applications, adding legacy to SMC toolbox, 788–789

G

H

Q

R

V

INTERNATIONAL CONTACT INFORMATION

AUSTRALIA
McGraw-Hill Book Company Australia Pty. Ltd.
TEL +61-2-9900-1800
FAX +61-2-9878-8881
http://www.mcgraw-hill.com.au
books-it_sydney@mcgraw-hill.com

CANADA
McGraw-Hill Ryerson Ltd.
TEL +905-430-5000
FAX +905-430-5020
http://www.mcgraw-hill.ca

GREECE, MIDDLE EAST, & AFRICA
(Excluding South Africa)
McGraw-Hill Hellas
TEL +30-1-656-0990-3-4
FAX +30-1-654-5525

MEXICO (Also serving Latin America)
McGraw-Hill Interamericana Editores S.A. de C.V.
TEL +525-117-1583
FAX +525-117-1589
http://www.mcgraw-hill.com.mx
fernando_castellanos@mcgraw-hill.com

SINGAPORE (Serving Asia)
McGraw-Hill Book Company
TEL +65-863-1580
FAX +65-862-3354
http://www.mcgraw-hill.com.sg
mghasia@mcgraw-hill.com

SOUTH AFRICA
McGraw-Hill South Africa
TEL +27-11-622-7512
FAX +27-11-622-9045
robyn_swanepoel@mcgraw-hill.com

SPAIN
McGraw-Hill/Interamericana de España, S.A.U.
TEL +34-91-180-3000
FAX +34-91-372-8513
http://www.mcgraw-hill.es
professional@mcgraw-hill.es

UNITED KINGDOM, NORTHERN,
EASTERN, & CENTRAL EUROPE
McGraw-Hill Education Europe
TEL +44-1-628-502500
FAX +44-1-628-770224
http://www.mcgraw-hill.co.uk
computing_neurope@mcgraw-hill.com

ALL OTHER INQUIRIES Contact:
Osborne/McGraw-Hill
TEL +1-510-549-6600
FAX +1-510-883-7600
http://www.osborne.com
omg_international@mcgraw-hill.com